Braided Rivers

Braided Rivers

EDITED BY

J. L. BEST
Department of Earth Sciences
University of Leeds, UK

&

C. S. BRISTOW
Department of Geology, Birkbeck College
Uiversity of London, UK

Published by
The Geological Society
London

THE GEOLOGICAL SOCIETY

The Society was founded in 1807 as The Geological Society of London and is the oldest geological society in the world. It received its Royal Charter in 1825 for the purpose of 'investigating the mineral structure of the Earth'. The Society is Britain's national society for geology with a membership of around 8000. It has countrywide coverage and approximately 1000 members reside overseas. The Society is responsible for all aspects of the geological sciences including professional matters. The Society has its own publishing house, which produces the Society's international journals, books and maps, and which acts as the European distributor for publications of the American Association of Petroleum Geologists, SEPM and the Geological Society of America.

Fellowship is open to those holding a recognized honours degree in geology or cognate subject and who have at least two years' relevant postgraduate experience, or who have not less than six years' relevant experience in geology or a cognate subject. A Fellow who has not less than five years' relevant postgraduate experience in the practice of geology may apply for validation and, subject to approval, may be able to use the designatory letters C Geol (Chartered Geologist).

Further information about the Society is available from the Membership Manager, The Geological Society, Burlington House, Piccadilly, London W1V 0JU, UK. The Society is a Registered Charity, No. 210161.

Published by The Geological Society from:
The Geological Society Publishing House
Unit 7, Brassmill Enterprise Centre
Brassmill Lane
Bath BA1 3JN
UK
(*Orders*: Tel. 01225 445046
         Fax 01225 442836)

First published 1993 as Geological Society Special Publication No. 75
Paperback edition 1998

British Library Cataloguing in Publication Data
A catalogue record for this book is available from the British Library.
ISBN 1-86239-006-1

Typeset by EJS Chemical Composition,
Midsomer Norton, Bath, Avon

Printed by Alden Press,
Oxford, UK

Distributors

USA
  AAPG Bookstore
  PO Box 979
  Tulsa
  Oklahoma 74101-0979
  USA
  (*Orders*: Tel. (918) 584–2555
           Fax (918) 584–0469)

Australia
  Australian Mineral Foundation
  63 Conyngham Street
  Glenside
  South Australia 5065
  Australia
  (*Orders*: Tel. (08) 379–0444
           Fax (08) 379–4634)

India
  Affiliated East–West Press PVT Ltd
  G-1/16 Ansari Road
  New Delhi 110 002
  India
  (*Orders:* Tel. (11) 327–9113
           Fax (11) 326–0538)

Japan
  Kanda Book Trading Co.
  Tanikawa Building
  3-2 Kanda Surugadai
  Chiyoda-Ku
  Tokyo 101
  Japan
  (*Orders*: Tel. (03) 3255-3497
           Fax (03) 3255-3495)

Contents

CONTENTS

Sponsors

The conference and foldout and colour printing in this volume have been supported by the following sponsors:

British Sedimentological Research Group
ARCO British Ltd
British Gas
BP Exploration Operating Company Ltd
Chevron UK Ltd
EE Caledonia
ESSO Exploration and Production
Hamilton Brothers Exploration and Production
Shell UK Exploration and Production
Ultramar Exploration Ltd
UNOCAL

Braided rivers: perspectives and problems

C. S. BRISTOW[1] & J. L. BEST[2]

[1] *Research School of Geological and Geophysical Sciences,*
Birkbeck College, Gower Street, London WC1E 6BT, UK
[2] *Department of Earth Sciences, The University, Leeds,*
West Yorkshire LS2 9JT, UK

Abstract: Progress towards a fuller understanding of the dynamics and deposits of braided rivers demands an interdisciplinary approach to a host of unresolved problems. Although many advances have been made within recent years in interpreting the mechanics of flow, transport of sediment and sedimentary architecture of braided rivers many key issues remain to be addressed. In particular, several areas demand attention: the mechanisms of braid bar initiation; confluence–diffluence dynamics, the nature of sedimentary facies over a range of grain sizes and the influence of flow stage and aggradational regime upon the depositional architecture over a range of channel scales. This paper focuses upon these issues and highlights several areas of fruitful future interdisciplinary collaboration.

Braided rivers form important topics of study for many scientists and one of the primary aims of this volume is to bring together work from many disciplines in an integrated approach to braided rivers. For the geomorphologist braided fluvial systems are abundant within upland and pro-glacial settings and are agents of considerable erosion and sediment transport. For engineers the high rates of sediment transport, deposition and erosion combined with frequent channel shifting and rapid bank erosion may pose considerable design problems both to within-channel structures, such as bridge piers (e.g. Mosley 1982a; Sutherland 1986) and braidplain edge constructions such as roads and railways Finally, for the geologist braided rivers form important agents of deposition that have been responsible for the accumulation of many sedimentary sequences that form valuable aquifers, hydrocarbon reservoirs and sites for heavy mineral accumulation. Because of these abundant and diverse applications, knowledge of the mechanics and deposits of braided rivers is vital within many areas and yet, when compared to the wealth of literature upon meandering systems, they have been comparatively under-studied. This may, in part, be due to the difficulty of measuring flow, sediment transport and morphology in the rapidly shifting braided river environment. Future progress in understanding the mechanics and morphology of braided rivers demands interdisciplinary collaboration and calls for a more integrated approach across the sciences than may have been present until comparatively recently. This paper highlights some specific areas upon which our knowledge of

braided rivers may be fruitfully extended by adopting such an interdisciplinary scope.

Zones of flow convergence and divergence

Braided rivers are characterized by 'having a number of alluvial channels with bars and islands between meeting and dividing again, and presenting from the air the intertwining effect of a braid' (Lane 1957). The division and joining of channels are essential features of braided rivers and, whilst the bars within these rivers have received attention from both geomorphologists and sedimentologists, the areas of flow convergence and divergence have not been incorporated into braided river depositional models. The flow dynamics and morphology of channel confluences have been studied by several researchers (e.g. Mosley 1976, 1982a; Best 1986, 1987, 1988; Best & Roy 1991; Roy & Roy 1988; Roy & Bergeron 1990; Roy et al. 1988), and recent attention has highlighted the abundant confluences within braided rivers (Ashmore 1982; Ashmore & Parker 1983; Klaassen & Vermeer 1988). However, the link between flow convergence and the downstream division of flow has been neglected, despite the fact that this transition is the area which may be of fundamental importance to the development of braid bars (e.g. Ashmore 1991; Ashworth et al. 1992). Although some depositional models of braided rivers are beginning to recognise and incorporate confluence scour and fill (Cowan 1991; Bristow et al. 1993; Bridge this volume; Huggenberger this volume; Seigenthaler & Huggenberger this volume), areas of flow divergence

From Best, J. L. & Bristow, C. S. (eds), 1993, *Braided Rivers*, Geological Society
Special Publication No. 75, pp. 1–11.

1

are less well understood and ignored in these models. In general, flow divergence is associated with flow deceleration and sediment deposition and, once deposition has been initiated, the sediment accumulation is likely to promote further flow division, deposition and bar formation. Divergent flow may also impinge on the bank at an increased angle leading to bank erosion, channel widening and a local increase in available sediment, all of which are likely to lead to the development of a new braid bar (Carson 1984; Thorne et al. this volume). The deposits of diffluence areas may therefore form the foundations of braid bars but there are no known descriptions of these deposits and their internal structure. It is possible that some sedimentation may occur by vertical or even upstream accretion in the diffluence areas in braided rivers (Ashmore this volume) and these must be manifested within the sedimentary record. Bed shear stress has been shown to increase in shallow flows over bar tops (Cheetham 1979) where a coarse bed armour may form. In coarse-grained braided rivers the bar heads may be characterized by coarse-grained sediments that are imbricated or laminated (Bluck 1979). There is a clear need for both an understanding of the fluid dynamics of the diffluence zone and how this may influence braid bar initiation and internal structure.

The influence of flow stage

The planform appearance of braided rivers can change radically with flow stage (see fig. 2 in Thorne et al. this volume). Indeed some authors (Doeglas 1962; Miall 1977) have proposed that fluctuations in discharge are a pre-requisite for braiding although this may often be discounted as has been demonstrated by the modelling of gravel-bed braided planforms in constant discharge scaled flume experiments (e.g. Ashmore 1982, 1991). Bluck (1979) suggests that bars may disappear at high flow stages, reforming as discharge falls, and similar observations have been reported by Smith (1974), Carson (1984) and Gupta & Dutt (1989). This may imply that some braided rivers act as single channels at bankfull stage and only adopt a characteristic braided pattern on the falling stage. However, these observations appear to be fairly unusual and most braided rivers retain their bars at both high and low flow stage (Krigstrom 1962; Coleman 1969; Smith 1970; Cant & Walker 1978; Collinson 1970; Church & Jones 1982; Bridge et al. 1986; Bristow 1987a). Where bars exist for periods of time in excess of a single flood event they will experience a complex history of

erosional and depositional modification related to changes in stage. At higher flow stages when the largest volumes of sediment are transported, the channels are often scoured, bars may be reduced in height or in some cases completely eroded. However, during falling stage maximum deposition occurs as discharge and flow competence are reduced. Channel beds aggrade, the high stage bedforms may be modified and new bars may be formed or enlarged as sediment is deposited. As discharge continues to fall, bars may become emergent and dissected by low stage channels. Additionally, the nature of the falling limb recession (rate and length of recession) will be important not only in the reworking of higher stage sediments, but also in the deposition and spatial distribution of the finer grained sediments (silts and clays) which may constitute discontinuous permeability barriers within braided alluvium. Classification of emergent areas based on their low stage appearance may be deceptive and care needs to be taken in determining which areas are bars, scaling with channel width, and those which are partially dissected bars or stranded collections of bars (Church & Jones 1982; Bridge 1985). Little data exists for the comparison of bar and channel morphology at different flow stages (but see Mosley 1982b) and this is an area in which controlled and correctly scaled flume models combined with field studies may contribute greatly to our understanding.

Channel hierarchies

The presence of a hierarchy of channels within braided rivers was first suggested by Williams & Rust (1969), who described three orders of channel in addition to a series of levels within the river which represented active and inactive parts of the channel system. These orders and levels of bar deposit may also be adjusted to the dominant discharge of the alluvial system (see Thorne et al. this volume). In the scheme proposed by Williams & Rust (1969) the entire river and active channels were termed the 'composite stream channel' and the 'stream channel' respectively adding two additional levels to the hierarchy. This system was modified by Bristow (1987a) to a three fold hierarchy and Bridge (this volume) suggests additional modifications to this view. If one accepts that the river can operate as a single entity with channels within it and that there may be different scales of channels which depend upon total discharge and discharge fluctuations, then a threefold hierarchy of channels is required. The first order comprises the whole river (see fig. 2 of Thorne *et al.* this volume, for an image of the Brahmaputra River in full flood). Second order channels are the dominant channels within the river whilst third order channels are primarily low stage features which modify the bars deposited by the second order channels. Lower order channels may also exist which modify the third order bars. One implication of viewing braided rivers as hierarchical systems is that individual ancient braided river sandstones should also show a hierarchy of channel dimensions, whereas stacking of a single channel river is more likely to produce similar sized sandbodies. The presence of different magnitude channels within a single sandbody may therefore be an indication of braiding. However, caution is required for, if the third order channels are dependent on stage changes, then the presence of several scales of channel could be due primarily to changes in stage. Therefore, a hierarchy of channel sandbody sizes is not an *a priori* indicator of a braided river but is a feature most likely to occur in braided rivers with fluctuating discharges.

Grainsize influences upon braiding

Within the geological and geomorphological literature there has been a long held distinction between gravel-bed braided rivers and sand-bed braided rivers. However, many natural gravel bed rivers include those with bedloads of sand, granule, pebble, cobble and even boulder grade material while fine-grained sand-bed braided rivers are held to contain less than 25% gravel (Bluck 1979). It is rare for a river to have only one type of bed material, and most rivers have a range of bed and bank material types. Although some small-scale alluvial bedforms show a clear grain size controlled stability (e.g. ripples, lower stage plane beds, particle clusters) many larger scale bar forms and the braided channel pattern appear similar in rivers of widely differing grain size. There has been little quantitative work comparing the planform characteristics of gravel and sand-bed braided rivers even though their apparent similarities may suggest important common processes (Fig. 1). Comparison of confluence scour in the sand-bed Brahmaputra River, for example, reveals similar relationships between confluence angle and scour depth to those found in gravel-bed rivers (Klaassen & Vermeer 1988). In a recent review of the differences between gravel and sand-bed rivers Simons & Simons (1987) concluded that 'gravel-bed reaches of a river system exhibit totally different morphological characteristics and in general, they will be less responsive to modest

changes in discharge and discharge duration than a sand-bed river'. While a clear distinction may be required when calculating sediment transport, there appears to be more morphologic similarity between sand and gravel bed rivers than differences between them. The depositional styles of gravel and sand bed braided rivers will directly affect the facies models that must be used to interpret ancient deposits. Investigation of the correlation between the classic sand-bed braided river depositional models (e.g. Cant & Walker 1978; Collinson 1970) with those derived for gravel-bed braided alluvium (e.g. Bluck 1979; Steel & Thompson 1983; Ramos & Sopena 1983; Ramos *et al.* 1986; Smith 1990) remains a high priority, both in terms of evolving realistic facies interpretation and in the feedback these schemes may provide into understanding the similarities and differences in depositional process between these rivers.

Braided channel morphology and scale

Studies of braided channel dynamics and deposits have ranged across at least five orders of channel size from small laboratory models (scaled field dimensions *c.* 2–20 m channel width), to natural braidplains several kilometres in width (e.g. Ashworth *et al.* 1992; Warburton *et al.* this volume) to the largest alluvial rivers such as the Brahmaputra (Coleman 1969; Bristow 1987*a*; Thorne *et al.* this volume) which have braidplain widths of up to 20 km, individual channel widths of several kilometres and maximum scour depths of up to 50 m. The issue of scaling depositional form and formative process across this range of braided channel sizes is rarely addressed yet is central when applying results and models from one channel size to a system of a completely different magnitude. Superficial examination (Fig. 1) often reveals a gross similarity to the appearance of braided systems of widely differing size, yet data is required, both on the planform and cross-sectional characteristics, to substantiate or refute this apparent similarity. The self-similarity of form across a range of scales or the scale dependent nature of the geometry of braided rivers has several fundamental applications. First, self-similarity across scales of braiding may shed light upon the processes inherent in causing braiding, bar formation and growth. Second, when applying models of braided alluvial architecture deduced from one system to another of a completely different size (for instance, in braided alluvial reservoir heterogeneity models) it is essential to know

(a)

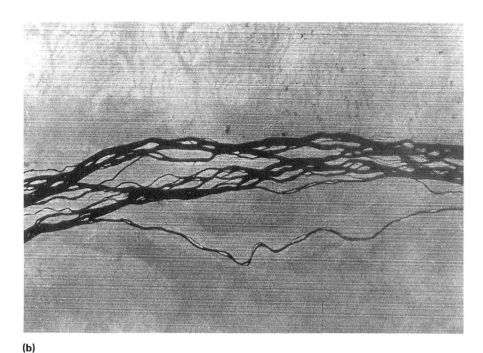

(b)

Fig. 1. Two scales of braided river. (**a**) Sunwapta River, Alberta, Canada with a one kilometre wide braidplain, 20–50 m wide channels and predominantly gravel bedload. Flow is from left to right. (**b**) The Congo (Zaire) River with a braidplain width of approximately 8 km and a sand bed. Flow is from right to left.

which geometrical attributes are scale invariant or scale dependent. Data on the morphology of the largest braided rivers is now becoming both more available and of sufficient resolution (e.g. the Flood Action Plan Studies upon the Brahmaputra, see Thorne *et al.* this volume) to enable this task to be tackled. The links between scale dependence and flow process will then pose the next research goal.

Facies models of braided alluvium

The vertical profile models of braided alluvium presented by Miall (1977, 1978) were based on the deposits of modern braided rivers and were therefore suitable models for the interpretation of ancient braided river deposits, given the proviso that these models only encompassed a certain range and type of depositional setting. However, the vertical profile is not unique and Jackson (1978) and Bridge (1985) have pointed out the convergence of coarse-grained braided river profiles and coarse-grained meandering river models. This realization led to the development of architectural analysis (Allen 1983) where lateral profiles are used to assess the geometry of deposits and reconstruct the original depositional channel form. This

approach became modified by Miall (1985) into architectural element analysis which switched the emphasis from the use of geometry as a primary discriminant to consideration of a hierarchy of bounding surfaces and the composition of depositional elements. The use of architectural element analysis is ably demonstrated by Miall (this volume) although the mechanics of the approach have been criticised by Bridge (in press).

Braided rivers may be envisaged as a series of channel segments which divide and rejoin around bars in a regular or repeatable pattern. The divisions, channel bends and confluences have characteristic forms and fluid dynamics which can be used to construct an improved model of braided river sedimentation. The evidence comes from both theoretical models of braid evolution where braided channels may evolve from straight channels with alternate bars (Bridge 1985), field studies of channel migration in modern rivers (Bristow 1987a) and statistical analysis of braiding parameters. Field studies of the low sinuosity braided Calamus River show that the channels on either side of a braid bar have flow characteristics similar to two curved channel segments (Bridge *et al.* 1986). From these observations it is predicted that braid bars,

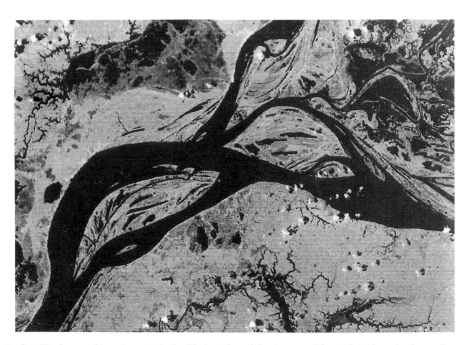

Fig. 2. Satellite image of bars in part of a braided section of the Amazon River. Note the paired accretion topography on the braid bars illustrating that braid bars may accrete laterally on both sides. Braidplain is approximately 10 km wide.

as well as migrating both downstream and across channel, may also accrete laterally in a manner similar to point bars in meandering rivers (Bridge this volume). This is confirmed by studies of accretion patterns in recent braided river deposits (Bristow 1987a) and the presence of paired accretion topography can be clearly seen in the satellite images of braided rivers such as parts of the Amazon River (Fig. 2).

In scale models of gravel bed rivers Ashmore (1991) has shown that braiding can be accomplished in four ways: accumulation of a central bar, chute cut-off of point bars, conversion of transverse unit bars to mid-channel braid bars and dissection of multiple bars. Preliminary observations indicate that similar braiding processes may also operate in sand bed braided rivers. It may now be possible to adopt a new approach to the development of braided river depositional model where form is just as important as fabric. Furthermore, the processes and their morphological expression may be independent of scale (see above) and common to braided rivers with a range of grainsizes. As a result these morphological elements may be useful tools for the recognition and interpretation of ancient braided river deposits. Cartoons of morphological elements from common braiding processes are shown in Fig. 3. The relative pro-

portions of the morphological elements may be derived from models of this type or from studies of modern rivers. In the Brahmaputra River, Bristow (1987a) found that exposed new mid-channel bars comprised 13% of deposits by area over a six year period, while lateral accretion to the bank and mid-channel bars amounted to 49%, upstream and downstream accretion were 7.5% and 15.5% respectively and the remaining 15% was formed through channel abandonment. However, additional channel fill and confluence scour elements which are submerged at low flows are missing from this analysis and should be incorporated into more complete models (see below). It can be clearly seen that lateral accretion will be an important component of braided river deposition although as Bridge (this volume) points out there is a continuum between upstream, through lateral to downstream accretion which may be difficult to resolve at outcrop without measuring the orientation of the accretion surfaces relative to palaeoflow.

Aggradation and preservation

A particular weakness of existing braided river facies models arises because they are largely based on sections measured from exposed bars

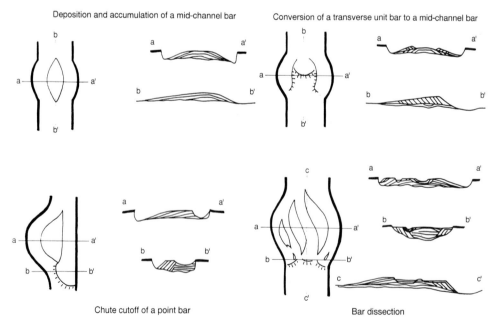

Fig. 3. Catoons of depositional morphology based on braiding processes derived from scale models of gravel bed braided rivers (Ashmore 1991) and observations of the Brahmaputra River :Bristow 1987b).

or river banks (Miall 1977, 1978; Williams & Rust 1969; Smith 1970; Cant & Walker 1978; Bristow this volume). It is possible to conjecture that bar top sequences should be preserved after avulsion or migration but in many cases the sandbody may be dominated by the deeper channel deposits as the upper, bar-top deposits are removed through subsequent erosion. Huggenberger (this volume) argues that low rates of aggradation will lead to the preferential preservation of the lower topographic (deeper) parts of a river. Studies in the Brahmaputra River (Klaassen & Vermeer 1988) indicate that the deepest natural scours occur at channel bends and confluences. Confluence scour and fill may therefore form an important element of the braided alluvium (e.g. see Huggenberger this volume, who describes junction deposits as a dominant depositional element of the Pleistocene Rhine gravels). Recent models of confluence sedimentation have been presented by Bristow *et al.* (1993) and are reviewed by Bridge (this volume). The scour associated with channel bends, nodal constrictions and obstacles should also not be ignored (Salter 1993).

It is also important to consider the short-term deposition rate as opposed to the long-term basin subsidence/aggradation rate in shaping what is preserved in the ancient deposit. Most alluvial sedimentary sequences represent long periods of non-deposition or erosion punctuated by rapid and short-lived depositional events. This is amply illustrated with reference to scour and fill at the Ganges–Brahmaputra confluence over a period of 12 years (Fig. 4) which shows periods of rapid incision and deposition at this site, with up to 9 m of deposition at the confluence occurring in one year. Hence, although we may calculate long-term basin aggradation/subsidence rates, it is the manifestation of the 'geologically instantaneous' processes (e.g. scour fill, bedform migration, anabranch avulsion) that will dominate the sedimentary fill of the channels. Bentham *et al.* (this volume) also highlight the importance of aggradation rate in determining the architecture of braided alluvial deposits and that it is a common misconception that braided alluvium does not contain appreciable quantities of fine grained sediment, this being dependent also upon the sediment supply, climate and tectonic regime. Preservation within braided rivers may be

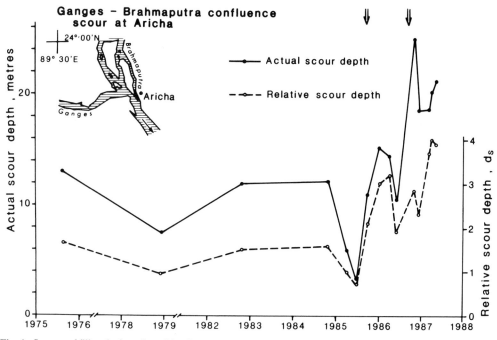

Fig. 4. Scour and fill at the junction of the Ganges and Brahmaputra rivers, Bangladesh. This plot, showing data collected over a 12 year period, shows the high rates of scour and fill present at this junction. Scour is given as an actual depth and as a relative depth, d_s, through division of the actual scour depth by the mean upstream channel depths. Double arrows indicate the approximate flood peaks in 1985 and 1986.

viewed as a function of the frequency of avulsion of the channel belt, the rate of lateral migration of the alluvial system and aggradation rate (Bridge & Leeder 1979). A schematic diagram of avulsion, migration and aggradation rate controls upon braided alluvial architecture (Fig. 5) illustrates that while the preservation of overbank and bar-top sediments increases with aggradation rate the nature of the channel deposits may not change appreciably. However, an increase in either the frequency of channel-belt avulsions (initiated either through major floods or tectonic events) or the rate of migration may radically alter the sandbody geometry, a feature revealed in alluvial simulation models (e.g. Bridge & Leeder 1979). Avulsion frequency appears to increase with high rates of sediment accumulation (Bridge & Leeder 1979), since this is most likely to lead to rapid establishment of local gradients favouring avulsion. The preservation of form may also be associated indirectly with a high rate of accretion produced under conditions of rapid aggradation which favour more frequent avulsion. Instantaneous avulsion of a river may result in complete form preservation. In reality this is an unlikely event and, through a combination of migration and aggradation, channel deposits will become reworked, superimposed and stacked to form multilateral and multistorey sandbodies. Multi-channel braided rivers are almost certain to form multilateral/multistorey sandbodies. Preservation style *within* the channel will be a function of the local rate of aggradation and the size and sequence of bedforms/scour surfaces that affect any particular spatial location.

Conclusions: the economic importance of braided rivers

Braided alluvial deposits form substantial hydrocarbon reservoirs (see Martin this volume), sites for the deposition and accumulation of heavy minerals (see Smith & Minter 1980; Slingerland & Smith 1986; Karpeta this volume) and important sand and gravel reserves. One central problem within all of these applications is an understanding of the internal heterogeneity of the braided alluvial architecture both in terms of sandbody connectivity, shale intercalations and the depositional controls upon subsequent diagenesis. Within all of these fields several topics demand urgent atten-

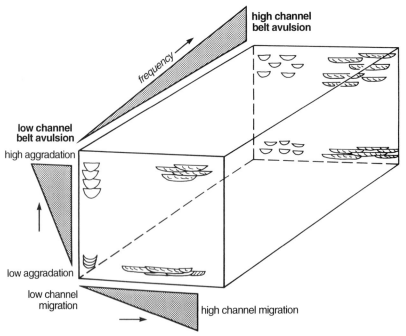

Fig. 5. A schematic diagram illustrating the preservation of braided river depositional morphology as a function of aggradation rate, lateral channel migration and channel-belt avulsion. The preservation of isolated channel sandbodies preserving morphology requires frequent avulsions as well as rapid aggradation.

tion in relating the depositional process to the preserved sediment. This is especially important for coarse-grained braided rivers where the recognition of depositional elements, especially in core, becomes far more problematical. Several key issues, which relate to some of the points raised previously, are evident.

(i) What depositional elements comprise braided alluvium and how is their relative abundance, three-dimensional geometry and spatial distribution influenced by both autocyclic (e.g. hydrograph type, local sediment transport) and allocyclic (e.g. aggradation rate, active tectonics) controls?

(ii) How does the depositional architecture of coarse and fine grained braided rivers differ? How widely is lateral accretion preserved in relation to downstream, upstream or vertical accretion?

(iii) Do the geometrical characteristics and sedimentary structures of braided alluvium show any scale dependence?

In addition to these more geologically related applications, braided rivers will continue to form zones of major threat to human life and settle-ment as well as posing regions of significant engineering complexity. The issues outlined above overlap directly with some of the pressing needs which can be highlighted for extension of our process knowledge base.

(i) What processes control the dispersal of sediment and bed/bank erosion at both channel confluences and diffluences?

(ii) What is the feedback between flow division, braiding, local sediment yield and channel shifting/bank erosion?

(iii) What controls the spatial and temporal variability of sediment transport at both the channel and braidplain scale?

(iv) What variables influence the depth and distribution of scour at key sites (bends, junctions, flow diversions)?

It is clear that progress towards possible solutions to these broad goals will only be achieved through interdisciplinary collaboration and the desire to cross traditional discipline boundaries in tackling these complex issues.

We would like to thank P. J. Ashworth, J. S. Bridge and T. Salter for the useful and stimulating conversations on some of the topics included in this paper which have helped shape our views on these issues.

References

ALLEN, J. R. L. 1983. Studies in fluviatile sedimentation: Bars, Bar-complexes and sandstone sheets (low sinuosity braided streams) in the Brownstones (L. Devonian), Welsh Borders. *Sedimentary Geology*, **33**, 237–293.

ASHMORE, P. E. 1982. Laboratory modelling of gravel braided stream morphology. *Earth Surface Processes*, **7**, 201–225.

—— 1991. How do gravel bed rivers braid? *Canadian Journal of Earth Sciences*, **28**, 326–341.

—— 1993. Anabranch confluence kinetics and sedimentation processes in gravel braided rivers. *This volume.*

—— & PARKER, G. 1983. Confluence scour in coarse braided streams. *Water Resources Research*, **19**, 392–402.

ASHWORTH, P. J., FERGUSON, R. & POWELL, M. 1992. Bedload transport and sorting in braided channels. *In*: BILLI, P., HEY, R. D., THORNE, C. R. & TACCONI, P. (eds) *Dynamics of Gravel Bed Rivers* Wiley and Sons, 497–513.

BENTHAM, P. A., TALLING, P. J. & BURBANK, D. W. 1993. Braided stream and flood-plain deposition in a rapidly aggrading basin: the Escanilla Formation, Spanish Pyrenees. *This volume.*

BEST, J. L. 1986. The morphology of river channel confluences. *Progress in Physical Geography*, **10**, 157–174.

—— 1987. Flow dynamics at river channel con-fluences: implications for sediment transport and bed morphology. *In*: THERIDGE, F. G., FLORES, R. M. & HARVEY, M. D. (eds) *Recent Developments in Fluvial Sedimentology*. Society of Economic Paleontologists and Mineralogists Special Publications, **39**, 27–35.

—— 1988. Sediment transport and bed morphology at river channel confluences. *Sedimentology*, **35**, 481–498.

—— & ROY, A. G. 1991. Mixing-layer distortion at the confluence of channels of different depth. *Nature*, **350**, 6317, 411–413.

BLUCK, B. J. 1979. Structure of coarse grained braided alluvium. *Transactions of the Royal Society of Edinburgh*, **70**, 29–46.

BRIDGE, J. S. 1985. Palaeochannel patterns inferred from alluvial deposits: a critical evaluation. *Journal of Sedimentary Petrology*, **55**, 579–589.

—— 1993. The interaction between channel geometry, water flow, sediment transport, erosion and deposition in braided rivers. *This volume.*

—— in press. Description and interpretation of fluvial deposits: a critical perspective. *Sedimentology.*

—— & LEEDER, M. R. 1979. A simulation model of alluvial stratigraphy. *Sedimentology*, **26**, 617–644.

——, SMITH, N. D., TRENT, F., GABEL, S. L. & BERN-STEIN, P. 1986. Sedimentology and morphology of a low-sinuosity river: Calamus River, Nebraska Sand Hills. *Sedimentology*, **33**, 851–870.

BRISTOW, C. S. 1987a. Brahmaputra River: Channel migration and deposition. *In*: ETHRIDGE, F. G., FLORES, R. M. & HARVEY, M. D. (eds) *Recent Developments in Fluvial Sedimentology*. Society of Economic Paleontologists and Mineralogists Special Publications, **39**, 63–74.

—— 1987b. *Sedimentology of large braided rivers ancient and modern*. PhD thesis, University of Leeds.

—— 1993. Sedimentary structures exposed in bar tops in the Brahmaputra River, Bangladesh. *This volume*.

——, BEST, J. L. & ROY, A. G. 1993. Morphology and facies models of channel confluences. *In*: PUIGDEFABREGAS & TOMAS (eds) *Alluvial Sedimentation*. Special Publications of the International Association of Sedimentologists, **17**, 91–100.

CANT, D. J. & WALKER, R. G. 1978. Fluvial processes and facies sequences in the sandy braided South Saskatchewan River, Canada. *Sedimentology*, **25**, 625–648.

CARSON, M. A. 1984. Observations on the meandering-braided transition, the Canterbury plains, New Zealand, part 1. *New Zealand Geographer*, **40**, 12–17.

CHEETHAM, G. H. 1979. Flow competence in relation to channel form and braiding. *Geological Society of America Bulletin*, **90**, 877–886.

CHURCH, M. & JONES, D. 1982. Channel bars in gravel bed rivers. *In*: HEY, R. D., BATHURST, J. C. & THORNE, C. R. (eds) *Gravel-bed Rivers*. Wiley, Chichester, 291–338.

COLEMAN, J. M. 1969. Brahmaputra River channel processes and sedimentation. *Sedimentary Geology*, **3**, 129–239.

COLLINSON, J. D. 1970. Bedforms in the Tana River, Norway. *Geografiska Annaler*, **52**, 31–56.

COWAN, E. J. 1991. The large scale architecture of the fluvial Westwater Canyon Member, Morrison Formation (Jurassic) San Juan Basin, New Mexico. *In*: MIALL, A. D. & TYLER, N. (eds) *The three-dimensional facies architecture of terrigenous clastic sediments, and its implications for hydrocarbon discovery and recovery*. Society of Economic Paleontologists and Mineralogists Concepts in Sedimentology and Paleontology, **3**, 80–93.

DOEGLAS, D. J. 1962. The structure of sedimentary deposits of braided rivers. *Sedimentology*, **1**, 167–190.

GUPTA, A. & DUTT, A. 1989. The Auranga: description of a tropical monsoon river. *Zeischrift für Geomorphologie*, **33**, 73–92.

HUGGENBERGER, P. 1993. Radar facies: Recognition of facies patterns and heterogeneities within Pleistocene Rhine gravels, NE Switzerland. *This volume*.

JACKSON, R. G. 1978. Preliminary evaluation of lithofacies models for meandering alluvial streams. *In*: MIALL, A. D. (ed.) *Fluvial Sedimentology*.

Canadian Society of Petroleum Geologists, Memoirs, **5**, 543–576.

KARPETA, W. P. 1993. Sedimentology and gravel bar morphology in an Archean braided river sequence: The Witpan Conglomerate Member (Witwatersrand Supergroup) in the Welkom Goldfield, South Africa. *This volume*.

KLAASSEN, G. J. & VERMEER, K. 1988. Confluence scour in large braided rivers with fine bed material. *International Conference on Fluvial Hydraulics*, Budapest.

KRIGSTROM, A. 1962. Geomorphological studies of sandur plains and their braided rivers in Iceland. *Geografiska Annaler*, **44**, 328–346.

LANE, E. W. 1957. *A study of the shape of channels formed by natural streams flowing in erodable material*. M.R.D. Sediment Series 9, United States Army Engineering Division, Missouri River, Corps Engineers, Omaha, Nebraska.

MARTIN, J. 1993. Braided fluvial hydrocarbon reservoirs: the petroleum engineer's perspective. *This volume*.

MIALL, A. D. 1977. A review of the braided stream depositional environment. *Earth Science Reviews*, **13**, 1–62.

—— 1978. Lithofacies types and vertical profile models in braided rivers: a summary. *In*: MIALL, A. D. (ed.) *Fluvial Sedimentology*. Canadian Society of Petroleum Geologists, Memoirs, **5**, 605–625.

—— 1985. Architectural-element analysis: a new method of facies analysis applied to fluvial deposits. *Earth Science Reviews*, **22**, 261–308.

—— 1993. The architecture of fluvial–deltaic sequences in the Upper Mesaverde Group (Upper Cretaceous), Book Cliffs, Utah. *This volume*.

MOSLEY, M. P. 1976. An experimental study of channel confluences. *Journal of Geology*, **84**, 535–562.

—— 1982a. Scour depths in branch channel confluences, Oahu River, Otago, New Zealand. *Proceedings of the New Zealand Society of Civil Engineers*, **9**, 17–24.

—— 1982b. Analysis of the effect of changing discharge on channel morphology and instream uses in a braided river, Ohau River, New Zealand. *Water Resources Research*, **18**, 800–812.

RAMOS, A. & SOPENA, A. 1983. Gravel bars in low sinuosity streams (Permian and Triassic, central Spain). *In*: COLLINSON, J. & LEWIN, J. (eds) *Modern and Ancient Fluvial Systems*. Special Publications of the International Association of Sedimentologists, **6**, 301–313.

——, —— & PEREZ-ARLUCEA, M. 1986. Evolution of Buntsandtein fluvial sedimentation in the northwest Iberian ranges (Central Spain). *Journal of Sedimentary Petrology*, **56**, 862–875.

ROY, A. G. & BERGERON, N. 1990. Flow and particle paths at a natural river confluence with coarse bed material. *Geomorphology*, **3**, 99–112.

—— & ROY, R. 1988. Changes in channel size at river confluences with coarse bed material. *Earth Surface Processes and Landforms*, **13**, 77–84.

——, —— & BERGERON, N. 1988. Hydraulic geometry and changes in flow velocity at a river confluence with coarse bed material. *Earth Surface Processes and Landforms*, **13**, 583–598.

SALTER, T. 1993. Fluvial scour and incision: models for their influence on the development of realistic reservoir geometries. *In*: NORTH, C. P. & PROSSER, D. J. (eds) *Characterization of Fluvial and Aeolian Reservoirs*, Geological Society of London Special Publications, **73**, 33–52.

SIEGENTHALER, C. & HUGGENBERGER, P. 1993. Pleistocene Rhine gravel: deposits of a braided river system with dominant pool preservation. *This volume*.

SIMONS, D. B. & SIMONS, R. K. 1987. Differences between gravel- and sand-bed rivers. *In*: THORNE, C. R., BATHURST, J. C. & HEY, R. D. (eds) *Gravel bed rivers*. John Wiley & Sons Ltd, 3–15.

SLINGERLAND, R. L. & SMITH, N. D. 1986. Occurence and formation of waterlaid placers. *Annual Reviews in Earth and Planetary Sciences*, **14**, 113–147.

SMITH, N. D. 1970. The braided stream depositional environment: comparison of the Platte River with some Silurian clastic rocks, North Central Appalachians. *Geological Society of America Bulletin*, **81**, 2993–3014.

—— 1974. Sedimentology and bar formation in the upper Kicking Horse River, a braided outwash stream. *Journal of Geology*, **82**, 205–224.

—— & MINTER, W. E. L. 1980. Sedimentological controls of gold and uranium in two Witwatersrand paleoplacers. *Economic Geology*, **66**, 114–150.

SMITH, S. A. 1990. The sedimentology and accretionary styles of an acient gravel bed stream: the Budleigh Salterton Pebble beds (Lower Triassic), southwest England. *Sedimentary Geology*, **67**, 199–219.

STEEL, R. J. & THOMPSON, D. J. 1983. Structures and textures in Triassic braided stream conglomerates ('Bunter' Pebble Beds) in the Sherwood Sandstone Group, North Staffordshire, England. *Sedimentology*, **30**, 341–368.

SUTHERLAND, A. J. 1986. Scouring at channel confluences. *In*: *Proceedings of the 9th Australasian Fluid Mechanics Conference, Auckland, 8–12 December 1986*, 260–263.

THORNE, C. R., RUSSELL, A. P. G. & ALAM, M. K. 1993. Planform pattern and channel evolution of the Brahmaputra River, Bangladesh. *This volume*.

WARBURTON, J., DAVIES, T. R. H. & MANDL, M. G. 1993. A meso-scale investigation of channel change and floodplain characteristics in an upland braided gravel-bed river, New Zealand. *This volume*.

WILLIAMS, P. F. & RUST, B. R. 1969. The sedimentology of a braided river. *Journal of Sedimentary Petrology*, **39**, 649–679.

The interaction between channel geometry, water flow, sediment transport and deposition in braided rivers

JOHN S. BRIDGE

*Department of Geological Sciences, State University of New York,
Binghamton, New York, 13902-6000, U.S.A.*

Abstract: Models of braided-river deposition must be detailed, fully 3D, and preferably quantitative to be of use in understanding and predicting the nature of ancient deposits. In order to construct and validate adequate predictive models it is necessary to have information on: (1) variation and interaction of channel geometry, water flow and sediment transport in time and space in modern channel belts, as these control erosion and deposition, the formation and migration of channels and bars, and channel abandonment and filling; (2) 3D variation of bed geometry, texture, sedimentary structures and paleocurrents throughout modern channel-belt deposits, including the age and spatial arrangement of preserved parts of bars and channel fills; (3) long-term (more than hundreds of years) trends in channel and floodplain geometry, flow and sedimentary processes in order to understand channel-belt movements such as avulsions, and the spatial arrangement of channel-belt deposits relative to overbank deposits. Such information is rare because: (1) it is difficult to study modern braided-river geometry, flow and sedimentary processes throughout a range of the all-important high discharges; (2) detailed reconstructions of braided channel and bar geometry and movement are only available for the past half-century and cannot readily be linked to causative mechanisms; (3) 3D documentation of modern deposits below the water table (especially large scale features like lateral-accretion bedding) requires extensive coring and dating of the deposits, and geophysical profiling. As a result of this lack of information, and because of the quality of analysis and presentation of the information available, existing braided-river facies models are virtually useless as interpretive and predictive tools. The nature of the information available is critically reviewed. Using information from recent detailed field and laboratory studies of the geometry, flow and sedimentary processes in braided rivers of simple geometry, in single river bends, in channel confluences, and using some theoretical reasoning, it has been possible to construct fully 3D qualitative and quantitative models of braided river deposits. These models can be used to provide sophisticated quantitative interpretations of palaeochannel geometry, hydraulics and migration, as illustrated by comparison with some particularly well described examples of ancient braided river deposits.

Channel geometry, water flow and sediment transport in braided rivers interact and vary in time and space, resulting in erosion and deposition, growth and migration of bars, and the formation, migration and filling of channel segments. An understanding of this interaction is important in modern environmental and engineering problems such as water supply and flood risk evaluation, dispersion of pollutants, disturbance of freshwater wildlife habitats, sedimentation in navigated channels and reservoirs, bank erosion and channel migration, construction of artificial channels, bridge piers, pipeline crossings, and stabilized banks, and sediment dredging operations.

A detailed knowledge of modern river deposits and their relationship to formative flow and sedimentary processes is critical for interpretation of ancient river deposits and predicting their subsurface geometry and facies. Braided river deposits are commonly associated with important resources such as water, oil, gas, coal, gold, sand and gravel. Fluvial reservoirs containing water, oil and gas are typically heterogeneous and definition of porosity and permeability variations requires, amongst other things, detailed and accurate facies models at a variety of scales. A particularly pressing concern is the widespread pollution of aquifers in Pleistocene braided river outwash deposits which blanket large areas of the northern hemisphere.

Depositional models of river channels abound in the sedimentological literature. Although they appear to be 3D, in reality the deposits are normally only represented in one or two vertical cuts through the channel belt; parallel and normal to the channel direction. The information shown in these 2D cuts lacks critical detail of the spatial variation of bed thickness and orientation, grain size, internal structures, paleo-

From Best, J. L. & Bristow, C. S. (eds), 1993, *Braided Rivers*, Geological Society Special Publication No. **75**, pp. 13–71.

13

currents, biological aspects and all the possible varieties of these features (Jackson 1978; Bridge 1985). The nature of preservation of super-imposed bars and channel fills in modern channel belts is virtually unknown. Further-more, the models are purely qualitative, and most do not contain even approximate scales. In short, existing facies models are of little use in interpreting ancient channel deposits to any reasonable degree of detail, and certainly cannot be used to predict spatial variations in porosity and permeability. This state of affairs is partly based on the method of analysis and presenta-tion of the primary data available, but is mainly based on the lack of primary data from modern rivers.

It is common practice in building fluvial facies models to combine observations of grain sizes and bedforms on channel-bar surfaces with reconstructed modes of channel migration to predict the distribution of grain sizes and sedimentary structures in 1D or 2D vertical sections (e.g. Bluck 1971; Jackson 1976a; and many others). In most published studies, grain sizes and bedforms on bar surfaces are observed at relatively low flow stages (when they can be seen), whereas it is commonly not known what is present at relatively high flow stages when observation is much more difficult. But it is at these high flow stages when most erosional and depositional activity (including channel migration) takes place, and is most difficult to document. Understandably, studies of the inter-action between flow, sediment transport and channel geometry in natural rivers over a range of high discharges are very rare. Modes and rates of channel and bar migration can be documented by direct observation for the duration of a field study, and for up to hundreds of years using maps, aerial photographs and radiocarbon dating of older surface deposits. However, the time resolution of these techniques decreases with increasing age. Long-term, large scale channel-belt movements like avulsion remain poorly known. Laboratory experiments have provided useful information about the nature and short-term evolution of braided rivers but direct application of this information to natural rivers must be treated with caution in view of simplified experimental conditions and scaling considerations (Ashmore 1982, 1991b).

Direct observations of sediment deposits in most river studies come from shallow trenches and cut-bank exposures, by necessity above the water table. Indeed, Bluck (1971, 1974, 1976, 1979) has divided river channel deposits into those that are above the low water table and can be observed (supraplatform) and those below

that cannot (platform). In perennial rivers, trenches and cut-bank exposures represent a very limited sample of channel-belt deposits. Although it is possible to expose more deposits in ephemeral streams, there have been no studies (for obvious environmental reasons) in which a channel belt has been completely dis-sected. Long cores through channel belt deposits are not available in most studies, and where available are not normally spaced closely enough. Critical information that is usually lacking is the age of the deposits and direct documentation of large-scale bedding surfaces (e.g. 'lateral-accretion' surfaces, basal erosion surfaces). Thus, facies models based on bed-surface sedimentary features, presumed modes of channel migration and limited exposure of deposits, are largely hypothetical.

The inadequate documentation of modern river deposits probably does not come as a great surprise to those who try to interpret ancient river deposits using modern analogues. Bridge (1985) indicated that it is not particularly easy to distinguish deposits of ancient single- and multi-channel sinuous rivers unless large-scale bedding features associated with channel bars and fills can be documented and understood. It is precisely this information which is lacking from modern river deposits. However, the dis-tinction between different ancient-channel patterns is critical for predicting the geometries and sedimentary characteristics of fluvial sand-stone bodies, and for quantitative reconstruc-tion of paleochannel geometry and hydraulics. Willis (1989) has clearly demonstrated that in order to understand any arbitrarily-oriented vertical section through a channel-bar deposit it is necessary to understand the distribution of grain size and bedforms over the whole surface of the bar during deposition, the mode and rate of bar migration, and the orientation of the cross-section relative to the direction of the channel and its migration. As an addendum to this, to fully understand the stacking and preservability of different bars and channel fills in channel belts, it is necessary to know more about the nature of channel migration (e.g. braided-channel diversions, meander cut-off, channel filling) in relation to net channel-belt aggradation.

Thus, in order to construct and validate adequate predictive models of channel-belt deposits it is necessary to have *all* of the follow-ing information for different channel-pattern types: (1) variation of flow, sediment transport and bed geometry in space and time, in order to understand and predict erosion and deposition associated with channel bars and fills; (2)

historic data on modes and rates of bank erosion, channel-bar migration, channel cutting and abandoned-channel filling; (3) 3D variation of bed geometry, grainsize, sedimentary structures, and palaeocurrents throughout the channel belt deposits, including the age and spatial arrangement of preserved bars and channel fills. Such data should preferably be quantitative, so that they can be incorporated into generalized mathematical models.

This paper is a review of current knowledge of the origin, geometry, flow, sediment transport, erosion and deposition of modern braided rivers, as gleaned from studies of modern rivers, laboratory experiments and theory. This information will be used to construct both qualitative and quantitative, 3D depositional models for braided rivers, and the use of such models in interpreting ancient braided river deposits is illustrated. The review will be limited to consideration of braided rivers at the scale of several bars over time periods of up to 10^2 years. Space and time limitations prohibit consideration of along-valley variations in braided rivers, associated floodplains or fans, long term ($<10^2$ years) processes associated with channel-belt avulsions, tectonism and climate change.

Definition and origin of braiding in rivers

Definition of braiding

The term 'braided river' denotes a channel pattern as seen in plan view. Leopold & Wolman (1957) defined a braided river as 'one which flows in two or more anastomosing channels around alluvial islands', whereas Lane (1957) stated 'a braided stream is characterized by having a number of alluvial channels with bars or islands between meeting and dividing again, and presenting from the air the intertwining effect of a braid'. Lane also used the term 'multiple-channel stream' to include both braided streams as defined above and anastomosing distributaries on deltas and alluvial fans (see also Chitale 1970). Brice (1964, 1984) also recognized the importance of defining the size of islands relative to channel width, and the difference between within-channel islands and those formed by river diversions. Schumm (1977) defined braided channels as single-channel bedload rivers which at low water have islands of sediment or relatively permanent vegetated islands, in contrast to multiple channel rivers (anastomosing or distributive) in which each branch may have its own individual pattern. The differences among these definitions raise a number of issues that require resolution. In particular: (1) the differ-

ence between 'bars' and 'islands' must be defined; (2) the appearance of bars or islands depends on flow stage; (3) there are different types of channel splitting, and the difference between the terms 'braided' and 'anastomosing' requires clarification; (4) the nature of the sediment load must be considered. Resolution of these issues will appear as it becomes known how the various channel patterns develop and why.

Formation of the continuum of channel patterns

Channel patterns and their associated flow and sedimentary processes form part of a continuum. This has been demonstrated in experimental studies of natural and laboratory channels (e.g. Leopold & Wolman 1957; Ackers & Charlton 1971; Schumm and Khan 1972; Ikeda 1973, 1975; Ashmore 1982, 1991b) and with theoretical models (e.g. Engelund & Skovgaard 1973; Parker 1976; Fredsoe 1978; Hayashi & Ozaki 1980; Blondeaux & Seminara 1985; Fukuoka 1989). As an illustration of this continuum, Fig. 1 shows how common types of channel pattern can evolve from a straight, erodible alluvial channel at constant water discharge, and from each other (see also Bridge 1985).

In the initial stages, the bed evolves towards a statistically constant geometry composed of single or multiple rows of bedwaves which are in equilibrium with the steady hydraulic and sediment transport conditions. In plan view, the water flow associated with these bedwaves follows a sinuous path, with a wavelength equivalent to that of the bedwaves in a particular row, and with a width equivalent to a bedwave width. Thus multiple rows of bedwaves have multiple rows of sinuous flow paths. Bedwave lengths are proportional to their widths (and thus to the widths of the sinuous flow paths), and their heights are comparable to flow depth. They are generally asymmetrical in alongstream cross section, may have an avalanche face on the downstream side, and generally migrate in the downstream direction.

The American Society of Civil Engineers Task Force on Bed Forms (1966) defined 'bedforms having lengths of the same order as channel width or greater, and heights comparable to the mean depth of the generating flow' as bars. The bedwaves under discussion are referred to as alternate bars because, within a given row, they occur on alternating sides of the channel with progression downstream. They are macroforms

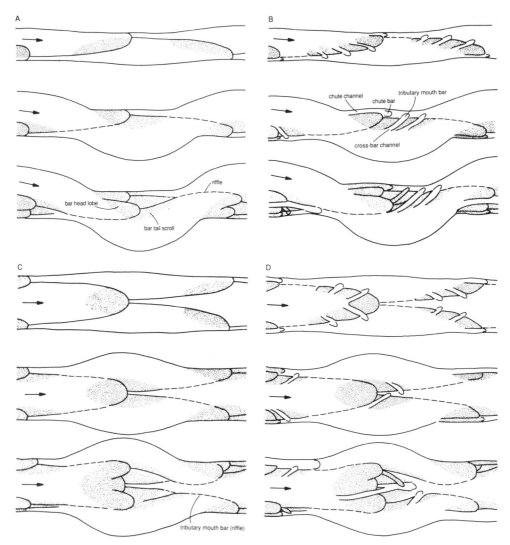

Fig. 1. Idealized evolution of channel patterns from straight alluvial channels resulting from bank erosion and channel widening. Deposition on evolving point or braid bars is shown as episodic accretion of unit bars (e.g. bar head lobes and bar tail scrolls), although such discrete features are not always present. The crestlines of unit bars (represented by solid or dashed lines) may or may not be associated with angle-of-repose avalanche faces. Arrows represent flow direction and stippled areas are topographic highs. (**A**) Single-row alternate bars (top) evolving into point bars (bottom). (**B**) As for (A) but with cross-bar channels and associated channel-mouth bars which may form at constant 'channel forming' discharge, or during falling stage. (**C**) Double-row alternate bars evolving into braid bars and point (side) bars. (**D**) As for (C) but with cross-bar channels and channel-mouth bars. See Bridge (1985) for models of the evolution of braid bars from multiple rows of alternate bars. This figure is based on numerous laboratory experiments and studies of rivers (e.g. Kinosita 1957, 1961; Krigström 1962; Stebbings 1964; Collinson 1970; Sukegawa 1970; Karcz 1971, 1972; Schumm & Khan 1972; H. Ikeda 1973, 1975, 1983; Bluck 1976, 1979; Lewin 1976; Parker 1976; Cant & Walker 1978; Ashmore 1982, 1991b; Mosley 1982b; Ferguson & Werritty 1983; S. Ikeda 1984; Jaeggi 1984; Bridge *et al.* 1986; Fujita 1989).

in the sense of Jackson (1975b) and Church & Jones (1982). Alternate bars or parts of them have also been referred to as unit bars, linguoid bars, side bars, transverse bars, cross-channel bars, and diagonal bars and riffles (Smith 1978; Church & Jones 1982). Some of the bedwaves which have been referred to as transverse bars or linguoid bars (e.g. Sundborg 1956; Collinson

1970; Boothroyd & Ashley 1975; Jackson 1976*b*) should probably be referred to as dunes (meso-forms) in that their equilibrium forms are apparently controlled by flow structures which scale with boundary-layer thickness (depth), and not flow width. Mesoforms such as dunes and bedload sheets are commonly superimposed on the alternate bars (macroforms), and during the initial stages of development may be the only bedwaves discernible (e.g. Fujita 1989; Ashmore 1991*b*).

The next stage in the evolution of channel patterns involves bank erosion and channel widening, which results in a drop in water level and emergence of the highest parts of alternate bars, all of which can be accomplished at constant discharge. Emergence of the highest parts of alternate bars and subsequent lee-side deposition allows recognition of three morpho-logical units which grade into each other: bar tail; riffle; bar head (terminology partly after Bluck 1971, 1974, 1976, 1979). The units repre-sent different positions on ancestral alternate bars.

If bank erosion is sufficiently rapid and inter-mittent, deposition may occur as recognizably distinct bar head and bar tail (scroll bar) units (Fig. 1). These accretionary units have been referred to as 'unit bars' (Smith 1974, 1978; Ashmore 1982, 1991*b*) and they appear to be directly analogous to the alternate bars that developed initially. Accretionary units can grow during steady flow stages in association with episodic erosion of an upstream thalweg and/or cut bank. The 'slug' of sediment thus produced migrates downstream and part of it may be deposited at a flow expansion as a discrete lobe with an avalanche face on the leading edge. If deposition is less rapid and more continuous, sheets of sediment without recognisable avalanche faces are produced.

The resulting accumulations of sediment in mid-channel or forming the banks on the inside of river bends are referred to as braid bars or point bars, respectively. Synonyms for braid bars include medial, longitudinal, crescentic, and transverse bars and sandflats, whereas point bars are also referred to as side bars and lateral bars (Smith 1978; Church & Jones 1982). Many refer to the incremental accretionary units on point or braid bars as bars also. As with the ancestral alternate bars, the basic geometry of point and braid bars is controlled by channel-forming discharge.

Bank erosion and bar deposition, still at con-stant discharge, create changing gradients of the bed and water surfaces, which in turn may lead to the formation of new channels which cut across braid bars and point bars (Fig. 1). Some of these channels may develop as a sheet of water starts to flow over a formerly emergent bar sur-face and progressively becomes concentrated into discrete channels which develop by head-ward erosion (e.g. Ashmore 1982). Other (chute) channels develop as the flow takes advantage of the low areas between adjacent bar head lobes or the 'slough' areas between adjacent bar tail scrolls. These cross-bar channels commonly develop their own bars (macroforms), the geometry of which is con-trolled by the flow and sediment transport con-ditions in these channels (Fig. 2). Where these channels join another channel, solitary delta-like deposits with avalanche faces commonly form (e.g. chute bars, tributary-mouth bars, Figs 1 and 2).

A cross-bar channel may be progressively enlarged at the expense of an adjacent channel, thus changing the location of the main channel segments. As such a channel develops, the pre-viously described evolutionary sequence recurs, but in a different place. Chute cut off is an example of such behavior. In other cases a channel on one side of a braid bar may become enlarged at the expense of the channel on the other side. In this way, braided channel seg-ments are commonly abandoned and filled, resulting in the accretion of a braid bar to the floodplain or to another bar. Channel diversions may also result in abandonment of a number of connected channel segments and bars. Previously abandoned channels are commonly reoccupied as the process of channel migration continues (Krigström 1962; Ferguson & Werrity 1983; Carson 1984*b*,*c*; secondary anastomosis of Church 1972).

Although these evolutionary patterns can be formed under constant discharge (Ashmore 1982, 1991*b*), they can all be found in natural rivers where discharge varies with time. How-ever, some geometries arise specifically as a result of changing discharge, particularly the dissection and modification of emerging alter-nate, point and braid bars (Fig. 1 B, D). Such features may give a braided appearance to a river at low-flow which does not exist at high flow stage. It is therefore very important to study rivers over a large range of stage over an extended time span, because their appearance is controlled by the history of changing flow stage. Bluck (1974, 1976, 1979) assigned the formation of certain morphological features of bars to specific flow stages based on their topographic elevation and cross-cutting structures within their associated deposits. Thus the topo-graphically high bar head was considered to be

Fig. 2. Example of a cross-bar channel through the downstream end of a side bar of the Brahmaputra River near Sirajganj. The main channel is in the far background, flowing to the right. The cross bar channel (where people are standing) has its own macroforms, and a dune-covered mouth bar (centre of photo) has built into the inner slough channel (foreground).

formed at high flow stage, whereas the lower bar tail and associated cross-bar channels were considered to form at lower flow stages. In general, the association of topographically low forms with low flow stage cannot be justified, and the high stage activity of bar tails and cross-bar channels can be demonstrated (e.g. Bristow 1987; Bridge & Gabel 1992).

In summary, the main braiding mechanisms that have been observed in laboratory and natural rivers are as follows.

(1) Development and emergence of individual or rows of alternate bars. This mechanism encompasses the mid-channel bar initiation described by Leopold & Wolman (1957) and cited in most standard texts which discuss braiding. However, initial deposition in mid-channel of relatively coarse grains is probably not associated with decrease in competence. Leopold & Wolman (1957) clearly show that the maximum bedload transport rate and grain size occurs over the crest of the developing mid-channel bar, as would be expected with an alternate bar under subcritical flow. This mechanism also encompasses the 'central bar initiation', 'transverse bar conversion' and 'multiple bar braiding' mechanisms of Ashmore (1991b). Bridge et al. (1986) and Ashmore (1991b) cite examples of this common type of braiding.

(2) Formation of cross-bar channels. This

mechanism complicates the relatively simple patterns of braid bars and channels produced from emergence of alternate bars in (1). As clearly shown by Ashmore (1982, 1991b) this mechanism does not require changes in flow stage. However, there are numerous examples in the literature where channels cutting across alternate, point or braid bars are associated with falling flow stage (e.g. Krigström 1962; Collinson 1970; Smith 1970, 1971a, 1974; Hein & Walker 1977; Rundle 1985a,b). A variant of this mechanism is the chute cut off of point bars or single-row alternate bars (Ashmore 1991b). Chute cut off (and the equivalent cutting of a new channel through the central upstream part of a braid bar) is enhanced by the deposition of bar head lobes and lack of filling of the low areas between these lobes, as discussed previously. Chute cut-off of point bars has been described by many workers (e.g. Friedkin 1945; Kinoshita 1957; Krigström 1962, Hickin 1969; Ikeda 1973; Hong & Davies 1979; Ashmore 1982, 1991b; Teisseyre 1977b; Ferguson & Werrity 1983; Bridge, 1985; Bridge et al. 1986, Lewin 1976; Carson 1986). There is no reason why cross-bar channels could not develop a braided pattern also. If a cross-bar channel is enlarged it may become very difficult to distinguish a cross-bar channel from a 'main channel'.

In subsequent sections, details of the

geometry, flow and sedimentary processes in braided rivers will be considered. However, first it is necessary to discuss the implications of the braiding mechanisms above to the description and classification of channel patterns, and their hydraulic controls.

Description and classification of channel geometry in plan

Leopold & Wolman's (1957) classification of channel patterns as straight, meandering and braided is unsatisfactory because the classes are not mutually exclusive and different parameters are used to define the different patterns (Chitale 1970; Kellerhals *et al.* 1976; Rust 1978*a*; Knighton 1984). It is necessary to consider at least the nature of channel splitting around braid bars or islands, and the sinuosity of the channel(s) in a descriptive classification of channel patterns (Kellerhals *et al.* 1976; Rust 1978*a*; Brice 1984).

Bars or islands?

Brice (1964) defined mid-channel bars as being unvegetated and submerged at bankfull stage, whereas islands are vegetated and emergent at bankfull stage. The degree of development of vegetation on mid-channel bars is related to the amount of time the bar surface has been exposed above the seasonal low-water mark, the nature of the sediment surface exposed, and the types of vegetation available for colonization. These are in turn controlled by the history of erosion and deposition, the sediment available to the river, and the climate. Depending on these factors, freshly emergent unvegetated bars may become progressively vegetated as they accrete vertically and laterally (e.g. Brice 1964; Bridge *et al.* 1986), thus it is difficult to assess when a 'bar' becomes an 'island'. Such a distinction also artificially separates depositional forms which may have a common geometry and genesis.

Brice (1964) further classified bars as 'transient' as opposed to 'stabilized' islands. These terms are analogous to the terms 'unstable' and 'stable' which are used by geomorphologists and sedimentologists to imply the degree of erosion and deposition within the channel and the rate of channel migration. None of these terms have been defined objectively, and there is every gradation in the rates of channel and bar movement among different rivers, irrespective of whether the sediment surfaces are vegetated. Therefore, terms such as 'transient', 'unstable' and 'stable' should

be replaced with quantitative measures of the lifespans, rates of creation, migration and destruction of bars.

Stage dependence of channel pattern

Bars generally exist for time periods in excess of a floodwave, and will therefore have experienced a complex history of erosional and depositional modification related partly to stage changes. Although the overall form of bars is controlled by near-bankfull flow patterns, certain geometrical features are related to falling flow stages (e.g. some cross-bar channels). It is essential to recognise that such falling stage features are genetically different from the overall, high-stage generated, bar morphology (see also Collinson 1970; Rust 1978*a*; Bristow 1987). Failure to do so will lead to errors in definition of the nature of braiding. Brice (1964) recognized that his 'transient' braiding index depends on flow stage, but the 'stabilized' index does not.

Ideally bars should be observed at their formative high discharges when falling-stage features are not present; however, this is very difficult to do. Kellerhals *et al.* (1976) recommended describing channel geometry at mean flow (noting also high and low flow geometries) because these have a high probability of occurring and being recorded on aerial photographs (see also Howard *et al.* 1970). Rust (1978*a*) similarly recommended definition of channel patterns at a stage approximately mid-way between bankfull and minimum discharge.

Hierarchies of bars and channels

Upon deciding at which flow stage(s) a channel pattern will be described, it is necessary to consider which of the channel segments and bars will be used to define the nature of channel splitting and channel sinuosity. For instance, should the relatively minor cross-bar channels be considered along with the relatively major channels around the main braid bars, even if all of the channels are active at the same flow stage? There appears to be no simple answer to this question in that any cross-bar channel may evolve into a 'main channel'. This dilemma has led to various attempts to assign different orders to channels and bars in multiple-channel rivers (e.g. Williams & Rust 1969; Rust 1978*a*; Bristow 1987; Fig. 3 A, B). Then description of channel geometry is referred to specific orders of channel.

The existing channel and bar ordering schemes are difficult to apply and are not defined consistently. For instance, in Rust's

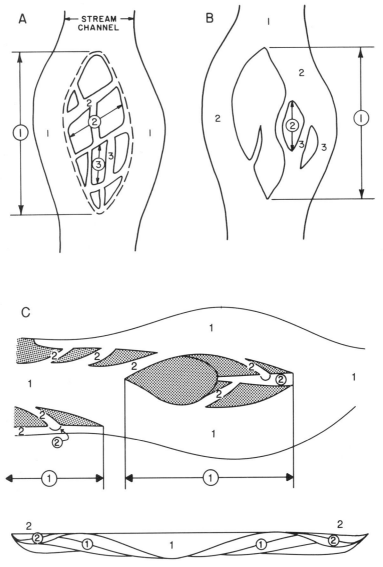

Fig. 3. Channel and bar ordering schemes of (**A**) Williams & Rust (1969), and (**B**) Bristow (1987). (**C**) Alternative channel and bar ordering scheme. Numbers in circles refer to bars, other numbers refer to channels. Cross section (lower figure) is from a confluence region, where a central channel (1) is bounded by side bars with cross bar channels (2).

scheme the difference between the second- and third-order (cross-bar) channels is not clear, and the second- and third-order bars are not bars in the true sense of the word; they are dissected segments of first order bars. Indeed, second- and third-order channels may have their own within-channel bars. In Bristow's scheme, all cross-bar channels are third-order because the main channels can be either first or second order.

Really, the main channels that flow adjacent to and over the largest scale of bars in the river should all be of the same order. A simpler, compromise scheme is shown in Fig. 3 C, where the largest scales of bar and adjacent channels are first order (following precedent), but all channels cutting across these bars are second order. The segments of first-order bars bounded by the second-order channels are not second-order bars. They *may* be partly eroded depositional units (bar heads, bar tail, scrolls etc.) associated with episodic deposition on first-order bars. Second-order bars are those that form within and at the terminations of second-order channels. It should be remembered that second-order channels may evolve into first-order channels.

Distinction between 'braiding' and 'anastomosing'

The term 'braiding' is generally taken to mean the splitting of channels around bars (islands).

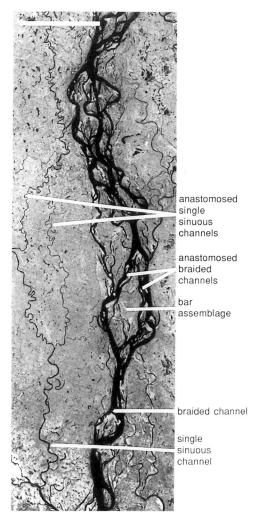

anastomosed
single
sinuous
channels

anastomosed
braided
channels

bar
assemblage

braided channel

single
sinuous
channel

Fig. 4. Landsat photograph (courtesy of C. S. Bristow) of the Brahmaputra River immediately north of its confluence with the Ganges showing various kinds of channel pattern. Scale bar is 20 km.

A different type of channel splitting has been recognized and referred to as anastomosing (Lane 1957; Smith 1976) or anabranching (Brice 1964, 1984). The characteristic, definitive feature of anastomosing (anabranching) channel segments is that they are longer than a curved channel segment around a single braid or point bar and their width-scale flow patterns behave substantially independently of adjacent segments, in contrast to braided channel segments around bars (e.g. Fig. 4). Thus anastomosed channel segments contain their own bars in accordance with imposed discharge and sediment load, enabling definition of braiding index and sinuosity for each segment. Anastomosing is therefore more akin to terms like distributive and tributive (e.g. Schumm 1985).

The classification of a river as anastomosing is clear cut if, for instance, the individual segments are undivided, sinuous channels separated by areas of floodplain much larger than the largest bars present (e.g. Fig. 4). However, the distinction between anastomosing and braiding is not as clear cut in braided rivers where, for instance, some second-order channel segments may have the characteristics of anastomosed segments as defined above, but first-order segments do not. A solution to this problem is to define anastomosing channels as those where the length of channel segments exceeds the length of first order channels around individual first-order bars. Nevertheless, many braided rivers appear to be both braided and anastomosing (Fig. 4). In the Brahmaputra, anastomosis is associated with bar assemblages (Coleman 1969; Bristow 1987; Fig. 4), which are analogous to what Church & Jones (1982) refer to as megaforms or sedimentation zones. Such anastomosed reaches are commonly taken to be associated with relatively large deposition rates (Smith 1976, 1983; Smith & Smith 1980; Rust 1981; Church & Jones 1982). As the land areas between anastomosed channel segments are generally not braid bars, the term anastomosing cannot be used to define channel patterns based on braiding index, as done by Rust (1978a) and Miall (1981).

The degree and style of braiding

Measures of the degree of braiding (see Table 1) generally fall into two categories: those that consider the mean number of active channels or braid bars per transect across the channel belt, and those that consider the ratio of the sum of channel lengths in a reach to a measure of reach length (referred to here as 'total sinuosity'). The first type of braiding index is more desirable for

Table 1. *Braiding indices*

Author	Braiding index
Brice (1960, 1964)	$\dfrac{2 \text{ (sum of lengths of bars or islands in a reach)}}{\text{centreline reach length}}$
Howard, Keetch & Vincent (1970)	Average number of anabranches bisected by several transects perpendicular to flow direction
Engelund & Skovgaard (1973), Parker (1876), Fujita (1989)	Mode = number of rows of alternate bars (and sinuous flow paths) = 2 times the number of braid bars and number of side (point) bars per transect
Rust (1978a)	Number of braids per mean curved channel wavelength = mode − 1 (see above)
Hong & Davies (1979)	Total sinuosity = $\dfrac{\text{length of channel segments}}{\text{channel belt length}}$
Mosley (1981)	Number of braids or channels in cross-section Braiding index = $\dfrac{\text{total length of bankfull channels}}{\text{distance along main channel}}$
Richards (1982), Robertson-Rintoul & Richards (this vol.)	Total sinuosity = $\dfrac{\text{total active channel length}}{\text{valley length}}$
Ashmore (1991a)	Mean number of active channels per transect. Mean number of active channel links in braided network.
Friend & Sinha (this vol.)	Braid channel ratio = $\dfrac{\text{sum of mid-channel lengths of all channels in reach}}{\text{length of mid-line of widest channel}}$

two main reasons. First of all it is related to the 'mode' of (ancestral) alternate bars. In order to express the degree of braiding in terms of 'mode' it is necessary to count point (side) bars as well as braid bars. Secondly, the total sinuosity is a combined measure of channel-segment sinuosity and degree of braiding. Thus braided rivers with relatively large numbers of channel segments of low sinuosity can have a similar total sinuosity to those with fewer, higher sinuosity channel segments (Fig. 5). Therefore it is desirable to determine separately the braiding index and average sinuosity of curved channel segments around bars (see below).

Brice's (1960, 1964) braiding index (Table 1) is a measure of the sum of bar or island perimeters relative to reach length and is strongly dependent on flow stage. More recently, Brice (1984; see also Brice *et al.* 1978) abandoned his braiding index and classified the *degree* of braiding as the proportion of the channel length in a each that is divided by bars and islands and the *character* of braiding in terms of whether the bars or islands are dominant and the plan shapes of islands. The degree of braiding cannot be compared with the braid-

ing indices discussed above, and the character of braiding cannot be defined objectively. Furthermore, in their classification of channel patterns, anabranched channels (where anabranching is arbitrarily defined as channel splitting where island width is greater than three times water width at average discharge) cannot clearly be distinguished from braided channels. Brice (1984) uses terms such as 'locally braided' and 'generally braided' based on arbitrary values of the degree of braiding. Rust (1978a) suggested the terms 'moderately braided' and 'highly braided' based on arbitrary values of his braiding parameter.

In Kellerhals *et al.*'s (1976) classification of channel splitting, the spatial distribution of islands in a reach is described but that of bars is not, and the shape of bars is described but not that of islands. Use of terms such as 'occasional', 'frequent', 'split', 'braided', to describe the distribution of islands mixes morphological terms with those having a time connotation. Some categories are objectively defined; others are not. Also, the terms do not have unambiguous meanings, in that 'braided' and 'split' could equally apply to all divided reaches.

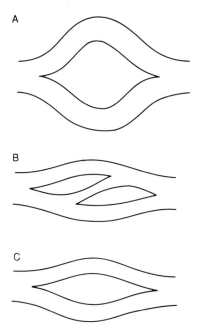

Fig. 5. Relationship between total sinuosity (ΣP), braiding index (Br) and mean sinuosity of channels (sn), where $\Sigma P = Br.sn$. (**A**) and (**B**) have the same ΣP but different sn and Br. (**A**) and (**C**) have the same Br but different sn and ΣP. (**B**) and (**C**) have the same sn, but different Br and ΣP.

Sinuosity of multiple-channel rivers

Sinuosity is defined as either channel thalweg length/valley length (Leopold & Wolman 1957; Rust 1978*a*), channel length/valley length (Brice 1984; Schumm 1985), or channel length/ channel-belt axis length (Brice 1964), the latter being useful for defining channel-belt sinuosity. Definition of sinuosity for multiple-channel rivers, as suggested by Rust (1978*a*), requires definition of some average thalweg length of channel segments of a given order at a given flow stage. Friend & Sinha (1993) use the centreline length of the widest channel in a braided river to define sinuosity. Based on precedent, Rust (1978*a*) used a mean sinuosity of 1.5 to separate 'low sinuosity' from 'high sinuosity' rivers. Brice's (1984) classification of braided rivers into 'sinuous' and 'non-sinuous' is not based on objective criteria.

Hydraulic controls of channel pattern

Empirical approaches using discharge, slope and bed material size

There are many myths about what controls channel pattern. It is generally accepted that they are controlled by the supply of water and sediment and, in the short term, by valley slope. Some have also invoked bank erodibility, especially as influenced by vegetation. Empirically, the degree of braiding (i.e. braiding index) and overall channel width/depth increase as water-discharge is increased for a given slope, or as slope is increased for a given discharge (e.g. Lane 1957; Leopold & Wolman 1957; Howard *et al.* 1970; Ackers & Charlton 1971; Schumm & Khan 1972; Chitale 1973; Mosley 1981; Richards 1982; Ashmore 1991*a*). However, channel pattern also varies with bed-material size, such that braiding occurs at lower slopes and/or discharges as grainsize decreases (Henderson 1961, 1966; Osterkamp 1978; Carson 1984*a*; Ferguson 1984, 1987; Ferguson & Ashworth 1991). Positive correlations between width/depth and water discharge are shown by Chitale (1970) and Leeder (1973). Width/depth is also strongly negatively correlated with sinuosity for streams of a given discharge (Schumm 1963; Chitale 1970) except for those near the transition from straight to sinuous, undivided channels.

Discrimination between different channel patterns using discharge (Q) slope (S) and bed-material size (D) is generally poorer if a large range of experimental data is used than if a smaller, specific data set is used (Ferguson 1984, 1987; Carson 1984*a*). This is partly due to different definitions of the experimental parameters and partly due to inappropriate choice of parameters. Discharge measures used have included the mean annual, bankfull, and mean or median annual flood. The most appropriate discharge to use is a flood discharge that does not depend on a reference to channel geometry, such as a frequency-based measure like the one or two year flood (Ferguson 1987; Carson 1984*a*). Valley slope should be used instead of channel slope, to avoid biasing the plotting positions of sinuous streams which have a lower channel slope than valley slope. In general, the definition of channel patterns has not been objective, and different workers have classified rivers near the meandering-braided transition in different ways.

Discharge variability

It is commonly held that channel geometry of alluvial rivers is dominated by flow and sedimentary processes operating over a range of high discharges. At seasonally low flows, sediment transport rates are relatively diminished and modification of the high-stage adjusted channel pattern is expected to be minimal. However, the increases in discharge, width/depth, and sediment transport associated with exceptional floods may precipitate a major change in channel pattern (e.g. increasing degree of braiding; Schumm & Lichty 1963) which may remain more or less intact for many years. Subsequent, long-term (many flood periods) reduction in flood discharge may eventually lead to modification of channel pattern (e.g. from braided to undivided; Werritty & Ferguson 1980; Ferguson & Werritty 1983; Schumm 1985). It is therefore important to be aware of the history of major flood events when assessing the hydraulic controls on channel pattern (see also Howard et al. 1970; Mosley 1981). Discharge variability does not exert a major influence on the existence of the different channel patterns because they can all be formed in laboratory channels at constant discharge, and many rivers with a given discharge regime show alongstream variations in pattern. That braided channels are associated with greater discharge variability than undivided channels is one of the myths. However, as demonstrated below, discharge variability does influence the detail of sediment transport, erosion and deposition in braided rivers and all other alluvial river types.

Discharge, slope, bed material size and sediment transport rate

Discriminators between unbraided and braided rivers of the form $S = aQ^{-b}$ (see Table 2) have been interpreted to represent a constant value of a hydraulic property at the channel pattern threshold. Parameter a controls the constant value of the hydraulic property, and the hydraulic property depends on the value of the exponent, i.e. $b = 0.33$ for bed shear stress, $b = 0.5$ for stream power per unit bed area, $b = 1.0$ for stream power per unit channel length (Antropovskiy 1972; Ferguson 1981, 1984, 1987; Begin 1981; Begin & Schumm 1984; Carson 1984a). The stream power per unit channel length also correlates weakly with braiding index (Howard et al. 1970; Mosley 1981) and total sinuosity (Richards 1982; Robertson-Rintoul & Richards this volume). These hydraulic measures are all known to be related to sediment transport rate, but this also depends on what type of sediment is available and what proportion of the total bed shear stress or power is available to transport sediment in the presence of rough banks and bedforms. Indeed, parameter a above must include these effects and therefore cannot be constant.

Table 2. *Hydraulic controls on braided channel patterns: discharge, slope and bed material**

Equation	Comments	Author
$S = 0.0007Q_m^{-0.25}$	Meandering sand-bed channels	Lane (1957)
$S = 0.0041Q_m^{-0.25}$	Braided sand-bed channels	
$S = 0.0125Q_{bf}^{-0.44}$	Meandering $\rightarrow$ braided	Leopold & Wolman (1957)
$S = 0.000196D^{1.14}Q_{bf}^{0.44}$	Meandering $\rightarrow$ braided	Henderson (1961, 1966)
$S = 1.4Q_{maf}^{-1}$	Meandering $\rightarrow$ braided	Antropovsky (1972)
$S = 0.0009Q_m^{-0.25}$	Mainly meandering sand-bed rivers in Kansas	Osterkamp (1978)
$S = 0.0017Q_m^{-0.25}$	Braided sand bed rivers in Kansas	
$S = aQ_m^{-0.25}$	Meandering $\rightarrow$ braided	
$S = 0.0016Q_m^{-0.33}$	Meandering $\rightarrow$ braided	Begin (1981)
$S = 0.07Q_{2f}^{-0.44}$	Sinuosity > 1.25 and meandering $\rightarrow$ Braided for gravel-bed rivers	Bray (1982)
$S = 0.042Q^{-0.49}D_{50}^{0.09}$	Meandering $\rightarrow$ braided for gravel-bed	Ferguson (1984, 1987)
$S = 0.042Q^{-0.49}D_{90}^{0.27}$	rivers†	
$S = 0.0049Q^{-0.21}D_{50}^{0.52}$	Meandering $\rightarrow$ braided using Parker's theory and hydraulic geometry	
$S \approx aQ^{-0.5}D^{0.5}$	Meandering $\rightarrow$ braided	Chang (1985)
$\Sigma P = 1 + 5.52(QS_v)^{0.38}D_{84}^{-0.44}$	Gravel-bed rivers	Robertson-Rintoul
$\Sigma P = 1 + 2.64(QS_v)^{0.4}D_{84}^{-0.14}$	Sand-bed rivers	& Richards (this vol.)

* S.I. Units.
† D in mm.

Discriminators of the form $S = aQ^{-b}D^c$ (Table 2), where D is some measure of bed sediment size, explicitly recognize at least one aspect of sediment supply (and erodibility of bed and banks) but a is still not likely to be constant. Values of $b = 0.33$ and $c = 1$ imply that the theshold between braided and unbraided rivers occurs at a constant value of dimensionless bed shear stress if a is constant (Begin 1981; Ferguson 1986, 1987; Carson 1984a). Henderson's (1961) approach with $b = 0.46$ and $c = 1.15$ is based on the stability of channels at the threshold of bedload motion and therefore cannot be correct in view of the requirement of sediment transport for channel bars to form.

The stream power per unit channel length (ϱgQS), where ϱ is fluid density and g is gravitational acceleration, controls the width-integrated sediment transport rate, depending on the grain sizes available for transport and the bedform drag. Thus an increase in QS for a given available sediment should be associated with an increased total sediment transport rate and braiding index. However, in natural rivers it is common for bedload grain size to increase with QS, whereas changes in bedform drag are more difficult to predict (e.g. Leopold & Wolman 1957; Osterkamp 1978; Prestegaard 1983; Ferguson & Ashworth 1991). If bedload grain-size and width/depth increase as QS increases, sediment transport rate per unit bed area is likely to be much more conservative than total sediment transport rate. If grainsize is held constant as in laboratory experiments an increase in QS will result inevitably in an increase in sediment transport rate per unit bed area unless the banks can be eroded, thereby resulting in an increase in width/depth and a change in channel pattern. Thus, as total sediment transport rate must equal sediment supply in an equilibrium river channel, an abrupt change in sediment supply to a reach of a river may result in a change in channel pattern, an increase in supply tending to induce braiding (e.g. Smith & Smith 1984). Ashmore (1991a) has documented periodic changes in braiding index due to periodic changes in sediment supply while discharge, slope and bedload size remained constant. Also, Hoey & Sutherland (1991) associate increase in braiding index with periodic aggradation (sediment storage in bars), and vice versa during degradation.

Empirical approaches using other parameters

Japanese empirical approaches to the hydraulic controls on the mode of alternate bars and braids are summarized by Hayashi & Ozaki (1980), Fukuoka (1989), and Fujita (1989). These approaches fall into two main groups, based on different combinations of dimensionless quantities: u_*/u_{*c} (flow intensity) and wS/d (channel form index); d/D and w/D (Table 3). Here, u_* is shear velocity, u_{*c} is shear velocity at the threshold of bedload movement, w is channel width, and d is mean flow depth. Ikeda's (1973) criterion for braiding (Table 3) was based on laboratory experiments. Ikeda's (1975) natural river data agree reasonably well with the wS/d criterion but do not appear to show a clear dependence on u_*/u_{*c}. As u_*/u_{*c} is proportional to $(dS/D)^{1/2}$, this criterion involves essentially the same variables as the approaches mentioned above, since w and d can be expressed in terms of discharge. Although this criterion correctly predicts the transition to braiding as w/d and S increase, it incorrectly predicts that, for a given channel-form index, braiding is favoured by a decreasing u_*/u_{*c}, hence sediment transport rate. The alternative braiding criterion has no dependence on slope, but otherwise the controlling variables are the same as those used by Ikeda. Chien's (1961) braiding criterion is based on multiple regression analysis of data from Chinese sandy rivers, but the reasons for the choice of variables is not given.

Channel patterns and bank stability

It has been suggested (Schumm 1963, 1971, 1972, 1977, 1981, 1985; followed by many sedimentologists) that rivers which transport large proportions of bedload relative to suspended load tend to have relatively low sinuosity and high braiding index. Such 'bedload streams' were associated with relatively easily eroded banks of sand or gravel, large channel slope and stream power, such that they were laterally 'unstable'. In contrast, rivers with relatively large suspended loads were postulated to be characteristic of undivided rivers of higher sinuosity. Such 'suspended load' streams were associated with cohesive muddy banks, low stream gradient and power, and lateral stability. However, the correlation between channel sediment size, type of sediment load and channel pattern is not generally supported, as recognized by Schumm (1981, 1985) in his more recent classifications of channel pattern (but unfortunately still not recognized by many sedimentologists). In fact, many braided rivers are sandy and silty and many single-channel, sinuous rivers are sandy and gravelly (Rust 1978b; Jackson 1978; Bridge 1985). Braided

Table 3. *Hydraulic controls on braided channel patterns: non-dimensional criteria*

Equation	Comments	Author
$\dfrac{U_*}{U_{*c}} = 1.4\left(\dfrac{wS}{d}\right)^{1/3}$	Meandering → braided	Ikeda (1973, 1975)
$\dfrac{(w/D)^{2/3}}{(d/D)} = 6.7$ for $1 < \tau_0/\tau_c < 12$	Meandering → braided	Muramoto & Fujita (1977)
$\dfrac{(w/D)^{2/3}}{(d/D)} = 3.5 \text{ to } 6.7$	Meandering → braided	Fujita (1989)
$2.2m^{2/3} < \dfrac{(w/d)^{2/3}}{(d/D)} < 6.7m^{2/3}$	m is mode (degree of braiding)	
$\left(\dfrac{\Delta Q}{0.5TQ_{bf}}\right)\left(\dfrac{d_{bf}S}{D_{35}}\right)^{0.6}\left(\dfrac{Q_{max} - Q_{min}}{Q_{max} + Q_{min}}\right)^{0.6}$ $\cdot \left(\dfrac{w_{rf}}{w_{bf}}\right)^{0.45}\left(\dfrac{w_{bf}}{d_{bf}}\right)^{0.3} = 5$	Transitional → braided*	Chien (1961)

* First term is dimensional, units days^{-1}.

channels have even been formed in muddy sediments on floodplains (Rust & Nanson 1986; Nanson *et al.* 1986), although the mud was probably transported in the form of sand-sized pellets.

Vegetation helps stabilize cut banks and bar surfaces (increasing tensile and shear strength) given adequate time and conditions for development (e.g. Brice 1964; Smith 1976; Witt 1985). Such stabilization allows the existence of relatively steep cut banks and may hinder lateral migration of channels. However, there is no conclusive evidence that vegetation has an important influence on the equilibrium channel pattern (contrary to the view held by Brice 1964). Early lithification of bank sediments (e.g. calcretes, silcretes) may have an effect on bank stability similar to vegetation (e.g. Gibling & Rust 1990).

Theoretical stability analyses

The theoretical stability analyses of Parker (1976) and Hayashi & Ozaki (1980) predict that channel pattern types are controlled by width, depth, slope and Froude number (*Fr*). Parker's (1976) criterion for braiding is $w/d \approx Fr/S$, which Ferguson (1984, 1987) reformulated as $S = Q/w^2(gd)^{1/2}$. Equations for w and d in terms of Q can then be substituted in order to produce the empirical criterion $S = aQ^{-b}$ where

a must depend at least on bed-material size. However, even when Parker's (1979) hydraulic geometry equations for gravel-bed rivers are used, this braiding criterion does not agree very well with field data. Parker's (1976) braiding criterion also does not agree with data from the Calamus River (Bridge & Gabel 1992) and that given in Hayashi & Ozaki (1980, pp. 7-28 and 7-29). Hayashi & Ozaki's (1980) braiding criterion, $2(wS/d)^{1/2} \approx Fr$, does agree with Calamus River data. It can be reformulated as $S = Q^2/4gd^2w^3$.

The theoretical analyses of Engelund & Skovgaard (1973), Fredsoe (1978) and Fukuoka (1989) all indicate that the major control on braiding is w/d (being > 50 for braiding to occur), with θ or (θ/θ_c) having a minor effect. θ is dimensionless bed shear stress, and θ_c is the value of θ at the threshold of bedload movement. In Fredsoe's analysis the type of bedform (i.e. flow resistance coefficient) also has a minor effect, and in Fukuoka's analysis slope has a minor effect (Table 4). Hayashi & Ozaki's braiding criterion can be recast as $w/d \approx 2/f$, where f is the Darcy-Weisbach friction coefficient. This agrees with Fredsoe's braiding criterion if f takes a value of approximately 0.04, and braiding can occur at lower w/d if flow resistance is increased. An unfortunate aspect of all of these theoretical approaches is that the main controlling variables (w,d) are not independent, but depend on the supply of water and sediment.

Table 4. *Hydraulic controls on braided channel patterns: theoretical stability analyses*

Equation	Comments	Author
$S/Fr \approx d/w$	Meandering $\rightarrow$ braided	Parker (1976)
$w/d \approx 50$	Meandering $\rightarrow$ braided Weak dependence on θ and f	Fredsoe (1978)
$2(wS/d)^{0.5} \approx Fr$	Meandering $\rightarrow$ braided	Hayashi & Ozaki (1980)
$\dfrac{S}{Fr^2}\left(\dfrac{w}{d}\right)^2 f(\theta) = constant$	Meandering $\rightarrow$ braided	Struiksma & Klaasen (1988)
$S^{0.2}w/d \approx 10$ to 20	Meandering $\rightarrow$ braided Weak dependence on θ/θ_c	Fukuoka (1989)

Minimum energy theories

Several approaches to the meandering-braided transition involve the concept of minimization of energy expenditure in transporting sediment (e.g. Kirkby 1972, 1977, 1980; Chang 1979, 1985; Bettess & White 1983; reviewed by Ferguson 1987). Both Chang and Bettess & White assume that discharge, valley slope and sediment supply are independent variables and then use regime theory (e.g. equations for flow resistance and sediment transport rate) to predict equilibrium channel slope, width, depth, and flow velocity. However, to predict channel pattern, the additional assumption of minimum stream power per unit channel length (or minimum S for a given Q) is also required.

According to Bettess & White, if the channel slope (S) equals the valley slope (S_v) the channel remains straight. If $S > S_v$ aggradation will occur in a non-equilibrium channel, whereas if $S_v > S$ the river is either meandering or braided. A braided pattern allows the slope of individual channels to approach the valley slope because the slope of small multiple channels is greater than that for a single large channel. Under these circumstances the choice between meandering and braiding is based on minimum stream power per unit channel length. Unfortunately, quantitative predictions with the model do not agree very well with natural data.

Chang's (1979) approach for sand-bed rivers results in four regions in plots of S against Q: (1) straight, (2) straight braided, (3) straight braided to meandering, (4) meandering to steep braided. Chang (1985; Fig. 6) slightly modified the positions and names of these four regions in

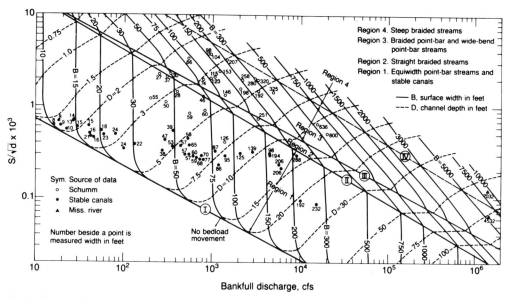

Fig. 6. Chang's (1985) theoretical prediction of channel patterns.

plots of $S/D^{1/2}$ versus Q: (1) stable channel and equiwidth point-bar streams, (2) straight braided, (3) braided point bar and wide-bend point bar streams, (4) steep braided. The transition from regions (1) to (4) as Q or S increases is clearly not as normally observed, the most glaring anomaly being region (2). The anomaly is probably based on Chang's criterion for braiding which is that an increase in S is associated with a large increase in w/d. Remarkably, however, Chang's (1985) region boundaries are lines of approximately equal w/d, and the middle of region (3) (which apparently marks the transition from meandering to braided rivers) has a w/d of 50 which is in close agreement with Fredsoe's (1978) criterion for braiding. Thus, if the discrimination between channel patterns is essentially in terms of w/d (as suggested by other theories) then the crux of the issue is finding out what independent variables control w and d. Chang's (1985) channel pattern discriminant lines have the approximate form $S \propto Q^{-0.5} D^{0.5}$, suggesting that the braiding theshold for sand-bed streams corresponds with some grain-size dependent threshold stream power per unit bed area (cf. Ferguson 1987). However, the exponents in this type of relationship are not likely to apply to gravel-bed streams, and there is much overlap in stream power per unit bed area for natural meandering and braided rivers (Carson 1984b,c; Ferguson 1987).

Geometry of braided rivers at the bar scale

Studies of the interaction between channel geometry, flow and sediment transport over a large discharge range for braided rivers are extremely rare. Those studies that do exist are only for the case of simple plan geometries. The essential features of flow in braided rivers are curved channel segments joined by zones of flow convergence (confluence) or divergence (diffluence). Flow around one side of a braid bar can be considered to be dynamically similar to flow in an undivided sinuous channel (Allen 1968, 1983; Bridge 1985; Bridge & Gabel 1992), and flow in river confluences can be considered to be dynamically similar to braided channel convergence zones (Best 1986). Therefore, it is

possible to piece together a picture of the 3D geometry, flow and sediment transport at the bar scale using limited field and laboratory data from braided rivers (e.g. Straub 1935; Abdullayev 1973; Ashworth & Ferguson 1986; Bridge & Gabel 1992; Ferguson et al. 1992; Ashworth et al. 1992a,b), the more extensive experimental data from undivided curved channels (e.g. Bridge & Jarvis 1982; Dietrich & Smith 1983, 1984; Jackson 1975a, 1976a,b) and confluence zones (e.g. Best 1986, 1987, 1988; Roy & Bergeron 1990; Roy & De Serres 1989; Ashmore et al. 1992) and some theoretical reasoning (e.g. Bridge 1992).

Channel geometry associated with multiple-row alternate bars at constant discharge is illustrated in Fig. 7, as a reference for comparison with the geometry of braided channels that may have developed from such alternate bars. When considering the geometry of braided channels it must be remembered that the channels may be developing and widening, or becoming abandoned and filling. Channel geometry may also change cyclically, as opposed to progressively, in response to cyclical discharge variations. Therefore, the geometry may not necessarily be in equilibrium with the flow and sediment transport at any particular flow stage. Nevertheless, there are clearly systematic and understandable variations in geometry that can be related to certain discharges.

Cross-sectional geometry of curved channel segments

Upstream of a typical braid bar a mid-stream thalweg splits, and the loci of maximum depth move towards the outer, cut banks with progression around the braid bar, depending in detail on flow stage (Figs 7 and 8). At high flow stage the channel segments near the upstream tip of the bar are deepest close to the bar, whereas further downstream they are deepest near the outer cut banks. The depth variation in a cross-section within a bend can be approximated by

$$d_1/d_c = (r_1/r_c)^a \qquad (1)$$

as long as the geometry is in equilibrium with the flow (details in Bridge, 1992). Here d_1 and r_1 are

---

Fig. 7. Idealized channel geometry for two simple braided channel patterns. Equivalent alternate bar patterns in straight channels are shown (upper diagrams) for comparison. Bankfull cross sections are smoothed (no mesoforms or cross-bar channels shown) and have vertical exaggerations (V.E.) of approximately 3 or 4. Dashed lines in cross sections represent low-flow stage geometry. Lines with solid or open arrows represent loci of maximum flow velocity for high and low flow stage, respectively. Single arrow and E represent potential locations of flow diversion and erosion in response to encroachment of the tributary bar (riffle) of the major channel.

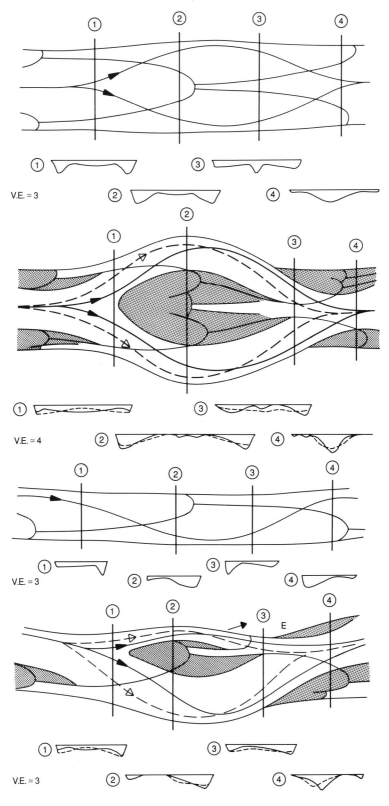

FLOW DEPTH

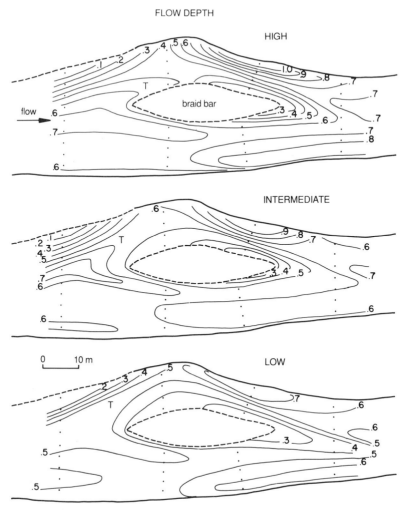

Fig. 8. Channel geometry at high, intermediate and low flow stages associated with a braid bar, Calamus River, Nebraska (from Bridge & Gabel 1992). Bed topography contours are in metres below a datum at approximately bankfull level. Dots are flow measurement stations. The thalweg of the left-hand channel near the upstream end of the bar (T) moves towards the left bank as stage falls.

local depth and radius of curvature respectively, d_c and r_c are centreline values, and the exponent a depends on the characteristics of the flow and sediment transport. In general, a increases as dimensionless bed shear stress and sediment transport rate increase, and as bed roughness decreases. Thus maximum cross-sectional asymmetry of curved channel segments increases as sinuosity increases, as bed sediment size decreases, and as flow stage increases. This kind of equation does not describe the detailed local relief of river cross-sections associated with mesoforms like dunes, and the discrete bar head lobes and bar-tail scrolls which are associated

with episodic deposition. Also, if bank erosion occurs, it takes a finite amount of time for the widened cross-section to approach equilibrium with the flow.

As discharge falls the thalwegs near the upstream part of the bar tend to move towards the outer banks in association with deposition near the upstream tip of the bar, and resulting in a tendency to reverse the cross-sectional asymmetry of the channels here (Figs 7 and 8; Bridge & Gabel 1992). In the channel segments adjacent to the bar, cross-sectional asymmetry may be reduced by deposition in the thalweg and erosion of the topographically high areas of the bar (Fig. 7). Such falling stage modification in channel geometry depends on the ability of the flow to erode and deposit. This may not be possible if the bed becomes armored or if shallow parts of channel segments become emergent. The changes in braided channel geometry with falling discharge described above are equivalent to decreasing height and trimming margins of (ancestral) multiple-row alternate bars. Conversely, increasing discharge would result in increasing alternate bar height and the tendency to migrate downstream.

'Hydraulic geometry' of curved channel segments

The 'at-a-station hydraulic geometry' (normally represented as log-log plots of water surface width (w), cross-section average depth (d) or flow velocity (V) versus discharge (Q)) for individual curved channel segments in braided rivers is similar to that for undivided sinuous channels (e.g. Church & Gilbert 1975). Thus, hydraulic geometry varies along the length of a segment and between segments in response to varying cross-sectional geometry and flow resistance, and in general log-log plots of hydraulic geometry are nonlinear (Knighton 1972; Nordseth 1973; Cheetham 1979; Eschner 1983; Bridge & Gabel 1992). The mean geometry of individual channel sections cannot necessarily be related to whole-stream discharge because the individual channel discharge and the whole-stream discharge may not vary congruently.

At-a-station hydraulic geometry of the entire braided cross-section is discussed by Mosley (1982b, 1983) and Ergenzinger (1987). Mosley (1982b, 1983) collected at-a-station hydraulic geometry data from a number of braided rivers for whole-river transects and individual anabranches. As discharge increased with time existing channels enlarged and merged, and new channels became active. For all cases, width, depth and velocity increase with discharge and were expressed as simple power functions as observed in other studies. However, the variability in hydraulic geometry relationships among different rivers, reaches of the same river, transects in a given reach, and different anabranches is so great as to be of little predictive value. This variability is clearly because discharge is not the sole control of hydraulic geometry, and because log-log plots may not be linear (see also Eschner 1983). Furthermore, as channels become enlarged or filled, hydraulic geometry will change with time (even as it is being measured!).

Downstream hydraulic geometry may also be expressed in terms of individual segments (Fahnestock 1963; Church & Gilbert 1975; Rice 1982) or the entire river (Ashmore 1991a). Ashmore's (1991a) results from a laboratory channel are broadly similar to those from single-channel streams. However, it is difficult to make a strict comparison because in real rivers downstream increases in channel-forming discharge are usually accompanied by decreases in slope and bed grain size, parameters held constant in Ashmore's experiments. Ferguson & Ashworth (1991) show that mean channel width in braided rivers (with braiding index less than 2) varies with discharge, slope and median bed-material size, and that rational regime theories are generally better predictors of channel width than are empirical equations.

It is well known that in single sinuous channels the width and wavelength are proportional to the square root of the channel-forming discharge. Thus the wave length/width ratio tends to equal approximately 10, or the riffle-riffle spacing is approximately 5. This also seems to be the case for braided river segments (e.g. Bridge et al. 1986). Also, the relative sinuosities of channels on either side of braid bars is commonly such as to give a braid length/maximum width of approximately 3–4, which represents a streamlined form according to Komar (1983, 1984).

In many natural rivers, the riffle-riffle spacing, and overall bar dimensions do not change appreciably as discharge falls seasonally below 'channel-forming' discharge. However, if a braided channel segment experiences a reduction in discharge over a long enough term (relative to erosion and deposition rate), a series of bars and bends may develop that have a shorter wavelength than the original segment. This will give the appearance of an anastomosing channel segment that has nothing to do with avulsion or high sedimentation rates. Indeed, many sinuous channel belts of undivided channels which contain smaller wavelength bends are probably related to such long-term reductions in discharge.

Geometry of confluence zones

Figure 9 illustrates the important geometrical features of confluence zones (see also Mosley 1976; Best 1986, 1988; Bristow et al. 1993; Ashmore this volume). Features of particular concern are: (1) the confluence angle; (2) whether the incoming channels are oriented symmetrically or asymmetrically relative to the confluence direction; (3) relative size of

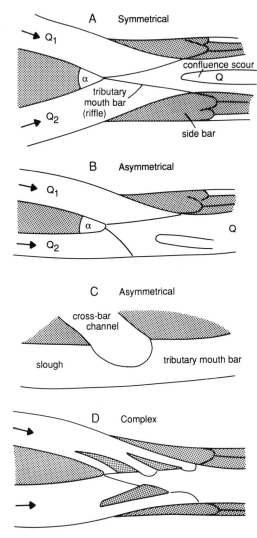

Fig. 9. Idealized plan geometry of different types of confluences at a given flow stage Q, Q_1 and Q_2 are discharges, and α is confluence angle.

incoming channels as measured by their widths, depths, cross-sectional areas, or discharges; (4) the maximum depth, width and length of the scour zone; (5) complications arising from the presence of more than two joining channels. These features are commonly difficult to define as they vary with time and discharge.

Relative discharge is defined in various ways, using different combinations of the incoming discharges and the combined discharge (Table 5). Changes in relative discharge with time can result during changes in overall discharge without any erosion or deposition in the joining

channels (Bridge & Gabel 1992). They will also result if one channel segment is being erosionally enlarged while the other is being filled. One channel segment may also lose discharge due to a channel diversion (avulsion) upstream of the confluence. In major tributary junctions relative discharge changes may be associated with upstream avulsions or incongruous flood peaks, possibly associated with ice jams or differing hydrological nature of drainage basins (e.g. Best 1986; Bergeron & Roy 1988; Alam *et al.* 1985; Reid *et al.* 1989).

Confluence angles are difficult to measure in natural channels (as opposed to laboratory models) because channels vary in curvature as they join. Common values of confluence angle range from 15° to 110°. An estimate of the confluence angle in terms of the sinuosity (sn) of the joining channels can be derived if the channel segments can be represented by a sine-generated curve (Langbein & Leopold 1966). As confluences tend to be associated with reversal in curvature of the joining channel segments (i.e. crossovers), and the deviation angle of the local channel direction at the crossover from the mean down valley direction is given in degrees as $126°[(sn-1)/sn]^{0.5}$, the *maximum* confluence angle possible is

$$126° \left[\left(\frac{sn_1 - 1}{sn_1} \right)^{0.5} + \left(\frac{sn_2 - 1}{sn_2} \right)^{0.5} \right] \quad (2)$$

where sn_1 and sn_2 are the sinuosities of the two channel segments. If the channel segments are assumed to be circular arcs, the constant in the above relationship is approximately 140°.

The geometry of confluence zones can be conveniently subdivided and described in terms of: (1) entering channels; (2) confluence scour zone (thalweg); (3) side (point) bars (Fig. 9). Braided channels entering confluence zones tend to be 'riffle' areas (e.g. Fig. 7) so that depth does not vary much across the channel width. However, with the channel geometry of Fig. 7, a thalweg is commonly present near the outer bank at high flow stage, but may be near the inner bank at low flow stage. Avalanche faces may be present where the entering channels pass into the confluence scour zone ('riffle' areas with avalanche faces are commonly referred to as tributary-mouth bars). Generally, their crestlines are oblique to the channel direction (as are the equivalent parts of ancestral alternate bars). This obliquity increases with cross-sectional asymmetry and flow stage and as one channel becomes dominant over the other. In the extreme case the avalanche face of the dominant channel may be almost parallel to its inner bank,

Table 5. *Measures of relative discharge of joining channels*

Measure	$Q_1 = Q_2$	$Q_1 \gg Q_2$	Author
$\dfrac{Q_1}{Q}$	0.5	1.0	Best & Reid (1984)
$\dfrac{Q_2}{Q}$	0.5	0.0	Best & Reid (1984)
$\dfrac{Q_2}{Q_1}$	1.0	0.0	Mosley (1976), Best (1986)
$\dfrac{(Q_1 - Q_2)}{Q/2}$	0.0	2.0	Ashmore & Parker (1983)
$\dfrac{(Q_1 - Q_2)}{Q}$	0.0	1.0	Bridge (This paper)

$$Q_1 > Q_2$$
$$Q_1 + Q_2 = Q$$

thereby blocking and/or migrating into the minor channel (e.g. Best 1986, 1987; Hein & Walker 1977; Krigström 1962; Lodina & Chalov 1971; Teisseyre 1975; Ashmore & Parker 1983; Bergeron & Roy 1988; Reid *et al.* 1989). This is an important process in the blocking of the downstream ends of channel segments which are becoming abandoned. If the channel being blocked is still active, this may lead to increased erosion of its outer bank or an upstream diversion (Fig. 9). Bluck (1979) referred to these channel blocking deposits as spits, erroneously assigning their origin to wave action. Where a cross-bar channel joins a larger main channel only one avalanche face may be present, associated with the tributary mouth bar of the cross-bar channel (Figs 1 and 2). According to Best (1987, p. 494) avalanche faces occur if confluence angle exceeds approximately 20°. In view of the above, the presence or absence of avalanche faces is also controlled at least by relative depth and discharge.

As discharge and relative discharge vary the tributary-mouth bars may grow forward or retreat, and change in crest height and orientation in plan (Best 1987; Bergeron & Roy 1988; Reid *et al.* 1989). The crests tend to increase in height and prograde during high flows, particularly near the outer banks where the flow velocities are highest, resulting in increasing obliquity of the crestlines relative to the flow direction (for the channel geometries of Figs 7 and 9). The crests tend to be eroded at low flow stages, and may become dissected, with higher parts emergent, resulting in a complicated confluence zone (Fig. 9D). These changes in channel geometry are entirely consistent with those that occur in single-channel rivers, where 'riffle' areas tend to be areas of deposition at high flow stages but areas of erosion at low flow stages (Lane & Borland 1954; and many others).

Confluence scour zones have received a lot of attention because the deep water in these zones is relevant to construction of bridge piers and pipeline crossings. The geometry and orientation of confluence scour zones are influenced once again by factors such as the confluence angle and the relative discharges of the entering channels. As the confluence angle increases the scour zone changes from trough shaped to more basin-like (Ashmore & Parker 1983; Best 1986). If the discharge of the entering channels are similar, the long axis of the scour tends to bisect the confluence angle (Best 1986). If one channel is dominant the scour zone tends to parallel the direction of this channel (Ashmore & Parker 1983; Best 1987; Figs 7 and 9).

The maximum depth of scour (d_s) is commonly expressed as a function of the average depth of the joining channels (d_1, d_2) at channel-forming discharge, i.e.

$$d_s^* = \frac{d_s}{(d_1 + d_2)/2}. \qquad (3)$$

When expressed in this way the dimensionless scour depth (d_s^*) commonly ranges up to 4, and may be as large as 6 (Mosley 1976, 1982a; Ashmore & Parker 1983; Best 1986; Kjerfve et al. 1979). However, with field measurement it is difficult to locate the maximum depth, and to be sure this geometry is in equilibrium with the flow.

Dimensionless maximum scour depth has been related to the confluence angle and the relative discharge of the entering channels (Mosley 1976, 1982a; Ashmore & Parker 1983; Best 1986, 1988). For a given relative discharge, scour depth increases with confluence angle and appears to approach an upper limit asymptotically (i.e. the relationship is nonlinear). For a given confluence angle, d_s^* increases as the discharges in the entering channels tend to equality. If one channel is overwhelmingly dominant the maximum scour depth must be equivalent to that in a single channel bend and the dependence on confluence angle is lost. There is a lot of scatter on plots of scour depth versus confluence angle and relative discharge using field data, suggesting that not all of the controlling variables are included. Mosley (1976) related d_s^* to sediment transport rate, and Mosley (1982a) related d_s^* to discharge for the Ohau River. Ashmore & Parker (1983) suggested that d_s^* might be related to a densimetric Froude number and the average water surface slopes of the entering channels, but field data did not support such correlations. It seems that the cross-sectional asymmetry of the entering channels, and the presence of multiple channels at the confluence may also influence d_s^*.

A simple, approximate model for the maximum equilibrium scour depth in confluence zones can be constructed if it is assumed that the joining channels can be represented by segments of sine-generated curves. In this model, the maximum scour depth is located approximately at the apex of the curved segments where the centreline radii of curvature (r_{c1} and r_{c2}) are at a minimum and the channels are orientated in the mean down valley direction. The upstream junction corner of the entering channels corresponds approximately to the crossovers in the sine-generated curves, where the channels have their maximum deviation angles (α_1 and α_2) from the down valley direction. The *maximum* conflu-

ence angle is given by

$$\alpha = \alpha_1 + \alpha_2 = \frac{1}{2\pi}\left(\frac{M_1}{r_{c1}} + \frac{M_2}{r_{c2}}\right) \quad \text{(radians)} \quad (4)$$

where M_1 and M_2 are the channel lengths in one wavelength, or four times the channel length from the crossover to the position of maximum scour depth. The deviation angles α_1 and α_2 are also related to channel segment sinuosity as

$$\alpha = 2.2\left(\frac{sn - 1}{sn}\right)^{0.5} \quad \text{(radians)}. \qquad (5)$$

Using equation (1), the maximum dimensionless scour depth for each channel segment is given by

$$\frac{d_s}{d_c} = \left(\frac{r_c + w/2}{r_c}\right)^a \qquad (6)$$

where d_c is the centreline depth of the segment, and w is its width. As the scour depth given by equation (6) will generally be different for each channel segment it is necessary to devise a way of determining a single value. In the absence of a more rigorous analysis, this value is assumed to be given by

$$d_s = \frac{q_1 d_{c1}}{Q}\left[1 + \frac{w_1}{2r_{c1}}\right]^a + \frac{q_2 d_{c2}}{Q}\left[1 + \frac{w_2}{2r_{c2}}\right]^a \qquad (7)$$

where Q_1 and Q_2 are the discharges of the joining channels, Q is combined discharge, $r_{c1} = M_1/2\pi\alpha_1$ and $r_{c2} = M_2/2\pi\alpha_2$. Equation (7) indicates that the maximum scour depth must depend on at least the confluence angle and the relative discharges of the joining channels, but also M and a. However, if common values of w/r_c of 0.5 to 0.33 and a of 4 to 6 are used in the case of equal sized channels, values of d_s^* of between 1.85 and 3.8 are obtained which are in the same range as common field values. This method does not take into account the effects of the shear layer between the joining channels, nor of flow separation downstream of avalanche faces or the equivalent alternate bars. However, the heights of alternate bars with avalanche faces and point bars evolved from them will be comparable.

As confluence angles and relative discharges will change with flow stage, the orientation and geometry of the scour zone will also change (Ashmore & Parker 1983; Bergeron & Roy 1988, Ashmore this volume). The confluence angle may be larger at low flow stages relative to high flow stages, and the position of the confluence may be further upstream (Figs 7 and 9). Thus, at high flow stages deposition may occur in the upstream end of the low-flow scour zone, whereas at low flow stages these high stage deposits are eroded and deposited downstream in the high stage scour zone. If one channel becomes dominant the maximum scour depth may be decreased and the scour zone moved towards the outer bank of the subordinate channel, possibly inducing bank erosion (Ashmore & Parker 1983; Fig. 7). The position of the confluence scour zone will shift in response to erosion of the outer banks of both entering channels and concomitant deposition near the downstream tip of the upstream braid bar (Ashmore this volume). The confluence scour will also change in orientation and geometry if there is avulsive shift of an upstream channel (Ashmore & Parker 1983).

The confluence scour zone passes laterally into topographically high bars which are directly analogous to point bars in single curved channels and represent parts of alternate bars in straight channels. There is only one bar present if the confluence is asymmetrical (one straight-through channel; Fig. 9). Longitudinal ridges of sediment on these bars extending parallel to the edges of the scour zone (Ashmore 1982; Ashmore & Parker 1983; Fig. 9) result from episodic deposition and are dynamically equivalent to the bar tail scrolls mentioned previously.

'Hydraulic geometry' of confluence zones

The widths and cross-sectional areas of the single channels at and downstream of confluence zones are generally less than those of the entering channels combined. This must mean that mean flow velocities in confluence zones are relatively large. Lyell (1830) explained this phenomenon in the case of tributary junctions as due to less flow resistance in the single channel which has a smaller wetted perimeter than the two entering channels. The differences in hydraulic geometry between the entering channels and the confluence zone and downstream are discussed by Roy & Woldenberg (1986), Roy & Roy (1988), and Roy et al. (1988).

Geometry of diffluence zones

Downstream of confluence scours the maximum depth decreases and in braided rivers the channel commonly widens and splits around a braid bar. In straight channels a mid-channel alternate bar would occur in this position (Fig. 7). Migratory lobes of sediment ('unit bars', Ashmore 1982) occur in this zone, possibly related to episodic bank erosion within or upstream of the confluence scour zone. If the diffluence angle is large and/or one dividing channel is dominant, there is a tendency for the upstream side bar to build into the subordinate channel from the outer bank thus tending to block its entrance (Chalov 1974; Bridge et al. 1986; Best & Reid 1987; Kasthuri & Pundarikanthan 1987).

Flow in braided rivers at the bar scale

Flow in curved channel segments

The flow in individual curved channels around braid bars is broadly equivalent to that in single-channel sinuous rivers, and can be approximated by simple flow models (Bridge & Gabel 1992; Bridge 1992; Figs 10–12). Curved flow around any type of channel bar results in a flow-transverse component of water surface slope towards the inner, convex bank, a spiral flow pattern, and convective accelerations and decelerations of the depth-averaged flow. The spiral flow pattern arises primarily because of an imbalance through the flow depth of curvature-induced centrifugal forces and the pressure gradient associated with the transverse-sloping water surface. The convective accelerations and decelerations are associated with spatially-varying bed topography and channel curvature and, to a lesser extent, with the spiral flow. These flow patterns cause the maximum depth-averaged velocity to cross from the inner, convex bank at the bend entrance towards the outer, concave bank with progression around the bend. Associated with this flow pattern is a net outward flow in the upstream segments of bends, and a net inward flow in the downstream segments (Dietrich & Smith 1983; Bridge & Gabel 1992; Figs 10–12). Bed shear stress tends to vary in a similar way to depth-averaged flow velocity. However, as flow resistance co-efficients tend to be controlled by local bed configuration rather than larger-scale bar topography, bed shear stress may not always have a simple relationship with depth-averaged flow velocity (Bridge & Jarvis 1982; Bridge & Gabel 1992).

In general, spatial variation in the magnitude of depth-averaged velocity, deviation of the depth-averaged velocity vector from the mean channel direction, magnitude of the spiral flow components, and transverse bed and water surface slopes all increase as the radius of curvature of the bend decreases, as dimensionless bed shear stress increases, and as the flow resistance

MEAN VELOCITY VECTORS

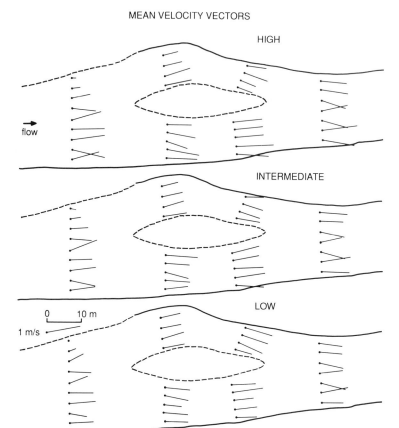

Fig. 10. Vertically-averaged flow velocity vectors for high, intermediate and low flow stages associated with a braid bar, Calamus River, Nebraska (from Bridge & Gabel 1992).

coefficient decreases. In the typically low sinuosity (<1.1) channel segments of braided rivers, the spiral flow and depth-averaged across-stream flow components are of the same order of magnitude, and are one or two orders of magnitude less than the along-stream flow components (Figs 11 and 12). At bend entrances the inward-directed near-bed spiral flow components tend to be counteracted by outward-directed depth-averaged flows, such that there is an overall outward flow increasing in magnitude from the bed upwards (Fig. 12). In the downstream parts of bends the inward-directed depth-averaged flow adds to the inward-directed spiral flow at the bed (Fig. 12). Deviation angles of these flow components from the mean downstream direction are generally only a few degrees, and normally less than 10°, which makes them very difficult to measure, especially in the presence of bedforms such as dunes (Bridge & Gabel 1992; Ashworth & Ferguson 1986).

In most braided channel segments the discharge will change as overall discharge changes, but it may not change in the same sense. All of the flow patterns mentioned above will change character with discharge, and new ones arise as a result of discharge variation. With falling discharge, the water flows in a more sinuous course around the emerging bar, resulting in relatively strong across-stream components of depth-averaged flow near the bend entrance, possibly enhanced magnitude of spiral flow, and rapid movement of the maximum depth-averaged velocity from the inner to outer bank. However, the magnitude of the spiral flow also increases as flow resistance decreases, and changes in flow resistance with discharge depend on changes in the relative roughness of bed forms and bed grains. In the sand-bed Calamus river, resistance coefficients at a point vary little with flow stage because maximum-steepness dunes were always present and more or less in equilibrium with the

MEAN FLOW VELOCITY VECTORS

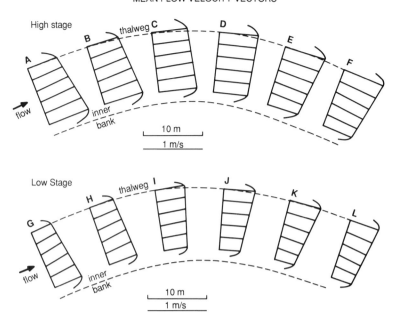

Fig. 11. Theoretical (see Bridge 1992) vertically-averaged flow velocity vectors at high and low flow stage for curved channel segments comparable to those in the Calamus River (Fig. 10). Channel cross-sections shown in Fig. 12.

flow (Bridge & Gabel 1992). In other sand-bed rivers large dunes in disequilibrium with falling flow, or a change from upper-stage plane beds to dunes as discharge falls, could increase resistance coefficients. In coarse sand-gravel rivers a transition from dunes to lower-stage plane beds as stage falls may decrease resistance coefficients. Alternatively, increasing relative roughness of falling flows over plane gravel beds may increase resistance coefficients. Thus, both flow velocity and bed shear stress patterns are likely to be difficult to predict in falling, disequilibrium flows.

New flow patterns may arise at high flow stages as new channels are cut, particularly where zones of high flow velocity can take advantage of topographically low areas. As an example, the relatively high water levels on the outside of curved channels may lead to spilling of water over a low section of bank, and possibly the development of a new channel transverse to the original channel (e.g. Ashmore 1982). Falling stage flow may also be diverted into low areas of the emerging bar topography, leading in some cases to incision of existing or new cross-bar channels.

As at-a-station hydraulic geometry normally varies among different channel segments (see previous section) cross-sectionally averaged flow velocity and depth will vary incongruently among channel segments as discharge varies (e.g. Cheetham 1979; Bridge & Gabel 1992). For example, higher velocities in chute channels relative to adjacent curved channels may occur at flood stage, but with similar or smaller velocities at lower stage. Such differences may lead to erosion of one channel and deposition in the other, which will result in a change in hydraulic geometry.

Flow in confluence zones

Very little detailed information is available on how the flow patterns in confluence zones vary in time and space. Most useful data come from flume experiments, and from river studies where measuring bridges were constructed (e.g. Mosley 1976, Ashmore 1982, this volume; Ashmore & Parker 1983; Best 1986, 1987, 1988; Best & Reid 1984, 1987; Best & Roy 1991; Roy et al. 1988; Roy & Bergeron 1990). However, other data are also available (e.g. Ashworth & Ferguson 1986; Davoren & Mosley 1986; Ashmore et al. 1992; Ferguson et al. 1992). Confluence flow has been compared to the flow

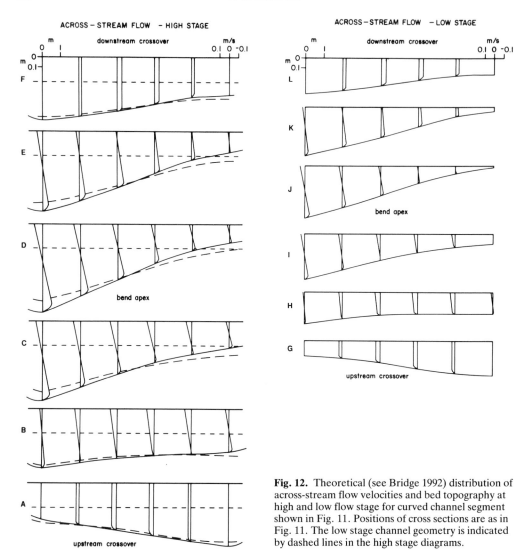

Fig. 12. Theoretical (see Bridge 1992) distribution of across-stream flow velocities and bed topography at high and low flow stage for curved channel segment shown in Fig. 11. Positions of cross sections are as in Fig. 11. The low stage channel geometry is indicated by dashed lines in the high stage diagrams.

in joining river bends and, because the cross-sectional area of the joined channels is less than the sum of the two joining channels, to wall jets (Mosley 1976; Ashmore & Parker 1983). Even in straight channels with double or multiple rows of alternate bars the water flows as a series of sinuous threads adjacent to each other (Fig. 1). The flow in confluences is discussed here in terms of three zones (cf. Best 1987): (1) entrance zones; (2) confluence mixing zone where the joining fluid streams become asymptotic and mix; (3) zones of flow separation with vertical axes near inner convex banks at the upstream tip of the confluence and associated with side bars adjacent to the confluence scour. Details of the

flow in these zones depends at least on the confluence angle and the relative discharges of the joining channels, which vary with flow stage.

Entrance zones are equivalent to the 'riffle' zones of curved channels, and downstream-dipping avalanche faces (tributary-mouth bars, chute bars) may be present. Such avalanche faces are typically present in natural channels where the confluence angle exceeds 20°. However, in straight channels with small width/depth ratios, the confluence angles associated with the confluence between adjacent alternate bars with avalanche faces may be less than 20° (Fig. 1). At the crest of the avalanche faces at high flow stage the depth-averaged flow velocities are expected to be greatest near the outer banks, and there should be a net across-stream component of flow towards the centre of the confluence throughout the flow depth as curvature-induced secondary flows are negligible (Figs 11 and 12). However, as the crestlines of the avalanche faces are generally oblique to flow, the separated and reattached flow downstream of the crestline will have a component of near-bed flow towards the banks, whereas the surface flow will continue to be directed towards the centre of the confluence (Fig. 13). At low flow stages shifts in the maximum velocity loci (Fig. 7) may result in changes in crest height and obliquity. Dissection of the crests of the avalanche faces may produce a complex, multichannel confluence zone (Fig. 9). The distance downstream from the crest of the

avalanche face to the reattachment zone is expected to be proportional to the height of the avalanche face, as with dunes. Thus, changes in the height and obliquity of the avalanche faces with discharge will influence the geometry of the scour zone associated with the reattaching boundary layer (Fig. 9).

The curvature of the joining channels in confluence zones should inevitably give rise to superelevation of the water surface in mid-channel and spiral flow with near-bed flow towards the outer banks (Mosley 1976, 1982a; Ashmore 1982; Ashmore & Parker 1983; Roy et al. 1988; Ashmore et al. 1992). The maximum water surface superelevation and the magnitude of the spiral flow tend to increase as the confluence angle (hence curvature) increase

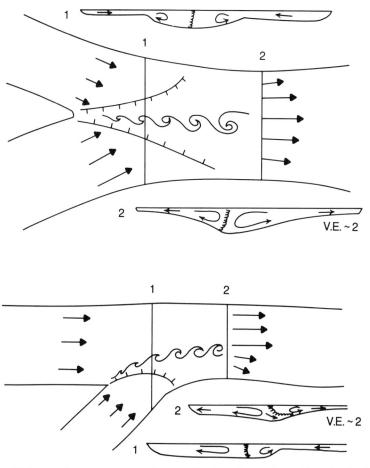

Fig. 13. Idealized high stage flow patterns at confluences showing tributary bars with avalanche faces, zones of Kelvin-Helmholtz instability at the interface of the joining streams, vertically-averaged flow velocity vectors (in plan) and cross-stream circulation patterns (in cross sections). Based on Best (1986) and Best & Roy (1991).

(Ashmore & Parker 1983) as expected. By analogy with flow in bends, the maximum high-stage flow velocity should occur near the centre of the confluence scour, with lower velocities near the outer banks (Fig. 11). The location and relative depth of the confluence scour zone is clearly influenced by the curvature-induced spiral flow, and migration of the loci of maximum depth-averaged velocity towards the centre of the channel. However, it is also influenced by: reattachment of the separated boundary layer downstream of the upstream avalanche faces; flow acceleration associated with a reduced cross-sectional area (possibly influenced by separation zones over side bars; Best & Reid 1984); enhanced turbulence in the mixing layer between the joining streams (Best 1986). At the time of writing, it is not possible to assess the relative importance of these factors.

The mixing zone between the two joining streams results from their velocity differential and can commonly be seen clearly if the suspended sediment loads of the two streams differ. Some mixing is inevitable in any turbulent flow. However, the existence of time-averaged relative velocity leads to a Kelvin-Helmholtz type instability and vortices with near-vertical axes form that become entrained in the faster moving flow (Fig. 13). The wavelength of these vortices is controlled by the relative velocity, densities and viscosities of the joining flows (i.e. dependent on Reynolds and Richardson numbers). If one stream is slower near the bed than the other, for instance due to flow separation in the lee of an upstream avalanche face, the mixing layer is distorted near the bed towards the slower stream (Fig. 13; Best & Roy 1991). This may result in upwelling of the fluid from one stream into the region occupied by the other (Fig. 13), which greatly affects the mixing of sediment from the joining streams.

Zones of flow separation with vertical axes of flow rotation are caused by adverse pressure gradients associated with curvature-induced transverse water surface gradients in combination with reduced downstream slope resulting from local flow expansion and deceleration. Such flows result in enhanced deposition on the downstream tips of braid bars and side bars adjacent to confluence scour zones, thereby reducing the effective local cross-sectional area of the channel. Note that flow separation *enhances* deposition on side bars rather than being the sole cause for their occurrence (cf. Bristow *et al.* 1993). These separation zones are most marked for large confluence angles. For the case of an asymmetrical junction the length and width of the separation zone increases with the confluence angle and the discharge of the tributary relative to the main channel (Best & Reid 1984).

During rising flow stages a partially abandoned braided channel segment may receive water from its downstream junction with an active channel. In other words, water flows upstream into the channel. This situation apparently occurs also in ephemeral rivers where water may start to flow in only part of a river system. This results in flow of water from an active tributary up the inactive tributary from their confluence (Alam *et al.* 1985; Reid *et al.* 1989).

Mathematical models of flow in confluences are not generally available because it is difficult to describe the complicated flow mechanics described above. Hager's (1984, 1987) flow model predicts well the geometry of the separated flow zone in Best & Reid's (1984) laboratory model of a tributary junction. However, some of the assumptions in this model (e.g. negligible friction loss, uniform flow, constant channel widths and depths) are unlikely to be applicable to natural rivers. Flow models of single river bends may be capable of giving at least a qualitative picture of the velocity field (e.g. Bridge & Gabel 1992; Bridge 1992). Indeed, as shown previously, such flow models predict confluence scour depths of the correct order of magnitude.

Flow in diffluence zones

Flow in diffluence zones is not known well (but see Straub 1935; Ashworth & Ferguson 1986; Davoren & Mosley 1986; Ferguson *et al.* 1992). By analogy with flow in curved channels, the maximum velocity locus, which is in mid-channel, starts to split in this zone such that each thread of maximum velocity is close to the upstream tip of the braid bar downstream. The mixing layer of the confluence zone does not exist as the relative velocity of the two streams is zero here (analogous to 'downstream recovery zone' of Best 1987). Bridge & Gabel (1992) observed relatively complicated patterns of convergence and divergence of local depth-averaged velocity in this zone, which were associated with bar-scale bed topography (see also Mosley 1976; Ashmore *et al.* 1992). In cases where the diffluence angle is large, as perhaps at the entrance of a channel that is being abandoned, a zone of flow separation with a vertical axis may occur near the outer bank of the channel entrance. Such a zone will enhance the deposition of sediment here. The width and length of this zone increase as the discharge into the filling channel decreases relative to the main channel (Kasthuri & Pundarikanthan 1987).

Sediment transport in braided rivers at the bar scale

It is very difficult to measure or calculate the total and local sediment transport in braided rivers because of its temporal and spatial variability, and obvious logistical problems. Some of the variability is associated with turbulence, the movement of sediment as bedwaves of various scales (e.g. ripples, dunes, unit bars, complete braid or point bars), random changes in sediment supply (e.g. bank slumping, breakup of 'armored' beds), local channel cutting and abandonment, weather-related changes in water discharge and sediment supply, and tectonically induced changes in sediment supply. Temporal scales of such variation range from seconds to many years, and spatial scales range from mm to km. Detection of any progressive or periodic changes in sediment transport must therefore depend on the time and space interval and extent of measurement. Most experimental studies of bedload transport are sufficient only to resolve time variations at a point on the order of hours (exceptionally minutes), and space variations on the bar and channel scale. Commonly, bedload transport samples taken over a minute or so at intervals of minutes or hours have a coefficient of variation of tens of percent (Bridge & Jarvis, 1982; Ashmore 1988; Gabel 1993; Bennett 1992). Typically, such measurements can reveal the growth and migration of dune-like bedforms, unit bars, and braid bar complexes (e.g. Griffiths 1979; Ashmore 1988, 1991*a*; Davoren & Mosley 1986; Kuhnle & Southard 1988; Bennett 1992; Ikeda 1983; Hoey 1992). The ensuing discussion is concerned mainly with grain size and rate of bedload transport at the bar scale over the lifespan of a bar. Then, the mode of sediment movement associated with smaller scale bedforms is considered.

Bedload transport at the bar scale

Studies of bedload transport in the curved channel segments adjacent to braid bars and point bars for the case of sandy rivers at high flow stage demonstrate that the loci of maximum bedload transport rate and grain size are similar to those of mean flow velocity and bed shear stress (e.g. Dietrich & Smith 1984; Bridge & Gabel 1992). With progression around a curved-channel segment the bedload grains larger than the average tend to move preferentially towards the outer bank, whereas those finer than the average tend to move towards the inner bank. In general, there is a small net component of bed-load transport towards the outer banks. However, for streams with a substantial gravel fraction, although the locus of maximum grain size follows that of bed shear stress, the locus of maximum bedload transport rate stays close to the centre of the channel (Bridge & Jarvis 1982; Dietrich & Whiting 1989; Bridge 1992).

The reason for this difference between sandy and gravelly streams lies in the fact that both mean grainsize and transport rate of bedload depend on what proportion of the total bed shear stress is available for bedload transport relative to that associated with immobile bed friction and bedform drag. For example, in mixed sand-gravel streams, gravel is transported only where bed shear stress is greatest. Bedload transport rates tend to be low here, however, as the bed shear stress is just above the threshold of grain motion and the bed may be armored. Thus, higher bedload transport rates can occur where lower bed shear stresses act on sandy beds. In sand-bed streams an increase in bed shear stress may result in an increase or decrease in bedform height/length (hence form drag) such that the bed shear stress effective in bedload transport may decrease or increase.

Despite these complications, high stage bedload transport rates and mean grain sizes agree well with theoretical models for steady, equilibrium flow conditions (Bridge 1984, 1992; Bridge & Gabel 1992). It is not possible at present to predict the sediment transport vectors of individual grain size fractions as these are a complicated function of the near-bed flow field and bed slope over bars and oblique-crested bedforms like dunes (Bridge & Jarvis 1982; Dietrich & Smith 1984; Bridge 1992).

Bed material normally fines downstream on the tops of both braid bars and point bars in modern sandy and gravelly rivers, but is relatively coarse in the thalwegs of the downstream segments (Straub 1935; Bluck 1971, 1974, 1976, 1979, 1982; Smith 1974; Jackson 1975*a*, 1976*a*; Bridge & Jarvis 1976, 1982; Lewin 1976; Deitrich *et al.* 1979; Crowley 1983; Ferguson & Werritty 1983; Ashworth & Ferguson 1986, 1989; Ashworth *et al.* 1992*b*). Thus the mean grain size of bed material reflects the distribution of bed shear stress and bedload grain size at high (channel-forming) discharges, as would be expected (Bridge & Jarvis 1982; Bridge & Gabel 1992).

As discharge changes, the changing patterns of bed shear stress, bed configuration and available bed material will result in complicated patterns of transport rate and grain size of the bedload. Mixed-size bedload transport models (e.g. Bridge & Bennett, 1992) clearly show how bedload size is controlled by both the flow conditions and the available sediment. Over a flood event, the size distribution of the available sediment and the bedload may vary as well as the bedload transport rate (e.g. Vogel *et al.* 1992). In general, relatively diminished bed shear stresses at low flow stages will result in smaller grain sizes and transport rates of bedload, or bedload transport may cease altogether. Static armor layers may develop. Limited deposition at these low flow stages results in veneers and patches of relatively fine grained sediments (e.g. Rust 1972; Bluck 1979; Boothroyd & Ashley 1975) and filling of openwork gravels with a sandy matrix (e.g. Minter & Toens 1970; Smith 1974; Beschta & Jackson 1979; Frostick *et al.* 1984).

Studies of bedload transport rate in confluences are rare (e.g. Davoren & Mosley 1986; Ashworth *et al.* 1992a,b; Ferguson *et al.* 1992) but suggest that the largest bedload transport rates generally occur where flow velocities and bed shear stresses are also largest, as long as sediment is available for transport (e.g. bed is not armored). Tracing the paths of seeded particles of various sizes (Best 1986, 1987, 1988; Roy & Bergeron 1990) clearly demonstrates that bedload particles travel more-or-less parallel to the channel banks and bed contours as they pass through the confluence scour zone (see also Ashmore & Parker 1983). This implies that bedload from the two joining channels experience very little mixing as it passes through the confluence zone. Best (1986, 1987) observed in his flume experiments that bedload moves along the sides of the confluence scour but not in its deepest part, and this separation of bedload became more marked as the scour depth increased. In contrast, Roy & Bergeron's (1990) observations of low-flow bedload transport in a low-angle natural confluence indicate that some bedload moves laterally down the sides of the scour zone. By analogy with the movement of bedload through single curved channels, the movement of grains more or less parallel to channel banks implies an approximate balance between the transverse gravity force into the scour zone and the fluid drag out of the scour zone at channel-forming discharges. Grains coarser than the mean are expected to have a small transverse downslope component of motion, whereas finer-than-average grains move preferentially upslope. However, as the forces on bedload grains are expected to vary with discharge, there should be times and places where most grains are moving downslope into

the scour zone (falling stage) or upslope out of it (rising stage).

Continuing the analogy with flow in bends, the mean grain size of bedload should increase with bed shear stress. Therefore, the largest mean grain sizes should occur in the base of the scour zone, whereas the finest grains should occur immediately upstream of the scour zone and near the banks adjacent to the downstream end of the scour zone (as observed by Best 1987, 1988). The absence of bedload in the deepest parts of the scour zone observed by Best (1987, 1988) may be due to armoring of the bed and/or the movement of all incoming bedload up the sides of the scour by spiral flows and intense turbulence.

Systematic detailed measurements of suspended sediment load have not been made in braided rivers. Suspended sediment distributions are likely to be very difficult to predict in confluence zones in view of the nature of the zones of mixing, upwelling and flow separation.

Bed configurations

Sediment is transported over braid bars and point bars as distinct bed configurations. These may be microforms, mesoforms or macroforms (terminology of Jackson 1975b). The occurrence and geometry of microforms (e.g. ripples) are controlled by inner-zone (viscous sublayer) boundary layer characteristics such as boundary Reynolds number or grain size. Mesoforms (e.g. dunes) are controlled by outer-zone boundary layer characteristics such as flow depth. Dunes include bed configurations that other authors have referred to as sand waves, megaripples, linguoid bars, transverse bars and so on (summary in Allen 1982; Bridge 1985; Ashley 1990). Macroforms (bars) scale with channel width, and their heights are comparable to mean depth of the formative flow. As discussed previously, solitary bedforms with or without slip facies occur on braid bars and point bars. These must be considered to be macroforms as well as the larger bars because they scale with the width of the channel segment in which they occur and have lifespans comparable with these channels. Thus solitary macroforms such as bar heads (Bluck 1971, 1976; Lewin 1976), riffles and tributary-mouth bars, and bar tail 'scroll' bars (Sundborg 1956; Nilsson & Martvall 1972; Jackson 1976b; Bridge & Jarvis 1982; Nanson 1980; Fig. 1) all represent various parts of alternate unit bars. The 'longitudinal ridges' adjacent to confluence scours described by Ashmore (1982) are also analogous to scroll bars. Chute bars and deltas occur at the end of channel segments as flow expands into a different segment (Collinson 1970; McGowen & Garner 1970; Smith 1974; Bluck 1976; Lewin 1976, 1978; Levey 1978; Gustavson 1978; Cant 1978; Ashmore 1982; Ferguson & Werritty 1983). The ephemeral 'chutes and lobes' of Southard *et al.* (1984) in shallow gravel-bed rivers are also macroforms. This section is concerned with mesoforms and microforms, the geometry, migration patterns and hydraulic controls of which are discussed at length in Allen (1982), Middleton & Southard (1984), and Southard & Boguchwal (1990).

At high flow stages the most common type of bed configuration on sandy braid bars or point bars is dunes with curved (sinuous and linguoid) crestlines (e.g. Harms & Fahnestock 1965; Coleman 1969; Bluck 1976; Smith 1971*a*; Jackson 1975*a*, 1976*b*; Blodgett & Stanley 1980; Cant 1978; Cant & Walker 1978; Bridge & Jarvis 1982; Crowley 1983; Bridge & Gabel 1992). Straight-crested forms are common on the higher parts of bars where flow velocity and depth are relatively low, and upper-stage plane beds occur locally in shallow areas of high velocity. Ripples are normally restricted to areas of slow-moving water near banks. In gravelly streams, high-flow bedforms include more straight-crested dunes, 'bedload sheets' (which are low-relief asymmetrical bedforms analogous to dunes; Hein & Walker 1977; Kuhnle &

Southard 1988; Whiting *et al.* 1988; Dietrich *et al.* 1989; Bennett 1992), lower stage plane beds and transverse ribs (analogous to antidunes; Koster 1978; Allen 1982; Ferguson & Werritty 1983). Pebble clusters are common on lower stage plane gravel beds (Dal Cin 1968; Teisseyre 1977*a*; Brayshaw *et al.* 1983; Brayshaw 1984, 1985; Naden & Brayshaw 1987) and static and mobile armor layers commonly develop. Discoidal and tabular gravel grains on lower stage plane beds and the backs of bedforms like bedload sheets are normally imbricated (dip upstream), whereas those that accumulate on the avalanche faces of dunes commonly dip downstream (pseudoimbrication).

Dune crestlines at high flow stage are commonly oblique to local channel direction, being particularly obvious for straight- and sinuous-crested forms (Fig. 14). This is due to across-channel variation in bedload transport rate and dune height, in turn associated with the flow pattern over braid bars. The orientations of dune crestlines mimic the orientations of alternate unit bars (Figs 1 and 14), indicating that the pattern of flow and sediment transport over ancestral alternate bars has not been modified greatly in the development of braid or point bars. Thus the crestlines of these bedforms are not in general normal to directions of sediment transport or near-bed flow velocity (Fig. 1). However, the orientation of spurs in dune

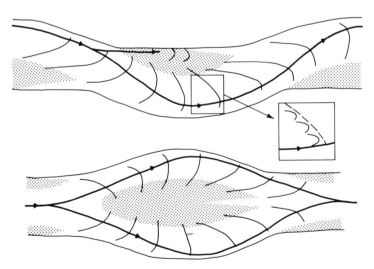

Fig. 14. Idealized pattern of dune crestlines and flow velocity in braided and unbraided channels at high flow stage, based on numerous studies of rivers (e.g. Hein & Walker 1977; Cant 1978; Cant & Walker 1978; Deitrich *et al.* 1979; Blodgett & Stanley 1980; Bridge & Jarvis 1982; Crowley 1983). Thick black lines with arrows are loci of maximum flow velocity and mean grain size. Dune crestlines are indicated schematically as sinuous to straight crested; however, the inset shows the equivalent orientation of linguoid dunes.

troughs is generally parallel to local flow direction. This has relevance to the orientation of cross-stratification, as discussed later.

The orientation of bedform crestlines under zones of flow separation with vertical axes may be highly oblique to local channel orientation, and the bedforms might even migrate upstream. Upstream migration of bedforms might also be associated with the downstream parts of some abandoned channel segments. In these cases, the crestline orientations are controlled by the orientation of local flow vectors, and not necessarily by across-channel variations in bedload transport rate and bedform height, as above.

Longitudinal bedforms (crestlines parallel to local flow direction) also occur in rivers (reviewed by Allen 1982). The most common are ribbons of sand moving over lower-stage plane gravel beds, but longitudinal sand ridges have also been reported on upper-stage plane beds (e.g. Coleman 1969).

At flow stages lower than bankfull, dunes are generally shorter and lower, and the proportion of curved crested dunes decreases relative to straight-crested dunes, ripples and lower-stage plane beds (Coleman 1969; Singh & Kumar 1974; Jackson 1975a, 1976b; Bridge & Jarvis 1976, 1982; Gustavson 1978; Crowley 1983). Dune geometry may not be in equilibrium with changing flow stage. Gabel (1993) studied the geometry and dynamics of dunes over changing flow stage in a braided reach of the sandy Calamus River in Nebraska. Dune heights, lengths, migration rates, creations and destructions were measured concurrently with bedload transport rates, flow depth, flow velocity, and bed shear stress during a series of day-long surveys. These surveys were conducted sequentially during changing discharge at different sites around a braid bar. Within each survey, individual dune heights, lengths and migration rates as seen in streamwise cross sections varied greatly with time, due to local changes in flow conditions and the 3D shapes of the dunes. Over periods of several days, mean dune geometry and migration rate changed in response to changing flow conditions with a small time lag. Because this time lag was small, mean dune lengths and steepnesses did not deviate much from theoretical and empirical equilibrium values (e.g. Yalin 1977; Fredsoe 1982). Theoretical models for changes in dune height and length with changing discharge (e.g. Allen 1976; Fredsoe 1979) performed with varying degrees of success, pointing to a need to substantially improve such models.

Large dunes are commonly not in equilibrium with rapidly falling stages, and this is particularly true in shallow areas with small transverse bed slopes which can become exposed rapidly by small decreases in water level. There has been a tendency to define emergent dunes or solitary dune-like macroforms as braid bars, and the channels that dissect these bedforms as braided channels (e.g. Smith 1971a, 1974; Blodgett & Stanley 1980). Actually, dissected dunes may superficially resemble solitary macroforms because dunes in disequilibrium cannot be expected to show regular repetitive patterns (Allen 1982). Furthermore, straight-crested dunes normally have long wavelength/height and extremely variable sizes (e.g. Costello & Southard 1981).

The emergence of braid and point bar areas during falling flow stages, the modification of flow patterns, and the dissection of emerging areas by small channels, results in a diverse orientation of the superimposed bedforms. The dendritic channel systems that develop parallel to the local slopes of emerging bars may terminate in small deltas. Desiccation cracks occur in local areas of mud deposition (e.g. in bedforms troughs and chute channels), and the encroachment of animals and plants on to emerging bar surfaces results in root casts, burrows and trails.

Finally, distinct bed configurations may occur locally in areas where net erosion is proceeding, especially in the thalwegs of channels where cohesive mud is present. Such erosional marks include flutes, gutter casts, rill marks and potholes (reviewed by Allen 1982).

Grain size-density sorting associated with bedforms

The size sorting of sand and gravel fractions associated with bedload sheets and dunes is discussed by Smith (1972, 1974), Allen (1982), Ikeda (1983), Iseya & Ikeda (1987), Kuhnle & Southard (1988), Whiting et al. (1988), Dietrich et al. (1989), Wilcock & Southard (1989), Chiew (1991), and Bennett (1992). At low sediment transport and supply rates the trough areas of bedforms are commonly relatively coarse grained and armored, whereas the finer grains comprise the moving bedforms. As sediment transport rate increases the coarser grains can be transported to the bedform crests. If sand supply is abundant the pore spaces between gravel grains are occupied by sand, especially in the bedform trough areas. Gravel beds with sand filling the interstices are relatively smooth, which facilitates the movement of the larger grains (e.g. overpassing).

Heavy minerals transported as bedload and

suspended load are commonly finer grained than associated light minerals. They may be concentrated where a flow which is powerful enough to entrain and transport all grain fractions decelerates and deposits some of them. The relatively small heavy minerals become protected from re-entrainment by the larger light minerals which can continue to move above them. Subsequent erosion may remove the larger light minerals but not the smaller heavies. Locations where such conditions prevail include the crestal and trough areas of a range of bedforms with or without flow separation (e.g. ripples, dunes, low-relief bedwaves such as bedload sheets, and bars) and in the lee of obstacles where deposition occurs (e.g. McQuivey & Keefer 1969; Brady & Jobson 1973; Slingerland 1977, 1984; Mosley & Schumm 1977; Minter 1978; Smith & Minter 1980; Buck 1983; Cheel 1985; Best & Brayshaw 1985; Slingerland & Smith 1986; Kuhnle & Southard 1990). Heavy mineral concentrations on the crests of bedforms are transient in view of the nature of bedform migration. However it is common to find heavy mineral concentrations above the erosion surfaces formed by migration of the trough regions of various scales of bedwave. At the bar scale, heavy mineral concentrations are common in channel thalwegs and bar heads (e.g. Smith & Minter 1980; Smith & Beukes 1983).

Erosion and deposition at the bar scale

Erosion and deposition at the bar scale are related to three main processes which are closely related to each other.

(1) Adjustments of the bed topography of braid and point bars as a result of seasonally changing discharge (e.g. Fig. 15). During rising flow stages erosion tends to occur in bend thalwegs, confluence scours and the upstream ends of bars, whereas these areas receive deposits during falling stages. In contrast, the downstream and topographically highest parts of bars tend to be areas of deposition at high flow stages, with erosion at low flow stages. It is important not to confuse the steep eroded downstream ends of bars with depositional avalanche faces.

(2) Bank erosion and deposition on adjacent bar margins (i.e. channel migration) are normally associated with (1). Such channel migration is episodic, and the deposition may be in the form of distinct unit bars (but not necessarily).

(3) Cutting of new channels, enlarging existing channels, abandonment and filling of others is closely associated with (2), as accreting bars commonly migrate into channel entrances, and

low areas adjacent to discrete unit bars are common conduits for diverted discharge. These processes are discussed below, followed by the nature of the deposited sediment.

Processes of erosion and deposition

In general, erosion and deposition are due to gradients of sediment transport rate, given by the sediment continuity equation:

$$-C_o \frac{\delta h}{\delta t} = \frac{\delta i_s}{\delta s} + \frac{\delta i_n}{\delta n} + \frac{1}{u_s}\frac{\delta i_s}{\delta t} + \frac{1}{u_n}\frac{\delta i_n}{\delta t}$$

(8)

where C_o is volume concentration of sediment in the bed, h is bed elevation, t is time, s and n are streamwise and across-stream space coordinates, i_s and i_n are streamwise and across-stream sediment transport rate by volume, and u_s and u_n are corresponding mean velocities of sediment grains. If bed topography is in equilibrium with a steady flow the term on the left hand side, and the last two terms on the right hand side, are zero when averaged over turbulence and bedforms of smaller scale than bars. As discharge varies, the bed topography is always potentially out of equilibrium with the flow. For example, as stage falls in curved channel segments, the cross-channel bed slope is too steep for the reduced flow and the transverse downslope gravity force on the bedload exceeds the upslope directed fluid drag. Thus, in the thalweg, the magnitude of $\delta i_n/\delta n$ exceeds $\delta i_n/\delta s$, the last two terms on the right hand side of equation (8) are generally negligible, and deposition occurs as described in (1) above. However, even in steady flows, $\delta i_s/\delta s$ and $\delta i_n/\delta n$ vary with time due to the passage of bedforms like unit bars, dunes, bank slumps, and so on.

The tendency for erosion in thalwegs near banks during floods leads to oversteepening and may induce failure (e.g. Turnbull et al. 1966; Thorne & Tovey 1981; Pizzuto 1984). The important factors governing bank erosion are the resistance of the banks to slumping and the ability of the flow to remove the slumped bank material. The shear strength of bank material, τ_s, is given by

$$\tau_s = C + P\mu_c$$

(9)

where C is cohesive strength, P is effective normal stress and ϕ_c is the static friction coefficient. The cohesive strength is increased by the presence of clay minerals, vegetation and cemented layers such as calcretes and silcretes. The effective normal stress depends on the weight of the potential slump and the excess

(A)

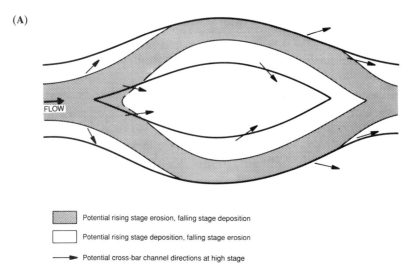

☐ (shaded) Potential rising stage erosion, falling stage deposition

☐ Potential rising stage deposition, falling stage erosion

→ Potential cross-bar channel directions at high stage

(B)   DOWNSTREAM PART OF CURVED CHANNEL OR CONFLUENCE

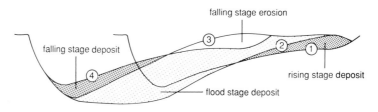

CURVED CHANNEL OR CONFLUENCE ENTRANCE

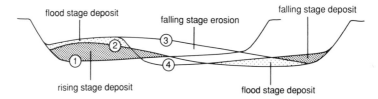

Fig. 15. (**A**) Theoretical locations of erosion and deposition in simple braided channel pattern during changing flow stage. (**B**) Cross-sections showing theoretical erosion and deposition during changing flow stage and channel migration. (1) low stage geometry; (2) flood stage geometry; (3) flood stage geometry following cut bank erosion and bar deposition; (4) final low stage geometry.

pore pressure. The excess pore pressure is increased (hence P is decreased) during falling flow stages when water flows out of the banks. The effect of undercutting is to increase the downslope component of the gravity force on bank material, which is the main force responsible for the downslope directed shear stress.

Slumps of bank material are typically on the order of $10^{-1}–10^{0}°$ m wide, $10^{0}–10^{1}$ m long (i.e. order of $10^{0}–10$ m^{3}) and occur periodically in time and space. Upon failure, slumps may remain coherent or disintegrate and become grain flows. The slumped material may be entrained by the flow and, if not, will contribute to armoring of the bed and protection of the bank against further erosion. Thus rates of bank erosion must depend on magnitudes of $\delta i_s / \delta n$

and $\delta i_n/\delta n$ at the toe of the bank, which must in turn be controlled by the spatial gradients of $\tau_o - \tau_c$, where τ_o is bed shear stress and τ_c is the critical entrainment stress. In the case of banks with large shear strength, providing large cohesive slump blocks, τ_c is expected to be large, thereby inhibiting erosion. Banks of cohesionless sand and gravel are the most easily erodible, and bank erosion rates can be the order of channel widths per year (i.e. 10^1–10^3 m a^{-1}) (e.g. Chien 1961; Coleman 1969; Bluck 1979; Werritty & Ferguson 1980; Ferguson & Werritty 1983; Ashworth & Ferguson 1986; Bristow 1987; review in Allen 1982).

A number of theoretical models relate bank erosion and channel migration in single curved channels to the nature of flow and sedimentary processes (e.g. Ikeda *et al.* 1981; Parker & Andrews 1986; Johannesson & Parker 1989; Hasegawa 1989; Odgaard 1989; Howard 1992). Largest erosion rates are normally associated with the largest near-bank velocity or depth, which normally occur just downstream of the bend apex. Unfortunately, these theoretical approaches are overly simplistic in that they do not consider flow unsteadiness and the unpredictable entrainment stresses of slump blocks. Furthermore, they normally contain empirical coefficients, the values of which must be 'fitted' to field data.

As channel geometry tends to be in equilibrium with high stage flow and sediment transport (Bridge 1984, 1992; Bridge & Jarvis 1982; Bridge & Gabel 1992) cut-bank retreat and associated flow expansion will inevitably result in deposition on adjacent bar surfaces. Likewise, if deposition occurs on a bar due to a local increase in sediment supply from upstream, narrowing of the channel cross section may induce erosion of the adjacent cut bank. Such depositional activity may be distinctly episodic as in the accretion of 'unit bars' to braid or point bars, but more gradual accretion may occur which does not involve 'unit bars'. The familiar 'accretion topography' results from the sequential accretion of unit bars (e.g. scroll bars).

There have been many studies of the patterns of channel migration for single curved channels (reviewed in Allen 1982; see also Elliott 1984; Ikeda & Parker 1989) but fewer for braided rivers (Coleman 1969; Bluck 1974, 1976, 1979; Werritty & Ferguson, 1980; Ferguson & Werritty 1983; Ashworth & Ferguson 1986; Bridge *et al.* 1986; Bristow 1987; Ashmore this volume). The nature of channel migration is critical to understanding the preservation of channel deposits. As flow patterns in curved channel segments vary with flow stage, so also

should channel migration patterns. For instance, if most erosion and deposition occurs around bankfull stage (e.g. gravel-bed streams), the large flow velocities near the outer banks of the downstream half of the bends should result in dominantly downstream bend migration. This would lead to preferential preservation of bar tail scrolls and erosion of bar heads. If substantial erosion and deposition are associated also with lower flow stages (e.g. sandy rivers) the largest flow velocities will also act upon cut bank locations all around the bend such that bend expansion may occur in addition to downstream translation. In this case, preservation of bar head units is possible, and abandonment of the curved channel by cut-off is more likely. If the upstream part of a bar is stabilized by vegetation, the bar may accrete and grow by lateral and downstream extension even if most erosion and deposition occur at high discharges (e.g. Calamus River; Bridge *et al.* 1986).

Confluence zones commonly migrate downstream in response to downstream migration of entering channels, especially for symmetrical confluences of similar channels (e.g. Ashmore, this volume). The lack of room for lateral migration of both side bars may lead to cutting of new (chute) channels, and the downstream migration of side bars may lead to blocking of the entrance of a downstream braid channel. Lateral migration of confluences is possible in the case of asymmetrical confluences, and those with entering channels of different discharge and/or geometry. Ashmore (this volume) also documents the expansion, rotation and obliteration of confluences in response to changes in the relative discharge or sediment supply of the entering channels.

Cutting and filling of channels is particularly characteristic of braided rivers although this occurs in all rivers to some degree. The processes are not well understood and no theoretical models are available. Channel diversion appears to be associated with high-stage scouring of thalwegs in curved channel segments and deposition of sediment as obstacles in braided channel entrances downstream (e.g. as riffles and bar heads) (Teisseyre 1977b; Ashmore 1982, 1991b; Bridge 1985). Once the process of channel abandonment is initiated the channel is progressively filled from the upstream end with bedload. Downstream migration of the adjacent enlarging channel causes blockage of the downstream end of the filling channel by the downstream tip of the enlarging channel's bar. In effect, this process represents the overriding of a stalled bar by an upstream bar, as happens with dune migration. The abandoned channel

may be reopened later, especially where a concave channel bank (with high water level)
approaches its entrance (e.g. Werritty &
Ferguson 1980; Ferguson & Werritty 1983;
Church's 1972 'secondary anastomosis').

According to Ferguson & Werritty (1983)
and Bristow (1987) channel migration by bar
erosion and accretion in braided rivers is
much more common than by channel switching.
Apparently, cross-bar channels are most
susceptible to switching position (Bristow 1987).
This is understandable as cross-bar channels
commonly occur between the discrete unit-bar

accretions to braid and point bars which form at
high flow stage. Examination of the accretion
topography in modern braided rivers and
adjacent floodplain areas (e.g. see photos in
Collinson, 1970; Mosley 1982b, Bridge et al.
1986; Cant & Walker 1978; Bluck 1979; Shelton
& Noble 1974) clearly indicates that bar accretion deposits are dominant over channel-fill
deposits, and that the downstream component
of bar migration is dominant over the lateral and
upstream components associated with bar
growth (expansion).

(A)

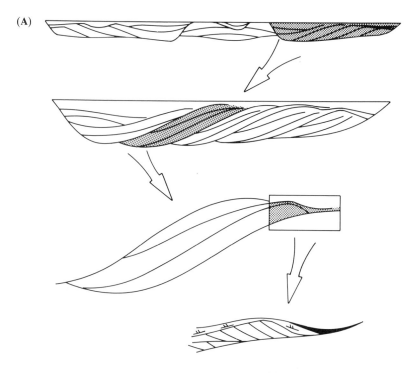

(B)   LEGEND

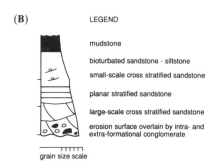

mudstone

bioturbated sandstone - siltstone

small-scale cross stratified sandstone

planar stratified sandstone

large-scale cross stratified sandstone

erosion surface overlain by intra- and
extra-formational conglomerate

grain size scale

Fig. 16. (**A**) Different scales of braided river deposits.
Top diagram is a cross section through the entire
channel belt showing four separate channel bar
deposits (storeys) and associated channel fills.
A single channel bar and fill (stippled) is expanded to
illustrate the seasonal accretionary units (bedsets).
These inclined bedsets are commonly referred to as
lateral-accretion deposits, although there is normally
a component of downstream accretion also. See
Fig. 15. The internal sedimentary structures
associated with part of a seasonal bedset are shown in
the lower diagram. The structures are associated with
flood stage migration of dunes and falling stage
migration of ripples. An organic rich mud drape
occurs in the swale adjacent to the accretionary ridge.
Symbols explained in legend. (**B**) Legend for Figs
16A, 18, 20, 24 to 26.

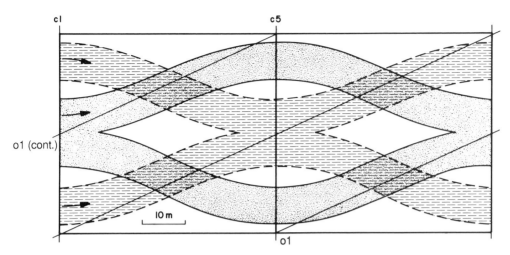

Fig. 17. Plan geometry of braided channel for the first model case. Initial channel position is stippled, whereas migrated channels are marked by dashed-line ornament. Cross-sections c1, c5 and o1 are shown in Fig. 18.

Quantitative depositional models

The previous discussion suggests that there should be different scales of depositional unit in braided rivers, depending on the scale of the associated topographic feature and the time over which deposition occurred (Fig. 16). For the purposes of this discussion four scales of deposition are recognized: (1) the complete channel belt; (2) the channel bar and adjacent fill deposits of major and minor channel segments; (3) seasonally controlled depositional increments on channel bars and fills; (4) increments of deposition associated with passage of discrete bed waves such as dunes, ripples, and bedload sheets.

An understanding of how these different scales of deposits are distributed in space requires detailed understanding of the bed geometry, flow, sediment transport and bed configurations during erosion and deposition, and the style of channel migration. Using the previously-discussed information on these

topics, and the somewhat limited direct observations of channel deposits from modern rivers, it has been possible to start the construction of both quantitative and qualitative depositional models. Although these models are simplified and do not predict the full details of deposition in braided channel belts, they represent a fundamental advance over previous models in that they are 3D, and include most of the main sedimentological properties that can be observed.

Quantitative models at present can only be constructed for the simplest channel geometries and modes of channel migration. In the first case a single braid bar is bounded by two identical curved channels placed side by side (Fig. 17). The bed topography, flow and sediment transport in these channels are described using Bridge's (1992) model for the case of steady, equilibrium flow in single curved channels. Bankfull flow conditions are assumed (details in Table 6). Such channel geometry and flow conditions were chosen as an analogue of the

Table 6. *Geometry and flow conditions for model channels*

	Initial channels in both models	Final channel in second model	
Channel width from thalweg to inner bank (m)	7.5	10.0	5.0
Centreline wavelength in one wavelength (m)	103.0	110.0	103.0
Sinuosity	1.03	1.1	1.03
Mean depth (m)	0.38	0.52	0.25
Centreline water surface slope at crossovers	0.00097	0.00091	0.00097
Darcy-Weisbach friction coefficient	0.1	0.1	0.1
Mean flow velocity (m s^{-1})	0.55	0.61	0.44

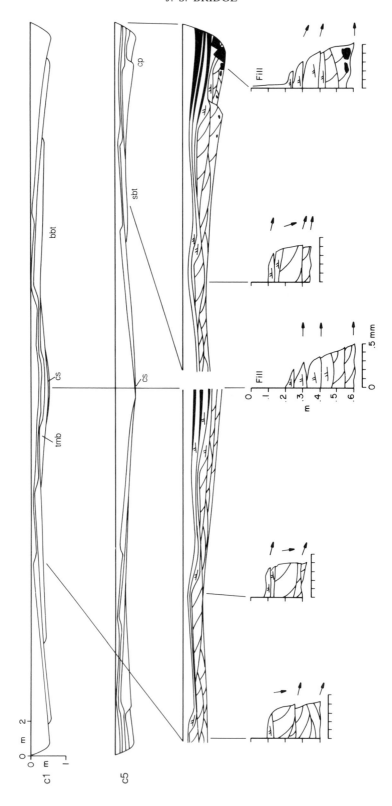

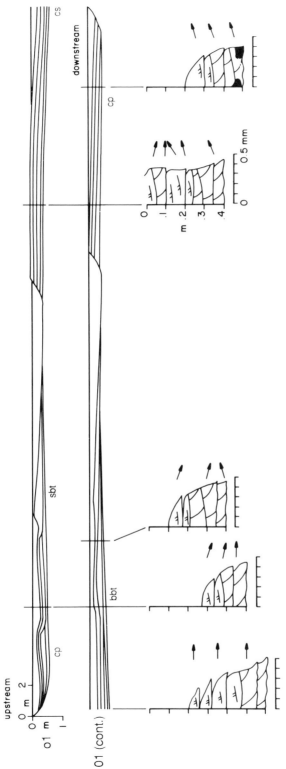

Fig. 18. Cross sections showing channel geometry and deposits formed by channel and bar migration shown in Fig. 17. The lines in the upper cross sections represent the high-stage bed surfaces at the end of each discrete increment of deposition (i.e. lateral and/or downstream accretion surfaces). For simplicity, these surfaces are smoothed (mesoform topography not shown), and cross-bar channels and falling-stage modifications are not shown. cs, confluence scour; tmb, tributary-mouth bar deposits; cp, counterpoint deposits; bbt, braid bar tail deposits; sbt, side bar tail deposits. More details of the spatial variation of mean grain sizes, internal structures and paleocurrent directions are shown in the lower parts of the diagrams. See Fig. 16B for legend.

Calamus River (Bridge *et al.* 1986; Bridge & Gabel 1992). The channels are then allowed to migrate downvalley in four discrete steps for a total distance of half a bend wavelength. During this downvalley migration channel geometry is held constant, and it is assumed that most deposition occurs during the constant bankfull flow conditions. In order to simplify the model, no cross-bar channels were included, and no net vertical deposition occurred.

The deposits are represented in Fig. 18 by two cross-stream sections and one oblique section which is almost alongstream. The deposits are primarily represented by the bounding surfaces which separate the four discrete depositional increments. The local waviness of these surfaces reflects the preservation of unit bars. The internal features of these depositional units are indicated in places by vertical logs or 2D sections. Internal structures reflect the meso-forms or microforms present during deposition, which were determined using Southard & Boguchwal's (1990) diagrams. Palaeocurrent orientations for trough cross strata are taken as parallel to local channel orientation whereas those for planar cross-strata reflect the crest-line obliquity of the formative straight crested bedform (e.g. scroll bars).

Section c1 (Fig. 18) represents the migration of the widest braid bar section into a confluence. The lowest, central deposits lie above the confluence scour, and the uppermost and marginal deposits are associated with the braid bar apex. Tributary-mouth bar deposits occur immediately above and to the side of the maximum confluence scour (Fig. 18) and braid-bar tail (including scroll-bar) deposits occur above and to the side of these deposits (compare with Bristow *et al.*'s (1993) model of confluence deposits). The thickness of the bar deposits can vary across the section by up to a factor of 2. The inclination of the major bedding surfaces increases outwards as predicted in Willis' (1989) point bar models. The widths of these surfaces vary as the projected channel widths vary. In general, the thickest depositional units bounded by these bedding surfaces are those where the change in bed elevation in a migration step is the greatest (e.g. associated with the downstream tip of the bar). If the migration rate was less there would be more depositional increments in a section, and the increments would be thinner. The vertical logs show either little vertical change in mean grain size or fining upwards.

Section c5 (Fig. 18) is where a confluence migrated into a widest braid bar section. The central parts of the section represent the confluence scour, whereas the outer parts are side

bar deposits. Although not shown in Fig. 18, these deposits may show evidence of large-scale flow separation (e.g. upstream-dipping cross strata). The outermost, lowest deposits are counterpoint deposits (e.g. Carey 1969; Taylor & Woodyer 1978; Hickin 1979; Lewin 1982, 1983; Page & Nanson 1982; Nanson & Page 1983; Smith 1987) which represent the most downstream parts of scroll bars.

In section o1 (Fig. 18) the lowest surface represents the downstream transition from channel margin at a bend apex through a cross-over to a confluence zone to another bend-apex channel margin on the opposite side of the channel belt. The deposits on the left hand side of the section represent the downstream migration of a side bar into the bend-apex section, and thus comprise mainly fining upward 'counterpoint' deposits. The central parts of the cross section represent the migration of the braid bar into the confluence. The vertical section in this region that fines upward then coarsens upward represents the upward progression from cross-over (riffle) to bar tail to bar head deposits. The right hand side of the section represents counterpoint deposits as seen in a view almost parallel to local flow direction.

If all of the palaeocurrent orientations in all of these vertical logs are considered (excluding those from straight crested bedforms like scroll bars) they give an accurate record of the range of channel orientations. However, the range of palaeocurrent orientations in single vertical logs does not.

In the second quantitative model, the initial conditions are the same as the first case. However, as the channels migrate downvalley by a quarter bend wavelength in two steps, one channel increases in sinuosity and width, whereas the other decreases in width (Fig. 19). The large-scale bedding patterns in section c3 (Fig. 20) are fairly similar to the younger deposits of section c1 in Fig. 18. The increase in inclination of the bedding surfaces and thickening of the deposits on the left hand side of section c3 reflect a change from a bar tail to a bar apex section and an increase in sinuosity and channel size. The increasing channel width may not be apparent in the widths of successive inclined bedding surfaces as these are apparent widths. The vertical log here shows little change in mean grain size. On the right hand side of section c3 the reduction in channel size here is reflected in a decreasing deposit thickness and inclination of large-scale bedding surfaces, and a fining upwards trend, even though a bend apex migrated over a bar tail region. Section c7 (Fig. 20) is similar to the central parts of section c5

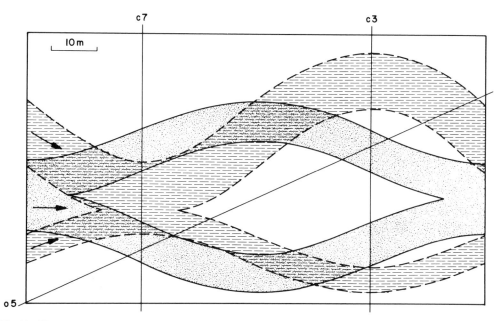

Fig. 19. Plan geometry of braided channel for the second model case. Initial channel pattern is stippled, whereas migrated channels are marked by dashed-line ornament. Cross-sections c3, c7 and o5 are shown in Fig. 20.

(Fig. 18) except for the markedly asymmetrical confluence scour in c7.

Qualitative depositional models

The two quantitative models are very specific, and more generality can only be achieved at present with qualitative models. The models in Figs 21 to 23 emphasize large-scale bedding geometry associated with episodic seasonal accretion on bars and in channel fills. For simplicity, cross-bar channels have not been included, there is no net vertical accretion, and the later stages of vertical accretion and channel filling (associated with channel-belt abandonment) have not been included. Figure 21 shows how downstream translation of bars results in preferential preservation of bar tail deposits, and erosional truncation of bar head deposits. With bar expansion and limited downstream translation (Fig. 22) bar-head deposits can be preserved, and erosional truncation of deposits is not as marked. Figure 23 shows how channel enlargement and filling results in subtle erosional truncations and changes in apparent channel geometry. In this example, the filling channel contains small bars and is being blocked at both ends by bar deposits. Detailed facies of these deposits are discussed below.

By reference to the quantitative models of Figs 17–20, fining upward sequences within bar deposits are expected to be most common and occur where point (side) bar tails build into bend apices, and where braid bar tails build into confluences (e.g. Shelton & Noble 1974). The vertical variation in mean grain size increases as channel sinuosity increases. Bar sequences with little vertical variation in mean grain size occur where bend apex areas build over bar tails. Such sequences may coarsen at the top if the bar head migrates over bar tail deposits (e.g. Bluck 1976).

The internal structure of the discrete accretionary units in sandy braid and point bars should be dominated by large-scale trough cross-stratification in view of the ubiquitous presence of curved-crested dunes mentioned previously (e.g. Harms *et al.* 1963; Allen 1965, 1982; Harms & Fahnestock 1965; McGowen & Garner 1970; Blodgett & Stanley 1980; Jackson 1976a; Bridge & Jarvis 1982; Bridge *et al.* 1986; Sarkar & Basummalick 1968). Gravelly deposits may have relatively more planar stratification (with imbrication) and planar cross-stratification (Williams & Rust 1969; Smith 1970, 1974; Rust 1972; Boothroyd & Ashley 1975; Bluck 1976, 1979; Boothroyd & Nummedal 1978; Gustavson 1978; Ferguson & Werritty 1983). Planar cross-stratification arising from straight-crested dunes is commonly described from the upper parts of braid bars and point bars (Sundborg 1956; Sarkar & Basumallick 1968; Smith 1970, 1971a, b, 1972; Jackson 1976b; Cant 1978; Cant

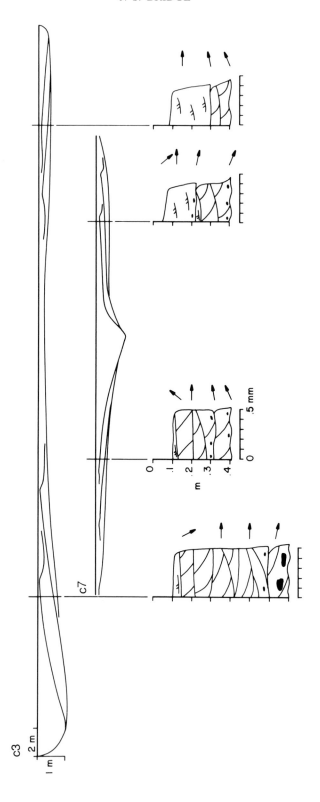

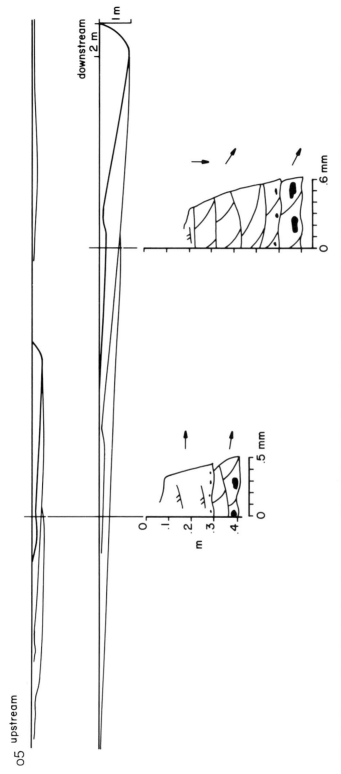

Fig. 20. Cross sections showing channel geometry and deposits formed by channel and bar migration shown in Fig. 19. See caption of Fig. 18 for explanation.

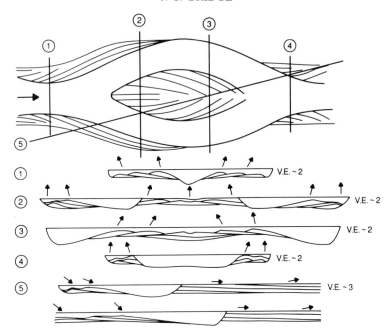

Fig. 21. Qualitative depositional model associated with a simple braided channel pattern and downstream migration, but no vertical deposition. Lines in plan and cross section are smoothed boundaries of seasonal accretionary bedsets (no mesoforms or cross-bar channels shown). Arrows represent channel orientation during deposition of uppermost bedset in the cross section (lower bedsets will have different orientations). The spatial variations in mean grain size can be reconstructed from Figs 17 to 20. Vertical exaggerations (V.E.) are approximately 2 to 3, and channel belt widths in nature will range from tens to thousands of meters.

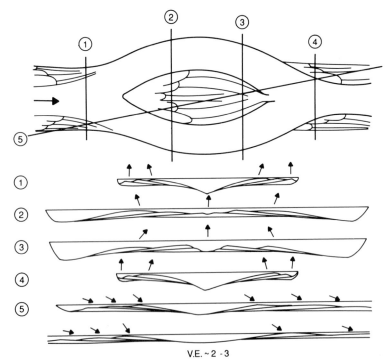

Fig. 22. Qualitative depositional model associated with a simple braided channel pattern, downstream migration and bend expansion. See caption for Fig. 21.

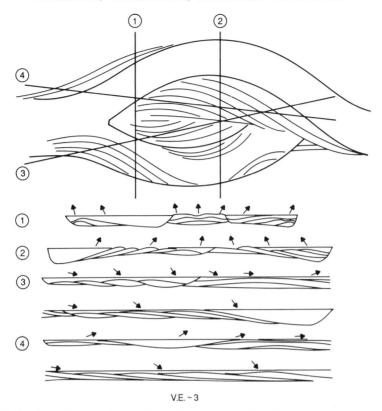

V.E. ~ 3

Fig. 23. Qualitative depositional model associated with a simple braided channel pattern, downstream migration, bend expansion, and channel switching. The lower channel has started to fill, and the upper channel is expanding. See caption for Fig. 21.

& Walker 1978; Crowley 1983) but it is not necessarily restricted to this position.

Exceptionally large scale, isolated sets of planar cross strata which comprise most of the thickness of an accretionary unit may represent parts of unit bars (i.e. bar heads, scroll bars) or chute and tributary-mouth bars. Examples of these structures where they have been dissected on the upper parts of bars are given by Collinson (1970), Jackson (1976b), Bluck (1976, 1979), Cant & Walker (1978), Blodgett & Stanley (1980), and Crowley (1983). Bar-head and scroll-bar planar sets tend to occur near the top of a bar sequence, whereas tributary-mouth bar (riffle) planar sets should occur nearer the base (e.g. Fig. 18, but compare with Bristow et al. 1993). If deposition is associated with down-stream migration of alternate bars with avalanche faces in straight channels it is expected that most of the deposits will be com-posed of a single set of planar cross-strata (e.g. Smith 1970, 1971a, 1972; Blodgett & Stanley 1980; Crowley 1983).

Planar strata are common in the tops of sandy braid and point bars (e.g. Harms et al. 1963; Sarkar & Basumallick 1968; Coleman 1969; Smith 1971b; Shelton & Noble 1974; Cant & Walker 1978; Bristow this volume) but there is little information on their occurrence elsewhere in a bar sequence. Cross laminated sand from ripple migration tends to be restricted to high areas near banks, and in other positions as falling stage deposits. Near banks, cross-laminated, bioturbated sand commonly occurs interbedded with vegetation-rich mud as cm-thick units ('accretionary bank deposits' of Bluck 1971).

The deposits of channel fills are poorly known from modern rivers and details are not included in the depositional models presented here. If the angle between the enlarging and filling channel segment is relatively small, as in low sinuosity rivers, flow is maintained in the filling channel so that bedload can be deposited particularly at the channel entrance. Although bedload may extend a considerable way into such filling channels the downstream ends will receive mainly fine grained, suspended sediment and organic matter from slowly moving water (e.g. Fisk 1947; Teisseyre 1977b; Bridge et al. 1986). With larger angles of divergence, both ends of the abandoned channel are quickly blocked so that most of the channel fill is relatively fine grained and organic-rich due to suspension deposition from ponded water (Fisk 1947).

Channel fills should generally fine upwards reflecting progressively weaker flows (e.g. Williams & Rust 1969; Bridge et al. 1986), and fine downstream reflecting progressive blockage at the entrance. The bedload deposits at the upstream end of a channel fill tend to fine upwards as they represent the progradation of bar tail deposits into the channel entrance (e.g. Bridge et al. 1986). Bedload deposits in channel fills may also show evidence of accretion on progressively smaller bars as discharge is reduced (Fig. 23). Deltaic deposits may be formed at the entrances of abandoned channels with ponded water (e.g. Gagliano & Howard 1984), and sediment gravity flows from cut banks may accumulate in thalwegs (Bridge et al. 1986). If suspended sediment loads are low, peat may accumulate in the ponded water of channel fills in humid climates. In arid climates, evaporitic tufas may form.

Evidence of changing stage during seasonal deposition on bars and channel fills includes fining of grain size and associated changes in sedimentary structure in the upper parts of accretionary units (e.g. Collinson 1970; Rust 1972; Bluck 1974, 1976, 1979; review in Allen 1982). Particularly common are reactivation surfaces in cross-stratified sets with current and wave ripples superimposed, and possibly mud drapes with abundant plant debris. Rill marks orientated parallel to depositional slopes represent falling stage drainage channels, and cross-stratified sand wedges represent the small deltas that form as these channels flow into standing water. Desiccation cracks occur in emergent mud drapes, and rooted plants can colonise areas exposed at low flow stage. Indeed the level of features such as these in channel sequences gives an indication of the low stage level. Burrowing and surface-browsing animals are most active above and below the water table following major erosional and depositional events, although escape burrows may occur within the main flood deposits. A detailed treatment of organic activity in braided rivers is not possible here.

Palaeocurrents

Palaeocurrent orientations observed in channel deposits must depend on: (1) orientation of the bedform (and associated sedimentary structure) relative to channel orientation, which varies with type of bedform, its position in the channel, and with river stage, and: (2) what part of the channel bar or fill is preserved. The orientations of structures like imbrication and various scales of cross-stratification from emergent parts of modern river bars correspond closely with *local* water flow directions (e.g. Harms et al. 1963; Steinmetz 1967; Coleman 1969; Bluck 1971, 1974, 1976, 1979; Shelton et al. 1974; Teisseyre 1975; Tandon & Kumar 1981) except in the case of planar cross stratification from straight crested dunes and unit bars (e.g. scroll bars) which are highly oblique to local flow directions (e.g. Rust 1972; Bluck 1971, 1974, 1976, 1979; Smith 1972; Jackson 1976b; Cant & Walker 1978; Bridge & Jarvis 1982). Also, imbrication near banks may be oblique to *local* channel direction (Teisseyre 1975) and downstream-dipping imbrication on bedform slip faces (pseudoimbrication) must be recognized as such. However, these local palaeoflow directions may be associated with deposition at a range of palaeoflow stages from flows of a range of strengths, and will not necessarily be parallel to the orientation of the high stage channels. As a result of this, the overall mean palaeocurrent azimuth for any particular structure may not be parallel to the mean channel orientation and the range of azimuths will probably greatly exceed the range of local channel orientations (e.g. Williams & Rust 1969; Bluck 1971, 1974, 1976, 1979; Schwartz 1978).

By virtue of the nature of channel migration discussed above, it is expected that flood stage palaeocurrents from the downstream parts of channel bars will be preferentially preserved in ancient deposits, which will reduce the variability evident in the studies of modern emergent channel bars. Thus observations of palaeocurrents from various sedimentary structures throughout a single, well-exposed braided channel-belt deposit will probably indicate the mean and range of channel orientations if analyzed correctly, but cannot generally be used to indicate sinuosity of individual segments (cf. Miall 1976). The sinuosity of individual segments and the mode of channel migration can, however, be reconstructed from very detailed observations from large outcrops and using 3D depositional models of the kind given previously (e.g. Willis 1993).

Discussion

The models described above are for braided channel belts with low braiding parameter; however, it would be conceptually simple to repeat the main features in the across valley direction, but practically difficult. Bridge (1985) speculated that the proportion of channel-fill deposits relative to bar-accretion deposits within a channel belt should increase with braiding parameter. Bristow (1987) challenged this based on the proportion of bar migration relative to channel cutting and filling in the Brahmaputra. In retrospect, if braided rivers can be looked upon as a series of single curved rivers placed side by side, there is no reason to think that my earlier speculation is correct. Indeed, the only definitive depositional evidence for braiding appears to be cross sections through braid bars with coeval channels, and confluences. Braided river facies models that show a series of overlapping channel fills associated with different scales of channels (e.g. Williams & Rust 1969) cannot be justified.

Vertical superposition of channel bar and fill deposits in single channel belts can be accomplished by superposition of a cross-bar channel on a larger bar and migration of one main channel bar over another. In the latter case, the degree of preservation of the overridden bar depends on the relative elevations of the two superimposed basal erosion surfaces. As is the case with dunes, the likelihood of preservation of the lower parts of the eroded bar increases with the vertical deposition rate relative to the lateral migration rate of the superimposed bar, and the variability of bar thicknesses (e.g. Allen 1982; Paola & Borgman 1991; Best & Bridge 1992). This kind of superposition of bars and fills could not be included easily in the models above because it is very difficult to predict how individual channel segments and bars will migrate and become superimposed on others within channel belts. Note that vertical superposition of channel bar and fill deposits can also result from superposition of distinct channel belts.

Other important aspects of braided river deposition which cannot be considered here include: (1) alongvalley variation of braided river geometry and processes (including on alluvial fans) associated with varying discharge, sediment supply and valley slope; (2) floodplain geometry, processes and deposits; (3) periodic avulsions of channel belts to other floodplain locations; (4) temporal changes in braided channels and floodplains associated with local and regional tectonism, climate and sea-level change.

Finally, the models presented here are largely hypothetical for reasons explained previously. In order to validate and extend these models it is necessary to undertake a detailed program of coring and geophysical profiling of modern channel belts, possibly supplemented by scale modelling of braided-river deposition. In the meantime, the next section is an examination of how and whether these models can further our interpretation and understanding of ancient river deposits.

Interpretation of ancient deposits: some examples

Willis (1993) has done a remarkable job of describing some Miocene fluvial deposits from the Siwaliks of northern Pakistan, where the rocks are exposed continuously along strike for many kilometers. He has also performed perhaps the most sophisticated qualitative and quantitative palaeoenvironmental interpretation of channel deposits to date. It is clear that to accomplish this considerable task the following are required: (1) very detailed description of large outcrops; (2) thorough understanding of the geometry, flow and sedimentary processes associated with modern channel bars and fills, and; (3) knowledge of how channel bar and fill deposits resulting from various modes of channel migration appear in variously orientated 2D sections. Regarding (3), Willis (1993) made use of diagrams similar to, but simpler than, those in Figs 21–23. Willis was able to quantitatively reconstruct the width, depth, mean velocity, slope, wavelength and sinuosity of individual channel segments, and remarkably, to estimate channel belt widths and braiding index. Channel bars migrated by downstream translation (mainly) and bend expansion, and by channel switching (cutting and filling of channels within the channel belt). Rates of channel migration could be estimated at up to the order of a channel width per seasonal flood period. Figures 24 to 26 show some examples of some of Willis' channel-belt deposits, in order to illustrate the usefulness of the facies models produced here. As indicated in the captions of Figs 24–26, all of the various channel bar and fill deposits in these examples can be explained by direct comparison with Figs 21–23. In most cases, Willis' interpretations are supported, but not always. It is commonly not easy to tell if a major bedding truncation in a braid-bar deposit is due to seasonal discharge changes or to channel switching.

Unfortunately, the majority of other studies of ancient river deposits do not show large enough outcrops with *details* of large scale bedding geometry, grain textures, internal structures and palaeocurrents to allow detailed

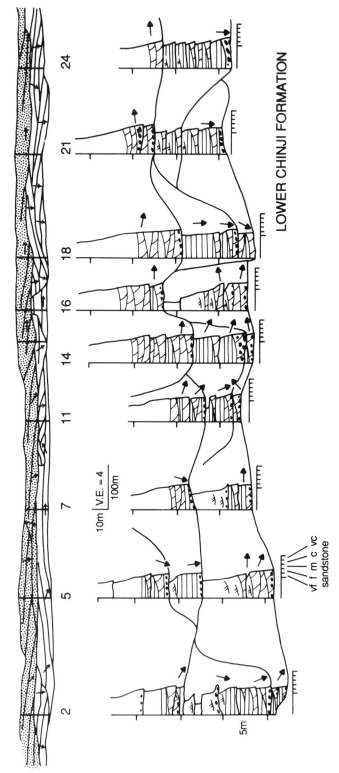

Fig. 24. Redrawn part of Willis' (1993) 2D bedding diagrams and selected vertical logs comprising a sandstone body from the Lower Chinji Formation, Pakistan Siwaliks. The bedding diagram shows major bedset and storey boundaries, and arrows represent paleocurrents relative to the outcrop (a downward pointing arrows indicates paleocurrents normal to, and out of, the outcrop). Symbols for vertical logs are explained in the legend (Fig. 16B), and arrows represent palaeocurrent directions relative to north (which is upwards). The storeys in the upper half of the sandstone body (shaded), and the lowest storeys on the left hand side are comparable to Fig. 23, section 3. The lowest storeys on the right hand side are comparable to parts of Fig. 21, section 3 and Fig. 23, section 2.

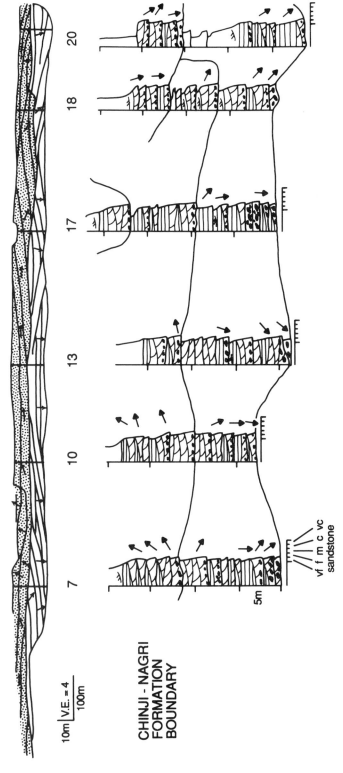

Fig. 25. Redrawn part of Willis' (1993) 2D bedding diagram and selected vertical logs for a sandstone body at the Chinji-Nagri formation boundary. See Fig. 24 caption for explanation. The upper storeys are comparable to Fig. 22, section 5 and Fig. 23, section 4. The lower storeys are comparable to Fig. 21, section 3 and Fig. 23, section 2.

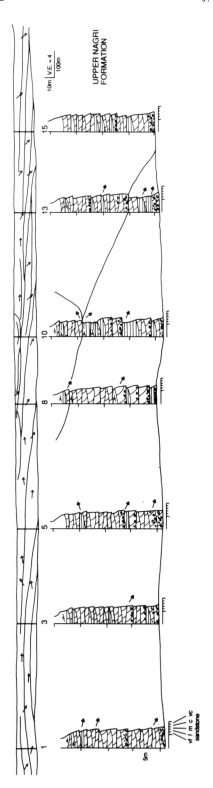

interpretations of the kind shown here. Indeed, many interpretations of ancient fluvial deposits as due to braided rivers have relied upon criteria which have been shown here to be mythical.

Concluding remarks

Substantial progress in our understanding of braided river processes will only come from a combination of: (1) field and laboratory studies of the variation and interaction of channel geometry, flow, sediment transport, erosion and deposition, and channel migration over spatial scales of several bars and time scales of decades, including sequential observations over large discharge ranges; (2) quantitative documentation of the 3D variation of all sediment properties of channel-belt deposits (including the age and spatial arrangement of preserved parts of bars and channel fills) and their relation to the causative processes; (3) development of theoretical models which can be tested using extensive data from braided rivers.

Such an ambitious undertaking would require a substantial commitment of resources over a relatively long period. In particular, collaboration of personnel with a wide range of expertise is essential. Innovative measuring equipment and techniques need to be developed. For instance, it is desirable to operate flow and sediment transport measuring equipment from stable positions, with automated deployment and recording. Channel belt deposits should be described using a combination of closely-spaced cores and a geophysical profiling method such as ground-penetrating radar or high-frequency seismic. A long-term program of sequential aerial photography and satellite imagery is required. Clearly, such a large scale, long term undertaking could not possibly be financed under the current mode of operation of government and private-sector funding agencies.

List of symbols

a	coefficient or exponent
b	exponent
c	exponent
C	cohesive strength

Fig. 26. Redrawn part of Willis' (1993) 2D bedding diagram and selected vertical logs for a sandstone body from the Upper Nagri formation. See Fig. 24 caption for explanation. This outcrop is comparable to Fig. 23, section 3.

C_o	volume concentration of bed sediment	Q_1, Q_2	discharges of channels entering a confluence
d	mean flow depth	Q_{2f}	two-year flood discharge
d_{bf}	bankfull mean flow depth	r_c	centreline radius of curvature
d_c	centerline depth	r_{c1}, r_{c2}	r_c values of channels entering a confluence
d_l	local flow depth	r_l	local radius of curvature
d_s	maximum confluence scour depth	s	streamwise spatial coordinate
d_s^*	dimensionless d_s	sn	sinuosity
d_1, d_2	mean depths of channels entering a confluence	sn_1, sn_2	sinuosity of channels entering a confluence
D	grain size	S	channel slope
D_{35}	35th percentile grain size	S_v	valley slope
D_{50}	median grain size	t	time
D_{84}	84th percentile grain size	T	duration of flood
D_{90}	90th percentile grain size	u_s, u_n	mean grain velocity in s and n directions
f	Darcy-Weisbach friction coefficient	u_*	shear velocity
Fr	Froude number	u_{*c}	critical u_* for sediment entrainment
g	gravitational acceleration	V	cross-section average flow velocity
h	bed elevation	w	channel width
i_s, i_n	volumetric sediment transport rate in s and n directions	w_{bf}	bankfull channel width
m	mode of alternate bars	w_{rf}	rare flood channel width
M	channel length in one curved channel wavelength	w_1, w_2	width of channels entering a confluence
M_1, M_2	M values for channels entering a confluence	α	confluence angle
n	across stream spatial coordinate	ΔQ	rise in discharge during flood
P	effective normal stress	θ	dimensionless bed shear stress
Q	discharge	θ_c	value of θ at threshold of sediment motion
Q_{bf}	bankfull discharge	μ_c	static grain resistance coefficient
Q_m	mean annual discharge	ϱ	fluid density
Q_{maf}	mean annual flood discharge	ΣP	total sinuosity
Q_{max}	maximum discharge in flood season	τ_0	bed shear stress
Q_{min}	minimum discharge in floor season	τ_c	value of τ_0 at threshold of sediment motion
		τ_s	shear strength

References

ABDULLAYEV, E. A. 1973. Experimental investigation of midstream bars on an erosible model. *Transactions State Hydrological Institute Trudy GGI*, **209**, 103–116.

ACKERS, P. & CHARLTON, F. G. 1971. The geometry of small meandering streams. *Proceedings of the Institution of Civil Engineers, Supplement* **XII**, 289–317.

ALAM, M. M., CROOK, K. A. W. & TAYLOR, G. 1985. Fluvial herring-bone cross-stratification in a modern tributary mouth bar, Coonamble, New South Wales, Australia. *Sedimentology*, **32**, 235–244.

ALLEN, J. R. L. 1965. A review of the origin and characteristics of recent alluvial sediments. *Sedimentology*, **5**, 89–191.

—— 1968. *Current ripples*. North Holland, Amsterdam.

—— 1976. Computational models of dune time-lag:

an alternative boundary condition. *Sedimentary Geology*, **16**, 255–279.

—— 1982. *Sedimentary structures: their character and physical basis, vol 1*, Elsevier, Amsterdam.

—— 1983. Studies in fluviatile sedimentation: bars, bar-complexes and sandstone sheets (low-sinuosity braided streams) in the Brownstones (L. Devonian), Welsh Borders. *Sedimentary Geology*, **33**, 237–293.

AMERICAN SOCIETY OF CIVIL ENGINEERS TASK FORCE ON BED FORMS IN ALLUVIAL CHANNELS, 1966. Nomenclature for bedforms in alluvial channels. *American Society of Civil Engineers Journal of the Hydraulics Division*, **92**, 51–64.

ANTROPOVSKIY, V. I. 1972. Quantitative criteria of channel macroforms. *Soviet Hydrology*, 477–484.

ASHLEY, G. M. 1990. Classification of large-scale subaqueous bed-forms: a new look at an old problem. *Journal of Sedimentary Petrology*, **60**, 160–172.

ASHMORE, P. E. 1982. Laboratory modelling of gravel braided stream morphology. *Earth Surface Processes*, **7**, 201–225.

—— 1988. Bed load transport in braided gravel-bed stream models. *Earth Surface Processes and Landforms*, **13**, 677–695.

—— 1991*a*. Channel morpology and bedload pulses in braided, gravel-bed streams. *Geografiska Annaler*, **73A**, 37–52.

—— 1991*b*. How do gravel-bed rivers braid? *Canadian Journal of Earth Sciences*, **28**, 326–341.

—— 1993. Anabranch confluence kinetics and sedimentation processes in gravel braided streams. *This volume*.

—— & PARKER, G. 1983. Confluence scour in coarse braided streams. *Water Resources Research*, **19**, 392–402.

——, FERGUSON, R. I., PRESTEGAARD, K. L., ASHWORTH, P. J. & PAOLA, C. 1992. Secondary flow in anabranch confluences of a braided, gravel-bed stream. *Earth Surface Processes and Landforms,* **17**, 299–311.

ASHWORTH, P. J. & FERGUSON, R. I. 1986. Interrelationships of channel processes, changes and sediments in a proglacial braided river. *Geografiska Annaler*, **68A**, 361–371.

—— & —— 1989. Size-selective entrainment of bed load in gravel bed streams. *Water Resources Research*, **25**, 627–634.

——, —— ASHMORE, P. E., PAOLA, C., POWELL, D. M. & PRESTEGAARD, K. L. 1992a. Measurements in a braided river chute and lobe: 2. Sorting of bedload during entrainment, transport and deposition. *Water Resources Research*, **28**, 1887–1896.

——, —— & POWELL, M. D. 1992*b*. Bedload transport and sorting in braided channels. *In*: BILLI, P., HEY, C. R. THORNE, C. R. & TACCONI, P. (eds) *Dynamics of Gravel-bed Rivers*. Wiley, 497–515.

BEGIN, Z. B. 1981. The relationship between flow shear stress and stream pattern. *Journal of Hydrology*, **52**, 307–319.

—— & SCHUMM, S. A. 1984. Gradational thresholds and landform singularity: significance for Quaternary studies. *Quaternary Research*, **21**, 267–274.

BENNETT, S. J. 1992. *A theoretical and experimental study of bedload transport of heterogeneous sediment*. PhD thesis, State University of New York at Binghamton.

BERGERON, N. & ROY, A. G. 1988. Les effets d'un embacle sur la morphologie du lit d'une confluence de cours d'eau. *Geographie physique et Quaternaire*, **42**, 191–196.

BESCHTA, R. L. & JACKSON, W. L. 1979. The intrusion of fine sediments into a stable gravel bed. *Journal of the Fisheries Research Board of Canada*, **36**, 204–210.

BEST, J. L. 1986. The morphology of river channel confluences. *Progress in Physical Geography*, **10**, 157–174.

—— 1987. Flow dynamics at river channel confluences: implications for sediment transport and bed morphology. *In*: ETHRIDGE, F. G., FLORES, R. M. & HARVEY, M. D. (eds) *Recent Developments in Fluvial Sedimentology*. SEPM Special Publication, **39**, 27–35.

—— 1988. Sediment transport and bed morphology at river channel confluences. *Sedimentology*, **35**, 481–498.

—— & BRAYSHAW, A. C. 1985. Flow separation — a physical process for the concentration of heavy minerals within alluvial channels. *Journal of the Geological Society, London*, **142**, 767–755.

—— & BRIDGE, J. S. 1992. The morphology and dynamics of low-amplitude bedwaves upon upper-stage plane beds and the preservation of planar laminae. *Sedimentology*, **39**, 737–752.

—— & REID, I. 1984. Separation zone at open-channel junctions. *Journal of Hydraulic Engineering, ASCE*, **110**, 1588–1594.

—— & —— 1987. Separation zone at open-channel junctions: closure. *Journal of Hydraulic Engineering, ASCE*, **113**, 545–548.

—— & ROY, A. G. 1991. Mixing-layer distortion at the confluence of channels of different depth. *Nature*, **350**, 411–413.

BETTESS, R. & WHITE, W. R. 1983. Meandering and braiding of alluvial channels. *Proceedings of the Institution of Civil Engineers*, **75**, 525–538.

BLODGETT, R. H. & STANLEY, K. O. 1980. Stratification, bedforms and discharge relations of the Platte braided river system, Nebraska. *Journal of Sedimentary Petrology*, **50**, 139–148.

BLONDEAUX, P. & SEMINARA, G. 1985. A unified bar-bend theory of river meanders. *Journal of Fluid Mechanics*, **157**, 449–470.

BLUCK, B. J. 1971. Sedimentation in the meandering River Endrick. *Scottish Journal of Geology*, **7**, 93–138.

—— 1974. Structure and directional properties of some valley sandur deposits in southern Iceland. *Sedimentology*, **21**, 533–554.

—— 1976. Sedimentation in some Scottish rivers of low sinuosity. *Transactions Royal Society of Edinburgh*, **69**, 425–456.

—— 1979. Structure of coarse grained braided alluvium. *Transactions Royal Society of Edinburgh*, **70**, 181–221.

—— 1982. Texture of gravel bars in braided streams. *In*: HEY, R. C., BATHURST, J. C. & THORNE, C. R. (eds) *Gravel-bed rivers*. Wiley, 339–355.

BOOTHROYD, J. D. & ASHLEY, G. M. 1975. Processes, bar morphology, and sedimentary structures on braided outwash fans, northeastern Gulf of Alaska. *In*: JOPLING, A. V. & McDONALD, B. C. (eds) *Glaciofluvial and Glaciolacustrine Sedimentation*. SEPM Special Publication, **23**, 193–222.

—— & NUMMEDAL, D. 1978. Proglacial braided outwash: a model for humid alluvial fan deposits. *In*: MIALL, A. D. (ed.) *Fluvial Sedimentology*. Canadian Society of Petroleum Geologists Memoirs, **5**, 641–668.

BRADY, L. L. & JOBSON, H. E. 1973. *An experimental study of heavy mineral segregation under alluvial flow condition*. US Geological Survey Professional Paper 562.

BRAY, D. I. 1982. Regime equations for gravel-bed rivers. *In*: HEY, R. D., BATHURST, J. D. & THORNE, C. R. (eds) *Gravel-bed rivers*. Wiley, 517–552.

BRAYSHAW, A. D. 1984. Characteristics and origin of cluster bedforms in coarse-grained alluvial channels. *In*: KOSTER, E. H. & STEEL, R. J. (eds) *Sedimentology of Gravels and Conglomerates*. Canadian Society of Petroleum Geologists Memoirs, **10**, 77–85.

—— 1985. Bed microtopography and entrainment thresholds in gravel-bed rivers. *Geological Society of America Bulletin*, **96**, 218–223.

——, FROSTICK, L. E. & REID, I. 1983. The hydrodynamics of particle clusters and sediment entrainment in coarse alluvial channels. *Sedimentology*, **30**, 137–143.

BRICE, J. C. 1960. Index for description of channel braiding. *Geological Society of America Bulletin*, **71**, 1833.

—— 1964. *Channel patterns and terraces of the Loup rivers in Nebraska*. US Geological Survey Professional Paper 422D.

—— 1984. Planform properties of meandering rivers. *In*: ELLIOTT, C. M. (ed.) *River Meandering*. American Society of Civil Engineers, 1–15.

——, BLODGETT, J. D. *ET AL*. 1978. *Countermeasures for hydraulic problems at bridges*. Federal Highway Administration Report FHWA-RD-78-162, Washington, D.C.

BRIDGE, J. S. 1984. Flow and sedimentary processes in river bends: comparison of field observations and theory. *In*: ELLIOTT, C. M. (ed.) *River meandering*. American Society of Civil Engineers, 857–872.

—— 1985. Paleochannels inferred from alluvial deposits: a critical evaluation. *Journal of Sedimentary Petrology*, **55**, 579–589.

—— 1992. A revised model for water flow, sediment transport, bed topography, and grainsize sorting in natural river bends. *Water Resources Research*, **28**, 999–1013.

—— & BENNETT, S. J. 1992. A model for the entrainment and transport of sediment grains of mixed sizes, shapes and densities. *Water Resources Research*, **28**, 337–363.

—— & GABEL, S. L. 1992. Flow and sediment dynamics in a low-sinuosity river: Calamus River, Nebraska Sandhills. *Sedimentology*, **39**, 125–142.

—— & JARVIS, J. 1976. Flow and sedimentary processes in the meandering River South Esk, Glen Clova, Scotland. *Earth Surface Processes*, **1**, 303–336.

—— & —— 1982. The dynamics of a river bend: a study in flow and sedimentary processes. *Sedimentology*, **29**, 499–550.

——, SMITH, N. D., TRENT, F., GABEL, S. L. & BERNSTEIN, P. 1986. Sedimentology and morphology of a low-sinuosity river: Calamus River, Nebraska Sandhills. *Sedimentology*, **33**, 851–870.

BRISTOW, C. S. 1987. Brahmaputra River: channel migration and deposition. *In*: ETHRIDGE, F. G., FLORES, R. M. & HARVEY, M. D. (eds) *Recent developments in Fluvial Sedimentology*. SEPM Special Publication, **39**, 63–74.

—— 1993. Sedimentary structures exposed in bar tops in the Brahmaputra River, Bangladesh. *This volume*.

——, BEST, J. L. & ROY, A. G. 1993. Morphology and facies models of channel confluences. *In*: MARZO, M. & PUIDEFABREGES, C. (eds) *Alluvial Sedimentation*. International Association of Sedimentologists Special Publication, **17**, 91–100.

BUCK, S. G. 1983. The Saaiplaas Quartzite member: a braided system of gold- and uranium-bearing channel placers within the Proterozoic Witwatersrand Supergroup of South Africa. *In*: COLLINSON, J. D. & LEWIN, J. (eds) *Modern and Ancient Fluvial Systems*, International Association of Sedimentologists Special Publications, **6**, 549–562.

CANT, D. J. 1978. Bedforms and bar types in the South Saskatchewan River. *Journal of Sedimentary Petrology*, **48**, 1321–1330.

—— & WALKER, R. G. 1978. Fluvial processes and facies sequences in the sandy braided South Saskatchewan River, Canada. *Sedimentology*, **25**, 625–648.

CAREY, W. C. 1969. Formation of floodplain lands. *Journal of the Hydraulics Division, American Society of Civil Engineers*, **95**, 981–994.

CARSON, M. A. 1984a. The meandering-braided threshold: a reappraisal. *Journal of Hydrology*, **73**, 315–334.

—— 1984b. Observations on the meandering-braided river transition, the Canterbury Plains, New Zealand: part one. *New Zealand Geographer*, **40**, 12–17.

—— 1984c. Observations on the meandering-braided river transition, the Canterbury Plains, New Zealand: part two. *New Zealand Geographer*, **40**, 89–99.

—— 1986. Characteristics of high-energy 'meandering' rivers: the Canterbury Plains, New Zealand. *Geological Society of America Bulletin*, **97**, 886–895.

CHALOV, R. S. 1974. Effect of side bars in riffles on river bank dynamics. *Soviet Hydrology: Selected Papers*, **1974 (4)**, 270–273.

CHANG, H. H. 1979. Minimum stream power and river channel patterns. *Journal of Hydrology*, **41**, 303–327.

—— 1985. River morphology and thresholds. *Journal of the Hydraulics Division, American Society of Civil Engineers*, **111**, 503–519.

CHEEL, R. J. 1985. Heavy mineral shadows, a new sedimentary structure formed under upper-flow regime conditions: its directional and hydraulic significance. *Journal of Sedimentary Petrology*, **54**, 1175–1182.

CHEETHAM, G. H. 1979. Flow competence in relation to stream channel form and braiding. *Geological Society of America Bulletin*, **90**, 877–886.

CHIEN NING. 1961. The braided river of the Lower Yellow River. *Scientia Sinica*, **10**, 734–754.

CHIEW, Y. M. 1991. Bed features in nonuniform sediments. *Journal of the Hydraulics Division, American Society of Civil Engineers*, **117**, 116–120.

CHITALE, S. V. 1970. River channel patterns. *Journal of the Hydraulics Division, American Society of Civil Engineers*, **96**, 201–221.

—— 1973. Theories and relationships of river channel patterns. *Journal of Hydrology*, **19**, 285–308.

CHURCH, M. 1972. *Baffin Island sandurs: a study of arctic fluvial processes.* Geological Survey of Canada Bulletin 216.

—— & GILBERT, R. 1975. Proglacial fluvial and lacustrine sedimentation. *In*: JOPLING, A. V. & MCDONALD, B. C. (eds) *Glaciofluvial and glacio-lacustrine sedimentation*, SEPM Special Publications, **23**, 22–100.

—— & JONES, D. 1982. Channel bars in gravel-bed rivers. *In*: HEY, R. D., BATHURST, J. C. & THORNE, C. R. (eds) *Gravel-bed rivers*, Wiley, Chichester, 291–324.

COLEMAN, J. M. 1969. Brahmaputra River: channel processes and sedimentation. *Sedimentary Geology*, **3**, 129–239.

COLLINSON, J. D. 1970. Bedforms of the Tana River, Norway. *Geografiska Annaler*, **52A**, 31–56.

COSTELLO, W. R. & SOUTHARD, J. B. 1981. Flume experiments on lower-flow-regime bedforms in coarse sand. *Journal of Sedimentary Petrology*, **51**, 849–864.

CROWLEY, K. D. 1983. Large-scale bed configurations (macroforms), Platte River Basin, Colorado and Nebraska: primary structures and formative processes. *Geological Society of America Bulletin*, **94**, 117–133.

DAL CIN, R. 1968. Pebble clusters: their interpretation and utilization in the study of paleocurrents. *Sedimentary Geology*, **2**, 233–241.

DAVOREN, A. & MOSLEY, M. P. 1986. Observations of bedload movement, bar development and sediment supply in the braided Ohau River. *Earth Surface Processes and Landforms*, **11**, 643–652.

DIETRICH, W. E. & SMITH, J. D. 1983. Influence of the point bar on flow in curved channels. *Water Resources Research*, **19**, 1173–1192.

—— & —— 1984. Bedload transport in a river meander. *Water Resources Research*, **20**, 1355–1380.

—— & WHITING, P. J. 1989. Boundary shear stress and sediment transport in river meanders of sand and gravel. *In*: IKEDA, S. & PARKER, G. (eds) *River Meandering.* American Geophysical Union Water Resources Monographs, **12**, 1–50.

——, KIRCHNER, J. W., IKEDA, H. & ISEYA, F. 1989. Sediment supply and the development of the coarse surface layer in gravel-bedded rivers. *Nature*, **340**, 215–217.

——, SMITH, J. D. & DUNNE, T. 1979. Flow and sediment transport in a sand-bedded meander. *Journal of Geology*, **87**, 305–315.

ELLIOTT, C. M. (ed.) 1984. *River Meandering.* American Society of Civil Engineers.

ENGELUND, F. & SKOVGAARD, O. 1973. On the origin of meandering and braiding in alluvial streams. *Journal of Fluid Mechanics*, **57**, 289–302.

ERGENZINGER, P. 1987. Chaos and order: the channel geometry of gravel bed braided rivers. *Catena Supplement*, **10**, 85–98.

ESCHNER, T. R. 1983. *Hydraulic geometry of the Platte River near Overton, south-central Nebraska.* US Geological Survey Professional Paper 1277C.

FAHNESTOCK, R. K. 1963. *Morphology and hydrology of a glacial stream — White River, Mt. Rainier, Washington.* US Geological Survey Professional Paper 422A.

FERGUSON, R. I. 1981. Channel form and channel changes. *In*: LEWIN, J. (ed.) *British Rivers.* Allen & Unwin, 90–125.

—— 1984. The threshold between meandering and braiding. *In*: SMITH, K. V. H. (ed.) *Proceedings of the 1st International Conference on Hydraulic Design.* Springer, 6.15–6.29.

—— 1986. Hydraulics and hydraulic geometry. *Progress in Physical Geography*, **10**, 1–31.

—— 1987. Hydraulic and sedimentary controls of channel pattern. *In*: RICHARDS, K. S. (ed.) *River Channels: Environment and Process.* Blackwell, 125–158.

—— & ASHWORTH, P. 1991. Slope-induced changes in channel character along a gravel bed stream: the Allt Dubhaig, Scotland. *Earth Surface Processes and Landforms*, **16**, 65–82.

—— & WERRITTY, A. 1983. Bar development and channel changes in the gravelly River Feshie, Scotland. *In*: COLLINSON, J. D. & LEWIN, J. *Modern and Ancient Fluvial Systems.* International Associated of Sedimentologists Special Publications, **6**, 181–193.

——, ASHMORE, P. E., ASHWORTH, P. J., PAOLA, C. & PRESTEGAARD, K. L. 1992. Measurements in a braided river chute and lobe: I. Flow pattern, sediment transport and channel change. *Water Resources Research*, **28**, 1877–1886.

FISK, H. N. 1947. *Fine grained alluvial deposits and their effects on Mississippi River activity.* Mississippi River Commission, Vicksburg, Mississippi.

FREDSOE, J. 1978. Meandering and braiding of rivers. *Journal of Fluid Mechanics*, **84**, 609–624.

—— 1979. Unsteady flow in straight alluvial streams: modification of individual dunes. *Journal of Fluid Mechanics*, **91**, 497–512.

—— 1982. Shape and dimensions of stationary dunes in rivers. *Journal of the Hydraulics Division, American Society of Civil Engineers*, **108**, 932–947.

FRIEDKIN, J. F. 1945. *A laboratory study of the meandering of alluvial rivers.* US Waterways Experimental Station, Vicksburg, Mississippi.

FRIEND, P. F. & SINHA, R. 1993. Braiding and meandering parameters. *This volume.*

FROSTICK, L. E., LUCAS, P. M. & REID, I. 1984. The infiltration of fine matrices into coarse-grained alluvial sediments and its implications for stratigraphical interpretation. *Journal of the Geological Society, London*, **141**, 955–965.

FUJITA, Y. 1989. Bar and channel formation in braided streams. *In*: IKEDA, S. & PARKER, G. (eds) *River Meandering.* American Geophysical Union, Water Resources Monographs, **12**, 417–462.

FUKUOKA, S. 1989. Finite amplitude development of alternate bars. *In*: IKEDA, S. & PARKER, G. (eds) *River Meandering*. American Geophysical Union, Water Resources Monographs, **12**, 237–265.

GABEL, S. L. 1993. Geometry and kinematics of dunes during steady and unsteady flows in the Calamus River, Nebraska. *Sedimentology*, in press.

GAGLIANO, S. M. & HOWARD, P. C. 1984. The neck cutoff oxbow lake cycle along the lower Mississippi River. *In*: ELLIOTT, C. M. (ed.) *River Meandering*. American Society of Civil Engineers, 147–158.

GIBLING, M. R. & RUST, B. R. 1990. Ribbon sandstones in the Pennsylvanian Waddens Cove Formation, Sydney Basin, Atlantic Canada: the influence of siliceous duricrusts on channel-body geometry. *Sedimentology*, **37**, 45–65.

GRIFFITHS, G. A. 1979. Recent sedimentation history of the Waimakariri River, New Zealand. *Journal of Hydrology (New Zealand)*, **18**, 6–28.

GUSTAVSON, T. C. 1978. Bedforms and stratification types of modern gravel meander lobes, Nueces River, Texas. *Sedimentology*, **25**, 401–426.

HAGER, W. H. 1984. An approximate treatment of flow in branches and bends. *Proceedings of the Institution of Mechanical Engineers*, **198C**, 63–69.

—— 1987. Separation zone at open-channel junctions: discussion. *Journal of Hydraulic Engineering, ASCE*, **113**, 539–543.

HARMS, J. C. & FAHNESTOCK, R. R. 1965. Stratification, bedforms and flow phenomena (with an example from the Rio Grande). *In*: MIDDLETON, G. V. (ed.) *Primary sedimentary structures and their hydrodynamic interpretation*. SEPM Special Publications, **12**, 84–115.

——, MCKENZIE, D. B. & McCUBBIN, D. G. 1963. Stratification in modern sands of the Red River, Louisiana. *Journal of Geology*, **71**, 566–580.

HASEGAWA, K. 1989. Studies on qualitative and quantitative prediction of meander channel shift. *In*: IKEDA, S. & PARKER, G. (eds) *River Meandering*. American Geophysical Union Water Resources Monographs, **12**, 215–235.

HAYASHI, T. & OZAKI, S. 1980. Alluvial bedforms analysis. I. Formation of alternating bars and braids. *In*: SHEN, H. W. & KIKKAWA, H. (eds) *Application of Stochastic Processes in Sediment Transport*. Water Resources Publications, Colorado, Ch 7, 1–40.

HEIN, F. J. & WALKER, R. G. 1977. Bar evolution and development of stratification in the gravelly, braided, Kicking Horse River, British Columbia. *Canadian Journal of Earth Science*, **14**, 562–570.

HENDERSON, F. M. 1961. Stability of alluvial channels. *Journal of the Hydraulics Division, American Society of Civil Engineers*, **87**, 109–138.

—— 1966. *Open channel flow*. Macmillan, New York.

HICKIN, E. J. 1969. A newly identified process of point bar formation in natural streams. *American Journal of Science*, **267**, 999–1010.

—— 1979. Concave bank benches in the Squamish River, British Columbia. *Canadian Journal of Earth Sciences*, **16**, 200–203.

HOEY, T. 1992. Temporal variations in bedload transport rates and sediment storage in gravel-bed rivers. *Progress in Physical Geography*, **16**, 319–338.

—— & SUTHERLAND, A. J. 1991. Channel morphology and bedload pulses in braided rivers: a laboratory study. *Earth Surface Processes and Landforms*, **16**, 447–462.

HONG, L. B. & DAVIES, T. R. H. 1979. A study of stream braiding. *Geological Society of America Bulletin*, **79**, 391–394.

HOWARD, A. D., KEETCH, M. E. & VINCENT, C. L. 1970. Topological and geometrical properties of braided rivers. *Water Resources Research*, **6**, 1674–1688.

—— 1992. Modeling channel migration and floodplain sedimentation in meandering streams. *In*: CARLING, P. A. & PETTS, G. E. (eds) *Lowland Floodplain Rivers: Geomorphological Perspectives*. Wiley, 1–41.

IKEDA, H. 1973. A study of the formation of sand bars in an experimental flume. *Geographical Review of Japan*, **46**, 435–452.

—— 1975. On the bed configuration in alluvial channels; their types and condition of formation with reference to bars. *Geographical Review of Japan*, **48**, 712–730.

—— 1983. *Experiments on bedload transport, bedforms, and sedimentary structures using fine gravel in the 4-meter wide flume*. University of Tsukuba, Japan, Environmental Research Center Paper No. 2.

IKEDA, S. 1984. Prediction of alternate bar wavelength and height. *Journal of Hydraulic Engineering, American Society of Civil Engineers*, **110**, 371–386.

—— & PARKER, G. (eds) 1989. *River meandering*. American Geophysical Union, Water Resources Monographs, **12**.

——, —— & SAWAI, K. 1981. Bend theory of river meanders. 1. Linear development. *Journal of Fluid Mechanics*, **112**, 363–377.

ISEYA, S. & IKEDA, H. 1987. Pulsations in bedload transport rates induced by a longitudinal sediment sorting: a flume study of sand and gravel mixtures. *Geografiska Annaler*, **69A**, 15–27.

JACKSON, R. G. 1975a. Velocity-bedform-texture patterns of meander bends in the Lower Wabash River of Illinois and Indiana. *Geological Society of America Bulletin*, **86**, 1511–1522.

—— 1975b. Hierarchical attributes and a unifying model of bedforms composed of cohesionless sediment and produced by shearing flow. *Geological Society of America Bulletin*, **86**, 1523–1533.

—— 1976a. Depositional model of point bars in the Lower Wabash River. *Journal of Sedimentary Petrology*, **46**, 579–594.

—— 1976b. Largescale ripples of the Lower Wabash River. *Sedimentology*, **23**, 593–623.

—— 1978. Preliminary evaluation of lithofacies models for meandering alluvial streams. *In*: MIALL, A. D. (ed.) *Fluvial Sedimentology*. Canadian Society of Petroleum Geologists Memoirs, **5**, 543–576.

JAEGGI, M. N. R. 1984. Formation and effects of alternate bars. *Journal of Hydraulic Engineering, American Society of Civil Engineers*, **110**, 142–156.

JOHANNESSON, H. & PARKER, G. 1989. Linear theory of river meanders. *In*: IKEDA, S. & PARKER, G. (eds) *River Meandering*. American Geophysical Union Water Resources Monographs, **12**, 181–213.

KARCZ, I. 1971. Development of a meandering thalweg in a straight, erodible laboratory channel. *Journal of Geology*, **79**, 234–240.

—— 1972. Sedimentary structures formed by flash floods in southern Israel. *Sedimentary Geology*, **7**, 161–182.

KASTHURI, B. & PUNDARIKANTHAN, N. V. 1987. Separation zone at open-channel junctions: discussion. *Journal of Hydraulic Engineering, ASCE*, **113**, 543–544.

KELLERHALS, R., CHURCH, M. & BRAY, D. I. 1976. Classification and analysis of river processes. *Journal of the Hydraulics Division, American Society of Civil Engineers*, **102**, 813–829.

KINOSITA, R. 1957. Formation of dunes on river beds — an observation on the condition of river meandering. *Proceedings of the Japan Society of Civil Engineers*, **42**, 1–21.

KINOSITA, R. 1961. *Study of the channel evolution of the Isikari River*. Bureau of Resources, Department of Science and Technology, Japan.

KIRKBY, M. J. 1972. Alluvial and nonalluvial meanders. *Area*, **4**, 284–288.

—— 1977. Maximum sediment efficiency as a criterion for alluvial channels. *In*: GREGORY, K. J. (ed.) *River channel changes*. Wiley, 429–442.

—— 1980. The streamhead as a significant geomorphic threshold. *In*: COATES, D. R. & VITEK, J. (eds) *Thresholds in Geomorphology*. Allen & Unwin, London, 53–73.

KJERFVE, B., SHAO, C. C. & STAPOR, F. W. 1979. Formation of deep scour holes at the junctions of tidal creeks: an hypothesis. *Marine Geology*, **33**, M9–M14.

KNIGHTON, A. D. 1972. Changes in a braided reach. *Geological Society of America Bulletin*, **83**, 3813–3822.

—— 1984. *Fluvial forms and processes*. Edward Arnold, London.

KOMAR, P. D. 1983. Shapes of streamlined islands on Earth and Mars: experiments and analyses of the minimum-drag form. *Geology*, **11**, 651–654.

—— 1984. The Lemniscate Loop-comparisons with shapes of streamlined landforms. *Journal of Geology*, **92**, 133–145.

KOSTER, E. H. 1978. Transverse ribs: their characteristics, origin and paleohydraulic significance. *In*: MIALL, A. D. (ed.) *Fluvial Sedimentology*. Canadian Society of Petroleum Geologists Memoirs, **5**, 161–186.

KRIGSTRÖM, A. 1962. Geomorphological studies of sandur plains and their braided rivers in Iceland. *Geografiska Annaler*, **44**, 328–346.

KUHNLE, R. A. & SOUTHARD, J. B. 1988. Bedload transport fluctuations in a gravel bed laboratory channel. *Water Resources Research*, **24**, 247–260.

—— & —— 1990. Flume experiments on the transport of heavy minerals in gravel-bed streams. *Journal of Sedimentary Petrology*, **60**, 687–696.

LANE, E. W. 1957. *A study of the shape of channels formed by natural streams flowing in erodible material*. Missouri River Division Sediment Series No. 9, U.S. Army Engineer Division, Missouri River, Corps of Engineers, Omaha, Nebraska.

—— & BORLAND, W. M. 1954. River bed scour during floods. *Transactions, American Society of Civil Engineers*, **119**, 1069–1080.

LANGBEIN, W. B. & LEOPOLD, L. B. 1966. *River meanders-theory of minimum variance*. US Geological Survey Professional Paper 422H.

LEEDER, M. R. 1973. Fluviatile fining-upwards cycles and the magnitude of paleochannels. *Geological Magazine*, **110**, 265–276.

LEOPOLD, L. B. & WOLMAN, M. G. 1957. River channel patterns: braided, meandering and straight. *US Geological Survey Professional Papers*, **262B**, 39–85.

LEVEY, R. A. 1978. Bed-form distribution and internal stratification of coarse-grained point bars, Upper Congaree River, South Carolina. *In*: MIALL, A. D. (ed.) *Fluvial Sedimentology*, Canadian Society of Petroleum Geologists Memoirs, **5**, 105–127.

LEWIN, J. 1976. Initiation of bed forms and meanders in coarse-grained sediment. *Geological Society of America Bulletin*, **87**, 281–285.

—— 1978. Meander development and floodplain sedimentation: a case study from mid-Wales. *Geological Journal*, **13**, 25–36.

—— 1982. British floodplains. *In*: ADAMS, B. H., FENN, C. R. & MORRIS, L. (eds) *Papers in Earth Sciences*. Geo Books, Norwich, 21–37.

—— 1983. Changes in channel pattern and floodplain. *In*: GREGORY, K. J. (ed.) *Background to Palaeohydrology*. Wiley, Chichester, 303–319.

LODINA, R. V. & CHALOV, R. S. 1971. Effect of tributaries on the composition of river sediments and of deformations of the main river channel. *Soviet Hydrology; selected papers*, **4**, 370–374.

LYELL, C. 1830. *The Principles of Geology, volume 1*. John Murray, London.

McGOWEN, J. H. & GARNER, L. E. 1970. Physiographic features and stratification types of coarse-grained point bars: modern and ancient examples. *Sedimentology*, **14**, 77–111.

McQUIVEY, R. S. & KEEFER, T. N. 1969. The relation of turbulence to deposition of magnetite over ripples. *US Geological Survey Professional Paper*, **650D**, 244–247.

MIALL, A. D. 1976. Paleocurrent and paleohydrologic analysis of some vertical profiles through a Cretaceous braided stream deposit, Banks Island, Arctic Canada. *Sedimentology*, **23**, 459–483.

—— 1981. *Analysis of fluvial depositional systems*. American Association of Petroleum Geologists Education Course Note Series No. 20.

MIDDLETON, G. V. & SOUTHARD, J. B. 1984. *Mechanics of sediment movement.* SEPM Short Course No. 3.

MINTER, W. E. L. 1978. A sedimentological synthesis of placer gold, uranium and pyrite concentrations in Proterozoic Witwatersrand sediments. *In*: MIALL, A. D. (ed.) *Fluvial Sedimentology.* Canadian Society of Petroleum Geologists Memoirs, **5**, 801–829.

MINTER, W. E. L. & TOENS, P. D. 1970. Experimental simulation of gold deposition in gravel beds. *Transactions of the Geological Society of South Africa*, **73**, 89–98.

MOSLEY, M. P. 1976. An experimental study of channel confluences. *Journal of Geology*, **84**, 535–562.

—— 1981. Semi-determinate hydraulic geometry of river channels, South Island, New Zealand. *Earth Surface Processes and Landforms*, **6**, 127–137.

—— 1982a. Scour depths in branch channel confluences, Ohao River, Otago, New Zealand. *Transactions, The Institution of Professional Engineers, New Zealand*, **9**, 17–24.

—— 1982b. Analysis of the effect of changing discharge on channel morphology and instream uses in a braided river, Ohau River, New Zealand. *Water Resources Research*, **18**, 800–812.

—— 1983. Response of braided rivers to changing discharge. *Journal of Hydrology (New Zealand)*, **22**, 18–67.

—— & SCHUMM, S. A. 1977. Stream junctions — a probable location for bedrock placers. *Economic Geology*, **72**, 691–694.

MURAMOTO, Y. & FUJITA, Y. 1977. Study on meso scale river bed configuration. *Annuals, Disaster Prevention Research Institute, Kyota Univ.*, **20B-2**, 243–258.

NADEN, P. S. & BRAYSHAW, A. C. 1987. Small and medium-scale bedforms in gravel-bed rivers. *In*: RICHARDS, K. S. (ed.) *River channels: environment and processes.* Blackwell, 249–271.

NANSON, G. C. 1980. Point bar and floodplain formation of the meandering Beatton River, northeastern British Columbia, Canada. *Sedimentology*, **27**, 3–29.

—— & PAGE, K. P. 1983. Lateral accretion of fine-grained concave bank benches in meandering rivers. *In*: COLLINSON, J. D. & LEWIN, J. (eds) *Modern and Ancient Fluvial Systems*, International Association of Sedimentologists Special Publication 6, 133–143.

——, RUST, B. R. & TAYLOR, G. 1986. Coexistent mud braids and anastomosing channels in an arid-zone river: Cooper Creek, central Australia. *Geology*, **14**, 175–178.

NILSSON, G. & MARTVALL, S. 1972. *The Ore River and its meanders.* Uppsala Universiteit Geologiska Institute Report 19, Uppsala, Sweden.

NORDSETH, K. 1973. Fluvial processes and adjustments in a braided river. The islands of Koppangsoyene on the River Glomma. Norsk Geografiska Tidsskrft, **27**, 77–108.

ODGAARD, A. J. 1989. River meander model.

I: Development. II: Applications. *Journal of Hydraulic Engineering, American Society of Civil Engineers*, **112**, 1117–1150.

OSTERKAMP, W. R. 1978. Gradient, discharge, and particle size relations of alluvial channels in Kansas, with observations on braiding. *American Journal of Science*, **278**, 1253–1268.

PAGE, K. & NANSON, G. C. 1982. Concave bank formation and associated floodplain formation. *Earth Surface Processes and Landforms*, **7**, 529–543.

PAOLA, C. & BORGMAN, L. 1991. Reconstructing random topography from preserved stratification. *Sedimentology*, **38**, 553–565.

PARKER, G. 1976. On the cause and characteristic scales of meandering and braiding in rivers. *Journal of Fluid Mechanics*, **76**, 457–480.

—— 1979. Hydraulic geometry of active gravel rivers. *Journal of the Hydraulics Division, American Society of Civil Engineers*, **105**, 1185–1201.

—— & ANDREWS, E. A. 1986. On the time development of meander bends. *Journal of Fluid Mechanics*, **162**, 139–156.

PIZZUTO, J. E. 1984. Bank erodibility of shallow sand bed streams. *Earth Surface Processes and Landforms*, **9**, 113–124.

PRESTEGAARD, K. 1983. Variables influencing water-surface slopes in gravel-bed streams at bankfull stage. *Geological Society of America Bulletin*, **94**, 673–678.

REID, I., BEST, J. L. & FROSTICK, L. E. 1989. Floods and flood sediments at river confluences. *In*: BEVEN, K. & CARLING, P. (eds) *Floods: Hydrological, Sedimentological and Geomorphological Implications.* Wiley, 135–150.

RICE, R. J. 1982. The hydraulic geometry of the lower portion of the Sunwapta River valley train, Jasper National Park, Alberta. *In*: DAVIDSON-ARNOTT, R., NICKLING, W. & FAHEY, B. (eds) *Research in glacial, glacio-fluvial and glacio-lacustrine systems.* Proceedings of the 6th Guelph Symposium on Geomorphology, Geo Books, Norwich, U.K. 151–173.

RICHARDS, K. S. 1982. *Rivers: form and process in alluvial channels.* Methuen, London.

ROBERTSON-RINTOUL, M. S. E. & RICHARDS, K. S. 1993. Braided channel pattern and paleohydrology using an index of total sinuosity. *This volume*.

ROY, A. G. & BERGERON, N. 1990. Flow and particle paths at a natural river confluence with coarse bed material. *Geomorphology*, **3**, 99–112.

—— & DE SERRES, B. 1989. Morphologie du lit et dynamique des confluents de cours d'eau. *Bulletin de la Societe Geographique de Liege*, **25**, 113–127.

—— & ROY, R. 1988. Changes in channel size at river confluences with coarse bed material. *Earth Surface Processes and Landforms*, **13**, 77–84.

——, —— & BERGERON, N. 1988. Hydraulic geometry and changes in flow velocity at a river confluence with coarse bed material. *Earth Surface Processes and Landforms*, **13**, 583–598.

—— & WOLDENBERG, M. J. 1986. A model for

changes in channel form at a river confluence. *Journal of Geology*, **94**, 402–411.

RUNDLE, A. S. 1985a. The mechanism of braiding. *Zeitschrift fur Geomorphologie, Supplement Band*, **55**, 1–13.

—— 1985b. Braid morphology and the formation of multiple channels, the Rakaia, New Zealand. *Zeitchrift fur Geomorphologie, Supplement Band*, **55**, 15–37.

RUST, B. R. 1972. Structure and process in a braided river. *Sedimentology*, **18**, 221–245.

—— 1978a. A classification of alluvial channel systems. *In*: MIALL, A. D. (ed.) *Fluvial Sedimentology*. Canadian Society of Petroleum Geologists Memoirs, **5**, 187–198.

—— 1978b. Depositional models for braided alluvium. *In*: MIALL, A. D. (ed.) *Fluvial Sedimentology*. Canadian Society of Petroleum Geologists Memoirs, **5**, 605–626.

—— 1981. Sedimentation in an arid-zone anastomosing fluvial system: Cooper Creek, Central Australia. *Journal of Sedimentary Petrology*, **52**, 745–755.

—— & NANSON, G. C. 1986. Comtemporary and paleochannel patterns and the Late Quaternary stratigraphy of Cooper Creek, Southwest Queensland, Australia. *Earth Surface Processes and Landforms*, **11**, 581–590.

SARKAR, S. K. & BASUMALLICK, S. 1968. Morphology, structure and evolution of a channel island in the Barakar River, Barakar, West Bengal. *Journal of Sedimentary Petrology*, **38**, 747–754.

SCHUMM, S. A. 1963. Sinuosity of alluvial channels on the Great Plains. *Geological Society of America Bulletin*, **74**, 1089–1100.

—— 1971. Fluvial geomorphology. *In*: SHEN, H. W. (ed.) *River Mechanics I*. Water Resources Publications, Colorado, 1–22.

—— 1972. Fluvial paleochannels. *In*: RIGBY, J. K. & HAMBLIN, W. K. (eds) *Recognition of Ancient Sedimentary Environments*. SEPM Special Publications, **16**, 98–107.

—— 1977. *The Fluvial System*. Wiley, New York.

—— 1981. Evolution and response of the fluvial system, sedimentologic implications. *In*: ETHRIDGE, F. G. & FLORES, R. M. (eds) *Recent and ancient nonmarine depositional environments: models for exploration*. SEPM Special Publications, **31**, 19–29.

—— 1985. Patterns of alluvial rivers. *Annual Reviews of Earth and Planetary Science*, **13**, 5–27.

—— & KHAN, H. R. 1972. Experimental study of channel patterns. *Geological Society of America Bulletin*, **83**, 1755–1770.

—— & LICHTY, R. W. 1963. Channel widening and floodplain construction along Cimarron River in southwestern Kansas. *US Geological Survey Professional Paper*, **352D**, 71–88.

SCHWARTZ, D. E. 1978. Hydrology and current orientation analysis of a braided-to-meandering transition: the Red River in Oklahoma and Texas, U.S.A. *In*: MIALL, A. D. (ed.) *Fluvial Sedimentology*. Canadian Society of Petroleum Geologists Memoirs, **5**, 105–127.

SHELTON, J. W. & NOBLE, R. L. 1974. Depositional

features of braided-meandering stream. *American Association of Petroleum Geologists Bulletin*, **58**, 742–749.

——, BURMAN, H. R. & NOBLE, R. L. 1974. Directional features in braided-meandering deposits, Cimarron River, North Central Oklahoma. *Journal of Sedimentary Petrology*, **38**, 747–754.

SINGH, I. B. & KUMAR, S. 1974. Mega- and giant ripples in the Ganga, Yamuna and Son Rivers, Uttar Pradesh, India. *Sedimentary Geology*, **12**, 53–66.

SLINGERLAND, R. L. 1977. The effects of entrainment on the hydraulic equivalence relationships of light and heavy minerals in sand. *Journal of Sedimentary Petrology*, **47**, 753–770.

—— 1984. Role of hydraulic sorting in the origin of fluvial placers. *Journal of Sedimentary Petrology*, **54**, 137–150.

—— & SMITH, N. D. 1986. Occurrence and formation of waterlaid placers. *Annual Reviews in Earth and Planetary Sciences*, **14**, 113–147.

SMITH, D. G. 1976. Effect of vegetation on lateral migration of anastomosed channels of a glacial meltwater river. *Geological Society of America Bulletin*, **87**, 857–860.

—— 1983. Anastomosed fluvial deposits: modern examples from Western Canada. *In*: COLLINSON, J. D. & LEWIN, J. (eds) *Modern and Ancient Fluvial Systems*. International Association of Sedimentologists Special Publications, **6**, 155–168.

—— & SMITH, N. D. 1980. Sedimentation in anastomosed river systems: examples from alluvial valleys near Bauff, Alberta. *Journal of Sedimentary Petrology*, **50**, 157–164.

SMITH, N. D. 1970. The braided stream depositional environment: comparison of the Platte River with some Silurian clastic rocks, north-central Appalachians. *Geological Society of America Bulletin*, **81**, 2993–3014.

—— 1971a. Transverse bars and braiding in the Lower Platte River, Nebraska. *Geological Society of America Bulletin*, **82**, 3407–3420.

—— 1971b. Pseudo-planar stratification produced by very low amplitude sand waves. *Journal of Sedimentary Petrology*, **41**, 624–634.

—— 1972. Some sedimentological aspects of planar cross-stratification in a sandy braided river. *Journal of Sedimentary Petrology*, **42**, 624–634.

—— 1974. Sedimentology and bar formation in the Upper Kicking Horse River, a braided outwash stream. *Journal of Geology*, **82**, 205–223.

—— 1978. Some comments on terminology for bars in shallow rivers. *In*: MIALL, A. D. (ed.) *Fluvial Sedimentology*. Canadian Society of Petroleum Geologists Memoirs, **5**, 85–88.

—— & BEUKES, N. J. 1983. Bar to bank flow convergence zones: a contribution to the origin of alluvial placers. *Economic Geology*, **78**, 1342–1349.

—— & MINTER, W. E. L. 1980. Sedimentological control of gold and uranium in two Witwatersrand paleoplacers. *Economic Geology*, **75**, 1–14.

—— & SMITH, D. G. 1984. William River: an outstanding example of channel widening and braiding caused by bedload addition. *Geology*, **12**, 78–82.

SMITH, S. A. 1987. Gravel counterpoint bars: examples from the River Tywi, South Wales. *In*: ETHRIDGE, F. G., FLORES, R. M. & HARVEY, M. D. (eds) *Recent developments in Fluvial Sedimentology*. SEPM Special Publications, **39**, 75–81.

STEBBINGS, J. 1964. The shapes of self-formed model alluvial channels. *Proceedings of the Institution of Civil Engineers*, **25**, 485–510.

STEINMETZ, R. 1967. *Depositional history, primary sedimentary structures, cross bed dips, and grain size of an Arkansas River point bar at Wekiwa, Oklahoma*. Report of the Pan American Petroleum Corporation Research Department. F67-G-3.

STRAUB, L. G. 1935. Some observations of sorting of river sediments. *Transactions of the American Geophysical Union*, **16**, 463–467.

STRUIKSMA, N. & KLAASSEN, G. J. 1988. On the threshold between meandering and braiding. *In*: WHITE, W. R. (ed.) *International Conference on River Regime*. Wiley, 107–120.

SOUTHARD, J. B. & BOGUCHWAL, L. A. 1990. Bed configurations in steady unidirectional flows. Part 2. Synthesis of flume data. *Journal of Sedimentary Petrology*, **60**, 658–679.

——, SMITH, N. D. & KUHNLE, R. A. 1984. Chutes and lobes: newly identified elements of braiding in shallow gravelly streams. *In*: KOSTER, E. H. & STEEL, R. J. (eds) *Sedimentology of gravels and conglomerates*. Canadian Society of Petroleum Geologists Memoirs, **10**, 51–59.

SUKEGAWA, N. 1970. Conditions for the occurrence of river meanders. *Journal of the Faculty of Engineering, University of Tokyo*, **30**, 289–306.

SUNDBORG, A. 1956. The River Klarälven: a study of fluvial processes. *Geografiska Annaler*, **38**, 127–316.

TANDON, S. K. & KUMAR, R. 1981. Gravel fabric in a sub-Himalayan braided stream. *Sedimentary Geology*, **28**, 133–152.

TAYLOR, G. & WOODYER, K. D. 1978. Bank deposition in suspended load streams. *In*: MIALL, A. D. (ed.) *Fluvial Sedimentology*. Canadian Society of Petroleum Geologists Memoirs, **5**, 257–275.

TEISSEYRE, A. K. 1975. Pebble fabric in braided stream deposits. *Geologia Sudetica*, **10**, 7–56.

—— 1977a. Pebble clusters as a directional structure in fluvial gravels: modern and ancient examples. *Geologia Sudetica*, **12**, 79–89.

—— 1977b. Meander degeneration in bed-load proximal stream: repeated chute cut-off due to bar-head gravel accretion — a hypothesis. *Geologica Sudetica*, **12**, 103–120.

THORNE, C. R. & TOVEY, N. K. 1981. Stability of composite river banks. *Earth Surface Processes and Landforms*, **6**, 409–484.

TURNBULL, W. J., KRINITSKY, G. L. & WEAVER, F. J. 1966. Bank erosion in soils of the Lower Mississippi Valley. *Proceedings of the American Society of Civil Engineers*, **92** (SM1), 121–136.

VOGEL, K. R. VAN NIEKERK, A., SLINGERLAND, R. L. & BRIDGE, J. S. 1992. Routing of heterogeneous sediments over moveable beds: model verification. *Journal of Hydraulic Engineering, American Society of Civil Engineers*, **118**, 263–279.

WERRITTY, A. & FERGUSON, R. I. 1980. Pattern changes in a Scottish braided river over 1, 30, and 200 years. *In*: CULLINGFORD, R. A., DAVIDSON, D. A. & LEWIN, J. (eds) *Timescales in Geomorphology*. Wiley, 53–68.

WHITING, P. J., DIETRICH, W. E., LEOPOLD, L. B., DRAKE, T. G. & SHREVE, R. L. 1988. Bedload sheets in heterogeneous sediment. *Geology*, **16**, 105–108.

WILCOCK, P. R. & SOUTHARD, J. B. 1989. Bed load transport of mixed size sediment: fractional transport rates, bedforms, and the development of a coarse bed surface layer. *Water Resources Research*, **25**, 1629–1641.

WILLIAMS, P. F. & RUST, B. R. 1969. The sedimentology of a braided river. *Journal of Sedimentary Petrology*, **39**, 649–679.

WILLIS, B. J. 1989. Paleochannel reconstructions from point bar deposits: a three-dimensional perspective. *Sedimentology*, **36**, 757–766.

—— 1993. Ancient river systems in the Himalayan foredeep, Chinji village area, northern Pakistan. *Sedimentary Geology*, in press.

WITT, A. 1985. Vegetational influences on intrachannel deposition: evidence from the Konczak stream, greater Poland lowlands, western Poland. *Quaestiones Geographicae*, **9**, 145–160.

YALIN, M. S. 1977. *Mechanics of Sediment Transport*. 2nd ed. Pergamon Press.

Understanding braiding processes in gravel-bed rivers: progress and unsolved problems

R. I. FERGUSON

Department of Geography, University of Sheffield, Sheffield S10 2TN, UK

Abstract: This paper is a review, from a geomorphologist's point of view, of recent progress in understanding the interrelationships between channel form, flow, bed texture, and bedload transport in braided gravel-bed rivers. The fundamental geomorphological units in such rivers are not bars alone but bar-pool units, usually associated with confluences and bifurcations. Braiding can develop not only by midstream deposition but by bar dissection and partial avulsion; the hydraulic conditions favouring different mechanisms deserve study. Braiding is highly dynamic, with rapid feedback between channel configuration, flow, and sediment transport. These interactions can profitably be observed in Froude-scaled flume models, and can to some extent be quantified by intensive field measurements, but numerical modelling is potentially the best approach. Sediment is sorted both laterally and longitudinally within pool-bar units, but some of the possible mechanisms have not been adequately studied. The downstream fining which occurs along entire braidplains can be explained by selective transport but associated changes in bar types may not follow any single sequence.

Braided rivers are distinctive because of their high power and consequent high rates of erosion, deposition, and channel change compared to other river types. This greater activity increases the potential for practical problems such as bridge scour and channel shifting. The activity of former braided rivers has also made a widespread and distinctive contribution to the rock record, with many ancient braidplain deposits forming important aquifers or hydrocarbon reservoirs. For all these reasons it is important to understand how braided rivers work.

There is a great deal of relatively recent literature which could be included in a review such as this. To keep things manageable I have concentrated on research on modern braided rivers and flume models rather than ancient deposits. Much of this research has a geomorphological perspective emphasizing understanding of how and through what mechanisms river morphology alters and evolves, and what the implications are for sedimentology and river engineering. This chapter is therefore less wide-ranging than Bridge's keynote contribution in this volume, and largely complementary to that of Martin which emphasizes the rock record. Furthermore, I deliberately concentrate on gravel-bed rivers and say little about sandy braided rivers, which are discussed at length by Bridge. I also omit the question of what hydraulic and environmental conditions favour the development of braiding rather than some other, less active, channel pattern, since this is reviewed well by

Bridge (1993) and was discussed in more detail by Ferguson (1987). It is, however, relevant to what follows that braiding is associated with high values of valley slope, stream power, shear stress, width/depth ratio, and bedload transport rate compared to other river types.

In reviewing progress in understanding how braided rivers work I focus on four questions.

(1) What are the basic morphological and sedimentological units in braided rivers?
(2) How in qualitative terms do these fundamental units develop?
(3) Can we quantify the processes acting in the development of braiding, either deductively or empirically?
(4) Can we explain and predict the lateral and longitudinal sediment sorting which occurs locally and more extensively in braided rivers?

In each case I highlight what I see as unsolved problems as well as progress achieved. My choices inevitably reflect my own research agenda, but several of the issues I raise are also recognized and addressed by other contributors to this volume. The research which I summarize and generalize from is partly field-based (including my own, in collaboration with several other British, American and Canadian workers), but important insights have also been obtained from flume studies. Miniature braided streams in the laboratory, using as bed material coarse sand or fine gravel some 3 or 4 phi units finer than in prototype braided channels, can be seen as generic Froude-scaled models which

From Best, J. L. & Bristow, C. S. (eds), 1993, *Braided Rivers*, Geological Society Special Publication No. 75, pp. 73–87.

73

retain the rough-turbulent flow and dimension-less morphometric and hydraulic characteristics of prototype gravel-bed rivers. The advantages over fieldwork are experimental control (notably of discharge), faster morphologic evolution, and above all easier observation and recording of pattern change. Ashmore (e.g. 1982a, 1993), Hoey & Sutherland (1991), and others have shown the value of this approach.

Fundamental morphological units

The complexity of braided river patterns is such that the natural reaction of reductionist scientists is to identify basic units or building blocks and study them in isolation. What then are the fundamental morphologic units in gravelly braided rivers?

Bars

Attention has traditionally been focused on the visible mid-channel bars which are the defining feature of the braided pattern. This is an obvious approach in reconnaissance fieldwork or when using air photographs or satellite imagery. There have been several attempts to classify braid bars using such criteria as elongation, symmetry, and presence or absence of a distal avalanche face; two of the best known are those of Miall (1977) and Church & Jones (1982). However, there is much disagreement over any such classification and unambiguous classification may well be impossible (e.g. Smith 1978, Ashmore 1982b, Ashley 1990). There are several drawbacks to excessive emphasis on visible bars as the basic units in braided rivers.

(1) The number and planform of visible bars is stage dependent.

(2) Visible bars not only appear to change because of stage variation, they also really change as sediment accretes to them, or as erosional trimming and dissection occur. Bars of initially symmetric planform can become skewed, and midchannel bars can become attached to one or other bank (e.g. Church & Jones 1982, fig. 11.4).

(3) Trying to understand braiding by looking only at visible bars is uncomfortably like trying to understand continental relief without considering what goes on beneath the oceans. Bar deposition requires sediment transport, and this generally originates in the deeper parts of channels. Important connections between channels and bars become apparent when one wades in small braided rivers, or observes braiding in the laboratory with the advantages of clear water and being able to drain the flume.

(4) Flume (e.g. Ashmore 1982a) and field (e.g. Ferguson et al. 1992) observations of bar development confirm what many sedimentologists have inferred from bar surface texture and imbrication direction: that the bars visible in braided rivers are mostly compound and of complex origin. Aggradation often occurs episodically through the accretion of individual gravel sheets or 'unit bars', and may be offset by erosion by flow over the top of the bar complex or past its tail.

Pool-bar units

Visible braid bars are instead often better understood as the distal or lateral rims of pools which become wider and shallower in the downstream direction, the whole making an elongated and often asymmetric unit. These units are seen by many fieldworkers and flume experimenters as common elements in gravel-bed rivers of all channel patterns, not just braiding. Three cases are sketched in Fig. 1, which is similar to diagrams in Bridge (1985, this volume), Dietrich (1987), and Ferguson (1987).

In low sinuosity single channels the bars are on alternate sides of the channel and have diagonal fronts (Fig. 1a). Under low flow conditions riffles slant across the rims of the pool-bar units, separating one pool from the next downstream. The flow convergence and acceleration through the riffle can cause local dissection of the bar front and small-scale delta construction in the pool head. In high flows these riffles are drowned out and flow converges into pool heads, which are liable to scour and thus cause deposition under the divergent flow over the next bar front (e.g. Ferguson & Werritty 1983).

In meandering channels the pool-bar units are wrapped round bends and overlap rather more (Fig. 1b). The distal limit of each unit is a diagonal riffle running from one point bar to the head of the next point bar on the opposite side of the channel. The head and tail of each point bar belong to successive pool-bar units, so that the point bar is a compound feature (Bridge 1985, this volume; Thompson 1986; Dietrich 1987).

In braided channels, the pool-bar units occur alongside each other in two or more parallel rows (Fig. 1c). The pools are linked by talwegs which define two or more back to back meandering traces, alternately converging and diverging. This view of braiding as consisting of multiple meandering talwegs is the same as is assumed in mathematical stability analyses of the conditions for development of meandering or braiding (e.g. Parker 1976). As Bridge (1985, this volume) has stressed, in this model each braid bar is part of

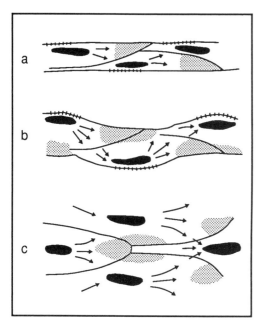

Fig. 1. Overlapping pool-bar units in gravel bed rivers of different channel pattern: (**a**) straight with single row of alternate bars, (**b**) meandering with point bars, (**c**) braided with medial bars composed of back to back double row of alternate bars. In each case pools are marked in black, cut banks by lines with tick marks, and bar fronts by curving lines. Stippled areas are 'bars' exposed at ordinary flow levels; note that in meandering and braided patterns they are compound features belonging to more than one pool-bar unit. Based partly on Bridge (1985, this volume), Dietrich (1987), Thompson (1986), and Ferguson (1987).

plain, anabranches cannot become very sinuous without intersecting and being captured by other channels.

Although curves and associated bank erosion should not be neglected as aspects of the mechanism of braiding, the most distinctive features of braided channels are confluences (junctions) and diffluences (bifurcations). These are the two main types of node in what by definition is a connected network of channels, as illustrated schematically in Fig. 2, as opposed to the tree-like network of a non-braided river in which there may be tributary junctions but not bifurcations. If one focuses on channels rather than bars, the distinctive parts of braided rivers are the localities containing channel nodes: Y- and reverse-Y-shaped junctions (J in Fig. 2) and bifurcations (B), and X-shaped pairs of junction followed by bifurcation. These X- or Y-shaped channel configurations have been adopted as the units for detailed study in all but one of the few attempts to date to make detailed process measurements in braided rivers (e.g. Davoren & Mosley 1986; Ferguson & Ashworth 1992). The exception is the pioneering attempt by Hein & Walker (1977) to make measurements during the evolution of small bars.

A third kind of node which may also be found in a braided river is a channel head (H in Fig. 2). These are formed either by incision of flow over a bar top or by blocking of one anabranch at a bifurcation. Channel heads formed by either mechanism are potential pathways for avulsion, in which case the head becomes a bifurcation.

This topological view of the plan form of braided rivers neglects the vertical dimension. In

three separate pool units and is thus a compound feature: the barhead is the distal part of one unit, and the left and right sides of the bar tail are lateral parts of two other units alongside each other.

Channel confluences and bifurcations

Individual channels in a braided river are subject to the same physical laws as in non-braided rivers, and the same processes and behaviour can be observed as in straight or meandering rivers. In particular, individual anabranches are usually curved to some extent, so that they resemble gentle meander bends. Bank erosion on the outsides of such bends can be rapid and an important cause of channel change, as well as an important source of sediment for bar construction (e.g. Ashworth & Ferguson 1986; Baumgart-Kotarba 1987; Thorne *et al.* 1993). However, except at the outer edges of a braid

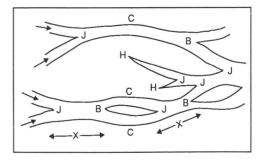

Fig. 2. Topological classification of channel nodes in a braided river with flow in the directions shown by the single arrows. The three types of node are junction (J) or confluence, bifurcation (B) or diffluence, and channel head (H). A junction followed by a bifurcation gives an X-shaped pattern of channels as marked at two places. Note also the characteristic curvature (C) of anabranches between nodes.

practice the convergent flow in braid junctions tends to be associated with scour pools, and the divergent flow at bifurcations with shallower channels and bar-head aggradation, as is clear from Fig. 1c. There is thus a link between the channel topology view of braiding and the pool-bar unit view. This reinforces the message that the basic units in braided rivers are three-dimensional not two-dimensional, and that we cannot expect to obtain a good understanding of bar development without considering channels and channel processes.

Mechanisms of braid development

It is increasingly clear that there is no single universal mode of braid development. Rather, braiding can be initiated either by deposition in midstream topographic lows or by erosional dissection of topographic highs. Ashmore (1991b) identified two types of central deposition (as midstream bars, or in chutes and lobes) and two erosional processes (chute cutoff and lobe dissection). To some extent the erosional mechanisms can be seen as consequences of a

preceding depositional phase, but at any given time an increase in the degree of flow division into separate talwegs can be achieved by either erosion or deposition. This is also true of avulsion, which is discussed here as a fifth mechanism but can in fact occur through either erosion or deposition and may either increase or reduce the degree of braiding.

Central bar deposition

This is the classic process in which an elongated, more or less symmetric, medial bar without a distal avalanche face develops in the middle of a channel expansion (Fig. 3a). The traditional explanation (e.g. Leopold & Wolman 1957) involves stalling of coarse bedload in the centre of a wide shallow channel. Although this is traditionally reported as the main process of braid development, Ashmore (1991b) found it was uncommon in his flume experiments: it occurred only in flume runs at shear stresses close to the threshold for bed movement, with a dimensionless bed shear stress of around 0.06. Since the shear stress is to a first order pro-

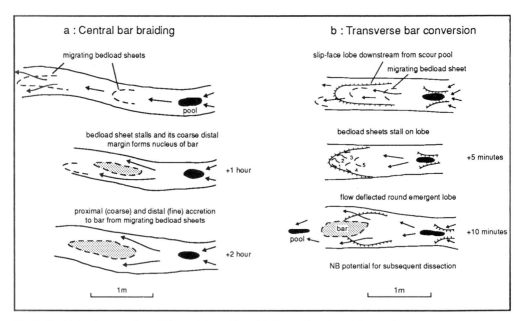

Fig. 3. Braid development by midchannel deposition. (**a**) Central bar deposition, as described by Leopold & Wolman (1957) and Ashmore (1991b). Cartoon based on flume photographs of Ashmore (1991b, fig. 5). Loss of capacity or competence in shallow channel causes coarse bedload to stall and accrete. Black patches are pools, stippled patches exposed bars, dotted lines bar margins without avalanche faces, and arrows show flow direction. (**b**) 'Transverse bar conversion' of Ashmore (1991b), also referred to as chute and lobe. Cartoon based on flume photographs of Ashmore (1991b, fig. 6). Symbols as in (a) together with ticked lines for avalanche faces and small numbers for successive positions of bedload sheets. Reduced transport capacity in flow expansion below chute causes lobate deposition; accreting gravel sheets form slip faces on either side of initial deposit.

portional to the product of flow depth and slope, the dimensionless stress varies with the ratio of depth (d) to grainsize (D). In shallow flows where the mean depth is only just sufficient for bedload transport, small absolute differences in depth can be large in relative terms and significantly reduce the dimensionless shear stress and thus the bedload transport capacity, possibly reducing it to zero for coarser particles: i.e. a loss of competence. Once a few coarse particles have lodged together, further bedload accretes both upstream and downstream of this cluster nucleus, to produce an elongated patch of coarse deposition. This is initially ill defined but may become more sharply defined if subsequent flow deflection around the patch causes incision of the anabranches and erosional trimming of the distal part of the emergent patch.

Chutes and lobes

The depositional development of mid-channel bars is not, however, restricted to situations in which the mean bed shear stress is so close to the threshold for motion that minor differences in depth cause stalling of bedload. A commoner situation is an overall streamwise reduction in shear stress and bedload transport capacity as flow expands out of a pool or chute, with increasing width and thus decreasing depth. The term 'chute and lobe' was coined by Southard et al. (1984) to describe a rather specific situation but has been widely adopted by others (e.g. Davoren & Mosley 1986; Ferguson et al. 1992). As originally described, the mechanism is characteristic of steep shallow channels (slope of several percent, flow typically supercritical) in which the lobes consist of coarse bed material, some of which protrudes above the water surface. These lobes are small features and very ephemeral, since they rapidly unravel and become dissected, creating new chutes and therefore new lobes.

Longer-lasting depositional lobes downstream from chutes or pools also occur in braided rivers which are less steep and shallow. This is probably a commoner situation and is illustrated schematically in Fig. 3b. Ashmore (1991b) termed it 'transverse bar conversion' and found it to be one of the two main modes of braiding in his flume experiments, observable whenever shear stress was appreciably above the threshold of motion and the ratio d/D_{90} of flow depth to coarse-particle diameter exceeded 2 or 3. In these conditions, pools at sites of flow convergence can scour appreciably, generating enough sediment for substantial deposition where the flow diverges. The gentler slope and

therefore greater depth than in the situation described by Southard et al. (1984) means that deposition may occur in water sufficiently deep for an avalanche face to develop. What then happens, according to Ashmore's observations, is that thin bedload sheets stall on the top or front of the lobe, which eventually emerges. Flow is then deflected off the edges of the lobe where a pair of diagonal slip faces can develop. The outcome is an approximately symmetric braid bar of the type shown in Fig. 1c, consisting of back-to-back alternate bars. The development of such a bar takes a finite time, being longer at lower values of the dimensionless shear stress and thus bedload transport rate (Fujita 1989; Ashmore 1991b).

Chute cutoff

Once diagonal bar forms exist, with flow obliquely across a wide shallow channel as in the single-row alternate bar scheme of Fig. 1a, the conditions are set for what Ashmore (1991b) regarded as the other main mode of braid development: chute cutoff (Fig. 4a). This is an erosional process, and involves headwards incision by flow taking a short cut across the bar. It also occurs on point bars in meandering gravel-bed rivers, and Schumm & Khan (1972) considered point bar cutoff to be the main way in which braiding developed in flume experiments. The more direct path has a steeper water surface slope than flow in the talweg, and thus a potential competitive advantage. But although chute cutoff involves erosion, Ashmore (1991b) argued that the increase in bartop flow to initiate incision is often due to aggradation of the outer channel towards the rim of the pool-bar unit, possibly through one of the mechanisms already described.

Multiple dissection of lobes

The fourth mode of braid development is also erosional, but instead of dissection by a single chute across a point or diagonal bar involves multiple dissection of a lobate bar (Fig. 4b) constructed in a preceding phase of deposition at a flow expansion. Rundle (1985a, b) considered this to be the characteristic braiding mechanism in New Zealand rivers and identified dissected lobes as basic morphologic units. They certainly occur in many gravelly braided rivers, but Ashmore (1991b) found them uncommon in his flume experiments. There are at least two possible reasons for this. One is inadequate flume width: the situation sketched in Fig. 4b involves a major expansion of the flow, which in

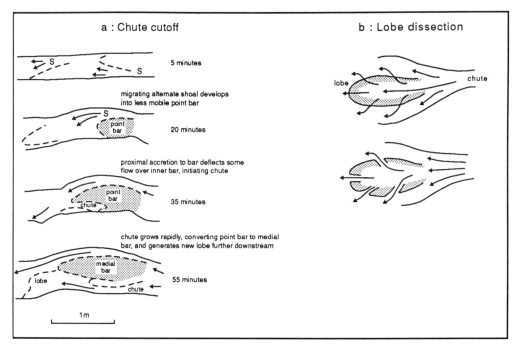

Fig. 4. Braid development by dissection. (**a**) Chute cutoff. Cartoon based on flume photographs of Ashmore (1991*b*, fig. 3). Arrows show flow direction, dotted lines denote diffuse bar margins, and stipple marks exposed bars. Flow over top of alternate or side bar incises into it, causing partial within-channel avulsion. (**b**) Multiple dissection of lobe. Cartoon based on Rundle (1985*a*,*b*). Symbols as in (a) plus solid lines for avalanche faces. Diverging flow over lobe below chute dissects lobe margin at one or more points, axial and/or lateral.

a flume may impinge on the sidewall where scour will then occur, leading to progressive capture of flow from the central and opposite parts of the lobe. This tendency for one of the multiple chutes to become dominant may well apply in unrestricted field situations too, but is accelerated in a narrow flume. Another reason for the scarcity of multiple lobe dissection in Ashmore's experiments is his use of steady discharge: in the field, the lobe may be generated by deposition at a high discharge and subsequently dissected under lower flows, in the same way that alternate bars tend to prograde during major floods but be dissected in minor ones (e.g. Ferguson & Werritty 1983).

Avulsion

The other mechanism characteristic of braiding is avulsion, the relatively sudden switching of course from one channel to another. Chute cutoff is of course a local, within channel, type of avulsion; but larger-scale switching of the main flow also occurs from time to time in all braided rivers.

One common situation is for ponding behind an aggrading bar to lead to overflow, often on the outside of a curve (Fig. 5a). If the overflow is into a topographic low such as an inactive channel (a channel head in the terminology of Fig. 2), the relatively steep gradient confers a competitive advantage which can cause headwards erosion and stream capture, as illustrated by Ashmore (1982*a*, Fig. 19) from flume experiments.

Avulsion into an adjacent inactive channel can also be triggered by bank erosion on curving segments of anabranches (Fig. 5b), as stressed by Carson (1984); as in Fig. 5a, the outcome is to reverse the direction of curvature. Leddy *et al.* (this volume) term the first mechanism (as in Fig. 5a) 'constriction avulsion' and the second (Fig. 5b) 'apex avulsion'. They also identified in their laboratory experiments a third mechanism, 'choking avulsion' (Fig. 5c), in which one anabranch at a bifurcation aggrades sufficiently to divert the entire flow down the other anabranch. In the field this often appears to follow a change in the discharge ratio of the channels entering the X-unit.

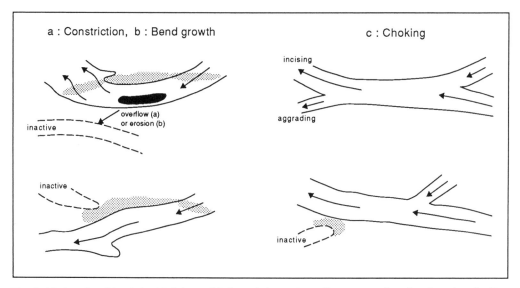

Fig. 5. Modes of avulsion in braided rivers. (**a**) Constriction and overflow: cartoon based on lines described by Ashmore (1982*a*, fig. 19), Ferguson & Werritty (1983), and Leddy *et al.* (this volume). Flow ponded behind an aggrading diagonal bar front in upper diagram goes overbank into adjacent inactive channel, then incises headwards causing abandonment of original channel as in lower diagram. (**b**) Bank erosion: an alternative mechanism having the same effect as in (a) is bank erosion towards the inactive channel (Carson 1984; Leddy *et al.* this volume). (**c**) Choking of one anabranch at a bifurcation causing it to be abandoned (Leddy *et al.* this volume).

The effect of avulsion can be to increase the degree of braiding, reduce it, or leave it unaltered. If the choking mechanism sketched in Fig. 5c proceeds completely it eliminates one anabranch, but the initial effect of the construction and bend growth modes of avulsion is to create a new anabranch. Presumably the generation of new anabranches and the elimination of others occur at the same long term average rate, since otherwise the degree of braiding of a reach would progressively alter over time. But there is very little published information addressing this question, the frequency of different types of avulsion, the speed with which they proceed, or the frequency with which avulsion proceeds to completion. The studies by Ashmore (this volume) and Leddy *et al.* (this volume) are therefore welcome contributions.

Progress and problems

The summary in this and the previous section of recent ideas on the basic morphologic units in braided rivers and the ways in which they develop leads to four conclusions.

(1) Braid bars should not be considered in isolation but in relation to the channels immediately upstream or alongside. It is useful to view them as parts of pool-bar units, though it is important to be aware that what looks like a single emergent bar may be part of more than one pool-bar unit.

(2) If bars should be seen in conjunction with pools, we need three-, not two-dimensional morphometric information. Simple planimetric maps of emerged bars and channel margins do not give this. Nor do aerial photographs and satellite images unless the water is sufficiently clear and shallow that its varying depth is indicated by tonal differences. What is needed is full topographic mapping of channel beds as well as exposed bars. Ways of achieving this are discussed in the next section.

(3) Braiding can develop in more than one way, and possibly by erosion as well as, or even instead of, deposition.

(4) There is some indication that different modes of braiding occur in distinctive, quantifiable hydraulic conditions, but more research is needed on this.

Quantitative studies of braiding processes

The generalizations in the last section about how braiding develops are based almost entirely on qualitative observation and description in flume experiments and in modern rivers. Such observations are instructive and indeed vital, but there has been increasing interest recently in supplementing the qualitative approach by making quantitative measurements. Such measurements are of greatest value if they embrace not just some, but all, of the inter-related factors involved in the behaviour of a mobile-bed channel: its three-dimensional channel geometry, the bed texture, the hydraulics of the flow through it, and the amount and grain size distribution of bedload transport. The channel geometry and bed texture, together with the imposed discharge, control the flow properties; these and the availability of sediment within the reach and supplied from upstream control rates of bedload transport; and any spatial or temporal imbalance in bedload transport causes erosion or deposition which alters the channel geometry and possibly also the bed texture.

Theoretical approaches

Quantitative formulations of these relationships are available, and have been used by various authors to predict the equilibrium morphology of straight single channels under given conditions ('rational regime theory'; see Ferguson 1986 for a review); the same approach has also been applied to meander bends (e.g. Bridge 1992). The problem in braided rivers is that individual anabranches are seldom in equilibrium, and indeed usually very unstable. There are several reasons for this instability.

(1) High stream power and bed shear stress, hence high bedload transport rates, with the possibility of more rapid erosion or deposition than in less mobile conditions.

(2) Pronounced convergence and divergence of flow at junctions and bifurcations, giving big streamwise fluctuations in bedload transport capacity.

(3) Low ratio of depth to grainsize (d/D), leading to rapid and sensitive feedback from local aggradation or degradation to flow depth and transport capacity, as already discussed in connection with the central deposition and chute cutoff mechanisms of braid development.

(4) The changing share of discharge between anabranches as the discharge of the whole river varies (Mosley 1983), and also as individual channels incise or aggrade. Changes in discharge may also be accompanied by changes in sediment load. If the balance of flow and/or load between anabranches changes there can be knock-on effects downstream, the extreme case being avulsion.

In principle, the inter-relationships in the system can be represented by some two-dimensional finite difference or finite element numerical model for vertically-averaged flow coupled to sediment transport and sediment continuity, updated at a short timestep. This approach has been applied fairly successfully to the transient behaviour of alternate-bar channels by Nelson & Smith (1989). There are no published implementations of such a model for actively braiding conditions, in which there is the complication of how to divide the flow at bifurcations as well as the above-mentioned sensitivity of feedbacks from topographic change to flow and sediment transport, but Paola & Wiele (pers. comm. 1992) are developing an analytical model and Richards & Lane (pers. comm. 1993) have applied a finite element numerical model to flow in a braid bifurcation.

Intensive field measurements

What has been attempted is integrated field measurement of flow variables, bedload transport, and channel change in individual X- or Y-shaped braid units, following the productive lead of Bridge & Jarvis (1982) and Dietrich (e.g. 1987) in making intensive measurements of the same variables from footbridges across single meander bends. The first serious attempts to apply this approach to braided rivers were made in the mid to late 1980s, by Bridge & Gabel (1992) using footbridges across the sandy Calamus River in the US, Davoren & Mosley (1986) using a jetboat as a measuring platform in the large Ohau River in New Zealand, and myself and others using wading in much smaller rivers in Norway, the US, and Canada (Ashworth & Ferguson 1986; Ferguson et al. 1989, 1992).

It is necessary to quantify spatial patterns and temporal changes in four aspects of the system.

(1) Three-dimensional channel morphology and change. In small rivers this can be achieved by repeated levelling (e.g. Ferguson et al. 1992). Sonic depth profiling is also valuable (e.g. Bridge & Gabel 1992), and trials of terrestrial photogrammetry are promising (Richards & Lane, pers. comm. 1993).

(2) Grain-size distributions of bed material and bedload, the latter by sieving and the former either by sieving or, in gravel-bed rivers, by pebble counts.

(3) Bedload transport rates. The only feasible way to investigate spatial and temporal varia-

tions in these is to use portable samplers, by wading or from bridges or boats.

(4) The magnitude and direction of local bed shear stress. The best available technique for estimating the magnitude of the stress appears to be fitting the law of the wall to detailed near-bed velocity profiles. The main alternative is the use of the full conservation of momentum equations, as done in meandering and alternate-bar channels by Dietrich (e.g. 1987) and Whiting & Dietrich (1991).

There are serious practical difficulties with most of these, as discussed by Ferguson & Ashworth (1992). It is hard to make detailed topographic surveys quickly enough to map an active braided reach before significant channel change occurs. Grain-size distributions determined by sieving and pebble counting are not necessarily comparable, but bulk sampling of bed material for sieve analysis is logistically demanding (Church et al. 1987). There is mounting evidence of major short-term sampling variability in bedload transport rates estimated using hand-held samplers (see Gomez 1991 for a review); this can be reduced by sampling for longer at each point, but it then becomes even harder to sample at enough points to map the field of sediment transport adequately before there is any change in either discharge or channel morphology. If the total catches used to estimate point transport rates are prone to high sampling variability, the same is likely to be true of bedload grain-size distributions calculated from the sampled transport rates of individual size fractions. Finally, estimation of local bed shear stress from velocity profiles in shallow coarse-bedded streams is sensitive to zero-plane displacement errors according to where the base of the current meter rests, it is difficult to obtain readings close to the bed but the law of the wall does not necessarily hold higher in the flow, and in the presence of bedforms local values may not be representative.

Notwithstanding these practical difficulties, intensive field measurements are beginning to throw light on braiding dynamics. Davoren & Mosley (1986) were able to show the extent of convergence and divergence of both the flow and the bedload transport in an X-pattern reach with a confluence followed by a bifurcation. Ashworth & Ferguson (1986) demonstrated that the spatial patterns of shear stress and of channel erosion or deposition can alter dramatically with an increase in discharge through a reach, causing drastic channel change or even avulsion. Ferguson et al. (1989) showed that local differ-

ences in bed texture can have a dramatic effect on shear stress and the mobility of coarse particles. Ferguson et al. (1992) were able to map flow and transport fields on successive days in an evolving reach and observe the self-limiting feedback whereby an aggrading lobe progressively deflected the flow and bedload transport.

Similar quantitative measurements in flume experiments are, paradoxically, very hard to make. This is because of the reduced spatial scale (e.g. velocity profiling is almost impossible) and accelerated timescale (features may change within tens of minutes, rather than hours or days). What can be done in a flume far more easily than in a river is to monitor the total sediment transport entering and leaving a reach. Field measurement campaigns, for example that reported in Ferguson et al. (1992), have suggested day-to-day changes in total bedload transport which have been tentatively attributed to fluctuations in discharge. The laboratory work of Ashmore (1991a) and Hoey & Sutherland (1991) revealed substantial fluctuations in total transport at an equivalent timescale (allowing for scaling), even though discharge was constant. This suggests that internal adjustments and changes are involved. Ashmore attributed the fluctuations to the migration of gravel sheets and bars out of reaches; Hoey & Sutherland pointed also to the development and later breakup of bed armour, as had previously been suggested by Davoren & Mosley (1986) to explain the big difference in point transport rates found in the same reach of the Ohau River on two different days.

Spatial and temporal variations in bedload transport rate imply changes in the storage of sediment within a reach. Conversely, it is possible to work backwards from measured channel change over a short interval of time to infer streamwise changes in total transport rate averaged over the same time interval. Ferguson & Ashworth (1992) found a reasonable match between transport rates inferred in this way and those estimated from point sampling in two small braided reaches, and speculated that the morphometric estimates may be more reliable. Griffiths (1979) and McLean (1990) had previously applied this method at a much larger scale.

Progress and problems

This discussion of process measurements in braided channels has indicated some progress but also several unsolved problems.

(1) The first attempts have been made to obtain integrated field measurements of the inter-related variables involved in braiding, and their spatial and temporal patterns as reaches evolve. Mapped patterns are, however, unreliable because of measurement difficulties, notably (but not only) the high short-term variability of bedload transport. Indirect estimation of transport rates from channel change may be helpful.

(2) There is evidence that gross bedload transport varies spatially and temporally as bars grow and pass or the bed armours and unravels. There is, however, much to learn about just how bedforms and patchy bed texture affect local flow and regulate sediment transport.

(3) Numerical modelling of the coupling between geometry, flow, and bedload transport has great potential if it can be implemented successfully for the more complicated situation of braided as opposed to single channels.

Sediment sorting in braided rivers

The final topic considered in this review is the sorting of sediment by size within braided rivers, both locally within reaches and at a more extended scale along braidplains. This is part of the more general issue of depositional models for braided rivers which is discussed at greater length by several other contributors to this volume. The emphasis here is on direct observations of processes and patterns in modern rivers, rather than inferences from the rock record which are unavoidably speculative.

Local sorting

It is well known that local sorting occurs along and across bars and channels in low-sinuosity gravel-bed rivers. For example Bluck (1976) mapped pronounced downbar and cross-bar fining in alternate- and lateral-bar reaches of Scottish rivers, associated with the divergence of flow from pools to bar fronts, and argued that bar progradation generates distinctive coarsening-upward deposits. Figure 6, based on measurements in another Scottish river, shows that systematic textural variation is characteristic of the entire pool-bar unit, not just the exposed bar. In the example shown, there is periodic coarsening and fining of median bed-material diameter along each side of the channel as the talweg swings from side to side across and around alternate bars. The out of phase behaviour along opposite sides of the channel corresponds to cross-stream fining where the cross-section is asymmetric, just as in a meander

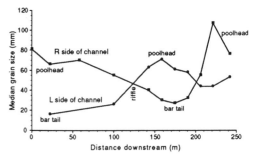

Fig. 6. Local size sorting within an alternate-bar channel: River Feshie, Scotland. Diameter is that of the median particle in a random sample of 100 pebbles at each point.

bend. In this case the down-pool and cross-pool fining was qualitatively similar to the pattern of measured bed shear stress at bankfull flow (Ferguson & Ashworth 1992, fig. 24.2).

A link between local textural differences and nonuniform channel geometry and flow pattern is of course well known in meandering channels (e.g. Bridge & Jarvis 1982; Dietrich 1987) and was found in a sandy braided river by Bridge & Gabel (1992). One obvious explanation for such links is the selective entrainment of particles of different size according to local differences in bed shear stress, though as discussed later there is strong evidence from recent research that entrainment from a mixed-size gravel bed is only slightly size-selective. There are, however, several additional mechanisms which may contribute to local sorting in braided rivers.

(1) Bluck (1982) observed that bar surface texture varies little over time and speculated that sorting occurs during deposition, with the initial surface texture of a bar acting as a template which traps similar-sized particles but allows coarser ones to overpass and finer ones either to overpass or to infiltrate beneath the surface. He also speculated that this depositional selection is in some way related to characteristics of flow turbulence over the rough bed. The possible connection has recently been explored by Clifford et al. (this volume), who show that local differences in surface texture, for example between pools and riffles, are reflected in the nature and intensity of turbulent fluctuations in the near-bed flow, which in turn has a bearing on entrainment.

(2) Some recent flume and field studies of channels with poorly sorted gravel/sand bedload have identified local segregation of relatively coarser and finer sediment associated with the passage of long low-amplitude dunes or 'bedload

sheets' (Iseya & Ikeda 1987; Whiting *et al.* 1988). The coarse dune fronts, it is argued, form 'congested' zones which tend to trap other coarse particles which have overpassed the smoother troughs and dune backs. Other sorting mechanisms associated with bedforms are discussed by Bridge (this volume).

(3) Ashmore (1982*a*) and Ashworth *et al.* (1992*b*) have drawn attention to the possible role of secondary circulation in braided reaches in assisting lateral sorting. The secondary circulation is envisaged as a back-to-back version of that in a meander bend, with two surface-convergent cells in a confluence. Ashworth *et al.* (1992*b*) therefore interpreted the relatively fine tail of a medial bar as analogous to two point bar tails prograding towards each other. This is also apparent in the double-row alternate bar view of braid morphology (Fig. 1c above) and is discussed further by Bridge (this volume).

(4) Another mechanism which should apply in braided as well as meandering channels is the differential effect of lateral bed slope on particles of different diameter D. The drag force of the flow varies as D^2 but the gravitational force down the lateral slope varies as D^3, so that larger particles tend to migrate downslope. The steepest lateral slopes in a braided channel are alongside scour pools at confluences. Coarse particles will tend to accumulate in the talweg here, in the same way that they accumulate in the pool alongside a meander point bar. This again is also discussed by Bridge (this volume).

The detailed sorting pattern in a braided reach must reflect the combined influence of local bed topography and the pattern of near-bed flow direction and bed shear stress. If coarse sediment does tend to accumulate in pools, because of the high stress there and also the sideslope effect, the bedload supplied from the pool towards the next barhead will also be coarse compared to that nearer the edges of the channel. Ashworth *et al.* (1992*b*) noted some evidence for this in flume experiments, and suggested that the coarse bedload tends to be deposited on the barhead whereas finer sediment is deflected around the bar where it may be deposited in the tail.

The recent attempts to make intensive field measurements in confluences and bifurcations which were discussed in a previous section have gone some way to testing these possible sorting mechanisms, though the cautionary remarks about sampling error in shear stress estimates and bedload grain size distributions must not be forgotten. In the Sunwapta River, Ashworth *et al.* (1992*a*) found that flow divergence and

shear stress reduction from confluence to bifurcation was associated with a general reduction in the maximum diameter of trapped bedload, suggesting the importance of entrainment thresholds. However, early in the development of the reach coarse sediment was found to be moving onto the distal barhead despite fairly low shear stress, in accordance with the ideas of Ashworth *et al.* (1992*b*). In other reaches of the same river Ashmore *et al.* (1992) used an electromagnetic flowmeter to measure primary and secondary circulation in braid confluences and confirmed the suspected pattern of surface-convergent back-to-back cells, dissipating downstream. The implications for sediment sorting were not however followed up in that study.

The pattern of flow and sediment transport in confluences, and the maximum scour depth, is known to depend on confluence geometry and discharge ratio (e.g. Mosley 1976; Best 1988; Ashmore & Parker 1983). Laboratory experiments, notably by Best (e.g. Best 1988; Best & Reid 1984), have yielded valuable insights into the way these controlling factors influence the actual flow structure in the confluence, and Best & Roy (1991) showed the complexity of flow separation and associated macroturbulence structure in the confluence of channels of different depth. It may be that the secondary circulation measured by Ashmore *et al.* (1992) is the time-averaged manifestation of intermittent shedding of large turbulent eddies from such a shear zone, and work is in hand to test this possibility. In making comparisons between confluences in laboratory and field, though, it has to be remembered that the latter are mobile rather than partly or wholly fixed, and have less abrupt breaks of slope. Both the geometry and the discharge ratio of natural confluences can change, as emphasized by Ashmore (1993), so that any particular flow pattern (and the associated pattern of sediment sorting) is unlikely to persist for long. Timelapse photography, or other forms of remote sensing, are probably required to obtain a coherent picture of how confluences evolve and how this evolution affects the channels immediately downstream and is itself affected by changes upstream.

Downstream sorting and its consequences

Sediment sorting in braided rivers does not only occur at the local scale. Downstream fining is usually apparent and can be very pronounced and rapid. For example, Dawson (1988) quantified and discussed a change over 10 km in the Sunwapta River (Canada) from cobbles and boulders to fine gravel and sand (with an anasto-mosing to sandy braided pattern). Downstream fining in this and other braided rivers can be orders of magnitude more rapid than can be accounted for by abrasion of and by bedload, so is conventionally attributed to selective transport.

There is, however, an ongoing debate as to whether bedload transport of mixed-size gravel is sufficiently selective to account for rapid downstream fining. A great deal of empirical, experimental, and theoretical research in the last decade has suggested that the threshold bed shear stress for entrainment of different sizes in a gravel mixture varies little, if at all, with particle size, at least at high excess stresses and transport rates (e.g. Parker & Klingeman 1982; Wiberg & Smith 1987; Wilcock & Southard 1989; Ashworth & Ferguson 1989). This is because the linear relation between particle diameter and critical stress for entrainment that is implied by the Shields criterion does not apply to individual particles in a mixture, which differ also in packing (friction) angle and protrusion into or hiding from the flow. The threshold stress to move one particle therefore depends far less on its size than on the average size of its neighbours. This has led some workers to seek alternative explanations for downstream fining. Paola (1989, pers. comm. 1992) has suggested that local equal mobility is not incompatible with overall selective transport if the bed contains finer and coarser patches developed by local sorting, giving local differences in entrainment threshold and thus bedload transport capacity. Others have demonstrated by numerical model-ling that only a slight degree of size selectivity is required to generate quite rapid downstream fining on a concave long profile (Parker 1991; Hoey & Ferguson in press).

Downstream fining obviously implies an eventual change from gravel to sand facies, and is likely to be associated with progressive changes in channel pattern and bar types. Characteristic sequences have been proposed by Bluck (1976) and Church & Jones (1982), and illustrated by Brierley (1991) and Ferguson & Ashworth (1991), though in each case attention was not restricted to braided channels. Smith (1974) found proximal–distal changes in the frequency of different types of braid bar, and Miall (1977) and Rust (1978) speculated that proximal and distal braid facies will differ, but there do not appear to have been any detailed quantitative studies. It seems likely that downstream changes in braiding style, while associated with decreases in grain size and slope, will not be directly explicable in these terms.

Rather, the discussion earlier in this paper of mechanisms of braiding suggested that local hydraulic properties and morphometric ratios are what directly control the mechanisms and thus the morphological and sedimentological style of braiding. They include the following.

(1) Dimensionless bed shear stress, which Ashmore (1991b) suggested differentiates central-bar braiding (characteristic of near-threshold stresses) from transverse bar conver-sion (at higher stresses).

(2) The flow depth to grainsize ratio d/D, which differentiates chutes and lobes as origi-nally described by Southard et al. (1984) from those described by other workers, including Ashmore's (1991b) 'transverse bar conversion'. It also determines the scope for development of slip faces, as noted above and by Hein (1987).

(3) The channel width/depth ratio. In channel pattern stability analyses (e.g. Parker 1976) this determines whether single or multiple-row alternate bars will develop, and in the latter case the degree of braiding likely to develop. It may also change over time, which could have a bearing on which braiding mechanisms operate: for example central bar deposition promotes channel widening and shallowing which may then trigger chute or lobe dissection.

It is likely that there is no universal down-stream sequence either of bar types or of channel pattern. In some rivers braiding gives way downstream to meandering (e.g. Ferguson & Ashworth 1991), in others to anastomosing (e.g. Dawson 1988). This is probably because one is looking at the net balance of opposing down-stream trends in different variables. The dimensionless shear stress, for example, is essentially the ratio of depth-slope product to grain size; depth tends to increase somewhat downstream, whereas slope and grain diameter tend to decrease considerably, but the balance of the three variables can tip different ways in different cases.

Progress and problems

Sediment sorting, as with other processes in braided rivers, is a topic in which there are new ideas and approaches, based on what is happening in channels as well as on bars. How-ever, several unsolved problems remain.

(1) The first integrated data sets have been obtained on spatial patterns of bed and bedload grain size distributions. But the bedload data are of doubtful reliability because of the great sampling variability in short-term transport rates.

(2) Hypotheses have been developed, and some laboratory and field confirmatory evidence obtained, about the possible roles of flow convergence/divergence and secondary circulation in local sediment sorting. But the relative roles of entrainment, transport, and deposition remain to be clarified.

(3) Numerical models have been developed which can generate the rapid downstream fining characteristic of braided rivers despite assuming only slightly size-selective transport. But these models have not yet been applied specifically to braided rivers, and the possible role of local lateral sorting in assisting downstream fining merits investigation.

(4) There have been no detailed, quantitative studies of downstream changes in bar types, and sedimentary facies generally, along braided rivers with concave long profiles and rapid downstream fining. This problem will best be tackled in the field though there is also scope for piecing sequences together from flume experiments using different combinations of slope and discharge.

Conclusions

Summaries of progress in understanding various aspects of braiding have been given at intervals throughout this paper together with an indication of pressing problems. Some common themes can be identified:

(1) the need to consider braid bars in association with the channels, and especially pools, through which bedload is supplied to bars;

(2) the need to understand the local spatial and temporal variability of hydraulic conditions, since these govern channel change and bed texture;

(3) the need to identify the range of hydraulic (and possibly other) conditions in which different braiding mechanisms occur; this is relevant also to the question of downstream facies change in braided rivers.

It is also possible to draw some methodological conclusions:

(4) there have been fewer flume experiments on braiding than field studies, but they have contributed a great deal to qualitative understanding;

(5) dynamic interactions exist between channel configuration, hydraulics, and bedload transport in braided river confluences and bifurcations; integrated field measurements of spatial patterns and temporal changes in these properties can provide important detail of the interactions, but there are substantial unresolved practical difficulties with such measurements;

(6) numercial modelling is potentially a much better way of investigating these dynamic interactions in evolving braid units, but is only just beginning to be implemented;

(7) finally, it is vital that researchers from different disciplines and adopting different approaches to the study of braiding take up opportunities to exchange ideas and results.

I thank J. Best, J. Bridge, D. Knighton, and K. Richards for comments on the first draft of this review, and NATO, NERC, and the Royal Society for assistance with field research.

References

ASHLEY, G. 1990. Classification of large-scale subaqueous bed-forms: a new look at an old problem. *Journal of Sedimentary Petrology*, **60**, 160–172.

ASHMORE, P. E. 1982a. Laboratory modelling of gravel braided stream morphology. *Earth Surface Processes*, **7**, 201–225.

—— 1982b. Discussion of Church & Jones, op. cit., 326–330.

—— 1991a. Channel morphology and bedload pulses in braided, gravel-bed streams. *Geografiska Annaler*, **73A**, 37–52.

—— 1991b. How do gravel-bed rivers braid? *Canadian Journal of Earth Sciences*, **28**, 326–341.

—— 1993. Anabranch confluence kinetics and sedimentation processes within gravel braided streams. *This volume*.

—— & PARKER, G. 1983. Confluence scour in coarse braided streams. *Water Resources Research*, **19**, 392–402.

——, FERGUSON, R. I., PRESTEGAARD, K. L., ASHWORTH, P. J. & PAOLA, C. 1992. Secondary flow in anabranch confluences in a braided, gravel-bed stream. *Earth Surface Processes & Landforms*, **17**, 299–311.

ASHWORTH, P. J. & FERGUSON, R. I. 1986. Interrelationships of channel processes, changes and sediments in a proglacial braided river. *Geografiska Annaler*, **68A**, 361–371.

—— & —— 1989. Size-selective entrainment of bed load in gravel bed streams. *Water Resources Research*, **25**, 627–634.

——, ——, ASHMORE, P. E., PAOLA, C., POWELL, D. M. & PRESTEGAARD, K. L. 1992a. Measurements in a braided river chute and lobe: II. Sorting of bedload during entrainment, transport and deposition. *Water Resources Research*, **28**, 1887–1896.

——, —— & POWELL, D. M. 1992*b*. Bedload transport and sorting in braided channels. *In*: BILLI, P., HEY, R. D., THORNE, C. R. & TACCONI, P. (eds) *Dynamics of gravel-bed rivers*. Wiley, 497–515.

BAUMGART-KOTARBA, M. 1987. Formation of coarse gravel bars and alluvial channels, braided Bialka River, Carpathians, Poland. *In*: GARDINER, V. (ed.) *International Geomorphology 1986, part I*, 633–648.

BEST, J. L. 1988. Sediment transport and bed morphology at river channel confluences. *Sedimentology*, **35**, 481–498.

—— & REID, I. 1984. Separation zone at open-channel junctions. *Journal of Hydraulic Engineering, ASCE*, **110**, 1588–1594.

—— & ROY, A. G. 1991. Mixing-layer distortion at the confluence of channels of different depth. *Nature*, **350**, 411–413.

BLUCK, B. J. 1976. Sedimentation in some Scottish rivers of low sinuosity. *Transactions of the Royal Society of Edinburgh (Earth Sciences)*, **69**, 425–456.

—— 1982. Texture of gravel bars in braided streams. *In*: HEY, R. D., BATHURST, J. C. & THORNE, C. R. (eds) *Gravel-bed rivers*. Wiley, 339–355.

BRIDGE, J. S. 1985. Paleochannels inferred from alluvial deposits: a critical evaluation. *Journal of Sedimentary Petrology*, **55**, 579–589.

—— 1992. A revised model for water flow, sediment transport, bed topography, and grainsize sorting in natural river bends. *Water Resources Research*, **28**, 999–1013.

—— 1993. The interaction between channel geometry, water flow, sediment transport and deposition in braided rivers. *This volume*.

—— & GABEL, S. L. 1992. Flow and sediment dynamics in a low-sinuosity river: Calamus River, Nebraska Sandhills. *Sedimentology*, **39**, 125–142.

—— & JARVIS, J. 1982. Dynamics of a river bend: a study in flow and sedimentary processes. *Sedimentology*, **29**, 499–550.

BRIERLEY, G. J. 1991. Bar sedimentology of the Squamish River, British Columbia: definition and application of morphostratigraphic units. *Journal of Sedimentary Petrology*, **61**, 211–225.

CARSON, M. A. 1984. Observations on the meandering-braided river transition, the Canterbury Plains, New Zealand: part one. *New Zealand Geographer*, **40**, 12–17.

CHURCH, M. & JONES, D. 1982. Channel bars in gravel-bed rivers. *In*: HEY, R. D., BATHURST, J. C. & THORNE, C. R. (eds) *Gravel-bed rivers*. Wiley, 291–324.

——, McLEAN, D. G. & WOLCOTT, J. F. 1987. River bed gravels: sampling and analysis. *In*: THORNE, C. R., BATHURST, J. C. & HEY, R. D. (eds) *Sediment transport in gravel-bed rivers*. Wiley, 43–88.

CLIFFORD, N. J., HARDISTY, J., FRENCH, J. R. & HART, S. 1993. Downstream variation in bed material characteristics in braided rivers: a turbulence-controlled form-process feedback mechanism. *This volume*.

DAVOREN, A. & MOSLEY, M. P. 1986. Observations of bedload movement, bar development and sediment supply in the braided Ohau River. *Earth Surface Processes & Landforms*, **11**, 643–652.

DAWSON, M. D. 1988. Sediment size variation in a braided reach of the Sunwapta River, Alberta, Canada. *Earth Surface Processes & Landforms*, **13**, 599–618.

DIETRICH, W. E. 1987. Mechanics of flow and sediment transport in river bends. *In*: RICHARDS, K. S. (ed) *River channels: environment and process*. Blackwell, 179–226.

FERGUSON, R. I. 1986. Hydraulics and hydraulic geometry. *Progress in Physical Geography*, **10**, 1–31.

—— 1987. Hydraulic and sedimentary controls of channel pattern. *In*: RICHARDS, K. S. (ed.) *River channels: environment and process*. Blackwell, 125–158.

—— & ASHWORTH, P. J. 1991. Slope-induced changes in channel character along a gravel bed stream: the Allt Dubhaig, Scotland. *Earth Surface Processes & Landforms*, **16**, 65–82.

—— & —— 1992. Spatial patterns of bedload transport and channel change in braided and near-braided rivers. *In*: BILLI, P., HEY, R. D., THORNE, C. R. & TACCONI, P. (eds) *Dynamics of gravel-bed rivers*. Wiley, 477–496.

—— & WERRITTY, A. 1983. Bar development and channel changes in the gravelly River Feshie, Scotland. *International Association of Sedimentologists Special Publications*, **6**, 181–193.

——, ASHMORE, P. E., ASHWORTH, P. J., PAOLA, C. & PRESTEGAARD, K. L. 1992. Measurements in a braided river chute and lobe: I. Flow pattern, sediment transport and channel change. *Water Resources Research*, **28**, 1877–1886.

——, ASHWORTH, P. J. & PRESTEGAARD, K. L. 1989. Influence of sand on hydraulics and gravel transport in a braided gravel bed river. *Water Resources Research*, **25**, 635–643.

FUJITA, Y. 1989. Bar and channel formation in braided streams. *In*: IKEDA, S. & PARKER, G. (eds) *River Meandering*. American Geophysical Union, Water Resources Monographs, **12**, 417–462.

GOMEZ, B. 1991. Bedload transport. *Earth Science Reviews*, **31**, 89–132.

GRIFFITHS, G. A. 1979. Recent sedimentation history of the Waimakariri River, New Zealand. *Journal of Hydrology (New Zealand)*, **18**, 6–28.

HEIN, F. J. 1987. Deep-sea and fluvial braided channel conglomerates: a comparison of two case studies. *In*: KOSTER, E. H. & STEEL, R. J. (eds) *Sedimentology of gravels and conglomerates*. Canadian Society of Petroleum Geologists Memoirs, **10**, 33–49.

—— & WALKER, R. G. 1977. Bar evolution and development of stratification in the gravelly, braided, Kicking Horse River, British Columbia. *Canadian Journal of Earth Science*, **14**, 562–570.

HOEY, T. B. & FERGUSON, R. I. In Press. Numerical simulation of downstream fining by selective transport in a highly concave gravel-bed river: model development and illustration. *Water Resources Research*.

—— & SUTHERLAND, A. J. 1991. Channel morphology and bedload pulses in braided rivers: a laboratory study. *Earth Surface Processes & Landforms*, **16**, 447–462.

ISEYA, F. & IKEDA, H. 1987. Pulsations in bedload transport rates induced by a longitudinal sediment sorting: a flume study of sand and gravel mixtures. *Geografiska Annaler*, **69A**, 15–27.

LEDDY, J., ASHWORTH, P. & BEST, J. 1993. Mechanisms of anabranch avulsion within gravel-bed braided rivers: observations from a scaled physical model. *This volume*.

LEOPOLD, L. B. & WOLMAN, M. G. 1957. River channel patterns: braided, meandering and straight. *US Geological Survey Professional Papers*, **282B**, 39–85.

McLEAN, D. G. 1990. *The relation between channel instability and sediment transport on Lower Fraser River*. PhD thesis, University of British Columbia.

MIALL, A. D. 1977. A review of the braided river depositional environment. *Earth Science Reviews*, **13**, 1–62.

MOSLEY, M. P. 1976, An experimental study of channel confluences. *Journal of Geology*, **84**, 535–562.

—— 1983. Response of braided rivers to changing discharge. *Journal of Hydrology (New Zealand)*, **22**, 18–67.

NELSON, J. M. & SMITH, J. D. 1989. Evolution and stability of erodible channel beds. *In*: IKEDA, S. & PARKER, G. (eds) *River meandering*. American Geophysical Union Water Resources Monographs, **12**, 321–377.

PAOLA, C. 1989. Topographic sorting (abstract). *Eos*, **70**, 323.

PARKER, G. 1976. On the cause and characteristic scales of meandering and braiding in rivers. *Journal of Fluid Mechanics*, **76**, 457–480.

—— 1991. Selective sorting and abrasion of river gravel I: Theory. *Journal of Hydraulic Engineering, ASCE*, **117**, 131–149.

—— & KLINGEMAN, P. C. 1982. On why gravel bed streams are paved. *Water Resources Research*, **18**, 1409–1423.

RUNDLE, A. S. 1985*a*. The mechanism of braiding.

Zeitschrift fur geomorphologie, Supplement-Band, **55**, 1–13.

—— 1985*b*. Braid morphology and the formation of multiple channels. *Zeitschrift fur Geomorphologie, Supplement-Band*, **55**, 15–37.

RUST, B. R. 1978. Depositional models for braided alluvium. *In*: MIALL, A. D. (ed.) *Fluvial sedimentology*. Canadian Society of Petroleum Geologists Memoirs, **5**, 605–626.

SCHUMM, S. A. & KHAN, H. R. 1972. Experimental study of channel patterns. *Geological Society of America Bulletin*, **83**, 1755–1770.

SMITH, N. D. 1974. Sedimentology and bar formation in the upper Kicking Horse River, a braided outwash stream. *Journal of Geology*, **82**, 205–223.

—— 1978. Some comments on terminology for bars in shallow rivers. *In*: MIALL, A. D. (ed.) *Fluvial Sedimentology*. Canadian Society of Petroleum Geologists Memoirs, **5**, 85–88.

SOUTHARD, J. B., SMITH, N. D. & KUHNLE, R. A. 1984. Chutes and lobes: newly identified elements of braiding in shallow gravelly streams. *In*: KOSTER, E. H. & STEEL, R. J. (eds) *Sedimentology of gravels and conglomerates*. Canadian Society of Petroleum Geologists Memoirs, **10**, 51–59.

THOMPSON, A. 1986. Secondary flows and the pool-riffle unit: a case study of the processes of meander development. *Earth Surface Processes & Landforms*, **11**, 631–641.

THORNE, C. R., RUSSELL, C. R. & ALAN, M. K. 1993. Planform pattern and channel evolution at the Brahmaputra River, Bangladesh. *This volume*.

WHITING, P. J. & DIETRICH, W. E. 1991. Convective accelerations and boundary shear stress over a channel bar. *Water Resources Research*, **27**, 783–796.

——, ——, LEOPOLD, L. B., DRAKE, T. G. & SHREVE, R. L. 1988. Bedload sheets in heterogeneous sediment. *Geology*, **16**, 105–108.

WIBERG, P. L. & SMITH, J. D. 1987. Calculations of the critical shear stress for motion of uniform and heterogeneous sediments. *Water Resources Research*, **23**, 1471–1480.

WILCOCK, P. R. & SOUTHARD, J. B. 1989. Experimental study of incipient motion in mixed-size sediment. *Water Resources Research*, **24**, 1137–1151.

Downstream variation in bed material characteristics: a turbulence-controlled form-process feedback mechanism

N. J. CLIFFORD[1], J. HARDISTY[1], J. R. FRENCH[2] & S. HART[1]

[1] *School of Geography & Earth Resources, The University of Hull, Hull HU6 7RX, UK*
[2] *Department of Geography, University College London, 26 Bedford Way, London WC1H 0AP, UK*

Abstract: Downstream changes in bed material characteristics represent an element of the sediment transport process which is of immediate geomorphological and economic significance. Particle size trends represent the joint effect of abrasion and sorting, often complicated by in situ weathering and variable sediment supply. In principle, the combined effects of abrasion and shorting can be explained if attention is paid to the role and characteristics of near-bed turbulence, via the mechanisms of 'abrasion in place' and the size-dependent particle acceptance or rejection involved in Bluck's 'turbulence template'. Field data describing spatially- and stage-dependent differences in turbulence characteristics by which the significance of such processes can be quantified are, however, lacking.

In this paper, high-frequency three-dimensional velocity data obtained with an ultrasonic current meter in a braided section of Langden Brook, Lancashire, are used to demonstrate significant variations in turbulence parameters at the bar-pool scale. These are related to grain abrasion, sorting and the arrangement of grains in surface microtopographic bedforms using a force-balance model which incorporates turbulent velocity components in two dimensions. Following Bluck, it is suggested that bar forms act as, and result from, sediment trapping phenomena, whose fundamental controls lie in the characteristics of turbulence at the bar surface. Variations in turbulence provide a physical rationale for differing values of sorting/abrasion coefficients used in descriptive models of longitudinal size contrasts. In contrast to single-thread channels, however, spatially- and stage-dependent variation in turbulence characteristics is more marked in braided environments. Consequently, greater research effort is required to fully incorporate this into a spatially-realized form-process feedback mechanism applicable at the reach-scale and beyond.

Longitudinal trends in particle characteristics continue to be of geomorphological and economic interest, indirectly, through the relationship between sediment size and channel slope and discharge, and directly, as a local factor in the determination of the rate, timing and manner of sediment transport. Longitudinal contrasts represent the joint effects of sediment abrasion and sediment sorting, the relative balance depending upon local lithological, morphological and flow conditions, as well as the spatial extent of any trends observed. A summary of many of the models describing downstream change is suggested by Knighton (1984), where the rate of an exponential decline in size (D) from an initial value (D_0) is given by:

$$D = D_0 e^{-\alpha L} \qquad (1)$$

This relationship is determined by α, representing the undifferentiated effects of sorting and abrasion over transport distance, L. Equation 1 is a derivative of 'Sternberg's Law' (Sternberg 1875), originally formulated in terms of particle weight.

Under active transport conditions, both sorting and abrasion contribute to observed downstream trends in particle texture, whereas between transport episodes, weathering of exposed deposits may be the controlling factor (Bradley 1970; Tricart & Vogt 1967). In general terms, the processes of selective transport, sorting and abrasion, as well as weathering, are all controlled by lithology (Richards 1982). Historically, abrasion and fracture have received most attention as mechanisms responsible for sediment size reduction (for review, see Pettijohn 1975), but increasing attention has been focused on the role of sediment sorting. This is mainly in response to abrasion tank experiments and some field studies which suggest that, in many cases, abrasion rates are much lower than those required to account for observed distance-dependent size diminution (Bradley *et al.* 1972; Kuenen 1956; Plumley 1948; Scott & Gravlee 1968), particularly the very rapid decline downstream from headwater areas which is frequently observed (e.g. Mills 1979). More-

From Best, J. L. & Bristow, C. S. (eds), 1993, *Braided Rivers*, Geological Society Special Publication No. **75**, pp. 89–104.

over, experiments with different bed material combinations indicate that abrasion rates are expected to decline with time/distance as bed sediments change from predominantly coarse gravels to sand-sized material providing less rough surfaces (Kuenen 1956), and because, in weak rocks, susceptibility to fracture is inversely proportional to size (Moss 1972).

Schumm & Stevens (1973), however, have suggested that abrasion may be important where turbulent lift and drag is responsible for essentially in situ particle jostling or vibration, without longitudinal particle transport. Their paper raises several issues of more general interest, particularly since in situ jostling is likely to be fundamental to the process of vertical winnowing (Parker *et al.* 1982), which is one mechanism by which coarse armour layers develop and stream beds are progressively stabilized. This accounts for an effective over-representation of coarser particles at the surface (Parker *et al.* 1982) and modifies entrainment to approximate the condition of 'equal mobility' (e.g. Andrews 1983). Jostling may, therefore, help to suppress longitudinal size-sorting which would otherwise result from selective entrainment of bed material. Significantly, studies which strongly support 'equal mobility' and the persistence of bed material particle size distributions before and after transport events also clearly show downstream fining in tracer particles (Andrews & Erman 1986). By implication, where marked longitudinal trends *are* apparent, some other mechanism must, therefore, operate to replace or supplement classic size-selective transport. Unfortunately, recent research into the nature of gravel beds and bedload movement also demonstrates the difficulties in relating flow to sediment characteristics in natural situations. Flume studies, for example, show that local supply considerations are vital in determining the evolution of surface characteristics which are themselves crucial in determining size-dependent entrainment (e.g. Wilcock &

Southard 1989), but supply is itself a dynamic characteristic in space and time, reflecting bar growth and decay (Davoren & Mosley 1986) and local surface characteristics and particle over-passing (Dietrich *et al.* 1989). With respect to observations of longitudinal particle size contrasts, it is very difficult to envisage 'initial conditions' from which a differential transport phenomenon might begin, or a 'final state' to which sediment distributions evolve. The relationship between sediment movement, the structure of bed surfaces and the growth and decay of bar forms under turbulent flow conditions requires much more research. In this paper, one aspect of the possible mechanism contributing to longitudinal particle contrasts is investigated, as proposed by Bluck (1987). From observations on alluvial fans, he presents a conceptual model in which longitudinal trends in particle characteristics represent the outcome of a particle transport-trapping mechanism operative at, and between, successive bar forms, associated with spatial differences in the local turbulent flow field.

The Bluck model

Bluck (1987) suggests that the fundamental control of longitudinal particle characteristics lies in turbulence at bar surfaces. The model is shown schematically in Fig. 1: bars are the primary loci of size change; as coarser material is temporarily trapped during bar head aggradation, finer bar tail material is more readily transported downstream. It is particle size differences within successive bar units which promote overall longitudinal trends, as downstream units are progressively starved of coarser material. Within the bar unit, a form-process feedback mechanism operates as a result of surface microtopographic differences:

> [Microtopographic] bedforms act as, and are the result of, a type of sediment trapping

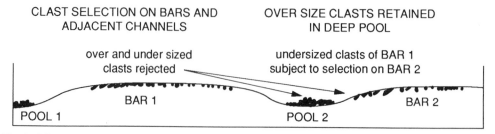

| CLAST SELECTION ON BARS AND ADJACENT CHANNELS | OVER SIZE CLASTS RETAINED IN DEEP POOL |

Fig. 1. Schematic representation of Bluck's transport-trapping model of longitudinal particle size trends which depend upon size-selection in sequential bar-pool units (re-drawn from Bluck 1987).

phenomenon which has its fundamental control in turbulence at the bar surface. Clasts are transported downstream until they reach a sufficient concentration to become established in the bed as the dominant coarse-grained fabric ... they control the size of clasts which may then accumulate near them... (Bluck 1987 p. 160).

Size selection occurs because

The difference in bed height created by different clast sizes ... generates a turbulence intensity and scale which in turn controls the sizes of clasts which can exist on the surface... (Bluck 1987, p. 171)

and therefore, small-scale flow-form interaction responsible for the creation of a 'turbulence template' is intimately related to larger scale morphology and dynamics. Importantly, the template is one of both particle acceptance and rejection: particles both larger and smaller than the locally dominant size pass to the next downstream bar unit. At any point in time and space, therefore, the range of the distribution of particles in transport is likely to be broad, which is consistent with the reduced significance of selective transport as conventionally described and reviewed above.

Bluck identifies a range of microtopographic bedforms, but greatest significance is given to transverse clast dams (the largest spanwise features responsible for a staircase-like appearance in the flow) which occur near to aggrading bar heads (Fig. 2). A growing literature on a variety of microform types is reviewed by Robert (1988), and a simple morphological distinction between spanwise ridges (larger dams and smaller ribs) and streamwise (cluster or ribbon) forms corresponds to local slope/energy criteria; transverse features are preferentially located in shallower, steeper and faster flow zones. The significance of various types of microform for surface bed structuring, and hence bedload transport, is reviewed in Richards & Clifford (1991) and it seems reasonable to conclude that all such forms have trapping potential, but to differing degrees, with transverse clast dams being the most important form on account of their size and relative stability, as assumed by Bluck.

Absent from Bluck's account, however, are quantitative flow measurements which substantiate the hypothesized relationship between particle size, bed relief and composition, and turbulence intensity. The purpose of this paper, therefore, is to investigate whether, in a braided environment, spatial differences do occur in turbulent flow characteristics which can be related to bar-scale and bed microtopography, and which can further be used to explain observed trends in particle size and sorting,

Fig. 2. View of Langden Brook, north Lancashire, looking upstream near the transition from sinuous/confined to braided planform. Note the association of the bar head with marked transverse clast dams (staircase-like appearance of flow), and the truncation of Holocene alluvial fans supplying abundant coarse material.

effectively providing a physical rationale for changing values of α in equation 1. The data presented here are limited to low flows, and were obtained from an environment where well-marked differences in relative roughness and microtopographic characteristics are already established. These circumstances provide the best test of the correlation between bed morphology and flow characteristics, which is essential to the Bluck hypothesis: if distinct associations cannot be shown, then the hypothesized mechanisms of clast acceptance-rejection cannot be sustained. However, the data do not provide information on the dynamic (formative) relationships between these. Further research is required both to establish the direction of the causative links between spatial patterns of flow characteristics and bed material size/arrangement, and also to assess any stage-dependency in these.

Data collection and methods

Data were obtained from a 2 km section of the Langden Brook, NW Lancashire [GR SD628510].

This is a third order tributary of the River Hodder, with a mean flow rate of 1.2–$2.5\,\mathrm{m^3\,s^{-1}}$. For most of its mid course, the river is confined to one side of its valley by relict braid bars, but where valley confinement is reduced in the lower course, the present channel braids freely (Fig. 2).

Two surveys were undertaken. In the first, overall particle size, shape and shorting trends were investigated for the entire reach. This involved the collection of 15 samples, taken at approximately 500 m intervals in a downstream direction. At each sample site, the Wolman grid-by-number sampling technique (Wolman 1954) was used to obtain size and shape measurements of surface clasts: an observer paced across the channel, measuring the axes of clasts immediately underfoot at each pace along a transect. To minimize operator variance, the same individual collected and measured all samples. Results from between three and five transects were combined and the median of the intermediate axes used to give an overall measure of particle size. In addition, indices of particle sphericity ($^3\sqrt{bc/a^2}$) and flatness ($(a + b)/2c$) were also calculated from the long (a), intermediate (b) and short (c) axes. The degree of sorting was assessed simply from the standard deviation of the particle size distribution.

In the second survey, flow measurements were made at contrasting locations in a single braid-

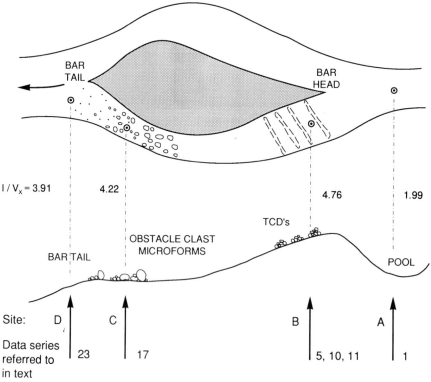

Fig. 3. Study reach, Langden Brook, in plan and profile. Also shown are normalized turbulent intensities (I/V_X), and the association between bed profile elevation and surface sediment microforms. Sites A–D exemplify differing zones of bed microtopography and turbulence structure/intensity. TCDs refer to transverse clast dams.

Fig. 4. Part of the study reach, Langden Brook, illustrating the association of mid-bar and bar-tail zones with 'cluster bedforms'.

bar reach (Figs 3 and 4). The bar is typical of the four units which occur downstream of valley widening: division of the flow occurs after an abrupt shallowing of the upstream pool, and in both subsequent channels, coarser bar head deposits occur, overlain by well-marked transverse clast dams. Mid-bar reaches are zones of shallow, but more uniform relief (cf.

gravel sheets of Bluck 1987), while bar tail reaches upstream of flow reattachment are zones of predominantly cluster bedforms interspersed with lower relief transverse ribs.

The locations were chosen to exemplify particular combinations of bed and flow characteristics. Here, data are presented from four of these as shown in

Fig. 5. The ultrasonic current meter and mounting rig.

Fig. 3: A, a zone of relatively low relative rough-ness (pool upstream of bar head); B, a zone between marked transverse clast dams; C, a zone amongst obstacle clast (stoss-wake) microforms; and D, a downstream relatively smooth bar tail zone of fast flow. In all, 27 data series were obtained, each comprising a 3 minute velocity record logged at 10 Hz.

Velocities were obtained using a Minilab 3-axis ultrasonic current meter (UCM) interfaced to a Macintosh II computer via National Instruments Ltd Labview hardware and software. The current meter and rig are shown in Fig. 5. This instrument allows simultaneous logging of three orthogonal velocity components at frequencies up to 36 Hz, with a maximum resolution of 0.001 ms^{-1} in the range $\pm 10 \text{ ms}^{-1}$. The instrument exploits the acoustic travel time difference principle, whereby a 4 Mhz signal pulsed between three orthogonal pairs of transducers at 100 bursts per second are accelerated or attenuated from still water velocities (c) by current velocity, V, such that

$$V = c^2 . \Delta T / 2L \quad (2)$$

where ΔT is the directional difference in travel time, and L is the transducer separation (0.03 m). Further details of operating principles and sensor charac-teristics are given in Hardisty (1990). At each location, measurements of instantaneous (mean plus turbulent components) were made at the same relative depth (approximately 60% of the depth measured from the water surface) by adjusting the current meter mounting, according to the following scheme: velocity parallel to channel mean flow ($V_x = <V_x> + V_x'$); transverse to mean flow ($V_y = <V_y> + V_y'$) and vertical to the bed ($V_z = <V_z> + V_z'$). The 60% depth measurement was chosen to provide the most repre-sentative and consistent single point measurement of boundary turbulence characteristics.

Results

Particle characteristics

Particle size, shape and sorting trends are sum-marized in Figs 6 and 7. Over a 2 km length, there is evidence of a downstream decline in median grain diameter. In addition, towards the

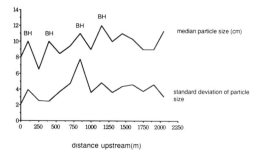

Fig. 6. Longitudinal particle size and sorting trends observed over *c.* 2 km distance in Langden Brook.

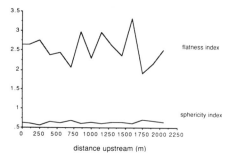

Fig. 7. Longitudinal variation in particle shape, Langden Brook over approx. 2 km distance (for definitions of shape indices, see text).

mid- and lower sections, there is some indication of the bar head/bar tail contrasts predicted by Bluck: particle size fluctuates in four marked peaks/troughs corresponding to the positions of the main lower course braid-bars (the bar head positions are marked BH on Fig. 6. The crude index of sorting, too, is suggestive of progressive downstream reduction in size variation, also as expected, but there is little or no evidence of any systematic trend in either of the particle shape indices (Fig. 7).

Reach-scale velocity and stress characteristics

Summary statistics describing reach-scale velocity and stress characteristics are given in Table 1. There are marked differences in the mean longitudinal velocity component, broadly confirming prior expectation of lower pool values, accelerating flow over the bar head, and deceleration towards the bar tail. The absence of similarly clear trends in the vertical component is noteworthy, and in all but one case, positive mean vertical components are indicative of lift, a phenomenon which is commonly recorded in these environments (Clifford 1990). The wide-spread occurrence of positive vertical velocities may reflect effluent seepage from the bed, which locally may account for 20% fluctuations in discharge in coarse-grained environments (Cherkauer 1973), but it may, in part, also reflect measurement bias. Obvious particle stoss and wake zones were avoided when locating the current meters, but in the tumbling flow (Herbich & Schulits 1964) common on bar sur-faces, local upward flow is very difficult to detect from visual field inspection. Downwelling, on the other hand, is more easily seen, possibly accounting for some locational bias in the results.

Table 1. Statistical characteristics of turbulent velocity and streamwise shear stress $(-\varrho V'_x V'_z)$ for data series obtained at contrasting locations in the bar-pool unit of Langden Brook (Fig. 2)

Data series	R_e	Velocity component						Shear stress	
		V_x		V_z		V_y			
		Mean (s)	Skew/kurtosis	Mean (s)	Skew/kurtosis	Mean (s)	Skew/kurtosis	Mean (s)	Skew/kurtosis
1	9.71×10^4	0.24(0.06)	0.21/0.87	0.04(0.04)	−2.68/17.71	0.02(0.06)	−4.75/42.3	1.86(6.01)	−10.77/164.4
5	1.67×10^5	0.59(0.05)	−0.61/3.9	0.14(0.06)	−4.28/39.30	0.11(0.11)	−4.90/41.84	16.7(31.32)	−26.77/914.29
10	1.27×10^5	0.45(0.08)	−0.16/0.34	0.09(0.04)	−0.62/1.61	0.08(0.05)	−0.71/8.73	58.99(164.90)	−5.61/64.58
11	8.24×10^4	0.36(0.08)	−0.30/0.18	0.08(0.04)	−1.46/4.84	0.06(0.05)	−1.27/12.11	39.04(84.08)	−5.83/58.13
17	1.36×10^5	0.66(0.07)	−0.87/3.71	0.14(0.08)	−3.17/17.38	−0.04(0.17)	−4.01/23.47	3.13(14.75)	−10.87/147.79
23	1.03×10^5	0.50(0.13)	−0.64/1.17	−0.02(0.17)	−1.63/3.34	−0.3(0.30)	−1.99/4.69	15.51(41.26)	−5.65/44.29

Velocity and stress terms in parenthesis (s) refer to RMS fluctuations. All velocity units are $m\,s^{-1}$, and all stress units are $N\,m^{-2}$. R_e is the flow Reynolds number.

Contrasts in three-dimensional turbulence characteristics most relevant to the Bluck model are, perhaps, better exemplified in the overall turbulent intensity, I, calculated as the sums of the three component RMS velocities

$$I = \tfrac{1}{3}(\sigma(V'_x) + \sigma(V'_y) + \sigma(V'_z)) \qquad (3)$$

normalized with respect to mean longitudinal velocity. The results (given on Fig. 3) again show clear spatial differences in the transition from relatively smooth to rough beds. In the upstream pool section, intensities are low (1.99), rising to a peak at the bar head (greatest relative roughness), and remaining high throughout the length of the bar.

A further measure of flow intensity which is commonly calculated is the streamwise turbulent shear stress, $-\varrho V'_x V'_z$, whose mean value and distributional characteristics are given in the final columns of Table 1. These again lend support for spatial zonations from pool to bar, but some caution is required in interpreting these values for at least two reasons. First, the relevance of this term to the transport of coarse particles in conditions of manifestly three-dimensional flow is questionable. This point is discussed in some detail by Clifford *et al.* (1991), but broadly, it should be remembered that this is only one of 12 turbulent stress terms in the Reynolds tensor, and more investigation is required to assess the relative importance of other terms, particularly the instantaneous mixed cross products involving mean and turbulent flow components. The few available coupled high frequency measurements of flow and sediment transport in gravel-bedded environments show very poor correlations between the streamwise turbulent shear term and gravel movement, but relatively good correlations between movement and the normal stress, $-\varrho V'^2_x$ (Williams *et al.* 1989), suggesting the dominance of drag forces over the shear term (at least as derived from a single point measurement). Second, it is apparent from Table 1 that the turbulent shear term is extremely difficult to characterize in terms of mean values. This arises since the distribution of turbulent stresses typically possess large standard deviations and extremely high kurtosis, evidence of intermittent momentum production. Lu & Wilmarth (1973) point out that this inevitably results when the turbulent velocity components are approximately normally distributed about a zero mean, and then cross-multiplied: most of the resulting values will be very small: On the other hand, for very short periods of time, very large stress values are recorded, which reflect the turbulent 'event structure' of near-bed flows (see below),

which again makes the comparison of mean values somewhat unreliable. Until more data are available to clarify these issues, therefore, further comparison will be limited to velocity and intensity characteristics.

Some additional insight into contrasting velocity behaviour may be gained from observing the structure of the velocity series, because this determines the nature of the energy expenditure between grain-, microform- and form-related energy losses (Clifford *et al.* 1992*b*). As an example Fig. 8 (upper plot) shows a 200 s time series of longitudinal velocity obtained between the transverse clast dams at the bar head (location B). In the second plot, a 50 s portion of the same series has been replotted at the larger scale to facilitate comparison with the vertical (V_z) and transverse (V_y) velocities at the same location. Three points emerge from these diagrams.

(i) The presence of more than one scale of structure: in the upper plot, there is the suggestion of a possible 35 second low period variation, and then as revealed in the other diagrams, an approximately 'saw-tooth' composition corresponding to *c.* 2–3 s.

(ii) It is evident that the absolute scale of variation in this very rough, high energy environment is comparable in many cases in all velocity components (typically $0.2\,\text{ms}^{-1}$) with peak fluctuations about the mean exceeding the value of the mean itself (see standard deviations in Table 1), confirming earlier observations of fluvial turbulence (Kalinske 1947; McQuivey 1973).

(iii) The presence of disruptions or 'events' which have been examined by a number of researchers in the context of assessing similarities/differences with laboratory flow models. Some comments on the appropriateness of these analogies and the significance of the 'burst-ejection' mechanism (Kline *et al.* 1967) in coarse grained environments have been made in Clifford *et al.* (1991) and will not be repeated here.

There is also strong evidence that the structure of velocity variation revealed in traces such as Fig. 8 is closely related to the physical characteristics of local bed conditions. In Fig. 9, for example, the longitudinal component of velocity (V_x) is contrasted for conditions near to the bar head (location A) where measurements were made around five obstacle diameters downstream of a large obstacle clast (upper plot), with measurements obtained once this clast was removed (lower plot). It is clear that while both traces share the 'saw-tooth' pattern referred to earlier (*c.* 2 s) that there is at least one

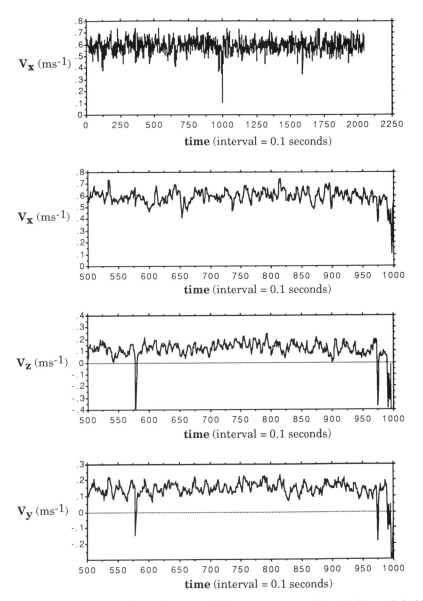

Fig. 8. Time series of fluctuating velocities (V_x longitudinal, V_y cross-stream, V_z vertical) recorded with ultrasonic current meter, Langden Brook, location B. For the longitudinal velocity component, plots are shown at two scales to aid visual identification of possible turbulent structures.

scale of variation in the upper trace (15 s, and even possibly another at *c.* 30 s) not present in the lower diagram.

Clear visual comparison between many different high-frequency series is obviously difficult to achieve. However, one way in which characteristic variation may be quantitatively summarized is to produce corresponding spectral density function of each velocity series. Here, the spectral density was estimated from the FFT routine within the Labview package, using a Hamming filter. Essentially, from the 78 records obtained, only two basic types of spectra were obtained, as shown in Fig. 10.

Type 1, characteristic of zones of lower relative roughness (essentially pool sections and bar

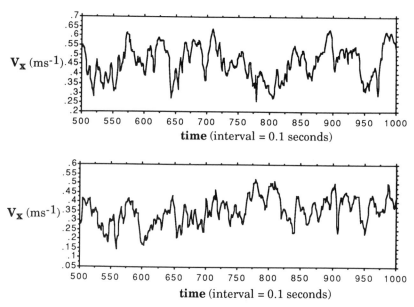

Fig. 9. Time series of fluctuating longitudinal velocities recorded with ultrasonic current meter, Langden Brook, location A. Upper plot refers to measurements in wake zone of a large particle; the lower plot refers to the same location, but with the large particle removed.

tail areas where the bed is well-compacted and devoid of obstacle clasts; Fig. 10a). These spectra exhibit smooth, exponentially-declining forms, occasionally with a single low frequency peak.

Type 2, characteristic of zones of very high relative roughness, i.e. between transverse clast dams and within areas of cluster bedforms (Fig. 10). These spectra are clearly multi-peaked about a broad, low to mid frequency 'shoulder', with a rapid decline thereafter.

Discussion

Particle-size sorting trends correspond well to the Bluck hypothesis despite the more complex sediment supply/transport/storage conditions associated with a braided river pattern. For example, a general decline in size is present, but this may be weakened by the many coarse inputs from valley sides, and from highly variable, stage-dependent floodplain source areas. Again, at several points, valley sides comprise

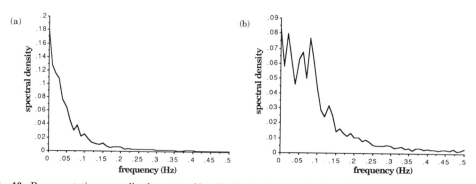

Fig. 10. Representative normalized spectra of longitudinal velocity series. **(a)** A 'Type 1' spectrum, characteristic of channel zones of low relative bed roughness; **(b)** a 'Type 2' spectrum, characteristic of zones of high relative bed roughness, with peaks indicating varying scales of turbulent structure.

truncated Holocene alluvial fans (see Fig. 2) and in at least one case, this may be responsible for augmenting bar head-tail differences as seen in Fig. 5. The absence of clear trends in particle shape is not unexpected, since the predominantly shale and marl lithology in this environment is probably responsible for the maintenance of shape as size declines, although further investigation into the interaction of particle shape and size and particle trapping would be of interest.

It is clear from the results presented above that, within the context of an overall longitudinal decline in particle size and an increase in particle sorting, there is a difference in both the visual and statistical representation of velocity behaviour which is location-dependent at the sub-bar scale. The basic form of the two types of spectra identified here can be related to clearly defined one-dimensional statistical models (Jenkins & Watts 1968), which may then be used to infer characteristics of the actual flow structure (e.g. French & Clifford 1992). Thus, the smooth, exponential decay of the Type 1 spectra are typical of first-order autoregressive processes, indicating that the flow has little time-dependent structure. A marked low frequency peak is characteristic of the free-stream, smooth bed shear flows observed in laboratory engineering models (Duncan et al. 1970). On the other hand, the broad shoulder underlying individual lower frequency peaks of the Type 2 spectra suggests a second order autoregressive process, signifying the increased importance of a time-dependent structure, and possibly pseudo-periodic behaviour. Pronounced individual peaks offer a further insight, since a peak in the spectrum indicate that particular frequencies of oscillation in the series are responsible for a large proportion of the variance. In the analysis of structure within naturally-occurring turbulent flows, the principal peak has, theoretically, been interpreted as the 'footprint' of a regular vortex formation (Gyr 1983; Prinos et al. 1985). Clifford et al. (1991, 1992b) and Clifford & French (in press) have provided evidence that vortex shedding from roughness elements dominates the flow structure over a coarse bed, together with the additional possibility of larger-scale eddying, scaling on channel and bedform dimensions. Where this is the case, as a first approximation, the Strouhal eddy-shedding relationship

$$S = \frac{fd}{V} \qquad (4)$$

may be rearranged to estimate the diameter d of the body held to be responsible for the vortex

structure of the flow. In equation 4, f is the frequency of shedding and V is the mean fluid velocity parallel to the eddy trajectory (taken here as V_x). For Reynolds numbers of the order 10^3, the Strouhal number (S) is approximately constant at 0.21, and varies between 0.18 and 0.21 for Reynolds numbers up to 10^5 (Schlichting 1979 pp. 31–32) which represents the range in the empirical studies described below (see Table 1). Peaks in the spectrum can be used directly in equation (4), and f may also be approximated from the 'periodicity' identified directly from plots of the velocity series, if values obtained in this way are divided by the mean longitudinal velocity.

Table 2 shows the results obtained when equation 4 is applied to the results shown in Figs 8 and 9. Also shown are the length scales obtained by multiplying period by mean velocity. In the case of the spectral analysis, peaks indicate the importance of relatively large scale motions, comparable in size to channel width (4–6 m). The largest motions indicated from this analysis and from the visual identification of periodicities might reflect the occurrence of large eddies in this zone immediately downstream from a pool section, induced by channel boundary irregularities. It is not clear that the Strouhal relationship is appropriate in the case of larger-scale motions, although interestingly, the mean spacing of the transverse clast dams at this location was recorded as 1.0–1.3 m. Unless turbulence is measured immediately downstream of a prominant obstacle, results must integrate the length scales of particles of a range of sizes and bar-scale features. Recent stability analyses (Chu et al. 1991) indicate that large scale turbulent motion scaling on channel width are generated by small-scale boundary disturbances, and the two kinds of turbulent structure can coexist in an unstable state. A variety of other possible causes of larger-scale motions in natural channel flows are reviewed in Clifford (1993).

Results from the visual analysis are easier to interpret: generally, length scales calculated from the Strouhal relationship compare well with particle sizes and/or with microtopographic bedform dimensions. In the upstream location for example, the smallest length scales are greater than those calculated in the downstream zone, which corresponds to observed particle size differences: $b_{50} = 0.10$ m and $b_{max} = 0.18$ m as against $b_{50} = 0.08$ m, $b_{max} = 0.12$ m, suggesting a grain-related effect. Similarly, transverse clast dam height was recorded as 0.27 m, whereas mean obstacle clast height was recorded as 0.23 m. Clifford et al. (1992b) show that the

Table 2. *Periods (seconds) identified from visual inspection of Figs 8–10, together with a length scale of eddying calculated directly from this (period × mean velocity), and a length scale derived from the Strouhal relationship given in equation 4*

Figure	Period	Mean velocity	Length scale (direct)	Length scale (Strouhal)
8	1.0	0.59	0.59	0.12
	2.5		1.48	0.30
	5.0		2.95	0.59
	30–40		17.7–23.6	3.9/4.72
9	1.0	0.45 and 0.35	0.45/0.35	0.09/0.07
	2.5		1.13/0.88	0.23/0.18
	5.0		2.25/1.75	0.45/0.35
	15.0	0.45	5.25	1.29
	(present only in Fig. 10a)			
10	3.3	0.66	21.78	6.60
	11		7.26	2.20
	8		5.45	1.65
	5		3.35	1.02

dominant scaling of vortex shedding in the near bed region corresponds well to a multiplier of grain size, with variation around seven times the median value. This could account for the intermediate length scales at both locations, although in more general terms, the precise mechanisms and characteristics of eddy growth and decay in natural coarse-boundary flows requires further investigation. The two dimensional, laboratory-derived relationship (equation 4) used here is but a first step to accurate interpretation, therefore. Nevertheless, as the velocity time series show, each location is characterized by relatively coherent flow behaviour at markedly contrasting scales. Since each scale represents a changing pattern of velocity fluctuation, and since it is this which determines the composition of forces at the bed, it seems reasonable to assume that high frequency velocity measurements provide direct evidence of grain-, microform-, and form-related energy losses which underlie the differential potential for sediment transport. In addition to Bluck's idea of changing turbulent intensity as the physical manifestation of the turbulence template, these results suggest that an additional factor, the changing balance of grain-related and form-related stress, is operative. Thus, in zones of high bed relief (near bar heads, in areas of marked transverse clast dams), form-related energy losses are higher, and potential transport lower, whereas in areas of lower relief, grain (i.e. transport)-related losses are higher, and hence the potential for sediment transport greater.

Where three components of the velocity field are logged simultaneously, it is possible more directly to assess the significance of local turbulent flow conditions which may be of significance to local particle movement, and in the context of this paper, to in situ vibration suggested as an important sorting control by Schumm & Stevens (1973). In Fig. 11, a resultant velocity

$$V_R = \sqrt{V_x^2 + V_y^2 + V_z^2} \qquad (5)$$

together with its two angular components (in the horizontal, ϕ; and in the vertical, θ)

$$\phi = \arctan(V_z/V_x) \qquad (6)$$

$$\theta = \arcsin(V_y/V_R) \qquad (7)$$

are plotted using the series obtained at location A (Fig. 3). Essentially, this demonstrates that, in a rough, relatively rapid flow regime, such are the magnitude of variations in all components, that the resultant direction of velocity shows appreciable unsteadiness, particularly at times of short-duration turbulent 'flow events', and that the magnitude of the resultant commonly varies by a factor of four or more. In addition to providing support for the possibility of in situ abrasion, such marked fluctuations in both the magnitude and direction of velocities may also be essential in the surface re-arrangement of particles, both with respect to vertical winnowing and, too, the creation of microforms (Clifford *et al.* 1992a). In principle, several flow models are available with which to test the correlation between turbulent flow characteristics and particle movement. Bridge (1981) and Bridge & Bennett (1992), for example, attempt

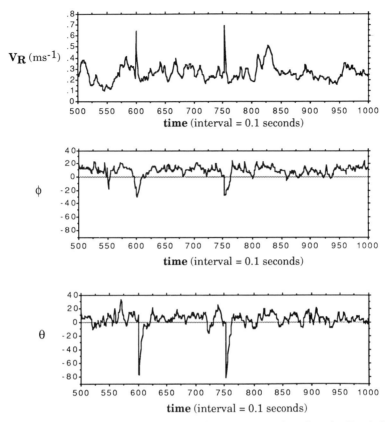

Fig. 11. Resultant velocity series calculated from ultrasonic current meter data, Langden Brook, location A. The upper plot shows the changing magnitude of the velocity, the lower plots deviations in the angle of the resultant velocity in the horizontal (ϕ) and vertical (θ) planes.

to model the distribution of sediment in transport based upon a partitioning of the turbulent shear stress distribution. However, these models are limited by their concentration on only a single turbulent stress term, and, given the findings reported here and more generally in the literature on turbulent flow, by the assumption that the stress term, rather than the velocity components, is also normally distributed. A simpler, but possibly more realistic model is that of Naden (1987). This has the advantage that it is based upon total (mean and turbulent) velocity, rather than stress distributions, and it utilises both the longitudinal and vertical component, thus incorporating a balance of instantaneous drag and lift as well as gravity forces. For a grain resting on the surface, motion begins when

$$V_x^2 + V_z^2 \tan \phi > 3.34 \left(\frac{\varrho_s - \varrho_w}{\varrho_w} \right)$$
$$\times gD \left(\cos \beta \tan \phi - \sin \beta \right) \qquad (8)$$

where V_x and V_z are the instantaneous (mean + fluctuating) velocities. Substituting a constant value for the friction angle (35°), appropriate values for gravitational acceleration and fluid density, assuming bedslope is small ($\cos \beta \to 1$, $\sin \beta \to 0$), and rearranging to solve for the diameter (m) of a grain D which moves for a given combination of U and W yields

$$D < \left(\frac{V_x^2 + 0.7 V_z^2}{37.8} \right). \qquad (9)$$

In the context of this paper, equation 9 can be used in conjunction with the UCM data in Table 1 to obtain the distribution of *potentially* mobile particle sizes under monitored near-bed flow, and hence as a guide to the possible effects of spatial variation in mean and fluctuating velocities responsible for the development of sediment structures/in situ movement.

The results of this analysis are shown for 3

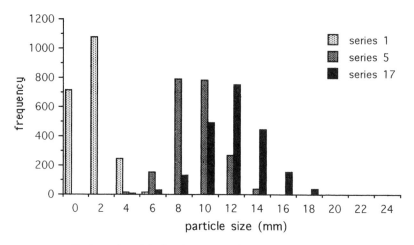

Fig. 12. Theoretical distributions of particle sizes in transport for contrasting locations in the bar-pool unit of Langden Brook derived from equation 9 based upon instantaneous lift and drag.

data sets in Fig. 12. Here, the data used represent pool (series 1), bar head (series 5) and bar tail (series 17) locations. It can be seen that in the pool, only relatively fine material, largely confined to sand sizes ($d_{75} = 2.1$ mm) is expected to move. Over the bar, however, larger material is expected to move, with characteristic (d_{75}) diameters of 10.8 mm and 13.4 mm respectively. Although in the absence of particle trapping, these results cannot be verified empirically, they do at least provide a plausible guide as to the likely sedimentological consequences of the varying turbulent flow characteristics recorded here, which is consistent with the expectation of greater sorting and jostling at, and over, bar surfaces. Further discussion of the Naden equation in the context of microtopographic bedform development and its association with macro-scale features is given in Clifford (in press).

More generally, the occurrence of manifestly three-dimensional flow behaviour has implications for those studies of field turbulence seeking to compare results with two-dimensional laboratory flow models. Resultant velocities might, for example, offer a more successful (and physically, more meaningful) basis on which to identify and categorize turbulent 'event structures', while greater use of three-component velocity sensors would appear to be essential, given the marked angular deviations of flow components which are not well-recorded by discoidal electromagnetic sensors (King 1977), which have become standard instruments in many cases.

Conclusions

Ferguson & Ashworth (1991) have emphasized that rapid declines in slope and bed material size in headwater streams are associated with *all* aspects of channel morphology, hydraulic processes and measures of channel activity, with boundary conditions of sediment supply and valley gradient inherited from immediate post-glacial conditions. Similar conclusions are appropriate in the case of Langden Brook, and reinforce growing demands (e.g. Richards 1988) for more physically-based explanations of channel form. In this context, evidence presented here of particle size-sorting patterns is consistent with the hypothesis presented by Bluck (1987) that sorting at a local (bar-form) scale contributes substantially to more general downstream trends. High frequency velocity measurements lend quantitative support to Bluck's qualitative observations that at the sub-bar scale, there is clear evidence for the presence of differing turbulence templates, or spectral footprints, which can be related to micro- and meso-scale location, and which drive the size-sorting mechanism. Whereas Bluck conceptualized significant differences solely with respect to changing turbulent intensity, these results suggest that the potential for size contrasts (clast acceptance/rejection) may also be related to the changing contribution of form and grain related flow resistance as evidenced in the differing structural properties of velocity time series. In addition, in rough turbulent environments, the magnitude and direction of turbulent flow is sufficiently great even at low to intermediate stage to provide for 'abrasion in place' and particle rearrangement, adding further insight into the physical mechanisms responsible for longitudinal sedimentological contrasts. Spatial differences in the structure and intensity of near-bed turbulence thus provide one component which might be incorporated into a physically-based model accounting for the evolution of sedimentological, channel bed and bar characteristics, and hence channel stability.

We are grateful for the permission of North West Water to gain access to the site at Langden Brook.

References

ANDREWS, E. D. 1983. Entrainment of gravel from naturally sorted riverbed material. *Geological Society of America Bulletin*, **94**, 1225–1231.

—— & ERMAN, D. C. 1986. Persistence in the size distribution of surficial bed material during an extreme snowmelt flood. *Water Resources Research*, **22**, 191–197.

BLUCK, B. J. 1987. Bed forms and clast size changes in gravel-bed rivers. *In*: RICHARDS, K. S. (ed.) *River channels environment and process*. Institute of British Geographers Special Publications, **17**, Blackwell, Oxford.

BRADLEY, W. C. 1970. Effect of weathering on abrasion of granitic gravel, Colorado River (Texas). *Geological Society of America Bulletin*, **81**, 61–80.

——, FAHNESTOCK, R. K. & ROWEKAMP, E. T. 1972. Coarse sediment transport by flood flows on Knik River, Alaska. *Geological Society of America Bulletin*, **83**, 1261–1284.

BRIDGE, J. S. 1981. Hydraulic interpretation of grain-size distributions using a physical model for bed-load transport. *Journal of Sedimentary Petrology*, **51**, 1109–1124.

—— & BENNETT, S. J. 1992. A model for the entrainment and transport of sediment grains of mixed sizes, shapes and densities. *Water Resources Research*, **28**, 337–363.

CHERKAUER, D. S. 1973. Minimization of power expenditure in a riffle-pool alluvial channel. *Water Resources Research*, **9**, 1612–1627.

CHU, V. H., WU, J. H. & KHAYAT, R. E. 1991. Stability of transverse shear flows in shallow open channels. *Journal of Hydraulic Engineering*, **117**, 1370–1388.

CLIFFORD, N. J. 1990. *The formation, nature and maintenance of riffle-pool sequences in gravel-bedded rivers*. PhD thesis, Cambridge University.

—— 1993. Formation of riffle-pool sequences: field evidence for an autogenic process. *Sedimentary Geology*, **85**, 39–51.

—— In press. Differential bed sedimentology and the maintenance of riffle pool sequences. *Catena*.

—— & FRENCH, J. R. In press. Field measurements of turbulence characteristics in gravel-bedded rivers: some technical and conceptual issues. *In*: CLIFFORD, N. J., FRENCH, J. R. & HARDISTY, J. (eds) *Turbulence: perspectives on flow and sediment transport*. John Wiley & Sons Ltd, Chichester.

——, MCCLATCHEY, J. & FRENCH, J. R. 1991. Discussion — Measurements of turbulence in the benthic boundary layer over a gravel bed, and comparison between acoustic measurements and predictions of the bedload transport of marine gravels. *Sedimentology*, **38**, 161–171.

——, RICHARDS, K. S. & ROBERT, A. 1992*a*. The influence of microform bed roughness elements on flow and sediment transport in gravel-bed rivers — comment. *Earth Surface Processes and Landforms*, **17**, 529–534.

——, ROBERT, A. & RICHARDS, K. S. 1992*b*. Estimation of flow resistance in gravel-bedded rivers: a physical explanation of the multiplier of roughness length. *Earth Surface Processes and Landforms*, **17**, 111–126.

DAVOREN, A. & MOSLEY, P. 1986. Observations of bedload movement, bar development and sediment supply in the braided Ohau River. *Earth Surface Processes and Landforms*, **11**, 643–652.

DIETRICH, W. E., KIRCHNER, J. W., IKEDA, H. & ISEYA, F. 1989. Sediment supply and the development of the coarse surface layer in gravel-bedded rivers. *Nature*, **340**, 215–217.

DUNCAN, W. J., THOM, A. S. & YOUNG, A. D. 1970. Mechanics of fluids, second edition. Arnold, London.

FERGUSON, R. I. & ASHWORTH, P. 1991. Slope-induced changes in channel character along a gravel-bed stream: the Allt Dubhaig, Scotland. *Earth Surface Processes and Landforms*, **16**, 65–82.

FRENCH, J. R. & CLIFFORD, N. J. 1992. Characteristics of near-bed turbulence in a tidal salt marsh creek. *Estuarine and Coastal Shelf Science*, **34**, 49–69.

GYR, A. 1983. Towards a better definition of the three types of sediment transport. *Journal of Hydraulic Research*, **21**, 1–15.

HARDISTY, J. 1990. *Acoustic measurements of bedload processes in turbulent flow: part 1 — data acquisition systems*. SGER Working Paper **12**, Univ. Hull.

HERBICH, J. B. & SCHULITS, S. 1964. Large-scale roughness in open channel flow. *American Society of Civil Engineers Journal of the Hydraulics Division*, **HY6, 90**, 202–230.

JENKINS, G. M. & WATTS, D. G. 1968. *Spectral analysis and its applications*. Holden-Day, San Francisco.

KALINSKE, A. A. 1947. Movement of sediment as bed load in rivers. *Transactions of the American Geophysical Union*, **28**, 615–620.

KUENEN, P. H. 1956. Experimental abrasion of pebbles. 2. Rolling by current. *Journal of Geology*, **64**, 336–368.

KING, C. R. 1977. *Performance of an electromagnetic current meter in oscillating flow.* Wallingford Report No. INT 157 HRS.

KLINE, S. J. W., REYNOLDS, W. C., SCHRAUB, F. A. & RUNDSTADLER, P. W. 1967. The structure of turbulent boundary layers. *Journal of Fluid Mechanics*, **30**, 741–773.

KNIGHTON, D. 1984. *Fluvial forms and processes.* Arnold, London.

LU, S. S. & WILLMARTH, W. W. 1973. Measurements of the Reynolds stress in a turbulent boundary layer. *Journal of Fluid Mechanics*, **60**, 481–511.

McQUIVEY, R. S. 1973. *Summary of turbulence data from rivers, conveyence channels and laboratory flumes.* USGS Professional Papers, **802B**.

MILLS, H. H. 1979. Downstream rounding of pebbles — a quantitative review. *Journal of Sedimentary Petrology*, **49**, 295–302.

MOSS, A. J. 1972. Initial fluviatile fragmentation of granitic quartz. *Journal of Sedimentary Petrology*, **42**, 905–916.

NADEN, P. S. 1987. An erosion criterion for gravel-bed rivers. *Earth Surface Processes and Landforms*, **12**, 83–93.

PARKER, G., KLINGEMAN, P. C. & McLEAN, D. C. 1982. Bedload and size distribution in paved gravel-bed streams. *American Society of Civil Engineers Journal of the Hydraulics Division*, **108**, 544–571.

PETTIJOHN, F. J. 1975. *Sedimentary rocks.* Harper & Row, London.

PLUMLEY, W. J. 1948. Black Hills terrace gravels: a study in sediment transport. *Journal of Geology*, **56**, 526–578.

PRINOS, P., TOWNSEND, R. & TAVOULARIS, S. 1985. Structure of turbulence in compound channel flows. *American Society of Civil Engineers, Journal of the Hydraulics Division*, **111**, 1246–1279.

RICHARDS, K. S. 1982. *Rivers: form and process in alluvial channels.* Methuen & Co, London.

—— 1988. Fluvial geomorphology. *Progress in Physical Geography*, **12**, 435–456.

—— & CLIFFORD, N. J. 1991. Fluvial geomorphology — structured beds in gravelly rivers. *Progress in Physical Geography*, **15**, 407–422.

ROBERT, A. 1988. *Statistical modelling of sediment bed profile and bed roughness properties in alluvial channels.* PhD thesis, Univ. Cambridge.

SCHLICHTING, H. 1979. *Boundary-layer theory,* 7th edition. McGraw-Hill, New York.

SCHUMM, S. A. & STEVENS, M. A. 1973. Abrasion in place: a mechanism for rounding and size reduction of coarse sediment in rivers. *Geology*, **1**, 37–40.

SCOTT, K. M. & GRAVLEE, G. C. 1968. *Flood surge on the Rubicon River, California — hydrology, hydraulics, and boulder transport.* USGS Professional Papers, **422-M**.

STERNBERG, H. 1875. Untersuchungen uber Langen- und Querprofil gescheibefuhrender Flusse. *Zeits. Chrif tur Bauwesen*, **25**, 483–506.

TRICART, J. & VOGT, H. 1967. Quelques aspects du transport des alluvions grossieres et du faconnements des lits fluviaux. *Geografiska Annaler*, **49A**, 351–366.

WILCOCK, P. R. & SOUTHARD, J. B. 1989. Bed load transport of mixed size sediment: fractional transport rates, bed forms, and the development of a coarse bed surface-layer. *Water Resources Research*, **25**, 1629–1641.

WILLIAMS, J. J., THORNE, P. D. & HEATHERSHAW, A. D. 1989. Measurements of turbulence in the benthic boundary layer over a gravel bed. *Sedimentology*, **36**, 959–971.

WOLMAN, M. G. 1954. A method of sampling coarse river-bed material. *Transactions of the American Geophysical Union*, **35**, 951–956.

Braiding and meandering parameters

P. F. FRIEND & R. SINHA

Department of Earth Sciences, University of Cambridge, Downing Street, Cambridge CB2 3EQ, UK

Abstract: Modifications to standard definitions of braiding and meandering are proposed to indicate the morphology of every river channel reach quantitatively, whether it has single channel or multiple channels. Sinuosity (P) is defined as, $P = L_{cmax}/L_R$, where L_{cmax} is the length of the midline of the channel (in single-channel rivers), or the widest channel (in multi-channel rivers), and L_R is the overall length of the reach. Braiding is a measure of channel multiplicity and a new term 'braid–channel ratio' (B) has been defined as, $B = L_{ctot}/L_{cmax}$, where L_{ctot} is the total of the mid-channel lengths of all the channels in a reach. Another expression for the braid–channel ratio which gives the same numerical result is, $B = P_{ctot}/P$, where the total sinuosity, $P_{ctot} = L_{ctot}/L_R$, and P has been defined above. Scatter plots on braid–channel ratio/sinuosity axes show a negative correlation between these parameters, as would be expected from the above relationships. Single-channel rivers ($B = 1$) have relatively higher sinuosities and the upper limit of these is the point at which cut-off becomes highly probable. For multi-channel rivers ($B > 1$), sinuosity remains low, reflecting the limiting effect of braid bars on the development of fully developed spiral secondary flow. Data analyses showing that increases in channel slope and bankfull discharge are associated with changes from meandering to braided morphology are diverting attention from the importance of the increased availability of bed-load-grade sediment as a control.

A variety of river systems supplying water and sediment to the Gangetic alluvial plains of India have been investigated. These alluvial plains are some of the most extensive in the world, so the examination has depended heavily on the use of topographical maps and satellite images. The degree of braiding and meandering displayed by these rivers varies greatly from river to river and along the course of particular rivers. One of the first steps has therefore been to devise methods of measuring the degree of braiding and meandering which can be applied to all the rivers, using maps and satellite images. With existing schemes, a river channel reach can either be expressed in terms of braiding or meandering (sinuosity). Although arguments have been developed against the 'thresholds' between braiding and meandering that were suggested by Leopold & Wolman (1957), there have been very few attempts at devising common parameters to quantitatively express the morphology of channels that vary from one type to the other.

The first part of this paper discusses definitions of braiding and meandering, and the modifications of these definitions that have been adopted. Variations of these numerical measurements are then illustrated, highlighting some of the factors that may be involved in causing the variation.

The meandering parameter (sinuosity)

Two minor modifications have been adopted to the procedures previously used in defining the sinuosity of channels (e.g. Leopold & Wolman 1957). Firstly, the channel length has been measured along a line that runs mid-way between the channel banks. This has allowed measurement readily from topographical maps, aerial photographs and satellite images, and also has the advantage that the channel length is unlikely to change in a major way with changes of river water level.

Secondly, the rivers in India show so many transitions between single-channel and braided morphologies that it was found necessary to abandon the hard and fast distinction between braided and meandering classes of rivers, and employ definitions of braiding and meandering that can each be applied to every river, no matter whether it has single or multiple channels, or both. Therefore, the meandering (sinuosity) parameter has been extended to multi-channel situations where it is based on the mid-channel length of the channel that is widest in each reach of the channel belt.

The modified sinuosity parameter, P, is defined as

$$P = L_{cmax}/L_R \tag{1}$$

From Best, J. L. & Bristow, C. S. (eds), 1993, *Braided Rivers*, Geological Society Special Publication No. **75**, pp. 105–111.

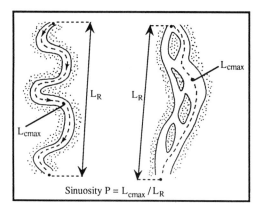

Sinuosity $P = L_{cmax}/L_R$

Fig. 1. Diagram representing the calculation of the Sinuosity for single-channel and multi-channel rivers.

where L_R is the overall length of the channel-belt reach measured along a straight line, and L_{cmax} is the mid-channel length for the same reach, or the mid-channel length of the widest channel, where there is more than one channel (Fig. 1).

Braiding parameters

Brice (1964) used a braiding index (BI), defined as follows:

$$BI = 2(\Sigma L_i)/L_r \qquad (2)$$

where ΣL_i is the length of all the islands and/or bars in the reach, and L_r is the length of the reach measured midway between the banks of the channel belt.

Brice rationalized this definition as a measure of the total amount of bank length, where most islands or bars have a significantly greater length

(parallel to the channel belt) than width, so that the total bank length will be approximated by doubling the island or bar length.

Rust (1978) introduced two modifications into the measurement of braiding. He was concerned about the variations of apparent island length that might be caused by fluctuations of water level (stage), and proposed that the channel talwegs be used to define a 'braid length' from upstream divergence to downstream convergence of the surrounding talwegs. He also proposed that a meander length should be measured for each channel belt (apparently taking the major channel in a braided reach), and that this should be used to characterize the channel belt.

The braiding parameter (B_p) discussed by Rust (1978, p. 188) appears to have been measured as follows:

$$B_p = \Sigma L_b/L_m \qquad (3)$$

where ΣL_b is the sum, in a reach, of the braid lengths, defined as above, between channel talweg divergences and confluences and L_m is the mean of the meander wavelengths in a reach of the channel belt.

The proposed 'braid–channel ratio' (B) in this paper builds clearly on some of the approaches used in both these parameters (Fig. 2). It also uses the idea of 'total sinuosity' developed by Richards (1982) to measure the braiding in some gravel-bed rivers. This paper adopts a similar use of the total active channel length which is as follows:

$$B = L_{ctot}/L_{cmax} \qquad (4)$$

where L_{ctot} is the sum of the mid-channel lengths of all the segments of primary channels in a reach, and L_{cmax} is the mid-channel length of the

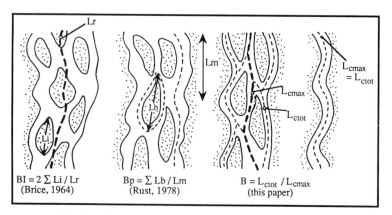

$BI = 2 \Sigma Li / Lr$
(Brice, 1964)

$Bp = \Sigma Lb / Lm$
(Rust, 1978)

$B = L_{ctot} / L_{cmax}$
(this paper)

Fig. 2. Diagram representing the calculation of the braiding indices of Brice (1964), Rust (1978) and this paper.

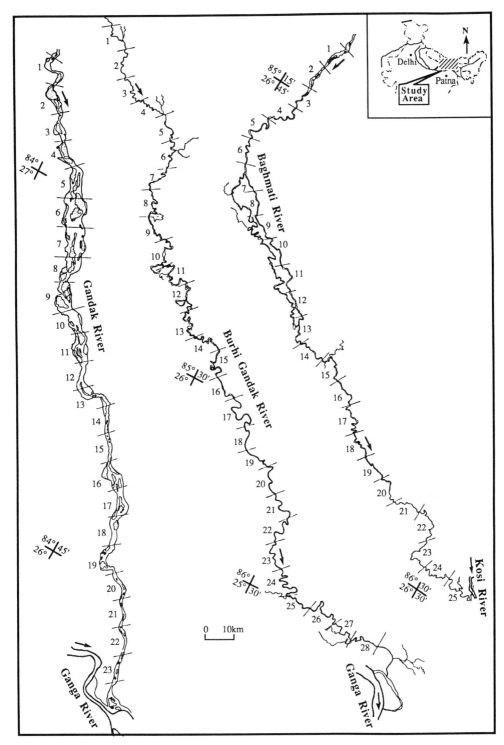

Fig. 3. Diagrammatic maps illustrating the alluvial reaches of three of the rivers of northern Bihar, India. These have been divided into 10 km reaches and the sinuosity (*P*) and braid–channel ratios (*B*) calculated.

widest channel through the reach, as defined for equation (1) above. The specification of primary channels recognizes that some braiding patterns display a scaling hierarchy of channel sizes (Rust 1978), and that only the major ones would be used for this measurement. The widest channel in a reach would be taken as the major channel.

In essence, the proposed braid–channel ratio measures the tendency of a channel belt to develop multiple channels in any reach. If a reach has only a single channel, with no braids, B will have a value of unity, and will thus compare with measurement of sinuosity (P) which will also have a minimum value of unity. Equations (1) and (4) may be combined, as follows:

$$B = L_{ctot}/(P \times L_R) = P_{ctot}/P \qquad (5)$$

which may be more convenient ways of measuring the parameter.

Variation patterns

Figures 3 and 4 provide some examples of the use of the braid–channel ratio (B) and sinuosity (P) in measuring the variable morphology of

three different types of Indian rivers. The three rivers all flow across the plains of north Bihar in eastern India and then join either the Ganges which is the main W–E-flowing axial river of the Himalayan foredeep, or the Kosi, the next main river to the east. For each river, the parameters have been measured for a continuous sequence of reaches, each reach being 10 km long. It may however be emphasized that some local or seasonal variations in the river channel morphology may not be reflected in this scheme; the reach length of 10 km may be rather large to record these effects. For most of the reaches, topographic maps of 1 : 63 360 scale have been used, dating between 1905 and 1947 except that, in a few cases, the only maps available were 1 : 253 440. For each river, the parameters have been tabulated (Table 1), and are also presented as scatter plots (Fig. 4).

The *Gandak* river rises in the high mountains of the Himalayas and is braided throughout its course between the point where it emerges in the plains to its confluence with the Ganga. The sinuosity values are generally low. The braid–channel ratio tends to be highest (up to 5.4)

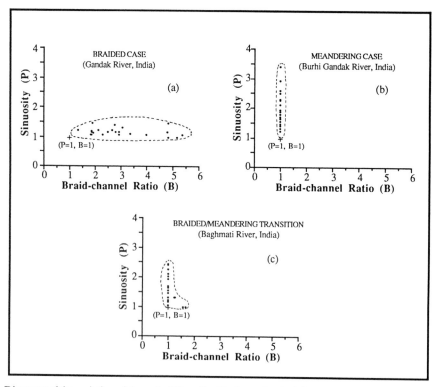

Fig. 4. Diagrams of the variation of sinuosity (P) and braid–channel ratio (B) for each of the three Indian rivers of Fig. 3.

Table 1. *Sinuosity variation in North Bihar rivers, India*

Reach No.	Gandak River (Braided)		Burhi Gandak River (Meandering)		Baghmati River (Braided/meandering)	
	P	B	P	B	P	B
1	1.45	3.21	1.53	1.00	1.0	1.67
2	1.21	4.83	1.85	1.00	1.0	1.58
3	1.45	1.33	1.93	1.00	1.29	1.25
4	1.09	1.89	1.45	1.00	1.61	1.00
5	1.13	3.38	1.69	1.00	1.45	1.00
6	1.0	4.79	1.93	1.00	1.29	1.00
7	1.0	5.17	1.37	1.00	1.21	1.00
8	1.05	4.83	2.25	1.00	1.53	1.00
9	1.05	5.38	1.61	1.00	1.03	1.00
10	1.21	2.92	1.93	1.00	1.29	1.00
11	1.37	2.67	3.38	1.00	1.29	1.00
12	1.13	2.76	1.93	1.00	1.03	1.00
13	1.21	2.50	2.57	1.00	1.61	1.00
14	1.13	2.13	2.25	1.00	1.29	1.00
15	1.05	2.50	2.28	1.00	1.61	1.00
16	1.13	1.85	1.29	1.00	1.13	1.00
17	1.05	2.93	2.09	1.00	1.69	1.00
18	1.29	4.00	1.61	1.00	1.93	1.00
19	1.13	3.06	1.21	1.00	1.13	1.00
20	1.13	2.79	1.69	1.00	1.61	1.00
21	1.18	1.86	1.45	1.00	1.45	1.00
22	1.10	1.88	1.77	1.00	2.01	1.00
23	1.05	1.94	1.53	1.00	2.25	1.00
24	—	2.31	2.90	1.00	2.09	1.00
25	—	—	1.37	1.00	2.41	1.00
26	—	—	2.49	1.00	—	—
27	—	—	2.09	1.00	—	—
28	—	—	1.45	1.00	—	—

in the upstream reaches. The *Burhi Gandak* originates within the plains and has a braid–channel ratio of unity throughout, i.e. it is not braided. Sinuosity varies considerably, and is highest in the middle reaches (reaches 8–15) where it flows across a distinct zone of the plains where there is a system of highly sinuous palaeo-channels and lakes that is very obvious on the satellite images. It seems likely that the high sinuosities in these reaches of the Burhi Gandak are due to the partial occupation of the highly sinuous palaeochannels, and to the influence of the variable substrate they have left. The *Baghmati* river rises in the foothills near Kathmandu in Nepal and cuts through the foothills before emerging onto the alluvial plains. It is braided for the three upstream reaches on the plains, though with a relatively low braid–channel ratio (1.7 to 1.3), but then becomes unbraided, and sinuous for the rest of its course to the Kosi. This restricted zone of upstream braiding seems typical of these rivers arising in the foothills, and probably reflects the heavy

monsoonal rains of the foothills zone, and the ready availability of sand-grade sediment from the foothills. In reaches 7 to 13 the Baghmati is clearly anastomosing, with a well-developed southwestern anabranch. Anastomosing is a different order of phenomenon than the channel bars and bends considered here. The question of anastomosing is not discussed further in this brief review. The sinuosity of the Baghmati river tends to be relatively high in the lowest reaches, just before the confluence with the Kosi.

Figure 5 is a highly schematic diagram summarizing the range of variability in data on the north Bihar rivers, generalizing the features that would be expected in any such scatter diagram. Theoretically, straight, single channels, with $B = 1$ and $P = 1$, provide an origin for the variation. As seen on Fig. 5, sinuosity and braid–channel ratio tend to correlate negatively, and this is not surprising in the light of equation (5), above. Channel belts developing along the single-channel, meandering arm of the scatter have higher sinuosities, and a natural limit on

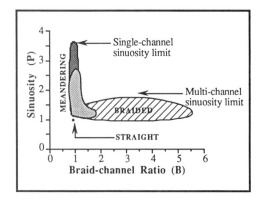

Fig. 5. Generalized diagram of the variation of range of variation of sinuosity (*P*) and braid–channel ratio (*B*) expected in natural rivers, with two limits discussed in the text shown.

the sinuosity values would be expected where it becomes increasingly inevitable that channel belts will intersect each other, thereby decreasing the sinuosity. Chitale (1970) presented some data on the limiting values of sinuosity (tortuosity ratio) and concluded that values greater than 5.5 are rarely met with in practice. In the case of the north Bihar rivers, using the parameters defined in this note, the limiting value is 3.5. However, measurements of lower reach lengths may yield a rather higher value. Channel belts developing in the braided arm have lower sinuosities, and here a natural limit on the degree of sinuosity may be provided by the tendency of braids and in-channel bars to inhibit the development of spiral secondary flow which will, in turn, limit the curvature of the channels.

Speculations on the controls

In suggesting modifications to the methods previously employed to measure the amount of braiding or meandering in rivers, the ultimate interest of the paper is not simply, of course, to quantify the patterns, but is to understand better the factors that produce the varying patterns, represented on a diagram like Fig. 5. Here, a few preliminary comments are offered in the hope that discussion may clarify the questions and improve future research approaches.

Leopold *et al.* (1964, p. 292) presented data

for about 100 river reaches, plotting a point for each reach against axes of $\log_{10}$ bankfull discharge, and $\log_{10}$ channel slope. A discriminant line on this scatter plot discriminated quite well between the braided reaches and the meandering (high sinuosity) reaches. Particularly for the intermediate values, relatively higher slope values, and/or higher discharge values clearly tend to be characteristic of the braided reaches. This plot has (unreasonably) encouraged a general belief that the particular variables, slope and discharge, determine on their own whether a river is braided or meandering.

In contrast, there is considerable evidence that braiding is strongly influenced by high *availability* of bed-load sediment, relative to suspended-load sediment. Chitale (1970) clearly showed that width–depth ratio and mean grain size of the bed material are closely correlated with channel pattern. Ferguson (1984, 1987) has discussed, much more fully than us, the discrimination of meandering and braided morphologies and concludes that a grain-size term should be incorporated with slope-discharge in the discriminant function. Carson (1984) also rejects the idea of any purely hydraulic threshold for channel pattern as this will vary significantly with the bed and bank material sediment.

Although the availability of different grain-size components is likely to be influenced by hydraulic factors, other factors, such as the previous geomorphological and geological history of the area, may be even more important. This is because the sediment available in any reach of a channel belt may include sediment supplied by:

(i)   the upstream reach of the same channel
(ii) tributary channels
(iii) overbank flows that drain into the channel belt and material entrained or eroded from older deposits in
(iv) the banks, or
(v)   the bed

Systematic surveys of the parameters suggested here in varying river reaches, like those of Fig. 3 in India, should also examine sediment availability, to provide a closer understanding of the controls over braiding and meandering.

We thank J. Best, R. Ferguson and A. Werrity for their constructive comments. This is Cambridge Earth Sciences Contribution No. 3087.

References

BRICE, J. E. 1964. *Channel patterns and terraces of the Loup Rivers in Nebraska.* United States Geological Survey Professional Papers, **422-D**.

CARSON, M. A. 1984. The meandering-braided river threshold: a reappraisal. *Journal of Hydrology*, **73**, 315–334.

CHITALE, S. V. 1970. River channel patterns. *Journal of Hydraulics Division, Proceedings of the American Society of Civil Engineers*, **96** (HY1), 201–222.

FERGUSON, R. I. 1984. The threshold between meandering and braiding. *In*: SMITH, K. V. H. (ed.) *Proceedings of the 1st International Conference on Water Resources Engineering.* Springer Verlag, Berlin, 6.15–6.29.

—— 1987. Hydraulic and sedimentary controls of channel pattern. *In*: RICHARDS, K. S. (ed.) *River channels: environment and processes.* Institute of British Geographers, Special Publications, **00**, 000–000.

LEOPOLD, L. B. & WOLMAN, M. G. 1957. *River Channel Patterns: Braided, Meandering and Straight. United States Geological Survey Professional Papers*, **282 B**, 39–84.

——, —— & MILLER, J. P. 1964. *Fluvial Processes in Geomorphology.* Freeman and Company, San Francisco.

RICHARDS, K. S. 1982. *Rivers: form and processes in alluvial channels.* Methuen & Co. Ltd., London.

RUST, B. R. 1978. A classification of alluvial channel systems. *Canadian Society of Petroleum Geologists, Memoir*, **5**, 187–198.

Braided-channel pattern and palaeohydrology using an index of total sinuosity

M. S. E. ROBERTSON-RINTOUL[1] & K. S. RICHARDS[2]

[1] ECOS Ltd, 26 Cameron Street, Stonehaven, Kincardineshire AB3 2HS, UK

[2] Department of Geography, University of Cambridge, Cambridge CB2 3EN, UK

Abstract: Channel patterns are commonly represented as discrete types (e.g. straight, meandering, braided) separated by threshold values of slope and discharge. However, for gravel-bed river patterns, an index of total sinuosity (ΣP) can be defined which varies continuously with both stream power per unit channel-belt length (represented as the product of mean annual flood and valley gradient) and median bed material diameter. An empirical relationship between ΣP and these controlling variables can be used to provide palaeo-hydrological reconstructions for braided stream traces on terrace fragments, as an alternative to methods based on bed material sizes and criteria for the threshold of grain motion.

Meandering and braided channel patterns have been separated on the basis of threshold values of slope (s_c) and discharge (Q) in many studies, resulting in threshold functions similar to that defined by Leopold & Wolman (1957)

$$s_c = 0.013Q^{-0.44} \qquad (1)$$

Both the constant and the coefficient in this function are known to vary with bed material size (Henderson 1961; Richards 1982, p. 216), bank sediment (Ferguson 1984, 1987), and the discharge criterion employed (Antropovskiy 1972). The threshold is blurred by the effects of these additional variables, as is implied by Begin and Schumm's (1984) probabilistic interpretation. Furthermore, this classificatory emphasis on pattern types ignores the similar nature of the physical processes occurring in both meandering and braided streams (bedload transport, energy dissipation, and bar construction: Parker 1976; Bridge 1985). An alternative approach to analysing channel patterns outlined in this paper therefore involves quantitative definition of parameters applicable to meandering and braided rivers (cf. Le Ba Hong & Davies 1979), and consideration of their continuous variation with controlling variables. Richards (1982, pp. 181–2) identified such a relationship, in the form

$$\Sigma P = 2.64(Qs_c)^{0.1} \qquad (\text{R}^2 = 0.41) \qquad (2)$$

where ΣP is a measure of total sinuosity (see below). However, this was based on a limited sample of rivers, lacked a rigorous operational definition for the total sinuosity index, and employed an index of power-per-unit-length (the discharge-channel slope product) which is not the most appropriate independent variable given that the channel slope itself depends on the channel pattern. This paper is therefore a more rigorous attempt to define this continuous relationship.

Once a relationship exists between a parameter such as ΣP and a discharge-related control variable, it can be used in palaeo-hydrological reconstruction. Equation 1, for example, would allow the discharge Q to be estimated if ΣP and s_c are known. This is an alternative to palaeohydraulic estimates of local flow velocity using threshold-of-motion and friction equations with the observed bed material clast sizes (Church et al. 1990), and which require the flow cross-section to be known in order to estimate discharge. Wide variation in the Shields entrainment function because of variable pivoting angle (Richards 1990) introduces problems in the application of this method to natural grain size mixtures. It is also difficult to apply if only part of the former channel is preserved on a terrace fragment, and flow reconstruction requires extrapolation of a water surface. Furthermore, the reconstructed discharge is of an unknown return period. Alternative palaeohydrological estimates have been obtained from empirical relationships between (palaeo)channel dimensions and discharges such as the mean annual flood, but only for meandering rivers (Schumm 1968). The advantage of the method developed in this paper and based on measurement of palaeochannel ΣP is that it reconstructs a representative discharge (the mean annual flood), can be applied to fragmentary remains of both meandering and braided palaeochannel traces on terrace

From Best, J. L. & Bristow, C. S. (eds), 1993, *Braided Rivers*, Geological Society Special Publication No. **75**, pp. 113–118.

surfaces, and does not require questionable assumptions about the former cross-section size of a partially-destroyed palaeochannel.

Quantifying the channel pattern continuum

Theoretical rationale

Alluvial rivers adjust their planform to prevailing water and sediment supply through a combination of bank erosion, bed material transport, and bar construction processes that vary in degree but not in kind between different patterns. With increasing stream power and bank erodibility, the channel width–depth ratio increases and the pattern of bar macro-forms varies systematically. Theoretical analysis suggests that meandering and braiding represent different degrees of a particular instability phenomenon (Engelund & Skovgaard 1973; Parker 1976), and flume and field studies support this (Ashmore 1982). Field studies of gravel-bed rivers illustrate sequences in which bank-attached lateral bars with chutes are replaced in high energy reaches by bars which are detached from the bank (Bluck 1976; Church & Jones 1982). There is also evidence of increasing braid complexity in high power environments (Howard *et al.* 1970). This trend in bar-channel characteristics is related to variations in width–depth ratio which occur as power-per-unit-length, bank erodibility, and bedload transport rates all increase (Bagnold 1977). Figure 1, based on data for 28 New Zealand gravel-bed rivers (Mosley, unpublished), shows

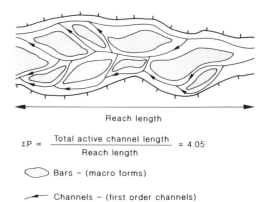

$$\Sigma P = \frac{\text{Total active channel length}}{\text{Reach length}} = 4.05$$

⬭ Bars – (macro forms)

⤙ Channels – (first order channels)

Fig. 2. Definition diagram for the measurement of total sinuosity P in braided rivers.

a systematic increase in width-depth ratio with increasing discharge-slope product (a power-per-unit-length index). Scatter in this plot reflects the influence of additional variables such as bed material size. However, the empirical trend indicates no discontinuity between meandering and braided rivers, although the latter pattern predominates above (Qs) of about $1 \, \text{m}^3 \, \text{s}^{-1}$, or a power-per-unit-length of about $9.8 \times 10^3 \, \text{Wm}^{-1}$ (cf. Carson 1984).

A quantitative index of pattern morphology

A quantitative index of channel pattern, such as the sinuosity, needs to be applicable to both meandering (Schumm 1963) and braided (Brice 1964; Rust 1978) rivers in order to be representative of the continuum suggested above. Le Ba Hong & Davies (1979) have suggested a total sinuosity index (ΣP) in which the cumulative length of all channels in a reach is divided by the reach length. This reduces to the conventional sinuosity index for single-thread rivers, but requires an explicit operational definition to enable its measurement for multi-thread rivers. Figure 2 indicates that measured channels are those diverted around the macro-forms (large bars or bar complexes), according to the consistent hierarchical classifications of Church & Jones (1982) and Parker (1976). These are the first-order channels defined by Williams & Rust (1969).

Figure 3 is a plot of total sinuosity against the mean number of braid channels averaged over 8 transects for 22 river reaches mapped in the literature, and indicates that the total sinuosity is a consistent measure of braiding intensity. It would therefore appear that meandering and braided streams should be comparable using a

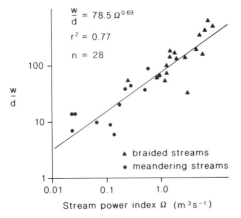

Fig. 1. Relationship between width–depth ratio and stream power index (discharge-slope product) for 28 New Zealand gravel-bed rivers, both meandering and braided.

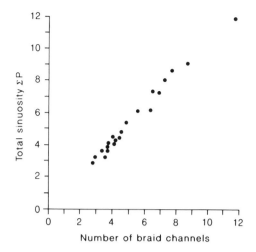

Fig. 3. Relationship between total sinuosity and mean number of braid channels in a cross-section.

common numerical sinuosity scale, with the latter having a higher ratio of active channel length to reach length. However, to be viable as an index, total sinuosity must be independent of short-term variations associated with bar inundation, as well as being representative of conditions at a 'formative' discharge (Kellerhals et al. 1976; Rust 1978). Mosley (1982) published five air photographs of the Ohau River, New Zealand at discharges ranging from 25 to 500 $m^3 s^{-1}$. At low flows, few channels are occupied and $\Sigma P = 5.3$; for flows of 57–240 $m^3 s^{-1}$, the variation of ΣP is between 7.3 and 8.0, reaching its maximum at the mean annual flood. At 500 $m^3 s^{-1}$, well above the mean annual flood, ΣP declines to 5.0. Thus the index is stable over a range of flows including the likely 'formative' or 'dominant' discharges. Fahnestock (1963) provided data for the White River, Alaska, which again indicate that at low flows (<6 $m^3 s^{-1}$) only a few channels are occupied, but that the average number of braids for three sampled sections fluctuates randomly about roughly constant values of 5.1 in 1958 and 3.6 in 1959 for a range of discharges including significant flood flows. It is thus reasonable to expect stable macro-forms and first-order channels in gravel-bed rivers such as these.

The data base

Data were gathered for a total of 60 rivers, of widely varying channel dimensions, bed material size, and pattern, and from North America, New Zealand, Scandinavia, and Britain (Church et al. 1981). Those selected were non-incised alluvial channels actively reworking their valley deposits. The sample included 39 gravel-bed rivers (24 valley-floor braided) and 21 sand-bed (6 braided). For each river, discharge (Q), valley gradient (s_v), bed material size (D_{84}), and a map from which ΣP could be measured had to be available. Although Carson (1984) suggested that discharges of a given frequency relate to channel forms in different ways in meandering and braided rivers, few data exist to define the frequency of formative flows in braided rivers and, as a first approximation, discharges of 1.5–2.3 years return period were identified for the sampled rivers; these range from 1.9 to 5500 $m^3 s^{-1}$. The indicator of stream power used is the product of this discharge estimate and the valley slope, since this defines the rate of potential energy expenditure for the flow prior to the morphological adjustments that determine the prevailing channel pattern (Ferguson 1987). Bed material size is an additional variable required for each reach, since it influences flow resistance and sediment transport. The D_{84} grain size was chosen as a representative measure. Values ranged up to 255 mm in the coarsest-grained gravel-bed river. Finally, ΣP was measured for each reach by digitizing channel centre lines around first-order bars in the case of braided rivers, defined on large-scale maps compiled from air photographs and either published or prepared specifically for this study. Sinuosities of single-thread reaches in the sample ranged from 1.3 to 2.78, while ΣP for multi-thread rivers ranged from 2.05 to 9.0.

Results of analysis

A constrained (zero-intercept) multiple regression was fitted to define the relationship between ΣP and the independent variables, by subtracting 1 (the limiting lower value) from each sinuosity, estimating power-law regressions which converge to $(\Sigma P - 1) = 0$, and adding 1 again. For the full data set ($n = 60$),

$$\Sigma P = 1 + 3.42 (Qs_v)^{0.40} D_{84}^{-0.04} \quad (R^2 = 0.74)$$
(3)

Partial correlations of both independent variables with the dependent variable are significant at $p = 0.05$. Separate analyses were performed for sand-bed and gravel-bed data. For sand-bed rivers, the relationship is

$$\Sigma P = 1 + 2.64 (Qs_v)^{0.38} D_{84}^{-0.44} \quad (R^2 = 0.48)$$
(4)

while for gravel-bed rivers it is

$$\Sigma P = 1 + 5.52(Qs_v)^{0.40} D_{84}^{-0.14} \quad (R^2 = 0.87)$$

(5)

Although the partial correlations are all significant at $p = 0.05$, these results suggest that a stronger relationship exists between ΣP and the independent variables in gravel-bed rivers, and that a single regression model is inappropriate. A significant difference occurs between the constants and the grain size exponents in Equations (4) and (5). The gravel-bed river data and Equation 5 are plotted in Fig. 4. Together, Figs 3 and 4 provide evidence of the continuum of channel pattern emphasized by Bridge (1985) in relation to sedimentology, since no discontinuity exists in the trends between meandering and braided channels. This suggests that pattern thresholds such as that implied by Equation (1) in part reflect this qualitative classification, rather than fundamental discontinuities in river behaviour. A continuum of increasing channel length is evident as stream power increases, uninterrupted by the qualitative change of pattern type, but affected by bed material size in that for a given power, the channel length is lower for coarser (rougher, less mobile) bed material.

That different equations describe the relationship between ΣP and the two independent variables (Qs_v and D_{84}) in sand- and gravel-bed rivers may be because the physical relevance of these control variables differs between these two sedimentary environments. In sand-bed rivers the bed is active at flows of higher frequency than the 1.5–2.3 year events employed in this analysis, and D_{84} may have less relevance as an index of flow resistance. Furthermore, although

the above analysis demonstrates the importance of bed material calibre, it does not address the role of the bank material in determining whether meanders or braids occur in a given reach (Ferguson 1984). In the sinuosity range 2.05 to 2.78, low complexity braids and highly sinuous meanders overlap in Fig. 4, and it may be the bank stability that determines the pattern type.

Applications in palaeohydrology

A pattern continuum for gravel-bed rivers which is related statistically to flow and sediment properties offers a potential new channel-scale approach to palaeohydrological reconstruction for braided channel traces on terrace surfaces. The ΣP of a modern gravel-bed river is related to power-per-unit-valley-length at approximately the mean annual flood. Thus, if reconstruction of ΣP from the channel trace preserved on a terrace surface is possible, together with estimates of terrace downstream gradient and grain size, approximate reconstruction of the mean annual flood should be possible from reformulation of Equation (5):

$$Q = (0.00045\Sigma P^{3.35} D_{84}^{0.64})/s_v \quad (R^2 = 0.87)$$

(6)

in which the power index is the dependent regression variable (Williams 1984).

Before Equation (6) can be applied, it is necessary to estimate ΣP for the palaeochannels being investigated. For a modern river, measurement of the total first-order channel length in the complete active channel zone of a study reach is relatively simple. A terrace fragment will not, however, preserve the full width of the former active zone because of post-

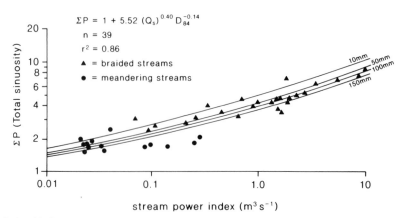

Fig. 4. Relationship between total sinuosity and stream power index (product of mean annual flood and valley gradient) for gravel-bed rivers, including single-thread and multi-thread streams.

Glen Feshie terrace palaeochannel networks

Palaeochannels – Fragment 36

Palaeochannels – Fragment 30

Palaeochannels – Fragment 32

Fig. 5. Examples of braided stream palaeochannel traces on terrace fragments in Glen Feshie, Cairngorms, Scotland.

Table 1. *Ages and palaeodischarges of braided channel systems on terrace surfaces, Glen Feshie, Cairngorms, Scotland*

Age in radiocarbon years BP	Discharge $(m^3 s^{-1})$
13 000	630
10 000	—
3600	180
1000	100
c. 100	130
Modern river	85
(95% confidence interval)	76–95

bed material and terrace gradient data are also available.

This method has been used to reconstruct flows in braided palaeochannels on terraces in Glen Feshie (Fig. 5), in the Scottish Cairngorm Mountains. Five terraces have been identified, and fragments have been dated and correlated using a soil chronosequence and ^{14}C dates (Robertson-Rintoul 1986). Estimated 'formative flows' (mean annual floods) for each dated surface are given in Table 1. These results indicate that the estimated mean annual floods associated with the late Holocene palaeochannels are similar to the present mean annual flood, and that the mean annual flood estimated by this method for the present river is close to that derived from the available gauging station data. The method therefore appears promising.

depositional erosion. Thus ΣP must be estimated without direct reference to the full active zone width. A composite dimensionless variable based on the product of channel density (D) and mean stream segment length (l_m), both of which can be measured from fragmentary evidence on terrace units, is therefore used to estimate ΣP for the palaeochannel. Being dimensionless, this index is unaffected by map scale.

For modern streams, the channel density is the total channel length divided by reach area (reach length, L times mean reach width, W). For palaeochannels the density is the palaeochannel length per unit terrace fragment area. Mean channel segment length (l_m) is obtained for a sample of complete braid channel links between nodes (junctions and bifurcations), for both modern or palaeochannels. A dimensionless relationship exists between ΣP and the product (Dl_m) for the 22 modern braided rivers used to produce Figure 3:

$$\Sigma P = 1.87(Dl_m) + 0.41 (R^2 = 0.92) \quad (7)$$

When D and l_m have been measured from braided palaeochannels preserved on a terrace fragment (Fig. 5), Equation 7 can be used to estimate ΣP even if only a partial trace remains, as long as it contains enough links to permit measurement of l_m. Equation (6) can then be used to reconstruct a flow approximately equivalent to the mean annual flood, provided that

Discussion and conclusion

Channel patterns are conveniently classified into a limited number of types, and to identify a channel by its ΣP value has less immediate meaning than to call it 'meandering' or 'braided'. However, these nominal classes are few in number, and therefore imply greater uniformity of morphology within the class than is the case in reality. There are many transitional channels whose patterns defy simple classification. A corollary of this is that slope-discharge threshold criteria (Equation 1) are based on data for clearly recognisable examples, and the 'threshold' thereby defined is at least in part an artefact of the use of nominal classes and the selection of data. The identification of a true threshold would follow discovery of discontinuous variation in continuously-measurable parameters, rather than identification of the conditions within which *a priori* discrete states exist.

The approach adopted in this paper requires further testing and refinement, but addresses at least two general issues.

(1) With suitable operational definitions and measurement and sampling procedures, it is possible to demonstrate a morphological continuum of channel pattern to parallel that discussed in relation to sedimentology by Bridge (1985).

(2) Palaeohydrological reconstruction may be undertaken using an empirical relationship between ΣP and stream power which is potentially applicable to both single- and multi-thread palaeochannels, and so does not require an arbitrary and undesirable change of method between pattern types.

References

ANTROPOVSKIY, V. I. 1972. Criterial relations of types of channel processes. *Soviet Hydrology*, **11**, 371–381.

ASHMORE, P. E. 1982. Laboratory modelling of gravel braided stream morphology. *Earth Surface Processes and Morphology*, **7**, 201–225.

BAGNOLD, R. A. 1977. Bed load transport by natural rivers. *Water Resources Research*, **13**, 303–312.

BEGIN, Z. & SCHUMM, S. A. 1984. Gradational thresholds and landform singularity: significance for Quaternary studies. *Quaternary Research*, **21**, 267–274.

BLUCK, B. J. 1976. Sedimentation in some Scottish rivers of low sinuosity. *Transactions, Royal Society of Edinburgh*, **69**, 425–456.

BRICE, J. C. 1964. *Channel patterns and terraces of the Loup River in Nebraska.* United States Geological Survey, Professional Papers, **422-D**.

BRIDGE, J. S. 1985. Palaeochannel patterns inferred from alluvial deposits: a critical evaluation. *Journal of Sedimentary Petrology*, **55**, 579–589.

CARSON, M. A. 1984. The meandering-braided threshold: a reappraisal. *Journal of Hydrology*, **73**, 315–334.

CHURCH, M. A. & JONES, D. 1982. Channel bars in gravel-bed rivers. In: HEY, R. D., BATHURST, J. C. & THORNE, C. R. (eds) *Gravel-Bed Rivers.* John Wiley & Sons, Chichester, 291–324.

——, MOORE, D. & ROOD, K. 1981. *Catalogue of alluvial river channel regime data.* Department of Geography, University of British Columbia.

——, WOLCOTT, J. & MAIZELS, J. 1990. Palaeovelocity: a parsimonious proposal. *Earth Surface Processes and Landforms*, **15**, 475–480.

ENGELUND, F. & SKOVGAARD, O. 1973. On the origin of meandering and braiding in alluvial streams. *Journal of Fluid Mechanics*, **57**, 289–302.

FAHNESTOCK, R. K. 1963. *Morphology and hydrology of a glacial stream — White River, Mount Rainier, Washington.* United States Geological Survey, Professional Papers, **422-A**.

FERGUSON, R. I. 1984. The threshold between meandering and braiding. *In*: SMITH, K. V. H. (ed) *Channels and channel control structures; Proceedings of the First International Conference on Hydraulic Design in Water Resources Engineering.* Springer Verlag, Berlin, 6.15–6.29.

—— 1987. Hydraulic and sedimentary controls on channel pattern. *In*: RICHARDS, K. S. (ed.) *River channels: environment and process.* Basil Blackwell, Oxford, 129–158.

HENDERSON, F. M. 1961. Stability of alluvial channels.

American Society of Civil Engineers, Journal of the Hydraulics Division, **87**, 109–138.

HOWARD, A. D., KEETCH, M. E. & VINCENT, C. L. 1970. Topological and geometric properties of braided streams. *Water Resources Research*, **6**, 1674–1688.

KELLERHALS, R., CURCH, M. & BRAY, D. I. 1976. Classification and analysis of river processes. *American Society of Civil Engineers, Journal of the Hydraulics Division*, **102**, 813–829.

LE BA HONG & DAVIES, T. R. H. 1979. A study of stream braiding., *Geological Society of America Bulletin*, **82**, 1251–1266.

LEOPOLD, L. B. & WOLMAN, M. G. 1957. *River channel patterns — braided, meandering and straight.* United States Geological Survey Professional Papers, **282-B**.

MOSLEY, M. P. 1982. Analysis of the effect of changing discharge on channel morphology and instream use in a braided river, Ohau River, New Zealand. *Water Resources Research*, **18**, 800–812.

PARKER, G. 1976. On the cause and characteristic scale of meandering and braiding in rivers. *Journal of Fluid Mechanics*, **76**, 459–480.

RICHARDS, K. 1982. *Rivers: form and process in alluvial channels.* Routledge, London.

—— 1990. Fluvial geomorphology: the initial entrainment of bed material in gravel-bed rivers. *Progress in Physical Geography*, **14**, 395–415.

ROBERTSON-RINTOUL, M. S. E. 1986. A quantitative soil-stratigraphic approach to the correlation and dating of Postglacial river terraces in Glen Feshie, Southwest Cairngorms. *Earth Surface Processes and Landforms*, **11**, 605–617.

RUST, B. R. 1978. A classification of alluvial channel systems. *In*: MIALL, A. D. (ed.) *Fluvial Sedimentology.* Memoirs of the Canadian Society of Petroleum Geologists, **5**, 187–198.

SCHUMM, S. A. 1963. Sinuosity of alluvial rivers on the Great Plains. *Geological Society of America Bulletin*, **74**, 1089–1100.

—— 1968. *River adjustment to altered hydrologic regimen — Murrumbidgee and palaeochannels, Australia.* United States Geological Survey, Professional Papers, **598**.

WILLIAMS, G. P. 1984. Palaeohydrologic equations for rivers. *In*: COSTA, J. E. & FLEISCHER, P. J. (eds) *Developments and applications of geomorphology.* Springer Verlag, Berlin, 343–367.

WILLIAMS, P. F. & RUST, B. R. 1969. The sedimentology of a braided river. *Journal of Sedimentary Petrology*, **39**, 649–679.

Mechanisms of anabranch avulsion within gravel-bed braided rivers: observations from a scaled physical model

J. O. LEDDY[1,2], P. J. ASHWORTH[1] & J. L. BEST[2]

[1] *School of Geography, The University, Leeds LS2 9JT, UK*

[2] *Department of Earth Sciences, The University, Leeds LS2 9JT, UK*

Abstract: The physical modelling of gravel-bed braided rivers, using a 1 : 20 Froude scale model, permits analysis of the types and relative occurrence of different avulsion mechanisms. Anabranch avulsion within braided rivers involves three main mechanisms: *choking avulsion* caused by blockage of one channel by a sediment lobe, *constriction avulsion* produced by deflection, confinement and subsequent diversion of the flow by a barform and *apex avulsion* following erosion at the outside of sinuous thalwegs and confined meander bends. Each avulsion mechanism is described and analysis of the abundance of each type illustrates choking avulsion to be predominant without braided rivers. Three factors are found to control anabranch avulsions, namely flow discharge, sediment flux and floodplain topography. These are briefly discussed together with the implications of avulsion type for the alluvial architecture of gravelly braided alluvium.

Avulsion within braided rivers occurs at all channel scales and is instrumental in dictating the spatial and temporal distribution of sediment within the braidplain. An understanding of the conditions which cause avulsion is important in many respects, such as the need to predict the likely loss of agricultural land (Gilvear this volume; Gilvear & Winterbottom 1992), the influence of avulsion upon the rates and location of bank erosion (Thorne *et al.* this volume) and the role of avulsion in preservation of sediment within ancient braided alluvium. Within hydrocarbon reservoirs that owe their origin to deposition within braided rivers (see Martin this volume), the type and frequency of channel avulsions may help determine the characteristics of heterogeneity, and hence permeability, within the reservoir.

Two basic types of avulsion can be defined in braided rivers: (i) those which involve a shift in the position of the *entire* braided river system, and (ii) those which concern shifts in the position of the anabranch channels *within* the active channel belt (see Richards *et al.* this volume). Large scale switches in channel network position may be due to both autocyclic processes (for example, local sediment supply at a nodal point in the network (Macklin & Lewin 1989) or ice-jams (Smith *et al.* 1989)), or allocyclic controls such as tectonic tilt or upstream alluvial fan progradation. This type of channel belt avulsion has been described in several case studies (Smith *et al.* 1989; McCarthy *et al.* 1992) and is the type of avulsion considered within several models of alluvial channel belt aggradation (Allen 1978;

Leeder 1978; Bridge & Leeder 1979; Bridge & Mackey 1993). Avulsion of individual anabranches *within* the braided river controls the short-term shifts in channel position and often involves processes which lead to the diversion of flow from an active channel into an inactive, older channel or area of topographically lower elevation. Anabranch avulsion usually involves temporal and spatial changes in the local sediment supply with subsequent feedback on the local channel cross-sectional geometry (Cheetham 1979; Ferguson & Werritty 1983; Ashworth & Ferguson 1986).

Despite the importance of avulsion within the braided network, few studies have been able to investigate the processes of channel switching. Knowledge upon avulsion is largely confined to very short term (i.e. flood by flood) observations with little opportunity for longer term observations across the entire braided system. Additionally, most field studies are necessarily limited to observations and measurements before and after the avulsion event and cannot document continuous change *during* avulsion, a problem compounded by the difficulty of observing planform changes in highly turbid, flood peak conditions. Scaled physical models offer an opportunity to overcome many of these problems and to document the mechanisms of avulsion over all the affected channels during an avulsion event. This paper describes observations and results from a scaled physical model of a gravel-bed braided river and identifies three basic mechanisms of anabranch avulsion. These mechanisms and their relative occurrence are

From Best, J. L. & Bristow, C. S. (eds), 1993, *Braided Rivers*, Geological Society Special Publication No. **75**, pp. 119–127.

described and some implications for braided river aggradation are discussed.

Physical modelling of gravel-bed braided rivers

The background of the physical model used in these experiments is not outlined in detail here. A full discussion of the principles of scale modelling, of the experimental equipment and model-prototype similarity is given in Ashworth *et al.* (1993). The experiments were conducted in a 5.5 m long × 3.5 m wide stream table (Fig. 1) which rests upon adjustable legs that allow setting of the downstream flume slope. Water and sediment are fed into the flume through a 0.40 m wide channel and exit through a wire

mesh to a sump tank. Discharge is controlled by a gate valve in the supply line. The field prototype of the Sunwapta River, Alberta, Canada was used as a basis for the scaling of grain size and channel geometries. A scale ratio of 1:20 was used in all experiments. In contrast to much past scale modelling, these experiments used a grain size scaling that encompassed the silt fractions of the prototype sediment through use of non-cohesive silica flour with a minimum grain size of 1 μm. The issue of grain size scaling is addressed fully in Ashworth *et al.* (1993). The grain size distribution used in these experiments had a D_{50} of 0.28 mm (equivalent to 5.6 mm in the field) and a sorting coefficient (Folk 1974) of 0.98.

All experiments followed the principles of Froude scale modelling which, by relaxation of

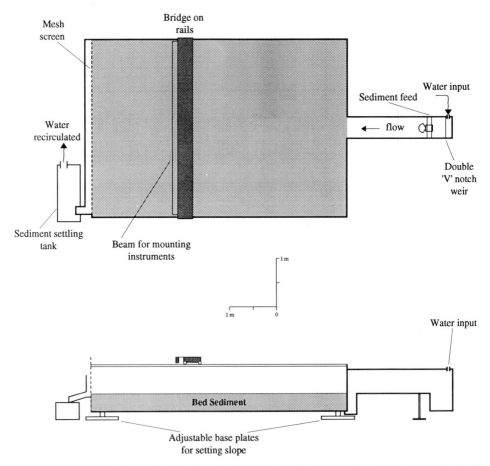

Fig. 1. Planform and sectional sketches of the Leeds stream table. Flow enters the channel over a double 'V' notch weir and exits through a mesh screen. Observations of the channel pattern are made using overhead and oblique time-lapse video cameras whilst bed and water surface measurements can be made from a point gauge mounted on the instrument trolley.

the similarity of the flow and particle Reynolds numbers, enables the Froude number to be kept in the same range between model and prototype. Froude scale modelling of braided rivers has been successfully used within past flume modelling studies (e.g. Ashmore 1982, 1991*a*, this volume; Davies & Lee 1988; Hoey & Sutherland 1991; Young & Davies 1991). Conditions within the model channels were found to closely replicate those within the field (mean values of flume variables: bed slope: 2%; Froude number: 0.50; flow Reynolds number: 2400; grain Reynolds number: 36; mean flow depth: D_{50} ratio: 42) with flows being largely subcritical although trains of standing waves did occur in the principal thalwegs, a feature also evident within the Sunwapta prototype at high stages.

A braided network developed naturally from an initial straight channel dredged down the centre of the flume. Braiding commonly progressed through development of alternate bar chute cut-offs and dissection of lobate bars, as found by Ashmore (1991*a*). Observations of changing channel planform and avulsion were recorded from video cameras located directly above the centre and obliquely to one side of the flume. Measurements of channel avulsion commenced only after a multichannel network had developed fully, typically after 6–9 hours, and concerned only those areas unaffected by entrance and exit effects of the flume (approximately a 2.5 m wide × 3 m long area). Analysis of the video records enables classification of the major types of anabranch avulsion and their relative abundance. The data reported here cover 10 experimental runs encompassing constant discharge experiments and others with simple, stepped hydrographs. Full details of the hydrograph type, model channel morphology and depositional niches are outlined in Ashworth *et al.* (1993).

Mechanisms of anabranch channel avulsion

Three principal mechanisms of channel avulsion within the braided network can be determined from the video records. These avulsions are termed choking, constriction and apex avulsion. Time-lapse sequences of each, taken directly from the video records, are presented and discussed below. A line diagram of each avulsion type is given using an example selected from the video records. These examples are, however, typical of the other avulsions within each avulsion grouping.

Choking avulsion (Fig. 2)

This mechanism involves choking and blocking of a channel through migration of a sediment lobe into an active channel and subsequent diversion of the main flow to a different course. It is associated with the chute-bar unit common to all braided rivers (Southard *et al.* 1984; Ferguson *et al.* 1992). When a sediment lobe passes through a confined and narrow deep chute and enters a zone of flow expansion, it decelerates with diverging flow transporting sediment to the lobate avalanche face (Fig. 2, T1). Such bar forms have been described as 'tongue' structures (Rundle 1985) and 'lobate bars' by Ashmore (1982) in the initial stages of braiding. Downstream migration of the lobe continues, perhaps through migration of avalanche slip-faces, until parts of the bar become emergent, thereby concentrating flow into several chutes which dissect the bar margin (Fig. 2, T2). Eventually, either through development of an asymmetry in flow (Fig. 2, T2), or ponding of flow behind the lobe, the flow seeks the lowest point on the active floodplain (and hence the highest lateral bed slope) and the discharge becomes concentrated on one side of the lobe (Fig. 2, T3), this leading to possible enlargement of the newly occupied channel as it receives more of the flow. Part of the original lobe of sediment which triggered the avulsion is preserved at the head of the former channel (Fig. 2, T4). Subsequent infill of the old channel will principally involve deposition of fine-grained sediment carried overbank and deposited from suspension in this new slack-water area. If subsequently preserved, the plug at the head of the former channel may have a vertical sequence of basal gravel lag, coarse-grained foresets (which may be graded) and overbank fines. The abandoned channel-fill downstream of this plug would consist of fines lying abruptly upon the old basal channel gravels.

This process of choking avulsion is probably the most commonly described channel switching mechanism (see later). Cheetham (1979) illustrated how two distributaries around a mid-channel bar compete with each other until one becomes a 'bottleneck' and infills. Ferguson & Werritty (1983) describe how aggradation of a riffle front (analogous to the lobe in Fig. 2) can promote ponding and subsequent diversion of flow to the side of the riffle crest, hence initiating avulsion into the favoured channel. Warburton *et al.* (this volume) also describe how sediment lobes may block and cause the abandonment of channels in gravel-bed rivers. A variant on the

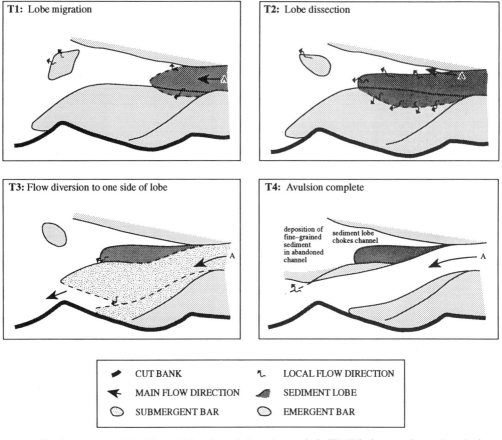

Fig. 2. The development of choking avulsion through four time periods (T1–T4). (see text for explanation)

choking avulsion mechanism occurs when the migration and aggradation of the sediment lobe is so rapid that the flow does not have time to rework or dissect the edge of the lobe. In this case, the entire channel is blocked by the incoming bar which leads to high rates of local aggradation and rapid switching of the channel to an entirely new course. Hence, choking avulsion need not be caused solely by *local* erosional and depositional processes but may also be influenced by upstream sediment fluxes and network development.

Constriction avulsion (Fig. 3)

This type of avulsion involves constriction of one channel by the inward movement of a lobe from an adjacent channel which forces deflection of flow, rapid bank erosion and channel diversion into a topographically lower area. The most favourable sites for constriction avulsion are channel junctions where one of the confluent channels may become dominant either in discharge or sediment supply (e.g. Krigström 1962; Hein & Walker 1977). This difference in discharge and/or sediment supply rate and the subsequent effects upon bed morphology is similar to junctions in single thread channels which suffer non-coincident floods from the contributing channels (e.g. Reid *et al.* 1989). Even in multi-braided rivers, individual channels respond to floods at different rates since the discharge in any one channel is determined by the direction and degree to which upstream low lying bars deflect the flow over them.

Constriction avulsion begins (Fig. 3, T1–T2) with encroachment of a bar avalanche face and/ or lobe from the most active channel (channel B) into the course of the other (channel A), possibly in response to upstream changes in local spatial/temporal sediment supply. Reduction in

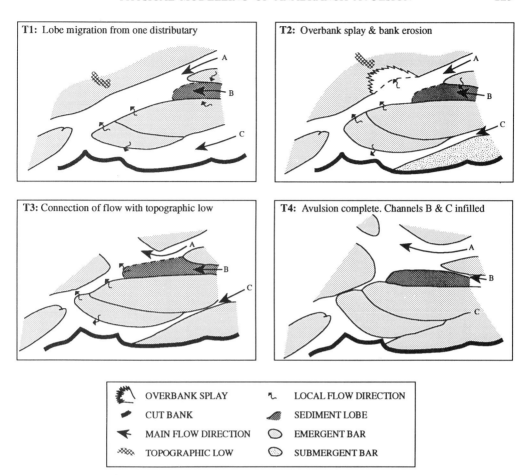

Fig. 3. The development of constriction avulsion through four time periods (T1–T4). (see text for explanation)

the cross-sectional area of channel A and flow deflection by the advancing lobe front initially promotes overspilling onto the outer banktop forming an overbank splay (Fig. 3, T2). Such overbank flows before avulsion have also been noted in the scale model experiments of Ashmore (1982). Continued constriction, flow deflection/acceleration and resultant rapid outer bank undercutting leads to the flow intersecting an older, topographically lower area (Fig. 3, T3). Once flow is diverted into this new course, the original anabranch channel is either blocked or infilled as shallow, diverging flow over the partly submerged lateral bars and lobe fronts seals the exit from the former confluence site (Fig. 3, T4). A field example of avulsion through constriction and erosion at nodes in the braided network is given by Warburton *et al.* (this volume).

Apex avulsion (Fig. 4)

Apex avulsion is connected with flow accelera-tion around a sinuous thalweg, subsequent lateral or point bar accretion on the inside of the bend and erosion and flow diversion on the out-side of the bend. Development of a locally sinuous thalweg (and therefore laterally accreted deposits which we have documented in planform and section (Ashworth *et al.* 1993)), promotes deposition of a point bar and bank erosion at the bend apex (Fig. 4, T1 & T2). The presence of meandering channel characteristics within the individual channels of braided systems has been well documented (e.g. Rundle 1985; Bridge 1985, this volume) and even flow around medial bars has been viewed and modelled as flow within two back-to-back meanders (Ashmore 1982; Ashworth *et al.* 1992;

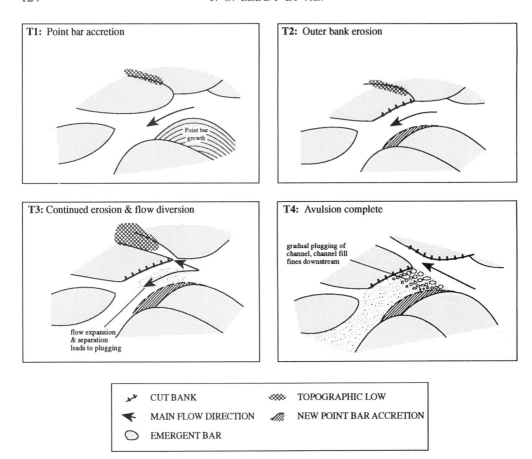

Fig. 4. The development of apex avulsion through four time periods (T1–T4). (see text for explanation)

Bridge & Gabel 1992). Evolution of the sinuous channel may lead to translation or extension of the thalweg accompanied by further point bar growth. Continued bank erosion leads to formation of an area of flow expansion downstream of the bend apex, usually accompanied by flow separation (Fig. 4, T3). The flow in the main channel becomes increasingly directed against the outer bank with deposition occurring within channel immediately downstream. Further bank retreat and reoccupation of an older channel/topographic low leads to a complete avulsion with the former channel eventually being blocked and filled with fines (Fig. 4, T4). Plugging and fill of the abandoned channel may therefore be contemporaneous with the avulsion process, this being in contrast to the choking avulsion described above.

Occurrence of anabranch avulsions

Video records for all the documented avulsions permit analysis of the relative occurrence of each type of anabranch avulsion mechanism for two orders of channel size (Fig. 5). The first order channel is defined as the inlet channel with second and third order anabranches being successively smaller channels that braid from the initial feeder channel. This histogram illustrates that choking avulsion is by far the dominant mechanism of avulsion within the gravel-bed model, accounting for over 70% of avulsions recorded in both second and third order channels. Constriction and rotation avulsion were much less common and each accounted for only 10–15% of the total avulsions. These similar results from both second and third order channels suggest that the mechanisms of anabranch avulsion may be scale independent and hence can be used as a classification scheme for all sizes of braided river channel. An explanation for the dominance of choking avulsion may lie in the numerical abundance of gravel lobes within the braided system that promote choking avulsion as compared to the number of sinuous reaches (for apex avulsion) and junctions with

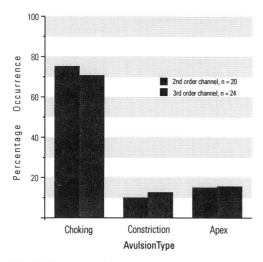

Fig. 5. Histogram of the occurrence of each avulsion type for second and third order channels. The inlet channel to the flume is defined as the first order channel.

unequal flow/sediment contributions from the confluent channels (often the principal sites of constriction avulsion). Bedload transport in the model was predominantly in the form of submerged lobate bars or gravel sheets, similar to previous observations in both natural channels (Hein & Walker 1977) and laboratory models (Ashmore 1982). Some of these lobes form continuous trains migrating down channel whilst others override each other and stack upon slower moving or stationary lobes. Since choking avulsion is the most common form of channel switching in braided rivers, it may be the case that the sedimentary architecture of avulsion fills will be dominated by coarse plugs of sediment which have blocked the channel and subsequent fine-grained fill in the abandoned channel.

Discussion

The observations detailed in this paper have sought to identify the principal mechanisms of anabranch avulsions within braided rivers. The controls upon avulsion are related to three factors: flow discharge, sediment flux and floodplain topography. The role of floodplain topography is clearly an important factor in influencing the probability of avulsion and in dictating the course of the new avulsive channel. Whilst the spatial and temporal variability of flow and sediment discharge are the ultimate

cause of the avulsion, these variations are often influenced largely by upstream channel changes. The reviews of Gomez *et al.* (1989) and Hoey (1992) clearly show that bedload transport occurs in a series of pulses at different temporal and spatial scales. These range from 'instantaneous' pulses associated with stochastic variations in entrainment due to turbulence, through to larger scale 'megaform' shifts in large sedimentation zones (Hoey 1992). The work of Ashmore (1988, 1991*b*), Hoey & Sutherland (1991) and Young & Davies (1991) all demonstrate large scale bedload pulses that are associated with bar creation, dissection and reworking in braided rivers. Such pulses may be several hours in duration in the field and can be expected to have a significant influence upon local sediment budgets and avulsion downstream.

One question that is not specifically addressed by these experiments is whether avulsion is a stochastic or deterministic process. Ferguson & Werritty (1983) suggest that whilst the potential for an avulsion may be recognized beforehand, prediction of the longer-term behaviour is 'almost impossible' (p. 192). Results from the current modelling experiments (Figs 2–4) illustrate that there may be characteristic trends to channel avulsion but that minor changes in channel pattern and local sediment flux may radically change the type of avulsion that occurs at any one site, a point evident from the field study of Laronne & Duncan (1992). Recognition of potential avulsion sites may be aided by repeated planimetric and cross-section surveys (Ferguson & Werritty 1983) or from evidence such as overbank flooding adjacent to sites which are undergoing constriction (Ashmore 1982; Fig. 3, T2, this paper).

Several numerical modelling approaches to predict long-term channel behaviour (e.g. Bridge & Leeder 1979; Bridge & Mackey 1993) assume a stochastic switching of channels which seek the lowest adjacent point on the floodplain. The present experiments support this contention and emphasise the strong influence of inherited floodplain topography on channel avulsion. These results also highlight the need to more fully understand the relationship between migration and aggradation of macroforms and the type, location and timing of channel avulsion. The number and relative occurrence of different avulsion mechanisms will largely determine the changing channel pattern within braided rivers and therefore control the dispersal of sediment in both the abandoned channels and in the active downstream channels and bars. The type of avulsion will also determine the nature of the abandoned channel fill, by providing cases in which waning flow sequences fill the channel (for instance in the gradual plugging of a channel in an apex avulsion), or provision of sites in which the channel is plugged at its entrance by a lobe of sediment (choking avulsion).

Recognition of the processes that may produce these different channel-fill patterns is important not only in the interpretation of ancient braided alluvium in outcrop (for example, the rapid abandonment and inhibition of channel-fill sequences in the Carboniferous South Bar Formation; Rust & Gibling 1990) but also in the recognition of different channel fill types in the subsurface (for an example in a meandering distributary channel, see Dreyer 1990). The geometry, abundance and type of fill within abandoned channels will, along with the prevailing aggradation regime, determine the nature of fine-grained heterogeneities in these depositional niches which may occur across all scales of channel. Physical modelling, especially if combined with simulation of aggradation within braided systems (e.g. Ashworth *et al.* 1993), may provide a suitable methodology by which to examine the controls upon the processes and products of avulsion within braided rivers. The physical modelling of aggradation may also provide guidelines for the recognition of avulsive fills within the ancient record.

We would like to thank British Petroleum for their funding of the research programme at Leeds. In particular, G. Geehan, M. Eller, P. Hirst and M. Dawson have been most constructive and supportive in their comments at various stages of this research. P.J.A. and J.L.B. thank the Royal Society for a grant which enabled purchase of the video camera system. J.O.L. acknowledges financial support from British Petroleum and the University of Leeds. We are grateful for the constructive reviews and suggestions of T. Hoey, C. Bristow and I. Reid which have improved the clarity of the paper.

References

ALLEN, J. R. L. 1978. Studies in fluviatile sedimentation: an exploratory quantitative model for the architecture of avulsion-controlled alluvial suites. *Sedimentary Geology*, **21**, 129–147.

ASHMORE, P. E. 1982. Laboratory modelling of gravel braided stream morphology. *Earth Surface Processes and Landforms*, **7**, 201–225.

—— 1988. Bedload transport in braided gravel-bed stream models. *Earth Surface Processes and Landforms*, **13**, 677–695.

—— 1991a. How do gravel-bed rivers braid? *Canadian Journal of Earth Sciences*, **28**, 326–341.

—— 1991b. Channel morphology and bed load pulses in braided, gravel-bed streams. *Geografiska Annaler*, **73A**, 37–52.

—— 1993. Anabranch confluence kinetics and sedimentation processes within gravel braided streams. *This volume.*

ASHWORTH, P. J. & FERGUSON, R. I. 1986. Interrelationships of channel processes, changes and sediments in a proglacial river. *Geografiska Annaler*, **68**, 361–371.

——, BEST, J. L., LEDDY, J. O. & GEEHAN, G. W. 1993. The physical modelling of braided rivers and deposition of fine grained sediment. *In*: KIRKBY, M. J. (ed.) *Process Models and Theoretical Geomorphology.* Wiley and Sons Ltd. In press.

——, FERGUSON, R. I. & POWELL, M. D. 1992. Bedload transport and sorting in braided rivers. *In*: BILLI, P., HEY, R. D., THORNE, C. R. & TACCONI, P. (eds) *Dynamics of Gravel-Bed Rivers.* Wiley and Sons Ltd, 497–513.

BRIDGE, J. S. 1985. Paleochannel patterns inferred from alluvial deposits: a critical evaluation. *Journal of Sedimentary Petrology*, **55**, 579–589.

—— 1993. The interaction between channel geometry, water flow, sediment transport, erosion and deposition in braided rivers. *This volume.*

—— & GABEL, S. L. 1992. Flow and sediment dynamics in a low sinuosity braided river: Calamus River, Nebraska Sandhills. *Sedimentology*, **39**, 125–142.

—— & LEEDER, M. R. 1979. A simulation model of alluvial stratigraphy. *Sedimentology*, **26**, 617–644.

—— & MACKEY, S. 1993. A revised alluvial stratigraphy model. *In*: MARZO, M. & PUIDEFABREGAS, C. (eds) *Alluvial Sedimentology.* International Association of Sedimentologists Special Publications, **17**, (in press).

CHEETHAM, G. H. 1979. Flow competence in relation to stream channel form and braiding. *Geological Society of America Bulletin*, **90**, 877–886.

DAVIES, T. R. & LEE, A. L. 1988. Physical hydraulic modelling of width reduction and bed level change in braided rivers. *Journal of Hydrology (New Zealand)*, **27**, 113–127.

DREYER, T. 1990. Sandbody dimensions and infill sequences of stable, humid-climate delta plain channels. *In*: *North Sea Oil and Gas Reservoirs - II.* Graham and Trotman, 337–351.

FERGUSON, R. I. & WERRITTY, A. 1983. Bar development and channel change in the gravelly River Feshie, Scotland. *In*: COLLINSON, J. D. & LEWIN, J. (eds) *Modern and Ancient Fluvial Systems.* International Association of Sedimentologists Special Publications, **6**, 181–193.

——, ASHWORTH, P. J., PAOLA, C. & PRESTEGAARD, K. L. 1992. Measurements in a braided river chute and lobe: I. Flow pattern, sediment transport and channel change. *Water Resources Research*, **28**, 7, 1877–1866.

FOLK, R. L. 1974. *Petrology of Sedimentary Rocks.* Hemphills, Austin, Texas.

GILVEAR, D. J. 1993. River management and conservation issues on formerly braided river systems: the case of the River Tay Scotland. *This volume.*

—— & WINTERBOTTOM, S. J. 1992. Channel change and flood events since 1783 on the regulated River Tay, Scotland: implications for flood hazard management. *Regulated Rivers: Research and Management*, **7**, 247–260.

GOMEZ, B., NAFF, R. L. & HUBBELL, D. W. (1989). Temporal variations in bedload transport rates associated with the migration of bedforms. *Earth Surface Processes and Landforms*, **14**, 135–156.

HEIN, F. J. & WALKER, R. G. 1977. Bar evolution and development of stratification in the gravelly, braided, Kicking Horse River, British Columbia. *Canadian Journal of Earth Sciences*, **14**, 562–570.

HOEY, T. B. 1992. Temporal variations in bedload transport rates and sediment storage in gravel-bed rivers. *Progress in Physical Geography*, **16**, 319–338.

—— & SUTHERLAND, A. J. 1991. Channel morphology and bedload pulses in braided rivers: a laboratory study. *Earth Surface Processes and Landforms*, **16**, 447–462.

KRIGSTRÖM, A. 1962. Geomorphological studies of sandur plains and their braided rivers in Iceland. *Geografiska Annaler*, **44**, 328–346.

LARONNE, J. B. & DUNCAN, M. J. 1992. Bedload transport paths and gravel bar formation. *In*: BILLI, P., HEY, R. D., THORNE, C. R. & TACONNI, P. (eds) *Dynamics of Gravel-Bed Rivers*. Wiley and Sons Ltd, 177–200.

LEEDER, M. R. 1978. A quantitative stratigraphical model for alluvium, with specific reference to channel deposit density and interconnectedness. *In*: MIALL, A. D. (ed.) *Fluvial Sedimentology*. Memoirs of the Canadian Society of Petroleum Geologists, **5**, 587–596.

MACKLIN, M. G. & LEWIN, J. 1989. Sediment transfer and transformation of an alluvial valley floor: the River South Tyne, Northumbria, UK. *Earth Surface Processes and Landforms*, **14**, 233–246.

MARTIN, J. 1993. A review of braided fluvial hydrocarbon reservoirs: the petroleum engineer's perspective. *This volume.*

MCCARTHY, T. S., ELLERY, W. N. & STANISTREET, I. G. 1992. Avulsion mechanisms on the Okavango fan, Botswana: the control of a fluvial system by vegetation. *Sedimentology*, **39**, 779–796.

REID, I., BEST, J. L. & FROSTICK, L. E. 1989. Floods and flood sediments at river confluences. *In*: BEVAN, K. & CARLING, P. A. (eds) *Floods: Hydrological Sedimentology and Geomorphological Implications*. Wiley and Sons, Chichester, 135–150.

RICHARDS, K. S., CHANDRA, S. & FRIEND, P. F. 1993. Avulsive channel systems: characteristics and examples. *This volume.*

RUNDLE, A. 1985. Mechanisms of braiding. *Zietschrift fur Geomorphologie Suppl.-Bd*, **55**, 1–14.

RUST, B. R. & GIBLING, M. R. 1990. Braidplain evolution in the Pennsylvanian South Bar Formation, Sydney Basin, Nova Scotia, Canada. *Journal of Sedimentary Petrology*, **60**, 1, 59–72.

SOUTHARD, J. B., SMITH, N. D. & KUHNLE, R. A. 1984. Chutes and lobes: newly identified elements in braiding in shallow gravelly streams. *In*: KOSTER, E. H. & STEEL, R. J. (eds) *Sedimentology of Gravels and Conglomerates*. Canadian Society of Petroleum Geologists Memoirs, **10**, 51–59.

SMITH, N. D., CROSS, T. A., DUFFICY, J. P. & CLOUGH, S. R. 1989. Anatomy of an avulsion. *Sedimentology*, **36**, 1–24.

THORNE, C. R., RUSSELL, A. P. G. & ALAM, M. K. 1993. Planform pattern and channel evolution of the Brahmaputra river, Bangladesh. *This volume.*

WARBURTON, J., DAVIES, T. R. H. & MANDL, M. G. 1993. A meso-scale field investigation of channel change and floodplain characteristics in an upland braided gravel-bed river, New Zealand. *This volume.*

YOUNG, W. J. & DAVIES, T. R. H. 1991. Bedload transport processes in a braided gravel-bed river model. *Earth Surface Processes and Landforms*, **16**, 499–511.

Anabranch confluence kinetics and sedimentation processes in gravel-braided streams

PETER ASHMORE

*Department of Geography, University of Western Ontario,
London, Ontario, Canada, N6A 5C2*

Abstract: Based on observations of channel changes and bar sedimentation in small-scale hydraulic models, it is argued that confluence zones play the key role in sedimentation patterns and processes in gravel-bed braided streams. The control is exerted because confluences are nodes in the channel network and therefore sedimentation and channel pattern downstream of a confluence are mediated by the response of the confluence to changes in discharge, bedload, and planform of the upstream confluent channels. Examples of confluence kinetics and sedimentation occurring over time-scales equivalent to days or weeks of competent flows in the prototype are described for the first time. Renewed braiding is directly associated with flow expansion downstream of confluences and triggered by migration of unit bars or bedload sheets through the confluence. Lateral translation of confluences may lead to the accretion of point bar complexes, while downstream translation often causes erosion or complete removal of existing bars. The effects of a change in position or orientation of one of the upstream channels are similar to those of confluence translation. In addition to the changes caused by progressive shifting of the confluence zone, a second group of adjustments involving changes in the discharge or bedload transport rate in the confluent channels is also common. These include: rotation of the scour axis redirecting flow and sediment movement downstream of the confluence and leading to downstream channel avulsion in some cases; a change in the total discharge of the confluence causing expansion or contraction of the scour zone; and the virtual abandonment of one of the confluent channels resulting in obliteration of the scour hole. Observing a confluence for several hours in the model leaves the visual impression of sediment being distributed downstream of the confluence rather like water spurting from a hose as it plays about. This descriptive synthesis of confluence kinetics provides the basis for analysis and quantitative modelling of confluence dynamics, which requires the acquisition of field data, as well as further laboratory experiments.

Despite recognition of the importance of confluence zones to the morphology and dynamics of braided rivers (Ashmore 1982, Davoren & Mosley 1986), until recently research has concentrated on the functional prediction of scour depth at confluences, to the exclusion of, perhaps more significant, aspects of anabranch confluence behaviour. Detailed field measurements of confluence flow structure, and patterns of shear stress and sediment transport, that might form the basis for comprehensive models of confluence dynamics (Davoren & Mosley 1986; Ashmore *et al.* 1992; Ferguson *et al.* 1992; Ashworth *et al.* 1992), have only just begun to appear. To these should be added the detailed studies of flow structure at fixed tributary confluences (Roy & Bergeron 1990) that may provide some insight into the behaviour of anabranch confluences. In the sedimentological literature, sedimentation processes at anabranch confluences have been largely ignored (Bristow *et al.* in press). None of these studies have provided data on the interaction of chang-

ing morphology and transport patterns in confluences. In addition, concentration on small-scale studies of confluence flow structure and sediment transport ignores the broader, and longer term, patterns of channel change and sedimentation associated with changes in confluence form and location. These longer term processes constitute a major component of the sedimentation processes in braided streams. Apart from the contribution to the fundamental understanding of braided river mechanics, the analysis of confluences zone processes may also have applications in economic geology because of the preferential accumulation of heavy minerals downstream of confluences (Mosley & Schumm 1977). Prediction of the location and extent of these placer deposits may be enhanced by knowledge of the patterns of channel migration and sedimentation associated with confluences.

While braided river anabranch confluences share many of the features of fixed tributary confluences, anabranch confluences are much more

From Best, J. L. & Bristow, C. S. (eds), 1993, *Braided Rivers*, Geological Society
Special Publication No. **75**, pp. 129–146.

129

variable in form and have one additional, and key, attribute: rapid adjustability to the changing discharge, bedload, position, orientation and morphology of the confluent channels. Thus, anabranch confluences can reorientate, translate laterally and downstream, and perhaps disappear and reappear in new locations. Fixed geometry confluences are much more restricted in their adjustability. In laboratory models these changes in form can take place in a matter of minutes or hours, which translate into periods of hours or tens of hours in the field prototype (Ashmore 1985). A variety of sedimentation processes and features are the direct product of this adjustability. The longer term behaviour of confluences (confluence kinetics) has not been described in detail. Ultimately, it might be possible to make an explicit link between the longer term kinetics, and models of confluence flow structure and bedload transport. There is an obvious analogy here with the contrast between descriptive models of meander evolution over decades and recently-developed quantitative models of flow and sediment transport in bends (e.g. Smith & McLean 1984).

The importance of anabranch confluences to braided river sedimentation processes arises because they are funnels for the movement of bed load between successive areas of sedimentation (Davoren & Mosley 1986; Ashmore 1991a) and the influence of bedload transport rate, the downstream distribution of transported sediment and local sorting patterns. They are also the areas of deepest scour of the bed and often have bars deposited immediately downstream, from which renewed braiding may develop (Smith 1973; Hein & Walker 1977; Ashmore 1982; Ashmore & Parker 1983; Davoren & Mosley 1986; Ferguson et al. 1992). They are one of the few places in gravel braided streams where flow is sufficiently deep to allow the development of avalanche faces at unit bar margins. The pool-bar (or chute-lobe) unit is now recognized as a fundamental building block of braided stream morphology (Ashmore 1982; Southard et al. 1984; Davoren & Mosley 1986), from which larger bar complexes (lateral and medial) grow (Bluck 1974; Smith 1974; Ashmore 1982). In addition, many sequences of avulsion and channel switching are initiated by confluence reorientation and migration (Ashmore 1985).

The connection between confluence kinetics and complex (braid) bar sedimentation has only been recognized in the literature in a very general sense (Coleman 1969). This aspect of confluence behaviour (distinct from short-term investigations of confluence flow structure in a

stable morphology) is a key element of braided river mechanics and must be incorporated into conceptual and mathematical models of braided river sedimentation, but the phenomena have first to be described in detail. The primary objective of this paper is to provide this descriptive base from which analytical work might proceed. This is preceded by a brief review of existing knowledge of the morphology, flow and sediment movement of anabranch confluences, which forms the basis for understanding the phenomena of confluence kinetics. The descriptions are based mainly on examples from small-scale hydraulic (Froude scaled) models of gravel braided streams in which confluences are completely self-formed. The laboratory examples are drawn from the photographic and video record of the experiments of Ashmore (1985) and supplemented by field examples from the Sunwapta River, Canada. The modelling principles and details of the flume are described in Ashmore (1985) and briefly in several subsequent papers. The model channels successfully reproduce the important features of confluence morphology and sedimentation. However, the model bed material is truncated at the fine tail and therefore the model does not reproduce the behaviour of the sand fraction of the prototype bed material.

Anabranch confluence morphology and kinetics

General considerations

Anabranch confluence geometry is highly variable (Fig. 1), and seldom do confluences resemble the classic Y shape which has been the subject of most quantitative work. Confluence morphology is strongly influenced by several variables including the total and relative discharges of the confluent channels, bedload delivery to the confluence, sediment mobility (boundary shear stress and particle size distribution) and plan geometry (confluence angle) (Mosley 1976; Ashmore 1982; Ashmore & Parker 1983; Best 1988; Bristow et al. in press). To this list should be added the potential for variation in the number of confluent channels and their relative position, which gives almost infinite possible arrangements. Description of these various forms may be a fairly arid pursuit, but recognition of the variability is important to the explanation of braided river dynamics. Presumably each form has a unique pattern of boundary shear stress and bedload transport, but from comparison of the dynamics of various

Fig. 1. Vertical and oblique photographs of Sunwapta River, Alberta, Canada, showing a variety of confluence planforms (some examples are highlighted by the short arrows). On the oblique photograph, scale is indicated by the two-lane road in the bottom left corner of the photograph. Long arrows indicate general flow direction.

forms some general predictive theory on confluence mechanics might emerge.

Despite the wide range of confluence form, for the sake of simplicity, and because there are few data on more complex forms, the typical features of confluence form are best described using the simple, symmetrical Y form. Best (1986), Roy & DeSerres (1989) and Bristow *et al.* (in press) provide summary descriptions and illustrations of the major features. Bed morphology

is dominated by a characteristic spoon-shaped (at relatively high confluence angle) or trough-shaped (at relatively low confluence angle) scour hole in the centre of the confluence (Ashmore & Parker 1983; Best 1986). Scour depth is primarily a function of confluence angle and discharge of the confluent channels (Mosley 1976; Ashmore & Parker 1983; Best 1988). Often one, or both, confluent streams build an avalanche face bar (similar to Krigström's (1962) tributary bar) into the confluence (Ashmore & Parker 1983; Best 1988). In laboratory confluences, the extent of progradation of avalanche faces is least when the two confluent channels are of similar size and the confluence angle if comparatively high (Best 1988). If the channels are of unequal size and the confluence angle is comparatively an avalanche face may prograde into the confluence (Best 1988) displacing the scour hole laterally. At unequal and low angle confluences scour depth is lower and avalanche faces are very subdued or absent.

It is also common to find pronounced bar development alongside the confluence ('separation zone bars' Best 1986, 1988; Bristow *et al.* in press) and downstream of the confluence (Smith 1973; Mosley 1976; Ashmore 1982; Davoren & Mosley 1986; Best 1988; Ferguson *et al.* 1992). Bristow *et al.* (in press) refer to this as a 'post-confluence bar'. Mosley (1976) observed that, in symmetrical laboratory confluences, pronounced mid-channel deposition and bifurcation usually only occurred downstream of confluences with an angle of greater than 60°. I am unaware of any subsequent confirmation of this observation. In the initial stages of bar emplacement, the scour and post-confluence bar are equivalent to a chute-lobe or pool-bar unit. Subsequently, bar accretion may cause renewed braiding and formation of a large medial complex bar.

In general, flow structure in the vicinity of the scour pool consists of two helical cells back-to-back with plunging flow in the centre (at the mixing zone or shear layer) and divergence at the bed (Mosley 1976; Ashmore & Parker 1983; Ashmore *et al.* 1992), although this may be complicated by horizontal separation vortices in the lee of the avalanche faces at the confluence entrance, and by more complex patterns at unequal depth confluences (Best 1988; Best & Roy 1991). Evidence for obliquely bankward flow at the bed can sometimes be seen in abandoned scour holes in the field, where it may be revealed by the orientation of bedforms and pebble fabric.

The changes in position of the avalanche faces, associated with changes in confluence angle and relative discharge described above, are one example of morphological change in response to changes in upstream flow. In addition to changes in the position of the avalanche faces, reorientation of the scour axis and the channel immediately downstream is also very common. Previous work suggests that confluence orientation (exit angle) is controlled mainly by relative discharge of the two anabranches (Mosley 1976; Ashmore & Parker 1983; Best 1988; Roy & De Serres 1989). When the two discharges are approximately equal the scour axis orientation bisects the confluence angle. As one channel becomes dominant the axis of scour becomes increasingly parallel to the larger of the confluent channels. Mosley (1976) used a momentum balance approach to explain this phenomenon and to predict the exit angle of the downstream channel.

Although less well documented, it is also apparent from observations of model anabranch confluences (Ashmore 1985, 1991a) that the passage of a pulse of bed load (independent of discharge fluctuation) down one channel will often force reorientation and lateral migration of the confluence. This fits with the more general observation that changes in braided river morphology occur episodically, even at constant discharge, in response to pulses in bedload (Ashmore 1991a; Hoey & Sutherland 1991).

The role of bedload pulses in confluence kinetics, independent of discharge, requires further experimental investigation. It is possible that information on local sediment budgets is required, in addition to the local momentum balance, in order to model confluence morphology. In other words, bedload pulses may be imposed from upstream (for whatever reason) independent of hydraulic conditions in the confluence.

The adjustability of confluence form has implications for the geomorphology and sedimentology of the whole river, not only the immediate vicinity of the confluence. As a particular confluence changes size, position and orientation, so the river morphology and sedimentation processes downstream change. In time-lapse films of braided streams, in which the processes are greatly accelerated, confluences can be seen shifting position and orientation constantly. As they do so water and sediment are distributed in a manner that gives the impression that they are nozzles of hoses playing across the flume. The following examples illustrate some of these changes.

Examples of confluence zone sedimentation and kinetics

Medial bar complex sedimentation. Bar sedimentation within or downstream of a confluence can usually be traced back to the passage of a pulse of bedload in the form of a distinct unit bar or gravel sheet. In the flume channels these sheets were often visible and were seen arriving at the entrance to the confluence and then emerging at the downstream end as a clearly-defined depositional lobe migrating downstream (Fig. 2). Bifurcation then proceeded by one of the several mechanisms of braid bar sedimentation described by Ashmore (1991b): transverse bar conversion, central bar deposition (in symmetrical cases), or chute cutoff of a diagonal unit bar or point bar complex. This process of braid bar initiation downstream of confluences is fundamental to the maintenance of the braided pattern.

Figure 3 illustrates the early stages of medial bar formation downstream of a large confluence. The upstream confluence (A) was formed by two channels of approximately equal size and had a fairly obvious scour hole. A sediment lobe (B) prograded through this confluence over a period of several minutes. In Fig. 3a the sediment lobe is emerging from the scour hole as a distinct sedimentation front. Several minutes later (Fig. 3b, B) it had prograded about 1 m

(a)

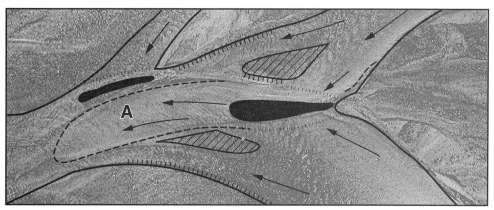

1 metre

(b)

Fig. 2. Model (**a**) and Sunwapta River (**b**) examples of a simple transverse unit bar (A) deposited downstream of a confluence. The distance between the arrow head and the letter A in the Sunwapta River photograph is approximately 40 m.

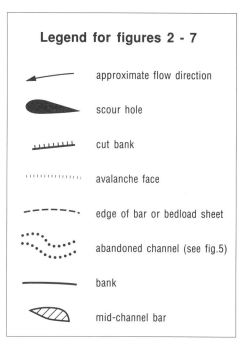

downstream, producing extensive aggradation in the process. The flow over the top of this unit bar had begun to divide at the distal end in the manner described by Ashmore (1991*b*) as 'transverse bar conversion'. This was the beginning of the formation of a complex medial bar.

If this medial bar formation process continues, the result is the large complex illustrated in Fig. 4a, A. The time-lapse films show that this bar originated in almost identical fashion to that shown in Fig. 3 — by the rapid progradation of a sediment pulse down the left confluent channel (B), followed by bifurcation on the bar top.

Coincidentally, flow in the right confluent channel (C) waned and a new confluence (D) formed further downstream. This new confluence controlled the subsequent growth of the medial bar complex (A). The bar grew by gradual lateral and headward accretion of gravel sheets emerging from the confluence. The resulting sedimentary structure, rather like two point complex bars back-to-back, has been

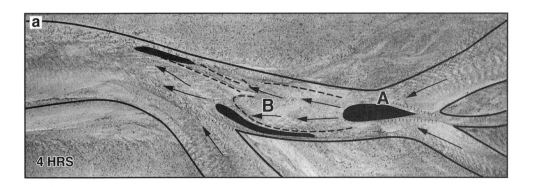

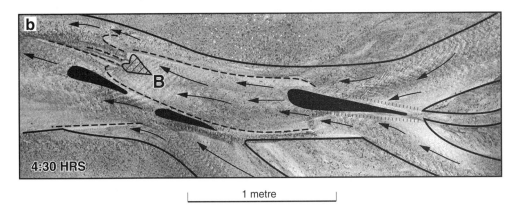

Fig. 3. Braid initiation by 'transverse bar conversion' downstream of a confluence. See text for explanation.

documented by Bluck (1974, 1979) and Ashmore (1982).

The role of the confluence in maintaining the downstream bar is dramatically illustrated later in the same sequence (Fig. 4b). The lateral migration of the confluent channels caused gradual downstream migration of the confluence zone (D). Eventually this triggered a massive avulsion through the bar complex, leaving behind only small remnants of the original bar structure (A). Thus, because the position of the bar complex is initially determined by the confluence zone, shifting of the confluence zone might also cause adjustment of the position of the bar or, as in this case, destruction of the bar.

Lateral bar complex sedimentation. Many confluences migrate laterally for a period of time. This is often the result of the lateral migration of the confluent channels where, for example, the confluence occurs on the outside of a bend in one of the anabranches. The process is essen-

tially one of point bar construction that is modified by the presence of the confluence. Alternatively, a change in the discharge ratio of the confluent channels might cause some lateral migration, as well as reorientation, of the confluence. These lateral (point) bar complexes that are deposited by lateral migration resemble those described previously by Bluck (1971), Lewin (1976) and others in low sinuosity gravel streams, and by Bluck (1974, 1979) and Ashmore (1982) in braided anabranches.

An example of the progressive construction of this type of bar complex is shown in Fig. 5a–c. The sequence begins (Fig. 5a) with two channels of approximately equal size, converging at a confluence (A). Erosion of the left bank of both channels immediately upstream of the confluence, caused gradual migration of the confluence towards the left, with simultaneous lateral accretion on the right side of the confluence (Fig. 5b and c, B). Temporary re-occupation of the chute channel on the inside of

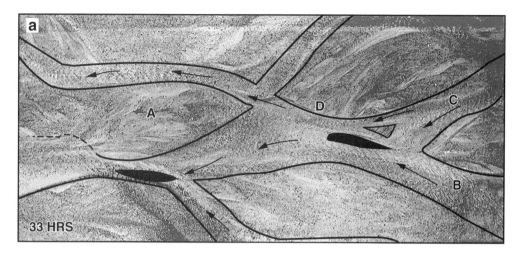

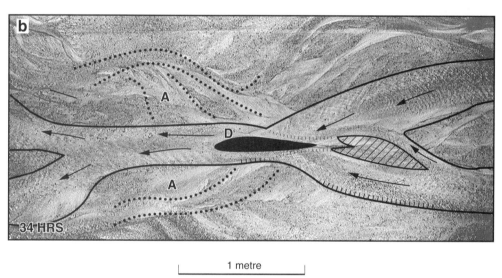

1 metre

Fig. 4. Medial bar destruction caused by longitudinal translation and change in total discharge of upstream confluence. See text for explanation.

the lateral bar (C) (due to a small temporary confluence upstream) interrupted the progressive lateral accretion of the bar which took place over the course of 4 hours in the model. Eventually the lateral complex was destroyed by avulsion, triggered by channel switching and confluence formation upstream. A field example is shown in Fig. 5d.

History of a confluence. Many confluences stay in approximately the same area for extended periods of time, but undergo constant adjust-

ment in size, orientation and position, with important consequences for sedimentation patterns downstream. Some of these processes of adjustment have been shown in the previous examples but in the following case history they are incorporated into a longer sequence of change that includes examples of other common processes of confluence shifting.

In the initial stage of the sequence (Fig. 6a) the channel pattern was dominated by a single large channel, with only small tributaries and a small scour hole at confluence 'A'. A change in

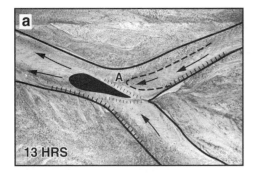

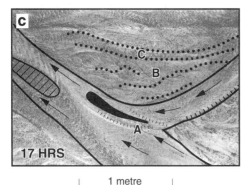

1 metre

channel pattern upstream resulted in enlarge-ment of the right tributary to confluence A and consequent dramatic increase in the size of the scour hole (Fig. 6b). This also caused rotation of the scour axis to the left. Simultaneously, a large sediment lobe emerged from the confluence and formed the nucleus for a complex medial bar deposited a short distance downstream (Fig. 6b, B). The process of medial bar forma-tion was essentially the same as that shown in Fig. 3. A new scour hole formed downstream of the medial bar (Fig. 6b, C).

One hour later (Fig. 6c) the right tributary to confluence A had become dominant. Tributary A and the whole confluence migrated towards the left, in the process depositing a lateral bar on the right side of the confluence (Fig. 6c, D) and causing diversion of the bulk of the flow around the left side of the medial complex (B) down-stream. Between 32 and 33 hours (Fig. 6c and d) the right confluent channel reoccupied a partially abandoned course (E), which resulted in confluence A shifting downstream slightly to A2. Scour hole A was infilled by rapid pro-gradation of a sediment lobe from the left con-fluent channel (F) and downstream shifting of this channel resulted in deposition of a large lateral complex (G). The progradation of the sediment lobes from channel F, and the waning of flow in channel E, caused the confluence (A2) to rotate to the right relative to the orien-tation of confluence A. Confluence A2 also migrated laterally towards the right side of the flume, resulting in deposition of a large lateral bar at H, and redirection of a large portion of the flow around the right side of medial bar B. This upstream reorientation of the confluence had the direct effect of causing the downstream confluence (C) to migrate towards the left.

Over the course of the next hour (Fig. 6d

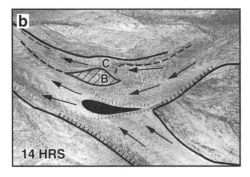

Fig. 5. (a–c) Lateral translation and point complex bar accretion. See text for explanation. (d) Example of point complex bar at an asymmetrical confluence in Sunwapta River. Photograph was taken at low flow in early October. Flow is left to right and scale is indicated by the two-lane road in the bottom left corner of the photograph. Note (i) true right confluent anabranch (A) is dry, (ii) the large avalanche face at the confluence entrance in the true left confluent anabranch, (iii) scour hole (darker tone) immediately downstream of the avalanche face, (iv) the gravel sheet at the left edge of the channel downstream of the scour hole, (v) cut bank, facing away from the camera, on the true right side of the confluence. This photograph also provides field examples of the many of the morphological features in (a)–(c) and Fig. 3.

and e) flow in channel F cut around the right side of the lateral complex G, and at the same time channel E migrated towards the left again and began to lose discharge. There were two consequences of these events. The first was to re-establish confluence A near its original position (Fig. 6, A3). The second was that several large sediment lobes, associated with the destruction of bar G and the waning of channel E, migrated through and largely filled, confluence A2. One of these (J) began to plug the channel around the left side of the medial bar complex B.

The final step in the sequence (Fig. 6f) shows further rotation of confluence A3 to the right as a result of the waning of channel E and the curvature of channel F. The net result was the restoration of the channel to a configuration almost identical to that shown at the beginning of the sequence. The medial bar (B) is incorporated into a large complex bar as a result of the loss of flow around the left side.

This sequence incorporates many of the features of confluence dynamics observed repeatedly in model channels: lateral migration following changes in upstream channel configuration or discharge; upstream and downstream shifting caused by relocation or gradual migration of the confluent channels; rotation of the scour axis; construction and destruction of lateral and medial bar complexes as a result of confluence shifting and rotation; progradation of large gravel lobes through abandoned or less active scour holes; and changes in the scale of the confluence (enlargement or reduction) caused by changes in discharge. In all cases the confluences mediate the pattern of downstream sedimentation resulting from the channel changes upstream.

Discussion

Figure 7 is a schematic synthesis of the typical changes in confluence morphology, and associated downstream changes in channel configuration and bar morphology, observed in the laboratory models and described in the preceding sections. Part A summarizes the initiation of braid bar sedimentation downstream of confluences (using the terminology of Ashmore 1991b) while Parts B and C illustrate the processes by which channel pattern and bar sedimentation may be affected by particular modes of adjustment of the upstream confluence. The diagram inevitably simplifies events. In Parts B and C it is assumed that the starting point in each case is a classic symmetrical X-form confluence–diffluence and the sedimentological detail of bar morphology and sedimentology is omitted to focus attention on the geometry of the channel changes. A distinction is made between those processes of channel change associated with the normal patterns of confluence migration under steady mean discharge and bed load (Part B) from those adjustments that depend on relative changes in the discharge and bed load of the two anabranches (C). In any particular sequence of events this distinction is probably rather difficult to make, and most examples involve some combination of the processes and results shown in Fig. 7. For example, the changes in confluence morphology and change depicted in Fig. 6 involve elements of rotation, longitudinal translation and expansion occurring simultaneously. Reference to the earlier examples (Figs 2–6) is included in Fig. 7 in order to tie together this schematic synthesis with the more detailed observations of the examples.

Figure 7 is not exhaustive; neither the list of processes, nor the possible results, is complete. For example, changes in confluence angle are common and have results similar to rotation and longitudinal translation. The possible range of downstream results of any confluence adjustment process is enormous and the exact downstream adjustment to any particular process depends on the bar morphology and channel geometry downstream. One of the most common consequences of confluence shifting is anabranch avulsion, triggered by the redirection of flow and bedload, which could be caused by any one of the processes illustrated, but particularly by confluence rotation or translation (Figs 4 and 6). Although the downstream effects are highly variable, some common features seem to arise and these are indicated in Fig. 7. Examples include the lateral accretion deposits resulting from lateral translation, rotation and obliteration, and bar head erosion following longitudinal translation or expansion. Note also that some of the processes may be reversed, for example, contraction instead of expansion, upstream instead of downstream translation and creation instead of obliteration. These possibilities were excluded from the diagram for the sake of simplicity.

The potential effects of falling stage at a particular confluence are not included in Fig. 7. These falling stage effects were not observed in the flume models which were run at constant discharge, and systematic field observations are not yet available. In my experience in the field, falling stage may result in dissection of avalanche faces and slight infilling of the scour hole. In addition, confluence angle may increase

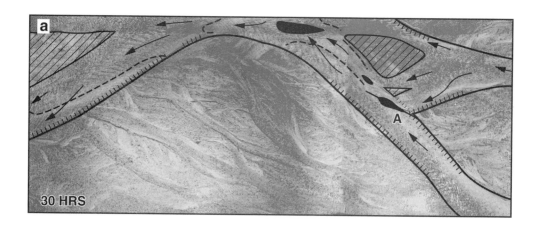

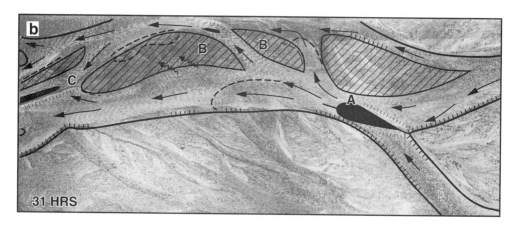

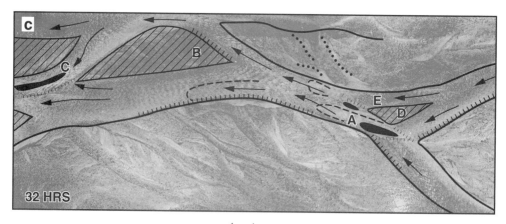

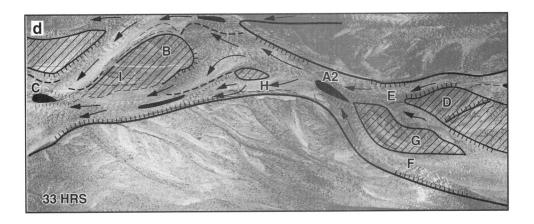

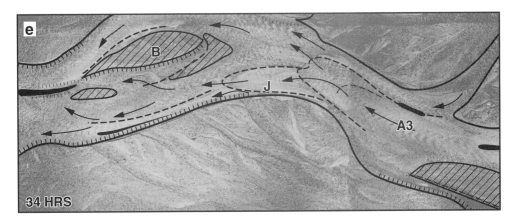

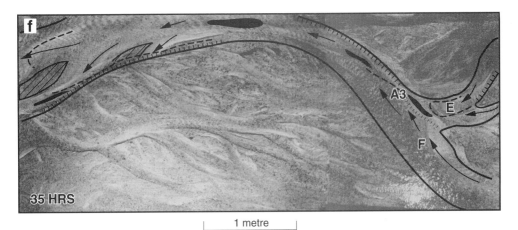

1 metre

Fig. 6. Example of complex pattern of confluence changes and sedimentation over 6 hours. See text for explanation.

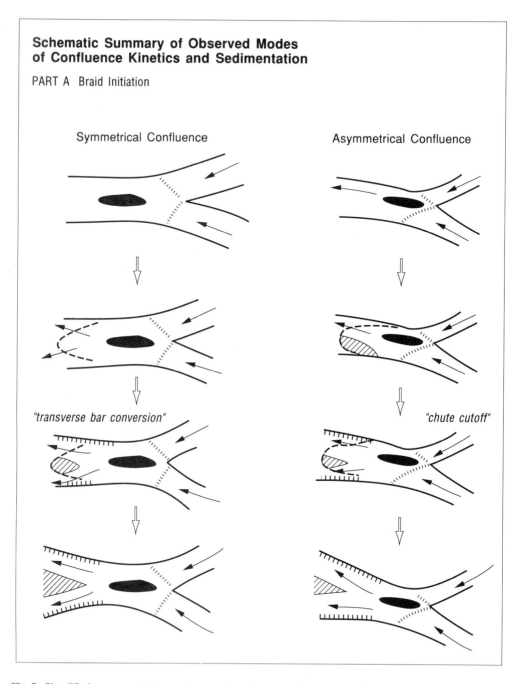

Fig. 7. Simplified summary of observed modes of confluence adjustment and the effect on channel pattern and bar sedimentation downstream (Figs 2–6). See text for further explanation and assumptions.

Schematic Summary of Observed Modes
of Confluence Kinetics and Sedimentation

PART B   Response to migration of confluent anabranches

LATERAL TRANSLATION

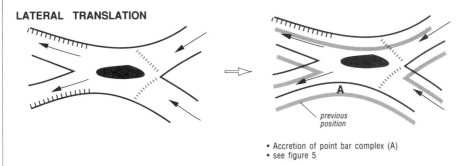

- Accretion of point bar complex (A)
- see figure 5

LONGITUDINAL TRANSLATION

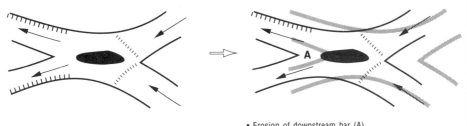

- Erosion of downstream bar (A)
- see figure 4 and figure 6/ 32-33 hrs (A - A2)

AVULSION OR BIFURCATION

- Multiple scour holes and new downstream bars
- see figure 6/ 31-32 hrs

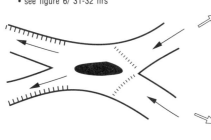

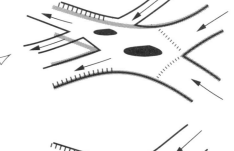

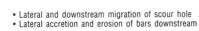

- Lateral and downstream migration of scour hole
- Lateral accretion and erosion of bars downstream

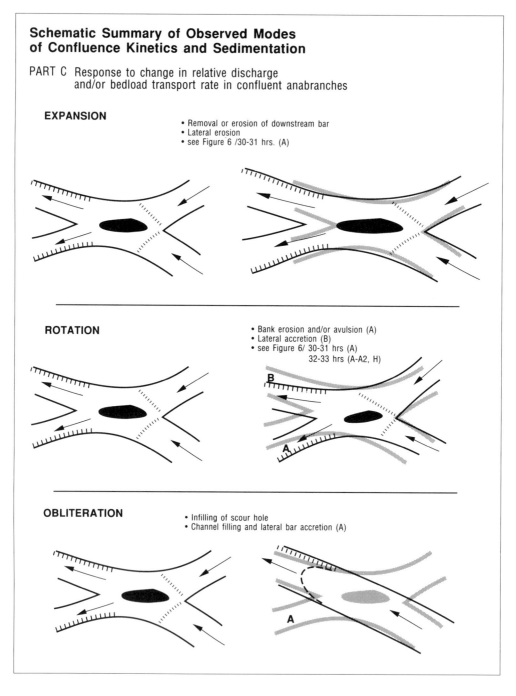

**Schematic Summary of Observed Modes
of Confluence Kinetics and Sedimentation**

PART C   Response to change in relative discharge
         and/or bedload transport rate in confluent anabranches

EXPANSION

• Removal or erosion of downstream bar
• Lateral erosion
• see Figure 6 /30-31 hrs. (A)

ROTATION

• Bank erosion and/or avulsion (A)
• Lateral accretion (B)
• see Figure 6/ 30-31 hrs (A)
               32-33 hrs (A-A2, H)

OBLITERATION

• Infilling of scour hole
• Channel filling and lateral bar accretion (A)

at lower stages because of the increased importance of topographic steering at the confluence
entrance. However, this normally coincides with
conditions below critical for gravel transport and
any modification to confluence form is minor
and quickly modified when stage rises again.

Many of the processes described here do not
occur in fixed geometry tributary confluences.
However, these observations do confirm some
of the results of experiments on small-scale fixed
geometry confluences, particularly the influence
of discharge ratio on the orientation of the scour

axis (Mosley 1976; Best 1988), and the role of confluences in triggering downstream bifurcation (Mosley 1976).

Although there is little published information, it seems likely that at least some of the features of braided river anabranch confluences will be duplicated in more stable transitional channel patterns, such as wandering, 'meanderthal' (Carson 1984) or split, and, perhaps to a lesser extent, at the junctions of stable single-thread streams. If confluence zones are key elements of braided patterns and provide vital information about the origin and maintenance of the channel pattern, presumably the same is at least partially true of these transitional patterns. However, in these cases it is likely that bank resistance and vegetation controls may cause some irregularity in confluence morphology and behaviour.

Field examples of sedimentation features at more stable confluences are few, but Best (1988) illustrates a small lateral bar in a gravel bed confluence which may be the result of slackwater or flow separation at the confluence corner. Presumably minor adjustments of confluence form are possible depending upon the variation in relative discharge and sediment load during storm events (Rhoads 1992). Over the time-span of significant channel migration, some of the rotation and translation processes may occur at alluvial junctions in freely-meandering streams, leaving extensive lateral deposits and perhaps influencing bend geometry and migration patterns downstream. Such changes may be revealed by sequential photography over years or decades. In this way, the kinetics of anabranch confluences may provide some clues to the longer term kinetics of more stable confluences.

Existing descriptive work on braided streams does not emphasise the aspects of confluence kinetics described here, except in a general way as nodes in the braided system, or in the context of pool-bar units (Chien 1961; Coleman 1969; Fahnestock 1963; Smith 1973; Ashmore 1982; Mosley 1982; Southard et al. 1984; Rundle 1985). Hein & Walker (1977) include sketch maps of channel changes which contain an example of scour hole infilling ('obliteration') due to waning flow in one of the two confluent channels. Similarly, some of the channel pattern changes mapped by Coleman (1969) on the Brahmaputra River appear to be related to, and controlled by, the upstream constriction or node. In one case (Coleman 1969, fig. 22) repositioning of the confluence due to upstream avulsion appears to be partly responsible for the massive erosion of the medial bar complex downstream. In the second example (Coleman 1969, fig. 23), the downstream changes can be seen to be the result of the abandonment of one confluent channel. In neither case does Coleman (1969) mention the role of the upstream confluence zone.

To date, our understanding of confluence morphology and processes derives mainly from laboratory models. Although modellers are aware of some of the limitations of the technique there has been no formal assessment of these restrictions. Thus, for example, the sand fraction appears to be a significant component of confluence zone deposition, yet most laboratory models have either not considered the explicit scaling criteria (Best 1988), or truncate the model bed material such that the sand fraction is not represented (e.g. Ashmore, 1985). Ashworth et al. (in press) have modelled the deposition of fine-grained sediment in braided streams, but the reliability of the scaling remains to be thoroughly evaluated in this case.

There is a limit to the utility of small-scale models in elucidating the dynamics of confluences. In many cases the models are too small (or the instruments too large!), and the confluences too unstable, to allow detailed measurement of flow and sediment transport. There is still potential for further functional understanding of confluences using scale models, but field measurements are required to provide confirmation of the range of behaviours described here, documentation of the effects of stage changes, as well as details of flow mechanics and sediment transport in anabranch confluences. Some data have been reported recently (Ashmore et al. 1992) but it is apparent to anyone who has attempted it, that field measurement of flow and bed load in gravelly braided streams is extremely difficult. In the case of confluences, problems abound and include: difficulty in locating confluences of a relatively simple geometry; difficulty in finding confluences in which lateral inflow and outflow do not occur (to establish a complete momentum balance for detailed hydraulic modelling); rapidity of morphological change that may be too great to monitor by routine surveying; rapidity of stage changes may preclude the completion of a set of measurements during a steady discharge; and occurrence of flows that are too violent for either the instruments or those carrying them. Some of these problems can be overcome (for instance high temporal resolution survey data may be obtained photogrammetrically) but, despite these difficulties, it appears that further progress on braided-river confluence mechanics cannot be made without tackling the problem in the field as well as the laboratory, and accepting that the precision and accuracy of the field data may fall short of that obtained in less testing conditions.

The detailed measurement of flow, shear stress and gravel transport in anabranch confluences, and particularly the form–process interaction, promises to provide insight into the geomorphology and sedimentology of confluence zones and also the braided-river system as a whole. This includes quantitative details of the bifurcation process downstream of confluences, as well as channel abandonment and avulsion, and bar complex sedimentation — in short, the suite of processes that constitute channel pattern changes in braided streams. It seems likely that changes in, for example, discharge ratio of the confluent channels could have observable effects on the flow structure and shear stress pattern in the confluence, causing adjustments in the channel form which are visible as rotation or migration of the confluence and which are the direct cause of the changes in channel pattern described in this paper. Thus, because of the rapidity of form adjustment, braided rivers may not be merely an interesting oddity in the realm of alluvial channel form, but an ideal river type in which to study more general issues of form–process interaction in alluvial channels, towards which much contemporary fluvial geomorphology is directed.

Conclusions

Observation and description of the kinetics of anabranch confluences in model braided streams, and the associated sedimentation processes, reveal an extremely complex set of phenomena which are not easy to describe, analyse or communicate. They may be categorized into various modes of confluence shifting, but this belies the enormous variety in detail. Confluence zones in braided streams are extremely dynamic and energetic. Their morphology is influenced by the discharge, bedload, geometry, planform, orientation and number of confluent channels. At flows above threshold, all of these variables are constantly changing, causing rapid, and complex, adjustments in confluence geometry. The rapidity and freedom of adjustment in form to prevailing flow conditions is much greater in anabranch confluences than in typical tributary confluences. The consequence is that anabranch confluences are characterized by a series of processes and fea-

tures not present in more stable types of confluences. This adjustability and rapid change appear to be responsible, either directly or indirectly, for most of the channel pattern and bar changes that characterise braided stream sedimentation.

The examples described herein demonstrate that there are several distinctive modes of sedimentation and channel pattern change associated with anabranch confluences that, as a group, encompass the full range of processes and forms that characterize sedimentation in braided rivers. These include: medial bar deposition and braiding initiation; lateral translation and point bar complex accretion; longitudinal translation, reorientation and upstream avulsion or bifurcation causing changes in position and size of the scour zone, and accretion or erosion of bar complexes; rotation, expansion or contraction and obliteration of the scour hole causing anabranch abandonment or avulsion downstream and associated bar construction or destruction. The time-scale of these processes is of the order of hours or tens of hours in the flume which scales to several days or weeks of competent flows in the field.

The central role of confluences in sedimentation and pattern change, and the various modes of adjustment, have not previously been described or emphasized in studies of braided river geomorphology and sedimentology. Recent detailed work on confluence mechanics encompasses neither the temporal or spatial scales of channel change described here, but should lead to a general model of process–form adjustment at confluence-diffluence zones, which might form the basis for the explanation of these longer-term processes of confluence kinetics and braid bar sedimentation.

The experiments from which the examples in this paper are drawn were originally carried out as part of my PhD research in the Department of Geography, University of Alberta. I am grateful to J. Shaw for research supervision. The research was funded by Natural Sciences and Engineering Research Council grants to J. Shaw and G. Parker. The experiments were carried out in the Graduate Hydraulics Laboratory in the Department of Civil Engineering with the technical assistance of S. Lovell. I am grateful to I. Craig (Zoology Department, UWO) for printing the photographs and to G. Shields (Geography Department, Cartographic section, UWO) for his conscientious work on the illustrations. Thanks also to T. Hoey for raising some useful issues in his review of this paper.

References

ASHMORE, P. E. 1982. Laboratory modelling of gravel braided steam morphology. *Earth Surface Processes and Landforms*, **7**, 201–225.

—— 1985. *Process and form in gravel braided streams: laboratory modelling and field observations*. PhD Thesis, University of Alberta.

—— 1991*a*. Channel morphology and bed load pulses in braided, gravel-bed streams. *Geografiska Annaler*, **73A**, 37–52.

—— 1991*b*. How do gravel bed streams braid? *Canadian Journal of Earth Sciences*, **28**, 326–341.

—— & PARKER, G. 1983. Confluence scour in coarse braided streams. *Water Resources Research*, **19**, 392–402.

——, FERGUSON, R. I., PRESTEGAARD, K. L., ASHWORTH, P. J. & PAOLA, C. 1992. Secondary flow in anabranch confluences of a braided, gravel-bed stream. *Earth Surface Processes and Landforms*, **17**, 299–311.

ASHWORTH, P. J., FERGUSON, R. I., ASHMORE, P. E., PAOLA, C., POWELL, D. M. & PRESTEGAARD, K. L. 1992. Measurements in a braided river chute and lobe 2. Sorting of bedload during entrainment, transport and deposition. *Water Resources Research*, **28**, 1887–1896.

——, BEST, J. L., LEDDY, J. O. & GEEHAN, G. W. in press. The physical modelling of braided rivers and deposition of fine-grained sediment. *In*: KIRKBY, M. J. (ed.) *Theoretical Geomorphology*.

BEST, J. L. 1986. The morphology of river channel confluences. *Progress in Physical Geography*, **10**, 157–174.

—— 1988. Sediment transport and bed morphology at river channel confluences. *Sedimentology*, **35**, 491–498.

—— & ROY, A. G. 1991. Mixing layer distortion at the confluence of channels of different depths. *Nature*, **350**, 411–413.

BLUCK, B. J. 1971. Sedimentation in the meandering river Endrick. *Scottish Journal of Geology*, **7**, 93–138.

—— 1974. Structure and directional properties of some valley sandur deposits in southern Iceland. *Sedimentology*, **21**, 533–554.

—— 1979. Structure of coarse grained braided stream alluvium. *Transactions of the Royal Society of Edinburgh*, **70**, 181–221.

BRISTOW, C. S., BEST, J. L. & ROY, A. G. 1993. Morphology and facies models of channel confluences. *In*: MARZO, M. & PUIDEFABREGAS, C. (eds) *Alluvial Sedimentation*. International Association of Sedimentologists Special Publication.

CARSON, M. A. 1984. Observations on the meandering-braided river transition, the Canterbury Plains, New Zealand. *New Zealand Geographer*, **40**, 12–17, 89–99.

CHIEN, N. 1961. The braided stream of the Yellow River. *Scientia Sinica*, **10**, 734–754.

COLEMAN, J. M. 1969. Brahmaputra River: channel processes and sedimentation. *Sedimentary Geology*, **3**, 129–239.

DAVOREN, A. & MOSLEY, M. P. 1986. Observations of bedload movement, bar development, and sediment supply in the braided Ohau River. *Earth Surface Processes and Landforms*, **11**, 643–652.

FAHNESTOCK, R. K. 1963. *Morphology and hydrology of a glacial stream. White River, Mount Rainier, Washington*. United States Geological Survey Professional Paper, **422A**.

FERGUSON, R. I., ASHMORE, P. E., ASHWORTH, P. J., PAOLA, C. & PRESTEGAARD, K. L. 1992. Measurements in a braided river chute and lobe 1. Flow pattern, sediment transport and channel change. *Water Resources Research*, **28**, 1877–1886.

HEIN, F. J. & WALKER, R. G. 1977. Bar evolution and development of stratification in the gravelly, braided Kicking Horse River, British Columbia. *Canadian Journal of Earth Sciences*, **14**, 562–570.

HOEY, T. B. & SUTHERLAND, A. J. 1991. Channel morphology and bedload pulses in braided rivers: a laboratory study. *Earth Surface Processes and Landforms*, **16**, 447–462.

KRIGSTRÖM, A. 1962. Geomorphological studies of sandur plains and their braided rivers in Iceland. *Geografiska Annaler*, **44**, 328–346.

LEWIN, J. 1976. Initiation of bed forms and meanders in coarse-grained sediment. *Geological Society of America Bulletin*, **87**, 281–285.

MOSLEY, M. P. 1976. An experimental study of channel confluences. *Journal of Geology*, **84**, 535–562.

—— 1982. Analysis of the effect of changing discharge on channel morphology and instream uses in a braided river, Ohau River, New Zealand. *Water Resources Research*, **18**, 800–812.

—— & SCHUMM, S. A. 1977. Stream junctions — a probable location for bedrock placers. *Economic Geology*, **72**, 691–697.

RHOADS, B. L. 1992. Flow patterns and bed morphology at an asymmetrical stream confluence. *Abstracts, Spring Meeting, American Geophysical Union*, 136.

ROY, A. G. & BERGERON, N. 1990. Flow and particle paths at a natural river confluence with coarse bed material. *Geomorphology*, **3**, 99–122.

—— & DESERRES, B. 1989. Morphologie du lit et dynamique des confluents de cours d'eau. *Bulletin de la Société Géographique de Liège*, **25**, 113–127.

RUNDLE, A. 1985. Braid morphology and the formation of multiple channels, The Rakaia, New Zealand. *Zeitschrift für Geomorphologie Supplement Band*, **55**, 15–37.

SMITH, D. G. 1973. Aggradation of the Alexandra–North Saskatchewan River, Banff National Park, Alberta. *In*: MORISAWA, M. (ed.) *Fluvial Geomorphology*. Allen & Unwin, London, 201–219.

SMITH, J. D. & MCLEAN, S. R. 1984. A model for meandering streams. *Water Resources Research*, **20**, 1301–1315.

SMITH, N. D. 1974. Sedimentology and bar formation in the upper Kicking Horse river, a braided meltwater stream. *Journal of Geology*, **82**, 205–223.

SOUTHARD, J. B., SMITH, N. D. & KUHNLE, R. A. 1984. Chutes and lobes: newly identified elements of braiding in shallow gravelly streams. *In*: KOSTER, E. H. & STEEL, R. J. (eds) *Sedimentology of gravels and conglomerates*. Canadian Society of Petroleum Geologists, Memoir **10**, 51–59.

Pleistocene Rhine gravel: deposits of a braided river system with dominant pool preservation

CHRISTOPH SIEGENTHALER & PETER HUGGENBERGER

Federal Institute for Water Resources and Water Pollution Control (EAWAG)
CH-8600 Dübendorf, Switzerland

Abstract: An example of a gravelly braided river deposit is described which exhibits a rather low structural diversity as compared to other ancient and modern braided river sediments. The presented model is based on a study of the Rhine gravel, formed in front of the Würm stage extension of the Rhine glacier (northern part of Switzerland). The observations in the Rhine gravel suggest that only processes which operate generally at a low topographic level of the braided river system generate a response in the geological record, i.e. (1) pool deposits produced at the junction of two channels (cross-bedded trough fills); (2) channel sediments which reflect thin bedload sheets deposited by moderate-magnitude flow stages with low suspension concentrations; (3) sheet flow deposits produced by extraordinary high-magnitude flow stages with high suspension concentrations, probably due to outbursts from glacial lakes.

Therefore, we postulate that in the Rhine gravel system only a limited number of braided river structures have a significant preservation potential: any deposit generated at an elevated geometric level, such as flood plain deposits or bars, are successively destroyed by channel formation and are replaced by channel deposits, which in turn may be reworked by pools which operate at the lowest geometric level. It is suggested that similar preservational hierarchies could eventually exist also in other braided river deposits.

Braided streams are characterized by divisions and rejoinings of flow around islands or bars composed of alluvial sediment (Smith 1978). The form and position of these islands and bars changes continuously while the channels that surround them migrate (Kellerhals *et al.* 1976; Smith 1978; Miall 1977). Miall (1981, 1985) elaborated a systematic approach for the description of ancient fluvial environments based on a set of standardized lithofacies assemblages, or 'architectural elements', some of them with a genetic connotation. A recent systematic approach on coarse alluvial fan deposits, based on Miall's principles, is presented by DeCelles *et al.* (1991). Whereas characteristic structural and lithological assemblages apparently exist in the study area, they exhibit a puzzling variety of lateral changes of lithofacies and erosional bounding surfaces. Therefore, any rigorous definition of types or architectural hierarchies appeared to be arbitrary and impractical. For these reasons we used a slightly different approach and tried to find a limited number of structural and textural elements, which we could interpret fluvio-dynamically, and which we consider to reflect braided river processes.

For this study we selected active quarries in the Rhine valley of northern Switzerland. The deposits in these quarries are 20 to 40 m thick,

gravelly glacial-outwash sediments that were deposited during the last glaciation. Rapid exploitation removes several metres of wall per day, and therefore provides excellent, although not accessible, outcrops up to 30 m high. A time series of photographs allowed us to reconstruct the three-dimensional aspect of the structures at a metre-scale and with a high level of confidence.

Geomorphological and hydrodynamical setting

The area is situated in front of the greatest Würm stage extension of the Thur and Glatt–Linth lobes of the Rhine glacier (Fig. 1). Imposing terminal moraine suites with heights up to 100 m above the outwash plain mark the end position of these lobes. Distal from the moraine, proglacial fluvial gravel from the catchment area of the Rhine glacier fills the east–west-trending Rhine valley cut through Tertiary sandstone and Jurassic limestone (Keller 1977). Farther down-valley, and outside the study area, the Rhine gravels merge with the outwash from the Rhone–Aar glacier. A carbon date, obtained from a bone fragment of a mammoth, gives an age of 17850 years BP (Hünermann 1985). This age corresponds with

From Best, J. L. & Bristow, C. S. (eds), 1993, *Braided Rivers*, Geological Society
Special Publication No. **75**, pp. 147–162.

147

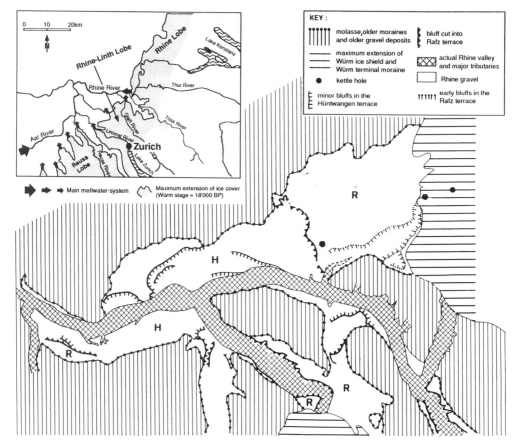

Fig. 1. Maximum extension of the ice cover during the last glaciation (Würm stage) in the northern part of Switzerland. The area studied is located in front of the Rhine and the Rhine–Linthlobe (marked with a star). Depositional levels (terraces) are separated by terrace bluffs in the glacial outwash deposit of the Rhine valley. R, Rafz terrace; H, Hüntwangen terrace.

the age of maximum Würmian ice extension in Europe, which is usually placed between 16 000 and 18 000 years BP (Welten 1978).

Several depositional terraces, dipping away from the moraines and separated from each other by terrace bluffs, exist in the glacial outwash of the Rhine valley. They can be used to establish the depositional history of the gravel during the greatest extent of the Würm glacier. Whereas the highest terrace must have been formed by aggradation, the lower ones are the result of degradation. The two most prominent terraces in the study area are an upper terrace (R, Fig. 1), which intergrades proximally with a slope of 0.4° into the terminal moraines, and a lower terrace (H, Fig. 1), cut into the former, with an average slope of 0.15°. The two terraces are separated by a prominent terrace bluff which can be as high as 20 m in proximal locations, but

diminishes in height to 5 m 8 km further downstream. The modern Rhine river is incised approximately 30 m into the lower terrace. At one location the smooth morphological contact between the upper terrace and the terminal moraines is interrupted by a more than 30 m deep kettlehole. This fact indicates that at least the uppermost 30 m of the gravel of the upper terrace (R in Fig. 1) has been deposited during the maximum extension of the ice-front, i.e. in a relatively short time.

The morphology of the outwash does not give direct evidence that a braided river system existed during deposition of the gravel. However, the fluvioglacial setting in front of the ice, the large volume of relatively large-sized clastics deposited in a relatively short time, and the steep gradient of the alluvial plain with slopes up to 0.4°, are favourable conditions for the estab-

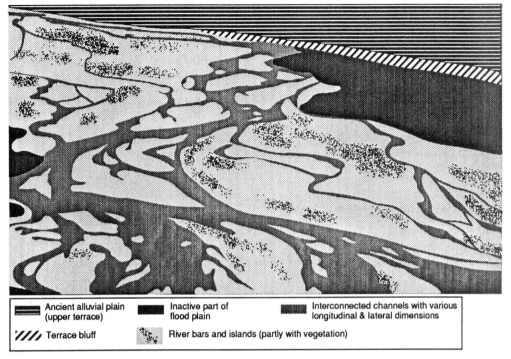

▬ Ancient alluvial plain (upper terrace)	▬ Inactive part of flood plain	▬ Interconnected channels with various longitudinal & lateral dimensions
▨ Terrace bluff	▨ River bars and islands (partly with vegetation)	

Fig. 2. Morphological components of a braided river system of an alluvial plain (Waimak River, Templeur Island, New Zealand, drawn from photograph courtesy of M. Jaeggi (VAW/ETH)).

lishment of a braided river regime, and no indications for other fluvial environments has been found in the sediment. In our conceptual model, the essential morphological components of a braided river system are (compare Fig. 2) as follows.

(i) Interconnected river channels with variable dimensions in space and time.

(ii) River bars, which are accumulations of bed material in river channels formed especially during high water flow. Active bars assume various geometric forms depending on the character of flow, sediment size and channel shape.

(iii) Scour pools at channel confluences, depending upon discharge, sediment load, channel shape and confluence angle, with important local channel scourings. The shape of the pool resembles a spoon with steep faces upstream and a rather flat distal end (Ashmore 1985; Mosley 1976; Best 1988). Sediment transport across the pool is mainly around rather than through the center of the confluence (Best 1988).

(iv) The flood plain or inactive section of the braided river system. This plain is the place of

eventual soil formation, of fine-grained aeolian sedimentation or flood and overbank deposition.

The hydrology of a braided river system is conceived to be highly variable in time.

At low-magnitude flow, water courses are restricted to a few interconnected individual channels. Bedform changes in the river bed are slow and the shaping of the overall morphology is insignificant. The flood plain is inactive: vegetation may thus grow there and soil forming processes are established.

At moderate-magnitude flow the alluvial plain is partly or wholly inundated and the morphology of the plain is locally reshaped, as a new channel system may be established.

At high-magnitude flow, caused e.g. by outbreaks of large dammed watermasses behind an ice front, the whole alluvial plain is covered by a flood sheet with high competence, which probably completely destroys the existing channel system and its bedforms as well as the flood plain and flood plain deposits. A completely new braided channel system is expected to be formed during the waning phase of the flood.

Lithofacies of Rhine gravel

Gravel types

Gravel of various grades dominate the deposits of the Rhine gravel, the remainder being sand and silt. Three types of gravels can be distinguished quite easily, nicknamed in the field 'brown gravel', 'grey gravel' (Fig. 3), and 'gravel couplets'. The first two gravel types differ from each other only texturally (Table 1), the third type, the 'gravel couplets' exhibits a specific structure.

'*Brown gravel*' (G1, Table 1) is a very poorly sorted sandy and silty gravel with massive horizontal bedding which contain larger clasts such as cobbles; all clasts are well rounded. The colour of the gravel is brownish due to the occurrence of silt and clay. The aspect of the horizontal bed boundaries is vague, and bedding thickness is thus difficult to estimate; it seems that most coarse-grained 'brown gravels' were deposited in 1 m to several metres thick horizontal beds. A significant feature is the entire absence of any armoured (paved) layer (i.e. of a monogranular surface layer of coarse imbricated clasts which is build up in the river bottom at steady flow conditions). Only single large clasts scattered in the 'brown gravel' often show preferred orientation with the apparent long axis dipping upstream.

'*Grey gravel*' (G2) is a moderately-sorted gravel containing coarse sand, granules, pebbles and, infrequently, cobbles. All gravel particles are well rounded. Clay and silt are missing, and fine and medium sand is practically absent, the gravel therefore has a greyish aspect. Preferred clast orientation can occur in horizontal beds, with the apparent long axis of the clast being parallel or oblique (dipping upstream) to the bedding (Fig. 3). Armoured layers are absent. Bedding thickness is in the order of 1 dm or less, but may reach several decimetres, individual beds being separated by a thin sandy layer or by a monogranular and sand-free gravel layer. Bedding may be horizontal or cross-stratified in large sets; seemingly massive horizontal beds are sometimes composed of vague and low-angle cross-beds.

A *gravel couplet (G3)* (Figs 4 & 5) is a fining-upward sequence made up of two beds: a bimodal gravel at the base (Fig. 5, 2) and an open framework gravel at the top of the couplet (Fig. 5, 1). *Bimodal gravel* consists of a framework of well-sorted pebbles and eventually cobbles with a matrix of well-sorted medium sand filling the interstices. Grain-size and bed thickness of the bimodal gravel are positively correlated (see also Steel & Thompson 1983, fig. 7). Preferred clast orientation is absent. Separate beds are 1–2 dm thick and occasionally up to 0.5 m. Horizontal or inclined beds occur as well. Although bimodal gravel beds are a component of gravel couplets, they may sometimes occur as solitary beds. *Open framework gravel* is completely free of sand and appears

Fig. 3. An example of a 'grey gravel' deposit containing variable amounts of 'brown gravel'. The top most bed consists of 'brown gravel' in which the clast orientation is poorly developed. Also shown are internal cross-bed sets with indistinct set boundaries and poorly organized cross-beds.

Table 1. *Summary of lithofacies in the late Pleistocene Rhine*

Textural gravel type	Composition and character	Interpretation

G1: Brown gravel	Poorly sorted, sandy and silty
	Clasts well rounded
	Larger clasts up to 0.5 m diameter
	Massive beds
		Rapid deposition
		High competence
		Regime interpreted as transitional
		  between debris flow and fluvial
		  bedload transport (e.g. Nemec &
		  Steel 1984)

G2: Grey gravel	Poorly sorted
	Containing coarse sand, granules,
	  pebbles and (cobbles)
	Clay and silt missing
	Fine sand in subordinate amounts
	Absence of armoured beds
	Bedding horizontal or cross-stratified
	  (long bottomsets)
		Deposition at higher flow stages which
		  destroy paved river beds
		Gravel transport in pulses (Reid &
		  Frostick 1986; Ashmore 1985)
		Diffuse gravel or bedload sheets
		  (Hein & Walker 1977; Whiting
		  et al. 1988)
		Traction carpet (Todd 1989)
		Cross-bedded grey level is
		  continuation of horizontal traction
		  carpets into trough (Carling 1987)

G3: Gravel couplets	Fining upward sequence of bimodal
	  gravel at the base and open-framework
	  gravel at the top
	
	Bimodal gravel
	Yellowish
	Framework of well sorted pebbles or
	  cobbles with a matrix of well sorted
	  medium sand
	Gravel particles well rounded
	Separate beds 1–2 dm thick (occasionally
	  up to 0.5 m))
	Horizontal or inclined beds
	
	Open framework gravel
	Greyish or brownish
	1–2 dm thick
	Well sorted
	Generally fining-upward grain size
	Well rounded
	Not occuring as separate beds
		Reflection of diurnal meltwater cycle
		  (Smith 1985)
		Stacking of size-segregated gravel and
		  sand sheets formed on bar surface
		  (Steel & Thomson 1983)
		Cross-stratified sets produced by
		  migrating gravel dunes (Carling &
		  Glaister 1987)
		coarse material at the base of the
		  slope
		sand from suspension by the counter
		  current or bedload in the form of
		  ripples moving up the channel in
		  separated reverse flow

Sand, silt and clay	Sand deposits rare
	Admixture in bimodal gravels
	As intercalations of gravel deposits
	Interfingering with gravelly cross-beds
	Few sandy-silty layers up to 100 m
	Local sand bodies with silty layers on
	  top of trough fills
		Sand bodies at diverse positions,
		  difficult to locate
		Back flooding of tributaries during
		  high magnitude floods (Kochel &
		  Baker 1982)
		Fine-grained slack-water sediment
		  accumulate in the valleys of the
		  tributaroes; mechanism responsible
		  for extensive sand and silt layers in
		  distinct levels of several pits

in 1 dm to several decimetres thick beds. The gravels are well sorted and fine upward. Occasionally clay and silt drape around the pebbles and cobbles, probably as a result of secondary clay transfer due to groundwater motion. Preferred clast orientation is absent. Open framework gravel beds are always coupled with bimodal gravel beds.

Gravel couplets are common strata in large-scale cross-bedded sets but may also appear as horizontal layers in the Rhine gravel. Obviously, gravel couplets are a widespread fluvial gravel type. A detailed description of gravel couplets in a Triassic Sandstone Group is given by Steel & Thompson (1983, their lithofacies A and B). Identical couplets seem to occur in very diverse

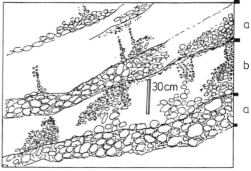

a: cobbles,pebbles + medium sand
b: cobbles without a fine fraction

Fig. 4. Two inclined cross-bedded gravel couplets (position given in Fig. 6). a: bimodal gravel consisting of pebbles and a well-sorted medium sand; b: open-framework gravel showing upward fining. The internal cross-bedded structure is not visible at this position.

settings such as the Buntsandstein in the Iberian Ranges, Spain (Ramos *et al.* 1986) or the deposits of the giant Missoula flood (Baker 1972, fig. 26), and we have seen them in large scale fluvial channel deposits in the Aquitanian Molasse of Switzerland. Similar, but probably more complicated gravel couplets in a Devonian fluvial conglomerate of Quebec have been described by Anketell & Rust (1990).

We think that a single gravel couplet is a covert cross-stratified set produced by migrating gravel dunes, as shown by Carling & Glaister

(1987) and Carling (1990). A similar mechanism was also suggested by Anketell & Rust (1990). Experimenting with gravel dunes in a current, Carling and Glaister obtained cross-bed sets with completely obscured foresets, which are almost exact replicas of horizontally bedded gravel couplets: (1) along the slip face formed downstream of an artificial step, particles segregated to concentrate coarser material at the base of the slope. Sand was supplied from suspension by the separation zone counter current but also as bedload in the form of ripples

Fig. 5. Gravel couplet (open framework (1) and bimodal gravel (2) with cross-stratification visible within the open-framework gravel in the upper part of the figure.

moving upward in the separated reverse flow. Thus, a mixture of coarse gravel and sand equivalent to the 'bimodal gravel' was deposited in the lowest position of the set. (2) In the upper part of the slip face the reverse flow was weak, much less sand was trapped in the interstitial spaces and a distinct and graded open frame-work texture was deposited above the 'bimodal gravel' which is identical to the 'open framework gravel'. This model explains the accumulation of both framework supported as well as of matrix supported bimodal gravels. The former type occurs in the Rhine gravel, whereas the latter has been described by Steel & Thompson (1983). In some cases we were able to reveal the conjectural cross-stratified structure of gravel couplets, especially in exposures cut obliquely to the supposed dune crest, i.e. with a flat apparent cross-stratification (Fig. 5).

The model of Carling & Glaister (1987) can explain convincingly horizontally bedded gravel couplets. In the study area gravel couplets also occur as cross-beds, and can build up complete cross-bed sets. We could not see any lithological or structural difference between horizontal and inclined gravel couplets, which are therefore thought to be formed by the same mechanism. Inclined gravel couplets could then be generated by gravel dunes migrating across an oblique plane, e.g. dunes migrating along the lateral trough wall.

Facies types

Structural and textural properties are used to define the three major lithofacies, which probably amount to roughly 90% of the total deposit in the quarries:

Troughs and trough fill deposits. This facies consists of large cross-bedded sets with trough shaped, concave upward and erosional lower bounding surfaces (Figs 6 & 7). The erosional lower surface appears as a clear-cut boundary, in some outcrops discontinuously overlain by a lag of cobbles. The lateral dimensions of the trough deposits range from a few metres up to more than 100 m and 0.5–6 m vertically. In sections roughly perpendicular to the general flow direction, the erosional bounding surface sometimes displays the shape of a circular-arc; the cross-beds are strongly curved and tangential to the lower set boundary giving the whole structure an onion-like appearance (Fig. 7). Under these circumstances it is not uncommon to see two interfingering cross-bed sets of different textural types and with apparently opposite growth directions (Fig. 8). In sections parallel or oblique to the general flow the surface is more asymmetrical and has a spoon-like aspect; in these sections the cross-beds are straighter but still often tangential to the lower set boundary, i.e. with long bottom-

Fig. 6. Shape and structure of depositional element A (troughs and trough fill deposits interpreted as junction pool deposits): trough shaped concave upward and erosional lower bounding surfaces (φ). Trough fill deposits consisting of tangential bottomsets with gravel couplet cross-beds (detail within frame is in Fig. 4).

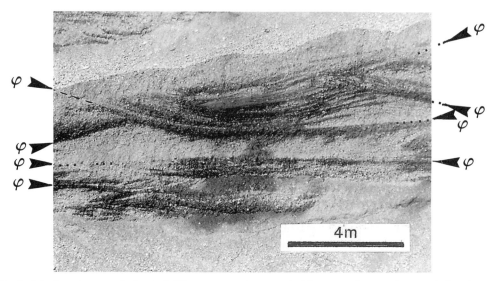

Fig. 7. Interfingering cross-bed sets of different textural types and with apparently opposite growth directions giving the onion-like appearance to the trough fill. φ, erosional bounding surfaces.

sets. A large variety of cross-bed sets (McKee & Weir 1953) may fill the troughs, but this variety can be regarded as a composite of three different set types, which are (ordered according to their importance) as follows.

(i) *Sets with gravel couplet cross-beds*. Individual couplets are 1 to 5 dm thick and form tabular cross-beds (angle of dip up to 25°), occasionally with short tangential bottomsets

(Fig. 6). Reactivation surfaces have not been observed.

(ii) *Sets with 'grey gravel' cross-beds* (Fig. 9). Individual foresets are vague and have thicknesses of 0.5 to 2.5 dm, mostly 1 dm, and are separated by thin stringers of sand or pebbles. The foresets are always tangential to the erosional boundary of the trough, and occasionally sigmoidal. Reactivation surfaces do occur.

Fig. 8. Interfingering of foresets and bottomsets with texturally different cross-beds, such as sand and grey gravel (section perpendicular to general flow). It reflects the difference in bedload in the two tributaries.

Fig. 9. Shape and internal structure of a trough-fill consisting of single sets with 'grey gravel' cross-beds.

Single cross-bed sets can be very large, up to more than 100 m long and 5 m thick.

(iii) *Sets with sandy cross-beds.* A single cross-bed is a compound of parallel laminated and ripple-laminated sets. Admixtures of granules and pebbles are frequent (Fig. 10). Bed boundaries cannot be delimited except in cases where sandy beds interfinger or intercalate with gravel cross-beds. Sandy cross-bed sets are not frequent.

Trough fills composed of different set types do occur, e.g. a set of 'grey gravel' cross-beds can be replaced laterally by a series of cross-beds composed of gravel couplets. Within a single trough one can find co-sets (McKee & Weir 1953) with interfingering cross-beds; such a configuration can only be observed between 'grey gravel' sets and sand sets (Fig. 8). At a few places the trough fill ends upwards with a rippled sandy deposit containing silt and clay laminae.

Fig. 10. Trough with single sets of sandy cross-beds interfingering with gravel cross-beds dipping in the opposite direction (length of rod is 2 m).

Horizontally bedded gravel. This lithofacies consists mainly of 'grey gravel' with occasional inclusions of single beds of bimodal gravels and of gravel couplets. Individual beds range in thickness from less than 1 dm up to several decimetres, typically 1–2 dm, the very thick beds being probably obscure low-angle cross-stratified sets (Fig. 3). Single beds extend laterally from a few metres up to several tens of metres. The bedded appearance is caused by: (1) textural modifications, especially within the 'grey gravel', e.g. by fining or coarsening upward sequences, or by thin sandy stringers between gravel layers, (2) vertical alternations of textural types, (3) thin interlayers of sand or of monogranular granule or pebble layers, or (4) discontinuous stringers of a coarse lag (pebbles and cobbles). Locally horizontal gravel beds can be replaced laterally by poorly organized horizontal cross-bed sets. Occasionally, horizontally bedded gravel beds abut without sedimentological modifications against a slightly inclined, older erosional surface, obviously a channel margin.

Massive and coarse-grained 'brown gravel' beds.

Laterally extensive massive beds are composed of 'brown gravels' with cobbles and small boulders. Single beds or sets of beds have thicknesses of up to several metres. Laterally the thickness may vary rapidly and the beds may locally vanish and reduce to a discontinuous lag of coarse cobbles due to subsequent fluvial erosion. Clast orientation is quite common, with the long axis of the clasts dipping roughly 15° upstream. Individual horizontal gravel couplets can be intercalated into the massive 'brown gravel' beds. Except for such patterns, the internal organization of 'brown gravel' beds is poor. They seem to be deposited in specific high stratigraphic levels of the Rhine gravel deposit. Convolutions of originally horizontally laminated sand may occur below a 'brown gravel' bed (Fig. 11).

Environmental interpretation

The environments of different morphological components of a braided river system, such as pools, channels, bars, flood plains, are all situated at distinct topographic levels in the braided river system (Fig. 2) and hence this con-

Fig. 11. Convolution structures (indicated by arrows) and deformed parallel-laminations in sand-layer overlain by a thick bed of coarse brown gravel. The top of this layer is partly removed by the pit activities.

cept suggests a definite hierarchical order of preservation potentials of the various braided river sediments.

Pool deposits are formed in the lowest geometrical, deepest, depositional levels and must therefore have an excellent chance of being preserved in a fluvial environment (Bristow *et al.* in press). Sedimentation in the pool is initiated

if a change of any flow or channel parameter in the confluence forces a shallowing or, more importantly, a lateral or a longitudinal shift of the pool. Ashmore (1979) and Ashmore & Parker (1983) have shown that the position and orientation of pools can be quite variable longitudinally as well as laterally. For reasons of geometrical continuity two distinct processes must contribute to the filling of the pool:

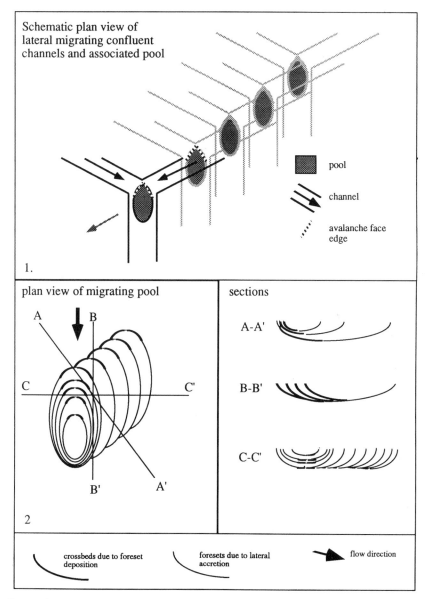

Fig. 12. Geometric model of lateral migrating pool and associated pool-fill structures depending on orientation of vertical section.

(1) foreset deposition at the upstream ends of the pool, e.g. avalanching at a slip face, possibly together with bottomset deposition. Foreset deposition must act during a longitudinal shift of the pool; and (2) lateral accretion along the flanks of the pool during a lateral shift of the pool. These two processes are independent of the way in which the material is transported across the pool, i.e. whether the material travels through the centre or along the sides (Best 1988; Reid *et al.* 1989). Any lateral shift of the pool must be accompanied by erosion on one side and deposition on the opposite side. From purely geometrical considerations and taking into account simple discharge modifications, a simple genetic scheme is formulated (Fig. 12).

In an aggrading braided river system the chances for the preservation of pool sediments are high, and all trough fill deposits in the Rhine gravel of the study area are interpreted as pool deposits.

Other interpretations of the trough deposits, such as the fill of abandoned minor channels, the toesets of large-scale dunes, or flute-like localized scours of the stream bed, have been abandoned for the following reasons.

(i) The large dimensions of a single trough deposit in longitudinal as well as in lateral directions (up to more than 100 m) seem to exclude any fill of (minor) channels or flutes. And only gigantic dunes could produce such large sets.

(ii) The intimate interfingering of the foresets and bottomsets in cases with texturally different cross-bed sets, such as sand and 'grey gravel' sets (Fig. 8). This structure indicates different bed-load sources and is not generated by dunes.

(iii) Concentrical fill of abandoned pools ('onion structure'). Occasionally, the very downstream end of the trough fill can be observed in the field. The cross-beds are then replaced by concentric, concave upwards gravel beds, obviously the filling and the abandonment of a negative bed form. A close correspondence exists between the anticipated pool structure and the actual trough fill (Figs 12 and 13). No fining upward occurs in this abandonment structure, which has therefore nothing to do with a decrease of flow competence, as e.g. in the case of the 'slough channel' (an abandoned pool in a river bend, Bluck 1979), or in the case of decrease of depth of dune troughs. Pools generated at confluences are filled if one of the channels gets innactive, an event which is not necessarily accompanied by an attenuation of the flow competence in the active channel.

Because individual cross-bedded gravel couplets never interfinger with sand or 'grey gravel' foreset-beds, gravel couplets probably do not act as real foresets. Instead, they could represent the lateral accretion deposit in pools, in an analogous manner as do dune sets which generate the lateral accretion in sandy point bars.

Fig. 13. Example of an inferred migrating pool deposit showing characteristic lateral accretion pattern and erosional bounding surface (φ) at the pool base.

Channels operate in a low level of the braided river system, but channel flow generally builds up complicated elevated depositional structures such as bars, islands and flood plains (see Bluck 1979) in or along the channels. In the large aggradational cycle which led to the thick Rhine gravel deposit, the highly transient network of the braided channels probably destroyed any elevated structure in and between the channels. Such structures are hence considered to have practically no chance of preservation and only channel deposits, or just the basal parts of bars, e.g. the unit bar or the bar platform in the notation of Smith (1974) and Bluck (1979), may escape destruction. The development of beds together with the absence of boulders and of material finer than medium sand suggests fluvial bedload transport at moderate-magnitude flows with less competence and with less silt and clay in the suspension as compared with high-magnitude flows. At such stages gravel transport may occur discontinuously in pulses (Reid & Frostick 1986; Ashmore 1985; as diffuse gravel bedload sheets, Hein & Walker 1977, Whiting *et al.* 1988). According to Todd (1989) a sheet a few grains thick of moderate- to well-sorted gravel is formed at moderate-magnitude river flow, with common imbrication of the large clasts. Such low-density bedload transport is dominated by fluid–solid momentum transfer (diffuse gravel sheets, Hein & Walker 1977). The 'grey gravels' are thus viewed as thin gravel sheets, each sheet being the product of a gravel pulse. Since the internal structure of 'grey gravel' beds is identical for horizontal and inclined beds, such cross-beds are not the result of avalanching along a slip face but must be simply the continuation of (horizontal) gravel sheets into a trough. Horizontal beds of gravel couplets, regarded as climbing translatent cross-strata, can be intercalated in the gravel sheets; the stream power was therefore high enough to produce gravel dunes in the channel bed.

Large and coarse-grained gravel sheets ('brown gravel'). During high-magnitude floods with high concentrations of suspended particles a thick 'traction carpet' (or high density bedload with dominant solid–solid momentum transfer) develops along the bed; sorting is then poor to moderate and large clasts often are imbricated. These coarse grained gravel sheets are considered to be formed rapidly by high-magnitude floods (Todd 1989). This is also indicated by the massive aspect, the large clasts, the very poor sorting of 'brown gravel', and the convolutions in sand layers at the base of the gravel sheets,

and which thus represent a striking contrast to other gravel types. Inclusions of individual gravel couplets attests a sporadic formation of gravel dunes during the flow. During glacial floods large fluctuations in discharge and sediment concentration that could allow such variations are likely to occur. Other bedforms such as bars or armored beds are probably eroded during the flow.

Intercalated pool deposits occur infrequently in the 'brown gravel' and seem to be restricted to the basal parts of the sheets, i.e. the flow is envisaged as a single sheet flow which was only partly conveyed in individual channels of the braid plain. Such a regime could be interpreted as transitional between a debris flow and a fluvial bedload transport (Nemec & Steel 1984; Smith 1986; Todd 1989), containing a large amount of fine-grained suspended particles. Laterally extensive sand and silt bodies in the Rhine gravel could also be attributed to large floods. According to Kochel & Baker (1982), high magnitude floods may produce backflooding, and fine grained slack-water sediments accumulate. The pattern of the meltwater system in front of the Würm glaciers (Fig. 1) would allow such backflooding.

No single structure in the Rhine gravel has been interpreted by us as a deposit of a complete bar. Similarly no indication of intraformational alluvial-plain deposits showing evidence of, pedogenesis, desiccation, or bioturbation phenomena, or of eolian or permafrost processes has been found in the Rhine gravel.

Discussion and conclusion

We propose a gravel braided river model for the late Pleistocene Rhine gravel, where only a few sediment types are preserved, i.e.

pool deposits generated at the junction of two channels (cross-bedded trough fills);

channel deposits generated at moderate-magnitude floods (horizontal 'grey' beds);

channel or sheet-flow deposits generated at high-magnitude floods (horizontal coarse 'brown gravel' beds);

and that, in particular, bar and flood plain sediments, which have been continuously destroyed by the lateral shift of the channels at moderate-magnitude flows and probably also by high-magnitude sheet floods, are absent in such deposits.

Pools and channels are both flow agents with erosional as well as depositional capacities, but they act at different topographic levels. Pools operate at the lowest level and, given a relatively low aggradation rate and/or relatively mobile channels and a high braiding intensity, they will reprocess the whole deposit, leaving only pool fills. On the other hand, for a high aggradation rate and/or immobile channels and low braiding intensity, channel sediments will predominate and pool fills would occur only sporadically; in the extreme case the preservation of bars or even flood plains could be imagined. Channel mobility and braiding intensity are probably correlated. Therefore, the ratio pool fill : channel deposit in braided river alluvium is suggested to be an expression of the ratio braiding intensity : aggradation rate. According to Ashmore (1985) the pattern of braided river channels varies under the influence of slope and discharge. Increases of these variables produce increased braiding intensity (see also Howard *et al.* 1970 and Maizels 1987). In the Rhine gravel the ratio of pool fill : channel deposits seems to vary according to the slope. In a pit less than 1 km beyond the former icefront, and with a high depositional slope, small pool deposits dominate and the lateral dimensions are in the 1–10 m range; 5 km farther downstream the dimensions are several tens of metres and pools account for up to approximately half of the deposit; another 4 km further down, at a position with a low depositional slope, the preserved pool fills are up to 100 m wide and probably account for less than one third of the deposit.

In our concept sedimentary structures of low-magnitude flow conditions are not preserved in the Rhine gravel, a possible exception being abandoned pools which are filled by fine-grained sediments (e.g. the slough channels of Bluck 1979). Instead, moderate-magnitude floods generated the bulk of the channel and pool deposits, and high-magnitude, probably sheet-like floods generated the coarse and thick 'brown gravel' beds. Exceptionally high-magnitude floods are postulated for the large-scale erosion of large portions of the alluvium and the shaping of terraces. To give an impression of the envisaged magnitude: the total

volume which would have been removed by the flood which formed the terrace H (Fig. 1) is in the order of $10^8 \, \text{m}^3$.

In our opinion similar deposits of gravel braided river systems have been described from ancient alluvial successions (e.g. Bluck 1967; Eynon & Walker 1974; Vos & Tankard 1981; Ori 1982; Steel & Thompson 1983; Ramos *et al.* 1986; Smith 1990). The interpretations given in these studies conflict in some important aspects with our braided river concept. The most striking disagreement concerns the depositional importance of bars. Most authors have considered them as important structures in the deposit, whereas we regard bars as sedimentologically insignificant in the Rhine gravel. Also controversial is the interpretation of some cross-bedded elements. Structures which resemble closely the pool fills in the Rhine gravel have previously been explained as channel deposits (Bluck 1967, fig. 2c; Ramos *et al.* 1986, fig. 3), as bar deposits (Ori 1982, figs 5 and 10; Steel & Thompson 1983, fig. 3), or as both (Smith 1990, figs 6,7,8 and 12). The conflicting views are clearly demonstrated by a comparison of the interpretation of Ramos *et al.* (1986, fig. 12), which gives a detailed environmental reconstruction of a gravelly Buntsandstein braided river deposit, and our interpretation of the very similar Rhine gravel. Whereas Ramos *et al.* (1986) envisage in the succession from the lower-cycle to the upper-cycle of the conglomerate an increase of the bar and channel dimensions and of the flow stability, we are inclined to see simply a rapid decrease of the ratio pool fill : channel deposits, and hence of the ratio braiding intensity : aggradation rate, which could be due to a decrease of the depositional slope or of the discharge.

B. Finkel, K. Kelts, A. Pugin and numerous other colleagues have discussed with us field results and conclusions of the present study. Figure 2 is drawn from a photograph with the permission of M. Jaeggi (VAW/ETH). We thank J. L. Best, P. A. Carling, P. G. DeCelles for reviewing previous versions of this manuscript, and also S. P. Todd and S. A. Smith, who reviewed the final version. Their helpful comments have significantly improved the manuscript.

References

ANKETELL, J. M. & RUST, B. R. 1990. Origin of cross-stratal layering in fluvial conglomerates, Devonian Malbaie Formation, Gaspé, Quebec. *Canadian Journal of Earth Sciences*, **27**, 1773–1782.

ASHMORE, P. E. 1979. *Laboratory Modelling of Braided Streams*. MSc thesis, University of Alberta.

—— 1985. *Processes and form in gravel braided streams: Laboratory modelling and field observations*. PhD Thesis, Dept. of Geology, Univ. Edmonton, Alberta.

—— & PARKER, G. 1983. Confluence scour in coarse braided streams. *Water Resources Research*. **19**, 392–402.

BRISTOW, C. S., BEST, J. L. & ROY, A. G. (in press).

Morphology and facies models of channel confluences. *International Fluvial Sedimentology Conference, Barcelona, 1989*.

BAKER, R. V. 1972. *Paleohydrology and Sedimentology of Lake Missoula Flooding in Eastern Washington*. Geological Society of America Special Paper, **144**.

BEST, J. L. 1988. Sediment transport and bed morphology at river channel confluences. *Sedimentology*, **35**, 481–498.

BLUCK, B. J. 1967. Deposition of some Upper Old Red Sandstone conglomerates in the Clyde area: A study in the significance of bedding. *Scottish Journal of Geology*, **3**, 139–167.

—— 1979. Structure of coarse grained braided stream alluvium. *Transactions of the Royal Society of Edinburgh*, **70**, 181–221.

CARLING, P. A. 1990. Particle over-passing on depth-limited gravel bars. *Sedimentology*, **37**, 345–355.

—— & GLAISTER, M. S. 1987. Rapid deposition of sand and gravel mixtures downstream of a negative step: the role of matrix-infilling and particle-overpassing in the process of bar-front accretion. *Journal of the Geological Society, London*, **144**, 543–551.

DECELLES, P. G., GRAY, M. B., RIDGWAY, K. D., COLE, R. B., PIVNIK, D. A. PEQUERA, N. & SRIVASTAVA, P. 1991. Controls on synorogenic alluvial-fan architecture, Beartooth Conglomerate (Paleocene), Wyoming and Montana. *Sedimentology*, **38**, 567–590.

EYNON, G. E. & WALKER, R. G. 1974. Facies relationships in Pleistocene outwash gravels, Southern Ontario: a model for bar growth in braided rivers. *Sedimentology*, **21**, 43–70.

HEIN, F. J. & WALKER, R. G. 1977. Bar evolution and development of stratification in the gravelly, braided, Kicking Horse River, British Columbia. *Canadian Journal of Earth Sciences*, **14**, 562–570.

HOWARD, A. D., KEETCH, M. E. & VINCENT, C. L. 1970. Topological and geometrical properties of braided rivers. *Water Resources Research*, **6**, 1674–1688.

HÜNERMANN, K. A. 1985. Eiszeit-Säugetiere aus dem Kanton Zürich. *Vierteljahresschrift der Naturforschenden Gesellschaft in Zürich*, **130**, 229–250.

KELLER, W. A. 1977. Die Rafzerschotter und ihre Bedeutung für die Morphogenese des zürcherischen Hochrheingebietes. *Vierteljahresschrift der Naturforschenden Gesellschaft in Zürich*, **122**, 357–412.

KELLERHALS, R., CHURCH, M. & BRAY, D. I. 1976. Classification and analysis of river processes. *Journal of the Hydraulic Division, American Society of Civil Engineers*, **97**, 1165–1180.

KOCHEL, R. C. & BAKER, V. R. 1982. Paleoflood hydrology. *Science*, **215**, 353–361.

MCKEE, E. D. & WEIR, G. W. 1953. Terminology for stratification and cross-stratification in sedimentary rocks. *Geological Society of America Bulletin*, **64**, 381–390.

MAIZELS, J. K. 1987. Large-scale flood deposits associated with the formation of coarse-grained, braided terrace sequences. *In*: ETHRIDGE, F. G., FLORES, A. M. & HARVEY, M. D. (eds) *Recent Developments in Fluvial Sedimentology*. SEPM Special Publications, **39**, 135–148.

MIALL, A. D. 1977. A review of the braided-river depositional environment. *Earth Science Reviews*, **13**, 1–62.

—— 1981. Alluvial sedimentary basins: tectonic setting and basin architecture. *In*: MIALL, A. D. (ed.) *Sedimentation and Tectonics in Alluvial Basins*. Special Paper of the Geological Association of Canada, **23**, 1–33.

—— 1985. Architectural Element Analysis: A new Method of Facies Analysis applied to fluvial Deposits. *Earth Science Reviews*, **22**, 261–308.

MOSLEY, M. P. 1976. An experimental study of channel confluences. *Journal of Geology*, **84**, 535–562.

NEMEC, W. & STEEL, R. J. 1984. Alluvial and costal conglomerates: Their significant features and some comments on gravelly mass-flow deposits. *In*: KOSTER, E. H. & STEEL, R. J. (eds) *Sedimentology of gravels and conglomerates*. Canadian Society of Petroleum Geologists Memoir, **10**, 1–31.

ORI, G. G. 1982. Braiding in meandering channel patterns in humid region alluvial fan deposits, River Reno, Po plain (Northern Italy). *Sedimentary Geology*, **31**, 231–248.

RAMOS, A., SOPENA, A. & PEREZ-ARLUCEA, M. 1986. Evolution of Buntsandstein fluvial sedimentation in the northwest Iberian Ranges (Central Spain). *Journal of Sedimentary Petrology*, **56**, 862–875.

REID, I. & FROSTICK, L. E. 1986. Dynamics of bedload transport in Turkey Brook, a coarse-grained alluvial channel. *Earth Surface Processes and Landforms*, **11**, 143–155.

——, BEST, J. L. & FROSTICK, L. E. 1989. Floods and Flood Sediments at River Confluences. *In*: BEVEN, K. & CARLING, P. (eds) *Floods: Hydrological, Sedimentological and Geomorphological Implications*. Wiley, 107–135.

SMITH, G. A. 1986. Coarse grained volcanoclastic sediment: Terminology and depositional process. *Geological Society of America Bulletin*, **97**, 1–10.

SMITH, N. D. 1974. Sedimentology and bar formation in the Upper Kicking Horse river, a braided outwash stream. *Journal of Geology*, **82**, 205–223.

—— 1978. Braided-stream deposits. *In*: FAIRBRIDGE, R. W. & BOURGEOIS, J. (eds) *Encyclopedia of Sedimentology*. Encyclopedia of Earth Sciences, **6**, 82–83.

SMITH, S. A. 1990. The sedimentology and accretionary styles of an ancient gravel-bed stream: the Budleigh Salterton Pebble Beds (Lower Triassic); southwest England. *Sedimentary Geology*, **67**, 199–219.

STEEL, R. J. & THOMSON, D. B. 1983. Structures and textures in Triassic braided stream conglomerates ('Bunter' Pebble Beds) in the Sherwood Sandstone Group, North Staffordshire, England. *Sedimentology*, **30**, 341–367.

TODD, S. P. 1989. Stream-driven, high-density gravelly traction carpets: possible deposits in the Trabeg Conglomerate formation, SW Ireland and some theoretical considerations of their origin. *Sedimentology*, **36**, 513–530.

VOS, R. G. & TANKARD, A. J. 1981. Braided fluvial sedimentation in the Lower Paleozoic Cape basin, South Africa. *Sedimentary Geology*, **29**, 171–193.

WELTEN, M. 1978. Gletscher und Vegetation im Lauf der letzten 100'000 Jahre. *Vorläufige Mitteilungen und Jahrbuch der Schweizerischen Naturforschenden Gesellschaft: Gletscher & Klima, Birkhäuser*, 5–18.

WHITING, P. J., DIETRICH, W. E., LEOPOLD, L. B., DRAKE, T. G. & SHREVE, R. L. 1988. Bedload sheets in heterogeneous sediment. *Geology*, **16**, 105–108.

Radar facies: recognition of facies patterns and heterogeneities within Pleistocene Rhine gravels, NE Switzerland

PETER HUGGENBERGER

Federal Institute for Water Resources and Water Pollution Control (EAWAG)
CH-8600 Dübendorf, Switzerland

Abstract: Pleistocene braided-river deposits in river valleys constitute a large fraction of natural groundwater reservoirs in Switzerland. A key for estimating the residence times of water and for determining the extent of macrodispersion, which describes large-scale mixing processes in the aquifers, is a knowledge of the distribution of hydraulic conductivities. In many contamination problems, sedimentological information is sparse and drill-core descriptions and pumping-tests only give a limited picture of the geometry of inhomogeneities. Ground-probing radar (GPR) offers the potential to resolve sedimentary structures and lithofacies in gravel deposits. For example, the geometry of characteristic sedimentary structures and the textures of late Pleistocene Rhine gravel are portrayed on GPR reflection images.

Because of the ability of the GPR method to detect changes in water content, the reflection image can be related to small changes in the degree of sediment saturation, which may also reflect a change in sediment composition. This allows a distinction between several characteristic lithofacies that are typical of late Pleistocene braided-river depositional systems. The main limitation of the GPR method is the rapid attenuation of electromagnetic waves in the ground, especially in clay-covered regions.

Fluvioglacial outwash of gravel of ancient braided river systems make up a large portion of the Quaternary valley-fills and more than two thirds of the aquifers in Switzerland. Because these gravel deposits are situated in the most densely populated regions, groundwater is very susceptible to contamination by chemical hazards, leaky landfills and infiltration by polluted rivers. Interest in the gravel deposits of the Quaternary fill of peri-alpine valleys has grown in response to the need for improved understanding of groundwater circulation systems in order to make short- and long-term predictions of various kinds of contaminant transport processes.

Mixing and transport of contaminants in groundwater are strongly controlled by advection, dispersion and, at larger scales, by macrodispersion (Bear 1979). The latter is mainly caused by the variability of hydraulic conductivity (e.g. Anderson 1989). Stochastic and deterministic approaches to the evaluation of large-scale mixing processes in heterogeneous deposits require some fundamental assumptions about the structure and composition of the subsurface. Stochastic theories assume statistical homogeneity and relatively small perturbations of hydraulic conductivity (Gelhar & Axness 1983). Deterministic theories presume perfect layering of the aquifer sediments (e.g. Molz *et al.*

1983). A commonly used method for determining the spatial structure of hydraulic conductivity is the single-well pumping test combined with flowmeter measurements (Hufschmied 1987). By using drill-core descriptions and pumping-tests by themselves, only a limited picture of the geometry of inhomogeneities and of the small-scale variability of hydraulic conductivity can be obtained (Jussel 1989).

Due to the selective sorting of sediments by fluvio-dynamic processes, changes in sediment composition in glacial outwash gravel and thus also changes of the hydraulic conductivities of several orders of magnitude may occur over short distances and depths. In particular, the relatively fast water-conduits observed in many gravel deposits (Huggenberger *et al.* 1988), reflecting a characteristic fluvial textural gravel type without a fine-material fraction (Steel & Thompson 1983), might be overlooked by the common testing methods in coarse unconsolidated sediments. This information can, however, be obtained visually by investigating fluvial deposits above groundwater level. Such studies turn out to be useful to gain an understanding of the dynamics of the ancient depositional system and for the recognition of the principal sedimentary structures and textures (Siegenthaler & Huggenberger this volume).

From Best, J. L. & Bristow, C. S. (eds), 1993, *Braided Rivers*, Geological Society
Special Publication No. **75**, pp. 163–176.

163

Unfortunately, in many practical contamination problems, outcrop information is normally not available.

The objectives of the present work are to examine whether and to what extent the characteristic lithofacies of the Pleistocene Rhine gravels can be recognized as mappable reflections or reflection patterns on ground-probing radar reflection profiles, in order to gain information about the geometry of inhomogeneities, the possible ranges of hydraulic properties, and the anisotropies in the subsurface.

Ground-probing radar: techniques and equipment

The appropriate geophysical exploration method to be applied is determined by the length-scale characteristics and variability of sediment composition and hydraulic properties on a metre to decimetre vertical scale (Fig. 1). In the reflection seismic and ground-probing radar methods, resolution increases with increasing frequency of the waves (see Eq. 1). Seismic methods are most sensitive to the mechanical properties of materials, whereas radar methods are sensitive to contained fluids and to the presence of electrically conductive materials (Steeples & Miller 1990). Generally, reflection methods and ground-probing radar

are similar in concept, but are almost mutually exclusive in terms of where they work well. Both methods use reflections of energy from underground features. Radar works well in the absence of electrical conducting materials near the earth's surface, but will not penetrate into good electrical conductors (e.g. clay rich materials). The seismic reflection methods, on the other hand, works best where the water table is near the surface and easily penetrates damp clays that are excellent electrical conductors (Steeples & Miller 1990). Previous experiments at the contact zone of proglacial and glacial deposits have shown that in the unsaturated zone dry gravels do not effectively transmit high-frequency seismic waves (Imhof 1991). Equally significant is the problem of masking of reflectors by seismic ground-wave, such that the top few meters often cannot be resolved (Steeples et al. 1985). Transmission frequencies commonly employed in ground-probing radar surveys range from 80 to 1000 MHz (megahertz). The electromagnetic-wave velocity, c ($cn\,ns^{-1}$) is equal to the product of the wavelength λ (cm) and the central frequency f (ns^{-1}):

$$c = \lambda f \qquad (1)$$

Velocities in the subsurface may be determined by common mid-point (CMP) experiments (Steeples & Miller 1990; Robinson 1983).

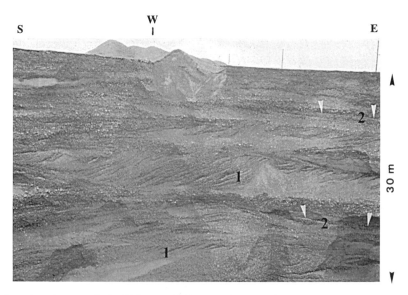

Fig. 1. Sedimentary structures in the Pleistocene Rhine gravels exposed in a 30 m high section showing lithofacies variability at the metre to decimetre scale. (Weiach, NE Switzerland). Pit-height c. 30 m. (1) Crossbed sets; (2) extended zones of high permeability gravel.

Velocities generally range from about 6 to 12 cm ns^{-1}, depending on whether measurements are from the saturated or unsaturated zone (a more detailed description is found in a later section). The resolution is ideally equal to about $\lambda/4$ (Sheriff 1984), but velocity uncertainties and waveform variations limit the practical resolution to about $\lambda/3$ to $\lambda/2$ (Trabant 1984). Therefore, using a 250 MHz antenna the expected resolution is of the order of 1–2.5 dm. Penetration of the radar signal generally decreases with increasing frequency (Davis & Annan 1989), but higher frequencies yield higher resolution information. Compared to the high resolution seismic methods which use frequencies of about 1000 Hz (Frei 1991), frequencies of ground-probing radar (GPR) systems are several orders of magnitude higher. Therefore, much higher resolution is expected from GPR methods. Because of the lithofacies changes observed in outcrops at the decimetre scale, higher resolution was preferred over deeper penetration for this project.

The GPR system applied in this experiment was a GEORADAR 1 from OYO (Hara & Sakayama 1985) consisting of transmitter and receiver antennae and a control unit. The system produces a short pulse of high-frequency electromagnetic energy emitted from the transmitting antenna at a rise time of the order of 10^{-9} s into the ground. At changes in the bulk electrical properties of the different subsurface lithologies, part of the energy is reflected. The reflected signals are recorded by the receiver antenna. The reflection or pulse delay times, which are the times between energy transmission and reception, are a function of the electromagnetic wave propagation velocities through the sediments and the depths to subsurface reflectors. Propagation velocities and penetration depths of electromagnetic waves depend on the complex dielectric constant ε, which is a measure of the response of the material to an applied electric field, such as an electromagnetic wave. This response is split into two factors: one that determines the propagation characteristics of the wave (i.e. its velocity and thus its wavelength in the material) and one that determines the energy loss (attenuation or absorption) as the wave travels through the material (Davis & Annan 1989, Eq. 4). These two factors are described by the real (ε') and imaginary (ε'') parts of the complex dielectric parameter (Schmugge 1985). The real part of ε (ε' term) for most dry geological materials range from 4 for quartz sand to 7 for shales and carbonates. Water, on the other hand, with ε' values of 80.3 at 20°C (*Handbook of Physics and*

Chemistry 1986) can radically alter the velocity of radar waves travelling through geological materials. Thus, saturated quartz sand may have ε' values of up to 30, and ε' for dry soils will rise from 8 to about 20 as they become wet (Schmugge 1985). In the following sections, 'dielectric number' refers to the real part (ε') only. According to Roth *et al.* (1990), the propagation velocity c of an electromagnetic wave in the ground may be approximated by the dielectric number ε' and the magnetic permeability μ (μ can be set to 1 for low-loss geological materials such as gravels; Hara & Sakayama 1985) as follows:

$$c = c_0/\sqrt{\varepsilon'_c \mu} \tag{2}$$

where c = electromagnetic wave velocity in the subsurface, c_0 = electromagnetic wave velocity in the air. Roth *et al.* (1990) relate the composite dielectric number ε'_c of a multiphase mixture of sediment, water and air to the dielectric numbers and volume fractions of its constituents. In addition, a functional relationship between the geometry of the medium and the direction of the applied electric field has been described by different authors (Tinga *et al.* 1973; Birchak *et al.* 1974; Roth *et al.* 1990). They introduce a geometry parameter α, where $\alpha = 1$ for electric field parallel to layering, $\alpha = -1$ for electric field perpendicular to layering and $\alpha = 0.5$ for random-oriented fabrics. The mixing law for the dielectric number of a three-phase system to describe wet soil was expressed by Roth *et al.* (1990) as:

$$\varepsilon'_c = (\theta\varepsilon_w{}^\alpha + (1 - \eta)\,\varepsilon_s{}^\alpha + (\eta - \theta)\,\varepsilon_a{}^\alpha)^{1/\alpha} \tag{3}$$

where η is the soils porosity, $1 - \eta$, θ, and $\eta - \theta$ are the volume fractions and ε_s, ε_w, ε_a are the dielectric numbers of the solid, aqueous and gaseous phases respectively. Thus, contrasts in the dielectric constants of subsurface materials are mainly due to differences in the volumetric water content.

The other principal physical factor influencing radar-wave interaction with geological materials is soil conductivity (part of the ε'' term; the other part is the frequency-dependent loss associated with the relaxation response phenomena of water; Davis & Annan 1989), which results in the attenuation of electromagnetic waves in earth materials.

Attenuation by geological materials is the principal factor for limited depth penetration of the electromagnetic waves. Considering the high frequency electrical properties of gravel at the test-site (resistivities in the 800 to 3000 Ωm range in the unsaturated zone and of the order of 120 Ωm in the saturated zone) the expected maximum penetration depth is of the order of 10–15 m.

Radar facies

Following Jol & Smith (1991) or Beres & Haeni (1991) depositional environments can be interpreted from radar records by analogy to seismic reflection interpretation methods. A radar facies is defined here as a mappable, three-dimensional sedimentary unit composed of reflections whose characteristics differ from adjacent units. Radar reflection signatures (patterns) that relate to lithologic and stratigraphic characteristics of sediments are given by Beres & Haeni (1991). However, there are some problems with the transferability and generalization of such signatures.

(1) The reflection pattern depends on the central frequency of the applied radar system, as clearly illustrated by Jol & Smith (1991).

(2) Reflections of electromagnetic waves are mainly caused by contrasts in the dielectric properties of the mixture sediment-water-air, and because water has the strongest influence on the dielectric constant, the degree of saturation is an important factor to be considered when interpreting radar reflection patterns. This also means that the same type of deposit (e.g. fluvial gravel deposits) may not only show different reflection patterns in the saturated and non saturated zones, but will also show differences under different humidity and salinity conditions. In this work, radar facies units are defined on the basis of the (1) types and geometries of major continuous reflections and (2) configurations of the reflection patterns within each distinct unit.

(3) A single reflecting surface will produce multiple events (peaks/troughs) on the reflection profile and care must therefore be taken in interpretation (Fig. 2).

Geological setting of test-site

The radar experiments were performed in a gravel pit within the Pleistocene Rhine gravels in NE Switzerland (Fig. 3). The pit is situated in front of the maximal Würm-stage extension of the Thur and Glatt-Linth lobes of the Rhine glacier. Imposing terminal moraine suites with heights up to 100 m above the outwash plain mark the end position of these lobes. Distally, proglacial fluvial gravel from the catchment area of the Rhine glacier fills the east–west-trending Rhine valley, which cuts into Tertiary sandstone and Jurassic limestone, and eventually into glacial deposits of the older Riss glacial stage, (Keller 1977). The gravels show the characteristic structures of braided-river deposition (Siegenthaler & Huggenberger this volume). The distance from the test-site to the former icefront is 6 km. The gravel pit is 20 m deep, more than 1 km long, and is exploited by the building industry. Those sections of the pits that are being excavated exhibit excellent outcrops with steep walls. GPR profiles were located at two different exploitation levels (the first in one of the upper levels and the second in the lower-

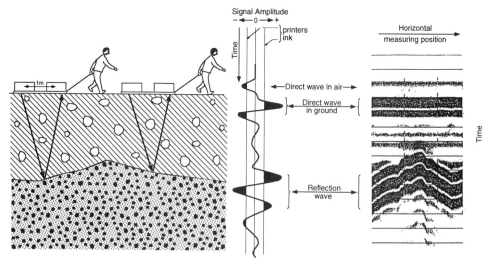

Fig. 2. Profiling method. Paths of electromagnetic waves with corresponding wave forms and radar profile (distance between receiver and transmitter fixed).

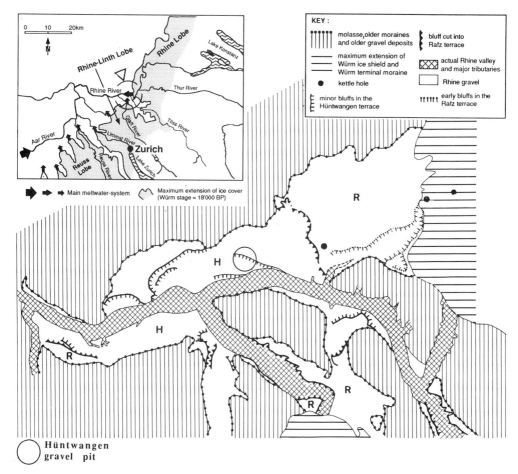

Fig. 3. Geological setting. The area studied is located in front of the Rhine and the Rhine-Linth lobe. Depositional levels (terraces) are separated by terrace bluffs in the glacial outwash deposit of the Rhine valley. R, Rafz terrace; H, Hüntwangen terrace.

most level) to allow investigations of the saturated zone about 3 m above the ground water level and 25 m above the valley bottom (Tertiary sandstone). Rapid exploitation of gravel gave an excellent and inexpensive opportunity to compare the GPR measurements of the upper level with the geological profile after excavation.

Sedimentological investigations and sampling

The description of the characteristic architectural elements and lithofacies of the Pleistocene Rhine gravels is based on sedimentological investigations by Siegenthaler & Huggenberger (this volume, table 1) and Huggenberger et al. (1988).

After exploration, sediment samples from the GPR profile were taken in the unsaturated zone from different lithofacies in order to determine the reflection coefficients of different lithofacies contacts. The parameters used to specify the dielectric numbers of the different lithofacies were: volumetric water content, porosity and temperature. The influence of temperature is small (Roth et al. 1990) and therefore it was neglected. Hydraulic conductivities of the distinguished lithfacies (see Siegenthaler & Huggenberger this volume) have been determined from undisturbed (Jussel 1992) and disturbed (Huggenberger et al. 1988) samples (Table 1).

Table 1. *Hydraulic conductivities of characteristic textural gravel types*

Textural gravel type	Hydraulic conductivity (m s^{-1})	$\sigma_{\ln K}$	
G2 'grey gravel'	1.4×10^{-4}	0.4	
G1 'brown gravel'	3×10^{-5}	0.6	
'Sand'	3×10^{-4}	0.3	
G3 'openframework gravel'	$c.\ 5 \times 10^{-1}$	≈ 1.0	
G3 'bimodal gravel'	1×10^{-4}–6×10^{-4}	(0.6)	(0.7)
'Silt'	$<1 \times 10^{-6}$		

Geometric mean and standard deviation of the natural logarithm of the measured (laboratory) and estimated (grain size distributions, Kozeny method) hydraulic conductivities (data from Jussel 1989, 1992 and Huggenberger *et al.* (1988). 1 m s^{-1} 1.04×10^4 darcy. For descrition of lithofacies see Huggenberger & Siegenthaler, in this volume.

Undisturbed samples have been taken by Jussel (1992) by freezing small blocks of sediments with liquid nitrogen, followed by stabilization with liquid paraffin. Measurements of hydraulic conductivity of undisturbed samples were used to calibrate the hydraulic conductivity of the disturbed samples derived from their grain-size distribution by different calculation methods (see e.g. Langguth & Voigt 1980). Porosity estimations (Fig. 4) are also based on measurements from undisturbed samples (Jussel 1992).

The volumetric water content was determined from samples of the different lithofacies (Table 2). Sediment sampling for the estimation of the volumetric water content took place a few days after the radar measurements. However, because sampling was done during a drought period of early 1990 it can be safely assumed that

the volumetric water content was not significantly influenced by changing hydrological conditions. For the estimation of the volumetric water content, sampling tubes of different sizes (diameter between 20 and 40 cm), depending on the grain-size of the sediment, were mounted on a bulldozer and pushed horizontally into the different lithofacies outcropping in the near-vertical pit-walls. Volumetric water content was then determined by gravimetric methods. It is likely that the disturbance of the sample and therefore the error in the volumetric water-content measurement increases with increasing grain size of the sampled textural gravel type. The time domain reflectometry (TDR) method (Roth *et al.* 1990), which was expected to give more accurate results, could not be applied because it was not possible to push the (TDR) probes into the pit-walls.

GPR profiles: results and description of radar facies

In the following sections the results of two experiments are presented, one performed in the unsaturated zone and the second in the lowermost level of the gravel pit that included the saturated zone. In each experiment, a description of the GPR profile and the character (geometry, pattern) of the reflections is given and then the reflection patterns are discussed in their sedimentological context.

The experiments were performed in a pro-filing mode; i.e. the distance between the trans-mitter and receiver antenna was fixed while they were moved along the lines. In this manner, a profile of horizontal survey distance in meters versus vertical two-way travel time in nano-seconds was obtained. Common mid-point (CMP; e.g. Jol & Smith, 1991) measurements

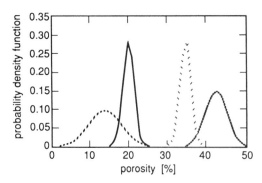

grey gravel (G2)
········· brown- and bimodal gravel (G1,G3)
⁗⁗ openframework gravel (G3)
sand lenses

Fig. 4. Measured total porosities from undisturbed samples (Jussel 1989).

Table 2. *Mean volumetric water content, porosity (see Fig. 2) and estimated composite dielectric number for the distinguished lithofacies (saturated and unsaturated zone)*

Gravel type	Mean volumetric water content (θ) [%]	Porosity (μ) [%] Jussel (1989)	ε (α = 0.5) Non-saturated zone	ε (α = 0.5) Saturated zone
Sand	8	43	5.1	26.8
Openframework gravel (G3)*	2	35	3.3	21.0
Grey gravel (G2)*	2	20	3.8	12.1
Bimodal gravel (G3)*	3	14	4.4	9.2

* Lithofacies G2 & G3 described by Siegenthalter & Huggenberger, this volume.
Calculation method after Roth *et al.* 1990. Parameters: geometry parameter $\alpha \approx 0.5$ (contact surface between different gravels). Temperature $\approx 10°C$, dielectric number for water = 80.3, dielectric number sediment ≈ 4.

(transmitter and receiver antenna moved in equal steps, in opposite directions from a fixed surface point) in experiment 2 resulted in a velocity–depth profile, which allowed the depth of the reflectors to be determined.

Experiment 1

The first experiment was performed in the unsaturated zone, which attains, at the measur-

ing position, a thickness of about 20 m. The profile length was 50 m, running north-south, perpendicular to the mean flow direction of the ancient fluvial system. The absence of major amounts of fine-grained sediments and the fact that the measurements were made within a period of prolonged drought imply that there was a relatively low water content in the unsaturated zone. The resulting reflection profile is given in Fig. 5a.

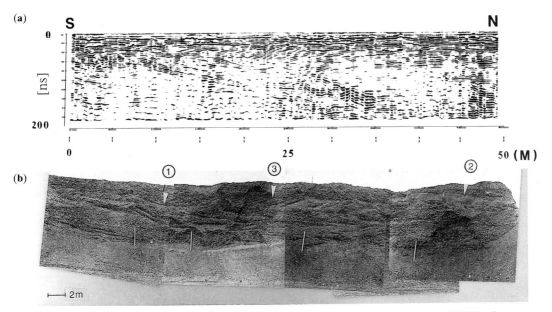

Fig. 5. (a) GPR profile (Experiment 1), N–S. Recording parameters: transmitter antenna 250 MHz, distance between transmitter and receiver: 0.8 m; recording time (200 ns); linear time dependent signal amplification; processing of the data included a time-dependent amplification of the signals and bandpass filtering between 70 & 250 MHz. (b) Geological profile along the GPR line after exposure by quarrying. Scale bars are 2 m long. (1) Trough structure, (2) sand horizon, (3) gravel couplets of Fig. 5.

Although reflections seem to become less pronounced with increasing depth due to attenuation of the electromagnetic waves, distinct reflections are found throughout the section. Oblique-tangential to oblique-parallel reflections dipping to the south can be recognized between 20 and 25 m at 20 to 50 ns. Overlying these reflections are more or less continuous subhorizontal, subparallel reflections that appear to truncate the underlying inclined ones. On the left side of the profile between 10 and 15 m at about 30 ns a suite of trough-shaped reflections are underlain by discontinuous, parallel reflections dipping to the north. To the left of the trough shaped reflections, between 0 and 10 m, reflection patterns are quite complex from 0 to 30 ns. A striking feature is the reflection free areas, or areas with only minor reflections without distinct terminations. Finally, there are continuous, parallel reflections, dipping shallowly to the north at 40 m and then approach the surface at about 37 m.

Correspondence between GPR and geological profiles

An initial visual comparison between the GPR-section (Fig. 5a) and the geological profile (Fig. 5b) after exploitation indicates significant correspondence. For example, Fig. 6 shows details of the central part of the geological profile (Fig. 5b), with parallel to tangential south-dipping sets consisting of bimodal-/openframework gravel cross-beds (a detailed description of this lithofacies is given by Siegenthaler & Huggenberger, this volume, Table 1). These sets are portrayed accurately on the GPR profile. Similarly, a correlation exists between the parallel reflections from 37 to 50 m and the sand-layer (Fig. 5b). The lithofacies G2, homogeneous, poorly sorted gravel with vague low-angle crossbeds (Siegenthaler & Huggenberger, this volume, table 1) seems to be related to the areas lacking major reflections. Finally, trough fills (Fig. 5b, left side), which always show erosional bounding surfaces, are clearly marked on the GPR profile.

What causes the reflections? According to theory, reflections in the unsaturated zone of low-conductive geological materials occur when electromagnetic waves meet boundaries between lithological units of contrasting dielectric constant. This can occur either at a change of water content within the same textural unit, or at a boundary between two distinct lithological units with the same or different volumetric water content. Transitions from low to high permeability sediments act as barriers to percolating waters at low volumetric water contents (Stauffer & Dracos 1985), which suggests that differences in moisture content at lithofacies boundaries with large permeability contrasts result in enhanced contrasts in dielectric numbers. The hydraulic conductivities and porosities of the characteristic lithofacies that exhibit little intergradation have been

Fig. 6. Gravel couplets consisting of openframework and bimodal gravel, central part of the geological profile Figure 4b (3).

determined by Huggenberger *et al.* (1988) and Jussel (1989, 1992; Table 1). The hydraulic conductivity of the openframework gravels is several orders of magnitude higher than the other lithofacies. Sand has the highest mean porosity, which obviously has some influence on the volumetric water content. These data, together with estimates of the volumetric water content, have allowed us to define a hierarchy of reflectivity of possible lithofacies contacts for non-saturated and saturated conditions (Table 3). In the unsaturated zone the highest contrasts are expected to occur at the transitions between sand and the openframework gravel and between the bimodal gravel and the openframework gravel. These transitions are expected to give the best reflection signals in the unsaturated zone; this is confirmed by this first experiment (e.g. correspondence between reflections and south dipping sets of openframework-bimodal couplets, or between the trough-shaped reflections which reflects the boundary between openframework and bimodal or homogeneous, poorly sorted gravel).

As the volumetric water content in the subsurface does not increase uniformly in all lithofacies during a wetting event, only a comparison between the specific conditions during the experiment with fully saturated conditions is provided (Table 2).

Experiment 2

Experiment 2 consists of 2 GPR profiles (profiling mode) running E–W parallel to the mean flow direction of the ancient fluvial system, one N–S profile perpendicular to the mean flow direction (Fig. 7a–c) and several CMP recordings. The experiment was located on the lowermost level of the Hüntwangen testsite, about 3.1 m above groundwater level (which could be extrapolated with an accuracy of ±5 cm from several observation wells located near the test-site). CMP data were collected in order to calculate reflector depths and the velocity profile. Velocities have been determined on the basis of a simple program presented by Steeples & Miller (1990). The program uses two or more time-distance pairs measured from a field CMP record as input data. It calculates, stores and displays zero-offset reflection times, velocities and depths to the reflecting interfaces and correlation coefficients. It assumes flat-lying reflectors. From this data the interval velocities have been estimated assuming a straight raypath (Robinson 1983). One of several CMP measurements is shown (CMP measurement at meter 15, profile 2) in Fig. 8 to illustrate the experiment and the related velocity profile.

In the N–S profile, four major continuous and numerous other reflections are recognized. The uppermost major reflection is relatively flat along the southern part of the line and is northward dipping along the northern part. Between 60 and 90 ns, two of the major reflections are near-horizontal to shallow north dipping. The lowermost of these reflections appears to truncate a package of curvilinear, mainly south-dipping reflections at the base of which is the fourth major reflection, a trough-shaped event between 90 and 120 ns. In E–W profile number 2 (Fig. 7b) there are two continuous reflections and in E–W profile 3 (Fig. 7c) there are four continuous reflections. These events can be correlated with those on the crossing N–S profile (Fig. 7a). Between the major reflections the

---

Table 3. *Reflection coefficient (R) at contact surfaces between different lithologies*

Lithological boundary	R Saturated conditions	R Non-saturated zone*
Sand/bimodal gravel	0.26	0.03
Openframework/bimodal gravel	0.20	0.08
Sand/grey gravel	0.20	0.06
Openframework/grey gravel	0.14	0.04
Sand/openframework gravel	0.06	0.1

* Estimates of volumetric water content from samples taken after a longer dry spell.

$$R = \left| \frac{\sqrt{\varepsilon 1} - \sqrt{\varepsilon 2}}{\sqrt{\varepsilon 1} + \sqrt{\varepsilon 2}} \right|$$

(Hara & Sakayama 1985).

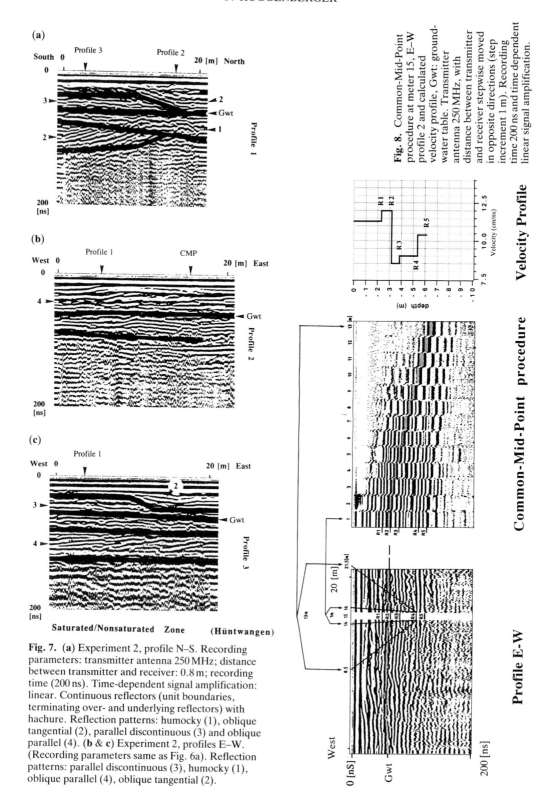

Fig. 8. Common-Mid-Point procedure at meter 15, E–W profile 2 and calculated velocity profile, Gwt: ground-water table. Transmitter antenna 250 MHz, with distance between transmitter and receiver stepwise moved in opposite directions (step increment 1 m). Recording time 200 ns and time dependent linear signal amplification.

Velocity Profile

Common-Mid-Point procedure

Profile E-W

Fig. 7. (a) Experiment 2, profile N–S. Recording parameters: transmitter antenna 250 MHz; distance between transmitter and receiver: 0.8 m; recording time (200 ns). Time-dependent signal amplification: linear. Continuous reflectors (unit boundaries, terminating over- and underlying reflectors) with hachure. Reflection patterns: humocky (1), oblique tangential (2), parallel discontinuous (3) and oblique parallel (4). (**b** & **c**) Experiment 2, profiles E–W. (Recording parameters same as Fig. 6a). Reflection patterns: parallel discontinuous (3), humocky (1), oblique parallel (4), oblique tangential (2).

following patterns are apparent:

Fig. 7a, N–S profile:
  hummocky (1)
  oblique tangential, trough shaped (2)
  parallel discontinuous (3)

Fig. 7b and 7c, E–W profiles:
  parallel discontinuous (3)
  hummocky (1)
  oblique parallel (4)
  oblique tangential, trough-shaped (2)

The velocity profile calculated from the CMP recordings with centre at 15 m (profile 2) shows a velocity drop of 12 to 8.5 cm ns^{-1} at a depth of 3.2 m (c. 60 ns). This depth corresponds to the groundwater level. The observed increase of velocity at a depth of 5.3 m could be due to low porosity cementation zones within the gravels, such as those previously observed in drillholes and inferred from the results of refraction seismic surveys (Frei 1991). Estimated velocities in the unsaturated zone of GPR experiment 1 are slightly lower (9–10 cm ns^{-1}) compared with those of experiment 2 (11 cm ns^{-1}). This can be explained by a slightly different water content in the unsaturated zone between winter and early summer 1990.

Discussion: environmental (sedimentological) interpretation of the observed radar facies

A striking reflection pattern, observed in both experiments, is the trough-shaped reflections that bound the packages of oblique-tangential and sigmoidal reflections. These patterns are recorded perpendicular to the ancient mean flow direction. The radar facies is interpreted to be due to trough-fill sediments above an erosional trough scour. Trough-fills are interpreted as pool-fill deposits, infilling channel confluences or alongside pre-existing bars (Siegenthaler & Huggenberger, this volume). Depending upon discharge, sediment load, channel shape and confluence angle, important scouring may occur at channel confluences. The shape of the scour surface generally resembles a spoon, with two steep avalanche faces upstream and a relatively low-angle distal end (Ashmore 1985; Mosley 1976; Best 1988). Sediment transport across the confluence scour is mainly around, rather than through the centre of the confluence (Best 1988). Scour-infill deposits evolve in the geometrically lowest depositional levels of a braided river system and hence have an excellent chance of being preserved in a fluvial environ-

ment. Examples of scour-fill were found on the geological profile after excavation (experiment 1); see for example, Fig. 7c, which shows a trough-shaped erosional bounding surface and fill consisting of single sets of gravel couplet cross-beds and tangential bottomsets formed by lateral accretion along the flanks of the pool during successive lateral shifts of the pool. The structural similarity between the trough-shaped radar reflection pattern (Fig. 7a, experiment 2) and the pool structure of Fig. 9 suggests that the structure on the GPR profile could correspond to a pool-fill deposit. This makes sense, since gravel couplets are expected to give the largest reflection contrasts (Table 3). From the radar sections parallel to the ancient flow direction, confluence scour infill deposits can rarely be clearly distinguished from inclined cross-beds formed in the active channel by migrating gravel dunes. However, in radar sections perpendicular to the mean flow direction, the characteristic form of the trough-shaped pool can be clearly identified.

The low reflectivity of homogeneous gravel allows the recognition of lithofacies G2 (grey gravel) in GPR profiles, at least in the unsaturated zone. Grey gravels are interpreted as thin gravel sheets in the active channels, either as the product of gravel pulses (Reid & Frostick 1986; Ashmore 1985) or as diffuse bedload sheets (Hein & Walker 1977; Whiting et al. 1988).

Finally, as shown on Fig. 5a & b, sand layers may produce continuous reflections. Sands are transported in different hydrodynamic regimes (see Huggenberger & Siegenthaler, this volume), but they mainly occur in the Rhine gravels as sandy cross-beds which alternate and interfinger with gravelly cross-beds or as

Fig. 9. Example of a migrating pool deposit, with characteristic lateral accretion structure and erosional surface at the pool base.

Configuration of GPR-reflection patterns   Interpretation

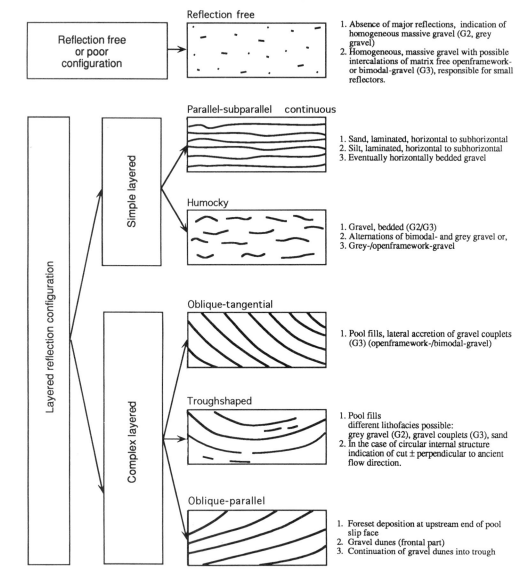

Reflection free

1. Absence of major reflections, indication of homogeneous massive gravel (G2, grey gravel)
2. Homogeneous, massive gravel with possible intercalations of matrix free openframework- or bimodal-gravel (G3), responsible for small reflectors.

Parallel-subparallel   continuous

1. Sand, laminated, horizontal to subhorizontal
2. Silt, laminated, horizontal to subhorizontal
3. Eventually horizontally bedded gravel

Humocky

1. Gravel, bedded (G2/G3)
2. Alternations of bimodal- and grey gravel or,
3. Grey-/openframework-gravel

Oblique-tangential

1. Pool fills, lateral accretion of gravel couplets (G3) (openframework-/bimodal-gravel)

Troughshaped

1. Pool fills
   different lithofacies possible:
   grey gravel (G2), gravel couplets (G3), sand
2. In the case of circular internal structure indication of cut ± perpendicular to ancient flow direction.

Oblique-parallel

1. Foreset deposition at upstream end of pool slip face
2. Gravel dunes (frontal part)
3. Continuation of gravel dunes into trough

Fig. 10. Chart relating configurations on the radar record to lithologic properties of the late Pleistocene Rhine gravel. Signatures modified. Mitchum *et al.* (1977) and Beres & Haeni (1991) for specific conditions of Pleistocene Rhine gravel and 250 MHz GPR antenna.

10–50 cm thick sand sheets that separate gravel beds.

Conclusions

Selective fluvio-dynamic sorting processes lead to a few distinct lithofacies, which exhibit little intergradation in the Pleistocene Rhine gravels. The textural differences cause variations in hydraulic conductivity, porosity and volumetric water content. The extremely high hydraulic conductivities of openframework gravel, at least three orders of magnitude larger than the hydraulic conductivities of all other textural gravel types, is inconsistent with the assumption of small perturbations of the hydraulic conductivity field. Therefore calculations of the macro-dispersivity coefficients of such braided river deposits by stochastic theories may involve significant errors.

The results of the GPR experiments demonstrate that information about the geometry of inhomogeneities can be obtained because of the rather big textural differences occurring within the Pleistocene Rhine gravels. In GPR profiling, changing water content at lithofacies boundaries results in the reflection of electromagnetic waves. Therefore, radar reflection patterns can often reproduce the geometry of sedimentary structures. In particular, confluence- or trough-scour geometry is clearly portrayed on GPR profiles. The dominant reflection patterns and types of reflection terminations are summarized in Fig. 10. It may also be concluded that the GPR method enables recognition of characteristic braided river architectures (scour-fill deposits, channel deposits) and lithofacies assemblages. Under certain conditions, prediction of the geometry of hydraulic inhomogeneities, anisotropies and the order of magnitude of hydraulic properties can be made. Finally, the method could potentially be used to estimate the pool-fill ratio or scour-fill, which is an expression of the ratio of braiding intensity/aggradation rate.

This work was supported by the Swiss Federal Institutes of Technology (project L + F 35 660). For practical support, helpful discussions and critical review of the manuscript I want to thank the following: E. Meier, C. Eggleston, A. Green and R. Collier.

References

ANDERSON, M. 1989. Hydrogeologic facies models to delineate large-scale spacial trends in glacial and glaciofluvial sediments. *Geological Society of America Bulletin*, **101**, 501–511.

ASHMORE, P. E. 1985. *Processes and form in gravel braided streams: Laboratory modelling and field observations.* PhD Thesis, Dept. of Geology, Univ. Edmonton, Alberta.

BEAR, J. 1979. *Hydraulics of groundwater.* McGraw-Hill, New York.

BERES, M. & HAENI, F. P. 1991. Application of Ground-Penetrating-Radar Methods in Hydrogeologic Studies. *Ground Water*, **29/3**, 375–386.

BEST, J. L. 1988. Sediment transport and bed morphology at river channel confluences. *Sedimentology*, **35**, 481–498.

BIRCHAK, J. R., GARDNER, C. G., HIPP, J. E. & VICTOR, J. M. 1974. High dielectric constant microwave probes for sensing soil moisture. *Proceedings of Electrical and Electronic Engineers*, **62**, 93–98.

DAVIS, J. L. & ANNAN, A. 1989. Ground-Penetrating Radar for high-resolution mapping of soil and rock stratigraphy. *Geophysical Prospecting*, **37**, 531–551.

FREI, W. 1991. Reflexionsseismik; eine praktische Wegleitung über ihre Möglichkeiten und Einschränkungen. *Workshop, Sismique de Haute Resolution, Geneva* 15–17, October, 37.

GELHAR, L. W. & AXNESS, C. L. 1983. Three-dimensional stochastic analysis of macro-dispersion in aquifers. *Water Resources Research*, **19**, 161–180.

HANDBOOK OF PHYSICS AND CHEMISTRY, 67th ed, 1986 CRC Press, Boca Raton, Fla.

HARA, T. & SAKAYAMA, T. 1985. *The applicability of ground probing radar to site investigations*, OYO, RP-4159.

HEIN, F. J. & WALKER, R. G. 1977. Bar evolution and development of stratification in the gravelly, braided, Kicking Horse River, British Columbia. *Canadian Journal of Earth Sciences*, **14**, 562–570.

HUFSCHMIED, P. 1987. *Ermittlung makroskopischer Transportparmeter am Beispiel des Grundwasserleiters im hydrothermischen Testareal Aelfligen.* Nationales Forschungsprogramm Wasserhaushalt, Teilbericht D, Wasser und Energiewirtschaftsamt des Kantons Bern (WEA).

HUGGENBERGER, P., SIEGENTHALER, CH. & STAUFFER, F. 1988. Grundwasserströmung in Schottern; Einfluss von Ablagerungsformen auf die Verteilung der Grundwasserfliessgeschwindigkeit. *Wasserwirtschaft*, **78/5**, 202–212.

IMHOF, M. 1991. *Seismostratigraphischer Beitrag zur Bestimmung von Kiesformationen im Rafzerfeld.* Diplom ETH.

JOL, H. M. & SMITH, D. G. 1991. Ground penetrating radar of northern lacustrine deltas. *Canadian Journal of Earth Sciences*, **28**, 1939–1947.

JUSSEL, P. 1989. Stochastic description of typical inhomogeneities of hydraulic conductivity in fluvial gravel deposits. *In:* KOBUS, H. E. & KINZELBACH, W. (eds) *Contaminant Transport in Groundwater*, 221–228.

—— 1992. *Modellierung des Transports gelöster Stoffe in inhomogenen Grundwasserleitern.* Institut fur Hydromechanik & Wasserwirtschaft, ETH Zürich, **R-29-92**, 323.

KELLER, W. A. 1977. Die Rafzerschotter und ihre Bedeutung für die Morphogenese des zürcherischen Hochrheingebietes. *Vieteljahresschrift der Naturforschenden Gesellschaft Zürich*, **122**, 357–412.

LANGGUTH, H.-R. & VOIGT, R. 1980. *Hydrogeologische Methoden.* Springer-Verlag, Berlin, Heidelberg, New York.

MITCHUM, R. M., VAIL, P. R. & THOMPSON, S. 1977. Seismic stratigraphy and global changes of sea level – part 6 – stratigraphic interpretation of seismic reflection patterns in depositional sequences. *American Association of Petroleum Geologists Memoirs*, **26**, 117–133.

MOLZ, F. J., GUVEN, O. & MELVILLE, J. G. 1983. An example of scale-dependent dispersion coefficients. *Groundwater*, **21**, 715–725.

MOSLEY, M. P. 1976. An experimental study of channel confluences. *Journal of Geology*, **84**, 535–562.

REID, I. & FROSTICK, L. E. 1986. Dynamics of bedload transport in Turkey Brook, a coarse-grained alluvial channel. *Earth Surface Processes and Landforms*, **11**, 143–155.

ROBINSON, E. A. 1983. *Seismic analysis and convolutional model*. International Human Resources Development Corporation, Boston.

ROTH, K., SCHULIN, R., FLÜHLER, H. & ATTINGER, W. 1990. Calibration of time domain reflectometry for water content measurement using a composite dielectric approach. *Water Resources Research*, **26/10**, 2267–2273.

SCHMUGGE, T. 1985. Remote sensing of soil moisture. *In*: ANDERSON & BURT (eds) *Hydrological Forecasting*, 101–124.

SHERIFF, R. E. 1984. *Encyclopedic dictionary of exploration geophysics*. 2nd ed. Society of Exploration Geophysics, Tulsa, OK.

SIEGENTHALER, C. H. & HUGGENBERGER, P. 1993. Pleistocene Rhine gravel: deposit of a braided river system with dominant pool preservation. *This volume*.

STAUFFER, F. & DRACOS, T. 1985. An advective transport model for recharge studies in layered soils. *International Association of Hydrologic Research, 21st congr. Melbourn, Australia*, 5.

STEEL, R. J. & THOMPSON, D. B. 1983. Structures and textures in Triassic braided stream conglomerates ('Bunter' Pebble Beds) in the Sherwood Sandstone Group, North Staffordshire, England. *Sedimentology*, **30**, 341–367.

STEEPLES, D. W., KNAPP, R. W. & MILLER, R. 1985. Field efficient shallow CDP seismic surveys. *55th Ann. International Meeting of the Society of Exploration Geophysists, Expanded Abstract*, 150–152.

STEEPLES, D. W. & MILLER, R. D. 1990. Seismic reflection methods applied to engineering, environmental and groundwater problems. *In*: WARD, S. H. (ed.) *Geotechnical & Environmental Geophysics. Investigations in Geophysics*, **5**, **Vol. 1**, SEG, Tulsa OK, 1–30.

TINGA, W. R., VOSS, W. A. G. & BLOSSEY, D. F. 1973. Generalized approach to multiphase dielectric mixture theory. *Journal of Applied Physics*, **44**, 3897–3902.

TRABANT, P. K. 1984. *Applied High-Resolution Geophysical Methods*. International Human Resources Development Corp., Boston.

WHITING, P. J., DIETRICH, W. E., LEOPOLD, L. B., DRAKE, T. G. & SHREVE, R. L. 1988. Bedload sheets in heterogeneous sediment. *Geology*, **16**, 105–108.

Braided stream and flood-plain deposition in a rapidly aggrading basin: the Escanilla formation, Spanish Pyrenees

PETER A. BENTHAM[1], PETER J. TALLING[2] & DOUGLAS W. BURBANK

Department of Geological Sciences, University of Southern California, University Park, Los Angeles, CA 90089-0740, USA

[1] *Present address: Africa and Latin America Area, Amoco Production Company, PO Box 3092, Houston, TX 77253, USA*

[2] *Present address: Department of Earth Sciences, University of Leeds, Leeds LS2 9JT, UK*

Abstract: Models of braided stream deposition have largely been developed from studies of regionally degrading and laterally confined alluvial environments. Glacial outwash streams, in particular, have supplied important and widely cited descriptions of intra-channel processes. These fluvial systems are typically confined within quite narrow valleys. It is felt that such systems have low long-term preservation potential and are unlikely to be present in the geologic record in large quantities. Therefore, the study of these modern laterally confined degradational systems may not provide holistic analogs of the larger-scale alluvial architecture developed in braided river environments in the ancient. The Escanilla Formation of the Spanish Pyrenees provides a well-exposed example of an Eocene fluvial system flowing axially within the Pyrenean foreland basin. Sedimentologic study shows coarse channelized deposits of braided character wholly enclosed within large amounts of fine-grained overbank mudstones and siltstones (>40% by volume), with both being deposited coevally across the Escanilla floodplain.

A new depositional model is proposed that combines facets of existing models derived from other fluvio-morphologic systems. This consists of a laterally confined channel belt, internally preserving a braided stream character, capable of rapid vertical aggradation on short geological time-scales (about a thousand years). Avulsion processes are used to explain finer sediment deposition in interfluve settings, as well as the large-scale architectural geometries within the lower Escanilla Formation. This new model illustrates that discrete channel belt avulsion, and the preservation of thick sequences of overbank material are not exclusively characteristics of higher sinuosity fluvial systems.

The development of braiding in fluvial systems can be shown to be the result of the complex interaction of a large number of independent variables (Leopold & Wolman 1957; Miall 1977; Ferguson 1987). Most importantly these include the amount and variability of stream discharge; the width, depth, and velocity of flow; the volume and grain-size distribution of the sediment load; and the slope and roughness of the stream bed. Extra-channel factors including bank material and the presence of bank vegetation also significantly control channel planform and, therefore, the resulting depositional geometries that are preserved (Ferguson 1987). Bridge (1985) emphasized the nature of the continuum of channel patterns that may be observed in recent fluvial systems, and stated the importance of viewing both channel systems and their associated overbank sediments when attempting to reconstruct such channel geometries in the geological record.

At the simplest level, braiding occurs as a consequence of a stream's episodic inability to move portions of its bedload. Sorting occurs, and deposition of coarser bedload results in shoaling and the subsequent initiation of within-channel barforms (Leopold & Wolman 1957). Most studies of lithofacies developed within modern braided rivers have concerned themselves with the channel deposits, while associated overbank or vertical accretion deposits have been largely neglected. Although in most widely cited modern examples (e.g. Miall 1978; Cant & Walker 1978) such deposits are volumetrically unimportant, a growing number of recent studies of ancient fluvial successions have described significant volumes of fine-grained material preserved in association

From Best, J. L. & Bristow, C. S. (eds), 1993, *Braided Rivers*, Geological Society Special Publication No. **75**, pp. 177–194.

177

with coarse channel systems of braided character (Raynolds 1980; Desloges & Church 1987; Jolley 1989; Reynolds 1987; Mack & Seager 1990; Eberth & Miall 1991; Mack & James 1993). In particular, studies of Plio-Pleistocene fluvial systems preserved in small extensional grabens within the southern Rio Grande Rift of southern New Mexico (Mack & Seager 1990; Mack & James 1993) and the Siwalik deposits of the Himalayan foreland of Pakistan (Raynolds 1980) may be used to question the wholesale applicability of established braided-stream facies models. The presence of large volumes of fine-grained material within braided stream deposits would be atypical according to most interpretations applying modern systems as analogs (Moody-Stuart 1966; Cant & Walker 1976; Miall 1977). Walker & Cant (1984) went so far as to say that the lack of fine-grained vertical accretion deposits may be a useful criterion when attempting to identify such ancient low-sinuosity systems. Most current braided stream depositional models are derived from modern fluvial systems that, on long time-scales (> 1000 years), are confined and actively degrading (glacial outwash streams in mountainous areas, for example). Although capable of aggradation for shorter periods in response to small changes

in discharge or local base-level (Schumm 1991), the deposits of such systems are unlikely to be preserved. Whether the deposits and alluvial geometries preserved in the short-term are truly representative of coarse fluvial systems that make up the geologic record will be addressed in the following discussion.

Fluvial sedimentological study of the Middle–Upper Eocene Escanilla Formation of the Southern Spanish Pyrenees has highlighted weaknesses inherent within established fluvial low-sinuosity depositional models (Miall 1978). Excellent exposures present along the western oblique ramp of the Pyrenean South-Central Unit thrust system has allowed the detailed description of the character and architectural geometries of coarse low-sinuosity channels and associated overbank material and has facilitated the construction of vertical and lateral variations of lithofacies (Bentham *et al.* 1991; Dreyer *et al.* 1993). The Escanilla Formation represents a particularly well exposed example that appears to contradict braided stream models that show only limited fine-grained sediment deposition (e.g. Walker & Cant 1984; Rust & Jones 1987).

As demonstrated by Allen (1983), Bridge (1985) and Miall (1985), high degrees of lateral variability of lithofacies in fluvial environments

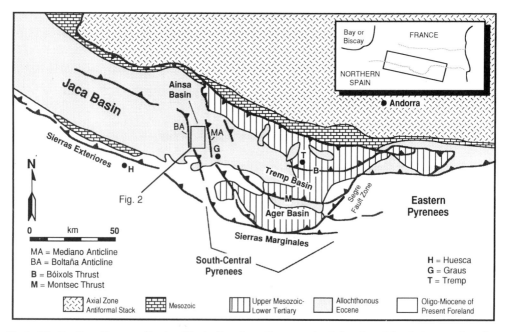

Fig. 1. The Southern Pyrenean Foreland Basin. Box shows the approximate location of the study area, along the western flank of the South-Central Unit thrust system, and the simplified configuration of the important structural elements discussed in the text.

preclude the wholesale application of vertical facies sequence models. In a review of paleo-channel reconstruction and its associated problems, Bridge (1985) suggested that existing facies models do not truly represent the variability of channel types and depositional facies that are observed in modern alluvial systems. He emphasized the importance of three-dimensional outcrop data and detailed palaeo-current information when attempting to perform such analysis. Such an approach is possible within the deposits of the Escanilla Formation,

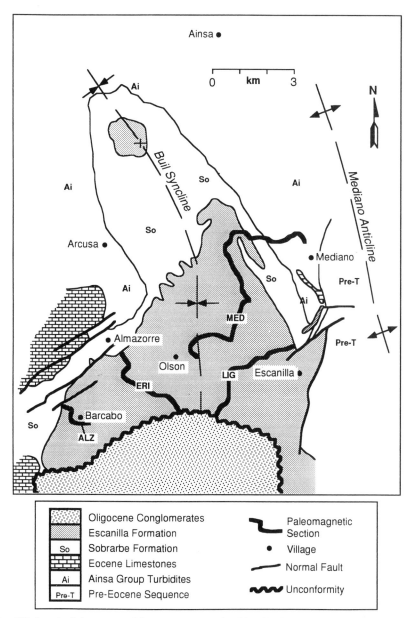

Fig. 2. Simplified geologic base-map of the western area, the Ainsa Basin or Buil Syncline, situated along the western oblique ramp of the South-Central Pyrenean thrust system. The location of villages within the study area; and the magnetostratigraphic traverses are shown, as are the important structural features within the basin. ALZ, Almazorre; ERI, Eripol; MED, Mediano; LIG, Liguerre.

and we feel that vertical and lateral facies sequence description within this system can be used to erect a significantly different depositional model than those currently used to 'characterize' braided stream deposition (Bentham *et al.* 1991).

Regional framework

The study area is situated across one of the major N–S-trending structural boundaries within the E–W-striking Pyrenean foreland basin system of NE Spain (Puigdefàbregas 1975; Cámara & Klimowitz 1985; Fig. 1). Excellent exposures of the Escanilla Formation fluvial deposits within the small, 20 km-wide, Ainsa Basin (Fig. 2), have allowed the detailed description of sedimentary facies and alluvial architecture within this Eocene drainage system (Bentham 1992; Bentham *et al.*, in press). The Escanilla system in the Ainsa Basin is underlain by the shallow marine and deltaic units of the Belsue Formation (Fig. 3), and unconformably overlain by the coarse alluvial conglomerates of the Oligocene-aged Collegats Group (Garrido-Meǵias 1973). Constituting the lower part of the Campodarbe Group of Puigdefàbregas (1975), the Escanilla sediments represent continental deposition within the south-central Pyrenees. Biostratigraphic and magnetostratigraphic data (Cuevas Gozalo 1990; Bentham 1992) suggest that the Escanilla Formation ranges from latest Lutetian to early Priabonian in age, and was deposited during a structurally dynamic phase of Pyrenean foreland basin development. At this time, the pre-existing flexural foreland began to detach as a series of laterally distinct piggy-back basins, and proximal parts of the foreland basin were incorporated into the south directed South Pyrenean thrust system. Alluvial architecture within the Escanilla Formation can be seen to vary spatially and temporally, and it is believed that this was largely controlled by lateral variations in tectonic subsidence rates (Puigdefàbregas 1975; Jolley 1989; Bentham 1992; Bentham *et al.* 1992). These variable subsidence rates can, in turn, be directly related to the continuing mid- to late Eocene structural development of the South-Central Pyrenees.

Architecture and facies descriptions

Four vertical stratigraphic sections (Figs 2 & 4a) were measured and described in lower Escanilla strata. These vertical sequences were combined with two-dimensional facies analysis based on aerial photography, photography of outcrops,

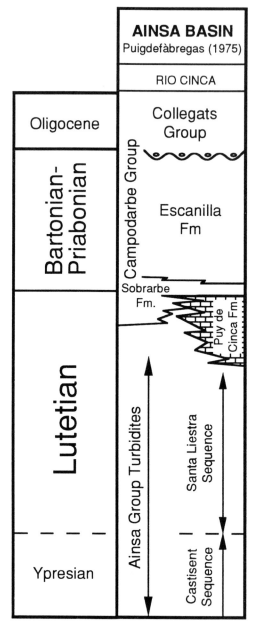

Fig. 3. The adopted stratigraphy applied during this study. The stratigraphic framework is essentially that of Puigdefàbregas (1975), but has been modified in the light of recent stratigraphic and magnetostratigraphic study (this study; Reynolds 1987; Cuevas-Gozalo 1989).

and physical tracing of extensive exposures in order to describe the overall lateral variability and geometries within the lower Escanilla alluvial system.

In most exposures, the outcrops are dominated by laterally extensive sandstone bodies interleaved with equal amounts of fine overbank material (Fig. 4a & b). Vertical sections typically traverse multiple channel systems and show nearly half of the section to be finer than fine- to medium-grained sandstone (Fig. 4a). Visible in small valleys cut at high angles to palaeoflow direction, the channel sand bodies can be seen to vary in width from 100 to 500 m and are 5–20 m thick. This yields width : thickness ratios typically in the range of 15–100 : 1. As such, they would be generally referred to as 'sheet' sandstones (Friend 1983). These sheets exhibit a complex internal architecture of vertically and laterally stacked lenses of coarse to pebbly sandstone and gravel, and as such are very similar to the multi-storey, multi-lateral lenticular sheets of Marzo *et al.* (1988). Although individual channel fills can be placed within one or two of Miall's (1977, 1978) vertical fining-upwards facies sequences resulting from deposition in a braided stream system (South Saskatchewan and Donjek facies models; Fig. 5b), a more complete description of the whole sequence, including intervening overbank sediments, highlights a significant difference. Simply, the Escanilla system preserves more fine-grained sediment than implied by existing braided stream facies models.

Facies descriptions and interpretations

Four important lithofacies are recognized: (i) gravel-dominated channel-fill sequences; (ii) sand-dominated channel-fill sequences; (iii) sheet sandstone splay deposits; and (iv) pedogenically modified overbank sediment. The minor lithofacies include white micritic limestones and mature calcic palaeosols or pedogenic calcretes. These are not common and are not discussed in detail below, except to note the implications of their absence or paucity.

(i) Gravel-dominated channel-fill facies. This gravel-dominated facies is preserved within wide (100–500 m) sheet and narrow (tens of metres) ribbon channel bodies that erosively overlie the reddened, root-mottled siltstones and mudstones of Lithofacies (iv). Clasts range in maximum diameter from 2 to 15 cm, and are typically sub- to well-rounded. They most commonly occur as lenses of clast-supported conglomerates (Fig. 6) that may be internally massive or cross-bedded. These cross-bedded units may show either low- (<20°) or high-angle (>30°) cross-sets. Low-angle sets are commonly 0.5–1.0 m high and consist of alternating

conglomeratic and coarse pebbly sandstone layers. These are preserved in the lower portions of the channel-fill sequences, immediately above the basal erosion surface, and the foresets usually dip at high angles to basal palaeocurrent indicators, such as gutter or groove casts. The more steeply dipping foresets are defined by coarse pebbly sandstones and subordinate gravels, and are preserved within irregular, erosively based lenses. These are surrounded by similarly sized lenses of coarse planar and trough cross-bedded sandstones which vary in dimensions, but are typically about 0.5 m thick and 4–5 m wide (Fig. 6). Palaeocurrent directions derived from these more common foresets have a greater variability, but normally reflect channel trends, and are in agreement with other palaeoflow indicators.

The massive, clast-supported conglomerates also occur in similar lensoidal geometries, with erosive upper and lower bounding surfaces (Fig. 6). Coarse sandstone lenses become more abundant towards the top of the channel-fill sequence, and a fining-upward trend is often present within them (Figs 5a & 6). Occasionally these channels preserve fine silt or clay 'plugs' up to 0.5 m thick within low, laterally restricted scours, or within minor channels at the top of the channel-fill sequence. In general, however, even though such fine-grained material wholly encloses the channelized bodies, it is rarely preserved within the channel-fill sequences themselves.

Interpretation. This facies and the overall facies association are the result of major trunk braided-stream deposition. Within the subdivision of the Escanilla Formation deposits offered by Dreyer *et al.* (1993), the gravel-dominated facies of this study would be equivalent to their Type 1 or Type 4 channel bodies. The lower-angle cross-bedded conglomerates most often preserved at the base of the channel-fill sequences are interpreted as coarse gravel transverse or bank-attached bar deposits, formed during the earliest stages of channel history. The dip of the cross-beds, at high angles to the apparent palaeoflow direction, suggests they represent coarsely defined lateral accretion surfaces developed by lateral bar migration within the developing channel. The massive conglomeratic lenses represent channel-lag deposits formed by shifting channel bars moving above a basal channel scour surface (Miall 1977). The lenses of crudely cross-bedded conglomerates and pebbly sandstones orientated parallel to palaeoflow direction are interpreted to reflect migrating linguoid bar deposition (Walker & Cant 1984; Bristow 1987).

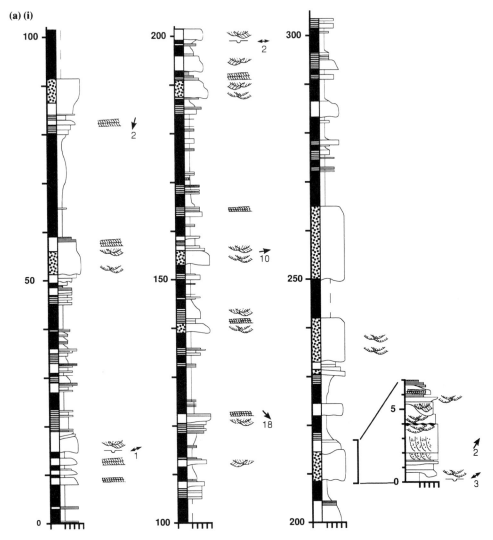

Fig. 4. (**a**) Examples of detailed lithological logs through the Lower–Middle Escanilla Formation: (**i**) Almazorre Log and (**ii**) Eripol Log. Arrows indicate average palaeocurrent directions, with the accompanying numbers indicating the number of measurements taken at a particular location. The legend is the same as that applied in Fig. 5a. The vertical scale in both logs is metres. (See Fig. 2 for the locations of the logs within the study area). (**b**) Sketch of a general view of the Escanilla Fm. exposures, south of Olsón. Note the wide multi-storey channel body wholly enclosed within fine-grained overbank material, and the interfingering geometries between the conglomerates and overbank siltstones along the left margin of the channel system.

These are in turn erosively overlain by the sandier lenses that are preserved within minor channels and scours. The major channels are interpreted to have been cut during the channel flood stages and then filled during succeeding phases of waning flow. The overall fining-up trend represents a phase of channel-system aggradation. Some channels show repeated aggradational cycles, rather than one single fill sequence. All channels are wholly enclosed

within finer grained lithofacies. The fine clay plugs may represent abandonment of the active channels within the braided stream channel belt and probably correspond with the final stages of an avulsion event, as the stream discharge is partly or wholly diverted into its new course. Suspension deposition and in-filling of existing topography within the old channel belt occurs prior to the establishment of overbank deposition in this abandoned region.

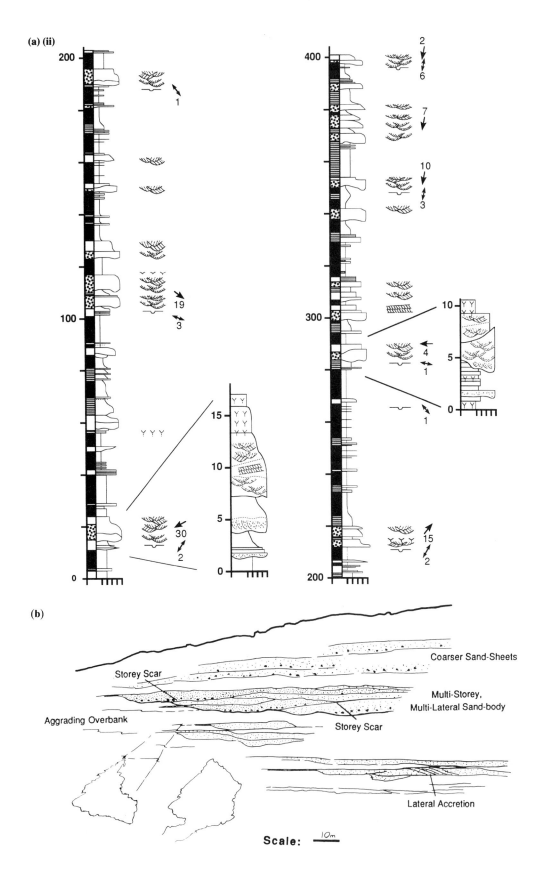

(a) (ii)

(b)

Coarser Sand-Sheets

Multi-Storey,
Multi-Lateral Sand-body

Storey Scar

Aggrading Overbank

Storey Scar

Lateral Accretion

Scale: 10m

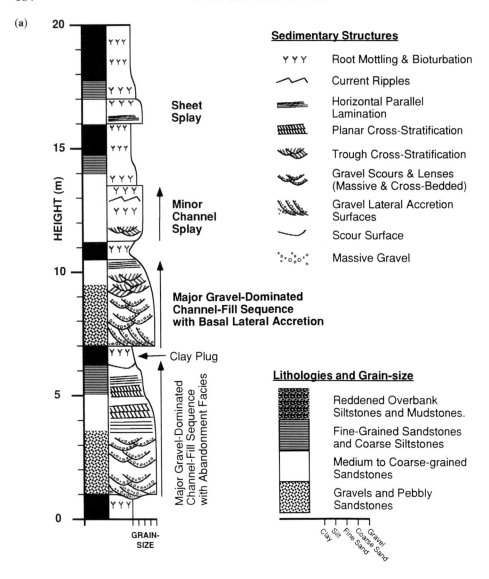

(a)

Sedimentary Structures

Y Y Y   Root Mottling & Bioturbation

Current Ripples

Horizontal Parallel Lamination

Planar Cross-Stratification

Trough Cross-Stratification

Gravel Scours & Lenses (Massive & Cross-Bedded)

Gravel Lateral Accretion Surfaces

Scour Surface

Massive Gravel

Lithologies and Grain-size

Reddened Overbank Siltstones and Mudstones.

Fine-Grained Sandstones and Coarse Siltstones

Medium to Coarse-grained Sandstones

Gravels and Pebbly Sandstones

Sheet Splay

Minor Channel Splay

Major Gravel-Dominated Channel-Fill Sequence with Basal Lateral Accretion

Clay Plug

Major Gravel-Dominated Channel-Fill Sequence with Abandonment Facies

HEIGHT (m)

GRAIN-SIZE

Clay / Silt / Fine Sand / Coarse Sand / Gravel

(ii) Sand-dominated channel-fill facies. This facies is most commonly preserved within laterally inextensive channel bodies (width : thickness ratios vary from 15–25 : 1 in channels that range from 75 to 150 m wide and 5 to 10 m thick). They are also distinguished by the lack of coarse, conglomeratic material above any basal lag deposits (Fig. 7a). Medium- to coarse-grained sandstones are most common and are preserved in a number of different geometries and this association also includes laterally continuous layers of both trough and planar cross-stratified sandstones (Fig. 7a). Troughs vary in size, but tend to decrease upwards to the top of

the channel-fill deposit from about 2–3 m wide down to less than 1 m. Thicknesses for both the troughs and planar sets are almost always less than 0.5 m. Palaeocurrent directions derived from planar cross-sets and plunge directions of trough axes are sub-parallel to the trend of the channels and the palaeoflow direction indicated by basal scour features. Upper parts of these sand-dominated channel sequences are typically composed of low, wide trough cross-bedded sands lying above a laterally extensive low-angle scour surface. The medium–coarse sandstones show a high degree of biogenic disturbance. They are pervasively colour-mottled, as a result

(b)

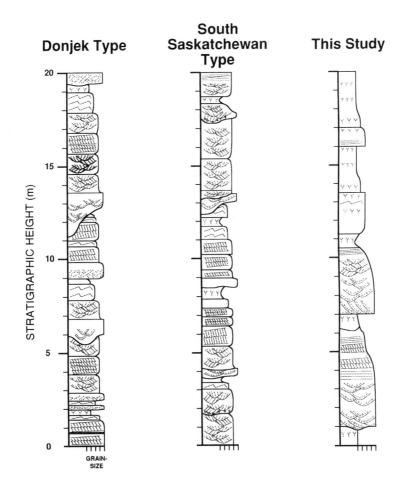

Fig. 5. (a) Generalized vertical lithologic log through the Escanilla Formation fluvial sequence. Interpretations of the various lithofacies are shown at the left side of the stratigraphic column, while grain-size and sedimentary structures are shown to the right. (b) Comparative general vertical lithofacies sequences showing the difference between the sandy braided river facies models of Miall (1977, 1978) and a general sequence through the Escanilla deposits. The three columns are drawn at the same vertical scale. The Donjek and South Saskatchewan type examples are redrawn from Miall (1978), using the legend presented in (a).

of extensive root and/or burrow invasion, and exhumed upper surfaces often show many cylindrical silt- or clay-filled root-casts weathered out in negative relief. The sand-dominated fill sequences also fine upwards similar to the gravel-dominated facies.

Interpretation. These ribbon sand bodies are interpreted to represent short-lived splay channels developed during the later stages of a major trunk-stream avulsion event (Stage III splays of Smith *et al.* 1989; Figs 5 & 7b). Dreyer *et al.* (1993) referred to these units as their Type 2 channel bodies. Developed as part of an evolving avulsion channel system and made up of

stable but short-lived channels, these fill sequences aggraded vertically rather than migrated laterally. The laterally extensive, low-relief scour surfaces present near the top of many channel-fill sequences are interpreted to be a 'Type 3' surface of Miall (1985), and represents low-stage reworking of larger bedforms or pre-existing channel belt topography. The planar and trough cross-stratified sands within these scours are interpreted to reflect the in-filling of basal channel scours by the migration of transitory dune bedforms (Singh & Bhardwaj 1991). The planar cross-sets represent the preservation of transverse bar forms or straight-

Fig. 6. Example of the gravel-dominated, channel-fill lithofacies association. Sand/Gravel lenses are present above a strong basal scour surface cutting into reddened overbank siltstones. Shallow foresets are present within the gravel lens at the lower left corner of the photograph. Channel body is 4 m thick.

Fig. 7. (**a**) Example of the sand-dominated, channel-fill lithofacies association. Sand lenses show complex trough and planar cross beds developed above a strong basal scour surface cutting into reddened overbank siltstones. Channel body is 3 m thick. (**b**)Distal view showing external morphology of a sand-dominated channel fill sequence. Note the strong ribbon geometry, and the lateral wing, traceable into fine overbank facies. This channel represents two stages of aggradation and filling. Channel sequence is 4 m thick.

crested dunes within the channel axis, that were migrating parallel to the channel axis (Cant & Walker 1976; Singh & Bhardwaj 1991). Upper surfaces of these channel-fill sequences are often pervasively bioturbated by vertical, tube-like root structures. These are interpreted to repre- sent the population of abandoned channels by thick grass and reed-like vegetation.

(iii) Sheet splay deposits. Developed as decimetre- to metre-scale sheets of massive medium–fine sandstone and siltstone, this

lithofacies shows gradational to planar, near-horizontal to slightly irregular erosive basal contacts above finer grained lithofacies (Fig. 8). Most commonly these sheet-splay deposits are seen as laterally extensive, and occasionally discontinuous beds that thin and pinch out laterally into the enclosing fines away from adjacent channels (Fig. 8, lower left sheet). Sedimentary structures within these layers are rare, although small asymmetric current ripples have been observed within some thin sandy sheets. Some fine sand sheets may also be traced laterally towards the coarse sand- and gravel-dominated channel sequences, and can be shown to be contiguous and contemporaneous with sandstone lithofacies of the channel-fill. The extent of erosion along the basal contact of these sheets seems, in part, to be related to their proximity to an adjacent channel, as only close to channel margins can one definitely observe basal erosion. Such units are also seen to fine markedly from sandstone to fine siltstone over a few 10's of metres from the major channel.

Interpretation. These massive sandstone and siltstones are interpreted as unconfined tabular splays developed during overbank flooding, or the early stages of major channel belt avulsion. (Stage I and II splays of Smith *et al.* 1989). The laterally continuous thin sand and silt lenses resemble the crevasse splays of other authors (e.g. Allen 1965; Kraus 1987). The lack of sedimentary structures is the result of extensive post-depositional reworking by flora and infauna, although rare preservation of current ripples suggests the coarser splays were deposited as shallow, partially-confined flows across limited parts of the Escanilla floodplain. Thicker units (<1 m) may represent multiple overbank depositional events that have subsequently been homogenized after deposition. The sheets that are contiguous with channel bodies represent break-out crevasse splay events that fine into and interfinger with overbank sediments. This relationship suggests rapid variations in flow velocity away from the active channel margin onto the surrounding floodplain. Flow was probably baffled or inhibited by vegetation on the floodplain and channel margins. The presence of vegetation is supported by the common rootlet development and color mottling at the upper surfaces of abandoned channel-fill sequences. The siltier units are interpreted to be evidence of splay abandonment and waning flow across the floodplain, or of deposition in more distal portion of the splay systems, well away from the causative channels (Smith *et al.* 1989).

(iv) Pedogenically modified overbank sediment. Extremely important by volume within the fluvial system (>40%), this facies association can be thought to be vertically and laterally gradational with the finer grained components of the overbank sheet splay events. The dominant lithofacies is reddened, pervasively bioturbated and mottled fine siltstones and silty

Fig. 8. Example of the sedimentary geometries present at the lateral margin of a sand-dominated channel fill sequence. Sheet-splay sandstones may be traced directly into lower channel body (lower left sheets traced to right). Splays commonly show a massive, tabular form with planar bases, while laterally equivalent channels erode down into underlying overbank materials.

mudstones. Calcified and sediment-filled root clasts have been observed, and these are often combined with the pervasive mottling. Mottling is expressed as purple, green or orange discolouration intermixed within the dominantly red and brown silt- and mud-stones. Distinctive bedding is very rarely preserved within these sediments, although a faint colour banding is often recognizable across hillslope outcrops. Mature calcic palaeosol horizons, although present in this lithofacies association, are generally quite rare. Thin micritic limestones (<10 cm) are occasionally seen within the reddened overbank material, but they are volumetrically insignificant and of limited lateral extent.

Interpretation. Deposition of this facies association is interpreted to occur as largely unconfined sediment-charged flows during times of widespread overbank flooding. Rates of deposition are likely to be extremely rapid and laterally variable during such events. Extensive wetland areas can also be established during avulsion events, and these may greatly contribute to trapping and deposition of large volumes of fine-grained material (Smith *et al.* 1989). Smith *et al.* (1989) also stress that fine-grained deposition in interfluve regions can occur during all stages of flow across the floodplain during channel avulsion. The presence of heavily vegetated channel flanks, as suggested by the presence of root-casts and colour mottling, could serve to inhibit flow within interfluve areas, inducing the fining trends away from the channels and favouring fine-grained deposition across wide parts of the floodplain. The lack of mature calcic palaeosols is taken to indicate relatively limited post-depositional pedogenesis of the fine portion of the section. The presence of such immature palaeosols is usually used to infer high rates of subsidence and sediment accumulation within the drainage basin (Kraus & Middleton 1987; Bentham 1992). Floodplain regions were generally not subject to long periods (>10 000 years) of emersion and non-deposition (Retallack 1986).

Proposed depositional model

The lower Escanilla Formation represents a coarse braided stream system dominated by the preservation of large amounts (>40% by volume) of fine-grained siliciclastic sediment (Figs 4 and 5a). Although in basic description, the lower Escanilla Formation may superficially appear similar to an 'anastomosing' fluvial system, we feel that the coarseness and typical sheet geometry of the channel bodies in combination with their complex internal architecture lacking evidence for channel-scale lateral accretion are all consistent with a braided stream interpretation.

The depositional model of the Escanilla fluvial system is best represented by a wide channel belt, internally showing a braided morphology of minor channels, wholly enclosed within finer grained overbank sediments (Fig. 9). Within the surrounding interfluve regions, aggradation is accomplished episodically, in response to overbank sheet, channelized splay, and flood-derived fines deposition (Smith *et al.* 1989). This mechanism infers significant lateral and temporal heterogeneity of sediments across a wide floodplain. The position of the active channel belt will vary through time, as the channel belt aggrades and then avulses (Fig. 9). Average rates of vertical accretion and avulsion, based on the lack of mature palaeosols, the low vertical and lateral interconnectedness of the trunk stream channel belts, and the large number of major channels preserved within the section, were high throughout lower Escanilla time. This is supported by the calculation of average (undecompacted) sediment accumulation rates across the study area using magnetostratigraphically-derived ages (Fig. 10). These rates are typically *c.* 250–350 mm per 1000 years (averaged over approximately 0.5–1 Ma) and are comparable with rates derived from modern fluvial settings showing gross architectural relationships (Leeder 1978). Note, however, that actual rates of deposition during any given event could certainly have been much higher.

In a way analogous with the present-day Brahmaputra and Rapti fluvial systems (Richards *et al.* this volume), but on a very different scale, the complex internal arrangement of sand and gravel lenses within the Escanilla channel sequences above basal scour surfaces resulted from the rapid switching and avulsion of smaller channels within the major trunk channel belt and by the lateral or downstream migration of low relief barforms (Bristow 1987). Small basal lateral accretion surfaces may be present, suggesting high-sinuosity morphologies immediately after new channel initiation or by gravel bar lateral migration. These are overlain by coarser grained lenses and scours that represent rather more energetic, less sinuous minor channel activity. These, in turn, are followed by fine-scale planar and trough cross-bedded sandstones deposited during low-stage flow. Channel-fill sequences terminate upward either with wholesale abandonment and deposition of fine silt and clay plugs within small-scale channels, or they show low-stage re-

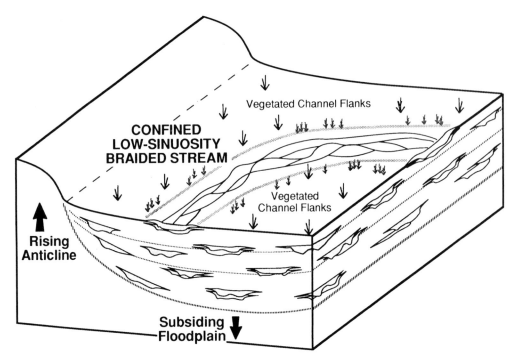

Fig. 9. Generalized block diagram showing the proposed depositional model. Note the low-sinuosity channel belt, internally braided in character, entirely enclosed by vegetated flanks and floodplain environments. Architectural geometries are shown in the vertical views.

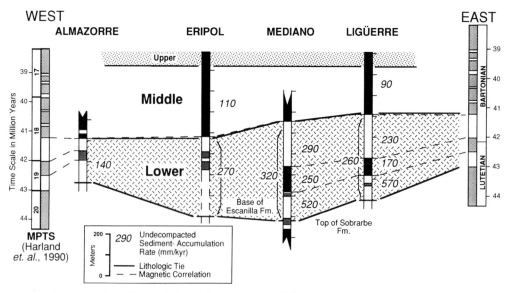

Fig. 10. Magnetostratigraphic correlation of the Lower and Middle members of the Escanilla Formation across the Ainsa Basin. Lithologic correlations confirmed in the field are shown as solid lines linking the magnetostratigraphic traverses. Correlations based on the comparison of the MPS's with each other and with the MPTS, are shown as dashed lines. Average undecompacted sedimentation rates (mm 1000 years) within the Escanilla system are shown, and are calculated using the ages of chron boundaries taken from Harland *et al.* (1990).

working of larger bedforms, producing the small-scale complex stratification above a laterally extensive irregular scour surface (Miall 1985).

Discussion

Intra-channel processes active during Lower Escanilla Formation deposition appear to have been comparable with those described by many other authors from modern 'sandy' braided stream systems (Moody-Stuart 1966; Miall 1978; Cant & Walker 1978; Desloges & Church 1987). However, the application of such models to the Escanilla system begins to break down when one considers the relationship between the channel-fill sequences and their enclosing overbank material. The importance of the detailed description of both channel-fills and intervening overbank sequences has been identified (Bridge 1985), and applied successfully in a number of different studies (Eberth & Miall 1991; Mack & James 1993).

The interfingering of channel deposits and the fine overbank is clearly seen along the channel margins where sheet splays can be traced laterally into the interfluve regions (Figs 7b and 8) indicating that splay deposition was contemporaneous with channel activity. Fine-grained deposition within floodplain settings was, therefore, occurring at the same time that much coarser grained material was being moved within the major trunk stream. The deposition of finer, more cohesive sediments along the flanks of active channels helped to confine the system laterally, as the erodibility of the bank material was decreased. Additionally, the presence of vegetation on these flanks would further impede lateral channel migration by bank erosion (Smith 1976). The Escanilla Formation and the other examples cited previously, therefore, represent peculiar associations that have not been widely identified by sedimentologists studying modern systems.

The study of Smith et al. (1989) offers possible explanation of the apparent partitioning and subsequent preservation of fine-grained material out of the braided channels into the interfluve settings. The short-lived splay systems of the avulsed South Saskatchewan River rapidly deposit large volumes of fine-grained material across its floodplain (Smith et al. 1989). The longer-lived splay channels are believed to have shown different hydrodynamic conditions for much of their history, and only the most stable, long-lived splay channel evolved to form the new trunk stream after the discrete avulsion event. The Escanilla splay lithofacies associ-

ations ((ii), (iii) and (iv)) represent a large volume of the total fluvial sequence preserved, and are interpreted to have been rapidly deposited during episodic avulsion or overbank flooding. Both mechanisms seem to have been important, and one does not preclude the other. The lack of mature palaeosol development suggests that significant breaks in deposition did not exist for very long periods (probably less than 10 000 years, Retallack 1986; Richards et al. this volume).

In overall geometry, the Lower Escanilla fluvial system seems to have produced deposits similar to those described by Desloges & Church (1987) in the Bella Coola River of British Columbia. Their 'wandering gravel-bed' river produces similar channel zones within finer associated overbank deposits. In both cases, the floodplain appears to have accreted vertically, at the same time that the channels were actively transporting much coarser grained material. However, the overbank deposits of the Escanilla system are significantly finer grained than those described by Desloges & Church. As such, the Bella Coola river offers a partial analog of deposition within the Escanilla system.

Low degrees of channel belt interconnectedness (Fig. 9) would suggest relatively high long-term rates of average sediment accumulation (after Bridge & Leeder 1979). The observed rates of c. 250–350 mm per 1000 years are of the same order as average un-compacted vertical accretion rates derived from the studies of floodplain deposits in a number of modern river systems (Leeder 1978). Schuster & Steidtmann (1987) also reported low-sinuosity channel deposits enclosed within finer overbank material, and they suggest the channels were fixed laterally, unable to migrate across the floodplain because of the rapid local rates of subsidence and sediment accumulation within a subsiding foreland basin. On the basis of comparison of the alluvial architecture from two related sequences formed in differentially subsiding regimes, Kraus & Middleton (1987) concluded that more rapidly subsiding floodplains tend to prevent the lateral migration of active channels, inhibiting the reworking of finer alluvium further down the fluvial network. This is because the channel belt and adjacent area must aggrade vertically in order to maintain grade as the region rapidly subsides. It is worth pointing out that rates of subsidence and vertical aggradation are still much slower than the potential rates at which a braided channel belt may laterally expand. This still, therefore, requires that the Escanilla channels were laterally confined and unable to significantly modify their widths during bankfull discharge.

This significant departure from 'traditional' braided stream depositional models may in part be a function of our currently available, and possibly biased, modern analogues. With the notable exception of recent studies from the Brahmaputra River (Bristow 1987), braided stream models have been based largely on the study of modern low-sinuosity rivers flowing in regionally degrading or neutral alluvial environments where erosion and transport are the dominant processes acting over geological time. Such rivers are not aggrading in response to long-term regional subsidence and, therefore, lack the preservation potential of fluvial systems seen within the geologic record. Due to the availability of exposures, and accessibility (many are drawn from examples on the North American continent), it appears that the braided stream data set has become unintentionally biased by examples from these confined degradational settings. Overbank material may be deposited within such a system for short time-scales, but slow vertical aggradation rates and rapid channel lateral migration promote the reworking and transportation of this material further downstream. It will seldom be preserved in association with coarser channel deposits (Cant & Walker 1976). Relatively rapid sedimentation and system aggradation within lower Escanilla time, combined with the presence of cohesive bank material, allowed the preservation of these overbank lithofacies, immediately adjacent to coarse, braided stream channel bodies. This preferential preservation is highlighted when facies sequences from the Escanilla deposits are compared to existing vertical facies models derived from streams flowing in such regionally degrading environments (Figs 4a & 5b).

Conclusions

Fluvial sedimentological study of the Lower Escanilla Formation highlights limitations of existing braided stream depositional models. In rapidly subsiding sedimentary basins, streams of braided character can produce deposits that have many characteristics of higher sinuosity river deposition, and only when the channel-fill sequences and their associated overbank materials are related to each other temporally, does this become evident. A new model for braided stream deposition is proposed, where a channel belt of internally braided character aggrades vertically rather than rapidly expanding laterally through time. The main channel belt changes position within the floodplain by episodic avulsion following a phase of floodplain aggradation. Large volumes of the preserved overbank material may well be deposited during these avulsion events.

Modern braided streams flowing in currently degrading regions and laterally confined within narrow valleys, therefore, while helping us to understand intra-channel processes are not useful as holistic analogs of the aggradational fluvial systems that are preserved within the geological records of active tectonic regions. We suggest that future studies of such systems be focused upon modern or recent fluvial systems deposited or flowing within young sedimentary basins. They may supply our best devices for analysing ancient coarse fluvial systems, and our best chance of deriving general predictive models of larger scale alluvial architecture.

This study represents a portion of the PhD dissertation work completed by P.A.B. at the University of Southern California under the guidance of D.W.B. The authors would like to thank NSF, AAPG Grants-in-Aid and the University of Southern California Graduate Student Research Fund for the financial support they provided during the course of this project. Additionally, the authors are grateful to J. Best, G. Mack, C. Bristow, and to reviewers N. Smith and A. Miall for numerous comments that helped to greatly improve this manuscript.

References

ALLEN, J. R. L. 1965. A review of the origin and characteristics of recent alluvial sediments. *Sedimentology*, **5**, 89–191.

—— 1983. Studies in fluviatile sedimentation: bars, bar-complexes and sandstone sheets (low-sinuosity braided streams) in the Brownstones (Lower Devonian), Welsh Borders, *Sedimentary Geology*, **33**, 237–293.

BENTHAM, P. A. 1992. *The tectonostratigraphic development of the western oblique ramp of the South-Central Pyrenean thrust system, Northern Spain*. PhD Dissertation, University of Southern California, Los Angeles, USA.

——, BURBANK, D. W. & PUIGDEFÀBREGAS, C. 1992. Temporal and spatial controls on alluvial architecture in an axial drainage system, Upper Eocene Escanilla Formation, Southern Pyrenean Foreland Basin, Spain. *Basin Research*, **4**, 335–352.

——, TALLING, P. J. & BURBANK, D. W. 1991. A new braided stream facies model — an aggrading and avulsing low-sinuosity system. *Geological Society of America Abstracts with Programs*, **23**, A462.

BRIDGE, J. S. 1985. Paleochannel patterns inferred from alluvial deposits: A critical evaluation. *Journal of Sedimentary Petrology*, **55**, 579–589.

—— & LEEDER, M. R. 1979. A simulation model of alluvial stratigraphy. *Sedimentology*, **26**, 617–644.

BRISTOW, C. S. 1987. Brahmaputra River: Channel migration and deposition. *In*: ETHERIDGE, F. G., FLORES, R. M. & HARVEY, M. D. (eds) *Recent Developments in Fluvial Sedimentology*. Society of Economic Paleontologists and Mineralogists Special Publications, **39**, 63–74.

CAMARA, P. & KLIMOWITZ, J. 1985. Interpretación geodinámica de la vertiente centro-occidental surpirenaica, (Cuencas de Jaca-Tremp). *Estudios Geológico*, **41**, 391–404.

CANT, D. J. & WALKER, R. D. 1976. Development of a braided fluvial facies model for the Devonian Battery Point Sandstone, Quebec. *Canadian Journal of Earth Science*, **13**, 102–119.

—— & —— 1978. Fluvial processes and facies sequences in the sandy braided South Saskatchewan River, Canada. *Sedimentology*, **25**, 625–648.

CUEVAS GOZALO, M. C. 1990. Sedimentary facies and sequential architecture of tide-influenced alluvial deposits. An example from the middle Eocene Capella Formation, South-Central Pyrenees, Spain. *Geologia Ultraiectina*, **61**, 1–152.

DESLOGES, J. R. & CHURCH, M. 1987. Channel and floodplain facies in a wandering gravel-bed river. *In*: ETHERIDGE, F. G., FLORES, R. M. & HARVEY, M. D. (eds) *Recent Developments in Fluvial Sedimentology*. Society of Economic Paleontologists and Mineralogists Special Publications, **39**, 99–110.

DREYER, T., FALT, L.-M., HØY, T., KNARUD, R., STEEL, P. & CUEVAS, J.-L. 1993. Sedimentary Architecture of field analogues for reservoir information (SAFARI): a case study of the fluvial Escanilla Formation, Spanish Pyrenees. *In*: FLINT, S. S. & BRYANT, I. D. (eds). *The geological modelling of hydrocarbon reservoirs*. International Association of Sedimentologists Special Publications, **15**, 57–80.

EBERTH, D. A. & MIALL, A. D. 1991. Stratigraphy, sedimentology and evolution of a vertebrate-bearing, braided to anastomosed fluvial system, Cutler Formation (Permian–Pennsylvanian), north-central new Mexico. *Sedimentary Geology*, **72**, 225–252.

FERGUSON, R. 1987. Hydraulic and sedimentary controls of channel pattern. *In*: RICHARDS, K. S. (ed.) *River channels; environments and process*. Methuen, London, 129–158.

FRIEND, P. F. 1983. Towards a field classification of alluvial architecture and sequence. *In*: COLLINSON, J. D. & LEWIS, J. (eds) *Modern and ancient fluvial systems*. International Association of Sedimentologists Special Publications, **6**, 345–354.

GARRIDO-MEGIAS, A. 1973. *Estudio geológico y relación entre tectónica y sedimentación del Secundario y Terciario de la vertiente meridional pirenaica en su zona central (prov. Huesca y Lérida)*. PhD Dissertation, University of Granada, Spain.

HARLAND, W. B., ARMSTRONG, R. L., COX, A. V., CRAIG, L. E., SMITH, A. G. & SMITH, D. G. 1990. *A geologic time scale 1989*. Cambridge University Press, Cambridge.

JOLLEY, E. J. 1989. Thrust tectonics and alluvial architecture of the Jaca Basin, Southern Pyrenees. PhD Dissertation, University of Wales (Cardiff), UK.

KRAUS, M. J. 1987. Integration of channel and floodplain suites: II. Vertical relations of alluvial paleosols. *Journal of Sedimentary Petrology*, **57**, 602–612.

—— & MIDDLETON, L. T. 1987. Contrasting architecture of two alluvial suites in different structural settings. *In*: ETHERIDGE, F. G., FLORES, R. M. & HARVEY, M. D. (eds) *Recent Developments in Fluvial Sedimentology*. Society of Economic Paleontologists and Mineralogists Special Publications, **39**, 253–262.

LEEDER, M. R. 1978. A quantitative stratigraphic model for alluvium, with special reference to channel deposit density and interconnected-ness. *In*: MIALL, A. D. (ed.) *Fluvial Sedimentology*. Canadian Society of Petroleum Geologists Memoirs, **5**, 587–596.

LEOPOLD, L. B. & WOLMAN, M. G. 1957. *River channel patterns, braided, meandering and straight*. United States Geological Survey Professional Papers, **282B**.

MACK, G. H. & JAMES, W. C. 1993. Control of basin symmetry on fluvial lithofacies, Camp Rice and Palomas Formations (Plio-Pleistocene), southern Rio Grande Rift, U.S.A. *In*: MARZO, M. & PUIDEFÀBREGAS, C. (eds) *Alluvial Sedimentation*. International Association of Sedimentologists Special Publications, **17**, 439–449.

—— & SEAGER, W. R. 1990. Tectonic control on facies distribution of the Camp Rice and Palomas Formations (Plio-Pleistocene) in the southern Rio Grande Rift. *Geological Society of America Bulletin*, **102**, 45–53.

MARZO, M., NIJMAN, W. & PUIGDEFÀBREGAS, C. 1988. Architecture of the Castisent fluvial sheet sandstones, Eocene, South Pyrenees, Spain. *Sedimentology*, **35**, 719–738.

MIALL, A. D. 1977. A review of the braided river depositional environment. *Earth Science Reviews*, **5**, 597–664.

—— 1978. Lithofacies types and vertical profile models in braided river deposits: a summary. *In*: MIALL, A. D. (ed.) *Fluvial Sedimentology*. Canadian Society of Petroleum Geologists Memoirs, **5**, 597–604.

—— 1985. Architectural-element analysis: a new method of facies analysis applied to fluvial deposits. *Earth Science Reviews*, **22**, 597–604.

MOODY-STUART, M. 1966. High- and low-sinuosity stream deposits, with examples from the Devonian of Spitzbergen. *Journal of Sedimentary Petrology*, **36**, 1102–1117.

PUIGDEFÀBREGAS, C. 1975. La sedimentación molásica en la cuenca de Jaca. *Pirineos*, **104**, 188 p.

RAYNOLDS, R. G. H. 1980. *The Plio-Pleistocene structural and stratigraphic evolution of the eastern Potwar plateau, Pakistan*. PhD dissertation, Dartmouth College, USA.

RETALLACK, G. J. 1986. Fossil soils as grounds for interpreting long-term controls on ancient rivers. *Journal of Sedimentary Petrology*, **56**, 1–18.

REYNOLDS, A. 1987. *Tectonically controlled fluvial sedimentation in the South Pyrenean Foreland Basin*. PhD Dissertation, Univ. of Liverpool, UK.

RICHARDS, K., CHANDRA, S. & FRIEND, P. 1993. Avulsive channel systems: characteristics and examples. *This volume*.

RUST, B. R. & JONES, B. H. 1987. The Hawkesbury Sandstone south of Sydney, Australia: Triassic analogue for the deposit of a large, braided river. *Journal of Sedimentary Petrology*, **57**, 222–233.

SCHUMM, S. A. 1991. The effects of base-level control on the fluvial system. *Geological Society of America Abstracts with Programs*, **23**, A170.

SCHUSTER, M. W. & STEIDTMANN, J. R. 1987. Fluvial-sandstone architecture and thrust-induced subsi-dence, Northern Green River Basin, Wyoming. *In*: ETHERIDGE, F. G., FLORES, R. M. & HARVEY, M. D. (eds) *Recent Developments in Fluvial Sedimentology*. Society of Economic Paleontologists and Mineralogists Special Publications, **39**, 279–286.

SINGH, A. & BHARDWAJ, B. D. 1991. Fluvial facies model of the Ganga River sediments, India. *Sedimentary Geology*, **72**, 135–146.

SMITH, D. G. 1976. Effect of vegetation on lateral migration of anastomosed channels of a glacial meltwater river. *Geological Society of America Bulletin*, **87**, 857–860.

SMITH, N. D., CROSS, T. A., DUFFICY, J. P. & CLOUGH, S. R. 1989. Anatomy of an avulsion. *Sedimentology*, **36**, 1–24.

WALKER, R. G. & CANT, D. J. 1984. Sandy Fluvial Systems. *In*: WALKER, R. G. (ed.) *Facies Models* 2nd Edition. Geoscience Canada Reprint Series, **1**, 71–90.

Avulsive channel systems: characteristics and examples

KEITH RICHARDS[1], SHOBHIT CHANDRA[1] & PETER FRIEND[2]

[1] Department of Geography, [2] Department of Earth Sciences,
University of Cambridge, Cambridge CB2 3EN, UK

Abstract: Fluvial processes in large subsiding sedimentary basins (e.g. tectonic foredeeps) must be adjusted in the long term to distribute sedimentation areally, although in the short term deposition is localized along the river courses. This means that the major long-term characteristic of the river pattern is that it is avulsion-dominated. Individual channels in an avulsive system display one of the conventional pattern types (e.g. meandering, braiding), but these patterns may reflect the behavioural relationships between the 'dominant' and 'secondary' channels in the system. These relationships change through time as aggradation along the dominant channel encourages avulsion into the course of former secondary channels, and the channels exchange roles. Thus, channel system behaviour is not explained by the variation of stream power used to analyse the behaviour of individual (meandering or braided) rivers, and palaeohydrological reconstructions for individual channels within such a system are of limited significance. Examples of avulsive systems are noted, including the northern Gangetic Plain.

Classifications of channel pattern commonly focus on a variant of the classic straight-meandering-braided distinction made by Leopold & Wolman (1957). However, this continuum of plan form reflects varying conditions of stream power and sediment resistance to transport, and is explicitly related to within-channel energy dissipation, sediment transport, and bar construction processes. Some apparently anomalous patterns fail to find a ready niche in a classification primarily based on local, within-channel fluid dynamic rather than basin-wide depositional processes; for example, the coexistent braiding-and-anastomosing pattern of Cooper's Creek, Australia (Rust 1981; Rust & Legun 1983; Nanson *et al.* 1986). These anomalous patterns require a classification defined in relation to channel *systems* rather than to conventionally-defined channel-scale attributes. This paper considers one such system, the 'avulsive channel system' in which the key depositional process involves the relationships *between* channels within the system rather than the behaviour and properties *within* any one channel. These relationships involve exchanges of role over time between 'dominant' and 'secondary' channels, when aggradation encourages avulsion. Typical conditions which appear to favour avulsive systems include tectonically-controlled sedimentation, and strongly seasonal monsoonal runoff regimes. Good examples of avulsive systems therefore occur in the northern Gangetic Plain (part of a foredeep basin), but others described in the literature occupy coastal and interior plains.

Modern avulsive systems represent analogues for the mud-dominated facies described, for example, from the Siwaliks by Tandon (1991) and in the Escanilla Formation in the southern Pyrenees by Bentham *et al.* this volume). These involve laterally extensive sand bodies with sedimentary structures comparable to those observed in braided rivers, but are dominated by mudstones (60–80% of their total volume) to a degree which textbook concepts of braided river sedimentology would not allow, given the common assumption that such rivers lack overbank fines.

Characteristics of avulsive channel systems

Interpretation of avulsive systems requires a different scale of analysis from that conventionally adopted in fluvial geomorphology and sedimentology, particularly in terms of palaeohydrology and Quaternary climate-controlled river adjustments. The form and behaviour of any one channel reflect its role in the system of periodically avulsing channels, and must therefore be analysed in relation to that system. Since the several channels continually interact to transport water and sediment, the 'pattern' of one channel is only understood in relation to the operation of the 'system' of channels.

Avulsive channel system behaviour

The first-order control of channel pattern characteristics in an areally-extensive sedimentary basin must be the conversion of linear

From Best, J. L. & Bristow, C. S. (eds), 1993, *Braided Rivers*, Geological Society Special Publication No. 75, pp. 195–203.

195

to areal sedimentation, in order that the basin fills relatively uniformly over timescales of several thousands of years. Deposition occurs along the courses of rivers delivering sediment from mountain sources. Such linear localization of sedimentation results in a developing but subtle elevation differentiation, at rates dependent on the relationship between channel bed and floodplain deposition. This drives a process of lateral channel avulsion into lower-lying areas (Allen 1965, 1978), with the result that those areas can then catch up topographically. Alluvial fans provide small-scale analogues of this process, which also occurs on the low-gradient mega-fans in large sedimentary basins. Numerical models (Price 1976; Hooke & Rohrer; 1979) show that the half-conical plan form of an alluvial fan can be generated by deposition along channel lines, as long as such radial lines can sweep through 180° when lateral elevation contrasts result in steeper lateral than radial slopes, and avulsion alters the channel path between the fan apex and toe. Channel shifts from the fan head may involve large-scale displacement ('nodal avulsion'; Leeder 1978), but may be less extensive from down-fan diversion points.

Similar underlying processes control the changing position of individual rivers in an avulsive channel system, in which linear sedimentation results in the river 'perching' above the topography on either side, and eventual diversion occurs during a flood period into the adjacent topographic low. This 'random avulsion' (Leeder 1978) has been modelled in vertical section by Allen (1978) and Bridge & Leeder (1979). Examples of present-day avulsive systems illustrate the mechanisms by which avulsive systems evolve. These include (1) linear aggradation by a combination of bed material accumulation along the channel alignment and overbank deposition of suspended sediment; (2) increasing but nevertheless subtle topographic differences and flood overspill; and (3) avulsion at scales from crevasse splays to complete channel switching, driven by the overspill but including self-diversion by river capture after headcut erosion in sub-parallel secondary channels. Such avulsion processes, by which channels step discretely in space, are poorly understood but control alluvial deposition over timescales of 10^1–10^3 years. At least five mechanisms are identifiable from the literature. (1) Progradation of a crevasse splay until intersection occurs with the main river downstream has been described by Smith *et al.* (1989). (2) Reoccupation of a 'palaeo'-channel by flood-

water overspill into its head from a dominant channel (see below) has also been observed (Richards *et al.* 1987). (3) Where channel perching occurs as a result of aggradation, both dominant and secondary channels may occupy alluvial ridges, and new channels may form in the intervening swales. Such a location for avulsion demands creation of a new channel, and this may be encouraged where the shear stress of overspill discharge exceeds a local erosion threshold (McCarthy *et al.* 1991). (4) The connection between such a newly-formed channel and the existing mainstream may then be made by headcut recession and eventual upstream capture. Finally, (5) it is possible for groundwater flow to initiate channel incision, and for the adjustment of the hydraulic potential field to result in positive feedback which increases subsurface flow towards the new channel, which then saps headward (McCarthy *et al.* 1991). These avulsion processes are not instantaneous, although treated thus in the models noted above (Allen 1978; Bridge & Leeder 1979). The rate of avulsion is an important influence on subsequent deposition, since rapid avulsion creates wetland areas such as ox-bow lakes and abandoned channels, while gradual avulsion results in underfit stream development (Wells & Dorr 1987).

Improved understanding of rates of aggradation and avulsion and scales of channel diversion requires field investigation of modern avulsive systems. For example, rivers in the Hadejia–Nguru wetlands of northern Nigeria (Adams & Hollis 1988) flow between degraded SW–NE fossil dune alignments, which are intermittently breached during floods after sedimentation has occurred along the troughs. The river pattern is then rearranged and the newly-occupied troughs silt up prior to the next autogenic diversion. When channel aggradation causes flood overspill towards adjacent, lower elevation, sub-parallel drainage lines, areas of erosion-susceptible surface in the intervening floodplain may experience incision and subsequent headcut recession.

The aggrading channel is thus eventually captured upstream from the centre of aggradation. This is observed in the Okavango delta fan, southern Africa (McCarthy *et al.* 1988, 1991, 1992). Avulsion can thus involve downstream overspill from a main channel, and headward capture by a minor one. One hypothesis to be tested is whether the former results in smaller-scale diversions (including chute and neck cutoffs and crevasse formation) around floodplain remnants legitimately referred to subsequently as 'islands', whereas the latter results in more radical restructuring of the drainage pattern.

Individual channel characteristics

The individual channels within an avulsive system have characteristics which reflect the proportion of total system discharge, suspended load and bedload that they carry at any time. A distinction can be made between 'dominant' and 'secondary' channels, pseudo-cyclic variations occurring in each type as system aggradation continues. The dominant channel may display some braided or wandering stream properties; or be a sandy-bedload meandering river with extensive point bars; or be a stable, sinuous suspended load river without point bars. The differences partly reflect local sediment supply and stream power conditions, but also depend on the stage reached in system evolution. Unstable bedload-dominated channels are likely to be dominants just after avulsion, into which discharge and bedload has recently been concentrated (for example, the Thomson River, Victoria, Australia; Brizga & Finlayson 1990), while more stable channels are late-cycle, pre-avulsion dominants which are losing significant proportions of peak flow to overspill. The dominant channel initially carries most flow and sediment, and is an active channel with eroding banks, bend migration, and unstable bar forms. As it aggrades and perches on an alluvial ridge (usually less than 10 m above adjacent flood basins), it loses flow, stabilizes, and the variance of its annual peak discharges decreases as discharge in excess of the channel capacity is diverted to lateral floodplain sloughs and secondary channels (Brizga & Finlayson 1990). After avulsion, it becomes a secondary channel which initially carries significant flow, but which gradually experiences within-channel siltation and becomes a classic underfit stream (Dury 1964). Later, as the dominant channel of its system begins to overspill, and it receives more flow again, its bed is incised and a narrow, deep cross-section develops, prior to its restitution as the dominant. The Rio Aguan, Honduras, illustrates this late stage (Richards et al. 1987). Its downstream reaches are stable, silty, narrow, deep, and meandering, and spill during flood periods into the adjacent Rio Chapagua. Flood overspill carries little bedload, and the Rio Chapagua is accordingly flushed and incised, while the loss of flow from the Rio Aguan without reduction of bedload further encourages its aggradation. Headcut migration along

tributaries of the Rio Chapagua may eventually result in reorganization of the channel system. Given the cyclic behaviour implied above, it follows that the stage in such an avulsive system cycle can be roughly gauged from the nature of its individual channels. A bedload-transporting dominant with a relatively large secondary channel carrying significant flow is in an early post-avulsion stage; when the secondary channel is clearly underfit, the system is 'mature'; and when the dominant is perched and losing overspill to a secondary which is being incised and flushed of its infill, the system is approaching another major avulsion event.

The channel sand units found in the mud-dominated facies described by Bentham et al. this volume) may be products of braided river deposition. However, dominant channels in avulsive systems with heavy loads of suspended sediment and sandy bedload may not be typically braided. Their braided behaviour is evident at low flow, often being observed during dry season fieldwork, or on satellite imagery obtained during the dry season. At bankfull flow, these channels may be sinuous and single-thread, with low-flow braid bars planed-off and deeply submerged, but reforming on the falling stage and dividing the flow at low stage. Falling stage flow is competent to transport sandy bedload, and significant bar construction may occur before dry-season minima are attained. The classic discrimination between meandering and braided patterns may be useful in distinguishing seasonal pattern changes in such rivers. This was originally based on a channel slope-bankfull discharge (s_c–Q_b) criterion (Leopold & Wolman 1957), where braided rivers plot above the discriminant function

$$s_c = 0.013 Q_b^{-0.44} \qquad (1)$$

However, the onset of braiding is favoured by mobile bed material and erodible banks, and this function must therefore be multivariate. A discriminant function based on discharge and bank material (Ferguson 1984; Richards 1982, p. 216),

$$s_c = 0.0028 Q_b^{-0.34} B^{0.90} \qquad (2)$$

where B is the silt-clay percentage in the banks, implies a higher threshold slope for braiding in channels with resistant muddy banks. When avulsive-system dominant channels are competent at falling-stage flows, sandy braided patterns may develop between sinuous muddy banks representing the high-flow pattern, if such flows are sustained sufficiently for self-formed patterns to develop. For example, a second low-flow modal discharge effective in net sediment transport in the Brahmaputra, illustrated by Thorne *et al.* (this volume, fig. 4) may be capable of constructing bar forms, rather than passively adjusting to or dissecting high-stage forms. The multivariate extension of the slope-discharge criterion may thus be used to account for seasonally-changing patterns in a single river. At high stages, suspended-load avulsive-system dominants are often confined by steep, high, muddy and relatively resistant banks. In spite of the higher discharge and slightly steeper gradient (the points labelled I in Fig. 1), the controlling threshold relationship is that for somewhat muddier banks, and the river plots in a 'meandering' region. At lower falling-stage discharges, and on a lower gradient because of the additional between-bank sinuosity imparted by the sand bars, the river nevertheless plots in a braided region because its banks are sandy (points II in Fig. 1). Such avulsive-system dominants may therefore act as natural two-stage channels, with different channel geometries at high and low stages. These are

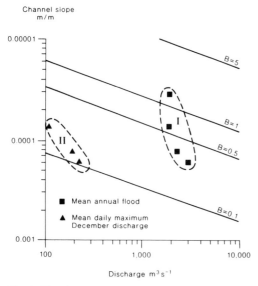

Fig. 1. The channel slope – discharge criterion distinguishing meanders from braids (the graph is contoured with values of bank mud percentage, *B*). Data from the River Rapti are superimposed on a slope-discharge-bank mud plot, showing that the transition from high flow (mean annual flood; points labelled I) to falling-stage-flow (mean maximum December discharge; labelled II) may be interpreted in relation to different bank materials (sandy for the low flow channel, less sandy for the high flow channel).

referred to as 'bi-level channels' by Wells & Dorr (1987) in a study of the Kosi River. Since conventional equilibrium relationships used in palaeohydrology assume a singular adjustment between dominant discharge and channel morphology, the abandoned channel traces of these rivers are ambiguous in terms of flow reconstruction. In particular, flow depths, velocities and shear stresses estimated from sedimentary structures relate to discharges below the peak, if the bed is plane at bankfull stage and the bedforms record falling-stage bar construction.

The secondary channels in avulsive systems also evolve as the system continues to aggrade. Some time after avulsion a secondary channel displays the classic characteristics of manifest underfitness (Dury 1964). Although their flow may be maintained by groundwater discharge during the dry season, these channels are often stagnant except when they carry significant flow and sediment load during flood periods, mainly because of overland flow on the adjacent low-gradient surfaces (overspill from the now dominant channel being inhibited until it is perched). The overland flow carries only suspended sediment load, which accretes against the banks of the formerly larger cross-section until the active cross-section has contracted to a capacity more appropriate for the locally-generated runoff. This is illustrated by Dury's (1962) seismic studies of sedimentary fills in underfit river valleys, and by the smaller-scale infill of minor channel sections in the anasto-mosing streams studied by Schumann (1989). The resulting depositional berms define a smaller channel which itself meanders between the banks of the former, larger cross-section. As the dominant channel aggrades, and the elevation difference diminishes, more over-spill of flood water occurs and the secondary channel may again become more active. Given that it is starved of bedload, it is unlikely to construct large point bars, but instead may develop forms typical of suspended load meandering rivers (Page & Nanson 1982). However, this phase is eventually replaced by a tendency to incision, when the proportion of overbank flow carried by the secondary channel increases as the aggradational ridge of the dominant channel develops.

The high stream power and concentration of sediment transport in a recently-occupied channel will delay the reversion of flow to the pre-avulsion alignment. However, the flood-plain retains evidence of two completely different meander patterns which reflect different channel-floodplain relationships, and whose different scale and geometry have no direct relationship with environmental conditions. This cannot, therefore, provide any reliable palaeohydrological estimates for the purpose of environmental reconstruction. In avulsive channel systems, because flood overspill occurs from one channel to another, the relationship between channel geometry, bankfull discharge, and catchment hydrology is opaque unless the interdependence of the channels can be established.

Avulsive systems in the northern Gangetic Plain

The Gangetic plain is the surface of a thick sequence of alluvium accumulating in the tectonically-controlled Himalayan foredeep basin. The unconsolidated alluvium may be 400–800 m thick (Raiverman et al. 1983), but is underlain stratigraphically by the Upper Siwalik Group which consists of indurated Plio-Pleistocene sediments of similar provenance and depositional environment, extending down to the Basement at depths of 6–10 km. Given this thickness of alluvium, largely of Quaternary age, a surface elevation range of only 20 m along 100 km sections across the Gangetic Plain perpendicular to the main river alignments seems the most remarkable topographic characteristic: a height range similar to that occurring between low and high flow water levels in the major rivers. Singh et al. (1990) have discussed the changing channel characteristics of the Ganga River during the late Quaternary. The present Ganga is considered to be braided, albeit with a low braiding index and a sinuous channel at bankfull stage. Meander scars and scroll bar features indicative of a different pattern occur on a low (T_1) terrace c. 5–10 m above the present floodplain, and tight abandoned meander bends also occur on a higher (T_2) surface 10–20 m above the floodplain. The pattern changes and terrace formation are attributed to the effects of Quaternary climatic change, via altered regimes of discharge and sediment load and/or base-level influences. While it may be the case that the Ganga has responded to these influences, the first-order control of channel behaviour throughout the Gangetic basin is likely to be rather different; avulsion between channel alignments is likely to have been necessary to distribute the sediments derived from the uplifting Himalayas to the north and the Archaean shield to the south across the surface of the basin. The rate at which this avulsion process has occurred may, of course, vary across the basin. The higher rates of sediment supply to the northern margin of the Gangetic Plain may result in more rapid aggradation, and more frequent channel shifts. The channel shifts on the Kosi megafan are well-known (Gohain & Parkash 1985), but occur equally on the Gandak megafan (Mohindra et al. 1992) and in the Kosi–Gandak inter-fan area. The axial Ganga probably experiences lower sediment supply per unit catchment area (Burbank 1992), much being trapped along the northern margin of the Plain. It therefore has less of an avulsive tendency, and a closer dependence on Quaternary environmental changes that have even caused river incision and terrace development. This implies that cycles of Quaternary climatic change have a temporal scale less than that of the major avulsion cycles where aggradation is less rapid in the centre of the basin, and therefore are dominant influences on the channels. Over longer timescales, however, competition between transverse and longitudinal drainage in the basin may also change with the balance between Himalayan uplift driven by either thrusting or isostatic recovery after erosion (Burbank 1992).

An example of the interdependency of channels in an avulsive system is provided by the River Rapti and its associated channels in the north-central Gangetic Plain. Figure 2 illustrates the main channels of this system; the Rapti has a large headwater area within Nepal north of the Siwalik Hills, and flows parallel to the Ghaghra trunk river. There is evidence of recent avulsion north of Bharaich (Fig. 3), where the Rapti has diverted southwards into the Bhakla (leaving a 1960 bridge identified as a Rapti crossing with only monsoon flood flow passing under it). However, the sub-parallel nature of the Rapti, Burhi Rapti, Ami and possibly the Kuwana are suggestive of larger-scale avulsion in the past. The Rapti itself is the present dominant in this system, and displays the channel-in-channel characteristics discussed above (Fig. 1). The River Ami, now a tributary of the River Rapti, provides a typical example of an underfit secondary channel with a contracted channel between lateral 'berms' deposited within a large former cross-section. The Burhi Rapti ('Old Rapti') collects the runoff and sediment delivered from the north-south flowing rivers draining the Siwalik Hills across a series of fans (the Terai). Ghosh & Singh (1988) have argued that deposition on fans such as these has expanded and contracted over the late Quaternary in response to climatic change. If this is true, the avulsions of the Rapti channel system may be seen to be a response to the competition

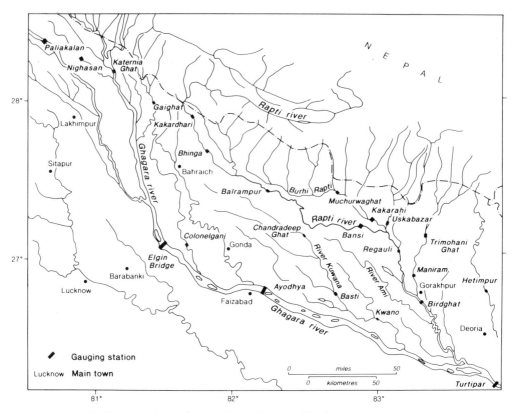

Fig. 2. A map of the River Rapti, showing its relationship to the Ghaghra trunk river, and its own 'secondary' channels (the Burhi Rapti, Ami, and possibly the Kuwana).

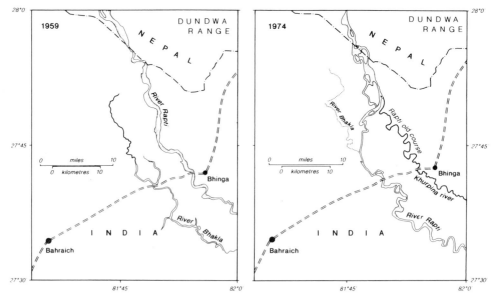

Fig. 3. Evidence of recent avulsion of the Rapti in its upper plains course, with the course of a small secondary (the Bhakla) being occupied at some time during the 1960s.

between sedimentation along the northwest–southeast line of the Ghaghra trunk river, and sedimentation along the north–south lines of the fans (a situation similar to that depicted in Allen 1965, fig. 36A). As the fans have encroached south, the Rapti has been forced to divert southwards, whereas progressive sedimentation along the Ghaghra trend has reversed this process (and, for example, the Ami alignment has been abandoned). Because the topographic differences and gradients are small, former main channels remain part of the channel system, to carry suspended sediment, flood overspill, and locally-generated monsoon runoff. This hypothesis suggests that Ghaghra and fan deposits should interfinger in the vicinity of the Rapti. To test this fully will require accurate elevations, and detailed three-dimensional stratigraphic data, in addition to the evidence of the channel system behaviour, and the historic minor avulsions.

Further investigation

Avulsions occur in a wide range of channel types, even in gravel-bed rivers with low suspended sediment loads and sedimentation rates. For example, in 'wandering' gravelly rivers, avulsions occur when bar migration occurs to a point where the upstream backwater effect causes overbank flow into palaeochannels or floodplain swales (Werritty & Ferguson 1980). In extreme floods, rivers with less active floodplains may re-activate palaeochannel alignments forming linear swales on the floodplain surface. Thus, Gilvear & Harrison (1991) observed floodwaters cutting new channels across the floodplain of the River Tay, when channelled by former courses which create linear depressions occupied by erodible sands and gravels. Avulsions also occur in anastomosing rivers (Smith & Smith 1980; Smith & Putnam 1980; Smith 1983, 1986; Schumann 1989), although a gradual transition may be observed between the avulsive systems discussed in this paper and anastomosing patterns. Possible differences, which need to be assessed more fully with data from a variety of river systems, include: (i) larger-scale tracts of land between channels in avulsive systems in unconfined sedimentary basin settings compared to confined valley settings; (ii) relatively more stable channels in anastomosing systems (Riley 1975), compared to the behaviour of dominant channels in avulsive systems; (iii) high sediment loads and rapid aggradation in avulsive systems, generating topographic differences relatively rapidly; (iv) large discharge ranges with sustained high flows in avulsive systems, encouraging large-scale channel diversion; and (v) a higher ratio of channel to overbank aggradation in avulsing systems, and rapid bed aggradation which results in channels perching above surrounding floodplain areas. These are suggested hypotheses, which would test the view that an anastomosing-avulsive system continuum exists which parallels the meandering-braiding channel continuum, and reflects different scales and rates of various depositional processes. This is consistent with the differences identified by Smith (1983) between the Columbia River and the Saskatchewan River. The former has a narrow, rapidly-aggrading sedimentary basin in which frequent crevasse-splay formation and avulsion occur, while the latter aggrades more slowly over a wider basin, and has more stable channels in a peat-covered floodplain with backswamps and lakes. Avulsion is clearly a widespread process, but in a rapidly-aggrading piedmont-fan or subsiding sedimentary basin setting it is the *dominant* long-term influence on sedimentary history and channel evolution.

The ideas discussed in this paper are rather speculative, but they are supported by the evidence of the behaviour and characteristics of modern rivers identified as examples. Further testing could be based on assessment of the sedimentological implications of the proposed model of interacting, avulsion-controlled, pseudo-parallel rivers that together constitute a depositional system. The geological record of such behaviour should include, on any time plane, a mixture of large and small sub-parallel sand bodies that represent the dominant and secondary channels, and which change more-or-less abruptly in the vertical direction (time-transgressively) from large to small and vice versa. Within these sand bodies certain vertical trends are also likely. The smaller should display gradual upward replacement of sand by silt and progressive narrowing, until truncation by a large channel fill that represents avulsion into a secondary channel. However, although the grain size of the sand grade material may generally be finer in the smaller channels at a given time plane, its mineralogy and provenance should be demonstrative of a unity in terms of source area for the rivers in a particular system, both dominant and secondary. Directional properties should assist in distinguishing the sub-parallel drainage lines oriented longitudinally within a sedimentary basin from the transverse channels draining low-gradient marginal fans, and these latter channels may also be distinctive in terms of mineralogy. Finally, the mud 'island' units that constitute the gradually aggrading surfaces between the channels are sufficiently stable to display frequent palaeosols, often with evidence of cumulative profile development (intermixed pedogenesis and sedimentation). Of course, these patterns may themselves be complicated by the superimposed effects of climatic and tectonic influences on the river depositional history. Many of these characteristics do appear to be qualitatively evident in, for example, the Siwalik Group (McRae 1990;

Badgely & Tauxe 1990), but it remains to test the ideas outlined as hypotheses in this paper more rigorously against the geological record. The significance of this study lies in the implications for interpretation of the palaeohydrology of channel fills in mud-dominated sediments. These channel fills may relate to their channel geometry and to each other in ways that are not accommodated in conventional models of the relationships between flow, transport, and channel characteristics.

References

ADAMS, W. M. & HOLLIS, G. E. 1988. *The Hedejia–Nguru Wetlands Project: hydrology and sustainable resource development of a Saharan floodplain wetland.* Unpublished Report for the Nigerian Conservation Foundation.

ALLEN, J. R. L. 1965. A review of the origin and characteristics of recent alluvial sediments. *Sedimentology*, **5**, 89–191.

—— 1978. Studies in fluviatile sedimentation: an exploratory quantitative model for the architecture of avulsion-controlled alluvial suites. *Sedimentary Geology*, **21**, 129–147.

BADGELY, C. & TAUXE, L. 1990. Paleomagnetic stratigraphy and time in sediments: studies in alluvial Siwalik rocks of Pakistan. *Journal of Geology*, **98**, 457–477.

BENTHAM, P. A., TALLING, P. J. & BURBANK, D. W. 1993. A revised braided stream depositional model: an aggrading and avulsing low-sinuosity system. *This volume.*

BRIDGE, J. S. & LEEDER, M. R. 1979. A simulation model of alluvial stratigraphy. *Sedimentology*, **26**, 617–644.

BRIZGA, S. O. & FINLAYSON, B. L. 1990. Channel avulsion and river metamorphosis: the case of the Thomson River, Victoria, Australia. *Earth Surface Processes and Landforms*, **15**, 391–404.

BURBANK, D. W. 1992. Causes of recent Himalayan uplift deduced from deposited patterns in the Ganges basin. *Nature*, **357**, 680–683.

DURY, G. H. 1962. Results of seismic exploration of meandering valleys. *American Journal of Science*, **260**, 691–706.

—— 1964. *Subsurface exploration and chronology of underfit streams.* United States Geological Survey, Professional Papers, **452-B**.

GHOSH, D. K. & SINGH, I. B. 1988. Structural and geomorphic evolution of the northwestern part of the Indo-Gangetic Plain. *Proceedings, National Seminar on Quaternary Studies in India, Baroda*, 164–175.

GILVEAR, D. J. & HARRISON, D. J. 1991. Channel change and the significance of floodplain stratigraphy: 1990 flood event, lower River Tay, Scotland. *Earth Surface Processes and Landforms*, **16**, 753–761.

GOHAIN, K. & PARKASH, B. 1985. Morphology of the Kosi Megafan. *In*: CHURCH, M. & RACHOCKI, A. (eds) *Morphology of Alluvial Fans — a field*

approach. John Wiley & Sons, Chichester, 151–178.

FERGUSON, R. I. 1984. The threshold between meandering and braiding. *In*: SMITH, K. V. H. (ed.) *Channels and channel control structures. Proceedings, First International Conference on Water Resources Engineering.* Springer Verlag, Berlin, 6.15–6.29.

HOOKE, R. leB. & ROHRER, W. L. 1979. Geometry of alluvial fans: effect of discharge and sediment size. *Earth Surface Processes*, **4**, 147–166.

LEEDER, M. R. 1978. A quantitative stratigraphic model for alluvium, with special reference to channel deposit density and interconnectedness. *In*: MIALL, A. D. (ed.) *Fluvial Sedimentology.* Canadian Society of Petroleum Geologists, 587–596.

LEOPOLD, L. B. & WOLMAN, M. G. 1957. *River channel patterns: braided, meandering and straight.* United States Geological Survey, Professional Papers, **282-B**, 39–85.

McCARTHY, T. S., ELLERY, W. N. & STANISTREET, I. G. 1992. Avulsion mechanisms on the Okavango fan, Botswana: the control of a fluvial system by vegetation. *Sedimentology*, **39**, 779–795.

——, STANISTREET, I. G. & CAIRNCROSS, B. 1991. The sedimentary dynamics of active fluvial channels on the Okavango fan, Botswana. *Sedimentology*, **38**, 471–487.

——, ——, ——, ELLERY, W. N. & ELLERY, K. 1988. Incremental aggradation on the Okavango Delta-fan, Botswana. *Geomorphology*, **1**, 267–278.

McREA, L. E. 1990. Paleomagnetic isochrons, unsteadiness, and non-uniformity of sedimentation in Miocene fluvial strata of the Siwalik group, northern Pakistan. *Journal of Geology*, **98**, 433–456.

MOHINDRA, R., PARKASH, B. & PRASAD, J. 1992. Historical geomorphology and pedology of the Gandak Megafan, Middle Gangetic Plains, India. *Earth Surface Processes and Landforms*, **17**, 643–662.

NANSON, G. C., RUST, B. R. & TAYLOR, G. 1986. Coexistent mud braids and anastomosing hannels in an arid-zone river: Cooper Creek, central Australia. *Geology*, **14**, 175–178.

PAGE, K. & NANSON, G. 1982. Concave-bank benches

and associated floodplain formation. *Earth Surface Processes and Landforms*, **7**, 529–543.

PRICE, W. E. Jr 1976. A random-walk simulation model of alluvial-fan deposition. *In*: MERRIAM, D. F. (ed.) *Random Processes in Geology.* Springer Verlag, New York, 55–62.

RAIVERMAN, V., KUNTE, S. V. & MUKHERJEE, A. 1983. Basin geometry, Cenozoic sedimentation and hydrocarbon prospects in North Western Himalaya and Indo-Gangetic Plains. *Petroleum Asia Journal*, **00**, 67–92.

RICHARDS, K. S. 1982. *Rivers: form and process in alluvial channels*. London, Methuen.

——, BRUNSDEN, D., McCAIG, M. & JONES, D. K. C. 1987. Applied fluvial geomorphology: river engineering project appraisal in its geomorphic context. *In*: RICHARDS, K. S. (ed.) *River channels: environment and process*. Basil Blackwell, Oxford, 348–382.

RILEY, S. J. 1975. Some differences between distributing and braided channels. *Journal of Hydrology (New Zealand)*, **14**, 1–8.

RUST, B. R. 1981. Sedimentation in an arid-zone anastomosing fluvial system: Cooper's Creek, central Australia. *Journal of Sedimentary Petrology*, **51**, 745–755.

—— & LEGUN, A. S. 1983. Modern anastomosing-fluvial deposits in arid central Australia, and a Carboniferous analogue in New Brunswick, Canada. *In*: COLLINSON, J. D. & LEWIN, J. (eds) *Modern and Ancient Fluvial Systems*. Special Publications of the International Association of Sedimentologists, **6**, 385–392.

SCHUMANN, R. R. 1989. Morphology of Red Creek, an arid region anastomosing channel system. *Earth Surface Processes and Landforms*, **14**, 277–288.

SINGH, I. B., BAJPAI, V. N., KUMAR, A. & SINGH, M. 1990. Changes in the channel characteristics of Ganga River during late Pleistocene-Holocene. *Journal of the Geological Society of India*, **36**, 67–73.

SMITH, D. G. 1983. Anastomosed fluvial deposits: modern examples from western Canada. *Special publication, International Association of Sedimentologists*, **6**, 155–168.

—— 1986. Anastomosing river deposits, sedimentation rates and basin subsidence, Magdalena River, northern Colombia, South America. *Sedimentary Geology*, **46**, 177–196.

—— & PUTNAM, P. E. 1980. Anastomosed river deposits: modern and ancient examples in Alberta, Canada. *Canadian Journal of Earth Science*, **17**, 1396–1406.

——, SMITH, N. D. 1980. Sedimentation in anastomosed river systems: examples from alluvial valleys near Banff, Alberta. *Journal of Sedimentary Petrology*, **50**, 157–164.

SMITH, N. D., CROSS, T. A., DUFFICY, J. P. & CLOUGH, S. R. 1989. Anatomy of an avulsion. *Sedimentology*, **36**, 1–23.

TANDON, S. K. 1991. The Himalayan foreland: focus on Siwalik basin. *In*: TANDON, S. K., PANT, C. C. & CASSHYAP, S. M. (eds) *Sedimentary basins of India: tectonic context*. Gyanadaya Prakashan Naintal, Delhi, 171–201.

THORNE, C. R., RUSSELL, P. G. & ALAM, M. K. 1993. Planform pattern and channel evolution of the Brahmaputra River, Bangladesh. *This volume*.

WELLS, N. A. & DORR, J. A. 1987. A reconnaissance of sedimentation on the Kosi alluvial fan of India. *In*: ETHRIDGE, F. G., FLORES, R. M. & HARVEY, M. D. (eds) *Recent developments in fluvial sedimentology: contributions from the Third International Geomorphology Conference*. SEPM Special Publications, **39**, 51–61.

WERRITTY, A. W. & FERGUSON, R. I. 1980. Pattern changes in a Scottish braided river over 1, 30 and 200 years. *In*: CULLINGFORD, R. A., DAVIDSON, D. A. & LEWIN, J. (eds) *Timescales in Geomorphology*. John Wiley & Sons, Chichester, 53–68.

Variability of late Holocene braiding in Britain

DAVID G. PASSMORE[1], MARK G. MACKLIN[1],
PAUL A. BREWER[2], JOHN LEWIN[2], BARBARA T. RUMSBY[1]
& MALCOLM D. NEWSON[1]

[1]*Department of Geography, University of Newcastle upon Tyne,
Newcastle upon Tyne NE1 7RU, UK*
[2]*Institute of Earth Studies, University College of Wales, Aberystwyth,
Dyfed SY23 3DB, UK*

Abstract: Braided channel patterns are relatively rarely found in contemporary British rivers, although site studies have been undertaken for reaches in catchments ranging in size from $2.6 \, km^2$ to $2850 \, km^2$ in area. Systematic study of two major British rivers, the Tyne ($2927 \, km^2$) and the Upper Severn ($1000 \, km^2$), reveal braiding at several sites, albeit at a limited scale. An examination of historical maps and air photographs shows, however, that braiding processes have been more widely active in the eighteenth and nineteenth centuries. Episodic braiding activity is discussed for selected sites. Floodplain stratigraphy shows significant channel aggradation and transformation to braided river planforms also occurred in the late Roman period and in the thirteenth and fourteenth centuries. Possible explanations are suggested in terms of flood frequency and magnitude variations (reflecting climatic fluctuations and land-use change), alterations in sediment supply (including the impact of historic mining activities), and channelization control.

Extensive braided river channels with multiple mobile mid-channel bars are a comparatively rare phenomenon in contemporary British fluvial environments; indeed, the Spey has been cited as the sole example of a major, actively braided river in Britain (e.g. Lewin & Weir 1977; Ferguson 1981). Elsewhere in the UK, published accounts of contemporary braiding are confined to smaller upland catchments in Wales, northern England and Scotland (see Table 1 for details), where divided channel patterns in trunk stream contexts (e.g. Lewin *et al.* 1977, 1983; Macklin & Lewin 1989) typically resemble those of 'wandering gravel rivers', as described by Neill (1973) and Church (1983), rather than the classic braided rivers such as are found for example in contemporary pro-glacial environments.

Reviews of the threshold (in the sense of Leopold & Wolman 1957) between single-thread and multi-thread channel configurations in a variety of fluvial environments have led workers to stress the importance of increased rates of coarse sediment yield (allied to higher stream powers) in promoting and maintaining braided channel forms (Carson 1984; Ferguson 1984; Ashmore 1991). These linkages have recently been demonstrated in several studies of upland gravel and cobble-bed British rivers, where locally divided channels are often associated with high rates of coarse sediment supply

from hillslopes, river banks or tributary streams (e.g. Harvey 1986, 1987, 1991; Wells & Harvey 1987; Ferguson & Werritty 1983), particularly following large flood events (e.g. Carling 1987; McEwan 1989).

Historical surveys of changing channel patterns in northern and western Britain have, however, occasionally revealed evidence of a locally greater incidence and intensity of braiding during the eighteenth and nineteenth centuries (e.g. Lewin & Weir 1977; Werritty & Ferguson 1980). This has been variously attributed to channel regulation (Gilvear & Harrison 1991), changes in flood frequency and magnitude (Lewin 1987; McEwan 1989), metal mining (Lewin *et al.* 1983; Macklin & Lewin 1989) and alluvial gravel extraction (Lewin *et al.* 1988).

Hitherto, studies of long-term channel change derived from historic maps and air photographs have focused on specific river reaches or small sub-catchments (e.g. Hooke & Harvey 1983; Macklin & Lewin 1989; Werritty & Ferguson 1980) or have randomly sampled reaches in a region (e.g. Hooke & Redmond 1989a; McEwan 1989). In this paper we document the occurrence and extent of *all* trunk stream braided reaches (i.e. reaches exhibiting fully bifurcated channels with at least one discrete medial bar) in the South Tyne and Tyne Rivers, northeast England, and the Upper Severn River

From Best, J. L. & Bristow, C. S. (eds), 1993, *Braided Rivers*, Geological Society
Special Publication No. **75**, pp. 205–229.

205

Table 1. *Published accounts of contemporary trunk stream braiding in Britain*

River	Catchment area (km^2)	Studies
Feshie (Highland Region)	235	Ferguson & Werritty 1983
		Werritty & Ferguson 1980
Scottish Highlands	N/A	Bluck 1976
Spey (Grampian Region)	2850	Lewin & Weir 1977
Nent (Cumbria)	25.6	Macklin 1986
Carlingill	2.6	Harvey *et al.* 1981, 1984
(Howgill Fells, Cumbria)		
West Allen (Northumberland)	50	Macklin & Aspinall 1986
South Tyne	800	Macklin & Lewin 1989
(Cumbria and Northumberland)		
Harthope (Northumberland)	N/A	Milne 1982
Langden Brook	15	Hitchcock 1977
(Forest of Bowland, Lancashire)		
Bollin-Dean (Cheshire)	N/A	Knighton 1972
Dane (Cheshire)	152*	Hooke 1986
Ystwyth (Dyfed)	193	Lewin *et al.* 1977, 1983
Tywi (South Wales)	747*	Blacknell 1982

N/A: not available.

* Catchment area at study reach.

in mid-Wales which are evident on historic maps and aerial photographs dating from *c.* AD 1710. In addition, patterns of episodic braiding during the late Holocene, prior to cartographic documentation, are investigated through geomorphic analysis of floodplain morphology and valley floor alluvial sedimentary sequences.

The potential causes and controls of late Holocene braiding are explored by comparing patterns of channel division and metamorphosis with (i) records of regional land-use and climate change which condition flood histories, catchment and reach sensitivity to erosion (e.g. Higgs 1987*a,b*; Macklin *et al.*, 1992*a*; Rumsby 1991; Rumsby & Macklin, in prep.), and rates of coarse sediment yields to trunk streams, and (ii) well-dated episodes of alluviation and channel incision at selected sites in the Tyne basin which provide detailed information on the timing and nature of vertical and lateral channel responses to variable flood and sediment supply regimes (Macklin *et al.* 1992*b, c*).

Study areas

Both the Tyne (drainage area 2927 km^2) and Upper Severn (drainage area 1000 km^2) catchments lie within the limits of the Late Devensian Dimlington Stadial and have a wide range of river valley environments. High catchment relief in the North Pennines (893 m, Fig. 1) is reflected in steep river gradients in upper reaches of the South Tyne between Garrigill and Coanwood

and in upland tributary valleys (e.g. Thinhope Burn, slope <0.01–$0.1 \, \mathrm{m \, m^{-1}}$). Gradients decrease between Coanwood and Haltwhistle (e.g. Lambley, slope $0.003 \, \mathrm{m \, m^{-1}}$) as the middle reaches of the South Tyne emerge from the North Pennine massif, and through lower reaches of the South Tyne between Haltwhistle and the confluence with the River North Tyne at Warden. Below the confluence gradients of the River Tyne decrease further through the upper reaches between Warden and Farnley (e.g. $0.019 \, \mathrm{m \, m^{-1}}$ at Broomhaugh Island) and middle reaches between Farnley and Wylam (e.g. $0.001 \, \mathrm{m \, m^{-1}}$ at Low Prudhoe), 2.5 km upstream of the present tidal limits. The Upper Severn River rises on the eastern flank of the Cambrian Mountains (610 m, Fig. 2), giving a relatively high gradient trunk stream (e.g. $0.018 \, \mathrm{m \, m^{-1}}$ at Llandidloes) and high gradient headwater tributaries (e.g. R. Clywedog, $0.015 \, \mathrm{m \, m^{-1}}$). Mean stream gradients steadily reduce downstream (e.g. $0.008 \, \mathrm{m \, m^{-1}}$ at Caersws).

The contrasting geologies of the Tyne and Upper Severn basins are representative of their respective upland regions; the Tyne basin is underlain by sandstones, limestones and shales with localised igneous outcrops, giving boulder, cobble and sand sediment loads, while shale lithologies that dominate the Upper Severn typically produce platy medium gravels together with silts and clays rather than sand grade material.

Currently braided reaches in both catchments

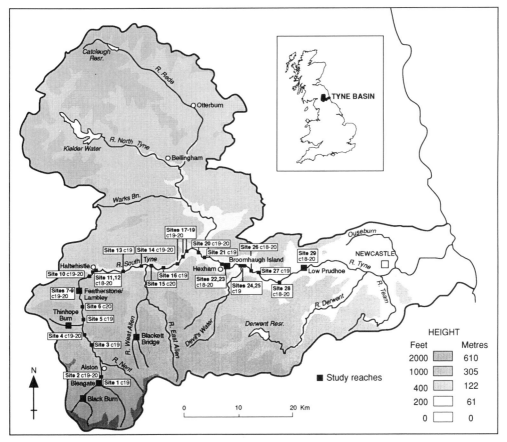

Fig. 1. Map of the Tyne basin showing relief, study sites and locations and dates (indicated by centuries, c) between which reaches in the South Tyne and Tyne Rivers were actively braiding. Site numbers correspond to Table 3.

are limited in number and largely confined to the middle and lower reaches of the South Tyne (Fig. 1), most notably at Featherstone (site 9), Broomhouse (site 10), Plenmeller (site 12) and Bardon Mill (site 14) and in middle reaches of the Upper Severn, particularly at Llandinam (Fig. 2, site 3). Typical contemporary channel and bar morphology is illustrated at Featherstone (Fig. 3, 1990) where channels are divided around overlapping (cf. Kellerhals *et al.* 1976) active gravel bars and occasionally larger, relatively stable vegetated islands that are characteristic of wandering gravel rivers.

Archive sources and methods of analysis

Cartographic and aerial photograph archives are commonly employed in geomorphic analyses of channel change patterns (e.g. Hooke & Kain 1982), although their applicability is subject

to certain qualifications. Ordnance Survey (County and National Grid Series) maps dating from the mid-nineteenth century are amongst the most accurate (Harley 1965, 1975), but in common with all map and aerial-photograph sources (unless specially-commissioned) they can only provide arbitrarily-timed 'snapshots' of channel morphology. Interpretation of channel change is inevitably constrained by flow-stage conditions (cf. Werritty & Ferguson 1980) and inconsistent surveying of channel and bar detail. These problems are likely to be greater in braided rivers which have relatively complex channel, bar and floodplain morphology (Hooke & Redmond 1989b). Despite these limitations, previous studies in the Severn (Lewin 1987) and South Tyne (Macklin & Lewin 1989) have demonstrated the utility of large-scale archive map- and aerial photograph-sourced analyses for evaluating long-term

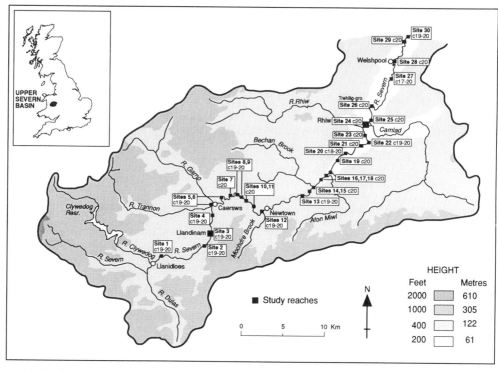

Fig. 2. Map of the Upper Severn basin showing relief, study sites and locations and dates between which reaches in the Upper Severn were actively braiding. Site numbers correspond to Table 4.

channel planform change in rivers with divided channels.

The primary archive record of historic channel changes used in this study are Ordnance Survey (County and National Grid Series) map editions at a scale of 1 : 10 560 and 1 : 10 000, available for dates spanning *c.* 1860–1975 in the Tyne basin, and from *c.* 1881–1982 in the Upper Severn, and

vertical aerial photographs dating between 1975 and 1981 (see Table 2 for details). Channel, active (unvegetated) gravel margins and vegetated islands throughout trunk streams in the South Tyne and Tyne Rivers and the Upper Severn River have been digitized and transformed to a common scale using ARC/INFO for each map edition and air photograph sortie.

Table 2. *Details of Ordnance Survey map and aerial photograph sources used in this study*

Basin	Map source	Date	Scale	A.P. source	Date	Scale
Tyne	1st edition	*c.* 1860	1 : 10 560	OS	1977–1978	1 : 8000
	2nd edition	*c.* 1900	1 : 10 560	ADAS	1976	1 : 10 000
	3rd edition	*c.* 1920	1 : 10 560			
	Provisional (National Grid)	*c.* 1960	1 : 10 560			
	National Grid	*c.* 1975	1 : 10 000			
Severn	1st edition	*c.* 1890	1 : 10 560	Meridion	1981	1 : 10 000
	2nd edition	*c.* 1902	1 : 10 560	Air Maps		
	Provisional (National Grid)	*c.* 1963	1 : 10 560			
	National Grid	*c.* 1983	1 : 10 000			

Maximum upstream and downstream reach limits of braiding over the survey period were identified for each site, and within these limits the active gravel area and number of discrete medial bars were obtained for each available date. In addition, some pre-OS map coverages dating between 1710 and 1828 are available which allow a qualitative assessment of braiding since the eighteenth century at some sites.

The general accuracy of digitized boundaries, and reliability of successive map transformations, can be gauged from overlays of channel margins in entrenched reaches known to have been laterally stable over the study period; these were found to plot consistently within a range of 3–4 m, and hence the boundaries of gravel areas and channel margins have been plotted with some degree of confidence. However, field verification of channel features denoted on OS maps as single large gravel bars in several of the large, formerly braided reaches show them to consist of multiple channels and barforms which had not been recorded during the survey. Thus, map-derived evidence of

channel changes are likely to *underestimate* braiding intensity. Furthermore, and contrary to Harley (1975), channel and bar detail in the latest (*c.* 1975) OS edition was found to be rather sparse and occasionally inaccurate. Accordingly, this coverage was supplemented with digitally-transformed data from vertical aerial photographs broadly contemporary with the OS map (Table 2). This most probably depicts a higher level of channel and bar detail than earlier maps. Nevertheless, we believe our estimates of active gravel area are sufficient to discern the major basin-scale patterns of braiding since the mid-nineteenth century.

A basin-wide survey of eroding river banks, together with detailed mapping, cross-profiling and machine-trenching of well-developed Holocene river terraces in the South Tyne valley at Featherstone (Figs 3 and 4), has identified a number of coarse-grained alluvial units which have sedimentary architectures and preserved palaeochannels characteristic of a multi-thread river and which pre-date OS cartographic records. These have been dated using ^{14}C and

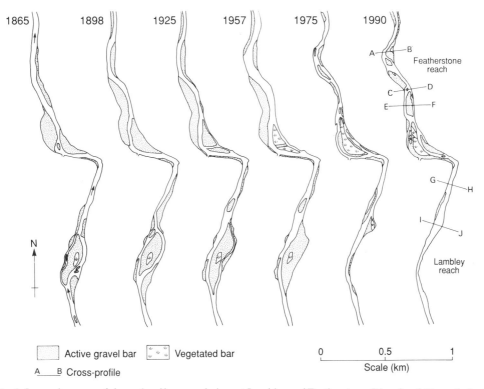

Fig. 3. Successive maps of channel and bar morphology at Lambley and Featherstone, River South Tyne, derived from cartographic, aerial photograph and field mapping (1990) sources. Locations of cross-sections shown in Fig. 4 are also indicated.

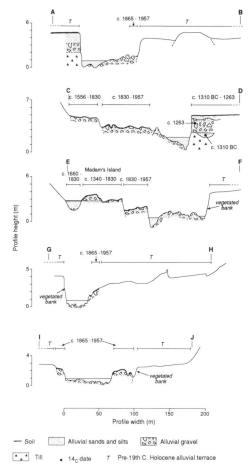

Profile height (m)

Fig. 4. Surveyed cross-sections at Lambley and Featherstone, River South Tyne, showing valley floor morphology, dated alluvial units (all dates are AD unless specified otherwise) and alluvial stratigraphy where exposed in cut-bank sections or machined trenches. For cross-section locations see Fig. 3.

palaeomagnetic techniques which show that some reaches in the South Tyne basin have experienced episodic braiding at least since late Roman times. Similar work is in progress on the Severn but is not reported here in detail.

Patterns of braiding on the Severn and Tyne: cartographic evidence

Analyses of historic maps and photographs show that 28 sites in the South Tyne and Tyne Rivers and 30 sites in the Upper Severn River have exhibited braiding tendencies over the last 300 years. The locations and dates between which

reaches were actively braiding are shown in Figs 1 and 2 respectively. Grid references, catchment areas, activity dates, size and morphological characteristics of each site are summarized in Tables 3 and 4. Former braided channels are evident throughout the study basins, particularly in the middle and lower valley of the South Tyne between Lambley (site 7, Fig. 1) and the confluence with the North Tyne River, and in middle and lower reaches of the Upper Severn between Llandinam and Trehilig-gro (sites 3 and 26, Fig. 2).

The largest braided reaches are located where valley floors are relatively wide with well-developed Holocene and Pleistocene alluvial terraces and are comparable to 'sedimentation zones', as defined by Church (1983). Figures 3–8 illustrate contrasting historic channel planform development at a series of sedimentation zones in the Tyne and Upper Severn basins. Late nineteenth and early twentieth century channel division at Lambley (South Tyne, Fig. 3), for example, is associated with multiple and variably sized overlapping mid-channel bars. Channel rationalisation at this site during the mid-late twentieth century and development of a single-thread reach coincides with increasing channel division about elongate medial bars 0.5 km downstream at Featherstone (Fig. 3), albeit within a narrower active valley floor than was present in the previous century.

By contrast, braiding at Broomhaugh Island (upper River Tyne, Fig. 5) has centred around a large vegetated gravel island formed by coalescence of overlapping mid-channel bars between 1769 and 1860. Progressive downstream migration of the island between 1860 and 1975 has resulted from upstream erosion and downstream accretion of successive sedimentary units. At Low Prudhoe (middle River Tyne, Fig. 6) channel division since 1720 has occurred over a 2 km reach, particularly at the confluence with Whittle Burn and at the distal end of the reach with eighteenth century development, and subsequent dissection during the nineteenth and twentieth centuries, of formerly vegetated and divided medial bars. In the middle part of the reach elongate vegetated and active gravel bars that developed during the eighteenth and nineteenth centuries had become attached to the southern bank of the river by 1895 and have since been colonized by vegetation. During the latter part of the twentieth century the active valley floor at Broomhaugh Island and Low Prudhoe, as is the case at Lambley and Featherstone, had narrowed appreciably.

Figures 7–8 illustrate contrasting patterns of historic channel planform development at two braided sites on the Upper Severn: Llandinam (Fig. 7) and Rhiw (Fig. 8). Multiple overlapping mid-channel bars at Llandinam during the late nineteenth and early twentieth centuries had been rationalized by 1983 to a largely single-thread channel with a single minor baid bar. However, transformation of this sedimentation zone coincides with establishment of a smaller braid zone (again with multiple overlapping medial bars) located immediately upstream which developed from a single late nineteenth century elongate gravel island. The Upper Severn at Rhiw (Fig. 8) demonstrates a different pattern of braid bar development, with a progressive increase in channel sinuosity between the confluences of the River Rhiw and River Camlad between 1836 and 1963, finally resulting in a meander cut-off and channel division. In contrast to these relatively large sedimentation zones, smaller-scale braiding at many sites in the Tyne and Upper Severn basins is restricted to bifurcation around a single large medial bar (Table 3 and 4).

As is the case in many wandering gravel rivers, braiding often occurs where large tributaries (for example at The Islands (Black Burn) and Knarsdale (Knar Burn) in the Tyne basin, and at Trehilig-gro (Rhiw and Camlad Rivers) in the Upper Severn) join the main channel (cf. Harvey 1987, 1991; McEwan 1989; Church 1983). However, many divided channel reaches in the Tyne (notably at Lambley) and Upper Severn (e.g. Llandinam and Llandinam Hall) coincide only with minor tributary streams or have no such association.

Divided channel zones in the South Tyne and Tyne are separated by laterally-stable, but presently entrenched, single-thread reaches which vary in length from 0.5 km (separating the Featherstone and Lambley sedimentation zones, Fig. 3) to 14 km (between The Islands and Williamstone, Fig. 1, sites 2 and 3). In the upper part of the South Tyne these reaches have steeper gradients than their braided counterparts and are typically confined by bedrock or Quaternary valley fills (Macklin & Lewin 1989). By contrast, braided channel zones on the Upper Severn are separated by a broad range of channel types, ranging from entrenched laterally stable single-thread reaches to highly sinuous laterally unstable channels, best developed at Caersws (Fig. 2, site 6).

Quantitative assessments of channel change in the South Tyne and Tyne for the period between c. 1860 and 1975 and in the Upper Severn for the period between c. 1890 and 1981 are depicted in Figs 9–12 which show variations in active gravel area (m²) and number of medial bars for each

braided reach over successive map and aerial photograph dates, plotted against valley distance (km) downstream from Garrigill (South Tyne) and Plynlymon (Upper Severn). Major trends in channel planform change and fluvial activity evident during this period are outlined below.

(1) Between 1860 and 1900 increases in active gravel area within braided reaches is evident throughout the Tyne basin, particularly in upper reaches of the South Tyne and in the River Tyne downstream of the confluence with Devil's Water (Figs 9 and 10). However, this trend was not always accompanied by increasing channel division, as evidenced by the decreasing numbers of mid-channel bars depicted on the respective maps at many sites in upper and middle reaches of the South Tyne (e.g. Lambley and Featherstone, Fig. 3, and Broomhaugh Island, Fig. 5), and most notably in the middle Tyne (e.g. Low Prudhoe, Fig. 6). The greatest decrease in active gravel area of braided reaches recorded over this period was in the River Tyne at Low Prudhoe and Corbridge. Widespread increases in active gravel area of braided reaches in the Upper Severn are also evident between 1890 and 1902, particularly in upper reaches above Llywn-y-brain (Figs 11 and 12). As is the case in the Tyne basin, increases in active gravel area did not necessarily correspond with an increase in channel division.

(2) The pattern of active gravel area change in the Tyne basin over the period 1900–1920 broadly mirrors that between 1860 and 1900, with the greatest increases evident in the middle and lower South Tyne below Broomhouse and notable decreases in upper parts of the South Tyne and in the lower Tyne (Fig. 9). A marked increase in channel division (despite a reduction in active gravel area) is evident at Knarsdale in the upper South Tyne (Fig. 10).

(3) Between 1920 and 1960 a basin-wide decrease in active gravel area occurred at many braided reaches in the Tyne basin (Figs 9 and 10) with pronounced reductions at sites in the upper and middle South Tyne above the confluence with the River Allen (e.g. at Featherstone, Fig. 3). Marked reductions in channel division are also evident in the upper South Tyne at The Islands and Coanwood. Only Haltwhistle experienced (minor) growth in active gravel area which coincides with the largest (albeit limited) increase in channel division. Below the River Allen confluence this period is generally characterized by little or no change in active gravel area and number of mid-channel bars, although notable decreases occurred at Broomhaugh Island (Fig. 5) and Low Prudhoe (Fig. 6).

Table 3. *Historical braided reaches on the South and Lower Tyne detailing locations, catchment areas, maximum area of braiding, activity dates and characteristics of channel division*

Site	Grid. Ref.	Max. area (km^2)	Catchment area (km^2)	Activity dates	Characteristics of channel division
1. Bleagate	NY 371543	0.04	56	1860–1896	Medial bars
2. The Islands	NY 371544	0.15	117	1860–1960	Sedimentation zone†, downstream migration of instability
3. Williamstone	NY 368551	0.05*	167	1820	Medial bar
4. Knarsdale	NY 367553	0.23	230	1860–1920	Sedimentation zone
5. Eals	NY 367555	0.06	254	1896	Medial bars
6. Whitwham	NY 368557	0.01	263	1920–1960	Medial bar
7. Coanwood	NY 367558	0.04	267	1896–1920	Medial bars
8. Lambley	NY 367559	0.07	268	1860–1920	Sedimentation zone, downstream migration of instability
9. Featherstone	NY 367559	0.09	276	1896–1992	Sedimentation zone, downstream migration of instability
10. Broomhouse	NY 368562	0.14	360	1820, 1896–1960	Sedimentation zone, downstream migration of instability
11. Haltwhistle	NY 370563	0.04	414	1769, 1960	Medial bar

12. Plenmeller	NY 371563	0.12	458	1769–1828, 1860–1896, 1960–1992	Sedimentation zone
13. Melkridge	NY 373563	0.12	468	1860	Medial bar
14. Bardon Mill	NY 378564	0.16	504	1896–1992	Sedimentation zone, downstream migration of instability
15. Lipwood	NY 381564	0.02	703	1960–1975	Medial bars
16. West Rattenraw	NY 382563	0.007	735	1860	Medial bar
17. Haydon Bridge	NY 384564	0.06	745	1860–1975	Medial bars
18. Allerwash Hall	NY 386565	0.006	760	1860–1960	Medial bar
19. Allerwash	NY 387566	0.01	761	1896–1960	Medial bars
20. Fourstones	NY 389566	0.02	789	1896–1975	Medial bars
21. Paper Mill	NY 390566	0.05*	795	1828	Medial bar
22. Hexham	NY 394564	0.26	1945	1769–1828, 1860–1975	Sedimentation zone, downstream migration of instability
23. Broomhaugh Island	NY 394564	0.30	1947	1769–1828, 1860–1992	Sedimentation zone
24. Widehaugh	NY 396564	0.15*	1960	1820	Medial bar
25. Devil's Water	NY 397564	0.25*	2100	1820	Confluence bar
26. Corbridge	NY 398564	0.14	2105	1769, 1828–1896, 1960–1975	Medial bars
27. Farnley	NZ 400563	0.08	2111	1860	Medial bars
28. Bywell	NZ 404561	0.17	2167	1769–1960	Meander apex, cut-offs
29. Low Prudhoe	NZ 408563	0.34	2252	1710, 1796, 1828, 1860–1992	Sedimentation zone

Site numbers correspond to Fig. 1.
* Estimated size.
† After Church (1983). See text for details.

Table 4. *Historical braided reaches on the Upper Severn detailing locations, catchment areas, maximum area of braiding, activity dates and characteristics of channel division*

Site	Grid. Ref.	Max. area (km^2)	Catchment area (km^2)	Activity dates	Characteristics
1. Morfodion	SN 974857	0.067	164	1836, 1948–1951, 1975–1981	Medial bars
2. Glanfeinion	SO 011864	0.025	188	1836, 1975–1981	Meander cut-offs
3. Llandinam	SO 024878	0.142	211	1836, 1884–1901, 1951, 1975–1981	Sedimentation zone*
4. Llandinam Hall	SO 027903	0.189	224	1836, 1884–1988	Sedimentation zone
5. Trannon/Garno	SO 026916	0.547	298	1884, 1969–1981	Tributary confluence
6. Caersws	SO 037920	0.111	372	1836, 1901–1948, 1960–1981	Sedimentation zone
7. Llywn-y-brain	SO 049925	0.005	379	1969–1981	Medial bar
8. Red House	SO 056925	0.018	404	1836, 1948–1969	Meander apex
9. Ty Mawr	SO 061925	0.009	404	1884	Medial bar
10. Penstrowed	SO 072916	0.156	406	1901–1988	Meander cut-offs
11. Doughty Bridge	SO 075911	0.011	414	1975–1981	Medial bar
12. Mochdre Brook	SO 086908	0.012	450	1884, 1972–1981	Tributary confluence
13. Glan Hafren	SO 132924	0.006	470	1884–1948	Medial bar
14. Freestone Lock	SO 140932	0.003	473	1901, 1963–1981	Medial bar
15. Aberbechan	SO 144934	0.006	526	1981	Medial bar
16. Maesderwen	SO 155945	0.009	529	1901–1988	Medial bar
17. Abermule Mills	SO 162951	0.008	580	1901–1963	Medial bar
18. Brynderwen	SO 163955	0.007	583	1981–1988	Medial bar
19. Upper Llegodig	SO 168961	0.008	584	1981–1988	Medial bar
20. Fron	SO 181974	0.081	599	1799, 1836–1884, 1981–1988	Sedimentation zone
21. Caerhowell Hall	SO 203982	0.023	606	1946–1988	Medial bar
22. Rhydwhyman	SO 208984	0.002	608	1884–1901	Medial bar
23. Llifior Brook	SO 204993	0.006	610	1981	Medial bar
24. Rhiw	SJ 205005	0.106	720	1960–1981	Tributary confluence
25. Lower Munlyn	SJ 211011	0.007	879	1981	Medial bar
26. Trehelig-gro	SJ 213026	0.094	895	1901–1981	Sedimentation zone
27. Coed-y-dinas	SJ 236064	0.052	915	1663, 1816, 1884–1901, 1960–1981	Medial bars
28. Welshpool	SJ 236078	0.005	939	1946, 1981	Medial bar
29. Mill Farm	SJ 255106	0.007	953	1946, 1981	Medial bar
30. Manor House	SJ 258117	0.007	956	1884–1901, 1960	Meander apex

Site numbers correspond to Fig. 2.
* After Church (1983). See text for details.

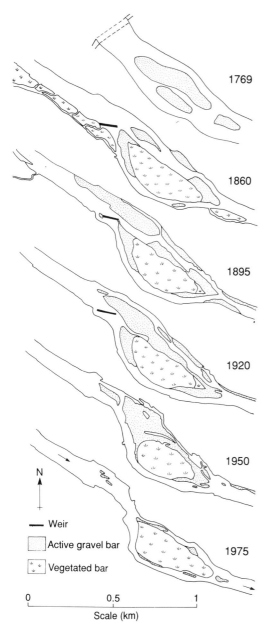

1769

1860

1895

1920

1950

N

— Weir

Active gravel bar

Vegetated bar

0   0.5   1

Scale (km)

1975

Fig. 5. Successive maps of channel and bar morphology at Broomhaugh Island, River Tyne, derived from cartographic and aerial photograph sources.

Between 1902 and 1963 increases in active gravel area in the Upper Severn are less marked than in the late nineteenth century (Figs 11 and 12), and a significant loss is observed at Llandinam (Fig. 7). Channel division remained unchanged or

increased slightly in the braided reaches with the exception of Llandinam and Coed-y-dinas.

(4)   High rates of channel change are evident over 1960–1975 with marked reductions of active gravel area throughout braided reaches in the Tyne catchment, most notably in the upper part of the South Tyne (coinciding with decreasing numbers of mid-channel bars) and in the lower reaches of the system below the North Tyne confluence (Figs 9 and 10). Downstream of Lambley this trend frequently coincided with marked increases in channel division, characterised typically by small, elongate medial bars in contrast to laterally-extensive multiple bar assemblages characteristic of the nineteenth and early twentieth centuries. This pattern of channel change is illustrated, for example, at Featherstone (Fig. 3), Broomhaugh Island (Fig. 5) and Low Prudhoe (Fig. 6). Increased active gravel area over this period is limited to reaches at Broomhouse and Low Prudhoe, while the reach at Lipwood became braided for the first time over the documented survey period. Patterns of channel planform change in the Upper Severn over the mid–late twentieth century are broadly comparable with that on the Tyne, with a significant decline in active gravel area between 1963 and 1983 coinciding with an increase in the number of small, elongate mid-channel bars.

Channel transformation and alluvial chronologies in the Tyne and Upper Severn basins since 1700

In Fig. 13 alluvial histories since AD 1700 (Macklin *et al.* 1992*b, c*; Rumsby 1991; Rumsby and Macklin, in submission) for selected reaches in both the South Tyne and Tyne catchments are presented where channel pattern change and phases of river erosion and sedimentation are relatively well dated. The main trends in temperature, precipitation, flood frequency and magnitude, land-use and channel modification in the Tyne catchment since AD 1700 are also plotted (after Rumsby 1991). Equivalent information for the Severn is only partly available; this will subsequently be discussed in the light of the Tyne chronology that follows.

c. *1700–1860*

Following a period of relatively mild climate and low flood frequencies in the first half of the eighteenth century, the Tyne basin between *c.* 1760–1800 experienced a phase of increased flood frequency and magnitude, corresponding

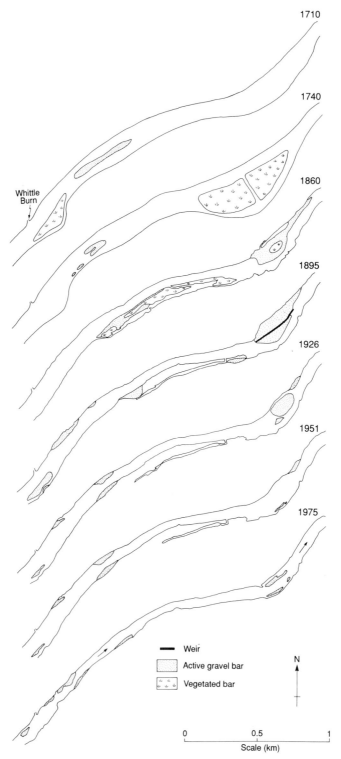

Fig. 6. Successive maps of channel and bar morphology at Low Prudhoe, River Tyne, derived from cartographic and aerial photograph sources.

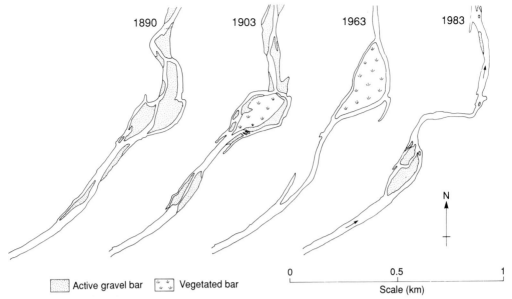

Active gravel bar Vegetated bar

0   0.5   1
Scale (km)

Fig. 7. Successive maps of channel and bar morphology at Llandinam, Upper Severn River, derived from cartographic and aerial photograph sources.

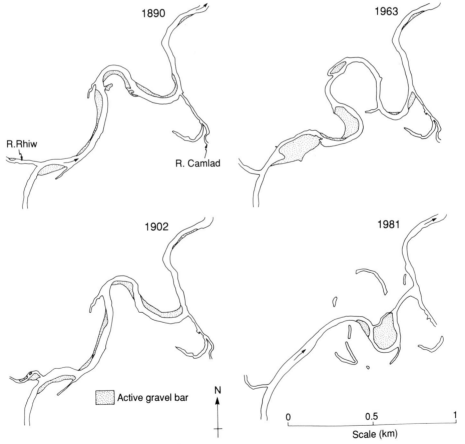

Active gravel bar

N

0   0.5   1
Scale (km)

Fig. 8. Successive maps of channel and bar morphology at Rhiw, Upper Severn River, derived from cartographic and aerial photograph sources.

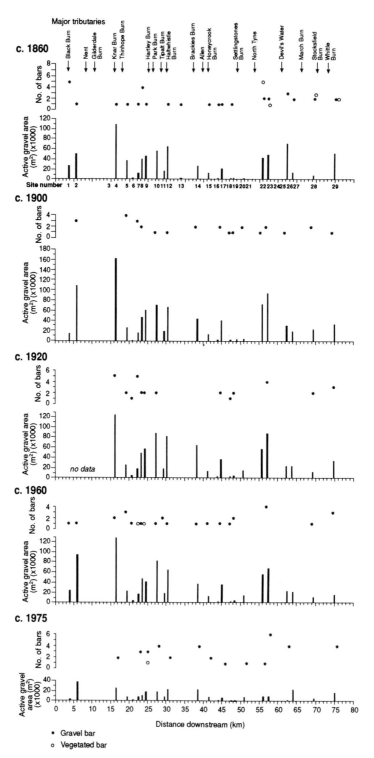

Fig. 9. Active gravel area (m²), number of gravel and vegetated mid-channel bars and distance downstream of each braided reach in the South Tyne and Tyne Rivers at various dates. Major tributaries are indicated with arrows and site numbers relate to Table 3. Note data does not include single-thread reaches.

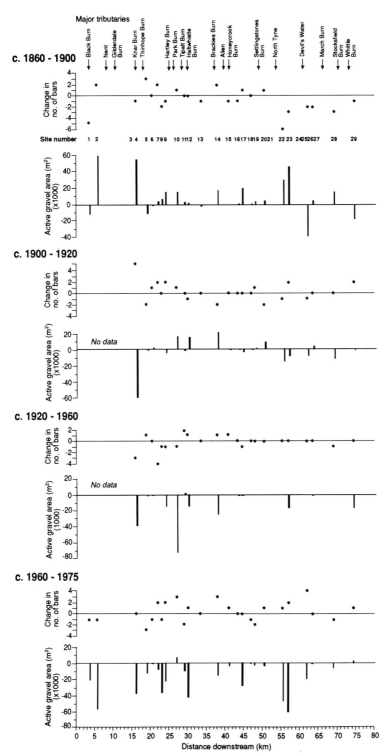

Fig. 10. Changes in active gravel area (m²) and number of mid-channel bars for each braided reach in the South Tyne and Tyne Rivers, plotted over four time periods against distance downstream. Major tributaries are indicated with arrows and site numbers relate to Table 3. Note data does not include single-thread reaches.

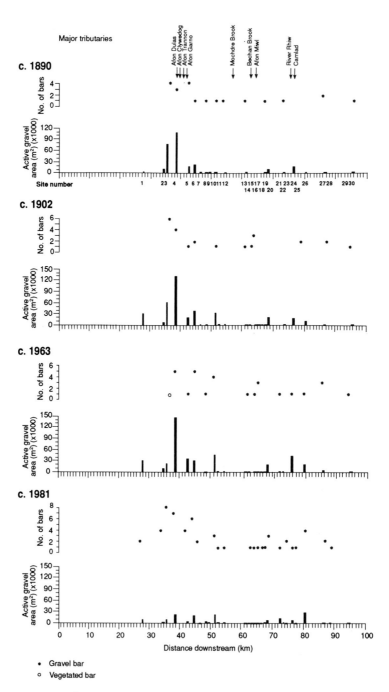

Fig. 11. Active gravel area (m²), number of gravel and vegetated mid-channel bars and distance downstream of each braided reach in the Upper Severn River at various dates. Major tributaries are indicated with arrows and site numbers relate to Table 4. Note data does not include single-thread reaches.

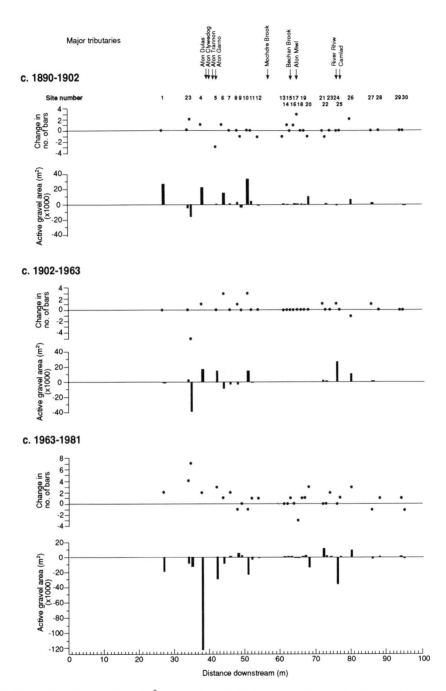

Fig. 12. Changes in active gravel area (m^2) and number of mid-channel bars for each braided reach in the Upper Severn River, plotted over three time periods against distance downstream. Major tributaries are indicated with arrows and site numbers relate to Table 4. Note data does not include single-thread reaches.

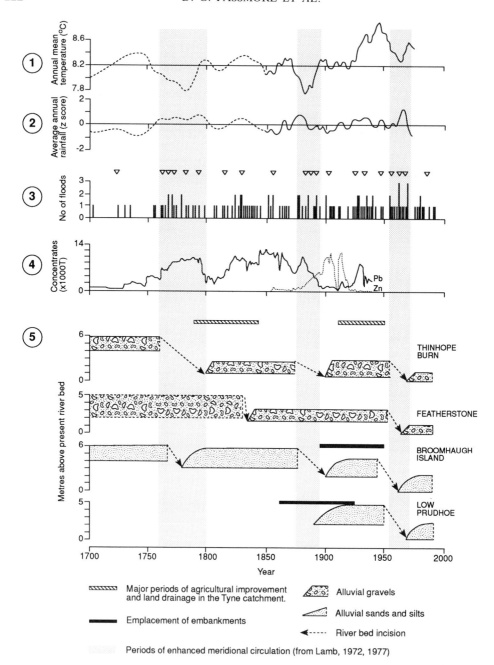

Fig. 13. Time–level diagram for alluvial units at Thinhope Burn and Featherstone, South Tyne catchment, and Broomhaugh Island and Low Prudhoe, Tyne catchment, 1700–1990, showing periods of river bed incision and alluvial sedimentation (redrawn from Rumsby & Macklin, in prep.). Key to numbered graphs as follows: (1) Annual mean temperature (from Lamb 1977; Harris 1985), (2) Average annual precipitation (from Lamb 1977 and Whittle Dene gauge in Tyne valley) Rainfall is given as a 2 score where $2 = x - (\bar{x}/\sigma)$ where x is average annual rainfall for one year, $\bar{x}$ is mean annual rainfall over the entire period and σ is the standard deviation of the rainfall records, (3) No. of floods/year and 20 largest floods (open triangles) recorded in documentary sources (Archer, unpublished; Jones *et al.* 1984) and (4) Production figures for heavy metal mining in the Tyne catchment (from Dunham 1990).

with the culmination of the Little Ice Age. Severe flooding (with several floods having return periods in excess of 100 years, Rumsby 1991) resulted in marked channel incision in many upland headwater tributaries (e.g. up to 4 m in Thinhope Burn, Macklin *et al.* 1992*b*) and some trunk streams, particularly in steeper reaches where channels are inset within bedrock or earlier Holocene and Pleistocene fills. Major sedimentation zones in the upper and middle reaches of the South Tyne, which are evident on late eighteenth and nineteenth century maps (Fig. 3), are therefore likely to have experienced broadly synchronous aggradation of coarse sediment generated from (i) incision of headwater tributaries (illustrated for example by Thinhope Burn), (ii) limited channel bed incision coupled with increased sediment delivery from bedrock valley walls (increased rock shattering, breakdown and falls as a result of greater freeze-thaw activity during the Little Ice Age) and till bluffs (slumping, mass-movement promoted by higher pore-water pressures caused by wetter and cooler climate) in laterally confined *trunk stream* reaches where these directly abut the river, and (iii) increased rates of local bank erosion (e.g. Carson, 1984). Tributaries joining the lower South Tyne and Tyne have comparatively low gradients and, with the exception of the River North Tyne and Devil's Water, do not appear to have delivered large coarse sediment loads to the main channel. Thus, downstream of Haltwhistle, localized bed and bank erosion during major flood events is likely to have been the principle factor in the development and maintenance of divided channels.

This period of severe flooding was followed by generally ameliorating climatic conditions during the early–mid nineteenth century, during which some formerly braided reaches in upper (Williamstone, Fig. 1, site 3) and particularly lower reaches of the South Tyne (Paper Mill, Fig. 1, site 21) and Tyne (Widehaugh and Devil's Water confluence, Fig. 1, sites 24 and 25) became single-thread channels. Local channel rationalization and limited incision suggests some reaches recovered relatively rapidly from instability initiated by exceptional flooding in the latter stages of the previous century (cf. Harvey 1991).

Nevertheless, widespread braiding depicted at many sites on the First Edition OS maps (*c.* 1860) suggests locally high rates of coarse sediment transfer persisted through the early–mid nineteenth century. Instability may have been sustained, at least in part, by a series of moderate floods between 1820 and 1840 (prob-ably enhanced by contemporary agricultural improvements and land drainage) which have been shown to be associated with lateral re-working and alluviation in Thinhope Burn (Macklin *et al.*, 1992*b*) and Broomhaugh Island (Rumsby 1991). However, a critical factor in promotion and maintenance of channel instability would have been influx of large quantities of fine sediment from tributary erosion and, particularly after the mid-eighteenth century, metal-contaminated fine sediment associated with escalating lead production in the Northern Pennine Orefield (Dunham 1990). This significantly impeded riparian vegetation growth, thus reducing the stability of channel banks and colonisation rates of gravel bars (Macklin & Lewin 1989; Macklin & Smith 1990), while generally high fine sediment loads at this time would have reduced bed armouring making coarser bed material relatively mobile.

c. 1860–1900

An increase in the frequency of high magnitude floods (with return periods in excess of 20 years) in the late nineteenth century, promoted further trunk stream and tributary incision, and bank erosion, albeit at a lesser scale than that of the late eighteenth century (Rumsby 1991; Rumsby & Macklin in prep.). Cartographic evidence indicates an increase in active gravel area in braided reaches throughout the Tyne system, most notably in the upper South Tyne and River Tyne immediately below the North Tyne River confluence, where by *c.* 1900 active gravel had reached its maximum extent during the period of map and aerial photograph documentation. However, this coincides with a decrease in the number of divided channels in the upper South Tyne and Tyne. Closing of less active side-channels in these areas appears to be partly the result of flood embankment construction (probably of only minor importance in the Tyne where flood embankments, for example at Low Prudhoe, were usually built some way back from the channel), but also by infilling with fine-grained sediment.

At some sites limited migration of instability zones and initiation of braiding in formerly single-thread channels is indicated by down-valley shift of extensive active gravel (see Table 3 and Lambley, Fig. 3). The onset of large-scale zinc mining in the North Pennines during this period would have further promoted instability by releasing phytotoxic metals (Zn, Cd) into the river system.

c. *1900–1920*

The early part of the twentieth century was a period of climatic warming with relatively few large floods, during which the majority of braided sites in upper and middle parts of the South Tyne and lower reaches of the River Tyne experienced some rationalization of channel morphology and a decrease in active gravel area. At Lambley, for example, the western branch of the formerly bifurcated river developed into the dominant channel of the reach (Fig. 3), while some previously braided sites in piedmont reaches between Plenmeller and Corbridge reverted to single-thread channels with large lateral gravel bars. Braided reaches experiencing some limited growth of gravel area during this period occurred largely in the lower part of the South Tyne, notably at Broomhouse, Haltwhistle and Bardon Mill, where localized reworking of bank and bar material appears to have been associated with downstream migration of channel instability.

c. *1920–1975*

Several high magnitude floods, notably in 1947 and 1955, initiated marked trunk stream degradation throughout the South Tyne and Tyne Rivers (Rumsby 1991; Rumsby & Macklin, in prep.). Accelerated incision during this period, however, was most likely exacerbated by the cumulative effects of:

(1) agricultural improvements and land drainage undertaken between and during the wars;
(2) local flood embankment construction (from the late nineteenth century) and closure of dead channels using stone embankments (particularly in the upper South Tyne, for example at Bleagate, The Islands, Knarsdale and Eals);
(3) alluvial gravel extraction which continued until 1966 (most notably in the middle and lower South Tyne and Tyne, for example at Broomhouse, Haltwhistle, Bardon Mill and Low Prudhoe);
(4) limited or no tributary incision between 1920 and 1975 and therefore limited sediment generation.

In contrast to incision phases in the late-eighteenth and late-nineteenth centuries (which were generally restricted to headwater tributaries in the upper part of the South Tyne, and to some extent laterally stable trunk stream reaches), channel incision in the mid-twentieth century took place throughout confined trunk stream reaches *and* sedimentation zones. Decreases in active gravel area at twelve sites throughout the Tyne basin between 1920 and 1960, most notably at Broomhouse and Knarsdale (South Tyne) illustrate the initiation of this trend which extended to virtually all braided reaches between 1960 and 1975. Contraction in the size of braided reaches was usually characterised by reduced active gravel width as previously active gravel bars became vegetated and upstanding floodplain benches and alluvial terraces. At Lambley and Featherstone, for example (Figs 3 and 4), the modern active valley floor is inset some 2–3 m below the nineteenth century channel bed and is currently incising locally into till deposits. A critical and widespread factor in this contraction of active gravel area was the *reduction* in supply of metal-contaminated fine sediment following the postwar cessation of mining activity which enabled trees and shrubs to colonize alluvial surfaces and stabilise channel banks (Macklin & Smith 1990).

Some former sedimentation zones were 'healed' during this period, for example at Lambley which between 1957 and 1975 reverted to an incised, single-thread channel (Fig. 3). Many sites, however, including Featherstone (Figs 3 and 4), remained braided but within a narrower entrenched active valley floor, while there is some localised evidence of emergent medial bars in formerly single-thread reaches (Whitwham and Lipwood, Fig. 1, sites 6 and 15). Sustained coarse sediment loads, from a combination of trunk stream incision and eroded banks (potentially releasing proportionally greater volumes of sediment following channel entrenchment and relative bank elevation, cf. Carson 1984), together with higher bed shear stresses (as a result of deeper flows) appear to have been locally sufficient to maintain, and in some cases initiate, channel braiding.

Available records for the Upper Severn indicate the hydrological regime on the Severn since the eighteenth century is broadly comparable with the Tyne. Five of the six largest floods recorded in the Severn basin occurred during the late seventeenth, late eighteenth and early part of the nineteenth century (Harding 1972; Wood 1987), while a period of severe flooding towards the end of the nineteenth century (Howe *et al.* 1967; Harding, 1972; Wood, 1987) may have been instrumental in initiating widespread braiding, for example at Llandinam (Fig. 7). Flood frequency and magnitude decreased through the early twentieth century prior to enhancement during the 1940s, 1950s and 1960s (Higgs, 1987*a,b*). However, in 1968 Clywedog Dam became fully operational as a flood regulator which has reduced the number of overbank flood events from 2.61 to 1.80 per annum and promoted the stabilization of gravel bars by vegetation colonization.

Episodic braiding in the late Holocene: stratigraphic evidence in the Tyne basin

Extensive survey of eroding river banks throughout the Tyne basin and a detailed investigation of palaeochannel and alluvial sedimentary sequences in the middle Tyne valley at Featherstone, has identified and dated a number of coarse-grained alluvial units associated with multi-thread channel morphologies that pre-date OS cartographic records. Summarized alluvial histories (spanning AD 0–1990) and a range of land-use, climate and proxy climate records are shown in Fig. 14.

Several major alluvial gravel units (between 1.5–2.5 m thick) identified in upper parts of the

South Tyne basin have been found to date (^{14}C assays on wood recovered from the base of gravel members) to the late-Roman period. These units are located immediately upstream of Bleagate (Fig. 1), where deposition occurred shortly after c. cal AD 290 (Beta-51820, calibrated after Stuiver & Pearson 1986), and in the tributary valleys of the West Allen at Blackett Bridge (Fig. 1) (aggradation shortly after c. cal AD 370, Macklin et al. 1992a) and Black Burn, 4 km upstream of the confluence with the South Tyne (Fig. 1) (aggradation shortly after c. cal AD 410 Beta-46297). Trunk stream aggradation was associated with significant incision in a number of upland tributaries in the South Tyne basin. This has been documented in some detail at Thinhope Burn (Macklin et al. 1992b) where channel entrenchment and metamorphosis in late Roman times represents the first major phase of Holocene valley floor erosion. Significantly, the initiation of enhanced erosion in the Northern Pennine uplands followed shortly after the first extensive phase

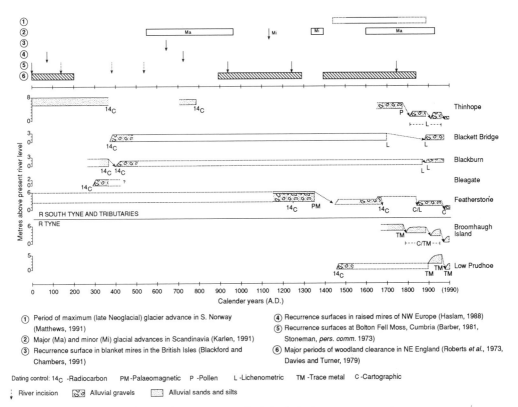

Fig. 14. Time–level diagram for dated late Holocene alluvial units in the South Tyne and Tyne basins, AD 0–1990, showing periods of river bed incision, alluvial sedimentation and methods of dating control. Selected independent proxy records of Holocene climatic change in Britain, Norway, Scandinavia and Europe, together with episodes of extensive woodland clearance in northeast England, are also presented.

of regional deforestation and agricultural expansion during late prehistoric and early historic times (Roberts *et al.* 1973; Davies & Turner 1979). However, the timing of incision likely owes more to a shift to wetter climatic conditions (with a concomitant increase in flood frequency and magnitude) in the fifth and sixth centuries AD, evidenced by humification changes in raised mire stratigraphies in western and northern Britain (Blackford & Chambers 1991; Barber 1981; R. Stoneman pers. comm.) as well as documentary records (Lamb 1977).

Radiocarbon dating of a coarse-grained bar and channel complex exposed in section at Featherstone to *c.* cal AD 1263 (Beta-45550) (Fig. 4, cross-section C-D) and a palaeo-magnetic date of *c.* cal AD 1340 from channel fill sediments on the surface of an equivalent terrace immediately upstream shows multi-thread, aggrading channels also existed in the middle South Tyne valley during the thirteenth-fourteenth centuries. Channel braiding during this period is broadly coeval with a shift to a cooler and wetter hydroclimate, and follows significant Medieval expansion of forest clearance (Davies & Turner 1979) and land under tillage (Lamb 1982) (Fig. 14) which would have enhanced run-off, flood flashiness and the sensitivity of hillslopes to erosion.

A subsequent phase of gravel aggradation at Featherstone is evidenced on the west side of the valley floor by an upstanding alluvial terrace, known as 'Madam's Island', comprising boulder and cobble lobate bars separated by narrow chute channels (Fig. 4, cross-section E–F). This terrace pre-dates the channel bed depicted on the First Edition (*c.* 1865) OS map and is truncated to the south and west by palaeo-channels dated by a combination of [14]C (assay on wood within channel fill sediments, Beta-45551), lichenometry and map evidence to between *c.* AD 1660 and 1830. Madam's Island thus reflects a further period of channel division in the middle South Tyne valley, most probably associated with major flooding during the Little Ice Age climatic deterioration (sometime between the fourteenth and early nineteenth centuries).

Discussion

The combination of climate and major land-use changes has clearly exercised a critical role in promoting episodic late Holocene braiding in the Tyne and Upper Severn basins. Deforestation, development of agriculture, metal mining and land drainage in the Tyne basin, for example, all appear to have reinforced the impact of climate fluctuations by making the Tyne more responsive to smaller magnitude shifts in temperature and precipitation than had been the case before human catchment interference. Indeed, accelerated basin erosion, higher run-off and sediment delivery in the Tyne catchment during the later Holocene may have been responsible for the development, in their present form, of sediment storage and transfer zones that currently regulate larger-scale and longer-term patterns of sediment transfer.

Differences in channel planform and cross-section response of braided reaches in the Tyne basin to increases in the frequency of major floods in the late eighteenth, late nineteenth and mid-twentieth centuries appears to reflect temporal and, to some degree, spatial variations of sediment supply to trunk rivers. Widespread channel aggradation and braiding in upper and middle reaches of the South Tyne during the late eighteenth and late nineteenth centuries resulted from effective stream sediment coupling between trunk streams and incising tributaries, combined with higher rates of sediment input from mass movement and rock-falls in laterally-confined reaches. In contrast, there appears to have been much weaker sediment coupling (certainly with respect to the coarse fraction) between tributaries and the main channel downstream in the lower South Tyne and Tyne where the principle source of coarse sediment to braided reaches appears to be bank erosion and transfer of sediment from partly entrenched reaches within (and upstream of) a sedimentation zone. Pollution of the Tyne by metal mining during these periods significantly promoted bank erosion and lateral instability by impeding riparian vegetation. During the mid-twentieth century, however, braided channel patterns have been associated with trunk channel entrenchment, partly as the result of alluvial gravel extraction and construction of embankments in some reaches, but more widely following stabilisation of former active gravel bars by vegetation and reduced coarse sediment input from tributaries and valley side walls in laterally confined reaches.

Elsewhere in northern and western Britain it is becoming increasingly evident that there were linkages between climate and river incision, alluviation and channel planform changes, such as those demonstrated in the Tyne and Upper Severn (see also Macklin *et al.*, 1992a for a longer-term perspective) during the later Holocene. The late eighteenth and nineteenth centuries appear to have been a period of particularly enhanced fluvial activity, both in terms of increased flood frequency and magnitude (McEwan 1990; Archer 1987; Wood 1987) and intensity of braiding (Lewin & Weir 1977;

Werritty & Ferguson 1980; McEwan 1989). Similarities in river planform histories are not confined to regions of north and west Britain; they are also evident in Continental Europe, where for example in Southern France (Bravard 1989; Bravard & Bethemont 1989) and Central Poland (Starkel 1991*a*, *b*) channel metamorphosis from meandering to braided morphologies, following climatic deterioration and severe flooding, has been documented in the fourteenth and eighteenth centuries.

Conclusions

Modern examples of spatially extensive braiding are comparatively rare in British rivers, particularly in larger trunk stream contexts, and with respect to the Tyne and Upper Severn basins are at present confined to relatively few sites. Cartographic and alluvial stratigraphic analysis, however, has demonstrated that the incidence and scale of braided reaches in these study catchments was greater in recent historic times, and we have charted the development and subsequent healing of several major sedimentation zones over this period. Significant channel aggradation and transformation to braided river planforms occurred in the late Roman period,

the thirteenth and fourteenth centuries and also the late eighteenth and nineteenth centuries.

Detailed studies in the Tyne basin suggest that episodic and localized river aggradation and channel division during the late Holocene was associated with increased rates of coarse sediment supply following tributary (mainly in upper and middle reaches of the South Tyne) and trunk stream incision and increased rates of bank erosion, with land-use changes accelerating runoff and increasing the sensitivity of hillslopes to erosion. Indeed, it seems likely that widespread deforestation in the late Roman period, in particular, may have set up the South Tyne basin for a period of relatively high fluvial activity extending through to the present day. Although over the eighteenth to twentieth centuries landuse changes and particularly metal mining played a major role in perpetuating channel instability, the *timing* of recent historic braiding, and earlier instability, appears to be related to changes in flood frequency and magnitude that are primarily governed by climate.

M.G.M., J.L. and M.D.N. are grateful to NERC for supporting investigations in the Tyne and Severn basins through a research grant (D.G.P., P.A.B.) and postgraduate studentship (B.T.R.).

References

ARCHER, D. 1987. Improvement in flood estimates using historical flood information on the River Wear at Durham. *Proceedings of the National Hydrology Symposium*. British Hydrological Society, 5.1–5.9.

ASHMORE, P. E. 1991. How do gravel rivers braid? *Canadian Journal of Earth Science*, **28**, 326–341.

BARBER, K. E. 1981. *Peat Stratigraphy and Climatic Change: A Palaeoecological Test of the Theory of Cyclic Peat Bog Regeneration*. Balkema, Rotterdam.

BLACKFORD, J. J. & CHAMBERS, F. M. 1991. Proxy records of climate from blanket mires: evidence for a Dark Age (1400 BP) climatic deterioration in the British Isles. *The Holocene*, **1**, 63–67.

BLACKNELL, C. 1982. Morphology and surface sedimentary features of point bars in Welsh gravelbed rivers. *Geological Magazine*, **119**, 181–192.

BLUCK, B. J. 1976. Sedimentation in some Scottish rivers of low sinuosity. *Transactions of the Royal Society of Edinburgh*, **69**, 425–456.

BRAVARD. J. P. 1989. La Métamorphose des Rivières des Alpes Francaises a la Fin du Moyen-age et a L'Epoque Moderne. *Bulletin de la Société Géographique de Liège*, **25**, 145–157.

—— & BETHEMONT, J. 1989. Cartography of Rivers in France. *In*: PETTS, G. E. (ed.) *Historical Change of Large Alluvial Rivers: Western Europe*, Wiley, Chichester, 95–111.

CARLING, P. A. 1987. Hydrodynamic interpretation of a boulder berm and associated debris torrent deposits. *Geomorphology*, **1**, 53–67.

CARSON, M. A. 1984. The meandering-braided river threshold: a reappraisal. *Journal of Hydrology*, **73**, 315–334.

CHURCH, M. 1983. Pattern of instability in a wandering gravel bed channel. *In*: COLLINSON, J. D. & LEWIN, J. (eds) *Modern and Ancient Fluvial Systems*. International Association of Sedimentologists Special Publications, **6**, 169–180.

DAVIES, G. & TURNER, J. (1979) Pollen diagrams from Northumberland. *New Phytologist*, **82**, 783–804.

DUNHAM, K. C. 1990. *Geology of the Northern Pennine Orefield, Volume 1: Tyne to Stainmore*. Second Edition, Memoir of the Geological Survey, HMSO, London.

FERGUSON, R. I. 1981. Channel forms and channel change. *In*: LEWIN, J. (ed.) *British Rivers*. Allen and Unwin, London, 90–125.

—— 1984. The threshold between meandering and braiding. *In*: SMITH, K. V. H. (ed.) *Channels and Channel Control Structures*. Spinger-Verlag, Berlin, 6.15–6.29.

—— & WERRITTY, A. 1983. Bar development and channel changes in the gravelly River Feshie, Scotland. *In*: COLLINSON, J. D. & LEWIN, J. (eds) *Modern and Ancient Fluvial Systems. International Association of Sedimentologists, Special Publications 6, 191–193*.

GILVEAR, D. J. & HARRISON, D. J. 1991. Channel

change and the significance of floodplain stratigraphy: 1990 flood event, Lower River Tay, Scotland. *Earth Surface Processes and Landforms*, **16**, 753–761.

HARDING, D. M. 1972. *Floods and droughts in Wales.* PhD Thesis, University of Wales.

HARLEY, J.B. 1965. The re-mapping of England, 1750–1800. *Imago Mundi*, **19**, 56–67.

—— 1975. *Ordnance Survey Maps, a Descriptive Manual.* Ordnance Survey, Southampton.

HARRIS, R. 1985. Variations in the Durham rainfall and temperature record, 1847–1981. *In*: TOOLEY, M. J. & SHEIL, G. M. (eds) *The climatic scene.* Allen and Unwin, London, 35–59.

HARVEY, A. M. 1986. Geomorphic effects of a 100 year storm in the Howgill Fells, Northwest England. *Zeitschrift für Geomorphologi, NF30*, 71–91.

——. 1987. Sediment supply to upland streams, influence on channel adjustment. *In*. THORNE, C. R., BATHURST, J. C. & HEY, R. W. (eds) *Sediment Transport in Gravel Bed Rivers*, Wiley, Chichester, 121–150.

—— 1991. The influence of sediment supply on the channel morphology of upland streams: Howgill Fells, Northwest England. *Earth Surface Processes and Landforms*, **16**, 675–684.

——, ALEXANDER, R. W. & JAMES, P. A. (1984). Lichens, soil development and the age of Holocene valley floor landforms: Howgill Fells, Cumbria. *Geografiska Annaler*, **66A**, 353–366.

——, OLDFIELD, F., BARON, A. F. and PEARSON, G. W. 1981. Dating of Post-Glacial Landforms in the Central Howgills. *Earth Surface Processes and Landforms*, **6**, 401–12.

HASLAM, C. J. 1988. *Late Holocene peat stratigraphy and climatic change - a macrofossil investigation from the raised mires of north-west Europe. PhD thesis, Southampton.*

HIGGS, G. 1987a. *Environmental change and flood hazard in the Upper River Severn.* PhD Thesis, University of Wales (Aberystwyth).

—— 1987b. Environmental change and hydrological response: flooding in the Upper Severn catchment. *In*: GREGORY, K. J., LEWIN, J. & THORNES, J. B. (eds) *Palaeohydrology in Practice.* Wiley, Chichester, 131–159.

HITCHCOCK, D. 1977. Channel pattern changes in divided reaches: an example in the coarse bed material of the Forest of Bowland. *In*: GREGORY, K. J. (ed.) *River Channel Changes.* Wiley, Chichester, 207–220.

HOOKE, J. M. 1986. The significance of mid-channel bars in an active meandering river. *Sedimentology*, **33**, 839–850.

—— & HARVEY, A. M. 1983. Meander changes in relation to bend morphology and secondary flows. *In*: COLLINSON, J. D. & LEWIN, J. (eds) *Modern and Ancient Fluvial Systems.* Blackwell, Oxford, 121–132.

—— & KAIN, R. J. P. 1982. *Historical Changes in the Physical Environment.* Butterworths, London.

—— & REDMOND, C. E. 1989a. River channel changes in England and Wales. *Journal of the Institute of Water and Environmental Management*, **3**, 328–335.

—— & ——. 1989b. Use of Cartographic Sources for analysing River Channel Change with Examples from Britain. *In*: PETTS, G. E. (ed.) *Historical Change of Large Alluvial Rivers: Western Europe.* Wiley, Chichester, 79–93.

HOWE, G. M., SLAYMAKER, H. O. & HARDING, D. M. 1967. Some aspects of the flood hydrology of the upper catchments of the Severn and Wye. *Transactions of the Institute of British Geographers*, **41**, 33–58.

JONES, P. D., OGILVIE, A. E. J. & WIGLEY, T. M. L. 1984. *Riverflow data for the UK: reconstructed data back to 1844 and historical data back to 1556.* Climate Research Unit Publication No. 8. University of East Anglia, Norwich, U.K.

KARLEN, W. 1991. Glacier fluctuations in Scandinavia during the last 9000 years. *In*: STARKEL, L., GREGORY, K. J. & THORNES, J. B. (eds) *Temperate Palaeohydrology*, Wiley, Chichester, 395–412.

KELLERHALS, R., CHURCH, M. & BRAY, D. I. 1976. Classification and analysis of river processes. *Journal of the Hydraulics Division, Proceedings of the American Society of Civil Engineers*, **102**, HY7, 813–829.

KNIGHTON, A. D. 1972. Changes in a braided reach. *Geological Society of America Bulletin*, **83**, 3813–3822.

LAMB, H. H. 1972. *British Isles weather types and a register of the daily sequence of circulation patterns 1861–1971.* Meteorological Office Geophysical Memoirs. **116**, HMSO, London.

—— 1977. *Climate: Past, Present and Future, Volume 2: Climatic History and the Future.* Methuen, London.

—— 1982. *Climate, History and the Modern World.* Methuen, London.

LEOPOLD, L. B. & WOLMAN, M. G. 1957. *River channel patterns: braided, meandering and straight*, US Geological Survey, Professional Paper 282E.

LEWIN, J. 1987. Historical channel changes. *In*: GREGORY, K. J., LEWIN, J. & THORNES, J. B. (eds) *Palaeohydrology in Practice.* Wiley, Chichester, 161–175.

—— & WEIR, M. J. C. 1977. Morphology and recent history of the lower Spey. *Scottish Geographical Magazine*, **93**, 45–51.

——, BRADLEY, S. B. & MACKLIN, M. G. 1983. Historical valley alluviation in mid-Wales. *Geological Journal*, **18**, 331–350.

——, DAVIES, B. E. & WOLFENDEN, P. J. 1977. Interactions between channel change and historic mining sediments. *In*: GREGORY, K. J. (ed.) *River Channel Changes.* Wiley, Chichester, 353–367.

——, MACKLIN, M. G. & NEWSON, M. D. 1988. Regime theory and environmental change - irreconcilable concepts? *In*: WHITE, W. R. (ed.). *International Conference on River Regime.* Wiley, Chichester, 431–445.

MACKLIN, M. G. 1986. Channel and floodplain metamorphosis in the River Nent, Cumbria. *In*: MACKLIN, M. G. & ROSE, J. (eds) *Quaternary river landforms and sediments in the Northern Pennines.* Field Guide, British Geomorphological Research Group/Quaternary Research Association, 19–33.

—— & ASPINALL, R. J. (1986). Historical floodplain sedimentation in the River West Allen, Northumberland: a case study of channel change in an upland, gravel bed river in the Northern Pennines. *In*: MACKLIN, M. G. & ROSE, J. (eds) *Quaternary river landforms and sediments in the Northern Pennines*. Field Guide, British Geomorphological Research Group/Quaternary Research Association, 7–17.

—— & LEWIN, J. 1989. Sediment transfer and transformation of an alluvial valley floor: the River South Tyne, Northumbria, U.K. *Earth Surface Processes and Landforms*, **14**, 233–246.

—— & SMITH, R. S. 1990. Historic vegetation succession of alluvial metallophyte plant communities in the Tyne Basin, North-East England, U.K. *In*: THORNES, J. B. (ed.) *Vegetation and Geomorphology*. Wiley, Chichester, 239–256.

——, PASSMORE, D. G. & RUMSBY, B. T. 1992*a*. Climatic and cultural signals in Holocene alluvial sequences: the Tyne Basin, Northern England. *In*: NEEDHAM, S. & MACKLIN, M. G. (eds) *Archaeology Under Alluvium*. Oxbow, Oxford, 123–140.

——, RUMSBY, B. T. & HEAP, T. 1992*b*. Flood alluviation and entrenchment: Holocene valley-floor development and transformation in the British uplands. *Geological Society of America Bulletin*, **104**, 631–643.

——, —— & NEWSON, M. D. 1992*c*. Historic overbank floods and vertical accretion of fine-grained alluvium in the lower Tyne valley, north east England. *In*: BILL, P., HEY, R., TACCONI, P. & THORNE, C. (eds) *Dynamics of Gravel-bed Rivers*. Wiley, Chichester, 564–580.

MATTHEWS, J. A. 1991. The late Neoglacial ("Little Ice Age") glacier maximum in southern Norway: new ^{14}C dating evidence and climatic implications. *The Holocene*, **1**, 219–233.

MCEWEN, L. J. 1989. River channel changes in response to flooding in the Upper River Dee catchment, Aberdeenshire, over the last 200 years. *In*: BEVEN, K. & CARLING, P. A. (eds) *Floods: Hydrological, Sedimentological and Geomorphological Implications*. Wiley, Chichester, 219–237.

—— 1990. The establishment of an historical flood chronology for the River Tweed catchment, Berwickshire, Scotland. *Scottish Geographical Magazine*, **106**, 37–48.

MILNE, J. A. *River channel change in the Harthope Valley, Northumberland, since 1897*. Department of Geography, University of Newcastle upon Tyne, Research Series No. 13.

NEILL, C. R. 1973. *Hydraulic and morphologic characteristics of Athabasca River near Fort Assiniboine*. Highway River Engineering Division Report, **REH/73/3**, Alberta Research Council, Edmonton.

ROBERTS, B. K., TURNER, J. & WARD, P. F. 1973. Recent forest history and land-use in Weardale, Northern England. *In*: BIRKS, H. J. B. & WEST, R. G. (eds) *Quaternary Plant Ecology*. Scientific Publications, Oxford, 207–221.

RUMSBY, B. T. 1991. *Flood frequency and magnitude estimates based on valley floor morphology and floodplain sedimentary sequences: the Tyne basin. N.E. England*. PhD Thesis, University of Newcastle upon Tyne, UK.

STARKEL, L. 1991*a*. The Vistula River Valley: A Case Study for Central Europe. *In*: STARKEL, L., GREGORY, K. J. & THORNES, J. B. (eds) *Temperate Palaeohydrology*. Wiley, Chichester, 171–188.

—— 1991*b*. Long-distance Correlation of Fluvial Events in the Temperate Zone. *In*: STARKEL, L., GREGORY, K. J. & THORNES, J. B. (eds) *Temperate Palaeohydrology*, Wiley, Chichester, 473–495.

STUIVER, M. & PEARSON, G. W. 1986. High precision calibration of the radiocarbon timescale, AD 1950–500 BC. *Radiocarbon*, **28**, 805–838.

WELLS, S. G. & HARVEY, A. M. 1987. Sedimentologic and geomorphic variations in storm-generated alluvial fans, Howgill Fells, northwest England. *The Geological Society of American Bulletin*, **98**, 182–198.

WERRITTY, A. & FERGUSON, R. I. 1980. Pattern change in a Scottish braided river over 1, 30 and 200 years. *In*; CULLINGFORD, R. A., DAVIDSON, D. A. & LEWIN, J. (eds) *Timescales in Geomorphology*, Wiley, Chichester, 53–68.

WOOD, T. R. 1987. The present-day hydrology of the River Severn. *In*: GREGORY, K. J., LEWIN, J. & THORNES, J. B. (eds) *Palaeohydrology in Practice*. Wiley, Chichester, 79–98.

River management and conservation issues on formerly braided river systems; the case of the River Tay, Scotland

DAVID J. GILVEAR

Department of Environmental Science, University of Stirling, Stirling, FK9 4LA, UK

Abstract: Although the present-day River Tay, Scotland is generally confined to a single course and exhibits limited lateral mobility, historical maps (1747–53) reveal that during the eighteenth and nineteenth centuries a braided river channel pattern was more characteristic of a number of reaches on the piedmont valley floor. Possible explanations of the change in channel pattern include flood embankment construction, flow regulation by impoundment and possibly a change in flood magnitude and frequency, and alterations in sediment supply.

Areas of former braiding isolated from the main channel by embankments or incorporated into the floodplain sediments, exhibit a greater susceptibility to erosion and are prone to flood embankment breaches. In contrast, river channel reaches still exhibiting unconfined braiding tendencies have been designated areas of high conservational value due to large expanses of gravel at different stages of vegetation colonization and high plant species diversity.

It is suggested that the identification of areas of former braiding and reaches prone to braiding is useful for land use management both for improved flood protection and floodplain habitat conservation.

Within the UK actively braided and wandering gravel-bed rivers are relatively rare although Werrity & Ferguson (1980) have shown the River Feshie, Scotland, to have both these characteristics. As a result little attention has been given to river management and habitat conservation issues within this type of fluvial environment. Recently, however, it has been demonstrated that wandering gravel-bed and braided rivers were probably more common in the eighteenth and nineteenth centuries. Macklin & Lewin (1992) suggest that the propensity towards more active braided rivers in the eighteenth and nineteenth centuries was due to an increase in flood frequency and magnitude together with sediment supply induced by climatic fluctuations and land use changes. The lack of currently active braided rivers and evidence of past river braiding in the UK is also due to channelization constraining rivers to relatively stable single channels (Gilvear & Winterbottom 1992) and floodplain agriculture masking morphological and sedimentological evidence of former channel patterns. Such changes, induced by channelisation, have been said to be typical for Western Europe (Petts *et al.* 1989). It appears that many UK rivers, draining upland areas, may lie close to the transitional boundary between single-thread and braided channels and may be highly sensitive to changes in flow regime, sediment supply and or river management practices. In other countries, for example Canada and New Zealand, where braided rivers are more frequent there has been more detailed study of braided rivers (e.g. Church 1989; Davies 1987) and the science of braided river management is more advanced. However, the complex and chaotic nature of changes in braid pattern still precludes accurate prediction.

This paper illustrates river planform changes on the River Tay, Scotland over the last 240 years. The study of river channel change was prompted by a large flood event in February 1990 which caused widespread damage due to bother overtopping and failure of flood embankments. The flood event prompted an improved flood warning scheme on the River Tay (Falconer & Anderson 1992) but no post-flood protection works (except for repair of flood embankment breaches) or land use zoning on the floodplain have been implemented. Smith & Bennett (in press), although not being able to discern a trend in flood frequencies and magnitudes, have noted a statistically significant increase in annual discharge over the last 20 years on the River Tay. It is therefore likely that river management and channel instability issues will continue to be the focus of attention on the River Tay.

Along the River Tummel and River Tay within the study area five Sites of Special Scientific Interest (SSSI), totalling 224.1 hectares in area, have been notified for the purpose of nature conservation; they contain extensive gravel islands in various stages of vegetation

From Best, J. L. & Bristow, C. S. (eds), 1993, *Braided Rivers*, Geological Society
Special Publication No. **75**, pp. 231–240.

colonization and are noted for their high plant species diversity. The gravel islands also form important breeding sites for birds including Ringed Plovers and Common Terns.

The purpose of the study is therefore to evaluate the significance of lateral instability and former braiding to riverbank protection schemes and floodplain habitat conservation. The con-

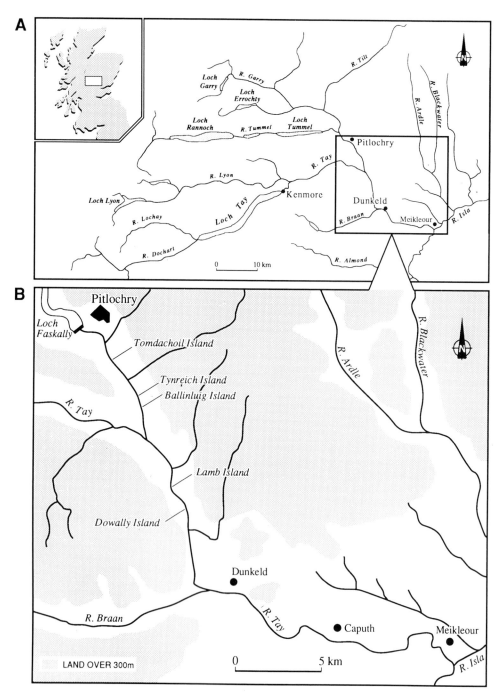

Fig. 1. The River Tay catchment and study area in Central Scotland. (*A*) The Tay catchment and location of the study area. (**B**) The study area

clusions are river specific and further research would be required to determine whether they are relevant for all UK Piedmont river systems.

The study area

The River Tay has a mean annual discharge of $160 \, m^3 \, s^{-1}$, the largest in the UK, and a catchment area of $4690 \, km^2$. The largest flood event recorded since gauging started at Caputh in 1951, took place in February 1990 and had an instantaneous peak discharge of $1747 \, m^3 \, s^{-1}$ $(0.54 \, m^3 \, s^{-1} \, km^{-2})$. Average annual precipitation in the headwater areas is high, over 1700 mm, but decreases to below 800 mm towards the lowland area to the east (Fig. 1A). The average annual precipitation for the whole catchment is 1255 mm with December being the wettest month (134 mm) and April the driest (80 mm). Much of the drainage basin lies in the Southern Grampian mountains and characteristically has thin soils and impermeable geologies. The geology of the River Tay catchment above its confluence with the River Isla (Fig. 1A) consists of metamorphic rocks including quartz–mica–schist, grit, slate and phyllite all of the Upper Dalradian. Within the piedmont valley floors, however, an extensive floodplain exists consisting of alluvium overlying sands and gravels of either fluvial or fluvio-glacial origin (Bremner 1939).

The area of study defined for this paper relates to the River Tummel downstream of Loch Faskally formed by Pitlochry Dam, completed in 1950, and the River Tay between the confluence of the River Tummel and the confluence of the River Isla; a channel length of 38 km (Fig. 1B). Upstream impoundments, for the purpose of hydro-electric power, regulate the flows of both the River Tummel and River Tay, but their effect on large flood events is minimal. Flood embankments have also been constructed over most of the length of both rivers within the study area. The first major period of flood embankment construction occurred after a large flood event in 1837 although estate records reveal that embankments were built as early as 1733.

Historical map sources

The earliest available maps allowing reasonably accurate identification of the location and planform of the River Tay are William Roy's Military Survey of Scotland (1747–53) and Stobie's map of Perthshire, 1783. From comparison with more recent maps , information can be gained on the position and planform at the time of survey, together with qualitative assessments of channel change. Evidence of later channel changes can be obtained by comparison with OS maps for different dates (at scales of 1 : 25 000, 1 : 10 560 and 1 : 10 000 dating from 1864/66, 1900 and 1962–69) and by comparison with aerial photographs (at scales of between 1 : 7500 and 1 : 27 000 for the period 1946 to 1988.

Evidence of former braided river channel patterns and historical channel changes

Examination of old maps dating back to 1747–53 illustrates that braided river channel patterns existed in the eighteenth and nineteenth centuries (Fig. 2). Within the context of this paper, river channel reaches with a number of channels, separated by gravel bars at low to medium flows, are defined as braided. The maps depict a reduction in the extent of braiding from 1747–53 to the present. For example, on the River Tummel between Tomdachoil Island and its confluence with the River Tay, the braiding index (Brice 1960) for 1753, 1783, 1863, 1897, 1946 and 1988 was 2.1, 1.73, 1.05, 0.58, 0.47 and 0.51 respectively. Associated with this reduction in braiding was flood embankment construction and in the twentieth century flow regulation for hydro-power. For example, Roy's military survey of 1747–53 shows 21 islands on the River Tummel, within the study area, but at present only one island exists (Fig. 2A). Twelve islands on Stobie's 1783 map of Perthshire are depicted, nine less than in 1753. This reduction in the extent of braiding may correspond with some of the earliest reports of flood embankment construction. The extent of the changes are such that it is thought that they cannot be explained by different definitions as to what constitutes an island on different map series. The use of these maps for accurately assessing river channel changes has been validated previously (McEwan 1989). A number of other vegetated gravel bars are currently not completely detached from the floodplain but the intervening abandoned channels are partially infilled confirming a change from a braided to single-thread pattern. At least ten major channel avulsions over the period 1747–53 to 1990 are evident as shown by changes in the location of channels between successive maps and field examination of the nature of the floodplain surface between any two successive channel locations. For example, an avulsion about 1900 resulted in the abandonment of a channel near Moulinearn resulting in Tynereich Island becoming attached to the floodplain with the old channel now forming a silted-up backwater (Fig. 2B). Avulsion is substantiated as the mechanism of channel change in this example, by a photograph taken in 1903

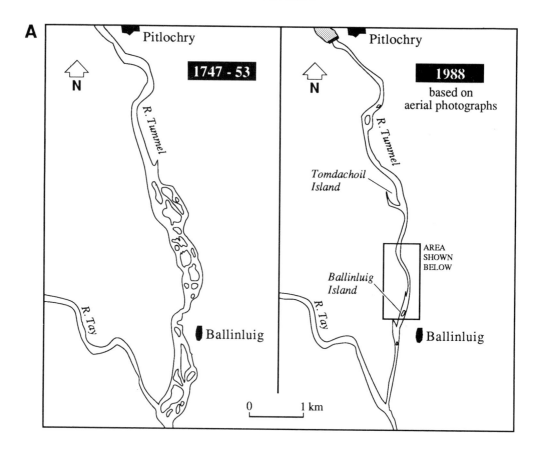

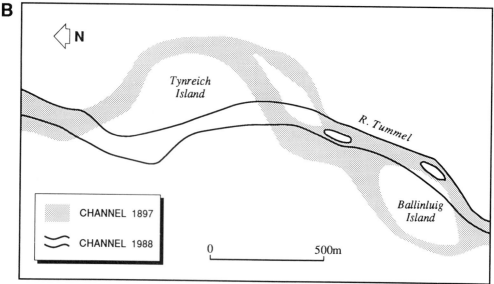

Fig. 2. Channel pattern changes on the River Tummel. (**A**) Comparison of the braided pattern as depicted on Roy's Military survey of 1747 with the 1988 river channel pattern. (**B**) Channel change in the vicinity of Tomdachoil Island

showing the River Tummel and mature vegetation on the floodplain in the area between the
old and new channel.

Currently much of the River Tay between
Pitlochry and the River Isla confluence is confined to a single course, with old channels
isolated from the main river behind flood
embankments. Many of the older isolated
channels have been infilled and surface evidence
obliterated by agricultural land use. More recent
cutoff channels, however, still contain water for
much of the year.

River channel reaches on the River Tay
exhibiting a braided pattern and lateral changes
in the position over the last 240 years, appear
to be confined to discrete reaches; the most
unstable reaches having moved back and forth
across the floodplain a number of times. In contrast, other reaches are single thread and have
remained in their present position over the same
timescale (Gilvear & Winterbottom 1992).
Given that some channel reaches appear to be
stable and yet other reaches are inherently
unstable, areas potentially at risk from future
erosion can be tentatively mapped.

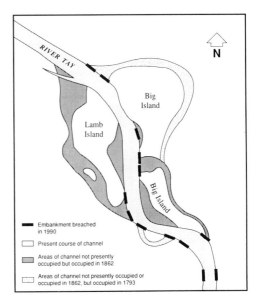

Fig. 3. Location of embankment breaches in the
vicinity of Lamb Island, River Tay, in relation to
former river channels now isolated from the main
river by flood embankments.

Avulsion and erosion hazards on the River Tay

Analysis of the geomorphic effects of historical
flood events in 1837, 1839, 1847, 1868, 1894 and
1903, using archived newspaper material and
articles in the *Proceedings of the Perthshire
Society*, together with a large flood event in
February 1990 demonstrates that lateral channel
shifts and flood embankment breaches have
occurred throughout the last 240 years on the
River Tay. For example, during the 1990 flood
over 20 embankment breaches occurred in the
study area. The major breaches in 1990 correspond with the locations of breaches in earlier
historic flood events (Gilvear & Winterbottom
1992). The location of the 1990 embankment
breaches corresponded, in all but three cases,
with the location of former river channels now
isolated from the main channel (Fig. 3); these
old channels may be identified on old maps, by
linear variations in floodplain markings on aerial
photographs and by depressions in the floodplain surface on the ground.

River bank erosion on the outside of bends is
also another recurring problem but is now
restricted only to short reaches by extensive use
of rip-rap (Fig. 4). It appears that active bank
erosion occurs along coarse-gravel riverbanks.
Observations before and after the 1990 flood
suggest that up to 5 m of bank erosion may have

occurred on unprotected river banks between
Tynereich and Ballinluig Island on the River
Tummel and close to Caputh on the River Tay.
In specific areas, bank retreat is threatening
man-made structures. For example, opposite
Tomdachoil Island SSSI, extensive rip-rap has
been used to protect the railway from rapid bank
retreat (Fig. 4, Fig. 5).

Analysis of the various maps dated between
1747–53 and 1990 indicate that approximately
15% of the total floodplain area has been
affected by river channel changes over the last
240 years. This value shows marked variability
along the course of the rivers Tay and Tummel;
on some reaches on the River Tummel almost all
of the floodplain has been affected by channel
change over the last 240 years but between the
confluence on the River Braan and Meikleour
the river has been essentially a stable low-
sinuosity channel.

Conservation value of braided river channel reaches

Within the study area, five Sites of Special
Scientific Interest have been designated by
virtue of their flora and fauna (Figs 5 and 6).
In total, they cover an area of 224.1 hectares.
These small SSSIs exist where the river exhibits

Fig. 4. The partially braided River Tummel in the vicinity of Tomdachoil Island SSSI showing the use of rip-rap to prevent further lateral bank erosion. Flow direction is from right to left.

lateral instability and/or braiding tendencies and is unconstrained by flood embankments.

The SSSIs consist of active unvegetated gravel bars and former bars in various stages of vegetation colonisation from bare shingle to mixed woodland (Fig. 5), together with old abandoned river channels with different degrees of siltation and infilling. These areas are noted for high plant diversity and have a number of rare species. They also form important breeding sites for a number of birds; for example, the Meikleour Area SSSI is of international importance as a Greylag Goose roost.

The conservational value of these sites may, in the long term, be threatened by river engineering outside of the SSSI boundaries. For example, the northwest section of Tomdachoil Island SSSI consists of a sequence of gravel bars, induced by the movement of the channel eastwards, at different stages of vegetation succession. Lateral movement eastwards of the channel has now been prevented by extensive rip rap in order to safeguard the adjacent railway (Fig. 4). The implication for the SSSI is that new areas of exposed gravel, allowing new vegetation colonization, will probably not be created while the existing colonized areas will move towards older stages of the vegetation succession sequence. Similarly if new channels do not form by avulsion the number of backwater channels will decrease due to siltation and infilling of older cutoffs leading to a reduction in environmental diversity.

Discussion and management implications

Flood hazard management

Floodplain areas once occupied by braided river channels, together with riverbanks containing former gravel bar deposits, appear suceptible to erosion. Along present-day river channel reaches on the River Tay bordered by flood embankments, breaches usually occur in locations where the embankment overlies an old course of the river. Moreover, in some cases, avulsion has occurred along the line of the former channel (Gilvear & Harrison 1991). Realisation of this enhanced vulnerability can be used to pinpoint areas of potential failure of existing embankments. Identification of former river channel braiding is also important at the design stage when deciding embankment locations and/or the type of embankment to be constructed.

It should also be realized that any change in river flows, or sediment supply may also trigger morphological changes in the river system that increase the likelihood of braided reaches forming and/or flood embankment breaches and avulsion.

Floodplain habitat conservation

Within the UK and Western Europe river regulation and channelisation has resulted in a reduction in the conservation value of flood-

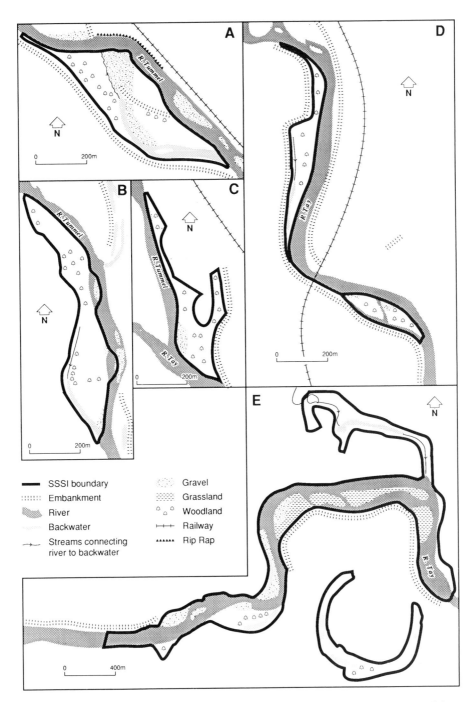

Fig. 5. The nature of the five areas designated as of high conservation value within the study area. (**A**) Tomdachoil Island SSSI; (**B**) Ballinluig Island SSSI; (**C**) Richards Islands SSSI; (**D**) Dowally Island SSSI; (**E**) Meikleour area SSSI.

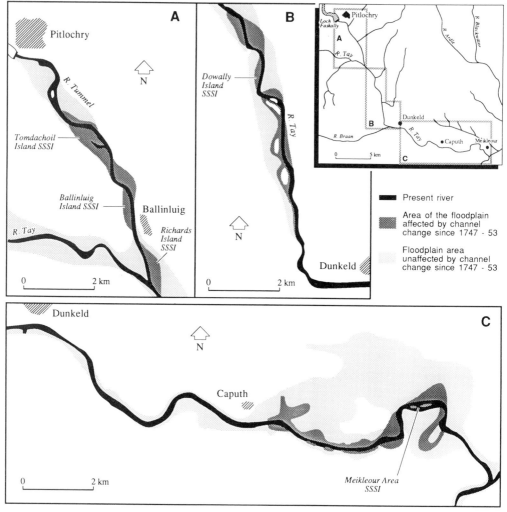

Fig. 6. A preliminary zonation of the floodplain according to areas of the floodplain that have been actively braided or affected by river channel change over the last 240 years. The map also shows the location of the five sites of special scientific interest (SSSI)

plains (Petts *et al.* 1989). Within Scotland, only 400 km of river have been notified as SSSIs (Brown & Howell 1992) out of an estimated total length of rivers in Scotland of 20 000 km. Realization that actively migrating and braided river channels induce habitats of high conservation value and that the building of flood embrankments, channelization and riverbank protection can threaten these areas is therefore of great importance. Forster & Green (1985) noted that on the River Dee, Scotland, river stabilization and bank protection leads to the destruction of shingle bars and islands and their natural vegetation. Werritty & Brazier (1991)

have stressed the need to maintain lateral instability to safeguard the conservational status of four braided river sections on the River Feshie, Scotland, which to date, has been largely unaffected by human activity.

Given the need for the conservation of floodplain habitats this paper supports the view that lateral channel mobility should be maintained in wandering gravel-bed rivers, thus maintaining habitat diversity. In view of this, setting back embankments within naturally unstable river channel reaches and allowing some lateral instability is a possible option for restoration of floodplain habitats that have previously been channelized to a single river course. Within Tomdachoil Island SSSI, areas once protected by embankments are now reverting to semi-natural vegetation due to channel change and flood embankment failure.

Holistic river management

The above examples demonstrate the importance of present-day and former braiding processes for flood hazard management and river conservation. In the case of the River Tay a sensible management strategy would be to locate flood embankments on the periphery of formerly braided sections. Implementation would, however, need the cooperation of landowners who may not personally benefit from such a scheme. In historically stable channel reaches, flood embankments would be located close to the present channel but in historically unstable reaches they would be located at some distance from the river; indeed over some short reaches the full floodplain width would have to be included.

Conclusion

Cartographic evidence has shown that the River Tay, had a braided channel pattern in the eighteenth and nineteenth centuries, confirming other reports of braiding in the UK during

the late Holocene (Macklin & Lewin 1992). Progressive building of flood embankments throughout the nineteenth and twentieth centuries, and possible flow regulation by impoundment in the twentieth century, has partially confined the channel to a more permanent and single course. Areas of the River Tay, not confined by flood embankments, and showing high lateral mobility and braiding have high botanical interest. Former areas of braiding now isolated from the main channel by flood embankments are vulnerable to erosion during flood events. A sensible river management strategy therefore appears to be to determine floodplain areas once exhibiting braided sections and to build flood embankments on the periphery of these areas. A number of advantages would accrue from implementation of such a management strategy: improved flood protection in remaining floodplain areas behind flood embankments, since floodplain inundation caused by breaches would be less likely; avoidance of expensive and often futile flood embankment repairs and creation of areas of high conservational value.

I wish to thank Scottish Natural Heritage for providing information on the Shingle Islands SSSIs and B. Jamieson for the cartography. The views expressed are those of the author and do not necessarily reflect those of organizations involved with the management of the River's Tay and Tummel.

References

BREMNER, A. 1939. The late glacial geology of the Tay basin from Pass of Birnam to Grantully and Pitlochry. *Transactions of the Edinburgh Geological Society*, **13**, 473–483.

BRICE, J. C. 1960. Index for description of channel braiding (abstract). *Geological Society of American Bulletin*, **71**, 1833.

BROWN, A. E. & HOWELL, D. L. 1992. Conservation of rivers in Scotland: legislative and organisational limitations. *In*: BOON, P. J., CALOW, P. & PETTS, G. E. (eds) *River Conservation and Management*. John Wiley and Sons, 407–424.

CHURCH, M. 1981. Pattern of Instability in a wandering gravel-bed channel. *International Association of Sedimentologists Special Publications*, **6**, 169–180.

DAVIES, T. R. H. 1987. Problems of bed load transport in braided gravel-bed rivers. *In*: THORNE, C. R., BATHURST, J. C. and HEY, R. D. (eds) *Sediment Transport in Gravel-Bed Rivers*. Wiley, 793–811.

FALCONER, R. H. & ANDERSON, J. L. 1992. *The February 1990 Flood on the River Tay and subsequent implementation of a flood warning scheme*. Paper presented at the Scottish Hydrological Group/ Institute of Water and Environmental Management Symposium on Floods in Scotland, Perth, March 31st 1992.

FORSTER, J. A. & GREEN, J. 1985. Vegetation of the valley floor of the River Dee. *In*: JENKINS, D. (ed.) *The Biology and Management of the River Dee, ITE Symposium*, NERC, 56–63.

GILVEAR, D. J. & HARRISON, D. J. 1991. Channel change and the significance of floodplain stratigraphy: 1990 flood event, Lower River Tay, Scotland. *Earth Surface Processes and Landforms*, **16**, 753–761.

—— & WINTERBOTTOM, S. J. 1992. Channel changes since 1783 on the regulated River Tay, Scotland: Implications for flood hazard management, *Regulated Rivers*, in press.

MACKLIN, M. G. & LEWIN, J. 1992. Holocene river alluviation in Britain. *In*; DOUGLAS, I. & HAGEDORN, J. (eds) *Geomorphology and Geoecology. Fluvial Geomorphology*. Zeitschrift fur Geomorphologie Supplement **85**.

MCEWAN, L. J. 1989. River channel changes in response to flooding in the Upper Dee catchment, Aberdeenshire, over the last 200 years. *In*; BEVAN, K. & CARLING, P. (eds) *Floods: Hydrological, Sedimentological and Geo-*

morphological Implications. Wiley, Chichester, 219–238.

PETTS, G. E., MOLLER, H. & ROUX, A. L. 1989. *Historical Change of Large Alluvial Rivers in Western Europe*, Wiley, Chichester.

SMITH, K. & BENNETT, A. M. in press. Recently increased wetness in Scotland: Effects on flow hydrology and some implications for water management, *Applied Geology*.

WERRITTY, A. & BRAZIER, V. 1991. *The Geomorphology, Conservation and Management of the River Feshie SSSI*. Report for the Nature Conservancy Council, Unpublished.

—— & FERGUSON, R. I. 1980. Pattern changes in a Scottish braided river over 1, 30 and 200 years. *In*; CULLINFORD, R. A., DAVIDSON, D. A. & LEWIN, J. (eds) *Timescales in Geomorphology*. Wiley, Chichester, 53–68.

A meso-scale field investigation of channel change and floodplain characteristics in an upland braided gravel-bed river, New Zealand

J. WARBURTON[1], T. R. H. DAVIES[2] & M. G. MANDL[3]

[1]Department of Geography, University of Leicester, Leicester LE1 7RH, UK
[2]Department of Natural Resources Engineering, Lincoln University,
Canterbury, New Zealand,
[3]Kulturtechnik und Wasserwirtschaft, Universität für Bodenkultur, Vienna, Austria

Abstract: Detailed data from active gravel-bed braided rivers over time periods greater than a decade is relatively sparse. The aim of this study is to establish a field site for examining channel change over an extended period (> 10 years) and determining the main mechanisms which produce the braidplain morphology. The prototype is the Ashley River, Lees Valley, New Zealand, which is 2.5 km in length, has an average braidplain width of 400 m and slope of 0.012 m m^{-1}. The flow regime is dominated by low flows (average flow 3.15 m^3 s^{-1}) with 2–3 winter flood events in excess of 25 m^3 s^{-1} per year. Planform information on this reach dates back to the 1860s with ten sets of maps/air photographs up to the present. Since 1989 the sedimentary and morphological characteristics of the braidplain have been carefully surveyed. There is a downstream decrease in sediment size which is accompanied by a reduction in bank height at the margin of the floodplain and a decrease in cross-section bed amplitude. Certain elements in the floodplain (vegetated bars, channels with coarse lag sediments and banks with armoured bank toes) persist while other features such as unconsolidated gravel banks and fine-gravel sheets do not. Channels are migrating towards the northern edge of the braidplain with old bars becoming vegetated on the southern margin. Channel patterns change most dramatically when the flood flows reoccupy old channel segments. Observations of channel change from flood to flood indicate that, although some channel segments switch dramatically, other segments are left intact and largely unaltered. Movement of small sediment lobes affected the flow at node-points within the channel (e.g. areas of flow divergence and convergence) causes avulsion. The dominant mechanisms of channel change are avulsion and bank notching/scalloping.

Braided rivers are often viewed as highly active channels which constantly traverse their gravel floodplains through the division and rejoining of their channels (Carson & Griffiths 1987). Although there is not a great deal of detailed data from prototype braided rivers over time periods greater than a decade (Griffiths 1979; Werritty & Ferguson 1980; Davies 1987), it appears that in braided rivers where the flow and sediment supply regimes are highly variable and there are significant periods between flood events, channels may be relatively stable (Carson & Griffiths 1987). The aim of this study is to document channel change in a braided river system with a view to: (1) establishing a field site for examining change over an extended period (>10 years); (2) identifying the main mechanism which determine the braidplain morphology; and (3) studying channel changes between fllods. These aims are important because in many braided river studies measurements have tended to focus on understanding of processes over short periods of time and at small spatial scales (e.g. Ashmore et al. 1992; Bridge & Gabel 1992). Unfortunately, scales relevent

to problems in braided river engineering are rarely addressed (see Church 1983 for an exception), yet it is the medium term and meso-scale behaviour or river reaches which is of importance in engineering applications such as changes in bed-levels (Griffiths 1979), erosion of braidplain margins and destruction of riparian habitat. Studies on timescales on the order of several years to decades are, however, often difficult to implement because there is no immediate return on the considerable investment of resources needed to collect data. As a consequence there are few formal measurement programmes at this scale and the only informal source of information is from the experience of river engineers.

In New Zealand investigations of channel change in braided rivers have involved studies of the effects of changing discharge on braided river morphology and geometry (Mosley 1979, 1981, 1982, 1983); observations of bar development (Rundle 1985a, b; Davoren & Mosley 1986) and of changes in channel planform (Carson 1986); and attempts to reconstruct the longer-term behaviour of braided river systems

From Best, J. L. & Bristow, C. S. (eds), 1993, *Braided Rivers*, Geological Society
Special Publication No. **75**, pp. 241–255.

(Beschta 1983; Griffiths 1979). Detailed attempts to investigate channel change in braided rivers over an extended period are absent from these investigations (Davies 1987; Carson & Griffiths 1987).

This study adopts the broad approach of examining the meso-scale geomorphology in order to identify small-scale problems that warrant detailed investigation by placing them in a proper temporal context. This approach is based on the belief that it is easlier to scale-down than to scale-up. This paper describes the first phase of this project and has two main objectives:

(1) to summarize historical channel development of the Ashley River at the study site;
(2) to identify the major mechanisms responsible for producing channel change at this site.

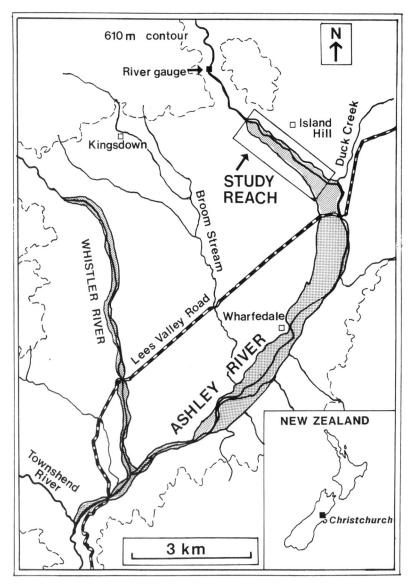

Fig. 1. The Ashley River, Lees Valley, Canterbury, New Zealand. The location of the study reach is indicated by the box. Flow in the study reach is from northwest to southeast.

Description of the Ashley River study site

The study reach is part of the Ashley River, New Zealand (Fig. 1) which rises on the eastern slope of the main divide of the South Island and drains from the Puketeraki Range through Lees Valley and Ashley Gorge across the North Canterbury Plains between Waimakariri and Hurunui Rivers. The length of the Ashley river from source to sea is approximately 90 km whilst the section studied here is in Lees Valley on the upper reaches, approximately 15 km from the source.

Lees Valley is a 17 km long southwesterly trending faulted intermontane basin sandwiched between the Puketeraki Range and the Mt Thomas foothills. The geology of the area consists of Cretaceous greywackes and argillites with minor volcanic outcrops. The basin has been infilled with Pleistocene periglacial gravels and Holocene cobble-gravel fan sediments to produce a valley plain with an average elevation of 450 m. The Puketeraki range was almost certainly never glaciated but was subjected to an intense frost climate (Bowden 1982). Present rates of uplift in the area are on the order of 0.5 to 1 mm a^{-1} (Wellman 1979). Soils are mostly shallow, stony and well-drained. Vegetation is dominantly short tussock grassland with some snow tussock, alpine scrub and native forest in the upper catchment (Bowden 1982).

This area was originally colonized by settlers in the 1850s to establish sheep runs and limited cattle grazing. In 1917–1918 the government subdivided the area into 3000–4000 hectare blocks which were balloted to returning servicemen. Partial drainage of the valley flats has occurred and much of the valley flat land is improved pasture. There has been little attempt to control the river. River protection has been piece-meal with the most significant works attempting to control erosion on the lower part of the study reach against the south bank. This involved the building of a gabion training groyne in the 1930s and more recently (c. 1970) the use of railway sleepers/wire fences and the planting of willow trees.

The study reach

The main study reach is 2.5 km in length, has an average braidplain width of 400 m and mean bed slope of 0.012 m m^{-1}. This is a small, low sinuosity ($P \approx 2$–3), braided stream. The river emerges from a bedrock gorge and flows southeast in an almost straight reach for 3 km where it turns and flows to the south (Fig. 1). Where the stream emerges from the bedrock gorge the braidplain immediately fans out in a fashion similar to the input conditions observed in many flume studies (Ashmore 1991).

River flow data

Precipitation varies between 1000 mm a^{-1} in Lees Valley to 1500 mm a^{-1} over the Puketeraki Range and is fairly evenly distributed with a peak in the winter months. Within the Ashley River system the only permanent water level recorder and gauging station is at Ashley Gorge Bridge 33 km downstream (installed April 1972). The gauge in Lees valley (a Foxboro water level recorder) is defined as a 'secondary gauging station' and was established 800 m upstream of the study reach in 1977. The site is visited infrequently and therefore the rating curve is only approximate. Records exist for the site since 1982 but the most reliable data comes from a two year series between 1988 to 1990 (Fig. 2). Analysis of the flow series, in period 31 October 1988 to 31 October 1990, reveals that the flow regime is dominated by low flows (average flow 3.15 m^3 s^{-1}), the minimum and maximum flows being 0.63 m^3 s^{-1}, and 55.19 m^3 s^{-1}, respectively with two or three winter flood events exceeding 25 m^3 s^{-1} (Fig. 2).

Historical changes in channel pattern and braidplain characteristics

For an upland braided river which has not been extensively disturbed by man, there is very good map and photo coverage. Planform information on this reach dates back to the 1860s with ten sets of maps/air photographs up to the present (six since 1979). The earliest available evidence dates back to a sketch map produced in the 1860s; this is followed by a settlement map in 1917, some oblique photographs in the 1930s and eight sets of air photographs between 1950 and 1992 (Figs 3, 4 and 5).

Historical maps and oblique photographs

The earliest evidence from the 1860s sketch map (Fig. 3) indicates the channel has the same general pattern as the present channel except in the lower part of the study reach where it prematurely cut the corner to the south. The lower part of the river also seems to have had a braidplain which was shifted to the northwest. A detailed map produced as part of the rural resettlement programme in 1917 shows that the overall form of the study reach was very similar to the present (Fig. 3). Downstream of the

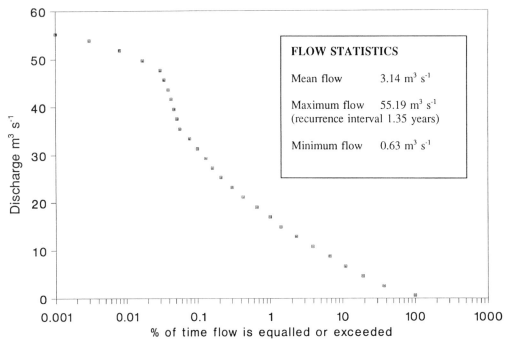

FLOW STATISTICS

Mean flow   3.14 m^3 s^{-1}

Maximum flow   55.19 m^3 s^{-1}
(recurrence interval 1.35 years)

Minimum flow   0.63 m^3 s^{-1}

Fig. 2. October 1988 to October 1990 flow series. The record is from the river gauge located 800 m upstream of the study reach (Fig. 1).

reach, however, the braidplain was relatively confined (Fig. 3). Local inhabitants maintain that the Ashley River used to have a much narrower braidplain in this reach. An oblique

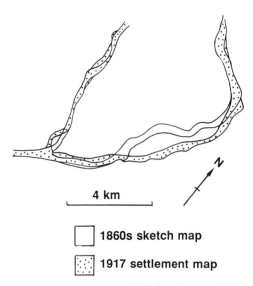

4 km

☐ 1860s sketch map

▦ 1917 settlement map

Fig. 3. Comparison of the 1860s sketch map and 1917 settlement map evidence for the extent and location of the Ashley River braidplain.

photograph of the Ashley River at a bridge site downstream of the confluence with the Whistler in the 1930s (which is 11 km downstream of the study reach; Fig. 4a), shows a wide braided system very similar to the present river (Fig. 4b). By comparing the clearance between the river bed and bridge piers common to both the 1930s and the 1990 bridge approximately 1–1.5 m of aggradation has taken place at this site. Direct evidence of similar rates of aggradation in the study reach is not available.

Air photographs

A series of air photographs from 1950 to 1992 reveal several important characteristics of the river (Fig. 5 and Table 1). However, it should be recognized that the air photographs are of variable style and quality. Colour photographs are particularly good for distinguishing gravel sheets and bars of different ages because colonisation and stabilization of bar surfaces by plants is rapid. However, the margins of the braidplain are diffuse and defining braidplain width is difficult. For this study the margin is defined as the point at which bare or sparsely vegetated gravels exist adjacent to a well vege-tated bank. Discharge at the time of the photo-graphs also varies although all are taken at low to

Fig. 4. The Ashley River at the middle bridge between the Whistler and Townshend tributaries, 11 km downstream from the study reach (Fig. 1). (**a**) The river *c.* 1930 and (**b**) the river in 1990. Based on estimates from burial depths around the bridge and aggradation against bank margins the site has aggraded by approximately 1.5 m in 60 years.

moderate flows and the overall legnths of the channel networks (the sum of all individual channel lengths) are similar in each case.

Firstly, the air photographs all show a low sinuosity braided channel (Table 1); and the 1960 photo shows a braidplain dominated by bare gravels with few vegetated bars (Table 1).

Since 1960 the channel in the upper reach has been pinned against the north bank; whilst the width of the braidplain has increased slightly since the 1950s/1960s. Several reach-scale avulsions are evident in many of the photographs e.g. from June 1989–February 1990– October 1990 the photographs show an avulsion

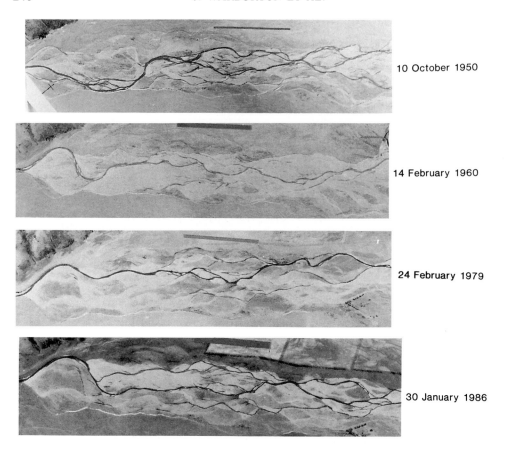

10 October 1950

14 February 1960

24 February 1979

30 January 1986

of the full reach followed by reoccupation of the old channel (Fig. 5). This process of avulsion–reoccupation is typical of the nature of channel change from flood to flood and results in a braidplain scarred by numerous avulsions and a

floodplain margin scalloped by bank notching (Carson & Griffiths 1987).

Although channel planform is only of limited value when considering the morphological development of a three dimensional braided

Table 1. *Changes in bar area, channel sinuosity and average braidplain width based on air photographs 1950 to 1992 (Fig. 5)*

Date	Bar area as a % of braidplain area	Sinuosity	Average braidplain width (m)	Total channel length (m)
1950	34	1.89	315 ± 39	4797
1960	16	1.77	340 ± 81	4486
1979	46	1.54	404 ± 55	3892
1986	40	2.74	401 ± 52	6928
1989	42	2.21	376 ± 32	5595
Feb. 1990	42	1.47	376 ± 32	3717
Oct. 1990	42	1.99	376 ± 32	5050
1992	42	2.73	376 ± 32	6918

Sinuosity is defined as total channel length divided by reach length. Between 1989 and 1992 there is little change in bar area and average width.

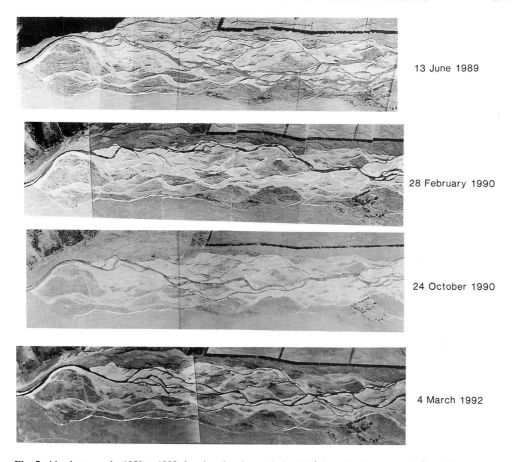

13 June 1989

28 February 1990

24 October 1990

4 March 1992

Fig. 5. Air photographs 1950 to 1992 showing the change in braided river planform morphology. The length of the reach is 2.6 km and the characteristics of the river in each photograph are given in Table 1.

system, it is often the only source of information available for assessing longer-term development. Based on this fragmentary air photo record it is possible to produce two maps.

(1) A composite map indicating all the channel positions recorded in the air photographs (Fig. 6a). Channel positions are mapped as centre-lines of all active channels and all major abandoned channels visible at the time of photography. Active channels are defined as channels transmitting streamflow (backwaters are not included). Major abandoned channels are those channels which have clearly been recently occupied by the flow. These can be distinguished on the basis of a lack of vegetation, sharply defined cut-banks and the presence of fines deposited along the bed of the channel. These fine sediment deposits can easily be mapped on colour air photographs.

(2) A map of vegetated bar areas indicating

the minimum age at which the bar stabilized (Fig. 6b). The last four sets of air photographs 1989 to 1992 show approximately the same bar areas and are therefore lumped into a single bar class 1989–1992. Mapping of bar areas is based on tonal and colour differences in the air photographs and is subject to errors due to photo-quality and seasonal differences in vegetation cover.

The composite map of channel centrelines shows three important features (Figs 6 and 7): (1) there is an increase in the number of channels downstream (Fig. 7); (2) there is a lack of channels on the south side of the braidplain; and (3) the majority of channels occur against the north bank with many channel branches corresponding to the clearly exposed notches in the river bank. For example during the period 1950 to 1992, 95% of the northern margin of the braidplain has been subjected to fluvial erosion

ASHLEY RIVER CHANNEL POSITIONS 1950 –1992

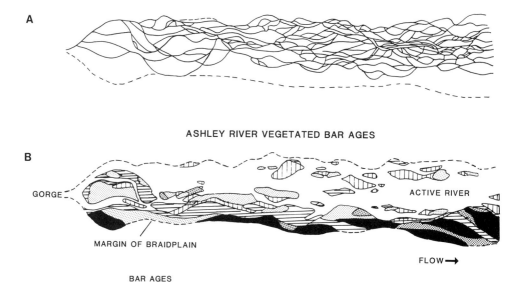

ASHLEY RIVER VEGETATED BAR AGES

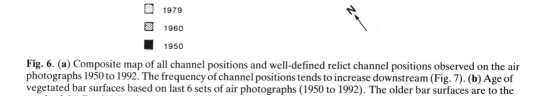

BAR AGES

▦ 1989 – 1992
▤ 1986
▢ 1979
▨ 1960
■ 1950

0   500   1000m

Fig. 6. (**a**) Composite map of all channel positions and well-defined relict channel positions observed on the air photographs 1950 to 1992. The frequency of channel positions tends to increase downstream (Fig. 7). (**b**) Age of vegetated bar surfaces based on last 6 sets of air photographs (1950 to 1992). The older bar surfaces are to the south of the floodplain with bare gravel (no shading) to the north.

whilst, over the same period, the southern margin has remained untouched. Based on this map (Fig. 6) it is possible to extract further information by determining the proportion of the channel network surviving between successive air photographs (Fig. 8). Figure 8 plots the time interval between a pair of air photographs and the proportion of the channel length which is common between the two photographs. This plot shows a decline over time but perhaps the most significant point is that some elements persist in the landscape for long periods e.g. the entrance bend to the reach has persisted since the 1960s (Fig. 5). In terms of storage the lower part of the braidplain has been traversed almost completely by channels over the last 40 years whereas the upper part of the reach has longer term storage elements. This suggests that the storage elements are not equally active along the reach over time as has

been suggested in some braided river models (Hoey 1989).

The ages of the vegetated bars (Fig. 6b) indicate that the oldest bars are on the south side of the braidplain while to the north of the braidplain consists of small young bars or bare areas of gravel. The main bar at the head of the reach has stabilized over time and results in the input channel being more likely to remain pinned against the northern side of the braidplain. Based on the fact that the braidplain has remained roughly the same width in this area of the reach then bar deposition and stabilisation on the south side and bank erosion on the north side indicate the active braidplain is slowly shifting north. During this period the position of the input channel at the entrance to the reach was on the north side and the northern margin of the braidplain was being actively eroded by fluvial processes.

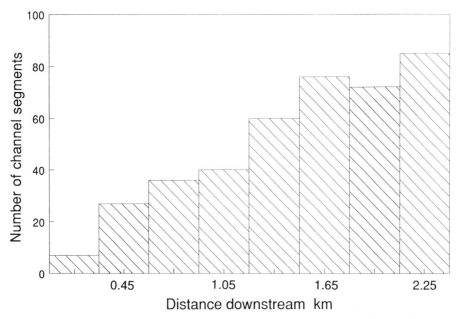

Fig. 7. Plot of the number of channels in 0.3 km segments of the main study reach with distance downstream.

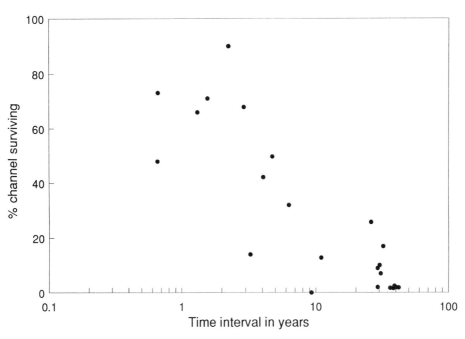

Fig. 8. Time-change plot of common channel lengths between air photographs. The time intervale between a pair of air photographs is plotted with the proportion of the channel length which is common between the two photographs.

Relations between sediment size, bank height and bed relief along the study reach

In order to characterize downstream variation in sediment size, surface samples were collected from unvegetated bar areas as close to the present channel at each of the 51 cross-section transects. At each site a 1 m² grid was set-up over the surface and the largest 25 clasts immediately below the grid points were sampled and classified using square openings in a template. The size of the river bed sediment shows a general decrease downstream (Fig. 9). From where the

channel emerges onto the braidplain down to the last cross-section (51) at 2.5 km downstream, sediment size decreases from a very coarse boulder gravel at the top end of the reach down to a small cobble gravel. The origin of this sorting is difficult to determine but it must reflect a combination of contemporary downstream sorting, minor abrasion and inheritance of a sorted profile from the older fan in which the braidplain is entrenched.

In quantifying changes in bed relief along the study reach, cross section data were used to construct a simple maximum bed amplitude index. A series of 51 permanent floodplain-wide cross-

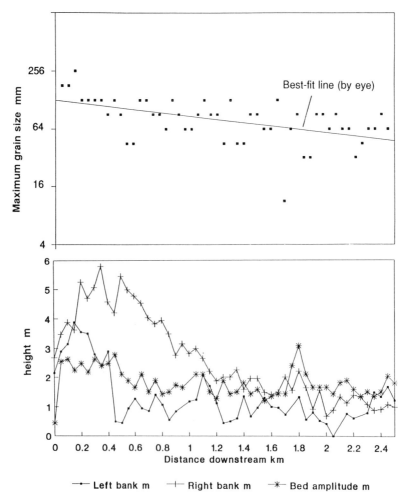

Fig. 9. Downstream changes in sediment size, bank height and bed amplitude in the study reach. Sediment samples were collected on the cross-section transects. All measurements of bank height and bed amplitude are in metres. Because the low point of the cross-section and the base of the bank are often a common point then both bed amplitude and bank heights can be referenced to a common datum.

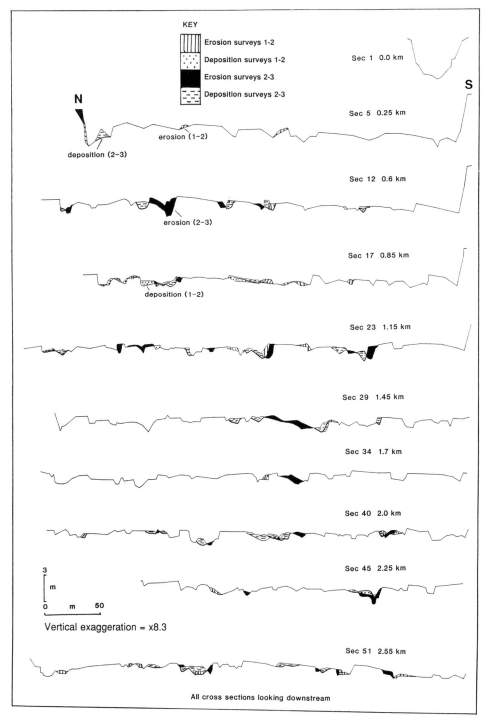

Fig. 10. River channel cross-sections. Data are from ten sections spaced approximately 250 m apart. Surveys were carried out at three separate times: (1) January 1990, (2) October 1990 and (3) February 1992. Changes between successive surveys (e.g. 1–2 and 2–3) are shown. Vertical exaggeration is 8.3 times the horizontal.

sections were set-out in 1989/1990 and surveyed
at each 50 m along the study reach (December to
January). Resurvey of ten of the cross-sections
has been repeated twice since: October 1990 and
February 1992 (Fig. 10). Sections were surveyed
using a Sokkia Set4B Total Station EDM with
errors determined from repeat measurements of
± 0.05 m in horizontal position.

The maximum bed amplitude index was calculated as the maximum height difference between
the lowest point in the profile and the highest bar
surface. Banks at the margin of the braidplain
were not included in the cross section for this
calculation. This was selected in preference to
more sophisticated bed relief indices because it
was the simplest means of determining whether
there was a large difference in relative relief
across the section. The purpose was to determine whether there were any systematic changes
in bed amplitude down the study reach which
may influence the relative stability of the
channel (Fig. 10). For example Section 5 in Fig.
10 shows a relatively high bed amplitude
(2.48 m) with the channel pinned against the
inner bank i.e. the channel is fixed by the intervening relief. In sections of lower relative relief
e.g. Section 40, Fig. 10, amplitude 1.65 m) the
pattern of erosion and deposition suggest a more
unstable channel. This interpretation is limited
since the two-dimensional relief expressed in
cross sections (spaced 50 m apart) will only contain a fraction of the information of the actual
three-dimensional relief of the floodplain.

Figure 9 shows that the downstream decrease
in sediment size is accompanied by a general
reduction in bank height at the margin of the
floodplain and a decrease in cross-section bed
amplitude. Because the low point of the cross-
section and the base of the bank are often a
common point then both bed amplitude and
bank heights can be referenced approximately to
a common datum. It therefore follows that lower
bed relief coupled with lower banks means that
the channel has the potential to more easily
migrate laterally or avulse locally because the
channel is less confined. Close examination of
Fig. 9 shows that from 0.4 km, bed amplitude is
greater than left bank height and remains so all
the way down the reach. However, on the right
bank bed amplitude does not exceed bank height
until approximately 1.8 km down reach. This
is significant because the geometry that this
describes explains why the northern left bank is
more susceptible to erosion whilst the southern
right bank is relatively stable (Fig. 6). It is
important to note that a large channel next to a
steep bank is often thought of as erosive, however if the bank is high enough and the banks

supply coarse material to the channel in large
enough quantities (i.e. a very coarse bank or tall
bank with proportionally more coarse elements)
then channel stability will result due to bed
armouring.

Recent developments and observations
of channel change

Evidence of recent channel development is
based on air photographs, cross section surveys
and field observations. The contemporary
channel pattern essentially consists of five
elements: straight channels, curved (meandering) bends, acute ('attack') bends, and diffluent
and confluent braided segments. Evidence from
the cross sections shows local small-scale piece-
meal erosion and deposition around the wandering channel thalweg. Figure 10 shows the detail
of ten cross-sections (vertical exaggeration is 8.3
times) looking downstream. Away from the
areas of active thalweg the cross-sections are
identical demonstrating that these areas are
inactive. Although there is local deposition,
there is no direct evidence of active reachwide
aggradation over the two years of monitoring.

There appear to be four main processes affect-
ing local erosion and deposition in the channel
(Fig. 11). Firstly avulsion of two main types
occurs involving channel erosion of a new part of
the braidplain or local erosion or deposition
within existing channels leading to the channel
flowing down an old channel in the braidplain.
The second mechanism is by far the most
important and generally involves a small sediment lobe moving down the main channel. This
lobe either blocks an old channel deflecting the
flow or locally constricts the flow causing bank
erosion and connection with an old channel (cf.
Lewis & Lewin 1983) in meandering rivers).
These mechanisms are highly localized, principally occurring at nodes in the network, but the
effects are widespread. Discharge is generally
shared between channels. Alternatively old
channels may be periodically reoccupied during
floods due to inundation without any major
change in the morphology. It therefore appears
that braiding here is primarily a function of
channel avulsion rather than a flow bifurcation
process forced by active medial bars. Braiding
exists not because the hydraulics are adjusted to
it but simply because of prior channels, with low
and intermediate flows insufficient to override
their imprint in the braidplain morphology.
Avulsion dominates because there is excellent
preservation of channel remnants in the braidplain between floods indicating little infilling of
the braidplain gravels.

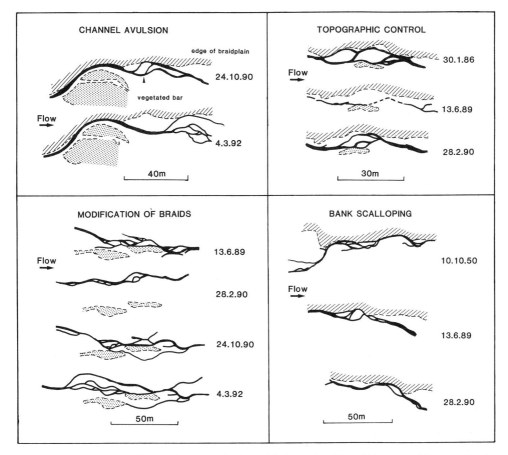

Fig. 11. Examples of recent channel change mechanisms: (**a**) channel avulsion, (**b**) topographic control by the pre-existing braidplain topography, (**c**) bar modification and (**d**) bank scalloping or notching.

Topographic control of channel pattern (Fig. 11), as indicated above under the avulsion section, may simply occur because of changes in river stage (Mosley 1983). As discharge increases larger parts of the floodplain become inundated by flow with spill-type avulsions commonly occurring. In moderate floods this is usually accompanied by only very local re-distribution of sediment.

A major part of research into braided channels has focused on the genesis of bar forms (Rundle 1985a, b; Ashmore 1991). How-ever, most braided rivers have a floodplain topography which is the result of prior flow events and it is the modification of the floodplain morphology by bank erosion and avulsion which is often important. Because of complex flow histories, bar/braid complexes rather than individual bar forms commonly develop. Braid

complexes are the areas of the channel which show the most evidence of channel change (Fig. 11). These areas consist of numerous conflu-ences and diffluences, whilst local redistribution of sediment within these complexes results in the loss of anabranches or avulsion onto new parts of the braidplain (Fig. 11).

Bank erosion of the braidplain margin pro-duces a characteristic 'notched' or 'scalloped' pattern (Fig. 11). There is no single dominant mechanism of bank erosion because there is evidence of premature inflection of the thalweg (Carson 1986), classical meander bends (with well-developed secondary circulation), and bends with very aggressive 'attack' angles causing intense flow convergence on the outer bank and rapid scour (Carson & Griffiths 1987). However, there is little overwidening of channels at the margin of the braidplain due to the vegetated banks. Bank erosion, although occurring on single bends against the margin of the braidplain, usually involves an anabranch of a braid complex. This is important because the anabranch will not evolve independently of the braid complex so that the situation, although geometrically similar to a classical meander, depends on the evolution of the entire braid complex.

These observations are consistent with Carson (1986) in as much as modification of channel form by bank erosion and deposition in the channels is periodically interupted by avulsions which redirect the active channel zone. These avulsions arrest bend development and keep the overall sinuosity of the channel relatively low.

Summary

Although existing records of channel change are incomplete and the long-term monitoring programme of the Ashley River has just begun, it is possible to draw several preliminary conclusions.

(1) Over a timescale of decades the braidplain is slowly migrating northwards due to bank erosion on the northern braidplain margin and bar stabilization to the south. This may be in response to long-term (large-scale) sedimentation cycles but the record is insufficient to distinguish these.

(2) There is a marked downstream decrease in grain-size accompanied by a reduction in bank height and bed amplitude. Much of this structure is probably inherited due to entrenchment of the braided system into the Pleistocene fan gravels.

(3) Some parts of the channel network and braidplain persist for long periods (>10 years) and help to stabilize parts of the braidplain.

Certain elements in the floodplain (vegetated bars, channels with coarse lag sediments and banks with armoured bank toes) persist in the braidplain while other features (such as unconsolidated gravel banks and fine-gravel sheets) do not.

(4) Channel erosion and deposition is a local phenomenon with most activity concentrated around the wandering channel thalweg as floods reoccupy old channels. Channel patterns change most dramatically when the flood flows reoccupy old channel segments. Observations of channel change from flood to flood indicate that, although some channel segments switch dramatically, other segments are left intact and largely unaltered.

(5) The dominant mechanisms of channel change are avulsion and bank notching/scalloping. Movement of small sediment lobes affects flow at node-points within the channel (principally areas of flow divergence) and causes avulsion down old channel segments. Small changes at critical points in the network may have a large effect on the channel pattern downstream. The mechanism of change is highly localized but the effect is widespread.

(6) It is important to investigate the mesoscale local geomorphology in order to understand river dynamics at a small-scale.

J.W. would like to acknolwege grant support from Lincoln University and provision of a Postdoctoral Fellowship from the New Zealand Universities Grant Commission. The survey would not have been possible would not have been possible without the assistance of D. Lees and L. Mlcoch. Flow data were supplied by Canterbury Regional Council. J. Lewin and J. Best provided useful constructive comments on an early version of the paper. Also our warm thanks to J. and A. Russell of Island Hill for their interest and support.

References

ASHMORE, P. E. 1991. How do gravel-bed rivers braid? *Canadian Journal of Earth Sciences,* **28**, 326–341.
——, FERGUSON, R. I., PRESTEGAARD, K. L., ASHWORTH, P. J. & PAOLA, C. 1992. Secondary flow in anabranch confluences of a braided gravel-bed stream. *Earth Surface Processes and Landforms,* **17**, 299–311.
BESCHTA, R. L. 1983. Long-term changes in channel widths of the Kowai River, Torlesse Range, New Zealand. *Journal of Hydrology (New Zealand),* **22**, 112–122.
BOWDEN, M. J. 1982. *The Water Resources of the Ashley Catchment.* North Canterbury Catchment Board and Regional Water Board, Christchurch, New Zealand.
BRIDGE, J. S. & GABEL, S. L. 1992. Flow and sediment

dynamics in a low sinuosity, braided river: Calamus River, Nebraska Sandhills. *Sedimentology,* **39**, 125–142.
CARSON, M. A. 1986. Characteristics of high-energy "meandering" rivers: The Canterbury Plains, New Zealand. *Geological Society of America Bulletin* **97**, 886–895.
—— & GRIFFITHS, G. A. 1987. Bedload Transport in Gravel Channels. *Journal of Hydrology (New Zealand) Special Issue,* **26**, 151.
CHURCH, M. 1983. Pattern of instability in a wandering gravel bed channel. *International Association of Sedimentologists, Special Publications,* **6**, 169–180.
DAVIES, T. R. H. 9187. Problems of bed load transport in braided gravel-bed rivers. *In:* THORNE, C. R.,

BATHURST, J. C. & HEY, R. D. (eds) *Sediment Transport in Gravel-bed Rivers*. John Wiley & Sons Ltd, Chichester, 793–828.

DAVOREN, A. & MOSLEY, M. P. 1986. Observations of bedload movement, bar development and sediment supply in the braided Ohau River. *Earth Surface Processes and Landforms,* **11**, 643–652.

GRIFFITHS, G. A. 1979. Recent sedimentation history of the Waimakariri River, New Zealand. *Journal of Hydrology (New Zealand),* **18**, 6–28.

HOEY, T. B. 1989. *An examination of the forms and processes associated with bed waves in gravel-bed rivers with special reference to the braided river type.* PhD thesis, University of Canterbury, New Zealand.

LEWIS, G. W. & LEWIN, J. 1983. Alluvial cutoffs in Wales and the Borderlands. *In*: COLLINSON, J. D. & LEWIN, J. (eds) *Modern and Ancient Fluvial Systems.* Basil Blackwell, Oxford, 145–154.

MOSLEY, M. P. 1979. Prediction of hydrologic variables from channel morphology, South Island rivers. *Journal of Hydrology (New Zealand),* **18**, 109–120.

—— 1981. Semi-determinate hydraulic geometry of river channels, South Island, New Zealand. *Earth Surface Processes and Landforms,* **6**, 127–137.

—— 1982. Analysis of the effect of changing discharge on channel morphology and instream use in a braided river, Ohau River, New Zealand. *Water Resources Research,* **18**, 800–812.

—— 1983. Response of braided rivers to changing discharge. *Journal of Hydrology (New Zealand),* **22**, 18–67.

RUNDLE, A. 1985a. The mechanism of braiding. *Zeitscrift für Geomorphologie, Suppl. Bd.* **55**, 1–13.

—— 1985b. Braid morphology and the formation of multiple channels The Rakaia, New Zealand. *Zeitscrift für Geomorphologie, Suppl. Bd.,* **55**, 15–37.

WELLMAN, H. W. 1979. An uplift map for the South Island of New Zealand and a model for the uplift of the Southern Alps. *In*: WALCOTT, R. I. & CRESSWELL, M. M. (eds) *Origin of the Southern Alps.* Royal Society of New Zealand Bulletin, **18**, 13–20.

WERRITTY, A. & FERGUSON, R. I. 1980. Pattern changes in a Scottish braided river over 1, 30 and 200 years. *In*: CULLINGFORD, R. A., DAVIDSON, D. A. & LEWIN, J. (eds) *Timescales in Geomorphology.* John Wiley & Sons, Chichester, 53–68.

Planform pattern and channel evolution of the Brahmaputra River, Bangladesh

COLIN R. THORNE[1], ANDREW P. G. RUSSELL[2]
& MUHAMMAD K. ALAM[3]

[1]*Department of Geography, University of Nottingham, Nottingham NG7 2RD, UK*
[2]*Sir William Halcrow & Partners, Burderop Park, Swindon SN4 0QD, UK*
[3]*Department of Civil Engineering, Bangladesh University of Engineering & Technology, Dhaka, Bangladesh*

Abstract: The Brahmaputra is one of the world's greatest rivers, ranking fifth in terms of discharge and eleventh in terms of drainage area. It also has a very high sediment discharge, ranking third in the world. The river is braided with meta-stable islands and nodal reaches, mobile sand bars, shifting anabranches and severe bank erosion. The dominant discharge is about 38 000 cumecs, which is a high in-bank flow. Islands have top elevations that are adjusted to bankfull discharge, with a spacing scaled on the width of the primary channel. Bar top elevations are adjusted to the dominant discharge and bars are scaled on the width of the major anabranches. The dominant bedforms are large dunes scaled on the third order sub-channels of the major anabranches. Sustained right bank erosion has occurred during the last 35 years, with average rates of about 90 m per year. The left bank shows both erosion and accretion that together produce relatively low rates of net movement. Erosion is faster in island reaches and slower in nodal reaches. Recognition of the geomorphic controls of bank erosion allows its spatial distribution to be related to the development of the braided pattern of the river and a tentative hypothesis is proposed to explain recent trends in both bankline movement and the evolution of the channel planform pattern.

The Brahmaputra (called the Jamuna in Bangladesh) is one of the greatest rivers in the world ranking fifth in terms of discharge (mean flow 12 200 cumecs) and eleventh in terms of drainage area (666 000 km^2). In Bangladesh the river enters the country from Assam (Fig. 1). It is joined by a major right bank tributary, the River Teesta and flows almost due south for approximately 220 km to its confluence with the Ganges. The combined flow of these two great rivers is called the Padma River. The Padma flows southeast for about 100 km before meeting the much smaller Meghna River. The Meghna estuary meets the open sea of the Bay of Bengal about 160 km to the south of this confluence (Fig. 1). This paper is concerned only with the reach of the Brahmaputra between the Teesta and Ganges confluences (Fig. 2).

The annual hydrograph of the Brahmaputra is characterized by low flows during the winter dry season and high flows during the summer due to snowmelt in the Himalayas and heavy local rainfall in the summer monsoon. The catchment supplies vast quantities of sediment from erosion of actively uplifting mountains of the Himalayas, slope erosion of the Himalayan foothills and movement of alluvial deposits stored in the Assam Valley. Consequently, the Brahmaputra in Bangladesh carries a very heavy sediment load of around 500 million tonnes annually. Most of this is in the silt size class, but around 15–25% is sand (Halcrow 1991) and the proportion of clay is very small.

The Brahmaputra usually peaks in late July or early August (mean annual peak flow 65 500 cumecs) and some overbank flooding usually occurs. When local monsoon rainfall is especially heavy and prolonged more serious flooding results, as in 1987 (Brammer 1990) (Fig. 2b). The Ganges peaks in late August or early September (mean annual peak flow 51 625 cumecs), also causing moderate to serious flooding. In most years between 20 and 30% of Bangladesh is flooded and this is quite acceptable to the population. However, on occasion the Brahmaputra peaks late, coinciding with the Ganges and leading to catastrophic flooding that is far more extensive and damaging. The last occurrence of flooding on this scale was in 1988, when nearly 60% of the nation was inundated (Brammer 1990). Suffering caused by the floods of 1987 and 1988 led to the establishment of the Flood Action Plan (FAP) concerned with the development of a strategic overall plan for water management in Bangladesh. In 1990 the Brahmaputra River Training Study (BRTS) was initiated with the aim of developing a master plan for training the Brahmaputra River, based

From Best, J. L. & Bristow, C. S. (eds), 1993, *Braided Rivers*, Geological Society Special Publication No. **75**, pp. 257–276.

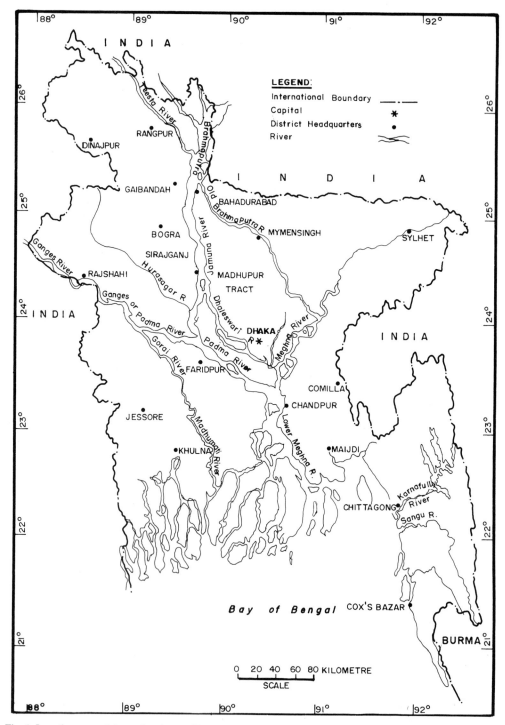

Fig. 1. Location map of the major rivers of Bangladesh.

on a thorough understanding of all aspects of the river and its catchment (Halcrow 1990). At present there are no substantial training structures in the study reach, and only short stretches of bank protection. These have, with the possible exception of town protection at Sirajganj, proved largely ineffective. Hence, there is at present (1993) no significant engineering impact on the overall morphology of the river.

In the 1960s the Brahmaputra Right Embankment (BRE), a substantial levee protecting the area west of the river from inundation during flood flow, was constructed from the Teesta to the Hurasagar confluences. When right bank erosion undermines the BRE breaches open rapidly, leading to catastrophic flooding (Fig. 2b). There is no similar embankment on the left bank, and substantial high flow spillage occurs via the Old Brahmaputra and Dhaleswari River distributaries (Fig. 2b). Hence, flood flows are not artificially constrained at present (1993).

Channel characteristics and dynamics

The Brahmaputra adopted its present course about 200 years ago. Prior to that time the river flowed to the east of a Pleistocene terrace, the Madhurpur Tract, along a course now occupied by the Old Brahmaputra (Fig. 1). In the study reach the river is braided, with numerous small bars and fewer, large islands, locally called chars, which divide the flow into sub-channels called anabranches (Fig. 2a). Braid bars are highly unstable and their size, shape and position change radically between each seasonal high flow (Coleman 1969; Bristow 1987), but the islands are relatively stable. Historical evidence demonstrates that islands are formed by the amalgamation of clusters of braid bars which build up to around flood plain level. Consequently, some reaches of the river can be classified as anastomosed rather than braided (Bristow 1987). The pattern of anabranches changes through time by lateral shifting of anabranches and through switching of flows between anabranches that drives rapid modifications of channel size and geometry.

Bristow (1987) identified three scales of channels within the braided river. The first order channel encompasses the whole river and has a variable number of second order channels within it. Each second order channel is itself a large alluvial stream termed an anabranch, and within the second order channels the flow divides and rejoins again to form third order sub-channels. Each size of channel has associated with it bars

that scale on the dimensions of the channel within which they are located. Changes in third order channels occur rapidly and within a season, while changes occur annually in the second order channels. No large scale avulsions of the first order channel have taken place recently, but evidence for such channel changes is evident in the historical record of maps and surveys, which dates back to Rennell's map (Rennell 1765). The first order channel has increased in width during historical time and there is evidence that it has migrated westwards through preferential erosion of the right bank (Coleman 1969). However, recent studies undertaken in connection with the proposal to construct a bridge over the Brahmaputra concluded that the apparent westward migration identified by Coleman was in fact an oscillation in the random shifting of banklines that it was unlikely to be sustained for long (JMBA 1988). This view is not shared by all engineers and scientists in Bangladesh. Hence, morphologically the river is known to be highly active at all scales, although numerous questions concerning the present direction of movement and future development of the planform are unresolved.

Morphological studies

Morphological studies focused on linking channel form and process. The hydraulic and sedimentary flow regime of the river was characterised using a dominant discharge analysis. This identified a dominant range of flows which were used as reference discharges and stages for the examination of the cross-sectional and planform features of the channel.

Dominant discharge analysis

The dominant discharge concept hypothesises that in stable alluvial rivers the geometry of the channel is determined by the flow which performs the most work. Work in this context was defined as sediment transport by Wolman & Miller (1960). Ackers & Charlton (1970) added to Wolman & Miller's original definition by showing that dominant discharge is also the steady flow that would produce the same meander wavelength as the observed range of flows. Wolman & Gerson (1978) extended the arguments concerning the effectiveness of sediment transport in doing work on the channel to include the morphological changes caused by erosion and deposition, and Hey (1975) demonstrated that in a degrading channel the flow

Fig. 2. (**a**) Satellite image showing the braided pattern of the Brahmaputra in the study reach on 7 February 1987. (**b**) Satellite image taken on 17 August 1987 near the peak of the 1987 monsoon flood (maximum daily discharge = 70 465 cumecs). Note breach in BRE just north of Kazipur. (Images supplied by ISPAN, FAP-19, Dhaka, Bangladesh).

doing most erosion (rather than sediment transport) would be the dominant flow, while an aggrading channel would adjust to the flow doing most deposition. Hey also showed theoretically that in rivers in dynamic equilibrium it is the flow doing most sediment transport that defines the dominant flow. In the BRTS study analyses of historical bed levels in cross-sections and long-profiles indicated neither aggradation or degradation over the last 40 years (Halcrow 1991). Hence, in the dominant discharge calculation it is appropriate to use the flow doing most sediment transport to define the dominant discharge.

Base data came from the Bangladesh Water Development Board (BWDB) gauging station at Bahadurabad at the upstream end of the study reach (Fig. 1). Daily discharge records for the period 1956/7 to 1988/9 were used to construct a flow frequency distribution (Fig. 3). Measured sediment transport data are also available for Bahadurabad, but not over the entire period of flow record. Available data consist of sand load for the period 1968–1970 and of both sand load and total measured load (that is sand plus silt load moving in suspension) for the period 1982–1988. The sediment rating equations are given by Halcrow (1991) as:

$$Q_{st} = 0.91 Q^{1.38} \text{ tonnes/day} \tag{1}$$
$$Q_{ss} = 0.93 Q^{1.25} \text{ tonnes/day} \tag{2}$$

$$S_i = 4.1 \times 10^{-6} Q^{1.38} \text{ m}^3 \text{ s}^{-1} \tag{3}$$

where Q = discharge (cumecs) and equation (1) refers to total measured sediment load for 1982–88 data, equation (2) refers to suspended sand transport for 1982–88 data and equation (3) refers to suspended sand transport for 1968–70 data.

The availability of several rating equations posed a question as to the selection of the one most appropriate for use in the dominant discharge calculation. Since the salient morphological features of the channel, the bars and the chars, are composed mostly of sand (Halcrow 1991), it is the erosion, transport and deposition of sand which is fundamental to the hydraulic shaping of the channel. The silt may then be viewed as 'wash load' passing through the channel without playing a significant role in forming it. However, an alternative view is that because the silt constitutes the much greater part of the total load, it cannot be ignored. In this study all three sediment rating curves were used to compute the sediment moved by a particular flow during the period of record. This was found by multiplying the sediment transport rate, in tonnes per day, by the frequency of that flow, in days to obtain a gross weight, in tonnes. The results are shown in Fig. 4.

Examination of the results shows that while the absolute amount of sediment moved

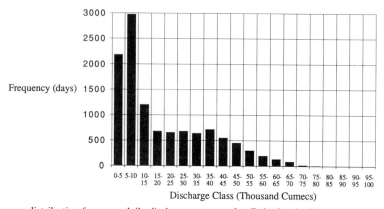

Fig. 3. Frequency distribution for mean daily discharge measured at Bahadurabad between 1956/7 and 1988/9.

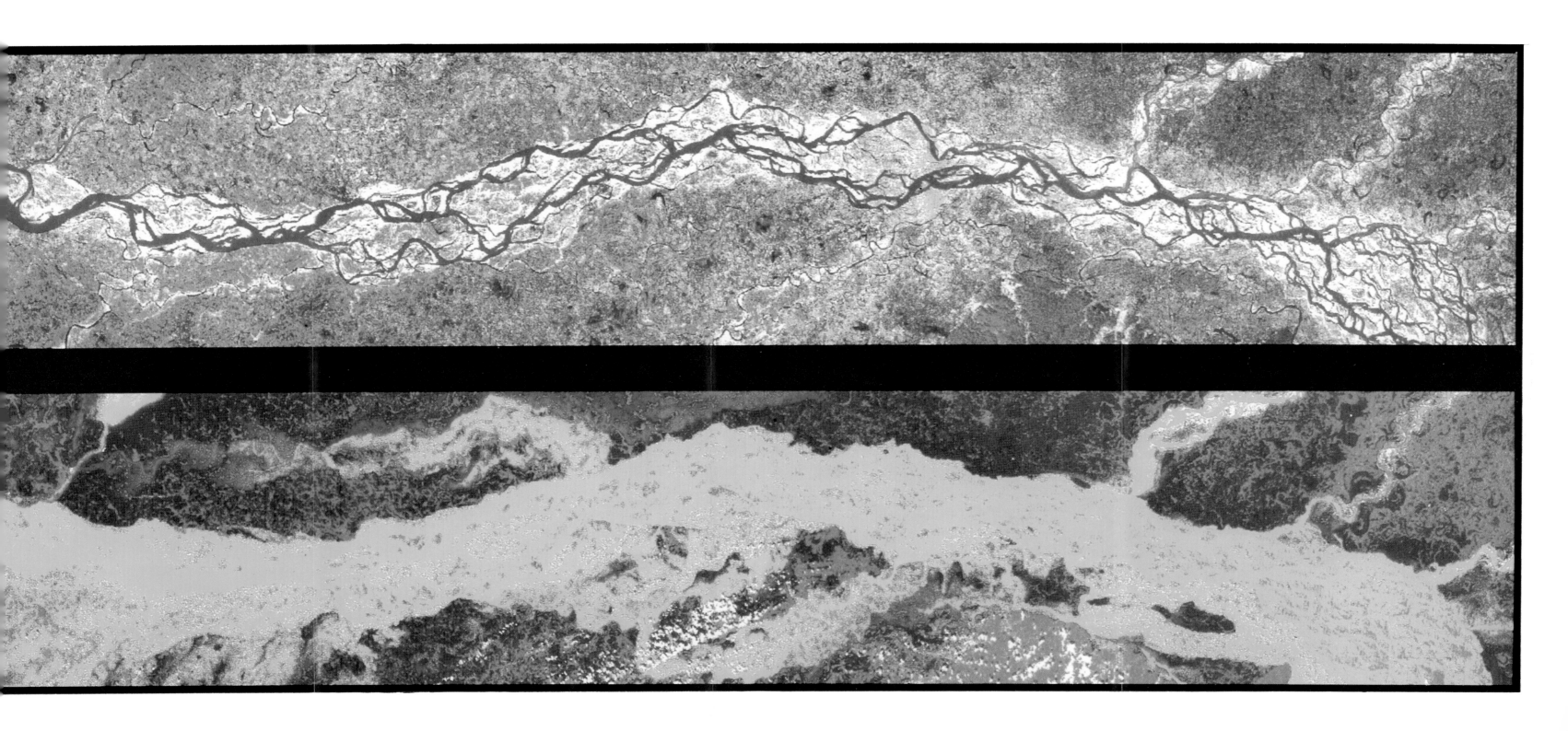

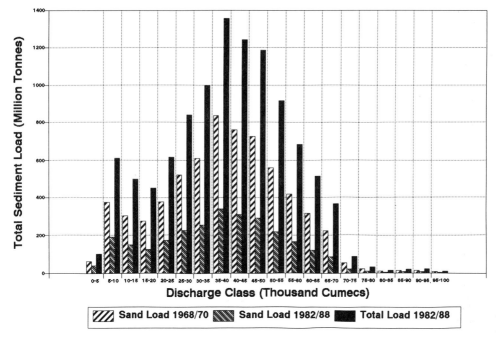

Fig. 4. Dominant discharge plot for the Brahmaputra at Bahadurabad.

changes, the choice of sediment rating curve has little impact on the shape of the histogram. In each case the distribution is bi-modal, with a major peak defining the dominant discharge at 38 000 cumecs. This discharge is equalled or exceeded 18% of the time. An independent study performed by the China–Bangladesh Joint Expert Team (CJET 1991) reached the same conclusion using a power law for the sediment rating curve rather than observed data. bankfull discharge is defined by the Bangladesh Water Development Board to be of the order of 60 000 to 65 000 cumecs in the study reach. Hence, dominant discharge is rather less than bankfull in the Brahmaputra. While dominant discharge has been found to coincide with bankfull discharge in many single-thread rivers (Richards 1982; Knighton 1984) it is not unusual for dominant flow to be less than bankfull in braided rivers (Lee & Davies, 1986). A small, secondary peak is associated with a flow of 7500 cumecs which corresponds to base, dry season flow for the river. Significantly, even though the period of record includes the catastrophic floods of 1987 and 1988 (peak discharge over 100 000 cumecs, return period 100 years) there is no discernible peak associated with these major floods. This analysis indicates that their contribution to the total mass of sediment moved during the 31 year period of record is comparatively small.

A cumulative plot of percentage sediment moved against discharge (Fig. 5) shows a characteristic 'S' shape, with a very steep, almost linear increase in cumulative sediment load for discharges in the range 32 500 to 60 000 cumecs. The dominant flow (38 000 cumecs) is also the median flow for sediment transport, as 50% of the load is transported by both greater and lesser flows. Although the river experiences discharges as low as 2500 and higher than 100 000 cumecs it is remarkable that 50% of the sediment is transported by flows in a range of discharges between about 25 000 and 50 000 cumecs. There is a very clear break of slope at around 60 000 cumecs, corresponding to bankfull discharge.

Low flows, less than 10 000 cumecs, together carry only 10% of the load, while large floods also contribute relatively little in terms of sediment movement. For example, flows greater than 60 000 cumecs transport less than 8% of the load, and those greater than 70 000 cumecs transport less than 2%. The return period for 70 000 cumecs is only about 3 years.

In the case of the Brahmaputra the data do not support the conclusion that great floods play the major role in transporting sediment over the medium to long-term. Conversely, the data clearly point to a range of discharges associated with high in-bank flows responsible for a disproportionately large percentage of the sedi-

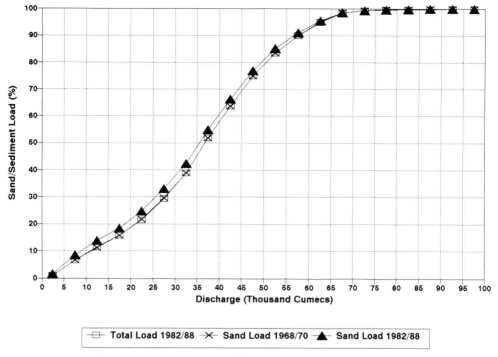

Fig. 5. Cumulative sediment transport curves for the Brahmaputra at Bahadurabad.

ment moved and work done. If this is actually the case then there should be evidence in the geometry of the channel that the main morphological features are adjusted to the dominant range of flows. The most prominent and important sedimentary features of the channel are the island chars and braid bars, which give it its characteristic, multi-channel cross-section, its braided planform, and its shifting nature. Therefore, the geometry and morphology of the braid bars were examined to determine whether there was a clear association between them and the dominant range of discharges.

Analysis of islands and braid bars

Analysis centred on the use of monumented, surveyed cross-sections supplied by the BWDB, together with water surface profile data generated by the BRTS team. Established sections are surveyed annually at low water by the BWDB, but in 1988/89, following the flooding of 1988, the intensity and detail of surveying was significantly increased. Hence the 1988/89 data were selected for this study. Moreover the availability of SPOT imagery supplied by the Flood Plan Coordination Organisation (FPCO) per-

mitted quality control checks to be carried out. Hydrographic surveys during the peak and post monsoon periods in 1990 (Halcrow 1991, 1992) demonstrated unequivocally that in the Brahmaputra the major topographic bed features formed during high flow are preserved at low flow, so that the BWDB surveys may be taken to represent the main features of the channel at formative flows.

The cross-sections for 30 locations spaced fairly evenly along the river in the study reach were obtained (Fig. 6). Preliminary examination confirmed that in cross-section most of the bars displayed flat, slightly saucer-shaped top surfaces as described by Coleman (1969) and Bristow (1987). This made it relatively easy to determine an average top elevation for each of the bars at each cross-section. It quickly became clear that while at some cross-sections the bar features all accorded to a single average elevation, many others showed both an upper and a lower elevation that differed by as much as 2 m. In some cases a further, very low bar height could be discerned, defining three levels of bar in all. For example, Fig. 7 shows a typical section in the centre of the study reach. The upper bar level corresponds to an island char and is charac-

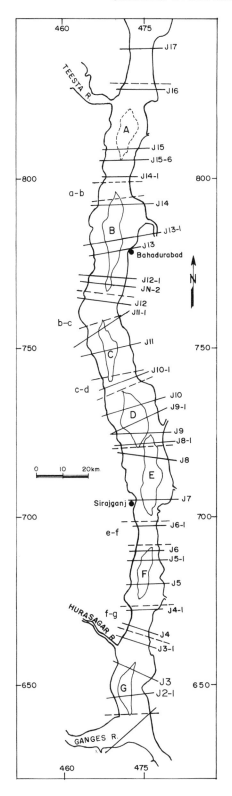

terised by mature, perennial vegetation, fully developed agricultural practices and permanent habitation. In terms of both elevation and land-use it is very similar to the flood plain outside the braid belt (Table 1, Figs 7 and 8). The second level corresponds to the braid bars that flank the main island in the satellite image (Fig. 8). These are quite different in appearance to the island. They are large sand bodies displaying loose sediment surfaces, immature and annual vegetation, seasonal cropping and no permanent habitation. The third, very low bar level is associated with dunes in the sub-channels flowing around the bars. These are much smaller features that remain inundated at all but the lowest flows and are not visible in Fig. 8. Echo-sounder records made by the BRTS team indicate that they are mobile at all flows and can migrate at speeds of up to 100 m per day, but that individually they play no significant role in forming the gross features of the channel. These constantly shifting and reforming features are truly bedforms rather than bars, and consequently do not merit further consideration in this analysis of channel macro-features. The upper, island top and lower, braid bar top elevations for all 30 cross-sections are listed in Table 1. The results of this part of the morphological studies are entirely consistent with the more detailed, sedimentary analysis of Bristow (1987) confirming the existence of a three level hierarchy of morphological features which scale on the first order channel, the second level, left and right bank anabranches and the various third level sub-channels.

Island and bar top elevations are plotted on a long-profile of the study reach in Fig. 9, together with the water surface profile for dominant discharge produced using a calibrated, one-dimensional hydraulic model. The water surface profile for dominant flow plots between the island and bar top elevations at almost all locations. Dominant flow over-tops the braid bars, which are active, but does not inundate the island chars, which are meta-stable, inhabited areas. In this respect the braid bars are 'adjusted' to the dominant flow and are the contemporary morphological expression of process-form inter-action. Dominant discharge of the Brahmaputra therefore corresponds to 'barfull' rather than bankfull discharge. The upper chars are islands that divide the flow even at the dominant range of flows and therefore

Fig. 6. Location of cross-sections and island/node sub-reaches used in morphological studies.

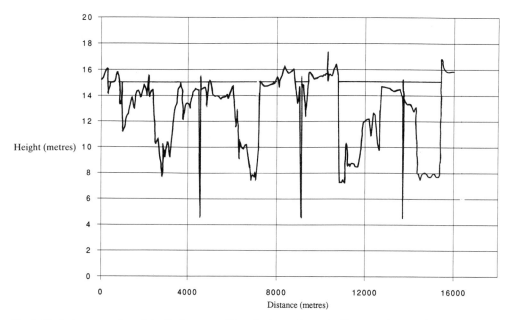

Fig. 7. Typical cross-section of the Brahmaputra River in the study reach: Cross-section J-10 just south of Kazipur (see Fig. 6 for precise location). Note that elevation of medial island is matched to flood plain height, while lower, flanking sand bars are just over topped at dominant flow. Dune bedforms are much lower and are covered at all flows.

their tops remain inactive except during high magnitude events, which also inundate portions of the flood plain. This requires a discharge above around 60 000 to 65 000 cumecs, corresponding to out of bank flow. This finding confirms that, at the first order level, reaches of divided flow around islands may be described as anastomosing rather than braided, as previously suggested by Bristow (1987).

Between around 30 000 and 60 000 cumecs the planform of the river is simplified because the braid bars have been drowned out, but the flow is still confined to the first order channel. In this range of flows the sediment stored in the braid bars becomes accessible to the river for sediment transport and the transport rate is large because of this free availability of loose sediment coupled with gains in hydraulic efficiency and transport capacity that occur when divided flows combine to reduce the number of anabranches and concentrate flow in a few, very large channels. Thus, discharges between barfull and bankfull are confirmed as being the dominant range of flows responsible for much of the sediment transport and for forming the major contemporary morphological features of the channel.

The distribution of the elevation difference between upper, island top and lower, bar top elevations is not random, but varies systematic-

ally along the channel (Fig. 9). The island and braid bar top points describe two sinuous profiles which alternately diverge and converge in a somewhat regular pattern. Sinuosity is more pronounced in the lower, bar top trace and its long profile displays a series of steps comprised of long, relatively steep reaches, where the elevation difference from the islands is greatest and the bars are well inundated at dominant flow, separated by short, flatter sloping reaches where the difference is much less and the bars are barely covered at dominant flow. The upper, island top trace is less sinuous, but still displays the 'whale-back' longitudinal profile of the islands quite clearly. Island reaches are high and dry at dominant flow, while intermediate, lower points are still just above the dominant flowline in Fig. 9, except at the confluence with the Ganges at the lower limit of the study reach. Here, all bar features are inundated at dominant flow and a single-thread, meandering channel predominates.

Planform analysis

Coleman (1969) qualitatively identified island reaches separated by nodes. In this study, SPOT and Landsat images were examined and the study reach was provisionally divided into island

Table 1. *Bank, island char, top, bar top and dominant discharge water surface elevations for cross-sections in the study reach*

Cross-section number	Chainage (km)	Dom. Q water surface elevation (m)	Bankfull elevation		Braid bartop elevation (m)	Island chartop elevation (m)
			Left (m)	Right (m)		
J-17	25.00	23.7	25.0	24.6	22.0	23.5
J-16	31.35	22.6	24.2	23.4	21.0	23.4
J-15	44.25	21.2	23.2	22.5	20.8	22.5
J-15-6	55.65	20.5	22.6	21.5	19.0	21.5
J-14-1	63.00	19.9	NS	NS	18.2	21.0
J-14	71.00	19.1	22.0	NS	18.3	20.0
J-13-1	81.70	18.6	19.8	NS	18.0	19.5
J-13	84.70	18.4	19.1	19.1	17.5	19.0
J-12-1	93.80	17.7	19.3	18.6	17.6	18.8
JN-2	95.50	17.6	18.2	18.6	17.3	18.8
J-12	100.50	17.3	19.0	18.2	17.0	18.1
J-11-1	108.90	16.8	18.3	18.0	16.8	17.5
J-11	117.75	16.0	17.9	16.6	14.8	16.8
J-10-1	126.50	15.5	15.8	16.8	14.6	15.8
J-10	134.30	14.9	15.3	16.5	14.6	15.5
J-9-1	139.00	14.5	15.3	15.0	14.4	14.9
J-9	142.45	13.9	15.3	14.8	13.8	14.8
J-8-1	145.40	13.6	14.3	14.2	13.5	14.3
J-8	149.50	13.3	14.3	14.0	13.8	14.0
J-7	162.35	12.4	15.0	14.7	13.0	13.0
J-6-1	170.75	11.8	13.3	13.3	None	12.5
J-6	177.70	11.0	14.0	12.5	11.3	12.0
J-5-1	180.60	10.9	13.0	12.5	11.0	11.0
J-5	188.20	10.3	12.0	12.0	9.8	11.7
J-4-1	195.75	9.7	11.6	NS	9.1	10.7
J-4	201.30	9.3	14.0	9.5	9.0	10.2
J-3-1	205.15	9.2	11.5	NS	8.6	10.55
J-3	213.20	9.1	10.0	NS	8.5	8.5
J-2-1	220.00	8.9	10.0	9.6	8.0	8.0
J-1-1	229.40	8.5	9.1	10.3	5.0	None

NS, not shown.

reaches and nodes on the basis of the width and braiding intensity variations, along the lines suggested by Coleman (Fig. 6). Island reaches are much longer than the nodes, although it was much easier to identify short 'nodal reaches' than it was to define precise nodal points. Islands are semi-permanent in that all seven are readily recognisable on available images dating back to 1973. Individual islands are subject to considerable dissection, erosion and accretion over this twenty year period, but they do not migrate appreciably. Over the longer timescales revealed by historical maps, some of the islands appear to have migrated slowly downstream (Halcrow 1991).

Church & Jones (1982) observed that most rivers may be divided into a series of sediment storage and sediment transmission zones. Under this classification the island reaches are sediment storage zones and the nodal reaches are sediment transmission zones. It is generally accepted that the length of a storage zone or bar is scaled on the width of the channel and Yalin (1977) has used dimensional analysis and theoretical fluid mechanics to produce the equation:

$$L = \pi w \qquad (4)$$

where, L = the length of the feature, π = 3.142 and w = the channel top width. Applying this rule to the Brahmaputra and taking an average top width for the first order channel as about 6 to 7 km (determined from measurements on satellite images), it would be expected that the islands should be about 20 km long. Table 2 lists the actual lengths of the seven islands observed in the study reach. The average length is in fact 20.6 km with a spread from 16 km for island C, to 25 km for Island B. The length of 31 km for

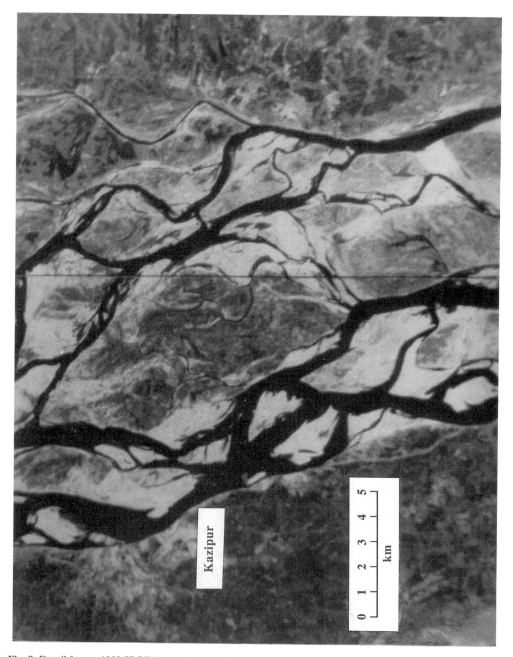

Fig. 8. Detail from a 1989 SPOT image showing the area around cross-section J-10 near Kazipur. The large medial island is island D. Note the smaller sand bars in the anabranches along each flank of the island. Embayments may be identified in both flood plain and island banklines due to flow deflection around growing sand bars.

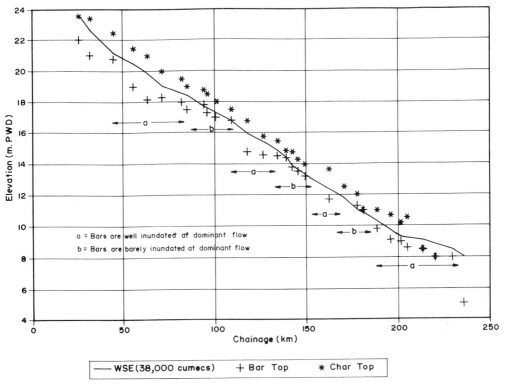

Fig. 9. Long-profile of Brahmaputra River showing island char, braid bar and dominant discharge water surface elevations.

Table 2. *Lengths of island reaches in the Brahmaputra River*

Island	Length (km)
A	31
B	25
C	16
D	18
E	18
F	18
G	18

reach A is distorted by the Teesta confluence and Fig. 6 shows that the actual island in reach A is about 20 km long. Hence, the length of the islands is not inconsistent with their being scaled on the first order channel of the Brahmaputra.

Comparison of the long-profile distribution of upper and lower bar elevations, together with the planform pattern of island and nodes in the river, shows that the sinuosity in the long-profiles is closely related to variations in plan-form pattern and channel width. Reaches where the upper and lower bar elevations differ markedly correspond to wide, island reaches and those where bar elevations converge correspond to narrower nodes. Viewed in this light, the long-profile and planform variability of the geometry are seen to be two expressions of a common, three-dimensional morphology which is spatially organised, temporally fairly stable and essentially non-random.

Examination of the planform using satellite images also extends to the active braid bars of the second level. Each large island has a series of smaller, lower braid bars along its flanks, in each of the major anabranches. Analysis of braiding intensity indicated that, if minor channels with a cross-sectional area of less than 5% of the total area were excluded, then the island reaches characteristically consist of large left and right bank anabranches, each divided by active braid bars (Halcrow 1991). Hence, a generalized cross-section for an island reach consists of a large island in the centre with a major anabranch on each side. Each major anabranch is divided by a braid bar, to produce four sub-channels (see section J-10 in Fig. 7, for example). In some locations one of the braid bars may be connected to the adjacent island or flood plain by lateral accretion to reduce this to three sub-channels. Usually, the connected bar assumes the form of a point bar and the anabranch containing it adopts a meandering, rather than a braided, pattern.

Following the logic used in consideration of the islands, braid bars should scale on the channel containing them. The major left and right bank anabranches of the Brahmaputra have widths of 1–2 km and so by Yalin's theory a braid bar should be of the order of 3–6 km long. This is not at all unreasonable for the braid bars observed in the satellite images (see bars in Fig. 8, for example). From the relative lengths of braid bars and islands, which are 3–6 km and 20 km long, respectively, it follows that there should be between three and six braid bars alongside each island. This too holds true qualitatively (see island D in Fig. 8, for example), but with the level of local variability that might be expected given the complexity of the system, the fact that braid bars may become attached to islands and the difficulty in differentiating between second level braid bars and third level bedforms at the low flow stage represented by the satellite image. Also, the sequence of flows occurring prior to the date of the image is important. The 1988/89 SPOT images which formed the basis for much of this analysis were preceded by two of the highest flows on record. They show a strong braiding intensity and a great deal of recent deposition on both braid bar and island surfaces. However, examination of the 1990/91 images, taken after two relatively low runoff years, shows the pattern to have simplified considerably, with a tendency for anabranches to become more meandering than braided.

The pattern that emerges is of a hierarchical series of process-form linkages in both time and space. Island and nodal reaches scale on the first order channel, are measured in tens of kilometres and evolve over decades and centuries. Islands themselves are formed from clusters of braid bars that combine, stabilise and gain a capping of silt. Erosion of the islands also occurs, mostly by embayment formation in the sides of the island due to braid bar growth and meandering tendencies in the adjacent anabranches, but also through dissection by sub-channels that etch out low points in the topography during high flows and, particularly, during the monsoon recession. As embayments are much shorter than islands, they produce the characteristic form of intact islands with a lenticular shape, but with cusps in the sides where embayments have formed (see Islands B and E in Figs 2 and 6 for example). Where embayments on opposite sides have broken through to split an island in two, or where sub-channel dissection is well advanced, only the outline of the former island can be traced around the periphery of a cluster of small island fragments (see island A in Fig. 2, for example). Silt deposition on the islands occurs by vertical accretion during over-bank flow and large areas of sediment deposited during the 1988 flood are clearly visible in the 1988/89 satellite images, but most growth occurs by the attachment of braid-bars which become joined to the flanks of an island when the channel separating the island and the bar is abandoned due to a chute cut-off, a channel avulsion, or an anabranch planform change from braided to meandering. Examination of old maps and satellite images shows that although levels of island erosion and accretion are high and radically alter the outlines of the islands, there remains a tendency for an island *feature* to remain easily identifiable over long periods through the preservation of a semi-permanent central core or cluster at about the same geographical location over years and decades.

Braid bars scale on the major left and right bank anabranches, are several kilometres long and change measurably during each annual hydrograph. They are rarely totally destroyed and reformed, but tend to persist in a given location for some years. They grow laterally by flank accretion and may tend to migrate downstream. As they grow they deflect the flow causing local bank erosion of the adjacent flood plain or island, and driving the development of bank embayments. Radical changes in the flow patterns around the braid bars are associated with bar connection to either an adjacent island or the flood plain.

Dune bedforms migrate freely through the anabranches and sub-channels at all discharges. They do not affect the planform of the river directly, but can cause rapid changes of flow direction in smaller channels that may eventually trigger new directions and trends in the evolution of the braid bars and, hence, the major anabranches, banklines and islands.

This morphological analysis of flow regime and channel form provides the basis for consideration of current bank erosion processes and bankline movements, which drive the short and medium term planform dynamics of the river.

Bank erosion studies

Bank characteristics and erosion processes

The banks of the Brahmaputra in the study reach are formed in weakly cohesive silty-sand. The primary process of bank erosion is toe scouring leading to mechanical collapse. Typically eroding banks display slab-type failure of the upper bank above the water surface generated by toe erosion and over-steepening due to undercutting at depth (Fig. 10). Failure blocks are poorly bonded by cohesion or root binding and upon failure they disintegrate rapidly to primary particles. Hence, there is practically no potential for even temporary stabilization of the bank through the accumulation of bank failure debris at the toe and the basal clean-out phase of bank retreat is very short. This combination of fluvial erosion, mass failure and basal cleanout is precisely that expected for weakly cohesive sediments (Thorne 1982) and is one of the most effective process-mechanism combinations in producing sustained and rapid bank retreat. Retreat is likely wherever fast flowing water approaches the bank and it is likely to be especially severe if bed erosion also produces deep scour close to the bank.

The composition of the bank materials is remarkably uniform throughout the length of the reach, although there are some clay deposits in a layer low in the right bank around Sariakandi. These are believed to be associated with the flood plain deposits of the Bangali River, which are intersected by the Brahmaputra in this area. Cohesive deposits of Pleistocene and Tertiary age may outcrop in the left bank near the ferry terminal at Bhuapur.

The eroded silt (about 40% of the bank sediment) constitutes 'wash load' for the Brahmaputra, for which there is almost unlimited sediment transport capacity and which is easily carried away in suspension. However, the sand fraction in the banks (60% by weight) goes into the bed material load. Preliminary estimates of the bank erosion sediment yield, island/bar deposition and erosion, and sediment input measured at Bahadurabad are listed in Table 3. They are based on channel changes observed between sections J-11–7 and J-5–6 during the period 1986 to 1987. Island and bar sediment samples collected during field surveys in 1991 indicate that on average chars are made up of 90% sand and 10% silt (Halcrow 1991). The size composition of the sediment load in transport is open to debate, depending on data that are accepted. Sediment records for Bahadurabad during 1986/87 describe the load as 95% silt and 5% sand. However, the ratio of 75% silt to 25% sand. It is not possible to resolve which ratio found in BRTS field measurements in 1991 indicates a perhaps more reasonable ratio better represents overall conditions, but the BRTS data are known to have had good quality control. The BRTS ratio of sand to silt was therefore used to split the total load for 1986/87 into the sand and silt fractions listed in Table 3. The results indicate that the bank erosion silt yield is less than 3% of the input load at Bahadurabad, but that the sand yield from bank erosion is 24% of the sand load supplied from upstream.

Given the uncertainty in the figures, it probably safe to concluded that the yield of sand from bank erosion is at least 10% and possibly 30% of the sand load input from upstream and this is almost certainly a significant input to an already heavily laden river. Morphological and sedimentary evidence support the hypothesis that the continued growth of island chars and bars is fuelled largely by the addition of sand to the channel through bank erosion. It is perhaps no coincidence that the rate of storage of sand in char growth appears to be closely related to the supply of sand by bank erosion. If this close link between bank erosion and char growth could be more clearly established it would have important implications for the explanation of the process-form linkage between bank erosion and braid bar deposition.

Bank erosion rates and distribution

Bangladesh survey maps and aerial photographs from the 1950s, together with the 1989 SPOT image, formed the basis for a preliminary assessment of bankline migration during the last three decades. An overlay map of bank movement is

Fig. 10. Typical slab failure of right bank north of Sirajganj on the right bank.

Table 3. *Sediment balance for the Brahmaputra River between cross-section J-11-7 and J-5-6 in 1986/87*

Sediment type	Sediment yield, storage and flux (10^9 kg)								Bank erosion as a percentage of upstream supply (%)		
	Upstream supply	Left bank yield	Right bank yield	Total bank yield	Island + bar deposition	Island + bar erosion	Net storage	Net addition to sediment load	Left bank yield	Right bank yield	Total bank yield
Sand	162	16	22	38	49	17	32	6	10	14	24
Silt	504†	11*	14*	25*	5*	2*	3*	22*	2	3	5
Total	672	27	36	63	54	19	35	28	4	5	9

* Assumes bank material is 60% sand, 40% silt, char material is 90% sand, 10% silt.
† Assumes total load is as measured but is 25% sand, 75% silt.

shown in Fig. 11. The study reach was divided into island and nodal reaches as shown in Fig. 6 and point measurements of right and left bank erosion distance were made at 0.5 km intervals, with erosion being measured as a positive distance and accretion as a negative distance. Offset distances were divided by the interval in years to give a mean erosion rate. Map updates were made between 1951 and 1957 and the rates listed in Table 4 reflect the best estimate of the actual date of the last map update for a reach. The sample distributions of bank erosion were used to generate average values of bank erosion for such sub-reach. The overall average rates for islands, nodes and the whole study reach were found by weighting the averages for the sub-reaches according to their lengths. These data are listed at the foot of Table 4.

The results show that over the entire study reach bank erosion during the period was more severe on the right than the left bank. The average right bank erosion rate is 90 m per year, with individual sub-reach rates as high as double this figure. The left bank exhibits a small net accretion rate overall, although reach scale erosion rates of over 90 m per year are also observed.

Comparison of the average erosion rates for island reaches with those for nodal reaches demonstrates that bank erosion tends to be greater adjacent to islands. For the right bank, the island average erosion rate is nearly three times that for the nodes, while for the left bank, island reaches show erosion at a relatively low rate. The data indicate that in island reaches the average width of the braided channel has increased markedly, since erosion of both banks together produces a net widening rate of about 120 m per year. Compared to this trend, the width at nodes is more constant, as right bank erosion and left bank accretion rates almost cancel out. This stability is, however, relative. A medium term average erosion rate of nearly 40 m per year for the right bank together with an accretion rate of nearly 50 m per year on the left bank indicates a very dynamic form of stability that leads to channel shifting. The bankline movement figures for the nodes support the conclusion that the river has migrated westwards during the last three decades.

There is marked variability in the rates of bankline movement along the length of the study reach. Island reach A showed moderate widening and westward shifting over the study period. Bank erosion is currently a problem in this reach and Kamarjani is a priority site for bank stabilization under FAP21/22. Node a/b was relatively stable. Island reach B widened

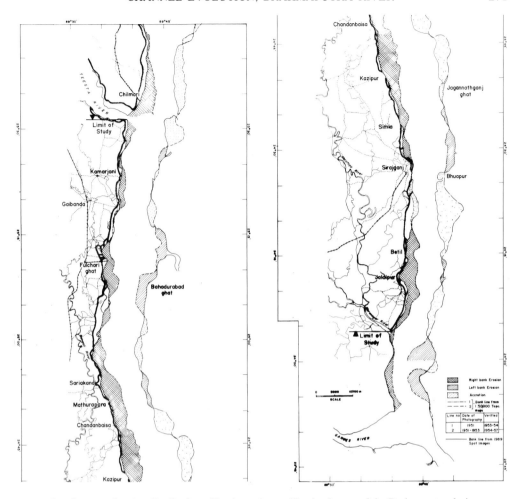

Fig. 11. Overlay map showing distribution of bank erosion and bank advance of the Brahmaputra during approximately the last three decades.

through retreat of both banks, while the next node (b/c), north of Sariakandi, was relatively stable, but with moderate westward migration.

Island reaches C and D migrated westwards and widened. Significantly, node c/d between these two islands also migrated westwards at rate only a little slower, whilst maintaining about a constant width. As a result the 40 km stretch of bank between Sariakandi and Simla/Sonali-bazar developed an almost straight alignment and experieneced severe, sustained bank retreat. No less than five priority bank stabiliz-ation sites are located in this reach.

Islands D and E are unusual in that they over-lap with no clear node between them. This reach widened quite rapidly through net erosion of both banks, resulting in priority sites for protec-tion at Simla/Sonalibazar and Sirajganj. Also, the left bank in this reach experienced the highest rate of left bank erosion in the study reach, causing problems in the Jamalpur Dis-trict.

Nodal reach, e/f, is the most prominent node on the river and includes the proposed site for the Jamuna Bridge (JMBA 1988). Up until 1989 this reach had been remarkably stable over the previous three decades, although erosion scars and accretionary deposits in the flood plain, especially to the east of the present course, demonstrate that there has been considerable lateral activity here in the past. Recently, bank erosion has begun on both banks in this reach.

Island reach F has a right bank erosion rate approaching 200 m per year. This underlines the

Table 4. *Bank erosion rates in island and nodal reaches between 1953/6 and 1988*

			Average erosion rate	
Reach	Period	Length (km)	Right bank (m/yr)	Left bank (m/yr)
Island A	1953–89	31	58.2	−18.8*
Node A/B	1953–89	5.5	−10.6	1.73
Island B	1953–89	25	59.2	65.6
Node B/C	1953–89	9.5	22.6	−8.36
Island C	1953–89	16	94.0	−16.6
Node C/D	1953–89	5	86.7	106.9
Island D	1953–89	18	165	−11.1
Island E	1953–89	18	151.4	73.0
Node E/F	1953–89	20.5	9.4	−36.7
Island F	1953–89	18	198.5	−34.2
Node F/G	1953–89	11.5	109	−98.1
Averages:				
Island reaches		21	111.6	10.2
Node		10.4	39.2	−47.8
Study reach		178	90.4	−6.7

* Negative erosion rates indicate bank accretion.

potential for sustained, rapid bank erosion on this scale to destroy large areas of flood plain land, infrastructures and personal property within a lifetime. Betil and Jalalpur in this reach are priority sites for bank stabilisation. The left bank has accreted, but at a slower rate, so that this reach is widening.

Node f/g has migrated rapidly westwards at constant width. This appears to be associated with a meandering tendency in the major ana-branch of the lower course of the river which, on occasion, carries nearly the entire flow of the Brahmaputra.

Further information concerning the distribution of bank erosion was obtained from historical records of retirements of the Brahmaputra Right Embankment, which have been documented since the embankment was constructed in the 1960s. When bank erosion destroys the berm between the flood embankment and the river, the embankment is exposed to deep, swiftly flowing water. This quickly leads to breaching that allows flooding behind the embankment (see Fig. 2b for example). Figure 12 presents a histogram showing the number of times that the embankment has had to be retired (that is replaced by a new section of embankment set back from the river edge) due to bank erosion at various points along the study reach. The distance of retirement is specific, but is usually of the order of 300 to 1500 m. Hence, the number of retirements is a qualitative indicator of the local rate of bank erosion and retreat.

It is clear from the histogram that while at

some locations chronic erosion has required multiple retirements, at other locations the original embankment, on its original alignment, is still in place. The location and spacing of spikes in the distribution are seen to closely match the island-node pattern and the scale of the second level braid bars, with spikes being about 6–10 km apart. This is consistent with the hypothesis that it is the growth and evolution of the active sand bars that drives bank erosion and determines the distribution of bankline retreat within the larger-scale framework of the island-node pattern.

These findings suggest that the distribution of severe bank erosion is related be the location and spacing of both the first order islands and the second order bar sand bars identified in the morphological study. This pattern is consistent with the explanation of the braiding process first put forward by Leopold & Wolman (1957) which attributes bank erosion to the growth and multiplication of medial bars that deflect the flow against the bank. As erosion progresses embayments develop in the banks on each side of the bar, providing space for consolidation and further growth of the original bar, allowing the formation of smaller, second generation bars and introducing curvature to the flow. Curvature promotes high near bank velocities and, consequently, high shear stresses on the bed and bank at the outside of the embayment. These high velocities produce deep scour and severe erosion of the noncohesive sands and silts in channel boundary, leading to more, rapid

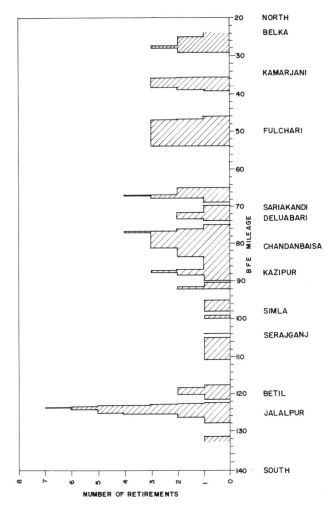

Fig. 12. Histogram of numbers of times the Brahmaputra right embankment has been retired at various locations along the study reach.

bank retreat. In this way the braided channel is able to continue widening as long as the flow at the outer bank can erode the bank and so create both the space for the bars and islands to expand and the excess sediment to fuel that expansion. In the case of the Brahmaputra the second order bars are about 3–6 km long and are spaced at about 6–8 km intervals. The characteristic length dimension of embayments in the bank was established by measuring embayment spacing in the right bank (Table 5). The mean spacing was found to be about 7 km.

Discussion and conclusions

The impact of bank erosion and island growth on the planform has been for the 'hour glass' shape

associated with an island–node–island geomorphological unit to become more pronounced through time. However, the nodes are also shifting and there are variations in the rate of migration of the nodes which may point to another facet of planform evolution at a scale greater even than that of the island-node pattern. To explain what may be happening, it is necessary to again consider the planform of the Brahmaputra River shown in Fig 2a and b.

When the channel, encompassing the islands, braid bars and anabranches is viewed as a whole, a degree of sinuosity can be identified in the planform. There are three curves between the Teesta and Ganges confluences. The first and longest curve is right (west) bank concave and extends from about Gaibanda to Kazipur. The

Table 5. *Spacing of right bank embayments in the 1989 SPOT image*

Embayment number	Spacing (km)	Location and comments
1	4.5	River Teesta distortion
2	6.5	
3	7.5	Kamajani
4	8.5	
5	8.5	Fulchari
6	6.0	
7	6.0	
8a	8.0	Embayment absent
8b	8.0	
9	8.0	Sariakandi
10a	7.0	Embayment absent
10b	7.0	
11	7.0	Kazipur
12	8.0	
13	7.5	Simla
14	7.5	Sailabari
15	8.0	
16a	8.0	Embayment absent
16b	8.0	Belkuchi
17	3.0	Betil
18	5.5	Jalalpur
19a	7.5	Embayment absent
19b	7.0	
20	2.5	
21	9.0	

Number of intervals: 24
Distance: 174.0
Mean spacing: 7.25 km
Standard deviation: 1.6 km

second curve is left bank concave and is shorter. It extends from Sonalibazar to around Bhuapur. The last curve is again right bank concave and extends from around Betil to the Ganges confluence.

Curvature is apparent in both the bank lines, but in Fig. 2 it is easier to pick out the sinuous curves in the line of the right bank than the left because left bank off-take channels tend to obscure the braid channel/flood plain boundary. The migration rates of the nodes listed in Table 4 take on new significance in the context of this sinuous planform to the braid belt.

Crossing a/b is located at the first inflection point and is almost static. Node b/c is close to the apex of the first curve which is right bank concave and is migrating westwards at 60 m per year. Node c/d is located at the downstream end of the right bank concave curve and is migrating southwest at nearly 90 m per year. In island reach E the left (east) bank concave curve displays the most severe left bank erosion in the whole reach, at 73 m per year. Node e/f is located

at the end of the second curve and is currently almost static. Node f/g is close to the apex of the third curve which is right bank concave. This node is migrating westwards at over 100 m per year.

In a meandering channel erosion is usually concentrated on the concave bank downstream of the bend apex and often at the bend exit. The distribution of bank erosion observed here is consistent with that general rule, except in the case of the left bank concave bend. The reason for the lack of eastwards migration through the retreat of the concave bank at the downstream end of this curve probably lies in the surficial geology. Bhuapur channel is the only reach of the present river which encounters more erosion-resistant deposits in the form of older, more consolidated sediments next to the Madhurpur Tract. It may be hypothesized that the eastward migration of the channel and development of this curve is being inhibited by more erosion resistant materials which act as a hard point.

It is not suggested that the sinuous curves of the braid belt are simply meanders of the type conventionally found in single-thread channels. This clearly is not the case, as with a width to depth ratio of nearly 700 at bankfull flow, the hydraulics and flow patterns in the Brahmaputra cannot be compared directly to those in a conventional river bend. However, it is proposed that the curves and inflections of the braid belt are in fact analogous to the meandering that is ubiquitous to most stream-cut river valleys (Richards 1982; Knighton 1984). These are known not to be the result of past mega-floods that turned the entire valley into a huge channel, but to be the result of interaction between the meander belt of the channel and the valley walls. The meander wavelength for the resulting valley meanders scales geometrically on the width of the valley rather than that of the channel. In a similar way it is proposed here that the curves of the braid belt are components of a meandering pattern formed by inter-action of the active braid belt with the flood plain that scales on the overall width of the braid belt. As bank erosion tends to occur predominantly on the outside of curves, and there are two concave curves in the right bank, this could explain the overall westward shifting of the Brahmaputra identified by Coleman. The eastward migration of the single left bank curve in the centre of the reach is unable to balance the amount of right bank retreat firstly, because it occupies a much shorter length of channel, and secondly, perhaps because of the restriction imposed by the erosion resistant flood plain materials north of Bhuapur.

This analysis of channel form and process has necessarily simplified and generalised what actually happens in the Brahmaputra in the study reach. Much of what has been described is tentative and certainly more work is required, particularly through quantitative treatment of the rectified and co-registered satellite images which are now becoming available from related studies in FAP-19. Also, semi-quantitative analysis of historical maps such as those of Rennell (1765) and Wilcox (1830) will shed useful light on longer-term channel evolution if their accuracy can be validated and accepted by the research community.

The research described here was directed by the authors while working on the Brahmaputra River Training Study. The Client is the Bangladesh Water Development Board and the sponsor of the project is the World Bank. The work was performed in the Dhaka offices of Sir William Halcrow & Partners Ltd and their associates on this study, Danish Hydraulic Institute, Engineering and Planning Consultants and Design Innovations Group. Some of the analyses were undertaken by staff of the Department of Civil Engineering, Bangladesh University of Engineering and Technology. Particular thanks are due to all those members of the Team who dedicated long hours in the field and office to this study and made important contributions. Any inaccurate speculations and errors are, however, entirely the responsibility of the authors.

References

ACKERS, P. & CHARLTON, F. G. 1970. Meander geometry arising from varied flows. *Journal of Hydrology*, **xx**, 230–252.

BRAMMER, H. 1990. Floods in Bangladesh: I. Geographical background to the 1987 and 1988 floods. *The Geographical Journal*, **156** (1), 12–22.

BRISTOW, C. S. 1987 Brahmaputra River: Channel migration and deposition, *In: Recent Developments in Fluvial Sedimentology*. ETHRIDGE, F. G., FLORES, R. M. & HARVEY, M. D. (eds). Society of Economic Paleontologists and Mineralogists Special Publications, **39**, 63–74.

CHINA-BANGLADESH JOINT EXPERT TEAM 1991. *Master Plan for Training the Brahmaputra River*. Final Report to the Government of Bangladesh, July 1991.

CHURCH, M. & JONES, D. 1982. Bar sedimentation. *In*: HEY, R. D., BATHURST, J. C. & THORNE, C. R. (eds) *Gravel-Bed Rivers*. Wiley, Chichester, UK, 291–338.

COLEMAN, J. M. 1969. Brahmaputra River channel processes and sedimentation. *Sedimentary Geology*, **3**, 129–239.

HALCROW, SIR WILLIAM AND PARTNERS 1990. *River training studies of the of the Brahmaputra River*. Inception Report to the Bangladesh Water Development Board, Dhaka Office, May 1990.

—— 1991. *River training studies of the Brahmaputra River*. Second Interim Report to the Bangladesh Water Development Board, Dhaka Office, December 1991.

—— 1992. *River training studies of the Brahmaputra River*. Draft Final Report to the Bangladesh Water Development Board, Dhaka Office, December 1992.

HEY, R. D. 1975. Design discharges for natural channels. *In*: HEY, R. D. & DAVIES, T. D. (eds) *Science and Technology in Environmental Management*, Saxon House, Farnborough, UK, 73–88.

JMBA 1988. *Jamuna Bridge Authority: Design Report, Volume II*. Rendel, Palmer and Triton, Final Report to the Bangladesh Water Development Board, Dhaka, Bangladesh.

KNIGHTON, D. 1984. *Fluvial forms and processes*. Arnold, UK.

LEE, A.-L. & DAVIES, T. R. 1986. *Analysis of Braided*

River Form and Process. Publication 9, Hydrology Centre, Ministry of Works of New Zealand, 220–229.

LEOPOLD, L. B. & WOLMAN, M. G. 1957. River channel patterns: braided, meandering and straight. *US Geological Survey Professional Papers*, **282B**, 39–85.

RENNELL, J. 1765. *A general map of the River Baramputrey, from its confluence with the Ifsamuty near Dacca towards Assam*. India Office Library and Records, London, UK.

RICHARDS, K. S. 1982. *Rivers*. Methuen, UK.

THORNE, C. R. 1982. Processes and mechanisms of bank erosion. *In*: HEY, R. D., BATHURST, J. C. & THORNE, C. R. (eds) *Gravel-Bed Rivers*. Wiley, Chichester, UK.

WILCOX, R. 1830. *Map of the Brahmaputra and Ichamati Rivers*. Reduced and drawn by M H Dias, India Office Library and Records, London, UK.

WOLMAN, M. G. & GERSON, R. 1978. Relative scales of time and effectiveness of climate in watershed geomorphology. *Earth Surface Processes*, **3**, 189–208.

—— & MILLER, J. P. 1960. Magnitude and frequency of forces in geomorphic processes. *Journal of Geology*, **68**, 54–74.

YALIN, M. S. 1977. *Mechanics of sediment transport*. Pergamon, Oxford, UK.

Sedimentary structures exposed in bar tops in the Brahmaputra River, Bangladesh

C. S. BRISTOW

Research School of Geological and Geophysical Sciences, Birkbeck College and University College London, Gower Street, London WC1E 6BT, UK

Abstract: The Brahmaputra River is one of the world's largest sand-bed braided rivers with a channel belt up to 15 km wide, a mean channel depth of 5 m and maximum scour depths of up to 40 m. The recorded discharge varies by around 60 000 cumecs every year following the annual monsoon, producing dramatic stage fluctuations with the water level falling between 7 and 8 m from bankfull to low flow stage. In the dry season large areas of bar top and channel bed are exposed and low flow channels cut natural sections through bar tops exposing the internal stratification. Elements of upstream, downstream and lateral accretion are identified, although the high width/depth ratio of channels (up to 500:1) results in extremely low depositional dips on bed bounding surfaces. Within the accretionary elements vertical and lateral changes in sedimentary structures are ubiquitous and varied but some patterns can be discerned. Channel deposits are dominated by sinuous-crested dunes and trough cross-stratification. Upper stage plane bed lamination, often with a very low angle depositional dip, has been observed in beds up to 4 m thick and is generally found at the base of the exposed bar top sections. Trough cross-stratification in bar tops occurs in sets from 0.1 m to 3 m thick with rapid vertical and lateral changes in set thickness. Very large sets of trough cross-stratification, >3 m thick, do not occur in the bar top sections. Current ripple lamination is most abundant on the tops of bars with very high rates of climb associated with high rates of sediment deposition. From these observations a generalised vertical sequence of bar top origin might include trough cross-stratification overlain by upper stage plane bed lamination, isolated sets of trough cross-stratification truncated and capped by current ripple lamination. This sequence, which is considered to represent the deposits of a single flood, may occur within the upstream, downstream or lateral accretion elements. However, it should be noted that vertical and lateral changes in facies are extremely abundant with many changes in sedimentary structures and reactivation surfaces within each depositional episode.

Most sedimentary models for braided rivers are based upon observations of relatively small, shallow or coarse grained rivers (Leopold & Wolman 1957; Krigström 1964; Williams & Rust 1969; Collinson 1970; Smith 1970, 1971a, 1974; Church 1972; Rust 1972, 1978; Bluck 1974, 1976, 1979; Boothroyd & Ashley 1975; Miall 1977, 1978; Blodgett & Stanley 1980; Church & Jones 1982; Crowley 1983; Bridge *et al.* 1986). Detailed descriptions of large sand-bed braided rivers are few and far between, yet many ancient sandstones appear to have been deposited by large sandbed braided rivers (Campbell 1976; Conaghan & Jones 1975; Kirk 1983), and large modern braided rivers such as the Niger, Indus, Brahmaputra and Yellow rivers account for a significant proportion of global alluvial sediment transport. Sedimentary models for this type of river are largely based on the South Saskatchewan (Cant & Walker 1976, 1978) and the pioneering study of the Brahmaputra by Coleman (1969). Furthermore, although early models of braided river sedimentation were

largely based on vertical sequences (Miall 1977, 1978), subsequent sedimentary interpretations of ancient alluvial sediments have become increasingly dependent on lateral profiling and architectural element analysis (Allen 1983; Miall 1985), and there are few correlative profiles from modern braided river deposits for comparison. In this paper, sedimentary structures exposed in bar tops in the Brahmaputra River are described and their vertical and lateral arrangement discussed to present a facies model for bars in large sand-bed braided rivers. This paper aims to fill two significant gaps in our understanding of fluvial sediments by providing detailed lateral profiles through bar tops in a very large sand-bed braided river, and presenting a new facies model which may be used to interpret bar top deposits from large, ancient sand-bed braided rivers.

The Brahmaputra is 2840 km long and drains an area of some 380 000 km^2 from Tibet to the Bay of Bengal. The mean annual discharge is around 7 200 000 cumecs which makes it one of

From Best, J. L. & Bristow, C. S. (eds), 1993, *Braided Rivers*, Geological Society
Special Publication No. **75**, pp. 277–289.

the world's largest rivers. In Bangladesh the river is a multichannel system with an overall braided appearance (Coleman 1969) although individual reaches show channel patterns which can be described as braided, meandering and anastomosed (Bristow 1987a). In the study area around Sirajganj (Fig. 1) the width of the river varies from 3 km to 18 km. Maximum channel depth is 40 m and mean channel depth is around 5 m, although this varies with stage fluctuations which are around 7–8 m per annum. Changes in stage are due to the monsoon climate in Bangladesh, India and Tibet, combined with snow melt in the Himalayan mountains, which produces a marked seasonal variation in discharge in excess of 60 000 cumecs. Annual maximum discharge is around 65 000 cumecs, annual minimum discharge is around 3800 cumecs. The surface slope of the Brahmaputra

in Bangladesh is 0.000077 decreasing to 0.00005 near the confluence with the Ganges. Bed material in the bar tops is mostly fine to very fine micaceous sand with some silt layers.

In the deposits of the Brahmaputra, Coleman (1969) described large- and small-scale trough cross-stratification, horizontal stratification, parallel stratification, ripple drift lamination and distorted stratification exposed in the river bank and bar tops. More recent papers on the Brahmaputra (Bristow 1987a; Klaassen & Vermeer 1988; Burger et al. 1988) have described the broad aspects of channel pattern and processes within the river. At low flow stage the river erodes into bar tops exposing natural cut bank sections up to 4 m high. The bar top sections described in this paper were examined in February 1986. A combination of cutbank and echosounder mapping of the river shows that the

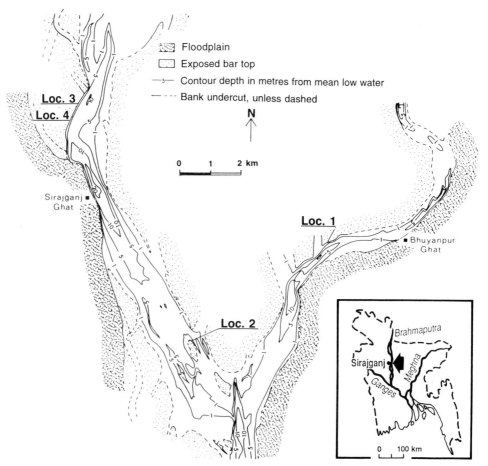

Fig. 1. Map showing the location of bar top sections 1–4 described in this paper and the location of the study area in Bangladesh.

sections described in this paper were all deposited during the previous flood, July–September 1985. Natural exposures were cleaned and logged at 10 m intervals in the field and logs from these sections were correlated with photomontages to produce two-dimensional facies diagrams of the sedimentary structures. In this paper, four bar-top sections near Sirajganj (Fig. 1) are used to describe the details of the sedimentary structures. These display typical vertical and lateral changes in facies encountered in the Brahmaputra. The sections are interpreted in a process framework and condensed to form a facies model for bar-tops in the Brahmaputra River. While it may be possible to infer something of the nature of sediments deposited deeper within the river from these observations it should not be assumed that all of the deposits of the Brahmaputra contain similar sedimentary structures.

Locality

Locality 1 is adjacent to two channels, the 'New' channel and the Bhuyanpur channel (Fig. 1). The Bhuyanpur channel has a relatively stable sinuous course along the eastern side of the channel belt and a well defined concave cut bank on the river left. The 'New' channel appears to have formed during or after the 1985 flood, dissecting a bar top. There are two vertical cutbank exposures oriented perpendicular to each other: section 1–2 is 60 m long and orientated north–south, parallel to the 'New' channel, whilst section 2–4 is orientated east–west parallel to the Bhuyanpur channel and is 250 m long. Diagrams of both sections are shown in Fig. 2. Note that the section 2–4 is in two parts and each section is described in turn. The base of section 1–2, parallel to the 'New' channel, (Fig. 2) contains flat parallel lamination, interpreted as upper stage plane bed lamination, overlain by sets of small (c. 10 cm) to medium (c. 50 cm) scale trough cross-stratification. Set size varies vertically and laterally and the sets of cross-stratification do not persist in a down-current direction for more than 20 m. The set size decreases slightly upwards and passes up into current ripple lamination indicating a decrease in flow velocity from the bottom to the top of the section. Some of the sets of cross-stratification dip down-current indicating an overall downstream accretion on the bar. There is no regular pattern to this accretion because the dunes were short lived suggesting constantly fluctuating flow on the downstream, depositional margin of the bar. The top of the section is almost flat and covered by linguoid current ripples indicating

flow to the south, parallel to the 'New' channel.

The base of section 2–4 is dominated by current ripple lamination indicating flow to the west parallel to the Bhuyanpur channel with some plane bed lamination. These strata are overlain by large sets of trough cross-stratification orientated north–south perpendicular to the Bhuyanpur channel. The sets are 3 m thick and are the largest sets of cross-stratification observed in this study. Some of the foresets contain current ripple lamination which climbs up and down the sides of the troughs produced by falling stage flow along the Bhuyanpur channel perpendicular to the foresets. There are no sedimentary structures in the north–south section 1–2 which correspond with the very large sets of trough cross-stratification. The large 3 m deep troughs appear to have formed as slipfaces on the downstream margin of the bar while linguoid current ripples were the dominant bedform on the bar top. It is interesting to note that the largest sedimentary structures observed in this study appear to be a waning stage deposit formed by avalanching on the downstream margin of a bar and not from very large dune bedforms.

Locality 2

Locality 2 (Fig. 1) is an exposed area on top of the tributary bar at the confluence of the Sirajganj channel and the Bhuyanpur channel. The exposed area comprises two curved crested forms approximately 100 m wide, 200–300 m wavelength and 4 m high. Hydrographic surveys by the Bangladesh Inland Waterways Transport Authority (BIWTA) show that the exposed area was deposited during the 1985 flood. The form of the area, with two large curve crested forms and another high area at the downstream end suggests exceptionally large dune bedforms modified by erosion on the falling stage. A natural exposure parallel to flow, 160 m long and up to 4 m high, was cut through the upstream end of the exposed area. The upstream end of the section (Fig. 3) shows upstream accretion with stacked scour fills younging upstream. However, most of the section is dominated by downstream accretion. Initial deposition on the bar top was upper stage plane bed lamination (UPB) which often dips slightly downstream at an angle of less than 10°. The UPB is overlain by a bed of massive sand with a sharp erosive base. The bed contains angular clasts of laminated sand up to 30 cm long which have been folded and reoriented and float in the fine grained structureless sand matrix. The top of the bed is marked by small extensional normal faults and

Fig. 2. Locality one cross section. The flow parallel section 1–2 shows upper stage plane bed lamination overlain by small to medium scale cross-stratification. Set size appears to decrease vertically and sets locally dip down-current towards the downstream margin of the bar. There are no structures in this section which correspond to the large trough forms seen in the Bhuyanpur section 2–4. The very large troughs appear to have formed on the downstream margin of the bar during the falling stage. The presence of current ripple lamination on the foresets indicates interaction between flow in the Bhuyanpur Channel and across the bar top. All of the sediments were deposited during the 1985 flood.

soft sediment deformation structures produced by dewatering. This bed has clearly been partially fluidized. The fluidization may have coincided with the development of the overlying bed of cross-stratification. There is no evidence for any tectonic activity during deposition which might otherwise have triggered fluidisation. The deformed bed is overlain by a bed of low-angle planar cross-stratification with small scale trough cross-stratification and current ripple lamination. The bed contains many low angle reactivation surfaces within a package of downstream accretion similar to that observed in bar tops in the Ganga River (Singh 1977). The top of this bed is strongly scoured by sets of trough cross-stratification which erode down by as much as 2 m and fill up within 20 m downstream. The scour fill starts with a single set of trough cross-stratification with an erosive base which passes into multiple small sets of cross-stratification separated by reactivation surfaces, and irregular down-current dipping cross-stratification. These are succeeded by climbing ripple lamination rich in cominuted plant fragments and mica which fill the scour. According to Fredsoe (1981) and Bridge & Best (1988) suspended sediment lag distance is approximately equivalent to flow depth. The large concentrations of suspended sediment in the scour fill features may imply very low flow depths at the time of formation. These cut and fill deposits at the top of the section are interpreted as falling stage deposits and are believed to be formed and filled very rapidly. It is suggested that the cut and fill is auto-cyclic because flow expansion within the scour leads to flow deceleration, suspended sediment deposition and scour fill under shallow decelerating flow conditions.

The top of the exposed area at locality two is covered by a layer of rippled fine sand. This bed truncates earlier structures and gives the exposed area a remarkably smooth surface with only a few subdued duneforms preserved. The current ripple lamination which caps the exposed area was deposited by waning flow as the water level fell. Dry sand on the top of the exposed bedforms was locally reworked by wind forming a thin veneer of wind ripple lamination on the bar top.

The overall vertical change in sedimentary structures from plane bed to cross-stratification followed by scour and fill and ripple lamination reflects a gradual reduction in flow power which suggests that deposition at locality 2 occurred during the falling stage. The geometry of the exposed section is best explained by downstream accretion from the migration of a very large low amplitude bedform with minor upstream accretion during falling stage. Similar structures have been described in bar top sediments in the Ganga River by Singh (1977). In the Ganga River the sediments were deposited as downstream accretion on a bar, whilst here the sands are believed to have been deposited within a very large dune. The abundant low angle cross-stratification may indicate that the bedform was formed at or near the dune/upper stage plane bed hydraulic boundary and that high suspended load damped turbulence in the lee of the bedform and prevented the formation of flow separation and a true slipface on the downstream margin of the dune (Saunderson & Lockett 1983; Bridge & Best 1988; Chakraborty & Bose 1992).

On the downstream margin of locality two (Fig. 3) climbing ripple lamination increases to more than 1 m thick (Fig. 4a). Using graphs given in Allen (1970), it is possible to estimate approximate rates of sedimentation from the ripple height and angle of climb. For the ripples shown in Fig. 4a the rate of climb increases from 9° to 24°, with a ripple height of 2 cm. Assuming a bulk density of $1.9 \, \text{g cm}^{-3}$ and deposition at the critical velocity, this indicates a rate of deposition rising from 19 cm per hour to just over 1 m per hour on the falling stage in the lee of a large bedform. An example from locality 1 (Fig. 4b) has an angle of climb of 65° with a ripple height of 1.6 cm. In this case the calculated rate of deposition is approximately 3.75 m per hour. This is an exceptional outcrop and deposition rates of this magnitude were almost certainly short lived.

Locality 3

Locality 3 is a flow-parallel section eroded through a midstream bar approximately 3.5 km north of Sirajganj (Fig. 1); echo-sounder surveys

Legend

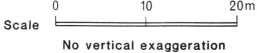

End on view of current ripples

Climbing current ripples

Down-dipping current ripples

Vertically accreting current ripples

Trough cross-stratification

Low angle plane bed
Plane bed

Soft sediment deformation

Structureless sand

Silts

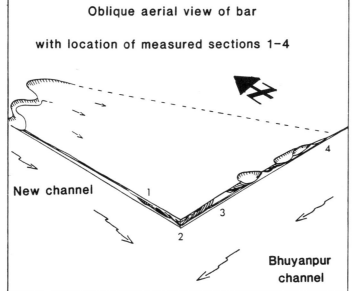

Locality 1

Oblique aerial view of bar

with location of measured sections 1-4

New channel

Bhuyanpur
channel

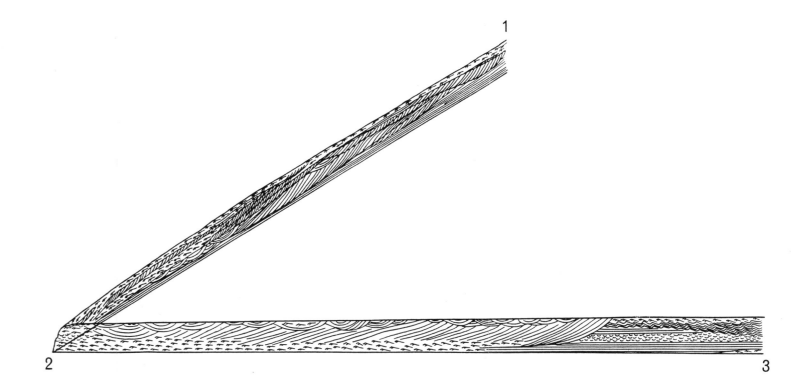

Scale

0   10   20m

No vertical exaggeration

LOCALITY ONE

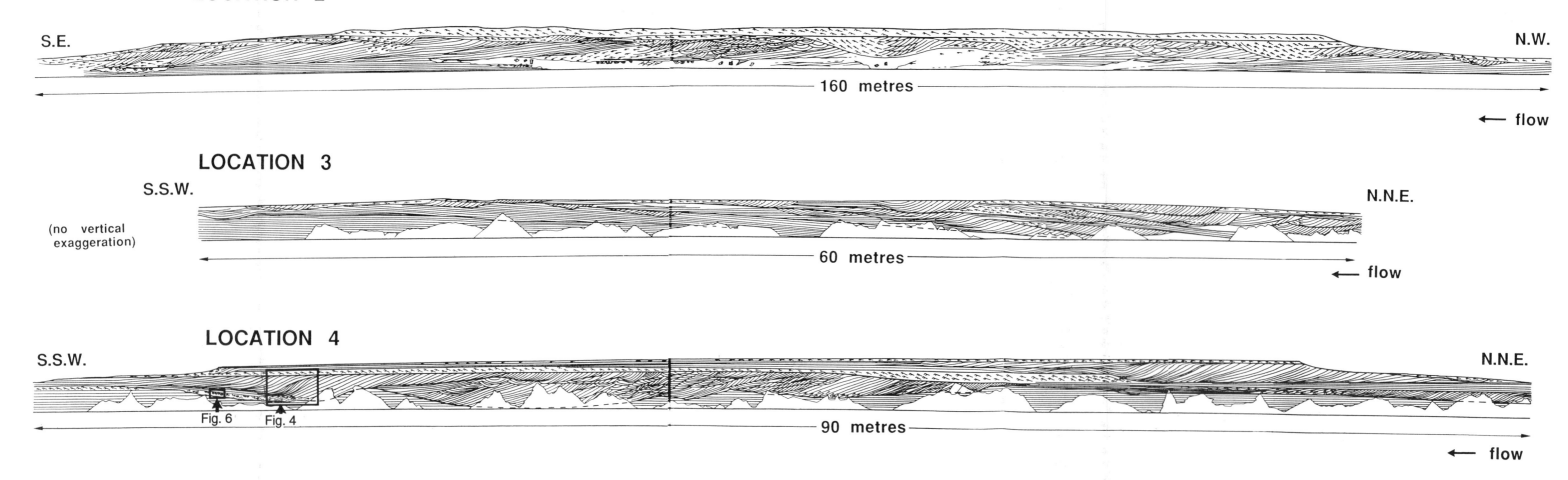

LOCATION 2

S.E.   N.W.

←——————————— 160 metres ———————————→

← flow

LOCATION 3

S.S.W.   N.N.E.

(no vertical
exaggeration)

←——————————— 60 metres ———————————→

← flow

LOCATION 4

S.S.W.   N.N.E.

Fig. 6   Fig. 4

←——————————— 90 metres ———————————→

← flow

Fig. 3. Outcrop diagrams of localities 2, 3 and 4. The form of the exposed area at locality 2 suggests that it may have been a very large dune at high flow stage. The sedimentary structures show that this is partially true but that the 'dune' did not develop a true slipface and is dominated by down-current dipping sets of cross-stratification and very low angle plane bed or 'swept out' cross-stratification. While the downstream section of the bar shows downstream accretion the upstream portion appears to have accreted upstream with stacked scour fills younging upstream. The base of the section is dominated by plane bed lamination overlain by a deformed fluidized bed which was deformed before or as the swept out dune form developed.

Locality 3 shows an upwards inclination in bedding in the downstream direction. This could be attributed to bedform climbing but since most of the section is upper stage plane bed lamination an upstream accretion model is preferred. The white areas at the bottom of the section are small talus cones formed by collapse of the bank.

Locality 4 shows a typical bar top section with plane bed lamination at the base overlain by irregular sets of trough cross-stratification and capped by current ripple lamination. Details of the sedimentary structures are shown in Figs 5 and 7. The white areas at the base of sections 3 and 4 are talus cones of bank collapse material which partially obscures the section, legend as in Fig. 2.

---

show that the sands were deposited by the 1985 flood. The base of the section is dominated by upper stage plane bed lamination which is inclined upstream parallel to flow in a downstream direction (Fig. 3). The upward inclination of bedding is a form of bedform climb which amounts to upstream accretion of the bar. Upstream accretion has also been recorded in the Brahmaputra from satellite studies of channel migration and deposition (Bristow 1987a). The overlying sets of medium scale trough cross-stratification have very tangential toesets which are also inclined upwards in the downstream direction. The cross-stratification is truncated by scour-fill which passes into current ripple lamination at the top of the bar. The vertical change in sedimentary structures from plane bed to cross-stratification, scour fill and ripple lamination reflects a gradual decrease in flow strength which suggests that deposition occurred during the falling stage of the flood. Tangential toesets indicate deposition of sand from suspension beyond the slipface of the dune. The implication is that fine sand as well as silt is carried in suspension in the Brahmaputra and forms part of the suspended load (wash load) implicated in the suppression of flow separation above. The upper surface of the bar is almost flat due to erosion during falling stage.

Locality 4

Locality 4 is 1 km downstream from locality 3 on the same midstream bar (Fig. 1). The base of the section (Fig. 3) is dominated by plane bed lamination deposited under upper stage flow regime conditions and overlain erosively by a 2.5 m thick bed of cross-stratification. This bed contains a large number of reactivation surfaces and passes from a single large set of trough cross-stratification into small sets of down-current dipping cross-stratification and further down-

stream reverts to a single set of cross-stratification (Fig. 3). In Fig. 5 a set of trough cross-stratification is shown with topsets, foresets and bottom sets preserved. The toesets contain current ripple laminated sands passing up into counter-current ripple laminated sands which pass into the foresets. The foresets flatten out downstream from angle of repose avalanche slipfaces to low angle surfaces and pass up into low angle dipping plane bed topsets. The presence of plane bedded topsets which pass into swept out foresets is typical of humpback dunes (Saunderson & Locket 1983) formed at the dune to plane bed transition. The presence of counter-current ripples on the toesets show that flow separation in the lee of the dune was present for at least some of the time but that as the dune became swept out and cross-stratification passes downstream into plane bed lamination there was no flow separation. The preservation of all parts of the bedform including counter current ripples on the toesets illustrates the astonishing rates of sedimentation in the Brahmaputra River. Beneath the cross-stratification described above, a 0.6 m layer of deformed sand is preserved (Fig. 7). This contains faintly laminated sand with an undulating base and an upward decrease in wavelength of deformation with convoluted lamination at the top. The deformation is attributed to dewatering with the upwards decrease in fold wavelength due to a decrease in viscosity of water saturated sediment at the top of the bed. It is interesting to note that the asymmetry of the fold structures is directed upstream rather than downstream, the reason for this is unknown. The bed of cross-stratification shown in Fig. 5 is overlain by a bed of climbing current ripple lamination which in turn is succeeded by a set or trough cross-stratification which passes downstream into plane bed lamination. 500 m further downstream the bar top sequence is dominated by

(a)

(b)

Fig. 4. (a) A 1.2 m thick bed of climbing ripple cross-lamination on the downstream end of locality 2 (Fig. 3) where the angle of climb increases vertically from 9° to 24° indicating an upwards increase in the rate of deposition during falling stage at the downstream margin of an exposed area. The maximum angle of climb suggests a rate of deposition of approximately 1 m per hour. (b) Climbing ripple cross-lamination at locality 1 with a ripple height of 1.6 cm and angle of climb of 65° which indicates a rate of deposition of approximately 3.75 m per hour. Flow left to right.

Fig. 5. Detail of locality 4 (Fig. 3) showing topset, foreset and bottomset preserved in a bed of trough cross-stratification. The topsets of upper stage plane bed laminae pass into foresets with 'swept out' tangential toesets containing counter-current ripples and current ripples overlying plane bed lamination.

plane bed lamination (Fig. 6) with only one very small set of trough cross-stratification. The top of the bar is capped by a 20 cm bed of climbing current ripple lamination. Both ends of the section described have been lowered slightly by erosion but otherwise the bar top is flat.

Down-current dipping cross-stratification

Down-current dipping cross-stratification occurs in three forms; downstream accretion on bars, regular cosets and irregular cosets. Down-current dipping cross-stratification on the

Fig. 6. Four metres of upper stage plane bed laminated sand exposed in a bar top 500 m downstream from locality 4.

Fig. 7. Detail of soft sediment deformation exposed at locality 4 (see Fig. 3). The wavelength of deformation decreases upwards with convolute lamination at the top (trowel for scale).

downstream margin of a bar (locality 1, Fig. 2 and locality 2, Fig. 3) is irregular, the angle of dip downstream is low, bed-bounding surfaces are on a larger scale than the sets of cross-stratification and sets rarely pass all the way down macroform surfaces. Sets of down-current dipping cross-stratification are shown in Fig. 3 (locality 4) where a large set of trough cross-stratification is filled by sets of small scale trough cross-stratification in an irregular fashion. These irregular cosets of down-current dipping cross-stratification have been produced by small dunes overtaking larger dunes, interpreted as the product of superimposed dune bedforms. Regular cosets of down-current dipping cross-stratification may occur where small dunes migrate across the top of larger bedforms (Banks 1973). The model of Banks requires that the downstream margin of the bedform is not slip-face bounded, or partially eroded by the over-lying dune (McCabe & Jones 1977). If the angle of the slipface is decreased, as in the Brahma-putra, it may be possible for small dune bed-forms to migrate down the slipface of a larger dune without significant erosion. In a flow parallel section this is likely to produce irregular down-current dipping sets bounded by reactiva-tion surfaces as described by Jones (1979). Large 3D dunes with curved crestlines usually have a scour pool and slipface at one point which passes into a depositional lobe or spur on either side. It may be possible to have coeval large sets of

cross-stratification formed in the scour pool and down-current dipping cosets of cross-stratification from superimposed bedforms descending the lobes or spurs beside the trough (Fig. 8). As a consequence large-scale sets of cross-stratification may pass laterally into cosets and the dip of the smaller foresets is often oblique to the set bounding surfaces. Both features are commonly seen in ancient cosets of down-current dipping cross-stratification (Jones 1979; Bristow 1987b, this volume).

Development of a facies model for bar top sedimentation in the Brahmaputra River

There are a wide variety of sedimentary struc-tures exposed in bar tops in the Brahmaputra River. A generalized vertical section would include upper stage plane bed lamination over-lain by sets of trough cross-stratification and capped by current ripple lamination. Upper-stage plane bed lamination (UPB) is very common in bar top deposits of the Brahmaputra. In one locality downstream from locality 4 it forms almost 100% of the exposed bar top section (Fig. 6). UPB most often occurs at the base of the exposed sections (Figs 2 & 4) which might suggest that UPB is the dominant sedi-mentary structure at high stage and at greater depth within the channels. However, echo-sounder profiles of the channels indicate that dunes are the dominant bedforms (Coleman

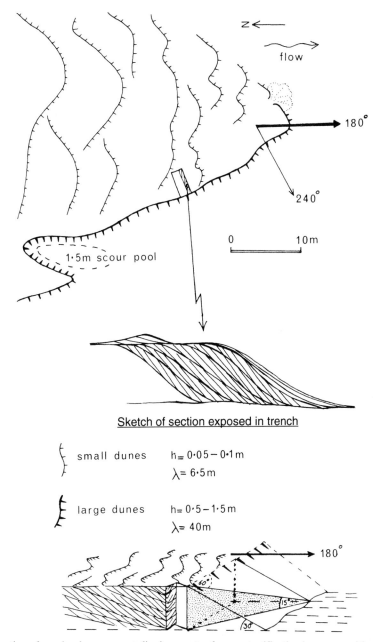

Fig. 8. Formation of regular down-current dipping cosets of cross-stratification by superposition of large and small dunes.

1969; Bristow 1987*b*). It is most likely that UPB is generated in shallow flows on bar tops because bed shear stress and sediment transport increases on the top of bars during falling stage (Cheetham 1979). Shallow flow is also believed to suppress dune formation and encourage the formation of very low relief bedforms which can produce planar lamination (Smith 1971*b*). Some of the laminae in Figs 6 and 7 are clearly discontinuous and vary in thickness suggesting that they may well have been formed by very low amplitude bedforms on an apparently flat bed as suggested by Bridge & Best (1988) and Paola *et al.* (1989). Trough cross-stratification produced by 3D dunes is very common in the deposits of the Brahmaputra. The thickness of sets of cross-stratification varies from 0.1 m to 3.0 m. The largest sets of trough cross-stratification observed in this study were 3 m thick but these were formed on the slipface of a bar (locality 1) rather than a very large dune. Sets often thicken and thin rapidly in a flow parallel section. Individual sets have been observed to scour down 2 m and fill up downstream within 20 m (Fig. 3) many of these sets are attributed to scour and fill rather than regularly repeating true dune forms. Scour and fill of this nature is frequently observed at the top of sections and may therefore be indicative of an overall waning flow regime. It is not uncommon for sets of trough cross-stratification in the Brahmaputra to preserve topsets, foresets and toesets indicating very high rates of sedimentation. Calculations of instantaneous rates of deposition from climbing ripple lamination indicates rates of sedimentation approaching 4 m per hour. Ripple lamination is particularly common on the downstream margins of medial bars, lateral bars and point bars. This is because during falling stage the flow velocity decreases in these areas and ripples replace dunes as the dominant bedform, sometimes migrating upstream in areas of flow separation.

The rapid changes in sedimentary structures with interbedded plane beds, ripples and dunes and the abundance of reactivation surfaces on the dunes might indicate that flow fluctuates considerably within the Brahmaputra. It is clear that the changes from plane bed through dune to ripple (shown in Fig. 5) illustrate a spatial lag in shear stress with maximum bed shear stresses upstream of the bedform crest and much lower bed shear stresses downstream. Local lag effects and flow parallel changes in bed shear stress related to bed topography can be considerable and rapid changes in sedimentary structures can, in part, be attributed to flow acceleration and deceleration over bedforms. Other changes in sedimentary structures can be related to lag effects or fluctuations in discharge, these include down-current dipping sets of cross-stratification and reactivation of bedforms. Reactivation surfaces were originally described by Collinson (1970) who attributed them to changes in stage. This observation was developed by Jones (1977) who related changes in sedimentary structures to flow regime and predicted that the long falling stage hydrograph of the Brahmaputra would result in extensive falling stage reworking and modification of high stage bedforms.

To some extent this theory is supported by the observations presented here, although Jones (1977) implied considerable falling stage dissection and erosion. The bar top sections show that falling stage in the Brahmaputra is characterized by deposition. In this paper, smaller fluctuations in flow on a time scale of hours or days, combined with bedform superimposition, rather than annual fluctuations, are believed to have generated the abundant reactivation surfaces since all the sections described were deposited in a single flood event. On a larger scale, patterns of upstream inclined, down-current dipping and laterally dipping bedding have been observed which are related to upstream, downstream and lateral accretion respectively. These observations are included in the facies model (Fig. 9).

Facies model for bar top sedimentation in the Brahmaputra

Figure 9 represents a generalized facies model for a hypothetical bar in the Brahmaputra River developed from observations of bar top sections exposed at low flow stage. Deeper channel deposits are not included in this model, although evidence drawn from outcrops not described in the text has been included. The upstream portion of the bar contains upstream accretion with trough cross-stratification and UPB lamination inclined upwards in a downstream direction. The upstream margins of bars are not always accretionary and many bars have erosive upstream margins. The model includes an erosive cut-bank with cantilever failure. Collapsed portions of the bar are reworked into intraformational mud pellet conglomerates. The central section of the model is characterized by vertical and lateral accretion. Sedimentary structures include UPB, trough cross-stratification and current ripple lamination. Vertical accretion dominates with an idealised sequence of plane beds overlain by trough cross-stratification and capped by current ripple lamination and occasional scour fill. Bars are often enlarged by lateral accretion (Bristow 1987*a*) with scroll bars migrating onto the bar flank. Channel width/depth ratios in the Brahmaputra are very high and lateral accretion surfaces are very low angle and barely discernible at outcrop. Lateral accretion leads to the development of ridge and swale topography on bar tops (Bristow 1987*a*). The tops of the active bars described in this paper are almost all flat or have very subdued topography due to falling stage modification. However, in

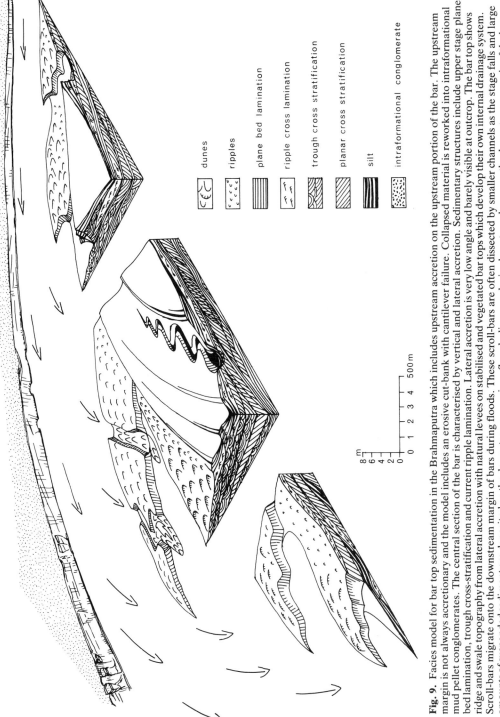

dunes

ripples

plane bed lamination

ripple cross lamination

trough cross stratification

planar cross stratification

silt

intraformational conglomerate

8
6
4
2
0 m

0 1 2 3 4 500 m

Fig. 9. Facies model for bar top sedimentation in the Brahmaputra which includes upstream accretion on the upstream portion of the bar. The upstream margin is not always accretionary and the model includes an erosive cut-bank with cantilever failure. Collapsed material is reworked into intraformational mud pellet conglomerates. The central section of the bar is characterised by vertical and lateral accretion. Sedimentary structures include upper stage plane bed lamination, trough cross-stratification and current ripple lamination. Lateral accretion is very low angle and barely visible at outcrop. The bar top shows ridge and swale topography from lateral accretion with natural levees on stabilised and vegetated bar tops which develop their own internal drainage system. Scroll-bars migrate onto the downstream margin of bars during floods. These scroll-bars are often dissected by smaller channels as the stage falls and large amounts of suspended sediment are deposited on the downstream margin as flow declines producing low stage drapes on the downstream margin of the bars.

Bangladesh the bars are rapidly vegetated and stabilized. Stabilized bars (chars) often have a broad saucer like topography with raised rims formed by natural levees. Bar top interiors are characterised by suspended sediment deposition but may develop their own internal drainage system as shown in Fig. 9. Floodplain deposition in the Brahmaputra is described in Bristow (1987b) & Bristow (in press). The downstream margin of bars varies considerably depending on the geometry of the downstream confluence and flow stage. With a low confluence angle bars tend to develop an accretionary platform on the downstream margin. At high stage dunes are the dominant bedform and scroll-bars sometimes migrate right around the downstream margin. At high stage downstream accretion occurs with bedforms migrating down low angle accretion surfaces. During the falling stage bedform migration is reduced and the bars accrete vertically. Downstream bar margins may become steepened to form avalanche faces. During the falling stage flow velocity decreases, large bedforms are modified and thick mud drapes are deposited. In some cases a zone of flow separation develops in the lee of the bar and flow circulates upstream. These currents are generally very sluggish and current ripples are the dominant bedform. With a high confluence angle tributary bars with distinct slipfaces are formed on either side of a confluence scour (see Bristow et al. in press). At low flow stage sandy areas on bar tops are reworked by wind ripples while muddy areas are planted as rice paddies. During low flow stage some of the bar top sections are incised. On bar tops low stage modification is relatively minor because the low stage discharge is only one twentieth of bankfull flow and is diverted into low flow channels leaving many bars exposed and preserved.

This paper is based on the author's PhD research undertaken at the Department of Earth Sciences, University of Leeds, supervised by M. Leeder and funded by TEXACO. The manuscript has benefited from discussions with J. Bridge and N. Smith and the comments of J. Best and T. Salter. The author is most grateful to everyone who helped shift sand.

References

ALLEN, J. R. L. 1970. A quantitative model of climbing ripples and their cross-laminated deposits. *Sedimentology*, **14**, 5–26.

—— 1983. Studies in fluviatile sedimentation: Bars, Bar-complexes and sandstone sheets (low sinuosity braided streams) in the Brownstones (L. Devonian), Welsh Borders. *Sedimentary Geology*, **33**, 237–293.

BANKS, N. L. 1973. The origin and significance of some downcurrent-dipping cross-stratified sets. *Journal of Sedimentary Petrology*, **43**, 423–427.

BLODGETT, R. H. & STANLEY, K. O. 1980. Stratification bedforms and discharge relations of the Platte braided river system, Nebraska. *Journal of Sedimentary Petrology*, **50**, 139–148.

BLUCK, B. J. 1974. Structure and directional properties of some valley sandur deposits in Southern Iceland. *Sedimentology*, **21**, 533–554.

—— 1976. Sedimentation in some Scottish rivers of low sinuosity. *Transactions of the Royal Society of Edinburgh*, **69**, 425–456.

—— 1979. Structure of coarse grained braided alluvium. *Transactions of the Royal Society of Edinburgh*, **70**, 29–46.

BOOTHROYD, J. C. & ASHLEY, G. M. 1975. Process bar morphology and sedimentary structures on braided outwash fans, northeastern Gulf of Alaska. *In*: JOPLING, A. V. & McDONALD, B. C. (eds) *Glaciofluvial and Glaciolacustrine Sediments*. Society of Economic Mineralogists and Paleontologists Special Publications, **23**, 193–222.

BRIDGE, J. S. & BEST, J. L. 1988. Flow, sediment transport and bedform dynamics over the transition from dunes to upper-stage plane beds: implications for the formation of planar laminae. *Sedimentology*, **35**, 753–763.

——, SMITH, N. D., TRENT, F., GABEL, S. L. & BERNSTEIN, P. 1986. Sedimentology and morphology of a low-sinuosity river: Calamus River, Nebraska Sand Hills. *Sedimentology*, **33**, 851–870.

BRISTOW, C. S. 1987a. Brahmaputra River: Channel migration and deposition. *In*: ETHRIDGE, F. G., FLORES, R. M. & HARVEY, M. D. (eds) *Recent Developments in Fluvial Sedimentology*. Society of Economic Paleontologists and Mineralogists Special Publications, **39**, 63–74.

—— 1987b. *Sedimentology of large braided rivers ancient and modern*. PhD Thesis, University of Leeds, UK.

—— 1993. Sedimentology of the Rough Rock: a Carboniferous braided river sheet sandstone in northern England. *This volume*.

—— in press. Overbank deposits of the 1984 Brahmaputra River flood in Bangladesh and other floodplain deposits. *Sedimentology*.

——, BEST, J. L. & ROY, A. G. in press. Morphology and facies models of channel confluences. *In*: MARZO, M. & PUIGDEFABREGAS, C. (eds) *Alluvial sedimentation*. Special Publications International Association of Sedimentologists.

BURGER, J. W., KLAASSEN, G. J. & PRINS, A. 1988. Bank erosion and channel processes in the Jamuna River, Bangladesh. *International symposium on the impact of river bank erosion, flood hazard and the problem of population displacement, Dhaka, Bangladesh*, 1–17.

CAMPBELL, C. V. 1976. Reservoir geometry of a fluvial sheet sandstone. *American Association of Petroleum Geologists Bulletin*, **60**, 1009–1020.

CANT, D. J. & WALKER, R. G. 1976. Development of a braided fluvial facies model for the Devonian Battery Point Sandstone, Quebec. *Canadian Journal of Earth Sciences*, **13**, 102–119.

—— & —— 1978. Fluvial processes and facies sequences in the sandy braided South Saskatchewan River, Canada. *Sedimentology*, **25**, 625–648.

CHAKRABORTY, C. & BOSE, P. K. 1992. Ripple/dune to upper stage plane bed transition: some observations from the ancient record. *Geological Journal*, **27**, 349–359.

CHEETHAM, G. H. 1979. Flow competence in relation to channel form and braiding. *Geological Society of America Bulletin*, **90**, 877–886.

CHURCH, M. 1972. *Baffin Island sandurs: a study of arctic fluvial processes*. Bulletin of the Geological Society of Canada, **216**.

—— & JONES, D. 1982. Channel bars in gravel bed rivers. *In*: HEY, R. D., BATHURST, J. C. & THORNE, C. R. (eds) *Gravel-bed Rivers*. Wiley, Chichester, 291–338.

COLEMAN, J. M. 1969. Brahmaputra River channel processes and sedimentation. *Sedimentary Geology*, **3**, 129–239.

COLLINSON, J. D. 1970. Bedforms in the Tana River, Norway. *Geografiska Annaler*, **52**, 31–56.

CONAGHAN, P. J. & JONES, J. G. 1975. The Hawkesbury Sandstone and the Brahmaputra River. *Journal of the Geological Society of Australia*, **27**, 275–283.

CROWLEY, K. D. 1983. Large scale bed configurations (macroforms) Platte River Basin, Colorado and Nebraska: Primary structures and formative processes. *Geological Society of America Bulletin*, **94**, 117–133.

FREDSOE, J. 1981. Unsteady flow in straight alluvial streams. Part 2. Transition from dune to plane bed. *Journal of Fluid Mechanics*, **102**, 431–453.

JONES, C. M. 1977. Effects of varying discharge regimes on bedform sedimentary structures in modern rivers. *Geology*, **5**, 567–570.

—— 1979. Tabular cross-bedding in Upper Carboniferous fluvial channel sediments in the southern Pennines, England. *Sedimentary Geology*, **24**, 85–104.

KIRK, M. 1983. Bar development in a fluvial sandstone (Westphalian "A"), Scotland. *Sedimentology*, **30**, 727–742.

KLAASSEN, G. J. & VERMEER, K. 1988. Channel characteristics of the braiding Jamuna River, Bangladesh. *In*: WHITE, W. R. (ed.) *International Conference on River Regime*. John Wiley & Sons Ltd, 173–189.

KRIGSTRÖM, A. 1962. Geomorphological studies of sandur plains and their braided rivers in Iceland. *Geografiska Annaler*, **44**, 328–346.

LEOPOLD, L. B. & WOLMAN, M. G. 1957. River and channel patterns: braided, meandering and straight. *United States Geological Survey Professional Papers*, **282**, 39–85.

MCCABE, P. J. & JONES, C. M. 1977. The formation of reactivation surfaces within superimposed deltas and bedforms. *Journal of Sedimentary Petrology*, **47**, 707–715.

MIALL, A. D. 1977. A review of the braided stream depositional environment. *Earth Science Reviews*, **13**, 1–62.

—— 1978. Lithofacies types and vertical profile models in braided rivers: a summary. *In*: MIALL, A. D. (ed.) *Fluvial Sedimentology*. Canadian Society of Petroleum Geologists, Memoirs, **5**, 605–625.

—— 1985. Architectural-element analysis: a new method of facies analysis applied to fluvial deposits. *Earth Science Reviews*, **22**, 261–308.

PAOLA, C., WIELE, S. M. & REINHART, M. A. 1989. Upper-regime parallel lamination as the result of turbulent sediment transport and low-amplitude bed forms. *Sedimentology*, **36**, 47–59.

RUST, B. R. 1972. Structure and process in a braided river. *Sedimentology*, **18**, 221–246.

—— 1978. Depositional models for braided alluvium. *In*: MIALL, A. D. (ed.) *Fluvial Sedimentology*. Canadian Society of Petroleum Geologists, Memoirs, **5**, 605–625.

SAUNDERSON, H. C. & LOCKET, F. P. J. 1983. Flume experiments on bedforms and structures at the dune plane bed transition. *In*: COLLINSON, J. D. & LEWIN, J. (eds) *Modern and Ancient Fluvial Systems*. Special Publications International Association of Sedimentologists, **6**, 49–58.

SINGH, I. B. 1977. Bedding structures in a channel sand bar of the Ganga River near Allahabad, Uttar Pradesh, India. *Journal of Sedimentary Petrology*, **47**, 747–752.

SMITH, N. D. 1970. The braided stream depositional environment: comparison of the Platte River with some Silurian clastic rocks, North Central Appalachians. *Geological Society of America Bulletin*, **81**, 2993–3014.

—— 1971a. Transverse bars and braiding in the lower Platte River, Nebraska. *Geological Society of America Bulletin*, **82**, 3407–3420.

—— 1971b. Pseudo-planar cross-stratification produced by very low amplitude sand waves. *Journal of Sedimentary Petrology*, **41**, 69–73.

—— 1974. Sedimentology and bar formation in the upper Kicking Horse River, a braided outwash stream. *Journal of Geology*, **82**, 205–224.

WILLIAMS, P. F. & RUST, B. R. 1969. The sedimentology of a braided river. *Journal of Sedimentary Petrology*, **39**, 649–679.

Sedimentology of the Rough Rock: a Carboniferous braided river sheet sandstone in northern England

C. S. BRISTOW

Research School of Geology and Geophysical Sciences, Birkeck College and University College London, Gower Street, London WC1E 6BT, UK

Abstract: The Rough Rock is a coarse-grained fluvial sheet sandstone which outcrops across northern and central England. It is interpreted as a braided river sandstone on the basis of sedimentary structures, internal erosion and growth surfaces. This study reveals that the Rough Rock represents more than a single phase of deposition and that internal erosion surfaces may indicate anabranch avulsions or more significant river avulsions. Detailed outcrop profiles are presented to try and distinguish the styles of deposition and the nature of internal bounding surfaces and channel geometry. The Rough Rock Formation contains a very large number of first and third order bedding contacts, which represent the migration of dunes and channels respectively, there are relatively few macroforms and bars preserved. The lack of second order surfaces within many outcrops could indicate that bars in the Rough Rock rivers were very large and therefore cannot be resolved at the outcrop scale. Similarly, the rivers which deposited the Rough Rock may have had such high width : depth ratios that the dip of second order bounding surfaces are too low to be identified. The large number of third order bounding surfaces indicates channel stacking which may have occurred in two ways: (1) relocation of rivers in the same area over time, or, (2) anabranch avulsion within a braided river within a hierarchy of channels. The problems associated with differentiating between these two mechanisms are discussed.

The Rough Rock is a very coarse grained, often granule grade, sandstone with occasional pebbles. It is predominantly cross-stratified with an erosive base, and has previously been interpreted as the deposits of a braided river (Shackleton 1962; Heath 1975; Bristow 1987*a*, 1988; Bristow & Myers 1989). The Rough Rock Formation occurs at the top of the Rough Rock Group (Fig. 1) which is equivalent to the Yeadonian stage of Hudson (1945), the base of the Group is marked by the *Gastrioceras cancellatum* marine band and the top of the Group is defined by the *Gastrioceras subcrenatum* marine band. The Yeadonian may be correlated with the lower part of the Bloydian Stage (USA) or part of the Bashkirian Stage (USSR) (Riley *et al.* 1987). Other named sandstone units within the Group include the Lower Haslingden Flags, the Upper Haslingden Flags and the Rough Rock Flags Formations which are not included in this paper. The group is the youngest in the Millstone Grit Series, a thick sequence of Lower Pennsylvanian and Upper Mississippian deltaic sediments in the Pennine Basin, northern England (Collinson 1988). At outcrop, the Rough Rock forms a low scarp on both limbs of the north–south-trending Pennine anticline, the 'backbone' of England. There are some natural exposures along the crest of the scarps but the majority of outcrops

are in old quarry workings. The Rough Rock is worked as a building stone and, after acid leaching, as a high quality quartz sand for glass making.

The Rough Rock is the most widespread and has the most uniform thickness of the Millstone Grit sandstones, forming a sheet sandstone approximately 15 m thick, outcropping over an area of 1000 km^2, with local thickness and facies changes. In the area between Sheffield and Coxbench [UK Ordnance Survey Grid Ref. SK 374 434] there are no coarse clastics within the Rough Rock Group. A corresponding lack of coarse clastics within the Rough Rock Group has also been recorded in the East Midlands Oil-field (Falcon & Kent 1960; Downing & Howitt 1969; Steele 1988). The Rough Rock reaches a maximum thickness of 60 m in the Rossendale area (Maynard 1992) due to increased differential intrabasinal subsidence (Bristow 1988).

The base of the Rough Rock is usually sharp and erosive, locally cutting down into the underlying Rough Rock Flags, Upper Haslingden Flags and associated shales. In the Rossendale area the Rough Rock is split into an upper and lower member by the Sand Rock Mine Coal which is not associated with any marine fauna (Wright *et al.* 1927). Corresponding splits and seatearths within the Rough Rock have been reported from other areas (Tonks *et al.* 1931) but

From Best, J. L. & Bristow, C. S. (eds), 1993, *Braided Rivers*, Geological Society Special Publication No. 75, pp. 291–304.

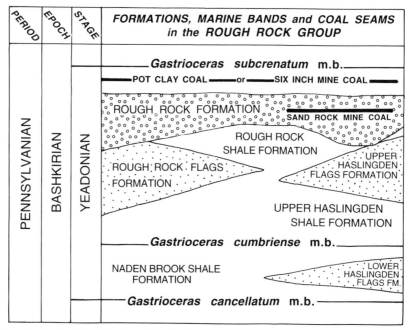

Fig. 1. Schematic stratigraphy of the Rough Rock Group.

the Sand Rock Mine Coal is only sufficiently well developed to be worked in the Rossendale Basin where it thickens and improves in quality towards the south. The top of the Rough Rock is generally sharp with little or no fining up beneath the overlying fine sands and silts which pass up into black carbonaceous mudstones, the Pot Clay Coal or the Six Inch Mine Coal. The coals are overlain by the *Gastrioceras sub-crenatum* marine band which is taken as the base of the Westphalian Series in Britain (Owens *et al.* 1983). The stratigraphy has recently been reviewed by Maynard (1992) who determined that the Rough Rock is a lowstand wedge overlying a highstand delta system and that the Yeadonian Stage corresponds to a parasequence in the terminology of the EXXON model (Vail *et al.* 1977) associated with a fourth or fifth order sea-level change.

Sedimentology

The Rough Rock is a very coarse-grained sandstone which contains a variety of primary sedimentary structures including trough cross-stratification, planar cross-stratification, down-current dipping cross-stratification, and occasional laminated or apparently structureless sands. Bedform terminology follows the guidelines set out in Ashley (1990). The cross-stratified sandstones are arranged in packages

defined by internal erosion surfaces and growth surfaces such as lateral accretion surfaces. Secondary, deformational sedimentary structures are rare. In this paper outcrop profile diagrams are presented and a hierarchy of bounding surfaces is identified. The bounding surface classification used here follows the work of Allen (1983), Miall (1985, 1988). First order bounding surfaces are formed by the migration of dunes or similar bedforms (mesoforms and microforms), second order bounding surfaces are formed where small scale bedforms (mesoforms and microforms) migrate over macroforms or bars, third order bounding surfaces are formed by channels.

Palaeocurrents

Palaeocurrents have been measured primarily from the trend of sets of trough cross-stratification and planar cross-stratification with occasional measurements from current ripple form sets and primary current lineation. A total of approximately 2000 measurements have been made at 150 different stations in this study. The number of measurements at each station varies from 6 to 600 (details can be found in Bristow 1987a), a vector mean for each outcrop has been calculated and these are plotted in Fig. 2. Each outcrop generally shows unidirectional palaeocurrents with relatively little dispersion.

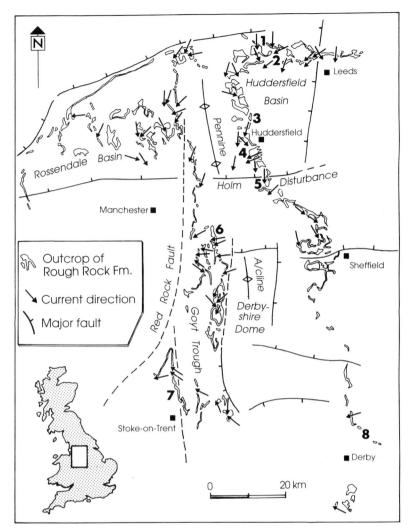

Fig. 2. Outcrop map of the Rough rock with palaeocurrent vector means for each outcrop, the numbers refer to localities shown in Fig. 3.

However, there are some marked palaeocurrent divergences within the Rough Rock over its whole outcrop which Bristow (1988) attributed to an underlying basement control on palaeo-geography. A mean of all the vector means is 218° illustrating the dominant palaeocurrent direction in the Rough Rock which is towards the southwest. This is consistent with the earlier observations of Shackleton (1962) and Heath (1975).

Trough cross-stratification

The dominant sedimentary structure in the Rough Rock is trough cross-stratification (Fig. 3) which occurs on a variety of scales from small to large (see Ashley 1990). The largest avalanche sets observed are 4 m high (Eldwick Crag [SE 124 424] and Honley Wood Quarry [SE 117 113] but these are exceptional and most sets of trough cross-stratification are between 0.5 and 1 m thick. Western outcrops at Cracken Edge [SK 037 836], Lantern Pike [SK 027 882], Combes Edge [SK 016 916], Cown Edge [SK 020 917] and Black Rocks [SJ 987 830] consist almost entirely of medium to large trough cross-stratification. In other outcrops trough cross-stratification occurs at the base of the section (e.g. Isle of Skye Quarry, Holmfirth [SE 146 084] or in the middle of the outcrop

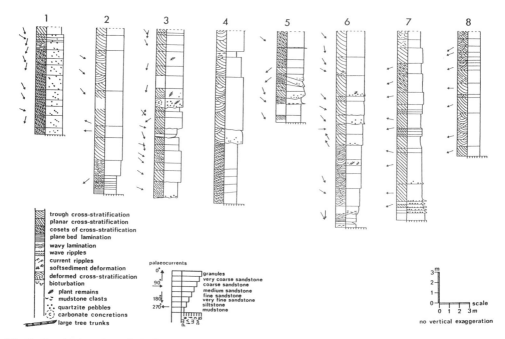

Fig. 3. Graphic logs through the Rough Rock Formation at: 1, Shipley Glen; 2, Baildon Bank; 3, Elland; 4, Johnsons Wellfield Quarry Crossland Hill; 5, Isle of Skye Quarry, Holmfirth; 6, Church Inn Quarry; 7, Knypersly Reservoir; 8, Coxbench Quarries; the locations of which are shown in Fig. 2 (modified after Bristow 1988).

(Baildon Bank [SE 150 390] (Fig. 4). In flow-parallel sections, such as the Elland Road cutting, individual sets of trough cross-stratification can be traced for more than 100 m (Bristow & Myers 1989) and set size and grain-size are remarkably consistant with relatively few reactivation surfaces. Trough cross-stratification is produced by curved crested 3D dunes which are produced by unidirectional flow in a variety of marine and non-marine sedimentary environments. The association with other lithofacies, sedimentary structures, lack of fauna and restricted flora indicate that these are river deposits as previously determined by Shackleton (1962), Heath (1975), Bristow (1987b, 1988) and Bristow & Myers (1989). Where trough cross-stratification dominates an outcrop (see above), the laterally discontinuous troughs often obscure larger scale growth or erosion surfaces making channel reconstruction very difficult. It is assumed that the trough cross-stratification represents undifferentiated channel deposits

because no macroform elements can be identified (Cant & Walker 1976, 1978). The lateral continuity of individual sets of trough cross-stratification, lack of reactivation surfaces and mud drapes in most outcrops suggests that the Rough Rock rivers had an almost constant discharge with only minor seasonal fluctuations. Small scale sets of trough cross-stratification can sometimes be found on larger amplitude bedforms which results in the development of downcurrent dipping cross-stratification, climbing dunes and lateral accretion which are discussed below.

Planar cross-stratification

Planar cross-stratification is rare in the northern outcrops of the Rough Rock although there are good examples exposed at the top of the outcrop at Shipley Glen [SE 130 390] and isolated examples occur within the outcrops at Elland

Fig. 4. Outcrop diagrams of the Isle of Skye Quarry, Holmfirth, and Baildon Bank, showing facies distributions within each outcrop. The geometries of major bounding surfaces are summarized in Fig. 6.

[SE 103 214], Lindley Moor [SE 097 187] and Erwood Reservoir [SK 012 750]. Further south, in Staffordshire, outcrops of Rough Rock at Rock End [SJ 898 586] and Knypersly reservoir [SJ 900 554] are dominated by planar cross-stratification, in these localities set size appears to decrease upwards (Fig. 5). Planar cross-stratification is interpreted as the product of straight crested 2D dunes which are common in shallow sandbed braided rivers. Straight crested dunes are generally considered to form at slightly lower current velocities than curved crested 3D dunes (Ashley 1990). The occurrence of this facies in distal, southwestern outcrops and at the top of more proximal, northern outcrops suggests that it is a lower energy facies deposited on bar tops and in the more distal portions of the Rough Rock river system. The upwards decrease in set size may indicate waning flow conditions on a mid channel bar as shown in Cant & Walker (1976, 1978) and Crowley (1983).

Cosets of down-current dipping cross-strata

Down-current dipping cross-strata are a common sedimentary structure in the Rough Rock and at Shipley Glen and the Isle of Skye Quarry, Holmfirth this facies forms almost 90% of the outcrop (Figs 3 & 4). The cosets contain regularly spaced sets of cross-stratification 10–20 cm thick on low angle bounding surfaces. The dip of the foresets often diverges strongly from the dip of the bounding surfaces by 30–60°, a characteristic feature noted in other Carboniferous sandstones in northern England (Banks 1973; McCabe & Jones 1977; Gardiner 1984). McCabe & Jones (1977) and Jones (1979) have described and interpreted similar structures from other formations in the Millstone Grit Series as reactivation surfaces produced by superimposed bedforms, although in their model there was no dip divergence between foresets and bounding surfaces. Gardiner (1984) noted a divergence in dip in similar beds from the Upper Border Group of Northumberland which he attributes to formation on alternate bars as suggested by Banks (1973). Jones (1979) suggested that downcurrent dipping sets could be formed by superimposed bedforms and this is the model preferred here. Trenching through large 3D, curved crested dunes with superimposed smaller dunes in the Brahmaputra River has revealed cosets of downcurrent dipping cross-stratification (Bristow, this volume). The range of coset dips and interbedding of large troughs with downcurrent dipping cosets in the Isle of Skye Quarry (Fig. 4) suggests that these cosets could have been formed in a similar setting. Large 3D dunes (megaripples) with superimposed small dunes are a common feature of shallow sandbed braided rivers (Collinson 1970; Smith 1970, 1971, 1972; Boothroyd & Ashley 1975; Blodgett

Fig. 5. Photograph of planar cross-stratified sandstones at the top of the Rough Rock in one of the most southwesterly outcrops at Rock End near Bidulph. The handle of the sledge hammer is almost 1 m long.

& Stanley 1980; Crowley 1983) and this is the most likely depositional setting for this facies.

Soft sediment deformation

There is very little soft-sediment deformation in the Rough Rock compared with some other Carboniferous fluvial sandstones in Northern England (Leeder 1987). Structures formed by dewatering occur at two localities, Meltham Moor [SE 077 088] and Coxbench Quarry [SK 374 434]. At Meltham Moor dewatering pipes around 1 m high have deformed very coarse to granule grade cross-stratified sandstones. The deformation has affected almost every outcrop in this area. At Coxbench Quarry dewatering pipes up to 3 m high have deformed medium to coarse grained cross-stratified sandstone. The dewatering pipes are more isolated in this outcrop and the majority of the formation is undeformed. The deformation at Coxbench is associated with thickness changes of 15 m in the Rough Rock and synsedimentary movement along the Horsly Fault System (Frost & Smart 1979). The deformation on Meltham Moor is associated with thickness changes across the Holm Disturbance (Bromhead et al. 1933) which also indicates contemporary tectonic movement.

Sand Rock Mine Coal

In the area of the Rossendale Basin, the Rough Rock is split by the Sand Rock Mine Coal (SRMC). The coal occurs almost exactly in the middle of the Rough Rock and thickens and improves in quality towards the south. At Scout Moor [SD 815 187] and Heys Britannia/ Whitworth Quarries [SD 872 203] the coal has been extracted by open cast mining which provides a good exposure of the coal. The base of the coal is almost flat, overlying a 20 cm thick clay with Sigillaria sp., the coal is approximately 50 cm thick and is erosively overlain by the base of the upper member of the Rough Rock. This surface locally preserves tree stumps and contains a large amount of tree trunks and wood clasts. The time taken to deposit this bed of coal can be estimated from present peat accumulation rates and compaction ratios. A bed of bituminous coal 0.5 m thick is equivalent to approximately 3 m of peat (Teichmuller & Teichmuller 1982) and might require 1000 to 3000 years to accumulate (Teichmuller & Teichmuller 1982; McCabe 1984). Using analogue data, Teichmuller & Teichmuller (1982) estimate that 1 m of bituminous coal probably represents accumulation over approximately 6000–9000 years. The SRMC is interpreted as an overbank swamp deposit and represents a major avulsion of the Rough Rock fluvial system. The SRMC provides unequivocal evidence of avulsion and relocation of the river in the same area over time. The interval between avulsions and the time taken to develop the SRMC must be greater than 1000 years and is more likely to be 3000–4500 years.

Internal erosion surfaces and macroforms

There are very few completely exposed channel forms in the Rough Rock. Most outcrops, on the other hand, contain several bounding surfaces which are either erosion surfaces or growth/ accretion surfaces which can be used to infer the larger scale channel geometry (Fig. 6). Each bounding surface is different but groups of bounding surfaces can be identified based on cross-cutting relationships, lateral continuity, geometry and association with sedimentary structures. This leads to a hierarchy of bounding surfaces (Allen 1983; Miall 1985, 1988), by tracing out bedform contacts on the outcrop diagrams in Fig. 3 it is possible to reconstruct the channels which deposited the Rough Rock. At Baildon Bank the lower part of the outcrop contains downcurrent dipping bounding surfaces which indicate downstream accretion, possibly on a midchannel bar. The structures in this unit indicate palaeoflow towards the west or southwest. The overlying beds contain large sets of cross-stratification with rare downcurrent dipping cosets of cross-stratification (Fig. 4), all with a similar westerly palaeoflow. These are interpreted as bar top deposits which appear to pass-downstream into the downstream accretion unit. The bar top deposits are overlain by sets of trough cross-stratification with a southerly palaeoflow out of the outcrop (Fig. 4). The change in palaeoflow is attributed to channel switching within a braided river system. A second internal erosion surface (third order bounding surface) occurs near the top of the section (Fig. 4) which is also accompanied by minor changes in sedimentary structures and palaeoflow. This could be due to short term channel switching or, possibly, longer term channel stacking. However, it is not possible to determine the amount of erosion or the time gap represented by this erosion surface from the outcrop at Baildon Bank.

At the Isle of Skye Quarry, Holmfirth (Fig. 4) the stacking pattern and the arrangement of erosion surfaces is rather different. The erosion surfaces are more closely spaced, usually only 1–1.5 m apart, and often cross-cut or join along

HOLMFIRTH

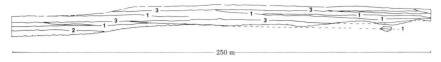

250 m

BAILDON BANK

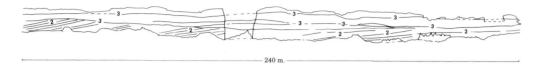

240 m.

ELLAND

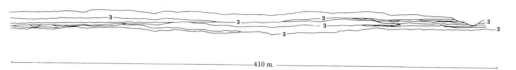

410 m.

Fig. 6. Bounding surfaces in three Rough Rock outcrops at Holmfirth, Baildon Bank and Elland. The detailed distribution of facies at Holmfirth and Baildon Bank are shown in Fig. 3 while the details of the Elland outcrop can be found in Bristow & Myers (1989). First order surfaces bound mesoforms (dunes), second order surfaces define macroforms (bars) and third order surfaces bound channels.

strike. The majority of these surfaces are bounding mesoforms within the river (first order bounding surfaces). However, some of the bounding surfaces appear to be more laterally extensive and divide beds and bedsets with slight changes in palaeoflow direction (Fig. 4). These are interpreted as third order bounding surfaces associated with channel switching (Fig. 6).

In the outcrop of the Rough Rock at Elland (Fig. 6) at least three channel sandbodies have been identified (Bristow & Meyers 1989). The individual channel sandstones can be separated by tracing out erosion surfaces and abandonment facies. In this outcrop there is a change in palaeocurrent direction between sandbodies and a marked change in sandbody geometry through the outcrop, the lower sandbodies are relatively simple concave lenses, while the upper sandbody is a broader sheet with several minor internal erosion surfaces. The change in sandbody geometry has enabled the coarse grained lithofacies to be interpreted as the deposits of two different channel systems (Bristow & Myers 1989). The lower sandbodies are interpreted as the deposits of relatively small (5–6 m deep, 100 m wide) low sinuosity distributary channels while the overlying sheet sandstone is interpreted as the deposits of a larger braided river at least 6.5 m deep and about 1 km wide. This

interpretation was aided by the presence of abandonment deposits within the outcrop, which are clear indicators of channel relocation over time.

Lateral accretion

Lateral accretion surfaces are well exposed in two outcrops in the Rough Rock in the Huddersfield area, at Greetland Quarry [SE 095 216] and Johnsons Wellfield Quarry, Crossland Hill [SE 118 144]. Figure 6 shows a 6.5 m high quarry face at Greetland with a series of 30 m long, low-angle bounding surfaces dipping at up to 15°, flattening out towards the west (Fig. 7). Cross-cuts in the quarry face show small scale sets of cross-stratification trending south out of the quarry face and perpendicular to the bounding surfaces. There is no evidence of fining upwards through the section as it is all coarse to very coarse sandstone. There is also no apparent vertical change in bedform size or type within the lateral accretion unit. Although the geometry of the deposits clearly indicates lateral accretion, the lack of fining upwards and the absence of an upwards decrease in bedform size or type distinguishes this outcrop from most conventional models of lateral accretion deposits

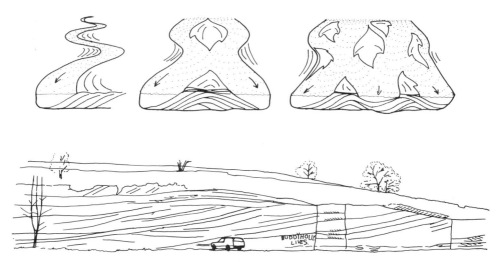

Fig. 7. Lateral accretion surfaces in the Rough Rock at Greetland Quarry, the quarry face is 6.5 m high and east–west orientated, perpendicular to palaeoflow which is out of the outcrop, accretion surfaces showing offlap and onlap can be traced along strike more than 30 m with cartoons showing how lateral accretion can be formed within a braided river as part of accretion on a medial bar, or as lateral accretion on a side or point bar.

associated with meandering river point bars (Allen 1965; Thomas *et al.* 1987). The lateral accretion surfaces appear to steepen towards the east and sedimentary structures increase in size in the same direction. At the eastern end of the outcrop there are several large sets of cross-stratification, equivalent to the lateral accretion unit, around which the bar may have nucleated. Due to lack of outcrop it is not possible to determine whether the lateral accretion surfaces formed part of a bank attached point bar or one half of medial bar (Fig. 7).

At Johnsons Wellfield Quarry, southerly dipping lateral accretion surfaces have been exhumed at the top of the outcrop, they can also be made out at the top of Fig. 8 which shows a north south section locally perpendicular to palaeoflow in the Rough Rock. The lateral accretion unit is approximately 10 m thick and shows only minor internal grainsize changes with no upwards fining. On an exumed accretion surface small dunes can be observed migrating up and around the bar in a westerly direction. The lateral accretion unit can be traced laterally in a flow perpendicular direction for 100 m with the lateral accretion surfaces gradually steepening up towards the south suggesting that the bend tightened as it migrated leading to a progressively steeper inner bank.

Fig. 8. Johnsons Wellfield Quarry, Crossland Hill, southerly dipping lateral accretion surfaces are exposed in the top 10 m of the outcrop, while the base of the section shows an unusual outcrop of climbing dunes.

River behaviour and lateral changes in facies

The Rough Rock Formation contains a very large number of first and third order bounding surfaces, which represent the migration of dunes and channels respectively, there are relatively few macroforms and bars preserved. The large number of third order bounding surfaces indicates channel stacking which may have occurred in two ways: (1) relocation of rivers in the same area over time, or (2) anabranch avulsion and deposition by a braided river with an hierarchy of channels. The problems associated with differentiating between these two mechanisms are discussed below. The logs in Fig. 3 show some of the variations within the Rough Rock across its outcrop which can be interpreted as proximal to distal facies changes. Many of the lateral changes in the Rough Rock are due to inherent variability within the braided river depositional system. Local changes in facies can be equal to regional changes in facies. Changes in facies within outcrops have been described above, and attributed to channel switching (anabranch avulsion) within a braided river or to channel stacking. One example of a lateral change in facies between outcrops is described below. In this case interpreting facies changes between outcrops presents additional challenges.

The outcrops at Shipley Glen (Fig. 3) and Baildon Bank (Fig. 4) are only 2 km apart, and yet they show no correlation of sedimentary structures. This could be due to a number of possible explanations and three scenarios are presented here. The outcrop at Baildon Bank contains sets of trough cross-stratification up to 3 m thick within a multistorey sandstone with several third order bounding surfaces representing the migration of channels with a minimum depth of 8 m. The outcrop at Shipley Glen contains stacked cosets of down-current dipping cross-stratification between 0.75 and 1.5 m thick, similar to that described from Holmfirth, overlain by 1 m thick sets of planar cross-stratification. There are very few changes in palaeocurrent through the outcrop and no evidence of channels or large scale macroforms. The outcrop at Shipley Glen is interpreted as the deposits of a relatively shallow braided river, probably 3–4 m deep, with small medial bars, superimposed 3D dunes and straight crested dunes on bar tops, while the outcrop at Baildon Bank appears to have been deposited by a larger (8–10 m deep) river with large (8 m thick) macroforms. The difference between the two outcrops could be explained by two sub-parallel

fluvial systems flowing across the alluvial plain at the same time (Fig. 9a). An alternative possibility is that the two outcrops were deposited at different times (Fig. 9b). In this case the change in facies could be explained as an evolution in fluvial style over time although it is impossible to date the outcrops and determine which came first. A third model (Fig. 9c) is proposed where the two different sequences were deposited contemporaneously within a single large braided river such as the Brahmaputra where a variety of styles of deposition can be observed within the river at any given moment in time (Bristow 1987b). In this case the section at Baildon Bank could be interpreted as the deposits of a relatively deep channel while the repeated cosets at Shipley Glen were deposited in an ajacent shallow channel or in a single channel with a stepped profile (Fig. 9c). There is no method for distinguishing the relative ages of the deposits at Shipley Glen and Baildon Bank, and the lack of intervening outcrops between these two localities makes it impossible to provide a definitive answer.

Interpretation of channel form and pattern

Bridge (1985) suggested that the most useful indicator of braiding should be 'the proportion of channel fills relative to lateral-accretion deposits, which increases with degree of braiding'. Using this criterion, the lack of preserved channel fills and the presence of lateral-accretion in the Rough Rock could be taken to indicate a meandering channel pattern. However, analysis of sedimentation patterns in a large braided river by Bristow (1987a, b) indicates that channel fill is a relatively minor component of braided river deposits (15%) and that the dominant component is accretion onto bars (53%). Sets of trough cross-stratification with beds arranged on a depositional dip in the Rough Rock indicate the presence of macroforms or bars. Within the Rough Rock these include lateral accretion surfaces exposed at Greetland (Fig. 7) and Johnsons Wellfield Crossland Hill Quarries (Fig. 8), and although lateral accretion surfaces are generally associated with meandering rivers they have also been observed in braided river deposits (Ori 1982; Allen 1983; Ramos & Sopena 1983; Ramos et al. 1986; Miall 1985, this volume; Bridge et al. 1986; Bristow 1987a, b). Downstream accretion has been identified at Baildon Bank while the outcrop at Holmfirth is dominated by vertical stacking of complex bedforms. Many outcrops do not show any clear evidence of macroforms, in which case the outcrop is

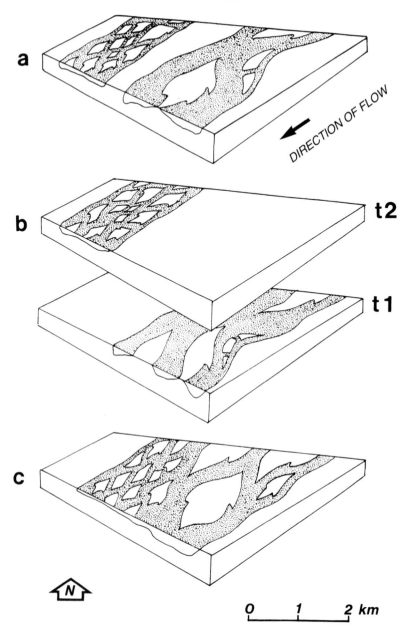

Fig. 9. The lateral variation in facies between Baildon Bank and Shipley Glen may be explained as the deposits of two contemporaneous but different braided rivers (**a**); two different braided rivers at separate times or an evolution of fluvial style over time t1–t2 (**b**); different styles of deposition within two channels in the same river or a single channel with a stepped cross-section (**c**).

interpreted as channel deposits. It is possible that outcrops with no macroforms are simply the deposits of channels with no bars or bar tops preserved. However, it is possible that channels or macroforms could not be identified because

the width : depth ratio of the channels was too high for low angle accretion surfaces to be identified at outcrop. Alternatively the bars may be too big to be identified at outcrop. High width : depth ratios are typical in braided rivers and this in itself could be a potential indicator of braiding. Another important indicator of braiding may be the presence of a hierarchy of channels (Williams & Rust 1969; Bristow 1987a, b, Bridge this volume) which may lead to the formation of different sized channels being preserved within the same sandbody, and potentially different styles of deposition within the same river. The lack of evidence for a break in deposition, change in bedforms, grainsize, or palaeocurrents within the outcrops at Holmfirth

(Fig. 4) and Shipley Glen suggests that stacking within a channel belt is quite possible. At Baildon Bank there are changes in sedimentary structures and palaeocurrents within the outcrop which might indicate a break in deposition and channel relocation over time. However, local changes in palaeoflow, channel geometry and fill should be expected within a braided river and it is not possible to determine the nature of the channel stacking in the Baildon Bank outcrop. Within the outcrop at Elland the presence of

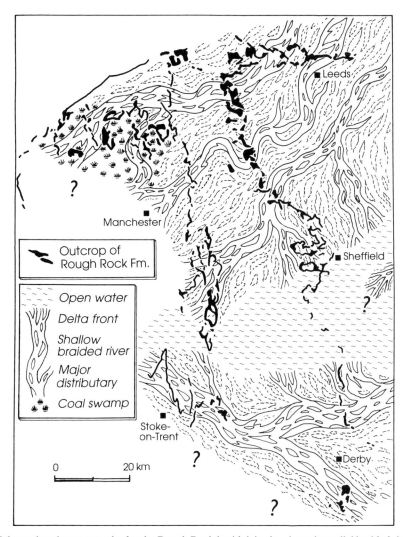

Fig. 10. Schematic palaeogeography for the Rough Rock braidplain showing subparallel braided river systems migrating across the delta top. The rivers contain a hierarchy of channels and are shown to change pattern locally as seen at outcrop. The presence of abandonment deposits within the Rough Rock indicates an overall avulsive control on sedimentation and suggests that only one of the channel belts is likely to have been active at any given time.

abandonment facies between mapped channels clearly shows that there were breaks in deposition between the relocation of channels in the same area. The Sand Rock Mine Coal also indicates a significant break in fluvial deposition between channel relocation in western outcrops and suggests an avulsive control on the Rough Rock river system.

In conclusion an overall model of braided river deposition on a delta top is preferred for the Rough Rock (Fig. 10). The palaeogeographic reconstruction incorporates local facies changes observed at outcrop together with regional facies changes and the occurrence of abandonment facies including the Sand Rock Mine Coal. It is suggested that any one of the major distributary systems was active at any one time and that avulsion of the river across the delta top played an important role in the development of the Rough Rock as a sheet sandstone. Accumulation of the Sand Rock Mine Coal indicates that relocation after avulsions occurred on a thousand year time scale. Proximal to distal changes in facies have been identified, although in many outcrops these are exceeded by local changes in facies attributed to the inherent variability of braided rivers. The use of lateral profiles at outcrop has assisted the interpretation of palaeochannel pattern by picking out laterally persistant erosion surfaces and internal sedimentary dips attributed to channel migration and macroforms respectively. Macroform elements include downstream-accretion and lateral-accretion on braid bars. The height of the macroforms enables channel depth to be estimated and possibly channel width although channel belt width cannot be calculated due to uncertainties over the number of channels within a given channel belt. Abandonment facies enabled channel stacking to be picked out in several outcrops. However, the absence of fines in many outcrops does not preclude channel stacking and many internal erosion surfaces may be due to either anabranch avulsion within the braided river or channel belt avulsions. It is not possible to determine the relative importance of these two mechanisms within the Rough Rock.

This study was undertaken as part of a PhD project at the department of Earth Sciences, University of Leeds supervised by M. Leeder and sponsored by TEXACO. The manuscript has been improved following reviews by M. Leeder and B. Turner.

References

ALLEN, J. R. L. 1965. The sedimentation and palaeogeography of the Old Red Sandstone of Anglesey, North Wales. *Proceedings of the Yorkshire Geological Society*, **35**, 139–185.
—— 1983. Studies in fluviatile sedimentation: Bars, Bar-complexes and sandstone sheets (low sinuosity braided streams) in the Brownstones (L. Devonian), Welsh Borders. *Sedimentary Geology*, **33**, 237–293.
ASHLEY, G. M. 1990. Classification of large-scale subaqueous bedforms: a new look at an old problem. *Journal of Sedimentary Petrology*, **60**, 160–172.
BANKS, N. L. 1973. The origin and significance of some downcurrent-dipping cross-stratified sets. *Journal of Sedimentary Petrology*, **43**, 423–427.
BLODGETT, R. H. & STANLEY, K. O. 1980. Stratification bedforms and discharge relations of the Platte braided river system, Nebraska. *Journal of Sedimentary Petrology*, **50**, 139–148.
BOOTHROYD, J. C. & ASHLEY, G. M. 1975. Process bar morphology and sedimentary structures on braided outwash fans, northeastern Gulf of Alaska. *In*: JOPLING, A. V. & McDONALD, B. C. (eds) *Glaciofluvial and Glaciolacustrine Sedimentation*. Society of Economic Mineralogists and Paleontologists Special Publication, **23**, 193–222.
BRIDGE, J. S. 1985. Palaeochannel patterns inferred from alluvial deposits: a critical evaluation. *Journal of Sedimentary Petrology*, **55**, 579–589.

—— 1993. The interaction between channel geometry, water flow, sediment transport, erosion and deposition in braided rivers. *This volume*.
——, SMITH, N. D., TRENT, F., GABEL, S. L. & BERNSTEIN, P. 1986. Sedimentology and morphology of a low-sinuosity river: Calamus River, Nebraska Sand Hills. *Sedimentology*, **33**, 851–870.
BRISTOW, C. S. 1987a. *Sedimentology of large braided rivers ancient and modern*. PhD Thesis, University of Leeds, UK.
—— 1987b. Brahmaputra River: Channel migration and deposition. *In*: ETHRIDGE, F. G., FLORES, R. M. & HARVEY, M. D. (eds) *Recent Developments in Fluvial Sedimentology*. Society of Economic Paleontologists and Mineralogists Special Publications, **39**, 63–74.
—— 1988. Controls on sedimentation in the Rough Rock Group. *In*: BESLY, B. & KELLING, G. (eds) *Sedimentation in a synorogenic basin complex*. Blackie, Glasgow, 114–131.
—— 1993. Sedimentary structures exposed in bar tops in the Brahmaputra River, Bangladesh. *This volume*.
—— & MYERS, K. 1989. Detailed sedimentology and gamma-ray log characteristics of a Namurian deltaic succession 1: Sedimentology and facies analysis. *In*: WHATELEY, M. K. G. & PICKERING, K. T. (eds) *Deltas: Sites and Traps for Fossil Fuels*. Geological Society, London, Special Publications, **41**, 75–80.

BROMHEAD, C. E. N., EDWARDS, W., WRAY, D. A. & STEPHENS, J. C. 1933. *The geology of the country around Holmfirth and Glossop.* Memoirs of the Geological Survey of Great Britain, HMSO London.

CANT, D. J. & WALKER, R. G. 1976. Development of a braided fluvial facies model for the Devonian Battery Point Sandstone, Quebec. *Canadian Journal of Earth Science*, **13**, 102–119.

—— & —— 1978. Fluvial processes and facies sequences in the sandy braided South Saskatchewan River, Canada. *Sedimentology*, **25**, 625–648.

COLLINSON, J. D. 1970. Bedforms in the Tana River, Norway. *Geografiska Annaler*, **52**, 31–56.

—— 1988. Controls on Namurian sedimentation in the central basins of northern England. *In*: BESLY, B. & KELLING, G. (eds) *Sedimentation in a synorogenic basin complex.* Blackie, Glasgow, 85–101.

CROWLEY, K. D. 1983. Large scale bed configurations (macroforms) Platte River Basin, Colorado and Nebraska: Primary structures and formative processes. *Geological Society of America Bulletin*, **94**, 117–133.

DOWNING, R. A. & HOWITT, F. 1969. Saline groundwaters in the Carboniferous rocks of the English East Midlands in relation to the geology. *Quarterly Journal of Engineering Geology*, **1**, 241–269.

FALCON, N. L. & KENT, P. E. 1960. *Geological results of petroleum exploration in Britain 1945–57.* Memoirs of the Geological Society of London, **2**.

FROST, D. V. & SMART, J. G. O. 1979. *Geology of the country north of Derby.* Memoirs of the Geological Survey of Great Britain, HMSO London.

GARDINER, A. R. 1984. A braided river sheet sandstone in the Lower Limestone Group of the Northumberland Basin. *European Dinantian Environments 1st meeting Abstracts*, 105–107.

HEATH, C. W. 1975. *A sedimentological and palaeogeographical study of the Namurian Rough Rock in the Southern Pennines.* PhD Thesis, University of Keele.

HUDSON, R. G. S. 1945. The Goniatite zones of the Namurian. *Geological Magazine*, **82**, 1–9.

JONES, C. M. 1977. Effects of varying discharge regimes on bedform sedimentary structures in modern rivers. *Geology*, **5**, 567–570.

—— 1979. Tabular cross-bedding in Upper Carboniferous fluvial channel sediments in the southern Pennines, England. *Sedimentary Geology*, **24**, 85–104.

LEEDER, M. R. 1987. Sediment deformation structures and the palaeotectonic analysis of extensional sedimentary basins. *In*: JONES, M. E. & PRESTON, R. M. F. (eds) *Deformation Mechanisms in Sediments and Sedimentary rocks.* Geological Society, London, Special Publications, 137–146.

MAYNARD, J. R. 1992. Sequence stratigraphy of the Upper Yeadonian of northern England. *Marine and Petroleum Geology*, **9**, 197–207.

McCABE, P. J. 1984. Depositional environments for coal and coal-bearing strata. *In*: RAHMANI, R. A. & FLORES, R. M. (eds) *Sedimentology of coal and coal-bearing sequences.* International Association of Sedimentologists Special Publications, **7**, 13–42.

—— & JONES, C. M. 1977. The formation of reactivation surfaces within superimposed deltas and bedforms. *Journal of Sedimentary Petrology*, **47**, 707–715.

MIALL, A. D. 1985. Architectural-element analysis: a new method of facies analysis applied to fluvial deposits. *Earth Science Reviews*, **22**, 261–308.

—— 1988. Architectural elements and bounding surfaces in fluvial deposits: anatomy of the Kayenta Formation (Lower Jurassic), southwest Colorado. *Sedimentary Geology*, **55**, 233–262.

—— 1993. The architecture of fluvial-deltaic sequences in the Upper Mesaverde Group (Upper Cretaceous), Book Cliffs, Utah. *This volume*.

ORI, G. G. 1982. Braided to meandering channel patterns in humid region alluvial fan deposits, River Reno, Po plain (northern Italy). *Sedimentary Geology*, **31**, 231–248.

OWENS, B., RILEY, N. & CALVER, M. A. 1983. Boundary stratotypes and new stage names for the Lower and Middle Westphalian sequences in Britain. *10th International Congress on the Carboniferous, Madrid*, **4**, 461–472.

RAMOS, A. & SOPENA, A. 1983. Gravel bars in low sinuosity streams (Permian and Triassic, central Spain). *Special Publications of the International Association of Sedimentologists*, **6**, 301–313.

——, —— & PEREZ-ARLUCEA, M. 1986. Evolution of the Buntsandstein fluvial sedimentation in the northwest Iberian ranges (central Spain). *Journal of Sedimentary Petrology*, **56**, 862–875.

RILEY, N. J., VARKER, W. J., OWENS, B., HIGGINS, A. C. & RAMSBOTTOM, W. H. C. 1987. Stonehead Beck, Cowling, North Yorkshire, England: A British proposal for the Mid-Carboniferous boundary stratotype. *Courier Forschungsinstitut Senckenberg*, **98**, 159–177.

SHACKLETON, J. S. 1962. Cross-strata of the Rough Rock (Millstone Grit Series) in the pennines. *Liverpool and Manchester Geological Journal*, **3**, 109–118.

SMITH, N. D. 1970. The braided stream depositional environment: comparison of the Platte River with some Silurian classic rocks, North Central Appalachians. *Geological Society of America Bulletin*, **81**, 2993–3014.

—— 1971. Transverse bars and braiding in the lower Platte River, Nebraska. *Geological Society of America Bulletin*, **82**, 3407–3420.

—— 1972. Some sedimentological aspects of planar cross-stratification in a sandy braided river. *Journal of Sedimentary Petrology*, **42**, 624–634.

STEELE, R. P. 1988. The Namurian sedimentary history of the Gainsborough Trough. *In*: BESLY, B. & KELLING, G. (eds) *Sedimentation in a synorogenic basin complex.* Blackie, Glasgow, 102–113.

TEICHMULLER, M. & TEICHMULLER, R. 1982. The geological basis of coal formation. *In*: STACH, E., MACKOWSKY, M.-TH., TEICHMULLER, M., TAYLOR, G. H., CHANDRA, D. & TEICHMULLER, R. (eds) *Stach's Textbook on Coal Petrology*. Berlin, Gebruder Borntraeger, 5–86.

TONKS, L. H., JONES, R. C. B., LLOYD, W. & SHERLOCK, R. L. 1931. *The geology of Manchester*. Memoirs of the Geological Survey of Great Britain, sheet 85, H.M.S.O., London.

THOMAS, R. G., SMITH, D. G., WOOD, J. M., VISSER, J., CALVERLY-RANGE, E. A. & KOSTER, E. 1987. Inclined heterolithic stratification — Terminology, description, interpretation and significance. *Sedimentary Geology*, **53**, 123–179.

VAIL, P. R., MITCHUM, R. M. Jr. & THOMPSON, S. 1977. Seismic stratigraphy and global changes in sea-level, part 4: global cycles of relative changes in sea-level. *In*: PAYTON, C. E. (ed.) *Seismic Stratigraphy — Applications to Hydrocarbon Exploration*. American Association of Petroleum Geologists Memoirs, **26**, 83–97.

WILLIAMS, P. F. & RUST, B. R. 1969. The sedimentology of a braided river. *Journal of Sedimentary Petrology*, **39**, 649–679.

WRIGHT, D. A., SHERLOCK, R. L., WRAY, D. A., LLOYD, W. & TONKS, L. H. 1927. *The geology of the Rossendale anticline*. Memoir of the Geological Survey of Great Britain, sheet 76, H.M.S.O., London.

The architecture of fluvial–deltaic sequences in the Upper Mesaverde Group (Upper Cretaceous), Book Cliffs, Utah

ANDREW D. MIALL

Department of Geology, University of Toronto, Toronto, Ontario M5S 3B1, Canada

Abstract: The Mesaverde Group is a clastic wedge that prograded eastward into the Western Interior Basin from the Sevier Orogen of central Utah during the Late Cretaceous. The Blackhawk Formation and the overlying Castlegate Sandstone represent tongues of fluvial-deltaic and shoreface strata that prograded far into the basin in response to pulses of tectonism.

The Desert Member of the Blackhawk Formation includes two fourth-order stratigraphic sequences and the Castlegate Sandstone represents the lower part of a third sequence. The upper two sequences begin with regional erosion surfaces, above which widespread fluvial blankets represent backfill deposits formed during periods of relative base-level rise. Transgressive and highstand deposits are poorly represented at the top of the Blackhawk Formation, having probably been removed by erosion prior to Castlegate sedimentation. The overriding tectonic control of this fluvial–deltaic wedge is demonstrated by regional changes in paleoslope and detrital sources. However, the sequence architecture indicates that this regional tectonism was modulated by short-term base-level changes, of tectonic or eustatic origin.

Architectural-element analysis of the fluvial units indicates deposition predominantly by large bars (macroforms) in braided river systems. The bars developed by lateral, oblique and downstream accretion. They combine laterally and vertically to form widespread sandstone sheets typically capped by thin mudstones and bounded by flat erosion surfaces. The sheets and their component bars thicken from an average of 4–6 m in the Price area to 6–9 m east of Green River, 140 km down palaeoslope, probably as a result of tributary amalgamation and consequent deepening of the river system. In the subsurface such sheets would define flow units for production purposes. However, they are not internally homogeneous, consisting of bar sandstones <400 m in lateral dimensions, and bar increments and small channels >120 m long and wide. Many of these heterogeneities are bounded by mudstone units, and contain dipping accretion surfaces which could act as baffles to lateral fluid movement.

The Mesaverde Group is a clastic wedge of Late Cretaceous (Campanian–Maastrichtian) age that prograded from the Sevier Orogen of central Utah eastward across the Western Interior Basin of Utah and Colorado (Figs 1 & 2). The Desert Member of the Blackhawk Formation, and the overlying Castlegate Sandstone Member of the Price River Formation, are two of several fluvial–deltaic units in the clastic wedge, all of which intertongue with marine strata of the Mancos Shale toward the east, revealing a repeated history of coastal-plain progradation and transgression throughout much of the Late Cretaceous. The Mesaverde Group is superbly exposed in the Book Cliffs of east-central Utah, where it has been widely studied for the examples of various shallow-marine and nonmarine depositional environments which it illustrates. In recent years developments in the study of sequence stratigraphy have renewed interest in the group.

The present study was undertaken in an attempt to combine two current strands of sedimentological research that concern themselves with the detailed architecture of clastic units. Firstly, recent developments in sequence stratigraphy (Wilgus *et al.* 1988) have led to uncertainties regarding the sedimentary controls of fluvial sedimentation within stratigraphic sequences (e.g. Miall 1991*a*). In successions of intertonguing marine and nonmarine strata, such as the Mesaverde Group, do the fluvial units represent relatively high or low stands of sea level? Is sea-level change (of tectonic or eustatic origin) the main control of fluvial progradation, or is progradation brought about primarily by tectonically-induced changes in slope and sediment supply? In other words, does the intertonguing seen in the Mesaverde Group

From Best, J. L. & Bristow, C. S. (eds), 1993, *Braided Rivers*, Geological Society Special Publication No. **75**, pp. 305–332.

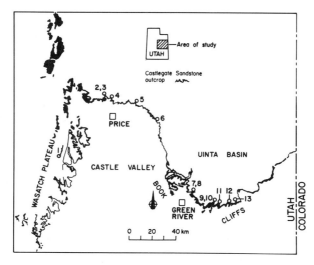

Fig. 1. Outcrop distribution of Castlegate Sandstone (after Van de Graaff 1972), and location of sections studied. Location numbers used in text are: 1, Joes Valley reservoir; 2, Castle Gate-A; 3, Castle Gate-B; 4, Willow Creek; 5, Soldier Creek; 6, Sunnyside; 7, Tusher Canyon-A; 8, Tusher Canyon-B; 9, Floy Wash-A; 10, Floy Wash-B; 11, Crescent Canyon; 12, Thompson Canyon-A; 13, Thompson Canyon-B. Precise location information is provided in the captions to each of the profiles.

represent upstream or downstream controls? This paper explores the recent sequence-stratigraphic analysis of the Castlegate Sandstone by Van Wagoner *et al.* (1990), and confirms and amplifies the main conclusions of that work.

Secondly, there has been a concerted attempt in recent years, particularly within some of the major petroleum companies, to improve our knowledge and understanding of the geometry of sandstone bodies by the collection of outcrop analogue data. This knowledge is applied to the study of reservoir heterogeneity in order to improve the efficiency of enhanced-recovery projects (Lake & Carroll 1986; Miall & Tyler 1991). To bring about improvements in pro-

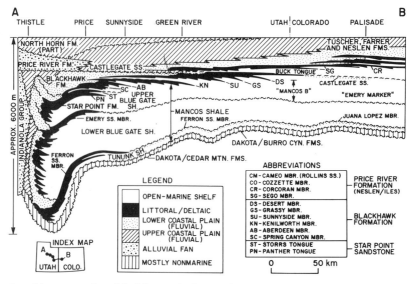

Fig. 2. Stratigraphic cross-section of the Mesaverde Group with associated strata, Book Cliffs (after Cole & Friberg 1989).

duction efficiency is typically the task of the reservoir engineer, who requires very specific, quantitative information on reservoir architecture. Such information is sparse. Petroleum geologists and sedimentologists have not, in general, paid enough attention to the three-dimensional geometry of sandstone bodies and their internal heterogeneities. This is particularly the case for fluvial reservoirs, which are difficult to correlate from field to field, and even within fields, and are difficult to break down into their component units because of the ubiquity of facies changes and the complex, three-dimensional geometry of most fluvial bodies. The Upper Desert Member and Castlegate Sandstone were selected for detailed architectural study because they offered the opportunity for the examination of well-exposed examples of fluvial architecture along a transect extending approximately 140 km down palaeoslope. Data reported here reveal some of the changes in fluvial style and consequent depositional architecture that take place across a sandy coastal-plain fluvial system, between the fringes of a belt of proximal conglomeratic alluvial fans and the deltaic marginal-marine zone. Architectural details of numerous individual macroforms are presented.

Regional setting and previous work

The Mesaverde Group is part of the sedimentary fill of the Western Interior Basin, a retroarc foreland basin that developed during the Sevier Orogeny (Jordan 1981; Fouch et al. 1983). The Castlegate Sandstone was named after prominent cliffs of the sandstone in the canyon of Price River, 7.5 km upstream from the railroad town of Helper, Utah (Spieker & Reeside 1925). A detailed stratigraphic study of the Castlegate Sandstone and the underlying and overlying units was carried out by Young (1955), who revised the system of member nomenclature applied to the numerous marine tongues. The Desert Member is named and defined in that paper. The first detailed sedimentological study of the Castlegate Sandstone was carried out by Van de Graaff (1972), who listed earlier stratigraphic work in the area. He recognized five main facies belts within the Castlegate Sandstone (Fig. 3): (1) a proximal piedmont conglomerate facies underlying the Wasatch Plateau in the west; (2) a broad fluvial belt extending from about 50 km west of Price eastward to Green River, (3) a narrow delta-plain and (4) shoreline facies belts occupying a combined zone about 35 km wide east of Green

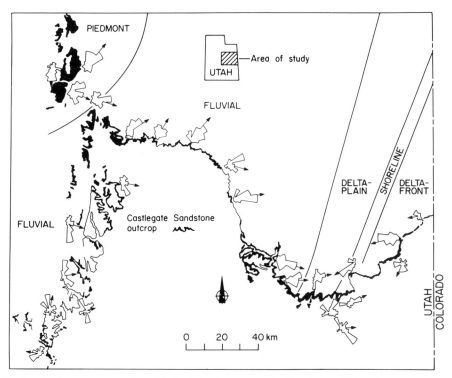

Fig. 3. Regional palaeocurrent trends and facies belts documented by Van de Graaff (1972).

River; (5) a delta-front zone extending east from there into Colorado. Van de Graaf (1972) also reported a regional paleocurrent study of the Castlegate Sandstone (Fig. 3). In the proximal area, north and west of Price, regional transport directions were toward the northeast, oblique to the generally NNE–SSW orientation of the Sevier orogen. Along the Book Cliffs east of Price, regional transport directions swing around to easterly, and become rather variable east of Green River, in the coastal zones.

Fouch et al. (1983) focused on the tectonic control of sedimentation in the basin, and attempted to improve the correlations between tectonic episodes in the Sevier Orogen and stratigraphic events in the foreland basin. This work was carried further by the detailed petrographic analysis of Dickinson et al. (1986), and Lawton (1985, 1986). These authors documented the shifts in detrital sediment sources during the Late Cretaceous and early Cenozoic, and related them to regional transport directions. It is clear from this work that the main control of the architecture of the Mesaverde Group is tectonism. In general terms, and in the detail of some of the major tongues of the clastic wedge, the development of clastic pulses can be correlated with the uplift of different parts of the Sevier orogen. Lawton (1986) was able to relate detrital modes in the Mesaverde Group and overlying Palaeocene North Horn Formation to changes in the structural evolution of the orogen and the foreland basin, with earlier units derived from the fold-thrust belt west of the basin, and later units derived in part from 'thick-skinned' basement uplifts within the basin. Changes in regional transport directions during the Late Cretaceous and early Cenozoic point to regional tilting caused by ongoing tectonism during sedimentation.

A quite different approach to the upper Mesaverde Group was taken by Van Wagoner et al. (1990). They applied the Exxon sequence models of Posamentier et al. (1988) and Posamentier & Vail (1988) to this and other units, in an exploration of the detailed stratigraphic response of coastal and marine clastic systems to base-level change. The interfingering of facies units documented by Young (1955), Van de Graaf (1972) and others was shown to be the result of repeated transgression and regression reflecting short-term (10^5 years) relative changes in sea level. Van Wagoner et al. (1990) interpreted the changes in sea level as eustatic in origin, but did not discuss the evidence for upstream tectonic control summarized in the preceding paragraph. They suggested as a general principle for the analysis of many basins that the 'higher-frequency eustatic overprint is superposed on the lower frequency or non-cyclic tectonic and sediment-supply controls'. This interpretation may apply to the Castlegate Sandstone, although the relative importance of the various controls has yet to be precisely evaluated.

Sequence stratigraphy

The Castlegate Sandstone and underlying Blackhawk Formation are Campanian in age. They range in combined total thickness from 470 m in the cliffs northwest of Price, to 50 m at Thompson Canyon. Most of this thickness decrease is the result of facies change of the Blackhawk Formation eastward into the Mancos Shale. Young's (1955) stratigraphic synthesis indicates that time-equivalent beds of the Blackhawk Formation actually increase in thickness eastward (deeper into the foreland basin), although he was not able to trace the base of the Blackhawk Formation along the entire Book Cliffs outcrop belt, and so the exact thickness increase cannot be determined. The Castlegate Sandstone decreases in thickness from 155 m at the type section, to 17 m at Thompson Canyon. Young (1955) concluded that the contact between the Blackhawk and Castlegate is a disconformity, an interpretation that is followed by Van Wagoner et al. (1990), who placed a sequence boundary there. Figure 4 is an adaptation of part of their cross-section of the Book Cliffs east of Green River (Van Wagoner et al. 1990, fig. 31), with additional sections measured by this writer, and a differentiation of various sandstone types on the basis of environmental interpretations, the basis for which is discussed later. The Castlegate Sandstone constitutes the lower part of sequence 3 of Van Wagoner et al. (1990). It rests on the Upper Desert Member, which constitutes sequence 2.

The synthesis of Van Wagoner et al. (1990) contains a radical reinterpretation of the stratigraphy reported by Young (1955). Both syntheses result from very detailed field work, with the tracing of beds and contacts by foot and on panoramic field photographs; but the sequence model of Van Wagoner et al. (1990) reinterprets an important contact within the Desert Member as a regional disconformity and sequence boundary, rather than as a series of local scour surfaces of different ages, as suggested by Young (1955). Young (1955, p. 195) noted that 'littoral marine sandstones' in the Desert Member have sharply defined tops, and that the tops rise stratigraphically to the east, especially in the area between Coal

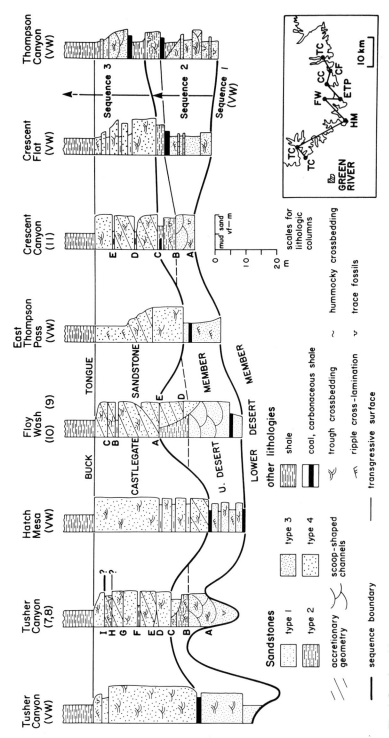

Fig. 4. Stratigraphic cross-section, Tusher Canyon to Thompson Canyon. Based on Van Wagoner et al. (1990) with additional sections by the writer. Sections from Van Wagoner et al. (1990) are indicated by (VW). Those forming the subject of this paper are shown by the location numbers. Major bounding surfaces in these sections are indicated by letters. The sequence interpretation and the differentiation into sandstone assemblage types are discussed in the text.

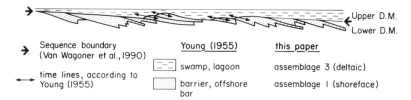

Fig. 5. Barrier bar-lagoonal interpretation of the Desert Member, according to Young (1955), and the sequence reinterpretation by Van Wagoner *et al.* (1990).

Canyon and Thompson Canyon. Figure 5 illustrates Young's (1955) interpretation of these sandstone tops. The overlying lenticular shales and sandstone with coals were interpreted as swamp and lagoonal deposits by Young (1955). They rest on the flat tops of the underlying sandstones, which were 'produced as subaerial gradation planes truncating successive beach planes as the land built seaward. The truncation was by currents transporting sand seaward, as testified by local channelling, and by the action of waves and ocean currents' (Young 1955, p. 195). The lagoonal and swamp deposits, in this interpretation, developed above each sandstone tongue as bar sedimentation stepped seaward, and are therefore contemporaneous with the sandstones. The new insight by Van Wagoner *et al.* (1990) is that these local scour surfaces in fact represent a single, continuous bounding surface, that they define as the contact between their sequences 1 and 2. The fine-grained clastics of the Upper Desert Member do not pass laterally into a bedding plane within the underlying sandstones, as Young's (1955) model would indicate (Fig. 5), but they rest on and drape over irregularities in the top surface of those sandstones. Local relief on the sequence boundary is at least 10 m, and, as shown by Van Wagoner *et al.* (1990, fig. 31), this surface cuts up across at least 60 m of beds between Tusher Canyon and Thompson Canyon. The detailed profile work by this writer has confirmed the utility of this interpretation (see later discussion).

Van Wagoner *et al.* (1990) did not distinguish fluvial from estuarine and other facies in their stratigraphic reconstruction of the Blackhawk and Castlegate succession. Detailed local examination by this author has permitted a subdivision into four types of sandstone-dominated lithofacies assemblages (Fig. 4), and has permitted some refinements of the sequence model. At Tusher Canyon (Loc. 8) beds of probable marginal-marine facies were mapped within the Castlegate Sandstone (between surfaces H and I, Fig. 4; environmental interpretation is dis-

cussed in the next section). Elsewhere this facies represents transgressive or highstand systems tract deposits (Van Wagoner *et al.* 1990). Its presence within the Castlegate suggests that this unit may not, in fact, consist of a single sequence, but represents a composite of more than one sequence of higher order. This stratigraphic configuration has not been recorded elsewhere along the Book Cliffs. However, in most of the Castlegate outcrops examined by this writer the member is characterized by prominent, laterally extensive bounding surfaces. While most of these surfaces are interpreted as channel scours some could be sequence boundaries, representing erosional events of regional significance (see, for example, discussion of Joes Valley, Castle Gate-B, and Willow Creek profiles, below). There would be little to distinguish these two types of surface in any single outcrop, and it would require extremely detailed mapping to check the hypothesis of intra-Castlegate sequences.

Methods of architectural analysis

Field methods employed for this study were those of architectural-element analysis, as developed by Miall (1985, 1988) from the pioneering work of Allen (1983). Outcrop analysis begins with the construction of photomosaics of the outcrop and tracing all field information onto an overlay in the field. Particular attention is paid to the drawing in of all internal bounding surfaces and locating as precisely as possible all paleocurrent measurements. Clean, vertical cliff faces in the Castlegate Sandstone provide excellent exposures of bounding surfaces, enabling reconstructions of internal element geometry in two dimensions to be carried out. However, such faces are typically not accessible for detailed sedimentological interpretations. It is therefore necessary to also select faces which are less precipitous, to permit ground observations. In such cases bounding surfaces may be less clear, and the shape of the exposure surface may introduce perspective problems and shape distortions in the resulting profile. Nevertheless, this method has been found to provide an extremely powerful tool for the reconstruction of the internal architecture (heterogeneity) of sandstone bodies.

Bounding surfaces are interpreted in the field or in the office on the basis of geometric information and, if available, palaeocurrent data. They are assigned rank designations from the hierarchy of depositional units and bounding surfaces listed in Table 1. Lithofacies are classified using the scheme of Miall (1977, 1978), as listed in Table 2. Architectural-element designations are made on the basis of their external and internal geometry, with the aid of palaeocurrent data (as discussed below). The main types of architectural element are listed in Table 3. The methodology of field work and interpretation was described more completely by Miall (1988), and the book edited by Miall &

Tyler (1991) contains several examples of the application of the methodology. Some examples of the interpretive arguments are included in the ensuing discussion, to illustrate the methods.

It has long been recognized that paleocurrent data are susceptible to analysis on a hierarchical basis, with the scale of the rock sample from which readings are taken corresponding to a particular level of variance within the depositional system (Allen 1966; Miall 1974). Such palaeocurrent analysis carried out within a framework of architectural-element analysis, as used here, provides a particularly powerful tool of geometrical and architectural analysis, providing, for example, the third geometrical dimension for two-dimensional outcrop profiles (the dip and orientation of accretion surfaces), and data on internal bar orientations and channel sinuosities. Sophisticated use can be made of limited date, if the date are properly

Table 1. *Hierarchy of depositional units in alluvial deposits*

Group	Time scale of proc. (a)	Examples of processes	Instaneous sed. rate (m/ka)	Fluvial, deltaic depositional units	Rank and characteristics of bounding surfaces
1	10^{-6}	Burst-sweep cycle		Lamina	0th-order lamination surface
2	10^{-5}–10^{-4}	Bedform migration	10^5	Ripple (microform)	1st-order, set bounding surface
3	10^{-3}	Bedform migration	10^5	Diurnal dune increment, reactivation surface	1st-order, set bounding surface
4	10^{-2}–10^{-1}	Bedform migration	10^4	Dune (mesoform)	2nd-order, co-set bounding surface
5	10^0–10^1	Seasonal events, 10-year flood	10^{2-3}	Macroform growth increment	3rd-order, dipping 5–20° in in direction of accretion. Downlaps on higher-order surfaces
6	10^2–10^3	100-year flood, bar migration	10^{2-3}	Macroform, e.g., point bar, levee, splay	4th-order, flat to convex-up macroform top. Downlaps on higher-order surfaces
7	10^3–10^4	Long term geomorphic processes	10^0–10^1	Channel, delta lobe	5th-order, flat to concave-up channel base
8	10^4–10^5	5th-order (Milankovitch) cycles	10^{-1}	Channel belt, sequence	6th-order, flat, regionally extensive, sequence boundary
9	10^5–10^6	4th-order (Milankovitch) cycles	10^{-5}–10^{-2}	Depo. system, alluvial fan, sequence	7th-order, flat, regionally extensive, sequence boundary
10	10^6–10^7	3rd-order cycles, tectonic and eustatic processes	10^{-1}–10^{-2}	Basin-fill complex	8th-order, regional disconformity

Modified from Miall (1988, 1991*b*).

Table 2. *Lithofacies classification from Miall (1977, 1978)*

Facies code	Lithofacies	Sedimentary structures	Interpretation
Gm	Massive or crudely bedded gravel	Horizontal bedding, imbrication	Longitudinal bars, lag deposits, sieve deposits
St	Sand, medium to v. coarse, may be pebbly	Solitary or grouped trough crossbeds	3D dunes (lower flow regime)
Sp	Sand, medium to v. coarse, may be pebbly	Solitary or grouped planar crossbeds	2D dunes (lower flow regime)
Sr	Sand, very fine to coarse	Ripple marks	Ripples (lower flow regime)
Sh	Sand, v. fine to v. coarse, may be pebbly	Horizontal lamination, parting or streaming lineation	Planar bed flow (upper flow regime)
Sl	Sand, v. fine to v. coarse, may be pebbly	Low-angle ($< 10°$) crossbeds	Scour fills, washed-out dunes, antidunes
Ss	Sand, fine to v. coarse, may be pebbly	Broad, shallow scours	Scour fills
Fl	Sand, silt, mud	Fine lamination, v. small ripples	Overbank or waning flood deposits
Fm	Mud, silt	Massive, desiccation cracks	Overbank or drape deposits
C	Coal, carbonaceous mud	Plant, mud films	Swamp deposits

located within the outcrop. The collection of large numbers of readings loosely located within large outcrops is no longer considered useful by this writer.

Palaeocurrent data for the Castlegate Sandstone are summarized in Table 4, including the regional azimuth means obtained from the study of crossbed orientations by Van de Graaf (1972). Statistics have been calculated using the method of Curray (1956). In most sections adequate data are available to permit separate calculations of mean azimuth and variance for some of the individual elements. Even where such data are not statistically significant, they can aid in element interpretation. The palaeo-current trends of Van de Graaf (1972) (Fig. 3, Table 4) are taken here to represent local average trends of the Castlegate fluvial system. They were collected from the entire thickness of the sandstone at each location, and can there-fore be considered representative of the long-term average, with the effects of local channel sinuosities smoothed out. In most cases the out-crop means derived from the present study are not significantly different from those of Van de Graaf (1972). Where there are large differences,

Table 3. *Architectural elements in the Castlegate Sandstone and upper Desert Member*

Element	Symbol	Principal lithofacies assemblages	Geometry and relationships
Channels	CH	Any combination	Finger, lens or sheet; concave-up erosional base; scale and shape highly variable; internal concave-up 3rd-order erosion surfaces common
Sandy bedforms	SB	St, Sp, Sh, Sl, Sr	Lens, sheet, blanket, wedge, tabular internal geometry; occurs as channel-fills, crevasse splays, minor bars
Downstream accretion macroforms	DA	St, Sp, Sh, Sl	Lens resting on flat or channelled base, with convex-up 3rd-order internal erosion surfaces and upper 4th-order bounding surfaces
Lateral accretion macroform	LA	St, Sp, Sh, Sl	Wedge, sheet, lobe; characterized by internal lateral-accretion 3rd-order surfaces
Overbank fines	OF	Fm, Fl	Thin to thick blankets; commonly interbedded with SB; may fill abandoned channels

Modified from Miall (1985, 1988). Lithofacies classification from Miall (1978).

Table 4. *Summary of palaeocurrent data*

Location	Loc. no.	Elements	n	Mean azimuth	Vec. mag. percent	Arith. variance	Rayleigh test	Regional mean*
Castle Gate-A	2	all	8	113	86	995	.2E − 02	030
Willow Creek	4	all	26	078	50	3906	.1E − 02	030
		3	3	158	92	506	.8E − 01	
		8	5	110	68	2746	.9E − 01	
Soldier Creek	5	12, 13	17	051	57	3230	.4E − 02	040
		all	26	027	71	2102	.2E − 05	
		1	7	033	85	1014	.6E − 02	
		3	16	013	70	3032	.2E − 03	
Sunnyside	6	all	51	106	53	3947	.5E − 06	110
		1	4	054	91	85286	.4E − 01	
		2	45	107	56	4403	.5E − 06	
Tusher Canyon-A	7	all	15	132	45	5014	.5E − 01	090
		2	9	153	93	467	.4E − 03	
		4	5	030	82	1256	.3E − 01	
Tusher Canyon-B	8	all	56	076	33	6087	.3E − 02	090
		1	3	124	18	27248	.9E + 00	
		2	7	011	94	14181	.2E − 02	
		3	15	028	88	10609	.9E − 05	
		4	15	146	40	20906	.9E − 01	
		5	9	150	71	7569	.1E − 01	
		6	7	131	78	1866	.1E − 01	
Floy Wash-A	9	all	43	141	75	2027	.3E − 10	080
		2	6	122	69	5869	.6E − 01	
		3	15	163	88	4780	.1E − 04	
		4	8	116	63	6569	.4E − 01	
		5	7	138	90	6906	.4E − 02	
		6	7	131	78	1866	.1E − 01	
Floy Wash-B	10	all	38	102	72	2356	.3E − 08	080
		1	16	128	82	7257	.2E − 04	
		2	12	074	64	4053	.7E − 02	
		3	10	086	92	3190	.2E − 03	
Crescent Canyon	11	all	34	103	83	1220	.6E − 10	076
		2	9	091	78	1561	.4E − 02	
		3	6	076	92	8025	.6E − 02	
		4	6	139	90	4225	.7E − 02	
		5	13	105	93	467	.1E − 04	
Thompson Canyon-A	12	all	8	322	46	4463	.2E − 00	088
		1	2	338	98	156	.1E − 00	
		3	5	339	33	5285	.6E − 00	
Thompson Canyon-B	13	all	23	189	56	18132	.7E − 03	088
		1	10	351	84	9578	.9E − 03	
		2	13	037	44	4293	.8E − 01	
Sagers Canyon	14	all	6	182	93	25990	.6E − 02	066

*Values in this column taken from Van de Graaff (1972).

it probably reflects the limited data available from the present study (Castle Gate-A, Thompson Canyon-A and -B, Sagers Canyon), and the weak trends displayed by the Castlegate where it becomes deltaic in facies to the east. In some cases (e.g., Floy Wash-A) large divergence between Van de Graaf's data and that of this study may indicate that the elements measured for this report all diverged from the regional mean. This is a feasible interpretation given the sinuosity of all fluvial systems, even those of braided type.

Interpretations of individual elements are made with the use of these data, plus measurements of the orientation of dipping second-, third-, and fourth-order accretion surfaces. These data are shown individually on the profiles and are discussed in the next section. It was not possible to collect enough of these measurements to treat them statistically. The method of interpretation is as follows. Where the orientation of the accretion surface and that of the cross-bedding within the same element are within about 60° of each other it indicates that the element grew by accretion in a direction parallel or oblique to *local* flow, and the element is designated a DA (downstream-accretion) unit, even if local flow is orientated at a high angle to the regional trend. Where the orientations of the accretionary surfaces and the cross-bedding are more nearly perpendicular (<60° difference) the element is designated an LA (lateral-accretion) unit. DA and LA geometries may be present in different parts of the same macroform and may consist of similar lithofacies (as at Floy Wash-B; see discussion below). These orientations may or may not be close to that of the regional mean, reflecting local sinuosities. For example, accretionary dips and cross-bed directions in DA units may be orientated at a high angle to the regional mean if the channel in which it formed has a locally high sinuosity (an example is illustrated later). The orientation of individual lateral-accretion surfaces may shown no relationship to regional mean, although if enough were studied to permit statistical treatment (as was not the case in the present study) their average orientation would be expected to approximate the regional mean.

In some outcrops elements defined as macroforms (LA or DA) are interbedded with sheets labelled SB. In such cases all bounding surfaces are horizontal in outcrop, suggesting accumulation of the element as a tabular sheet. However, it is possible that the outcrop is parallel to the strike of dipping accretion surfaces, in which case the designation SB is incorrect. This possibility should be borne in mind when examining the profiles. A good example was identified at Tusher Canyon, and is described below.

On the profiles, where adequate data are present to justify classification of bounding surfaces and elements, they are assigned identifying codes. Bounding surfaces of fifth- and sixth-order rank are lettered from base to top of the outcrop in capital letters. Elements are numbered in the same order, and, where possible, the number is followed by the two-letter element code given in Table 3. In places elements may contain distinct third- and fourth-order surfaces, which are designated by Roman numerals. The element so subdivided is labelled parts A, B etc. For example, the code designation 2B-LA would indicate the second unit to be deposited within element 2, and which is interpreted as a lateral-accretion deposit. Although this coding seems complex, once the user is familiar with it, it facilitates quick 'reading' and comprehension of profiles.

Lithofacies assemblages

Four main lithofacies assemblages can be differentiated, based primarily on study of the sandstones in the Upper Desert Member and the Castlegate Sandstone.

Lithofacies Assemblage 1. This assemblage is dominated by sandstone, which is fine-grained, thick-bedded, with horizontal and wavy laminae, oscillation ripples, hummocky cross-stratification, rare trough cross-bedding, and feeding trails. Following Van Wagoner et al. (1990) this type of sandstone is interpreted as the deposit of shoreface environments, or of wave-influenced shoals. The beds beneath the sequence boundary at the base of sequence 1, constituting the upper part of the Lower Desert Member in the Green River area, are typically of this assemblage. A tentative identification of the assemblage was also made in the Upper Desert Member at Tusher Canyon-B profile, below bounding surface C (Fig. 4).

Lithofacies Assemblage 2. This assemblage consists of very fine-grained, thin-bedded sandstone, which is laminated, and contains abundant ripple cross-lamination (lithofacies Sr), Trough cross-bedding (St) is rare to common. Horizontal feeding trails and other trace fossils are typically present. The beds are interpreted as low-energy marginal-marine in origin, forming in such environments as lagoons or estuarine-interdeltaic shoals.

Lithofacies Assemblage 3. Sandstone, fine-grained, interbedded with shale, abundant St, deformed cross-bedding, water-escape structures, trace fossils, oyster beds. The assemblage is characterized by clinoform units up to at least 20 m thick, and scoop-shaped channels. The channels typically have erosive bases which incise up to 10 m into the underlying beds. This assemblage was formed as distributary channels, and as channel-mouth Gilbertian deltas.

Lithofacies Assemblage 4. Sandstone, in sheets several metres thick, thin- to thick-bedded, typically fine-grained, but may be very fine- to medium-grained. Lags of plant fragments are common at the base of units. St abundant, Sp, Sh and Sr rare. Evidence of lateral and downstream accretion is common. Minor associated lithofacies include interbedded shale and siltstone beds, carbonaceous shale, and thin coals. Sideritic nodules, and dinosaur bones and footprints are locally common, especially in associated fine-grained beds. This assemblage is interpreted as fluvial in origin. The element assemblage includes DA, LA and SB, and is characteristic of braided fluvial environments.

Summary of profiles

A brief description of the main features of each profile (Figs 6–18) is presented in this section, in order to indicate how the main element and bounding-surface classifications have been carried out, and to clarify the sequence model shown in Fig. 4. All profiles are of the Castlegate Sandstone. In some, underlying beds of the Desert Member have also been included. Palaeocurrent data are summarized in Table 4. Thicknesses of sandstone sheets defined by fifth-order bounding surfaces at each location are summarized in Table 5. Note the general increase in sheet thickness toward the east. An example of the development of an environ-

mental interpretation from profile data is given in Fig. 19. Photographs of important outcrop features are shown in Fig. 20.

Joes Valley Reservoir (Location 1; Fig. 6)

This section is largely inaccessible because of the steepness of the cliff. It is included here because the outcrop illustrates at least two types of major bounding surface. The top of the Blackhawk Formation is interpreted regionally as a sequence boundary, and it is therefore of sixth-order rank.

The Castlegate Sandstone consists here of assemblage 4. In general it is characterized by numerous horizontal or near-horizontal bounding surfaces traversing the entire cliff. They have been designated surfaces A to M, but it is likely that in some intervals, notably between surfaces J and L, additional major surfaces are present but have not been made visible by weathering. Surfaces A to M are interpreted as channel-scour fifth-order surfaces. A few of the sheet-like elements defined by these surfaces display evidence of internal accretion, with third- and fourth-order surfaces in evidence. The outcrop is oriented approximately parallel to regional palaeocurrent trends of Van de Graaf (1972) (no data collection was possible from the actual cliff face), and the easterly (along-cliff to the right) dip of most of the accretion surfaces may therefore indicate downstream accretion.

It is possible that some of the major bounding surfaces in this outcrop represent erosional breaks more significant than those between individual braided channels. Gentle tectonic tilting could produce pauses in sedimentation, or subtle changes in palaeoslope orientation. The results would be surfaces of sixth-order rank, separating distinct nonmarine stratigraphic sequences. At Joes Valley, surface E truncates surfaces C and D at a very acute angle, and

Table 5. *Summary of element thicknesses*

Location	Loc. no.	Range (m)	Average (m)	*n*
Castle Gate-A	2	1.4–7.9	4.1	9
Willow Creek	4	3.5–7.5	4.4	10
Soldier Creek	5	2.8–10.6	5.9	6
Sunnyside	6	4.6–13.6	7.5	4
Tusher Canyon	7, 8	2.4–12.6	5.7	9
Floy Wash	9, 10	3.1–14.8	8.8	3
Crescent Canyon	11	7.0–8.2	7.6	2

(Units defined by 5th-order surfaces, Castlegate Sandstone only).

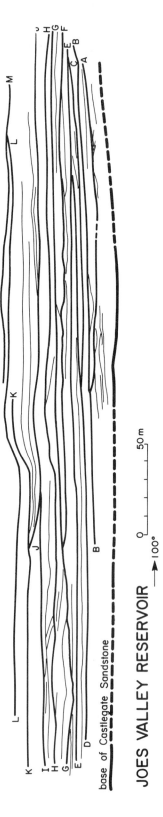

comes close to truncating surface B, which would add up to a total of about 10 m of section cut out over a lateral distance of less than 200 m. Such angularity, if continued for a few kilometres, would strongly suggest that surface E is a sequence boundary of sixth-order rank.

Castle Gate-A (Location 2; Fig. 7)

This outcrop is orientated oblique to regional palaeocurrent directions, although the outcrop mean calculated from the limited data collected by the writer indicates a mean nearly parallel to the outcrop face. The difference of 83° between the means probably reflects the limited data obtained during the present study (most of the cliff is inaccessible). The outcrop consists entirely of lithofacies assemblage 4, and is characterized by prominent horizontal bounding surfaces, which gives the rocks their sheet-like appearance (Fig. 20a). These are interpreted as fifth-order channel scour surfaces, and are designated local surfaces A to L.

The fifth-order surfaces A to L define 11 elements, averaging 4.1 m in thickness. Several contain laterally persistent internal bounding surfaces that are designated as fourth-order in rank, because they subdivide the element into discrete sub-elements, but are truncated by the fifth-order surfaces. Many of these fourth-order surfaces have an irregular trace across the outcrop, and are locally convex-up or concave-up,

---

Fig. 6. Joes Valley Reservoir profile. Loc. 1, Cliff face opposite dam, above Highway 29 (Locations for this and subsequent profiles are given in Fig. 1. Architectural-element and bounding-surface designations are explained in the text).

LEGEND FOR OUTCROP PROFILES

BOUNDING SURFACES

— A — sixth order (sequence boundary)

— B — fifth order (sheet, major channel)

— c^i — fourth order (sub-sheet, macroform, minor channel)

— D^{ii} — third order (minor erosion, macroform reactivation)

——— first and second order (set and coset boundaries)

ELEMENTS AND FACIES

2B-CH   element number and type

St,Sr   lithofacies type

m   mudstone bed

ORIENTATIONS

⊤   dip and strike of accretion surface

↗   paleocurrent direction (relative to outcrop face. paleocurrent north indicated at base of profile)

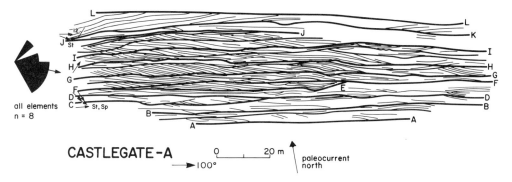

Fig. 7. Castle Gate-A profile. Loc. 2. East side of Price River valley, 600 m north of the Castle Gate.

suggesting an origin as a bar growth surface or as a local channel scour, respectively. It is this irregular shape of the fourth-order surfaces, and the fact that none are as prominent in a weathered cliff face as the fifth-order surfaces (because of an absence of lithologic change across them) that permits the distinction between the fourth- and fifth-order ranks to be made. All the elements contain internal inclined accretion surfaces, indicating that the elements represent large bar complexes (macroforms, in the terminology of Jackson 1975). In elements 2 to 10 apparent accretionary dips are along the cliff face to the east (no orientation measurements were possible), which is in the same quadrant as the regional palaeocurrent direction. These elements are probably, therefore, DA units, developed by downstream to oblique accretion. Element 11 shows accretionary dips in the opposite direction, and this is confirmed by a single orientation measurement on a second-order surface, of 315°. This is at a high angle

to palaeocurrent trends, and the element may be a LA unit.

Castle Gate-B (Location 3; Fig. 8)

No palaeocurrent data could be collected from this outcrop. It is included here because it shows an interesting contrast to the previous outcrop, which represents the same stratigraphic interval 600 m to the north. Prominent horizontal bounding surfaces are present throughout, as at Castle Gate-A, although none can be recognized in the thick interval defined by surfaces B and C, which is undoubtedly a multistorey unit. Several of the elements contain fourth-order surfaces comparable in shape and weathering character to those at Castle Gate-A. Few accretion surfaces can be identified. This is probably because the cliff face is orientated nearly perpendicular to that at Castle Gate-A, and is therefore parallel to the strike of the accretion surfaces.

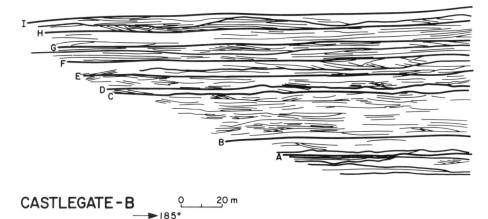

Fig. 8. Castle Gate–B profile. Loc. 3. North face of the Castle Gate, east side of Price River valley.

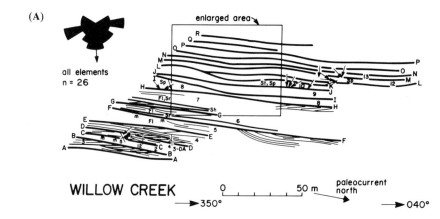

WILLOW CREEK

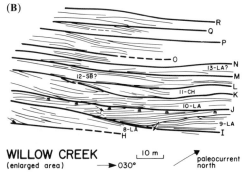

WILLOW CREEK
(enlarged area)   → 030°   paleocurrent north

Fig. 9. Willow Creek profile. Loc. 4. North side of valley, above Highway 33, 3.8 km (in straight line) NE of railroad crossing at Castle Gate Coal Mine #1. (**A**) Entire profile, (**B**) enlargement of upper part of profile.

Willow Creek (Location 4, Fig. 9)

This outcrop displays a variety of element styles, indicating a more variable fluvial system than at Castle Gate, although Willow Creek is only 4 km east of (down palaeoslope from) those outcrops. The beds are entirely of assemblage 4, and are stratigraphically higher than those at Castle Gate.

At least 18 fifth-order surfaces are present in this outcrop, although poor exposure may obscure others, such as between surfaces E and F. The underside of surface J reveals large wood impressions up to 1 m long, suggesting the transport of waterlogged plant debris as a channel-floor lag. Some minor but extensive fine-grained beds are present, below surfaces C and F, and constituting the upper part of element 6. Elements 7 and 8 consist of interbedded thin, in places carbonaceous, shale, and fine-grained sandstone.

A few elements can be interpreted with some degree of confidence. The lower part of element 3 contains accretion surfaces with dips orientated at 140°, and yielded a crossbed mean azimuth of 158°. This suggests that the element is a DA unit, although it is oriented approxi-

mately perpendicular to outcrop and regional means. Element 8 contains accretion surfaces with apparent dip along the cliff face to the north, whereas the cross-bed mean azimuth is 110°, suggesting that this is a LA unit. Element 9 displays a similar configuration, although the accretion surfaces dip in the opposite direction, obliquely into the cliff. The accretionary beds consist of a heterolithic assemblage of thin sandstones and shales (cf. IHS of Thomas *et al.* 1987). A cross-cutting third-order reactivation surface is present toward the right side of the exposure. The unit grades up into a bed of dark grey shale 40 cm thick immediately below surface J. The composition and geometry of this element is therefore typical of a fine-grained point bar (Miall 1985, model 7). Element 12 consists of a tabular sandstone sheet with abundant planar-tabular crossbedding (lithofacies Sp), and is designated a SB unit. A comparison with the simple Platte model (Miall 1977, 1985, model 9) is suggested. The combined mean azimuth for elements 12 and 13 is 051°, which is close to the regional mean.

Element 4 contains a distinctive style of load structures, as seen in cross-section; these are tentatively interpreted as dinosaur footprints (similar to those illustrated in Fig. 20c).

Soldier Creek (Location 5, Fig. 10)

This outcrop consists entirely of assemblage 4. It exposes seven major bounding surfaces, enclosing six architectural elements. Elements

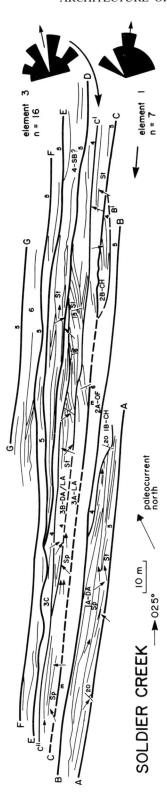

SOLDIER CREEK

paleocurrent
north

10 m

025°

1, 2 and 3 can be subdivided by the presence of internal fourth-order surfaces.

Element 1A contains accretion surfaces dipping toward the ENE (one reading of 070°), and a cross-bed mean azimuth of 033°. It is therefore interpreted as a DA unit. Surface A^i, which caps it, has an erosive, concave-up shape, suggesting channel incision, possibly during falling water (cf. Kirk 1983), and the overlying element 1B is therefore designated a CH unit. Element 2 is largely recessive, although small mudstone exposures are present beneath surface C at the south end of the profile. A minor channel (element 2B-CH) is incised into the top of this unit. Element 2 probably represents local floodplain and crevasse-channel facies.

Element 3 is a composite unit, containing two internal fourth-order surfaces, C^i and C^{ii}. Units 3A and 3B are interpreted as LA and LA/DA elements, respectively. Four readings were obtained on second-order accretion surfaces, indicating accretion directions ranging from southeast to southwest. The crossbed mean azimuth for element 3 is 013°, close to the outcrop and regional means; but this is at a high angle to the accretion directions, suggesting lateral to downstream accretion. In detail element 3A is probably a LA unit throughout, whereas element 3B may vary from DA to LA from left to right across the centre of the profile, as accretion directions swing from ENE to S.

Sunnyside (Location 6, Fig. 11)

The fluvial style in this outcrop is similar to that at Soldier Creek. At least six elements defined by fifth-order surfaces are present, although data are adequate for interpreting only two of these in detail.

Element 2 is characterized throughout by dipping minor (first- and second-order) accretion surfaces. It also contains at least five internal minor bounding surfaces, which downlap onto each other and onto surface A, and are truncated by surface B. Surface A^i separates elements 2A and 2B, in which the accretion directions are opposed (SSW–SSE versus NW–NNE, respectively). It is therefore interpreted as a fourth-order surface, separating distinct macroforms within the same sheet sandstone body. Surface A^i curves downward to the south, parallel to underlying bedding and downlaps onto surface A. This is characteristic

---

Fig. 10. Soldier Creek profile. Loc. 5. West side of valley 900 m south of junction with Ping Canyon.

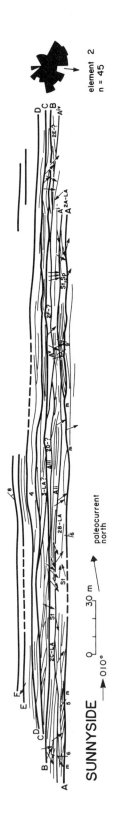

Fig. 11. Sunnyside profile. Loc. 6. West side of valley, 400 m north of Sunnyside mine gate.

of a fourth-order 'growth' surface — one of active accretion, abandoned with little or no erosion as a result of a channel-avulsion event. Surface A^{ii}, by contrast, separates elements with similar accretion directions, and is in part parallel to the minor accretion surfaces in both elements 2B and 2C. It is therefore interpreted as a third-order reactivation surface — a surface representing a pause in the accumulation of a macroform, possibly at a time of flood erosion. The mean crossbed azimuth for element 2 is 107°, identical to the regional mean. Elements 2A, 2B and 2C are interpreted as LA units. Elements 2D, 2E and 2F are considered to be eroded fragments of indeterminate type. Element 3 is probably also a LA unit, but palaeocurrent data are not available to confirm this interpretation.

Tusher Canyon-A (Location 7, Fig. 12)

This outcrop provides a good exposure of the sequence boundaries between sequences 1, 2 and 3 of Van Wagoner *et al.* (1990). Most of the field observations recorded on this profile relate to the Upper Desert Member (sequence 2), between surfaces A and C. Palaeocurrent mean directions from the Desert Member (elements 2, 3) and the Castlegate Sandstone (element 4) are different by 123°, suggesting a shift in dispersal directions across the sequence boundary (surface C), although this divergence is no greater than that present *within* some fluvial and deltaic systems.

Element 1 (in sequence 1) consists of fine-grained sandstone with hummocky cross-bedding, interbedded with thin shales and very fine-grained sandstones containing oscillation ripples and feeding trails (lithofacies assemblage 1). This assemblage is interpreted as lower shoreface deposits by Van Wagoner *et al.* (1990).

Element 2 (in sequence 2) consists of assemblage 3, comprising thin-bedded, fine- to very fine-grained sandstone, with abundant trough crossbedding and ripple marks. Vertical burrows, carbonaceous debris, plant fragments and plant impressions are locally abundant. The most distinctive feature of these elements is the abundance of numerous minor concave-up bounding surfaces, interpreted as channel scour surfaces. These fill and drape over erosional relief of the sequence boundary, surface A. The few accretion directions available for this element indicate southerly channel filling directions, which is confirmed by the average crossbed azimuth of 153° for element 2.

Surface B is laterally extensive and nearly flat in this outcrop. It presumably represents a pause in sedimentation. Element 3 is poorly exposed, but outcrops at the right end of the profile are of assemblage 2. Around the corner, At Tusher Canyon-B, beds at this level below the Castlegate Sandstone are interpreted as shoreface and marginal-marine sandstones of assemblages 1 and 2. Surface B therefore represents a transgressive surface, with the beds above constituting the transgressive systems tract of sequence 2 (an exposure of these beds somewhat further west than recorded by Van Wagoner *et al.* 1990). A small channel occurs at the top of element 3 and is designated element 3B-CH. It is filled with thin-bedded, fine-grained sandstone and siltstone with carbonaceous plant material and plant impressions, and represents a fragment of a fluvial succession that occurs at the top of sequence 2. These sequence-2 fluvial beds are better exposed at Floy Wash.

Element 4 is largely inaccessible in this outcrop. It was studied in more detail around the corner of the cliff to the northwest, in Tusher Canyon profile B.

Tusher Canyon-B (Location 8, Fig. 13)

This profile provides an excellent exposure of the Castlegate Member. It occurs at a bend in the cliff above Tusher Wash, and the profile changes orientation from NNW at the left, to ENE at the right. Seven major bounding surfaces have been mapped, including the basal sequence boundary, surface C. Elements and surfaces can be correlated around the corner between Tusher Canyon profiles A and B, and the bounding surfaces are annotated accordingly, using the same letters for both profiles. They are mostly sharp and flat, and the immediately overlying beds commonly contain large plant or wood fragments in the basal few centimetres, that probably were transported as channel-floor lags. In places, underlying surfaces F and G, there are shale beds up to about 1 m thick, with plant rootlets and scattered and weathered dinosaur bone fragments. Castlegate elements are numbered 1 to 6 in profile B. They consist of assemblage 4, except for element 5, as noted below.

Element 2 contains an internal bounding surface, E^i, which separates increments showing opposite accretion directions (in the left-hand half of the outcrop). It is therefore interpreted as a fourth-order surface. Accretion surfaces at the left-hand end of the outcrop in element 2A dip NNW and NNE, while the mean crossbed azimuth from the same beds is to the NNE (011°). These data indicate that element 2A is a DA unit, accreting obliquely downstream at about 70° to the outcrop mean (Fig. 19). Element 2B appears to be accreting in the opposite direction, but it was not possible to obtain any orientation or palaeocurrent measurements to confirm this. In the right-hand part of the outcrop (around the bend) the internal structure of element 2 consists of two macroforms separated by surface E^{ii}. Accretion surfaces in element 2B appear to dip in opposite directions at either end of the profile, but this is probably because the profile bends through 90° from left to right. The true accretionary dip of element 2B is, therefore, likely to be in the quadrant that represents the bisector of the outcrop orientations, that is, toward the ESE.

Element 3 contains no major accretion surfaces in the left-hand half of the profile, although these could be striking parallel to the outcrop. The mean azimuth, at 028°, is about 50° from the outcrop mean. The unit is tentatively interpreted as a SB element. It contains, near the bend in the outcrop, a small channel incised into its top (surface F^{ii}). This is orientated in a northwesterly direction, about 110° from the outcrop mean, and is probably a minor channel formed by surface bar run-off during falling water. Surface F^i is interpreted as a cutbank marking the eastern (right-hand) edge of this element, or scour into a midchannel macroform. Note that the dip of this surface is continued, down to the left, by surface F, suggesting that surfaces F and F^i at this point were both formed by channel scour cutting down into element 2. Bedding surfaces above and below F^i indicate accretion to the left.

Element 4 contains accretion surfaces dipping in several directions, and appears to have a complex internal structure. The element mean azimuth is 146°, which is 70° from the outcrop mean and 118° from the mean of element 3, below. Dispersion is, however, high. The element is tentatively interpreted as DA, with the difference in means between elements 3 and 4 possibly indicating the magnitude of local channel sinuosity.

Element 5 is of different facies, consisting of fine-grained sandstone weathering a white colour, paler than the yellowish-brown of the other elements. It contains abundant ripple cross-lamination (lithofacies Sr) and scattered trace fossils, and is assigned to assemblage 2. In the profile this element appears to contain no dipping accretion surfaces, and was initially

Fig. 12. Tusher Canyon–A profile. Loc. 7. Cliff on north side of canyon, sec. 8, T20S, R17E, 7.2 km (in straight line) due east of Green River.

Fig. 13. Tusher Canyon-B profile. Loc. 8. Cliff on north side of valley, immediately upstream and around a bend from Loc. 7.

designated a SB unit. However, exposures of element 5 behind the cliff face reveal an internal accretionary geometry, with accretion surfaces dipping westerly (280°; striking within 20° of orientation of cliff face, which is why they were not seen at first), whereas the crossbed mean azimuth for this element is 150°. The element is tentatively interpreted as LA. As noted earlier, the unit may represent a marginal-marine tongue, with the LA element forming as a bar in an estuarine or distributary-channel-mouth environment (cf. Yang & Nio 1989).

Floy Wash-A (Location 9, Fig. 14)

This outcrop spans a similar stratigraphic interval to Tusher Canyon-A. The lower part of the section is in the Upper Desert Member. The sequence boundary with the Lower Desert Member is not exposed here (it can be picked up by tracing the beds downstream to the south). The sequence boundary with the Castlegate Sandstone occurs in the middle of the outcrop (surface E). Of interest is that the beds of the Desert Member here (elements 2 to 4, in particular) are of fluvial character (lithofacies assemblage 4), comparable to those of the Castlegate Sandstone. This is the only outcrop studied by the writer where the Desert Member contains fluvial beds with large macroform elements.

Element mean azimuths in both the Desert Member and Castlegate Sandstone are all within 25° of the outcrop mean of 141°. This indicates relatively low sinuosity, and consistency of transport directions across a sequence boundary. The outcrop mean is oriented 60° from the regional mean of Van de Graaf (1972), but his data become very dispersed in his eastern facies belts, and there may be no significance to such a divergence.

Element 2 contains accretion surfaces oriented at about 50° to crossbed directions, and is interpreted as the product of oblique downstream accretion (DA). Element 3 consists of at least three separate units, separated by fourth-order surfaces C^{iii} anc C^{iv}. The lower one contains two dipping third-order erosion surfaces, C^{i} and C^{ii}, suggesting accumulation by accretion, or local channelling. This element is provision-

ally designated SB, as there are inadequate data to subdivide the element and to define individual macroforms. Element 4 is a compound macroform, containing several internal third-order erosion surfaces D^{ii} to D^{vii}. Four measurements of accretion-surface orientation were taken, ranging from 110° to 160°. The element crossbed mean is 116°. This element therefore developed by downstream to oblique-downstream accretion, and is labelled 4-DA. It appears to climb over an earlier bar remnant to the left of centre of the outcrop, where surface D^{ii} develops an apparent dip to the right. Element 5 is an indeterminate LA/DA unit (dipping accretion surfaces are present, but their geometry is unclear), and element 6 contains accretion surfaces dipping at 015°, a difference of 116° from the element crossbed mean, suggesting a LA configuration.

Floy Wash-B (Location 10, Fig. 15)

Detailed study of this outcrop was confined to the Castlegate Sandstone, although there are good exposures of the Upper Desert Member below. They consist of assemblage 2, unlike the fluvial beds at the same stratigraphic level in Floy Wash-A. The lateral facies change is interpreted as the result of scour by the fluvial beds forming the top of the upper Desert Member at Floy Wash-A (Fig. 4).

There are three elements in the Castlegate Sandstone, the lowermost being one of the thickest sandstone sheets observed during this study. Element 1 is a large but relatively simple macroform up to 15 m thick. It consists of cosets of trough and planar crossbedding (lithofacies St, Sp, mainly the former) separated by third-order bounding surfaces (Fig. 20b). Although the base of the element is a sixth-order surface defining the base of the Castlegate Member, the shape of this surface is, in places, determined by the scour that accompanied the formation of the third-order surfaces. This is particularly clear where surface A^{i} merges downwards with surface A at the centre of the profile. Dip azimuth on the third-order accretion surfaces ranges from 035° to 145° (NNE–SSE), a range of 110°, with a mean of 093°. This is 38° from the element crossbed mean of 128° and close to the

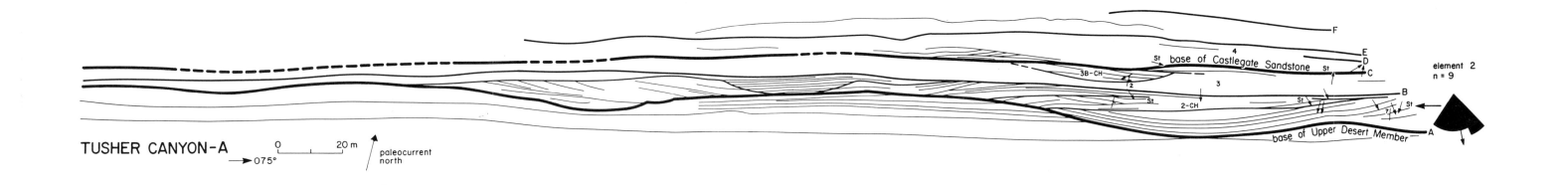

TUSHER CANYON-A   0   20 m   paleocurrent north

→ 075°

base of Castlegate Sandstone

base of Upper Desert Member

element 2 n = 9

3B-CH   2-CH

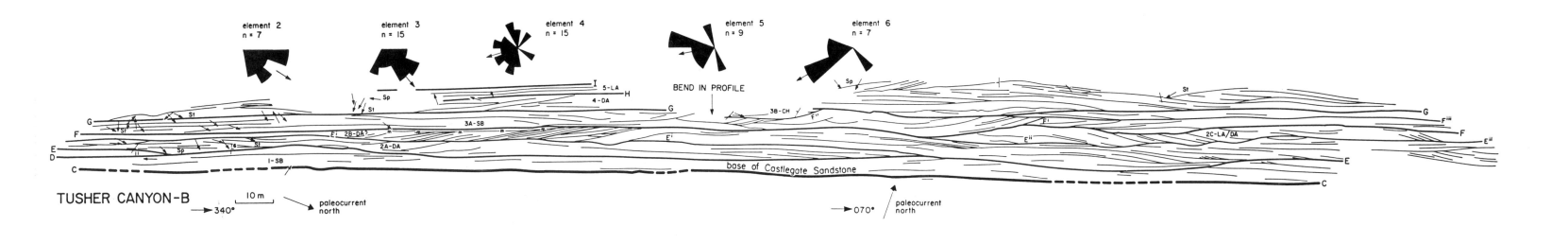

element 2 n = 7   element 3 n = 15   element 4 n = 15   element 5 n = 9   element 6 n = 7

BEND IN PROFILE

5-LA   4-DA   3A-SB   2B-DA   2A-DA   1-SB

3B-CH   2C-LA/DA

base of Castlegate Sandstone

TUSHER CANYON-B   10 m   paleocurrent north

→ 340°

→ 070°   paleocurrent north

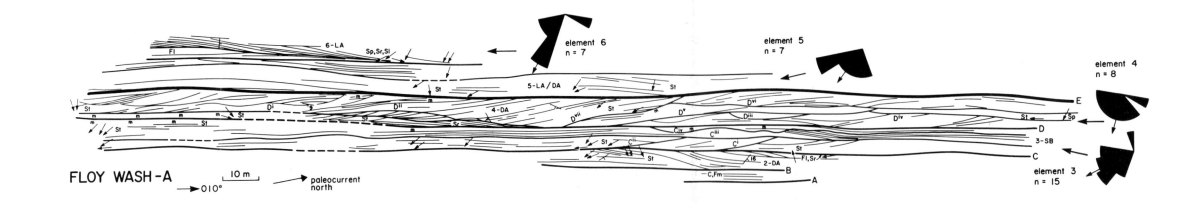

FLOY WASH-A   ├──┤ 10 m   → paleocurrent north
→ 010°

element 6
n = 7

element 5
n = 7

element 4
n = 8

element 3
n = 15

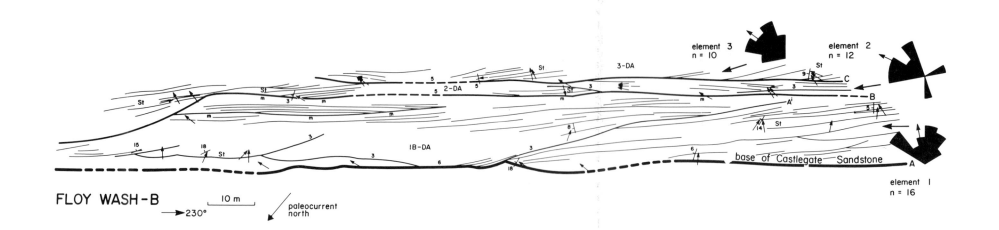

FLOY WASH-B   ├──┤ 10 m   ↙ paleocurrent north
→ 230°

base of Castlegate Sandstone

element 3
n = 10

element 2
n = 12

element 1
n = 16

Fig. 14. Floy Wash-A profile. Loc. 9. Cliff on northwest side of valley, sec. 5, T21S, R19E, 2.3 km (in straight line) upstream from junction between Floy Wash jeep trail and Thompson Pass trail.

Fig. 15. Floy Wash-B profile. Loc. 10. Cliff on southeast side of valley, opposite Loc. 9 and 100 m downstream.

outcrop mean of 102°. The element therefore was deposited by oblique accretion, and may represent an alternate bar within a major channel. In detail accretion directions shift from ENE in element 1A to ESE in element 1B, while crossbed directions remain similar (ESE) throughout. This, therefore, is an example of a macroform which shows lateral and downstream accretion in different parts of the same unit. Earlier beds (element 1A) constitute a lateral-accretion (LA) unit, and at surface A^i there is a change in internal geometry to a DA unit (element 1B).

Element 2 is in part a tabular unit 3 m thick tentatively interpreted as DA unit. To the left it thickens dramatically into a hollow 10.5 m thick, which has the shape of a scoop-shaped scour fill. The accretion surfaces within this unit dip at 070°, identical to the element crossbed mean of 074°. There is no obvious break or transition between the two components of element 2, suggesting that the two parts interfinger and formed simultaneously. The hollow may represent a zone of enhanced scour such as those described from the Morrison Formation by Cowan (1991).

Crescent Canyon (Location 11, Fig. 16)

The profile exposes the Upper Desert Member and the Castlegate Sandstone. Detailed work was carried out mainly in the latter, which here consists of three elements ranging from 7.0 to 8.2 m in thickness. This is nearly double the typical element thicknesses in the western Book Cliffs, suggesting an amalgamation of tributary braided systems into fewer, deeper rivers.

Element 3, which comprises the lower Castlegate Sandstone, consists of two macroforms oriented in opposite directions, and separated by a fourth-order surface C^i. Unit 3A contains accretion surfaces dipping at 210–260°, which is 134–184° from the element crossbed mean, suggesting very oblique, possibly local upstream accretion. Element 3B developed by accretion at 015°, which is a difference of 61° from the element crossbed mean, suggesting formation as a LA unit. Element 3 therefore represents at least two lateral-accretion units developed more or less side-by-side as a result of lateral channel migration. Load structures interpreted as dinosaur footprints occur near the top of element 3B (Fig. 20c).

Element 4 is a typical LA unit. It contains accretion surfaces dipping at 040–065°, which is approximately perpendicular to the element crossbed mean of 139°. The lower bar deposits have a massive weathering character, similar to element 1 at Floy Wash-B, but they pass upward, laterally, into much thinner bedded sandstones. At the right end of the outcrop the element scours about 5 m down into element 3.

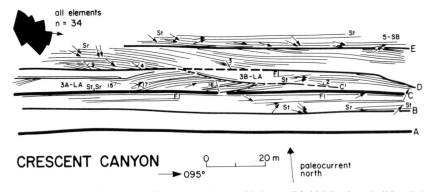

Fig. 16. Crescent Canyon profile. Loc. 11. Exposures above and below trail (which has been bulldozed along coal and shale beds at top of Desert Member, surface C), sec. 10, T21S, R19E, 4.2 km (in straight line) NE of junction of this trail with Thompson Pass trail.

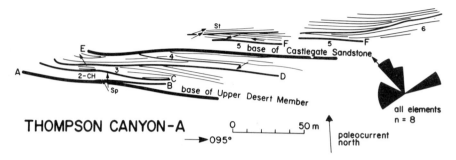

Fig. 17. Thompson Canyon-A profile. Loc. 12. Exposures on east side of valley at petroglyphs monument, sec. 33, T20S, R20E, 400 m south of junction of Thompson and Sego canyons.

Thompson Canyon-A and -B
(Locations 12, 13, Figs 17, 18)

The cliffs above the petroglyphs, on the east side of the valley, expose a complete section from the Upper Desert Member to the top of the Castlegate Sandstone. The outcrop is readily accessible, but architectural details are less well exposed than in the other exposures between this canyon and Green River. The Upper Desert Member, corresponding to sequence 2, consists of a succession of thin-bedded deltaic/estuarine sandstones (elements 1–3 in profile A, element 1 in profile B) overlain by a sheet sandstone body (elements 4, 2, respectively) of probable deltaic origin (assemblage 3). Element 1 contains broad, scoop-shaped hollows similar to those at Tusher Canyon-A (Fig. 12). They are filled by clinoform units, containing minor internal erosion surfaces of third-order type. Trace fossils and oyster beds indicate a marine to brackish-water influence during deposition, but there is no evidence of tidal action, in the form of tidal bundling of crossbedding, nor of open

marine conditions in the form of marine body fossils.

Profile B (Fig. 13) provides an excellent exposure of one of the clinoform units. The strata dip at an azimuth of between 005° and 015°, at an agle of 9°. They consist mainly of fine- to very fine-grained sandstone interbedded with minor thin shales and siltstone beds (assemblage 3). Lithofacies include Sp, St, Sh and Sr. Mean azimuth calculated from all sedimentary structures in this element is 351°, indicating oblique-downstream accretion of this unit. It is interpreted as a Gilbert-type delta building out from a channel mouth. Profile A (Fig. 12) exposes a distributary channel at the base of this element (unit 2-CH), where it incises into the underlying shoreface sandstones of sequence 1. The beds here consist of thin- to medium-bedded, fine-grained sandstone with deformed cross-bedding and water-escape structures. Element 3 in this outcrop consists of interbedded fine-grained sandstone, thin carbonaceous shales and coal. Burrows were observed in one bed of sandstone. These beds are

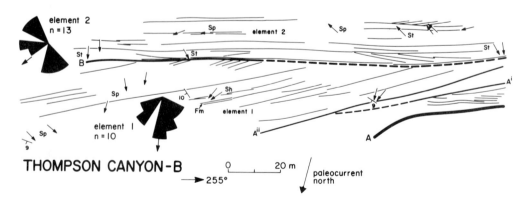

Fig. 18. Thompson Canyon-B profile, Loc. 13. Exposures on south side of side valley, 100 m SE of Loc. 12.

interpreted as deltaic levee or overbank deposits.

The uppermost unit in sequence 2 (element 4 in profile A, element 2 in profile B) is a sheet sandstone body consisting of fine- to medium-grained sandstone with abundant cross-bedding (lithofacies Sp, St; assemblage 2). Feeding trails are present on some bedding planes, and an oyster bed was observed near the top of the element at Location 13 (profile B). At this location the base of the unit is sharp and probably erosional, and contains large mudstone clasts up to 45 cm long in the lowermost beds. The basal bounding surface clearly truncates element 1. Palaeocurrent readings have a high dispersion, with a mean of 037°, oblique to the regional mean. An accretionary geometry is visible in part of profile A. The element may be a delta abandonment facies, as suggested by Cole and Friberg (1989).

The Castlegate Sandstone is present at the top of profile A (elements 5, 6). Element 6 consists of scoop-shaped deltaic channels of assemblage 3 similar to those of elements 1–3. This indicates an important facies change from the fluvial assemblage of the Castlegate Sandstone a few kilometres to the west.

Fluvial styles

Several of the profiles, particularly that at Castle Gate-B, could be described as showing a characteristic fluvial style that has been termed 'sheet-braided' by many authors (e.g. Cotter 1978). Most braided systems contain prominent fifth-order bounding surfaces that collectively give outcrops this appearance. However, in this case it is clear that the term is misleading, because it conveys no information regarding the presence of the accretionary geometries within the elements. Field work by the writer is indicating that such geometries are extremely common in sandy braided systems, so the term should be used with caution. An important question remains regarding the significance of the prominent horizontal bounding surfaces. Are they all simply fifth-order channel scours, or are some of them regionally extensive erosion surfaces comparable to sixth-order sequence boundaries? They may record shifts in regional dispersal patterns reflecting subtle tectonic tilting, or pauses in sedimentation brought about by a relative fall in base level.

Lithofacies Assemblage 4 is dominated by lateral-accretion (LA) and downstream- to oblique-downstream accretion (DA) units. Sheet-like elements (SB) are present in some outcrops, but in some cases these may, in fact, be accretionary macroforms exposed in strike section. Minor channels (element CH) are present in a few outcrops. Shales and siltstones (element OF) are present in minor amounts. These elements combine laterally into successions of sandstone sheets bounded by fifth-order surfaces. Sheet thicknesses increase down palaeoslope from west to east (Table 5). In the west they range from 1.4 to 13.6 m, but average between 4 and 6 m in thickness. In the east thicknesses range from 2.4 to 14.8 m, with an average of between 6 and 9 m. Much thicker macroform units are present in the east, such as the LA–DA unit comprising element 1 at Floy Wash-B, and LA elements 3 and 4 at Crescent Canyon.

Assemblage 4 is similar to that comprising model 10 of Miall (1985), and is interpreted as the product of sandy braided rivers with large, mid-channel bars (sand flats). The modern South Sakatchewan River is a good modern analogue, although the original descriptions of the sedimentology of that river (Cant & Walker 1978) did not include a description of the internal geometry of the macroforms. Other ancient deposits with comparable, complex element geometries have been described by Allen (1983) and Ramos et al. (1986). Figure 19 illustrates a reconstruction of a South Saskatchewan-type river from element and palaeocurrent data at Tusher Canyon.

Fluvial styles are not consistent in detail between outcrops within the project area, nor, in some cases, even within the same outcrop. For example, compare the Castlegate Sandstone outcrops at Castle Gate, with that at Willow Creek, only 4 km down paleoslope to the east. At Castle Gate the sandstone is dominated by DA units showing a fairly consistent style, whereas at Willow Creek (at a slightly higher stratigraphic level) the fluvial style is quite variable, including DA and LA units, a hetero-lithic point bar comparable to the IHS units of Thomas et al. (1987; model 7 of Miall 1985), and crossbedded sheet units with tabular internal geometry similar to the deposits of much of the modern Platte River (model 9 of Miall 1985). The explanation for this variability is that local fluvial style is influenced by local conditions, such as the merging of tributaries, the nature of local bank materials, and the occurrence of 'dynamic events' (in the sense of Jackson 1975), such as floods. Carson (1984a, b, c) has shown that the development of braiding is very dependent on the availability of easily erodible bank materials, such as loosly consolidated sand. Braiding will be less likely to occur where a channel incises into consolidated floodplain

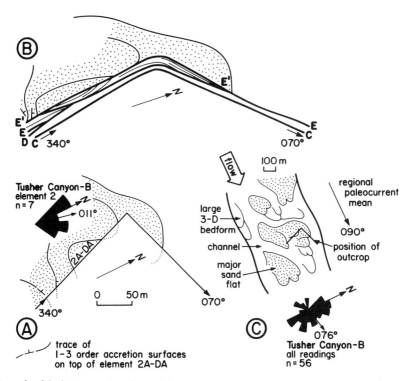

Fig. 19. Example of the interpretation of an architectural element using orientation data from crossbedding and accretion surfaces. (**A**) Orientation of Tusher Canyon-B section, showing measured accretionary dip directions and interpreted accretion surfaces on the top of element 2A-DA, and current rose diagram obtained from measurement of crossbed orientations in element 2. (**B**) Perspective view of element 2A-DA. (**C**) Interpretation of braided river that deposited the Tusher Canyon section. Note the position of the Tusher Canyon-B section. The river is oriented according to the regional palaeocurrent mean (Table 4). The rose diagram for this outcrop is also shown. Note the slight divergence between the outcrop mean and the regional mean, which may reflect the dominance of channels and macroforms oriented oblique to the main channel trend at the Tusher Canyon outcrop. Note also the large divergence between the element-2 palaeocurrent mean and the outcrop mean, reflecting the locally high divergence of accretion directions from the mean channel trend. Accretion in element 2A is interpreted as DA rather than LA because of the *within-element* similarity between indicated palaeoflow and accretionary dip directions.

muds. These bank conditions can change within a few metres downstream, as the river meanders through the complex of its own alluvial deposits, and fluvial style may therefore be expected to show many small changes. It is also possible that the Willow Creek outcrop is a transect through several nonmarine stratigraphic sequences, in which the changes in fluvial style reflect subtle variations in regional slope.

As summarized in Table 5, sandstone sheet thicknesses undergo a gross increase from west to east across the Book Cliffs exposures. For the most part sandstone elements in the project area probably preserve close to the original depositional thickness (disregarding compac-

tion) for the following reasons: (1) they may be capped by thin shales, probably of floodplain origin; (2) in most cases, even where sandstone rests on, and appears to incise into sandstone, there is little evidence of truncation of underlying bedding by fifth-order surfaces. Accretion surfaces commonly curve over and lap out upward rather than undergo truncation. If this is the case, and following Allen's (1965) argument regarding the significance of the thickness of epsilon crossbed sets, element thickness can be used to approximate channel depth.

There are some exceptions to the general rule of minimal truncation. For example, in the Soldier Creek profile (Fig. 10) elements 3B and

4 wedge out across the outcrop, so that at the left-hand end of the profile element 5 rests on element 3, and a minimum of 13 m of section is absent, much of which is probably a result of erosion.

Given the exceptions noted in the previous paragraph, the increase in sheet thickness across east-central Utah can be interpreted as a reflection of a downstream deepening of fluvial channels, as tributary streams merged into fewer, larger rivers.

This interpretation contrasts with that of Cowan (1991), who argued that, in the Westwater Canyon Member of the Morrison Formation, element tops are rarely preserved, with deep, scourfill hollows having increased preservation potential. The fluvial style of the Westwater Canyon Member is distinctly different from that described here, with the scour hollows described by Cowan (1991) rare in the Castlegate Sandstone. The greater abundance of large scours in the Westwater Canyon Mamber may be related to the more flashy discharge of the rivers that deposited that unit. The lack of preservation of element tops (if Cowan's interpretation is correct) may reflect a subtly different balance between sedimentation, lateral channel migration, and subsidence rates relative to that which prevailed during Castlegate sedimentation.

Controls on sequence architecture

In broad terms the major clastic tongues of the foreland-basin fill in Utah (Blackhawk Formation, Castlegate Sandstone, North Horn Formation) are stratigraphic sequences of third-order magnitude, that is to say they are within the range of 1–10 Ma in duration. The overriding tectonic control of these units is clear. The clastic tongues can be correlated, in broad terms, with orogenic pulses in the Sevier orogen (Fouch et al. 1983). Changes in detrital composition and in regional palaeocurrent directions between these tongues can only be explained by changes in source areas and in regional tilts brought about by tectonism (Lawton 1985, 1986). There is no obvious correlation of these clastic pulses with the third-order cycles of Weimer (1986), which he attributed to eustasy. Regional tectonism as a cause of many third-order cycles has been discussed by Galloway (1989), Embry (1990), and Miall (1991b). Cloetingh (1988) proposed a possible mechanism, relating continental tilting to stresses transmitted across plate interiors from regions of

extensional or compressional stress at plate boundaries. Such tilting can account for widespread changes in base leve, simulating eustasy within the confines of a single plate, and it can also explain broad changes in sediment source areas and in sediment supply, such as those discussed by Galloway (1989) and Embry (1990).

It is not yet clear what mechanism generates the shorter term cycles, such as the sequences within the Desert Member and Castlegate Sandstone identified by Van Wagoner et al. (1990) and discussed in this paper. The disconformities defined as sequence boundaries probably represent times of low relative sea level, when the sea retreated to the east, and the basin was exposed to subaerial erosion (Van Wagoner et al. 1990). This would account for the erosional relief on the disconformity surfaces, and the regional truncation of underlying strata. The subsequent fluvial or deltaic/estuarine sedimentation then comprises the record of renewed base-level rise. Marine transgressive and highstand deposits form the top of each sequence, although these beds have been removed by erosion from much of sequence 2. The Quaternary fluvial sequences of the Gulf Coast are a good analogue for this style of sedimentation (Suter et al. 1987).

The sequences of the Upper Desert Member and Castlegate Sandstone are dominated by deepening-upward successions, recording the drowning of broad, possibly estuarine erosional valleys during the gradual rise of base level. In the Castlegate sequence the fluvial deposits occur at the base of the sequence, and are overlain sharply by the transgressive-marine beds of the Buck Tongue (Fig. 4), in contrast to the sequence models of Swift et al. (1987) and Posamentier et al. (1988), in which fluvial deposits occur at the top of shallowing-upward, progradational wedges. In the Desert Member at Floy Wash-A there is a fluvial succession at the top of sequence 2, above deltaic channel-fill deposits, suggesting local progradation. Another possible remnant of this fluvial succession is a small channel, designated element 3B-CH, at Tusher Canyon-A. These fluvial remnants occur above transgressive deposits of lithofacies assemblages 1-3 at these two locations, and probably represent progradational deposits formed at a time of highstand. Such highstand deposits are absent from the Castlegate sequence. Is this simply a question of preservation, with progradational sequence tops having been lost to erosion during each base-level drop? Or did the coastal plain not advance into the area during each highstand? Most other stratigraphic sequences described from foreland

(A)

(B)

basins are dominated by progradational, high-stand deposts (e.g. Plint *et al*. 1986). The under-lying Lower Desert Member (sequence 1) in the Green River area also contains thick, pro-gradational, marine highstand deposits (Van Wagoner *et al*. 1990). This architecture suggests a rapid rise in base level followed by a long period of highstand or slow fall, whereas the architecture of the Castlegate and Upper Desert Member sequences suggests slow rise followed by a relatively short period of highstand and base-level fall.

The sequence architecture is probably in part a reflection of sediment-supply considerations. The sequence boundaries described by Plint *et al*. (1986) are blanketed by sparse or patchy conglomerate beds supplied by limited fluvial input and reworked by marine processes during rising base level. In the case of the Castlegate Sandstone the extensive fluvial blankets over-lying the sequence boundaries suggest that fluvial sediment supply was adequate to keep pace with the increase in accommodation space brought about by rising base level, allowing

(C)

Fig. 20. Outcrop photographs. (**A**) Type section of the Castlegate Sandstone, near Castle Gate, showing the characteristic sheet-braided appearance of the formation. (**B**) View of the base of a DA unit, element 1B, Floy Wash-B. Stratigraphic horizontal corresponds to edge of picture. Dipping surfaces are third-order bounding surfaces C. Load structures, probably representing dinosaur footprints, near top of element 3B, Crescent Canyon.

erosional valleys to fill with widespread fluvial deposits. The deltaic channels so well exposed in the Desert Member at Tusher Canyon and Thompson Canyon, and in the Castlegate Member at the latter locality, represent the distal, marginal-marine fringe of this backfill blanket.

Could sediment-supply controls alone generate the Castlegate and upper Desert Member sequences? From the time of the original stratigraphic synthesis of the Mesaverde Group by Young (1955) it has been known that the Castlegate Sandstone is an unusually extensive sandstone sheet, relative to the rest of the clastic wedge. It may be that the allogenic mechanisms included a strong component of tectonism at this time. The fourth-order cyclic base-level changes, of possible eustatic origin, that controlled sequence development during deposition of the Mesaverde Group and overlying Tertiary beds, were overprinted during deposition of the Upper Desert Member and Castlegate Sandstone by the effects of tectonic instability and increased sediment supply, arising from a pulse of crustal shortening and uplift in the Sevier orogen.

As noted earlier in this paper, there is some evidence of intra-Castlegate sequences, suggesting very short-term events of change in base

level. There is a need for considerable detailed mapping and regional correlation of the subtle facies variations and major bounding surfaces within these rocks, to test this possibility. Tracing of major bounding surfaces within thick fluvial successions, such as the Castlegate Sandstone west of Green River, though difficult, would be worthwhile, revealing whether an entirely nonmarine succession consisted of more than one stratigraphic sequence.

Reservoir architecture

The sandstone units defined by fifth-order surfaces are essentially tabular in external form, and could be used as the basis for a subdivision of a subsurface braided sandstone deposit into flow units, for production purposes. In the Castlegate Sandstone they vary in thickness from an average of 4–6 m to an average of 6–9 m, over a downstream distance of about 140 km (the east-west distance down paleoslope from Castle Gate to Crescent Canyon). This thickness change probably reflects river amalgamation and consequent increases in discharge and channel depth. The pattern of change may have predictive value in other fluvial systems.

Even given the large outcrops in the Book Cliffs, little reliable information is available on the lateral extent of sandstone and mudstone bodies. Few lateral element terminations were mapped, suggesting that sandstone-body widths are considerably greater than the 400 ± m width of the typical outcrop. One element at Castle Gate-A (Fig. 7) is completely exposed, and is 90 m in length, as measured along the outcrop. The element is probably a DA unit, exposed approximately parallel to the outcrop palaeo-current direction. At Joes Valley surfaces C, D, and E define a sandstone sheet fragment 180 m in length. Most element terminations that have been observed, where a fifth-order surface trun-cates the one below (Castle Gate-A, Tusher Canyon-A, Soldier Creek) reveal a gradual wedging out, rather than a sharp truncation at a cutbank.. Examples of termination at probable cutbanks are seen at Willow Creek (Fig. 9); surface K, where it is terminated by surface L, and the possible channel truncated by surface F.

Almost all the fifth-order surfaces that define sandstone sheets overlie a few decimetres of mudstone or siltstone. In places these fine-grained units exceed 1 m in thickness. It is the persistent presence of these recessive beds that causes the surfaces to weather out in outcrop, and thus permit their tracing on the profiles. In the subsurface it is the presence of such fine-grained beds that divides a sandstone unit into tabular flow units, with little vertical permea-bility communication between them. However, no consistent variations in mudstone thickness or extent could be determined. Many shale units associated with fifth-order surfaces can be traced for the full width of the outcrop, and are there-fore at least a few hundred metres in lateral extent. In a few instances sandstone sheets rest on each other at a fifth-order surface without intervening fine-grained beds. In such cases the bounding surface may be difficult to trace across the outcrop. Surface D in the Tusher Canyon-B profile (Fig. 13) is a good example. Its course across the outcrop is unclear in several places. These sandstone-sandstone contacts across major bounding surfaces are rare, and in the subsurface would provide vertical fluid communication between the sheets. Such vertical communication may cause problems where attempts are being made to produce successive sheets at different flow rates.

As noted earlier, fluvial style shows many local changes, which could reflect local vari-ations in channel and bank materials, discharge, and slope. The possibility of intra-Castlegate sequences has also been noted earlier, as a possible cause of vertical changes in fluvial style.

The internal geometry of the sandstone ele-ments (those bounded by fifth-order surfaces) indicates an abundance of dipping first- to third-order bounding surfaces resulting from down-stream, oblique, and lateral accretion through-out the Castlegate fluvial system. The importance of these architectural components in a braided 'sheet' sandstone has rarely been emphasized. Third-order surfaces are normally visible in outcrop because of a lithofacies heterogeneity, such as a mudstone bed below the surface, or poorly-sorted sandstone with intraclasts immediately above. They may, there-fore, be of some importance as baffles to lateral fluid movement, and production models should take them into account. As in the case of fifth-order surfaces (as noted above), in some cases macroform increments defined by third-order surfaces rest on each other without intervening fine-grained units, providing for unimpeded horizontal fluid communication. Element 1 at Floy Wash-B (Fig. 15) is a good example. Three third-order surfaces are indicated. Only one can be traced (with difficulty) through the entire element.

Successive DA and LA elements may have comparable crossbed mean azimuth directions (all within 25° of the outcrop mean at Floy Wash-A), but accretion directions are typically highly variable, even within the same element, varying laterally by up to 90° within the same element and 180° between successive elements. In a few instances individual macroform increments are completely exposed in one of the profiles, allowing measurements of lateral extent. For example, in the Floy Wash-B profile (Fig. 15) the major DA unit forming element 1B at the base of the Castlegate Member consists of several increments separated by third-order surfaces. One of these, in the centre of the profile, is completely exposed, and is 120 m long, in an oblique downstream direction. In Floy Wash-A (Fig. 14) a macroform fragment defined by third-order surfaces D^v, D^{vi}, and D^{vii} is 90 m in length. Several minor channels, prob-ably bar-top channels formed during falling water, are exposed in other profiles, and range from 30 to 60 m in width.

This limited information on the geometry and lateral extent of sandstone elements, minor channels, and macroform increments, indicates the scales of heterogeneity that must be allowed for in reservoir engineering. Braided sandstone 'sheets' cannot be expected to be amenable to simple production modelling, as if they were internally homogeneous. In fact, the term 'sheet-braided' may be inappropriate and mis-leading as applied to most braided systems, except some of those formed by ephemeral flash-flood processes (fluvial styles 11 and 12 of Miall 1985). Information from seismic tomography, horizontal seismic data, and horizontal boreholes may be required for the evaluation of reservoir heterogeneity.

Thanks are due to my wife, Charlene, for her field assistance in 1990, and to M. Stephens for assistance during 1991. Diagrams were drafted by S. Shanbhag.

Field work was funded from an Operating Grant awarded by the Natural Sciences and Engineering Research Council, Canada. This paper was prepared while the author was on sabbatical leave at the University of Oxford, UK. I am grateful to The Chairman, J. Dewey, for affording me the facilities of the department during my stay, and to P. Allen for helping me to find my way around. I have benefitted from discussions of sequence stratigraphy with D. Nummedal, B. Galloway, H. Posamentier, J. Van Wagoner, J. Suter, and P. Allen and his sedimentology seminar groups.

References

ALLEN, J. R. L. 1965. The sedimentation and palaeogeography of the Old Red Sandstone of Anglesey, North Wales. *Yorkshire Geological Society Proceedings* **35**, 139-185.

——. 1966. On bed forms and paleocurrents. *Sedimentology*, **6**, 153–190.

——. 1983. Studies in fluviatile sedimentation: bars, bar complexes and sandstone sheets (low-sinuosity braided streams) in the Brownstones (L. Devonian), Welsh Borders. *Sedimentary Geology*, **33**, 237–293.

CANT, D. J & WALKER, R. G. 1978. Fluvial processes and facies sequences in the sandy braided South Saskatchewan River, Canada. *Sedimentology*, **25**, 625–648.

CARSON, M. A. 1984*a*. The meandering-braided river threshold: a reappraisal. *Journal of Hydrology*, **73**, 315–334.

—— 1984*b*. Observations on the meandering-braided river transition, the Canterbury Plains, New Zealand. *New Zealand Geographer*, **40**, 12–17.

—— 1984*c*. Observations on the meandering-braided river transition, the Canterbury Plains, New Zealand. *New Zealand Geographer*, **40**, 89–99.

CLOETINGH, S. 1988. Intraplate stresses: a new element in basin analysis. *In*: KLEINSPEHN, K. & PAOLA, C. (eds) *New Perspectives in basin analysis*. Springer-Verlag, New York, 205–230.

COLE, R. D. & FRIBERG, J. F. 1989. Stratigraphy and sedimentation of the Book Cliffs, Utah. *In*. NUMMEDAL, D. & WRIGHT, R. (eds) Cretaceous shelf sandstones and shelf depositional sequences, Western Interior Basin, Utah, Colorado and New Mexico. 28th International Geological Congress, Washington, D.C., Field Trip Guidebook **T119, 13–24.**

COTTER, E. 1978. The evolution of fluvial style, with special reference to the central Appalachian Paleozoic. *In*: MIALL, A. D. (ed.) *Fluvial sedimentology*. Canadian Society of Petroleum Geologists Memoirs, **5**, 361–383.

COWAN, E. J. 1991. The large-scale architecture of the fluvial Westwater Canyon Member, Morrison Formation (Jurassic), San Juan Basin, New Mexico. *In*: MIALL, A. D. & TYLER, N. (eds) *The three-dimensional facies architecture of terrigenous clastic sediments, and its implications for hydrocarbon discovery and recovery.* Society of Economic Paleontologists and Mineralogists Concepts in Sedimentology and Paleontology, **3**, 80–93.

CURRAY, J. R. 1956. The analysis of two-dimensional orientation data. *Journal of Geology*, **64**, 117–131.

DICKINSON, W. R., LAWTON, T. F. & INMAN, K. F. 1986. Sandstone detrital modes, central Utah foreland region, stratigraphic record of Cretaceous-Paleogene tectonic evolution. *Journal of Sedimentary Petrology*, **56**, 279–293.

EMBRY, A. F. 1990. A tectonic origin for third-order depositional sequences in extensional basins — implications for basin modelling. *In*: CROSS, T. A. (ed.) *Quantitative dynamic stratigraphy.* Prentice-Hall, Englewood Cliffs, 491–501.

FOUCH, T. D., LAWTON, T. F., NICHOLS, D. J., CASHION, W. B. & COBBAN, W. A. 1983. Patterns and timing of synorogenic sedimentation in Upper Cretaceous rocks of central and northeast Utah. *In*: REYNOLDS, M. & DOLLY, E. (eds) *Mesozoic paleogeography of west-central United States.* Society of Economic Paleontologists and Mineralogists, Rocky Mountain Section, Symposium, **2**, 305–334.

GALLOWAY, W. E. 1989. Genetic stratigraphic sequences in basin analysis II: Application to northwest Gulf of Mexico Cenozoic basin. *American Association of Petroleum Geologists Bulletin*, **73**, 143–154.

JACKSON, R. G. II 1975. Hierarchical attributes and a unifying model of bed forms composed of cohesionless material and produced by shearing flow. *Geological Society of America Bulletin*, **86**, 1523–1533.

JORDAN, T. E. 1981. Thrust loads and foreland basin evolution, Cretaceous western United States. *American Association of Petroleum Geologists Bulletin*, **65**, 2506–2520.

KIRK, M. 1983. Bar developments in a fluvial sandstone (Westphalian "A"), Scotland. *Sedimentology*, **30**, 727–742.

LAKE, L. W. & CARROLL, H. B. (eds) 1986. *Reservoir characterization.* Academic Press Inc., Orlando.

LAWTON, T. F. 1985. Style and timing of frontal structures, thrust belt, central Utah. *American Association of Petroleum Geologists Bulletin*, **69**, 1145–1159.

—— 1986. Fluvial systems of the Upper Cetaceous Mesaverde Group and Paleocene North Horn Formation, central Utah: a record of transition from thin-skinned to thick-skinned in the foreland region. *In*: PETERSON, J. A. (ed.) *Paleotectonics and sedimentation in the Rocky Mountain region, United States*. American Association of Petroleum Geologists Memoirs, **41**, 423–442.

MIALL, A. D. 1974. Paleocurrent analysis of alluvial sediments: a discussion of directional variance and vector magnitude. *Journal of Sedimentary Petrology*, **44**, 1174–1185.

—— 1977. A review of the braided river depositional environment. *Earth Science Reviews*, **13**, 1–62.

—— 1978. Lithofacies types and vertical profile models in braided river deposits: a summary. *In*: MIALL, A. D. (ed.) *Fluvial Sedimentology*. Canadian Society of Petroleum Geologists Memoirs, **5**, 597–604.

—— 1985. Architectural-element analysis: A new method of facies analysis applied to fluvial deposits. *Earth Science Reviews*, **22**, 261–308.

—— 1988. Reservoir heterogeneities in fluvial sandstones: lessons from outcrop studies. *American Association of Petroleum Geologists Bulletin*, **72**, 682–697.

—— 1991*a*. Stratigraphic sequences and their chronostratigraphic correlation. *Journal of Sedimentary Petrology*, **61**, 497–505.

—— 1991*b*. Hierarchies of architectural units in clastic rocks, and their relationship to sedimentation rate. *In*: MIALL, A. D. & TYLER, N. (eds) *The three-dimensional facies architecture of terrigenous clastic sediments, and its implications for hydrocarbon discovery and recovery*. Society of Economic Paleontologists and Mineralogists Concepts in Sedimentology and Paleontology, **3**, 6–12.

—— & TYLER, N. (eds) 1991. *The three-dimensional facies architecture of terrigenous clastic sediments, and its implications for hydrocarbon discovery and recovery*. Society of Economic Paleontologists and Mineralogists Concepts in Sedimentology and Paleontology, **3**.

PLINT, A. G., WALKER, R. G. & BERGMAN, K. M. 1986. Cardium Formation 6. Stratigraphic framework of the Cardium in subsurface. *Bulletin of Canadian Petroleum Geology*, **34**, 213–225.

POSAMENTIER, H. W. & VAIL, P. R. 1988. Eustatic controls on clastic deposition II - sequence and systems tracts models. *In*: WILGUS, C. K., HASTINGS, B. S., KENDALL, C. G. ST. C., POSAMENTIER, H. W., ROSS, C. A. & VAN WAGONER, J. C. (eds) Sea-level research: an integrated approach. Society of Economic Paleontologists and Mineralogists Special Publications, **42**, 125–154.

——, JERVEY, M. T. & VAIL, P. R. 1988. Eustatic controls on clastic deposition I - conceptual framework. *In*: WILGUS, C. K., HASTINGS, B. S., KENDALL, C. G. ST. C., POSAMENTIER, H. W., ROSS, C. A. & VAN WAGONER, J. C. (eds) Sea-

level research: an integrated approach. Society of Economic Paleontologists and Mineralogists Special Publications, **42**, 109–124.

RAMOS, A., SOPEÑA, A. & PEREZ-ARLUCEA, M. 1986. Evolution of Buntsandstein fluvial sedimentation in the northwest Iberian Ranges (Central Spain). *Journal of Sedimentary Petrology*, **56**, 862–875.

SPIEKER, E. M. & REESIDE, J. B., JR. 1925. Cretaceous and Tertiary formations of the Wasatch Plateau, Utah. *Geological Society of America Bulletin*, **36**, 55–81.

SUTER, J. R., BERRYHILL, H. L. & PENLAND, S. 1987. Late Quaternary sea-level fluctuations and depositional sequences, southwest Louisiana continental shelf. *In*: NUMMEDAL, D., PILKEY, O. H. & HOWARD, J. D. (eds) *Sea-level fluctuation and coastal evolution*. Society of Economic Paleontologists and Mineralogists Special Publications, **41**, 199–219.

SWIFT, D. J. P., HUDELSON, P. M., BRENNER, R. L. & THOMPSON, P. 1987. Shelf construction in a foreland basin: storm beds, shelf sandbodies, and shelf-slope depositional sequences in the Upper Cretaceous Mesaverde Group, Book Cliffs, Utah. *Sedimentology*, **34**, 423–457.

THOMAS, R. G., SMITH, D. G., WOOD, J. M., VISSER, J., CALVERLEY-RANGE, E. A. & KOSTER, E. H. 1987. Inclined heterolithic stratification — terminology, description, interpretation and significance. *Sedimentary Geology*, **53**, 123–179.

VAN DE GRAAF, F. R. 1972. Fluvial-deltaic facies of the Castlegate Sandstone (Cretaceous), east-central Utah. *Journal of Sedimentary Petrology*, **42**, 558–571.

VAN WAGONER, J. C., MITCHUM, R. M., CAMPION, K. M. RAHMANIAN, V. D. 1990. *Siliciclastic sequence stratigraphy in well logs, cores, and outcrops*. American Association of Petroleum Geologists Methods in Exploration Series 7.

WEIMER, R. J. 1986. Relationship of unconformities, tectonics, and sea level change in the Cretaceous of the Western Interior, United States. *In*: PETERSON, J. A. (ed.) *Paleotectonics and sedimentation in the Rocky Mountain region, United States*. American Association of Petroleum Geologists Memoirs, **41**, 397–422.

WILGUS, C. K., HASTINGS, B. S., KENDALL, C. G., ST. C., POSAMENTIER, H. W., ROSS, C. A. & VAN WAGONER, J. C. (eds) 1988. *Sea-level changes: an integrated approach*. Society of Economic Paleontologists and Mineralogists Special Publications, **42**.

YANG CHANG-SHU & NIO, S.-D. 1989. An ebb-tide delta depositional model — a comparison between the modern Eastern Scheldt tidal basin (southwest Netherlands) and the Lower Eocene Roda Sandstone in the southern Pyrenees (Spain). *Sedimentary Geology*, **64**, 175–196.

YOUNG, R. G. 1955. Sedimentary facies and intertonguing in the Upper Cretaceous of the Book Cliffs, Utah-Colorado. *Geological Society of America Bulletin*, **66**, 177–202.

A review of braided fluvial hydrocarbon reservoirs: the petroleum engineer's perspective

JOHN H. MARTIN

Department of Geology, Imperial College of Science, Technology and Medicine, London SW7 2BP, UK

Present address: Reservoir Geological Consultant, 150 Croxted Road, London SE21 8NW, UK

Abstract: Braided fluvial reservoirs form some of the world's giant oilfields and are found in many petroleum provinces. At best, they have excellent characteristics, but where non-net intervals (shales and siltstones) form higher proportions, they are more difficult to appraise and develop. Geological characterization (lithological correlatability, vertical sequence and porosity/permeability variability) must be communicated effectively to the reservoir engineer, whose role is to formulate a development plan and predict the production profile for a field, and to monitor and optimise day-to-day field performance. He has at his disposal other techniques: cased hole neutron logging to monitor contact levels; well testing to determine reservoir flow capacity, boundary and layering effects; production logging to assess well inflow performance or injectivity; wireline pressure profiling, field pressure and production history analysis to define vertical permeability and to reveal reservoir compartmentalization and/or communication with aquifer or injected fluids.

Computer reservoir simulation modelling, now an essential tool for management of most major fields, has provided the impetus for advances in geological reservoir characterization. The question is: how can we adequately represent braided fluvial reservoirs in such models? At one end of the spectrum, sheet sands (although laterally variable) can be adequately mapped and modelled as 'layered' systems based on conventional approaches. At the other are multiple low-sinuosity channel sand reservoirs which, being uncorrelatable at well spacings typical during appraisal of offshore fields, may be suitable targets for stochastic or network - type approaches.

Although the behaviour of a hydrocarbon reservoir must be controlled at least in part by its sedimentological characteristics, the engineer's view of a field may be somewhat different to that of the geologist. This is as true for braided fluvial reservoirs as for those of other environmental origin. The geologist and reservoir engineer must be fully aware of each others' data, analytical methods and objectives in order to avoid wasted effort. In the future, despite greater computing power and better modelling software, specialist technical disciplines must not loose sight of the overall objectives of field development.

Small-scale geological variability affects the viability of enhanced recovery processes such as miscible flooding. However, at the development planning stage, more generalized parameter assessments may be sufficient. Reservoir characterization at the small scale, such as geostatistical outcrop analogue studies, should be balanced by more geological involvement in the planning and interpretation of well tests, which often provide the only dynamic data available during the appraisal and development planning of offshore fields. Greater cross-disciplinary understanding of reservoir characteristics could in turn ensure that an engineer would not develop an incorrect view of a braided fluvial reservoir, perhaps by correlating shaley intervals which just happen to be present at about the same location in the section.

This paper discusses some engineering aspects of braided fluvial reservoirs at the appraisal and development planning stage and during development. Its objectives are:

(i) to summarize the reservoir characteristics of braided fluvial sands;
(ii) to illustrate the use of engineering data in monitoring field behaviour, with particular reference to fluvial reservoirs;
(iii) to discuss the use of reservoir simulation methods in development planning and management, focusing where possible on braided and low-sinuosity channel reservoirs.

It addresses the need for collaboration between the geological and petroleum engineering professions, and indicates some possible future trends. It is aimed at readers unfamiliar with petroleum engineering practise.

From Best, J. L. & Bristow, C. S. (eds), 1993, *Braided Rivers*, Geological Society Special Publication No. **75**, pp. 333–367.

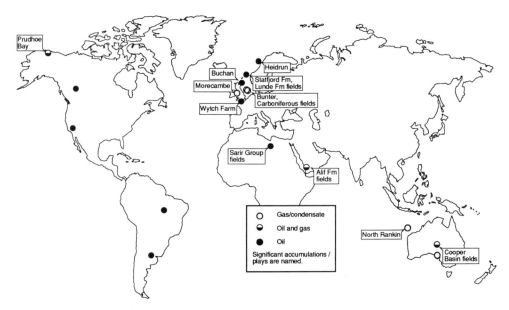

Fig. 1. Location of braided fluvial reservoirs. See Tables 1 and 2 for details of fields.

Reservoirs

Published data provides basis for review

Braided fluvial and related reservoirs indicated on Fig. 1 are summarized in Tables 1 and 2. In the space available it is not possible to discuss individual fields in reservoir trends. Information on many fields is, in any case, not freely available. From English language publications it is currently impossible to make confident interpretations of even the most significant fields within the former Soviet Union, which doubtless include a number of braided fluvial reservoirs. Screening of the many hundreds of onshore oilfields in North America proved impractical, as in the petroleum engineering literature which formed the main data source for this review, environmental interpretations of many individual fields are either vague or omitted entirely.

Braided fluvial sands: high quality with major reserves

Significance. Developed or appraised oil fields in which major reservoir units are of braided fluvial origin probably contain remaining proven recoverable oil reserves of at least well over 30 000 MMSTB in petroleum provinces including Alaska, the North Sea and the Sirte Basin of Libya. (Tables 1 and 2; Fig. 1). This is approximately equal to original UK total oil reserves, or

about 4% of world cumulative oil production. Remaining proven gas reserves are more difficult to quantify but may be at least 40 TSCF; comparable to around 2% of world cumulative gas production (extrapolated from Tiratsoo 1990).

The largest braided fluvial reservoir, and the fifteenth largest of all oil fields, is the supergiant Prudhoe Bay Field (Wadman *et al*. 1978; Atkinson *et al*. 1988, 1990) recently producing at a rate equivalent to around 70% of that of the entire United Kingdom Continental Shelf and supplying up to 15% of the oil consumed in North America. The second largest, the Sarir C-Main Field (Sanford 1970) has contributed approximately 0.2% of the world's cumulative oil production, while the nearby Messla and Bu Attifel Fields (Table 2) are just two of some 16 separate fluvial Sarir Group pools in the Libyan Sirte Basin. In the Arabian peninsula, the Alif Sand forms a prolific recently discovered reservoir trend; the 700 MMSTB Alif Field has produced at a peak rate approaching 200 MSTBD. Although little is published, its smaller neighbour, the Azal Field (Table 2) has the same reservoir. In the Cooper Basin of Australia Permian braided fluvial sands flow gas. A braided fluvial sand also produced the highest gas test rate recorded in South Australia (Malavazos & McDonough 1991). More significantly, braided fluvial facies contribute much of the natural gas liquids produced from Australia's North West Shelf (Harris 1981).

Some of the J-Sand reservoirs in the Malay Basin are likewise interpreted to be of braided fluvial origin (J. Stiles, pers. comm.).

In the UK the Sherwood Sandstone reservoir of the Wytch Farm Field (Dranfield et al. 1987; Bowman et al. 1993), now producing at some 60 MSTBD, makes it the largest onshore oil field in Western Europe. The same reservoir produces gas in the offshore East Irish Sea Basin (Bushell 1986; Stuart & Cowan 1991). Bunter sands (Table 1) are significant producing gas reservoirs in the southern North Sea (Ketter 1991; Cooke-Yarborough 1991) whereas development of Westphalian channel gas sands (Green & Slatt 1992; Ritchie & Pratsides 1993) is scheduled.

Characteristics. Braided fluvial reservoirs are usually sheet-like with high net/gross ratios, porosity and permeability. Oil recovery factors are generally high (up to more than 50% of STOOIP) either by natural depletion (which typically takes advantage of strong regional aquifer support) or by 'engineered' recovery using fluid injection (Tables 1 and 2). Reservoirs mainly are in internal pressure communication with common field-wide contacts (e.g. Azal, many Sarir Group fields). Separate fault block compartments are observed in only a few of the fields listed. In many, pressure drops due to production propagate across intra-field faults, indicating their non-sealing or only partially sealing nature. Vertically separated reservoir 'flow units' (that is, distinct horizons whose production characteristics differ from those of other intervals) occur only if laterally continuous non-fluvial shales are interbedded (Geehan et al. 1986). Most low permeability layers within channel sands are laterally discontinuous and effective vertical permeability is generally good (e.g. Bu Attifel Field; Table 2). In the Pulai Field of the Malay Basin sandy intervals are separated by layers of continuous shales such that separate development of the reservoirs is required (J. Stiles pers. comm.). Although the sands have high net/gross ratios there are shaley streaks and it would be easy to assume that vertical flow might be restricted. However, the combination of short permeability barriers within the braided fluvial section and more continuous shales between sands provides effective gravity drainage. Oil drains vertically through the reservoir sands and collects on the shales from where it continues to drain down-structure to the producers.

There are exceptions to these generalizations but most result from non-sedimentological features.

(i) Differential diagenesis above and below a palaeo gas–water contact controls the pro-duction behaviour of the Morecambe Field (Woodward & Curtis 1987). Although sedi-mentological studies indicated considerable depositional heterogeneity, for field manage-ment purposes a much simpler model has so far been adequate.

(ii) The low expected recovery of the Aracas Field (Nascimento et al. 1982) is probably partly a result of poor aquifer pressure support which has not been compensated by sufficient injected water.

(iii) Partial barriers between the oil leg and aquifer in the Prudhoe Bay and some Sarir Group Fields are caused by geochemical effects rather than sedimentary characteristics.

(iv) The production performance of the Amal Field in Libya and Buchan in the Moray Firth (Table 1; Edwards 1991; Benzagouta & Turner 1992) is controlled by natural fracturing, which is responsible for increasing the productivity of otherwise low permeability rock matrix caused by deep burial and/or diagenesis.

Thus it appears that many braided fluvial reservoirs, although laterally variable, can be adequately mapped and modelled as 'layered' systems (reservoirs which consist of vertically stacked sheets of different properties) based on conventional geological approaches (Weber & Van Geuns 1990) although stochastic approaches may be useful for modelling dis-continuous shales (see below). Simple con-ceptual models (Richardson et al. 1987b) may be appropriate for engineering purposes.

Alluvial fan reservoirs: more variable

The distinction between 'fluvial' and 'fan' models is somewhat arbitrary (e.g. Esmond Complex; Table 1) so few reservoirs can be reliably assigned to this category. The Barrancas Formation of the Vacas Muertas Filed in Argentina (Table 2) is poorly sorted with a high clay matrix but nevertheless has performed well, whereas the Haima Group of south Oman (poorly described in the literature; parts may have been deposited on an extensive fan) con-tains thick stacked sequences of fine-grained, laminated or occasionally channelized sands. Although oil-bearing in a number of major fields including Marmul, well productivities are typically modest as a result of high fines content.

Transitional channel types: complex reservoirs

Several fluvial reservoirs which have a higher proportion of non-net silts and shales are interpreted as being composed of partly discrete

Table 1. *Selected braided fluvial reservoirs, Northwest Europe*

Field	Brent	Buchan	Caister B	Caister C	Esmond Complex	Heidrun
Location	Offshore UK	Offshore UK	Offshore UK	Offshore UK	Offshore UK	Offshore Norway
Age	U. Triassic–L. Jurassic	Devono-Carboniferous	Triassic	Carboniferous	Triassic	M. Jurassic
Group	—	U. Old Red Sandstone	Bacton	Coal Measures	Bacton	Fangst
Formation	Statfjord	—	Bunter Sst	—	Bunter Sst	Garn
Status	Developed	Developed	Appraisal	Appraisal	Developed	Appraisal
Type	Gas & oil	Oil	Gas	Gas	Gas	Oil & gas
Drive mechanism	Edge water	Depletion/water	Depletion	Depletion	Depletion	Gas cap expansion?
Area (sq km)	39	14	7.5	15	39	40
STOOIP (MMSTB)	580	466	—	—	—	n/a
Estimated oil recovery	54%	18%	—	—	—	'high'
Max. prodn (MSTB/D)	200	28	—	—	—	'high'
GIIP (BSCF)	3241	—	156	230	n/a	1000
Estimated gas recovery	1215 BSCF	—	75%	81%	533 BSCF	n/a
Max. prodn (MMSCF/D)	n/a	—	280†	280†	200	n/a
No. of wells	46	12	n/a	3	21	8
Well spacing (m)	750–1500	700–1500	n/a	n/a	300–2000	1000–3000
Engineered recovery	Flank water drive/miscible gas	—	—	—	—	Water injection?
Net/gross ratio	0.35–0.9	n/a	0.84–1.00	0.67–0.80	0.70–0.95	n/a
Porosity (fraction)	0.16–0.29	0.07–0.11	0.11–0.30	0.06–0.15	0.09–0.24	0.27–0.35
Permeability (mD)	20–10 000	0.1–2 (matrix)	1–1000	0.1–400	n/a	9000
Interpretation	Braided/meandering	Braided	Channel/sheetflood	Braided/low sinuosity	Braided/alluvial fan	Braided/meandering
Fluvial facies importance	Dominant	Dominant	Dominant	Dominant	Dominant	Subordinate
References	Johnson & Krol (1984) Struijk & Green (1991) Keijzer & Kortekaas (1990)	Benzagouta & Turner (1992) Edwards (1991)	Ritchie & Pratisides (1993)	Ritchie & Pratisides (1993)	Ketter (1991)	Harris (1989)

Description is specific to braided fluvial part of mixed reservoirs.
Well spacing quoted is that at date of most significant published information.
Oil and gas in place values are those assigned to fluvial parts of reservoir only.
All figures are approximate.
Interpretation is based on published accounts.
* Gas storage scheme implemented.
† Figures not separately assigned.
n/a: data not available (or cannot be assigned to fluvial part of reservoir).
— not present, not appropriate or not applicable.

sand bodies. These correspond to the 'labyrinth' reservoir type of Weber & Van Geuns (1990); that is, a reservoir in which flow paths are extremely tortuous and probably unpredictable using conventional geological techniques. The Statfjord Formation (Table 1) is the best-known North Sea example: as a result of the relative complexity of its internal architecture, often

Hewett	Morecambe	Murdoch	Snorre	Snorre	Statfjord	Wytch Farm
Offshore UK	Offshore UK	Offshore UK	Offshore Norway	Offshore Norway	Offshore UK/ Norway	Onshore UK
Triassic	Triassic	Carboniferous	L. Triassic	L. Jurassic	U. Triassic– L. Jurassic	Triassic
Bacton	—	Coal Measures	—	—	—	—
Bunter Sst Developed Gas Depletion	Sherwood Sst Developed Gas Depletion	— Appraisal Gas —	Lunde Appraisal Oil Water (weak)	Statfjord Appraisal Oil Water (weak)	Statfjord Developed Oil Edge water (weak)	Sherwood Sst Developed Oil Water (weak)
190 —	170 —	n/a —	50 2080†	30 2080†	35 1500	34 350
—	—	—	21–41%	32–42%	42%	n/a
—	—	—	—	—	250	60
n/a 'very good'	6750 80%	n/a n/a	— —	— —	— *	— —
n/a	1220	280†	—	—	*	—
30 300–500	17 (40) 500–4000	n/a n/a	11 2000–4000	11 2000–4000	30 1000–2000	49 n/a
—	—	—	Water injection	Water injection	Miscible gas (Water injection)	Water injection
0.88–98 0.19–0.23	0.56–0.85 0.14–0.15	n/a n/a	0.35–0.68 0.19–0.29	0.4–0.63 0.19–0.29	0.50–0.72 0.18–0.23	n/a 0.16
250–1000	1–100	1–400	320–535	1300–2000	1500	50
Alluvial plain	Braided	Braided	Braided	Braided/ low sinuosity	Braided/ meandering?	Braided
Dominant	Subordinate	Dominant	Dominant	Dominant	Dominant	Dominant
Cooke-Yarborough (1991)	Bushell (1986)	Green & Slatt (1992)	Stanley et al. (1990) Nybråten et al. (1990) Hollander (1987)	Stanley et al. (1990) Nybråten et al. (1990) Hollander (1987)	Buza & Unneberg (1987) Roberts et al. (1987) Haugen et al. (1988)	Dranfield et al. (1987) Bowman et al. (1993)

uncorrelatable at well spacings typical during appraisal of offshore fields, it has been the subject of recent studies which aim to predict sand body connectivity and fluid flow characteristics using unconventional methods (Martin et al. 1988; Keijzer & Kortekaas 1990; Stanley et al. 1990). Interpretation of the formation, which forms an important reservoir in two of the largest North Sea fields, is the subject of some debate: Johnson & Krol (1984) suggested a meandering channel origin in Brent Field, whereas in other fields a low sinuosity to braided interpretation is favoured (e.g. Martin et al. 1988; Buza & Unneberg 1987). Whatever its interpretation, good reservoir management is required to avoid poor reservoir sweep (poor displacement of oil by aquifer influx or injected fluids) and/or premature aquifer or injected water breakthrough. Nevertheless, moderate recoveries (at least 20–40% of STOOIP) should be possible. In fact the Statfjord reservoir of the Statfjord Field is used for temporary storage of

Table 2. *Selected braided fluvial reservoirs, rest of world*

Field	Aracas	Azal	Bu Attifel	Katnook	Messla
Location	Onshore Brazil	Onshore Yemen	Onshore Libya	Onshore Australia	Onshore Libya
Age	U. Jurassic	Cretaceous	L. Cretaceous	n/a	L. Cretaceous
Group	—	—	Sarir	n/a	Sarir
Formation	Sergi	Alif	—	Pretty Hill Sst	—
Status	Developed	Developed	Developed	Developed	Developed
Type	Oil	Oil & gas	Oil	Gas	Oil
Drive mechanism	n/a	Gas cap expansion/ water	n/a	Depletion	Water
Area (sq km)	8	13	55	4	230
STOOIP (MMSTB)	113	n/a	n/a	—	3000
Estimated oil recovery	8%	142 MMSTB	15% to date	—	50%
Max. prodn (MSTB/D)	n/a	n/a	n/a	—	100 (per well)
GIIP (BSCF)	—	n/a	—	n/a	—
Estimated gas recovery	—	5.7 BSCF	—	n/a	—
Max. daily prodn (MMSCF/D)	—	n/a	—	n/a	—
No. of wells	37	20	40	3	100
Well spacing (m)	n/a	500–1000	1000–2000	n/a	2000–4000
Engineered recovery	Water injection	Gas injection	Water injection	—	—
Net/gross ratio	0.95	n/a	n/a	n/a	n/a
Porosity (fraction)	n/a	0.16–0.18	0.80–0.16	n/a	0.17
Permeability (mD)	n/a	500–1200	1–1000	11–250	500
Interpretation	Braided	Braidplain/ channel fill	Braided	Braided	Braided
Fluvial facies importance	Dominant	Dominant	Dominant	Dominant	Dominant
References	Nascimento et al. (1982)	Huurdeman et al. (1991)	Erba et al. (pers. comm.)	Malavazos & McDonough (1991)	Clifford et al. (1979)

Notes: see Table 1.

produced gas from the Brent Group (Buza and Unneberg 1987). Gas storage is only possible in good quality reservoirs.

The Peco Field (Table 2) is interpreted as a braided fluvial system (Gardiner *et al.* 1990) but its elongate sand body geometry could perhaps favour a single composite channel. Unusually low net to gross ratios (0.3) and estimated recovery factor of only 10% of STOOIP does not correspond to the general pattern. Poor reservoir performance is due to severe diagenesis. While stimulation can increase the production from individual wells by increasing the effective permeability in the wellbore area, the permeability in the bulk of the reservoir, which controls the displacement process, remains low.

Mixed reservoirs: complex but ultimately predictable?

Other fields produce from sequences which comprise a variety of depositional environments, and thus correspond to the 'jigsaw puzzle' reservoir type of Weber & Van Guens; that is, different shaped units of different properties interleaved in a complex, but ultimately predictable, fashion. The fluvial Garn Formation of Heidrun (Table 1), currently awaiting development, is the best reservoir in the field. Interpretation is controversial (Harris 1989): some workers favour a meandering fluvial origin although from the engineering point of view, this distinction may be irrelevant as the formation is extensive. The mature South

North Rankin	Peco	Prudhoe Bay	South Belridge	Sarir C-Main	Vacas Muertas
Offshore Australia	Onshore Canada	Onshore Alaska	Onshore USA	Onshore Libya	Onshore Argentina
Trias-L. Jurassic	Cretaceous	Permo-Trias	Pleistocene	L. Cretaceous	Cretaceous
n/a	—	Sadlerochit	—	Sarir	—
n/a	Belly River	Ivishak Sst	Tulare	—	Barancas
Developed	Developed	Developed	Developed	Developed	Developed
Gas condensate	Oil & gas	Oil & gas	Oil	Oil	Oil
Depletion	Solution gas/ gas cap expansion	Gravity drainage/ gas cap expansion	Solution gas/ gravity drainage	Bottom water	Depletion/water
50	19	1140	50	800	n/a
—	34	21 5000	n/a	8000	400
—	10%	56%	1200 MMSTB	25% to date	38.5% to date
—	4	1450	170	350	—
n/a	n/a	46 500	—	—	—
7700 BSCF	n/a	7000 BSCF (to date)	—	—	—
n/a	n/a	n/a	—	—	—
14 (50 planned)	61	900	6100	300	n/a
500–4000	400	569–805	61–152	1000	n/a
Gas recycling	Fraccing	Water injection Water alternating gas	Steam flooding	Water injection (suspended)	Water injection/ ? caustic flooding
0.75–0.83	0.3	0.87	0.3–0.7	0.5–0.95	n/a
0.17–0.21	0.06–0.13	0.22	0.32–0.42	0.13–0.17	17.5
500–1500	1–150	400	100–10 000	30–600	217
Braided	Braided/single channel	Braided	Braided	Braided	Alluvial fan
Dominant	Dominant	Dominant	Subordinate	Dominant	Dominant
Barker & Vincent (1988) Beston (1986) Harris (1981)	Gardiner et al. (1990)	Atkinson et al. (1990) Atkinson et al. (1988) Wadman et al. (1978)	Gates & Brewer (1975) Miller et al. (1990)	Sanford (1970)	Simlote et al. (1985)

Belridge Field (Table 2) comprises separate accumulations within stacked fluvio-deltaic sands (some braided) whose distribution and depositional origin is interpreted from the extremely dense well control, dating back to 1911. Recovery of the viscous oil is poor, but shallow burial and high permeability have made the field an attractive candidate for EOR steam injection projects, which demand good understanding of the geometry of target zones.

The petroleum engineer's role

Dynamic modelling requires synergy

The reservoir geologist describes a hydrocarbon reservoir's external geometry, lithological correlatability, vertical sequence and porosity/ permeability distribution (e.g. Johnson & Stewart 1985; Van der Graaf & Ealey 1989 and references therein). This produces a *static* model. Engineering techniques, on the other hand, predict and monitor dynamic (pressure and fluid flow) behaviour (Archer & Wall 1986). Since the 1970s oil companies have understood that the two disciplines must adopt a synergistic approach (Halbouty 1976; Richardson *et al.* 1977; Harris & Hewitt 1977; Wadman *et al.* Archer 1983).

Field appraisal focuses on reservoir continuity

An oil company requires cash flow, which in turn relies on field development (Corrigan *et al.* 1990). Future income generated from a field is a

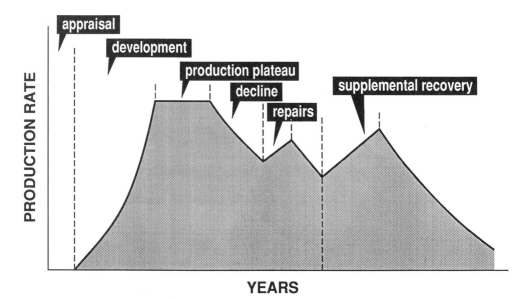

YEARS

Fig. 2. Idealized production profile (modified from Dake 1978). The initial part of the profile showing rapid build-up to a production plateau is typical of offshore development, whereas the long decline period with secondary or enhanced recovery is more typical of onshore fields.

function of its production profile (Fig. 2) predicted by the petroleum reservoir engineer from a reservoir model. Engineering analysis carried out on a new discovery must establish its size and commercial viability. The engineer must establish the likely reserves (Garb & Smith 1989) and production rate of the field, its depletion mechanism (the processes which allow the production of hydrocarbons) and well numbers required for efficient production. At this stage reservoir continuity is one of the main causes for uncertainties: the main problem is characterizing inter-well space from a limited number of observation points (Fig. 3).

In the earliest stages a 'rule of thumb' recovery factor may be applied to determine an order of magnitude for the potential reserve based on knowledge of similar situations (Arps 1967; Fielding & Crane 1987; Garb & Smith 1989). This will be refined as appraisal/development drilling and reservoir performance data become available. The geometry and the geology of the reservoir are of the first importance, and the engineer depends very heavily on the accuracy of reservoir description given by the geophysicist and geologist (e.g. Barker & Vincent 1988). In many situations the engineer has available more computational power than can be used effectively, the limitation in models is often the physical description of the reservoir in terms of corre-

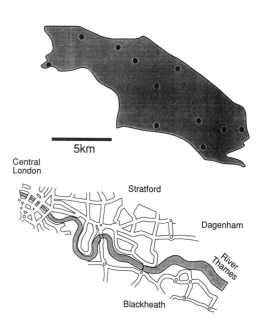

Fig. 3. Location and spacing of appraisal wells on the Snorre Field, offshore Norway (after Nybråten *et al.* 1991) compared with a map of part of central and east London, showing motorways and trunk roads. As a crude analogy, predicting the geometry of individual channel sands in the reservoir from limited well data may be likened to an attempt to draw this road map based on observations made at a few random locations.

lation and continuity of sand and shale layers (e.g. Nybråten *et al.* 1990). Monte Carlo techniques are frequently used at this stage to gain a feeling for possible uncertainties (Haldorsen & Damsleth 1990).

Development planning often requires 'engineered recovery'

Field development is a plan to optimize economic recovery from a reservoir or reservoirs. The development plan defines the capital investment required for the field. This includes the number of wells, the processing requirements and requirements for fluid injection. In the past, development of an onshore oilfield could be divided into three phases.

Primary: in which oil recovery relies on the natural drive mechanism of the reservoir, including natural aquifer influx or gas cap expansion etc. (e.g. Sanford 1970; Exploration Staff of the Arabian Gulf Oil Company 1980).

Secondary: in which production is boosted by pressure maintenance schemes; mainly water flooding (e.g. Yusun *et al.* 1985, 1989; Zhiwu *et al.* 1989) or gas injection.

Tertiary: in which declining production is countered by the use of enhanced oil recovery (EOR) methods such as steam flooding (e.g. Gates & Brewer 1975). Onshore fields typically show a long decline period, during which time EOR projects may be designed to recover (relatively small amounts of) incremental oil (e.g. Rupp *et al.* 1984; Simlote *et al.* 1985). Well spacings associated with EOR schemes (particularly pilot projects) may be very small (Fig. 4).

However, modern practice (particularly offshore where rapid return on investment is demanded) has blurred these distinctions. These days 'engineered recovery' schemes requiring some form of fluid injection may be scheduled very soon after field production startup (e.g. Johnson & Krol 1984; Buza & Unneberg 1987). Development offshore is much more sensitive to uncertainty than development onshore, particularly when development wells are 'pre-drilled' through a subsea template prior to platform installation, to shorten the build-up to plateau production. The development plan must be determined without the benefit of substantial dynamic data (in contrast to onshore fields, in which pilot production from the first wells can provide information in order to fine-tune the overall development).

Gas field development. Gas reservoirs pose different problems (Simpson & Weber 1986)

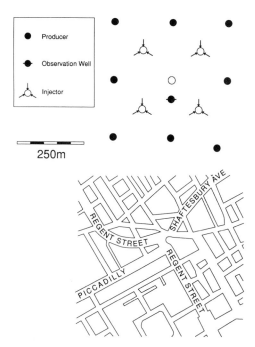

Fig. 4. Well locations of an EOR pilot (Martin & Cooper 1984) superimposed on a detailed street plan of the Piccadilly Circus area, London. The geologist and engineer will have much data with which to evaluate connectivity between injectors and producers, but the flow pathways must be characterized in detail.

particularly because of contract requirements which may impose penalty clauses in the case of non-achievement of agreed sales volumes. Most development offshore NW Europe has been restricted to those reservoirs with good properties and high well productivity (Bushell 1986; Stuart & Cowan 1991). Many have been considered to be homogeneous 'tanks' which allowed development wells to be clustered at structural culminations, and completed high above potentially troublesome gas-water contacts (e.g. Esmond, Forbes and Gordon Fields; Ketter 1991). One result of this is lack of geological control on field flanks: in such cases it may be more accurate to estimate gas initially in place (GIIP) from material balance (Dake 1978, p. 25) than from geological maps, especially where water influx is absent or limited. Problems arise, however, during equity determination of fields which straddle licence block boundaries as flank structure controls the areal *distribution* of GIIP, and thus the share of reserves and production allocated to each owner. Furthermore, lack of peripheral wells can also leave no way to monitor contact movements on the flanks (see below).

Production optimization maximizes economic recovery

After initial development, the engineer's task is to monitor reservoir performance and to maximise economic recovery through planning of infill wells (wells drilled to decrease the overall grid spacing of producers), recompletions (modifications to perforated intervals), secondary and advanced recovery methods. As reservoir data become available, understanding of reservoir continuity increases, and supplements stratigraphic and lithogical information (Knutson 1976; Lorenz et al. 1975; Chancellor & Johnson 1988). Offshore, this may be too late for major investment decisions, but will control redrilling and recompletion plans.

Engineering tools

Well test analysis helps reservoir characterization

Background. Drill stem tests (DSTs), effectively temporary completions of exploration and appraisal wells; and production tests of permanent completion intervals in development wells have for many years been used to determine fluid type, well productivity rate, productivity index and identify wellbore damage (Dake 1978; Archer & Wall 1986). Boundary and layering effects can be determined by analysis of pressure response (Gringarten 1987; Ehlig-Economides 1987; Horne 1990; Ayestaran & Karakas 1990). Many methods consider the pressure build-up following a flow period normally of a few hours or days duration.

Major recent advances in well test design and interpretation include:

(i) higher precision, high frequency data, both for flow rate and pressure;
(ii) software data presentation and interpretation using graphical presentations to identify different characteristic flow periods (Matthews 1986) during a test;
(iii) use of pressure derivative plots, which provide simultaneous presentation of $\log \Delta p$ versus $\log \Delta t$ and $\Delta t \log \partial p/\partial t$ versus $\log \Delta t$ (Fig. 5);
(iv) non-linear regression methods (automated type curve matching).

Well tests are increasingly used for reservoir characterization, through computer analysis and simulation of model test responses. Well tests can be used to estimate bulk reservoir properties (which control well and field behaviour) because they are relatively insensitive to local heterogeneities. Test analysis is an inverse problem: model parameters are inferred by analysing model response (pressure transient) to a given input (flow rate transient). The main drawback, however, is that a model may act like the reservoir even though physical assumptions are invalid.

A powerful analytic tool made possible by computer-aided interpretation is non-linear regression, or automated type-curve matching. This differs from graphical techniques in that it uses a mathematical algorithm to match data to a chosen reservoir model. Matching is achieved by changing the values of unknown reservoir parameters until the model and the data fit as closely as possible. However, non-linear regression analysis must be complemented by visual diagnosis of the data so that the engineer can select the most appropriate reservoir model. Geological input is critical.

Test design. The test period has to be sufficient to reach that part of the reservoir response which is of interest. The analyst must determine whether the maximum flow rate attainable will provide sufficient pressure change over the part of the reservoir most diagnostic of the unknown reservoir parameters. One of the best approaches to design is to perform a computer simulation of the test with prospective values of the reservoir parameters, and then examine the simulated data to see if it is able to provide valid estimates of the required parameters. Tests can be designed to validate the depositional geometry of a reservoir interval interpreted by the geologist, or alternatively to help differentiate between two possibilities.

Sequential DSTs in which the perforated interval is successively increased can be very useful if planned and interpreted with care (Schlumberger 1992a). Unfortunately in older fields a high proportion of tests is commonly uninterpretable due to technical problems, insufficient pressure response or co-mingled production from several perforated inervals.

Application. Despite sedimentological complexity as observed in core or outcrop (Rudkiewicz et al. 1990; Miall 1988) test response from some braided fluvial reservoirs shows that the engineer may consider them to be essentially homogeneous within the region of investigation (Fig. 5).

This behaviour, however, differs from

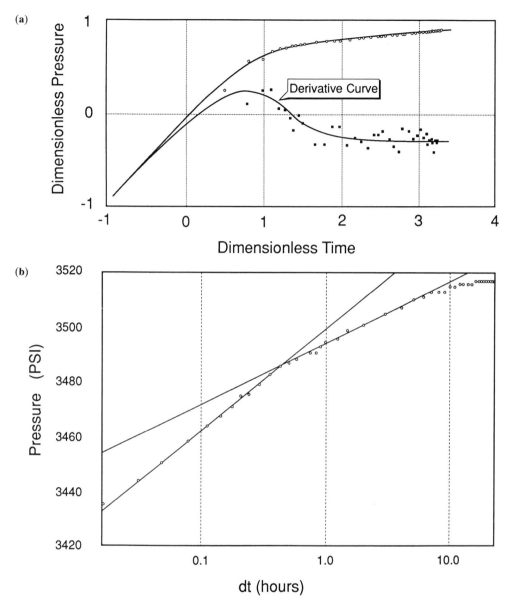

Fig. 5. (a) Pressure build-up test analysis from a braided fluvial reservoir, showing features typical of a homogeneous reservoir, with a radial flow pattern. 'Dimensionless variables' (Horne 1990) are used in test analysis to reduce the number of unknowns, and provide solutions that are independent of any particular units system. Dimensionless pressure and time are linear functions of actual pressure and time. The shape of the derivative curve can be used to infer the best model from which to seek the best interpreted solution.
(b) Logarithmic plot of pressure versus build-up time for a less typical test in the same field. The diagnostic change in slope is interpreted as the effects of heterogeneity (a homogeneous reservoir would yield a single straight line on this type of plot).

responses from low sinuosity channels within a Statfjord Formation interval in which pressure response conformed to a linear inflow pattern, rather than radial flow typical of extensive reservoirs (Martin et al. 1988). Well tests were used to estimate characteristic channel width (below 100 m, for 3 m thick channels). This provided independent support for the geological

a) GEOLOGICAL SCHEMATIC

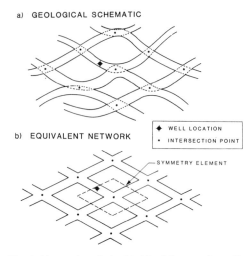

b) EQUIVALENT NETWORK

◆ WELL LOCATION
• INTERSECTION POINT
— SYMMETRY ELEMENT

Fig. 6. Abstraction of a braided fluvial system for well test analysis and simulation: plan view (after Martin *et al*. 1988).

FULL WELL MODEL

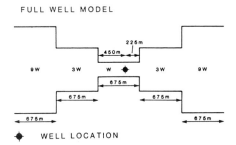

◆ WELL LOCATION

Fig. 7. 'Expanding flow' model for well test analysis using computer methods; derived from Fig. 6 (after Martin *et al*. 1988). The value for W was derived from conventional test analysis. The repeat length was modified iteratively until a satisfactory match was obtained between measured and predicted pressure. The offset well location with respect to the first expansion was also suggested by iterative pressure matching.

interpretation. However, single channel models were not sufficient to account for pressure response during the latest period of build-up, which indicated a degree of interconnectedness (Fig. 6). Although more than one model could account for this pattern, an 'expanding flow' network of channels was geologically defensible (Figs 7 & 8). Well test analysis software was used to establish typical 'repeat lengths' between successive expansions.

Well tests have also been used to estimate the dimensions of southern North Sea Carboniferous channel reservoirs (P. Haynes, pers. comm.) and in Australia (Malavazos & McDonough 1991). Wadsley *et al*. (1990) describe a successful match of a long term (6 month) production test followed by a 3 month build-up using computer test analysis combined with stochastic channel modelling (see below).

Well tests can also determine the effective radius of a non-correlatable permeability barrier observed in a well (Fig. 9). Some testing techniques have more general applicability: let us imagine that there are two sandy intervals separated by a shale whose lateral extent is in question. One can investigate this by perforating the sand with the lower permeability × height product (the 'flow capacity' of an interval is the product of permeability, k, and interval height h). This kh term, expressed in mD ft or mD m, is a fundamental property of a perforated interval which can be determined independently by appropriate test analysis. Perforations can then be added in the other sand, with the initial perforation still open. The well would again be tested, and the kh again interpreted. If the two kh values are the same, it is quite likely the shaley interval is not laterally continuous. Conversely, different kh values would suggest that it was continuous for some distance.

Well tests can also be used to estimate vertical permeability. This is done by perforating the

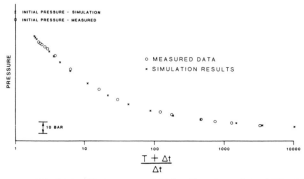

Fig. 8. Excellent pressure match obtained between model (Fig. 7) and raw data. (After Martin *et al*. 1988).

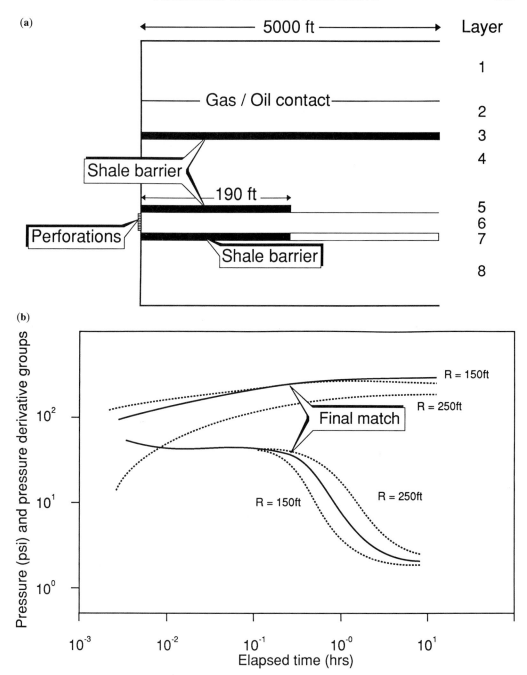

Fig. 9. Use of non-linear regression techniques for estimating the length of a permeability barrier penetrated by a well (after Ayestaran *et al.* 1989). (**a**) Well test simulation model. (**b**) Sensitivity analysis on length of barrier.

poorer section of an interval and running a welltest for a long period, maybe a day or two (depending on the permeability level). The shape of the pressure plot will differ depending whether or not the pressure transient 'feels' the

contribution from the other interval. If it does, there are analytical techniques to calculate vertical permeability from such a test.

However, one must remember that the volume of reservoir 'interrogated' by a test depends on factors including its duration, and the permeability of the reservoir. Most tests only provide information on average reservoir characteristics up to several hundred metres away from the wellbore. Nevertheless, properly conducted and interpreted tests provide much independent data with which to characterize dynamic reservoir behaviour.

Interference testing can establish reservoir communication

In an interference (or pulse) test one well is produced and pressure is observed in a different well or wells, to evaluate either the degree of lateral communication (Britt *et al.* 1991) or the

vertical communication between units. The technique has particular value in planning EOR projects, in which it is critical to establish whether producers and injectors communicate. Pressure changes at a distance from the producer are much smaller than at the well itself, so interference tests require sensitive pressure recorders and long duration. The technique is not appropriate to all reservoirs: the fluid system should have low compressibility, well spacing should be small, and pressure perturbations from surrounding areas should be minimal. Although no readily accessible account of interference testing in a braided fluvial reservoir is in the public domain, such reservoirs are attractive candidates for interference testing as their high permeability will allow shorter flow periods.

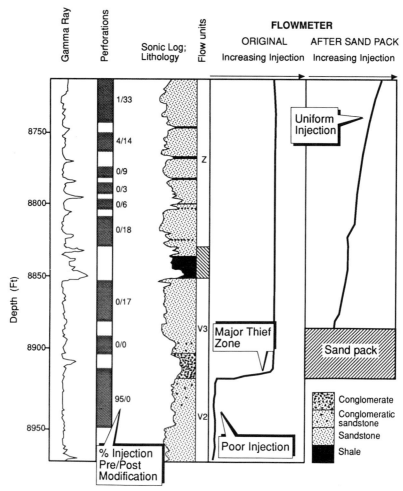

Fig. 10. Flowmeter log showing restriction of injectivity to highly permeable intervals, Prudhoe Bay Field. Track A shows original flow profile dominated by high permeability thief zone which takes 95% of injected water. Following profile modification with sand pack, injection profile is more uniform. (After Atkinson *et al.* 1990).

Production logging demonstrates flow contribution of individual zones

Background. Cased hole wireline flowmeter surveys (Schlumberger 1989) quantify the relative proportion of total flow entering the casing from specific perforated intervals. Other measurements allow the interpreter to determine the nature of the fluid in the wellbore. Flowmeters and/or temperature logs can also be run in injector wells to check on where the fluid is entering the reservoir, and can thus form part of a surveillance package for waterflood operations (Thakur 1991).

Application. Flowmeter logs are often directly related to medium scale reservoir heterogeneity observed from cores or logs. Interpreted flowmeter surveys from braided fluvial reservoirs (Figs 10 & 11) show high permeability zones dominating flow. The *kh* term (defined above) is proportional to the amount of fluid flowing out of (or into) an interval. The reservoir geologist is concerned with predicting which intervals will dominate flow. Unfortunately many geologists display measured or predicted permeability vs. depth plots on semi-logarithmic scales. However, linear plots are more useful as they give a much better representation of flow capacity (Fig. 11).

Wireline formation pressure profiling establishes differential depletion

Background. The wireline repeat formation tester (RFT; Schlumberger 1981) and similar tools allow the engineer or geologist to investigate pressure communication in partially depleted reservoirs (Stewart & Ayestaran 1982; Gunter & Moore 1987; Dickey 1989). The tool is positioned at successive points across a reservoir interval and direct fluid pressure readings obtained. Offsets in fluid pressure gradients in infill wells in partly depleted reservoirs indicate permeability barriers or partial 'baffles' (Fig. 12). Correlation schemes must take into account RFT surveys, as they will indicate the presence of separate flow compartments (although RFTs must be interpreted with care, as the pressure profile will reflect production: if pressure decline in two adjacent but non-communicating reservoirs is balanced, no differential will be observed). Although now standard in the North Sea since its introduction in the mid-1970s, in many operating areas the RFT is not used as much as it should be.

Application. RFT responses in braided fluvial reservoirs (Fig. 13) show good vertical communication in most sand bodies, with only localised evidence for compartmentalisation, particularly in sequences with higher proportions of overbank deposits. Normally, fine-grained intervals do not form pressure barriers within individual sands (as most shales are relatively short, except for intercalations of lacustrine facies between channel sands). The RFT is the best way of identifying any continuous shales.

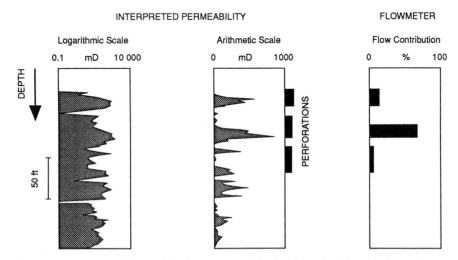

Fig. 11. Comparison of permeability profiles (from cores and logs) with productivity of perforated intervals (from flowmeter) in a braided fluvial reservoir. Note restriction of flow to high permeability intervals.

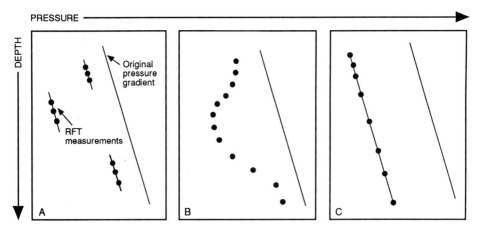

Fig. 12. Schematic RFT pressure profiles in infill wells from partially depleted fields. (**a**) Effect of two permeability barriers; (**b**) 'baffle zone'; (**c**) fully communicating (after Schlumberger 1981).

Cased hole nuclear logging monitors contact movement

Background. The engineer needs to know if the oil–water contact (OWC) in a reservoir moves over time (Westaway *et al.* 1979; Libson *et al.*

1985). The thermal decay time (TDT) tool (Schlumberger 1989), and other pulsed neutron tools are through-casing chlorine detectors: provided that formation water is salty, and reservoir quality good, sequential runs of this tool will allow changes of OWC with production to be

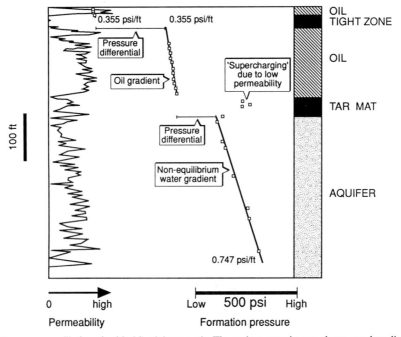

Fig. 13. RFT pressure profile from braided fluvial reservoir. The main reservoir zone shows good quality partly depleted sands in pressure communication. At the top there is an isolated sand. Note the pressure offset between the oil leg and aquifer due to permeability reduction by a geochemical barrier. Aquifer pressure gradient indicates disequilibrium possibly associated with the effect of a baffle zone caused by discontinuous low permeability streaks (channel abandonment drapes and overbank deposits) observed in the permeability profile.

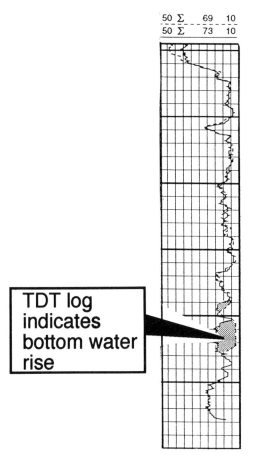

TDT log indicates bottom water rise

Fig. 14. Two TDT logs run in a braided fluvial reservoir showing evidence for bottom water rise: the second log, run four years after the first, does not overlay it across the lower part of the reservoir.

monitored. This involves logging wells at different times and overlaying the logs to detect differences. Today a wide range of cased hole nuclear tools (Schlumberger 1989) is used to monitor OWC and gas–oil contact (GOC) behaviour.

Application. The TDT log of Fig. 14 shows a typical response of a braided fluvial reservoir with an extensive aquifer. Despite sedimentological variability, in this field OWC rises predictably in line with production. This is typical of a bottom water drive reservoir. Only limited evidence of bypassed oil (Felder 1988) is found (in any case, bypassed oil observed on a TDT log could actually be producible from an up-dip well location). In contrast, isolated channel sand reservoirs may show evidence of lateral water encroachment due to unfavourable permeability profile leading to poor vertical sweep efficiency (Fig. 15). In fact the permeability profiles associated with different depositional environments play a great role in determining recovery under different drive mechanisms: this can be demonstrated by the use of simple simulation models (Poston & Gross 1984).

Johnson & Scanlon (1991) describe the use of pulsed neutron logging in the Esmond Complex. Haugen *et al.* (1988) used case hole neutron logs to monitor the growth of a secondary gas cap in the Statfjord Formation of the Statfjord Field. Logging techniques to monitor the movement of gas caps are also used routinely in the Prudhoe Bay Field, where high pressure drawdowns have led to gas 'cusping' beneath extensive shale barriers (Fig. 17). More typical of braided sequences, however, are discontinuous barriers

FINING-UPWARD SEQUENCE

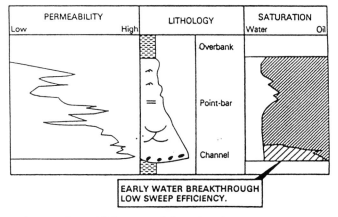

Fig. 15. Water encroachment at base of fining-upward channel sand.

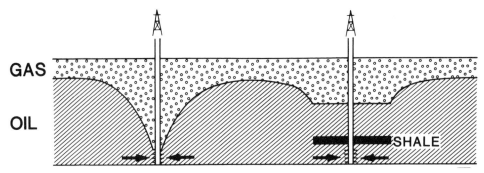

Fig. 16. Gas coning. Arrows indicate perforated intervals, which act as a pressure sink. A shale protects the perforations from downward gas movement. An analogous situation may occur at an oil–water contact, where wells may be completed above tight streaks to prevent upward water coning.

which do not extend between production well spacings. Such barriers can nevertheless be of extreme importance in limiting either gas or water 'coning' (Fig. 16; Richardson *et al.* 1987*a*) even if they extend only relatively short distances: well completion design should take advantage of any such intervals.

Pressure and production history trends help reservoir understanding

Review of field pressure history since production start-up, based on regular measurements of pressure from dedicated observation wells (completed across a reservoir sand but used neither for production nor for injection) or field-wide pressure surveys made while wells are not producing (shut-in) will reveal reservoir compartmentalisation or communication with aquifer or injected fluids. Many braided fluvial reservoirs are in good pressure communication (Fig. 18) as a result of good rock quality, the low permeability streaks not forming significant pressure barriers. The geologist is, however, cautioned against over-interpretation of field-wide or single well pressure v. time plots: mechanical problems such as communication between reservoir and shallow aquifers (recognized or unrecognized) can cause pressure anomalies and equipment failure or transcription errors can sometimes not be excluded. Close co-operation with the reservoir engineer is required.

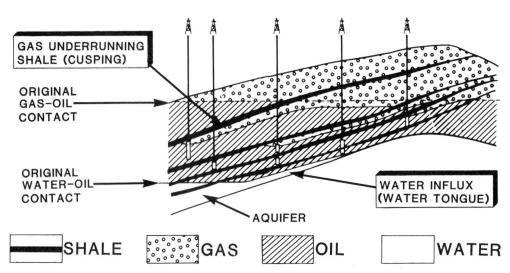

Fig. 17. Gas cusping and water tongues in the Prudhoe Bay Field resulting from extensive shales (lacustrine intervals). Note how early gas and water breakthrough occurs despite perforations some distance from OWC and GOC. (After Haldorsen & Chang 1986).

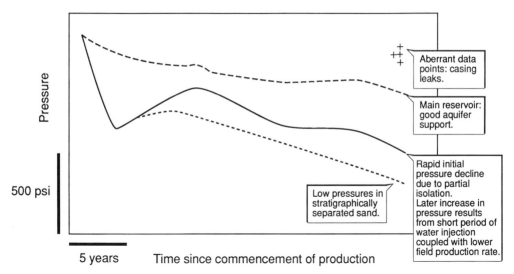

Fig. 18. Pressure trends in a braided fluvial field.

Production decline curve behaviour of individual wells can be investigated to determine remaining oil reserves or productive life (Garb & Smith 1989). Cumulative production and time are selected as independent variables. Of the many dependent variables that can be considered, the rate of production is most appropriate when production is not restricted. If wellbore and mechanical conditions are satisfactory, a declining production trend can be extrapolated to predict remaining recoverable reserves if there is a long production history and the drive mechanism is unlikely to change. However, the technique is inappropriate if production/injection distribution or drive mechanism changes and although the engineer will inspect production data to monitor problems caused by water or gas breakthrough into perforated intervals (e.g. Chancellor & Johnson 1988), computer reservoir simulation models are now more regularly used to predict future performance.

Reservoir simulation: conventional approach

Why simulate reservoirs?

Computer reservoir simulation incorporates multi-dimensional, multiphase reservoir analysis to investigate the behaviour of discrete field regions over time, taking into account changes in saturation resulting from pressure drops induced by production (Arnovsky et al.

1985; Archer & Wall 1986; Fisher 1989; Coats 1989; Dalton & Mattax 1990 and references therein).

Grid points or nodes are each assigned a value for permeability, thickness, porosity, fluid content, elevation and pressure at pre-production conditions. Initial rates for produced fluid phases are assigned to the wells in the field. Then, for a finite time difference new saturations and pressures for each of the grid nodes are calculated, which in turn allows new rates for each of the producing wells to be estimated. This process is repeated for a number of time steps, to calculate rate and pressure histories for each well in the system, as well as saturation and pressure histories for each grid node.

A reservoir simulator allows the engineer to investigate various operating schemes, select the optimum from the cases which were run and produce answers which could not have been arrived at intuitively:

(i) determine field performance under depletion or fluid injection operations;
(ii) predict the effect of well spacing, flood pattern or producing rate on recovery;
(iii) calculate critical well rates for water or gas coning;
(iv) evaluate the benefits of workovers, stimulation or gas lift.

Simulation modelling has been a significant advance in field development planning, and allows sensitivity analysis (evaluation of uncertainties in input parameters) and prediction which would not otherwise be possible. However, it is simply a 'tool' for use alongside other geological and engineering methods. It is too easy to get carried away by the numerical and graphical output of a reservoir simulator: mistakes have been made as a result of faith in simulator output, without critical evaluation of uncertainties in key input data.

Different model types address specific problems

Single well models have radial geometry consisting either of a single sector or a cylinder extending away from the well bore. Cell radii decrease logarithmically or geometrically towards the well bore to give greater detail close to the perforations. Single well models are usually employed to investigate coning and cusping phenomena and to design production rates to limit encroachment of undesirable fluid phases; also to design and simulate well tests or determine optimum completion policy. The required geological reservoir description is location-specific and more detailed than for other model types.

Cross-section models allow the representation of detailed layering effects and structural dip of the reservoir, to:

(i) calculate and validate averaged permeabilities for application in coarse grid models, along with a simplified vertical grid description;
(ii) investigate mechanisms of pressure support (both natural and assisted) and the influence on the vertical efficiency of the displacement process caused by layer and inter-layer properties;
(iii) evaluate completion method.

They require careful interwell, layer and inter-layer reservoir description in terms of capillary pressure, relative permeability and vertical/horizontal permeability.

3D models. Sector or full field models (Barnes 1989) are usually based on rectilinear or distorted grids and can combine results from more detailed models into a coarse areal and vertical description, which includes all interwell effects. Full field models are used to determine overall field performance (Starley *et al.* 1991; Wood & Young 1991) but may not be detailed enough to adequately represent small-scale effects. They should, however, be re-usable throughout development and subsequent production of a field.

Despite the value of simulation, many engineers use hand calculations and analytical techniques to obtain answers to many reservoir questions. In general one should use the simplest model possible to solve a particular problem and only go on to more complex models if required. For example, in braided stream reservoirs, gas or water coning (defined below) can be a critical question and single well models may be adequate early on. If the reservoir is layered by the presence of continuous shales, cross-section models may give answers to most of the major questions. Thankfully, one does not necessarily need a full field simulation model to solve every problem.

Steps in performing a simulation study

Geological input is critical

Layering. Fluid movement during drainage is principally controlled by permeability; thus the correct distribution of permeability is the major factor in successful modelling. Ideally, the actual permeability profile from each well should be used in modelling, but except in finely gridded single well or cross-sectional models, this is impracticable.

The reservoir is instead broken down into a manageable number of layers, each of which must be provided with the key parameters of the reservoir, not only at the position of the wells but extrapolated between them. The process of layering the reservoir is purely for the convenience of engineering analysis and inevitably leads to loss of detail. The reservoir geologist must try to ensure that all critical parameters are retained during this process. Layers may follow a sedimentary facies or be purely artificial (e.g. in a complex, uncorrelatable reservoir in which 'slice mapping' may be adopted). The vertical dimension of layers must be determined with regard to the nature of the reservoir and of the model required. For example in a cross-sectional model it may be possible to explicitly represent layers on a metre scale, whereas in full-field models layer thicknesses may typically be on a 10 m scale.

The layering process requires permeability to be averaged across specific zones. How do we generate these averages? The first step is to ensure that permeabilities derived from well tests are broadly in line with those determined from cores or predicted using some combination of log response. In braided fluvial sequences without fracturing or delicate clay mineral morphologies this should not be a major problem bearing in mind that results are unlikely to be exactly equal due to differences of scale or possible sample bias.

We then have to determine which type of average is most appropriate. For modelling horizontal flow in a layered system, an arithmetic average will probably be most suitable. For modelling vertical flow, a harmonic average, which produces a result biased towards the lowest values, may be chosen. However, this model assumes lateral continuity of low permeability beds: clearly inappropriate in the case of most braided fluvial sands containing uncorrelatable shales (Martin & Cooper 1984). In such reservoirs it is most appropriate to choose layer boundaries at any continuous (lacustrine?) shales which form pressure barriers. Within the layers effective vertical permeability (on the scale of the simulator unit) can be very difficult for the geologist and engineer to specify. It is unlikely to be equal to vertical permeability determined from core plug analysis. Many methods for determining vertical permeabilities have been proposed: some rely on statistical techniques discussed below (e.g. Begg & King 1985; Begg et al. 1985; King 1990). However, most engineers still rely on the simple method of assigning one or more vertical/horizontal permeability ratios to the layers within a model. The sensitivity of simulation results to changes in vertical/horizontal permeability ratio is normally evaluated.

Mapping. For 3D simulation, structural and reservoir property maps are required for each of the simulation layers. However, the simulation model may at best only be able to handle a fraction of the complexity of a full reservoir description. The most important map which is required is that of permeability. A plot of porosity against the logarithm of permeability is often used to assign permeabilities in uncored wells. However, where significant differences exist between core- and test-derived estimates, this method gives an entirely false precision. Note that the facies of high permeability zones may have a different orientation compared to other permeability layers, and permeability itself may be directional, especially in channel sands.

The account above, based largely on Corrigan et al. (1990) is only a brief introduction; further descriptions of geological support required for simulation studies are given by Harris (1975), Archer (1983, 1987) and Weber & Van Geuns (1990). A repeated theme is that of scaling: of geological heterogeneity and of geological, petrophysical and engineering tools (Haldorsen

1986; Van der Graaf & Ealey 1989; Slatt & Hopkins 1990).

How to use the model

History matching. Once a model is constructed and running it is necessary, wherever possible, to validate assumptions and input data. History matching is the procedure of adjusting reservoir description (as given in a simulation model) to fit observed data (pressure, field or well performance). Historical information is available as well rates of individual phases and flowing/static pressures. With the advent of the RFT tool layer pressures in new wells are also available: these make very good layer-specific match criteria, whilst flowmeter data can assist in ascribing flowrates and phase contributions from individual reservoir layers. Obviously, history matching cannot be performed before production commences, which is why simulation modelling is less reliable at the field appraisal stage.

History matching gives the engineer the opportunity to adjust some of the least well-defined parameters against actual performance before predictions are made. As more reservoir history becomes available, so simulation models become more reliable representations. History matching is not a unique process since several variables could usually be modified to obtain a match. Each modification must be both geologically and in engineering terms both reasonable and defensible: history matching should be collaborative.

Neither the engineer nor the geologist should be fooled into believing that assumptions made have given a unique solution: matches can often be made by several combinations of reasonable data. Even a 'good' history match does not guarantee a successful prediction. History matching can be one of the most contentious issues during an engineering study, and considerable man- and computer-time can be expended in trying to achieve an acceptable match. Experience shows that accurate reservoir description, and co-operation between all relevant technical specialists will speed this process.

Prediction. This encompasses the simulation of individual well and total field production profiles with corresponding hydrocarbon recovery. It will usually include alternative development strategies. The most attractive strategies would be refined with further runs incorporating fine tuning adjustments. The optimum exploitation strategy would be selected on the basis of economic evaluation of a few cases.

Application to braided fluvial reservoirs

Evaluation of well performance

Huurdeman *et al.* (1991) use single well models to investigate how halite-cemented layers in a sand control water and gas coning (Fig. 19). Layer rock properties were derived from logs and cores from several wells, while different possible configurations of reduced permeability halitic zones were tested against observed pressure, gas–oil ratio (relative volumes of gas and oil flowing) and watercut (water production expressed as a percentage of total liquid flowing). Martin *et al.* (1988) used single well models to attempt to match DST results in several appraisal wells: these models used a standard radial and concentric grid, but stochastic techniques (see below) were used to assign values for rock properties.

Scaling-up flow effects

Tollas & McKinney (1991) used cross-section models to define 'pseudofunctions' for use in a full-field model (see below). Further discussion of pseudofunctions is outside the scope of this paper: 'rock curves' of relative permeability and capillary pressure (important properties which control fluid flow and displacement) derived from core plug measurements are often inappropriate for use in field calculations (Dake 1978, ch. 10) so they may be replaced by values calculated to represent gravity and scale effects.

3D models to predict field performance

Sector models. Johnson & Krol (1984) describe the integrated geological and engineering approach necessary to achieve a satisfactory reservoir simulation of the Statfjord Formation during the early stage of development of the Brent Field. The main problem was to adequately represent the contrast between channel sands and overbank shales. Grid block thicknesses (4.5–9 m) were chosen to be representative of individual channel dimensions determined by sedimentological study. Although by modern standards the model was small (4000 grid blocks) it had a relatively fine vertical definition (12 layers) which allowed the inactive channel and overbank shales, which together form (largely discontinuous) permeability barriers, to be incorporated into the simulation in some detail. The model predicted the inter-

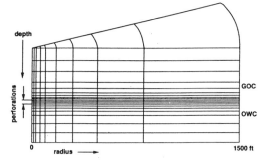

Fig. 19. Single well model (after Huurdeman *et al.* 1991). The diagram shows the radial grid construction, plus the fine layering adopted to model fluid flow in the region of the perforated interval.

connected nature of the reservoir both areally and vertically (Fig. 20): since confirmed by pressure surveys.

Full-field models of fluvial reservoirs adopt a more generalized approach. A more recent model of the Brent Group and Statfjord Formation in the Brent Field (Tollas & McKinney 1991) comprised 34 000 grid blocks (30 east/west and 54 north/south; dimensions 150 × 300 m within the oil leg, with larger aquifer blocks). The Statfjord Formation was divided into four layers (pressure history match of one of these layers is shown in Fig. 21a). Tollas & McKinney (1991) show clearly how the results of the simulation (e.g. Fig. 21b) were used to optimise future field performance. It became clear that several of the platforms would be constrained by gas handling capabilities for some time: upgrades were put in hand following the study.

Buza & Unneberg (1987) review the results of the first and second post-production simulation exercises of the Statfjord reservoir of the Statfjord Field, which matched production periods of 21 and 44 months respectively. Gas–oil ratio, water cut and RFT pressure gradients in infill wells were used as matching parameters. The models correctly predicted the time of first gas breakthrough. Haugen *et al.* (1988) used a later model (11 000 active grid-blocks in seven layers) to ensure that oil production was maximized, and overpressuring by gas injection avoided. Full field modelling of the Prudhoe Bay Field was particularly difficult because of the high number of wells. In such cases, a more generalized approach to history matching well performance is often adopted (O'Brien *et al.* 1984).

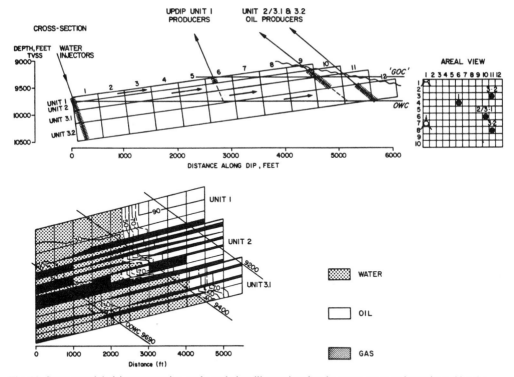

Fig. 20. Sector model: (**a**) cross-section and areal view illustrating development strategy investigated by the model. (**b**) Cross-section illustrating predicted fluid saturations following production period (Johnson & Krol 1984). Reproduced with permission of the Society of Petroleum Engineers.

Non-conventional reservoir characterization and simulation

Stochastic models can quantify uncertainty

Background. Since Haldorsen & Lake (1984) suggested that stochastic modelling could be an effective tool in reservoir modelling, techniques have been refined particularly to estimate effective vertical permeability in reservoirs containing discontinuous shales (Martin & Cooper 1984; Begg & King 1985; Haldorsen & Chang 1986; Haldorsen *et al.* 1987). 2D (or more recently 3D) 'realizations' are created, based on geological input data including length distribution statistics derived from outcrop analogues, and observations of permeability barrier location and thickness from cores. Having created one or more realization(s) the detailed model(s) are translated into a reservoir simulation. This has been attempted using simple 'building blocks' (Martin & Cooper 1984) or shale frequency maps and statistical procedures (Begg & King 1985; Begg *et al.* 1985). Where production history has been available it

has been found that the stochastic model gives only a starting point for history matching, although it can be speeded by the initial stochastic approach.

Two points must be stressed.

(i) There is no justification for using stochastic techniques unless the geologist is unable to derive a convincing deterministic correlation. Successful models must in fact be hybrid: based on any overall deterministic framework, and honour (i.e. be 'conditioned' to) observed well data.

(ii) A realization is not 'reality'. Early models suffered from lack of computing power, time and lack of an interface between the stochastic model and the simulator. For this reason, insufficient realizations were constructed or tested. However, recent advances have made it much simpler to create and simulate more realizations, to obtain a better idea of the uncertainty range of the predictions.

Shale distribution models for fluvial reservoirs. Many braided fluvial reservoirs are basically

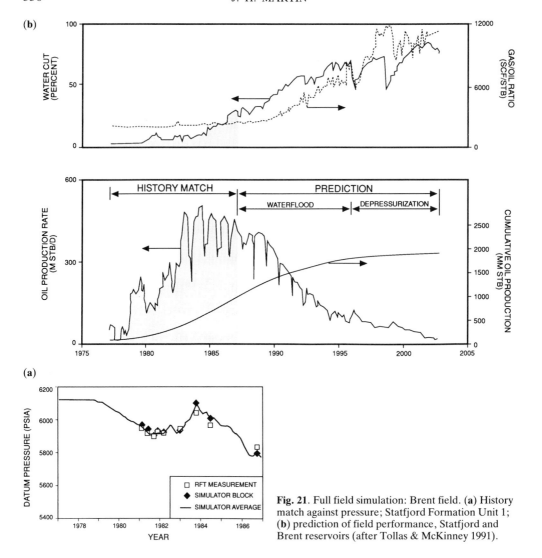

Fig. 21. Full field simulation: Brent field. (**a**) History match against pressure; Statfjord Formation Unit 1; (**b**) prediction of field performance, Statfjord and Brent reservoirs (after Tollas & McKinney 1991).

sheet sands with intercalated permeability barriers, many of which are discontinuous and uncorrelatable on a well spacing of several hundred to thousands of metres. This is the basic model followed in studies of the Prudhoe Bay Field (Geehan *et al.* 1986; Haldorsen & Chang 1986) Dranfield *et al.* (1987) built a more complex hybrid model, which incorporated the distribution and properties of reservoir facies as well as shales, during appraisal of the Sherwood Sandstone reservoir of the Wytch Farm Field (Fig. 22). With development drilling, however, it has become clear that the overall continuity of reservoir facies is higher than originally envisaged, and a more deterministic model has recently been introduced (Bowman *et al.* 1993).

Channel models. Partly isolated low sinuosity ribbon sands developed in non-reservoir matrix form the other end of the spectrum. Development planning of the Statfjord and Lunde Formations (and distributary sands in the Ness Formation of the Brent Group) in offshore prospects with well spacing of several thousands of metres has been difficult. This led to considerable interest, particularly by the Norwegian oil industry, in integrated stochastic channel sand software modelling packages.

(i) 'SISABOSA' (Augedal *et al.* 1986; Stanley *et al.* 1990) which creates a reservoir by placing 3D parallelepipeds of permeable sand into a volume of impermeable mudstone until a prescribed sand content and sand content variation

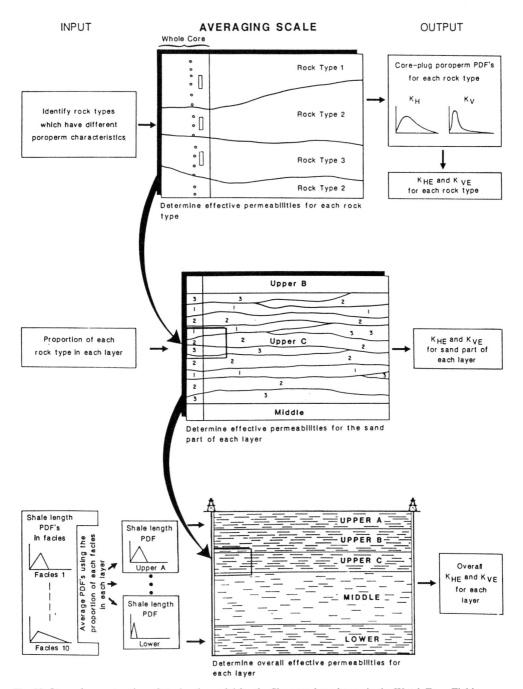

Fig. 22. Stages in construction of stochastic model for the Sherwood sandstone in the Wytch Farm Field (Dranfield *et al.* 1987). PDF, probability density function; K_H, horizontal permeability; K_V, vertical permeability; K_E, effective permeability. Reproduced with permission of Graham and Trotman.

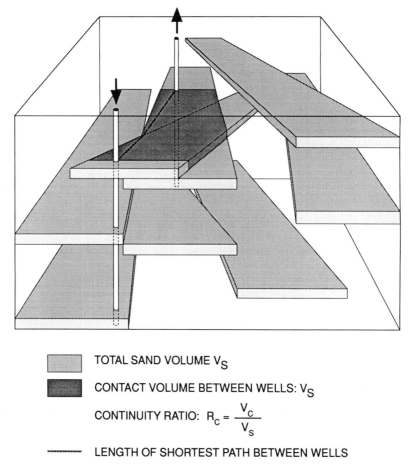

TOTAL SAND VOLUME V_S

CONTACT VOLUME BETWEEN WELLS: V_S

CONTINUITY RATIO: $R_c = \dfrac{V_c}{V_s}$

----------- LENGTH OF SHORTEST PATH BETWEEN WELLS

Fig. 23. Stochastic model of channel sands: schematic representation (after Nybråten *et al.* 1990).

is achieved (Fig. 23). Sandbody length is considered infinite; thicknesses are determined by a probability distribution; widths from a conditioned probability distribution that may be tied to thickness, while orientation is also determined probabilistically.

(ii) 'FLUREMO' (Clemetsen *et al.* 1990): a development of SISABOSA which allows individual sand bodies to be clustered within channel belts. It calculates measures of interconnectedness and continuity ratio for describing the reservoir potential of each realisation, and is able to transfer reservoir realisations to a grid form suitable for input to reservoir simulators.

(iii) 'SESIMERA' (applied to a fluvial system by Gundesø & Egeland 1990) which uses high-resolution 3D grids for hybrid modelling of heterogeneous reservoirs. As in all approaches a problem remains; how to effectively reduce the

high degree of detail to a simulation grid? Wadsley *et al.* (1990) offer one solution.

(iv) Shell's MONARCH 3D reservoir modelling package, which primarily allows the operator to interactively create a deterministic sand architecture scheme, also has stochastic capabilities (Keijzer & Kortekaas 1990).

Caution must be exercised before applying such models to braided fluvial systems. Input requirements are summarized by Martin *et al.* 1988: in my experience two of the most important parameters controlling model behaviour: (a) channel width (or width–thickness relationships) and (b) channel sinuosity are often hugely uncertain.

There are to date few published examples of the practical use of such approaches in field scale simulation for development planning: a major study of the Snorre Field by Nybråten *et al.* (1990) and a briefer account of a revision to part of the Brent Field model by Keijzer & Kortekaas (1990) which indicates that the stochastic model gives a better history match owing to a more realistic shale distribution.

Network models incorporate dynamic data

Stochastic modelling is not the only channel modelling technique which deserves mention. Martin *et al.* (1988) attempted unsuccessfully to validate single well stochastic models against observed test response, before matching test pressure histories against an idealized 'expanding flow' network (see above). This concept was then used to create a very simple 3-layer areal model (each layer, e.g. Fig. 24, was again matched against well-test response) to construct a simple simulation model of a low sinuosity channel sand reservoir, with which to investigate sensitivity of a planned water injection project to different well spacings. The key was to use well test results to independently verify sector model characteristics, in the absence of established production history, prior to prediction. The approach was geared towards reduction of uncertainty, rather than quantification of uncertainty.

Geostatistics, conditional simulation and fractals: current research topics

Rudkiewitcz *et al.* (1990) apply the HERESIM software system to reproduce 2D macro-scale heterogeneity of fluviodeltaic outcrops using variogram-based geostatistical methods. As with all the other techniques discussed above, the objective of geostatistic outcrop-based studies is to develop workable practical techniques which may allow the geologist and engineer to predict subsurface lithofacies (or more importantly, permeability) distribution between isolated well control points.

Outcrop minipermeameter studies show that within even sands considered relatively homogeneous, horizontal correlation lengths for permeability are normally only a few metres, and less than a metre vertically. At present this level of heterogeneity can not be incorporated within workable field-scale simulators, although research interest in techniques for scaling up such detail commenced with demonstrations some six years ago (e.g. Lasseter *et al.* 1986). An exception has been the application of geostatistical models and fractal theory to establishing realistic levels of heterogeneity within 2D models for simulation of EOR processes (Hewett & Behrens 1988; Mathews *et al.* 1989; Payne *et al.* 1991; summarized in Schlumberger 1992*a*, *b*). Changing correlation lengths of permeability domains in a simulation model affects the performance of a miscible flood such as CO_2 injection (Fayers 1991). Small scale heterogeneity clearly does have greater (detrimental) effects on miscible flooding than on other recovery processes (Khataniar & Peters 1992): this has implications for EOR in Prudhoe Bay and other Alaskan fields. Fingering of flood fronts in reservoirs which contain discontinuous shales is especially difficult to model using large grid blocks without introducing explicit permeability barriers. Interestingly, the presence of small shales now appears to have little detrimental effect on at least some conventional oil recovery processes (Thomas 1990).

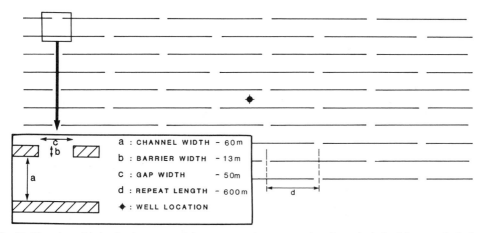

Fig. 24. Plan view of a simple element model to represent interconnecting channels derived from geological representation in Fig. 6. Parameters which gave a satisfactory match are shown (Martin *et al.* 1988).

Discussion

Geologists and reservoir engineers need to communicate more

Studies reviewed above illustrate the synergy which should exist between the reservoir geologist and engineer during any field evaluation study. However, day-to-day relationships between the two may not always be optimal. Of the work undertaken by the specialist sedimentologist (particularly core description and interpretation) many engineers believe, rightly or wrongly, that only a limited amount is of practical use:

> But the truth is, we engineers can't use a lot of information that geologists provide. Geologists do a great service in explaining the nature of the rocks, the depositional environment, the petrology - information that we don't use. Conversely, a number of things we really *do* want to know, geologists can't or don't routinely provide. So our job is to educate them. We need to make sure that the earth scientists we work with know enough about reservoir simulation inputs, operations and outputs — not in tremendous detail — to know which of their tools will be most useful. (D. N. Meehan *in* Anon. 1990, p. 27).

Whether or not one agrees with Meehan's viewpoint, he demonstrates the need to more effectively 'sell' the implications of geological efforts to a wider audience. With this aim, I list below several practical tips.

(1) *Make geological results accessible to non-specialists*. The main results of development geology studies must be expressed simply, clearly and briefly.

(2) *Environmental classification is interpretation, not fact*. A non-genetic facies scheme (e.g. Miall 1978) is preferable at least during the early stages of studies. This should avoid scepticism when an environmental 'label' is changed as a result of additional information, or simply disagreed.

(3) *Do not overstress idealised models*. Except within the pages of basic textbooks fluvial sequences can not be 'pigeonholed' into neat categories. Despite generalizations, exact correlations between depositional environment and reservoir quality, geometry and (especially) size are rarely observed. The geologist should carefully explain the relationships between local tectonics, sea level fluctuations and sedimentation rates which control the preserved rock record.

(4) *Be aware of the limitations of subsurface geological techniques*. The main task of the geologist is to predict the 3D geometry of a reservoir. We believe that the best way to do this is to interpret its depositional environment by vertical sequence analysis of core. Yet how does the geologist approach an outcrop study? Without doubt he would examine all 3D exposures before feeling confident about his interpretation. This is particularly important in the assessment of channel type. Thus there is an element of circular argument in geological work.

(5) *Predict large-scale permeability trends in the reservoir*. Directional permeability is often related to palaeocurrent trends. Yet with few exceptions (Stanley *et al.* 1991; Green & Slatt 1992; Cowan *et al.* 1993) we are not good at predicting palaeocurrent direction before drilling development wells, or in advance of problems (e.g. preferential water breakthrough) for which anisotropic permeability is responsible. The new generation of high-resolution dipmeter tools should be beneficial, especially when combined with interactive systems for selecting features for dip computation rather than relying on automatic correlation techniques.

The petroleum engineer should, in turn undertake the following.

(1) *Inspect cores (or at least, core photographs)* as this is a very effective method for gaining a 'feel' for the reservoir. Brief visits to appropriate outcrops will also usually give a better understanding of heterogeneity than simple models described in geological textbooks.

(2) *Give the geologist specific guidelines* for information that will be critical and agree mutually on the level of detail that will be required.

(3) *Ensure that assumptions made in analytical studies are reasonable* and consider also the uncertainty range.

(4) *Accept that geological studies are beneficial*. Although it is reasonable to expect the geologist to quantify his observations and predictions, the study of geology relies on inferences made from limited data. It is unwise to be sceptical of the value of geological studies because two or more geologists disagree (engineering calculation methods and data themselves do not always give unequivocal answers!). Different or uncertain interpretations often point to the requirement for further data to be acquired specifically to resolve the problem, or for further studies to be undertaken.

Future trends favour the technological approach

Forecasting trends is always dangerous, and it is enlightening to compare yesterday's predictions (e.g. Chierci 1985) with today's reality. During the early 1990s the structure of the oil industry changed dramatically. 'Down-sizing' and 'out-sourcing' have been dominant trends. Oil company reservoir engineers and geologists now act more to co-ordinate, commission and analyse results of specialist studies performed by subcontractors. Geologists, especially, must be very clearly aware of the cost/benefit of the work which they recommend to be performed.

Reservoir description. Ideally, the petroleum engineer would like a seismic tomographic technique which will allow the reservoir to be visualised on a metre scale (Haldorsen & Damsleth 1991; Hill-van Beek 1991). This would allow him to concentrate on recovering hydro-carbons from a perfectly constrained rock volume. Despite advances in geophysical tech-niques this is over-optimistic. More achievable would be further reduction of uncertainty through the application of integrated geological, petrophysical and fluid dynamic studies; in particular, better planned and executed well testing (including long term production testing) with accurate pressure measurement and down-hole fluid flow monitoring.

Geological modelling. Geological work practices will change in line with new engineer-ing capabilities. During the 1980s the transfer of data (maps, correlations etc.) from the geologist to the engineer was often a bottleneck. Current integrated software packages which should make this transfer virtually 'invisible' have some drawbacks: the next generation (e.g. Van *et al.* 1991) should allow common data sharing between disciplines. In the mid-1980s geologists realized that the computing power of reservoir simulators was starting to outstrip our capacity to provide quantified input data (particularly of permeability distributions): this led to efforts to quantify and model heterogeneity levels from outcrops. In the next five years we shall see how, and if, this information can be used in practical day-to-day field management. Despite interest in their application the day-to-day use of expert systems (e.g. Maher 1991) will probably take longer.

Reservoir simulation. As computing power becomes cheaper, simulation models increase in size and complexity: a million grid block model should be possible within five years. In parallel, mathematical techniques are now established which (a) remove the need for grid blocks to be constrained to cartesian geometry, allowing much better areal representation of geological detail, and (b) allow greater flexibility in order to optimise model runs, by refinement of model structure in near-well regions, or gathering of blocks in non-critical areas. It should become possible to 'embed' detailed single well models within more generalized 3D models, and switch seamlessly between the two to investigate different aspects of production performance.

Reservoir surveillance. Integration of flowmeter data with reservoir description is a very powerful reservoir surveillance technique. One should run flowmeters to define the distribution of production and injection in a layered reservoir. In addition one should have a knowledge of the permeability distribution in each well. Then, with a knowledge of the pressure distribution the expected flow distribution can be calculated, based on the permeability model. This should then be compared with flowmeter results. Large differences can identify intervals which are damaged and need to be stimulated. However, we need improvements in technology which will allow the engineer to accurately define the distribution of flow in highly deviated or hori-zontal wells producing multiple fluids. Currently most flowmeters in horizontal wells are useless once water breakthrough occurs (J. Stiles pers. comm.)

Horizontal drilling. Horizontal wells have become a viable alternative to conventional vertical production wells (Freyss & Burgess 1991). Annual activity is increasing at some 250%, (although this represents only about 1% of total drilling world-wide). Costs of drilling horizontally have reduced to some 1.5 times that of a conventional well. In clastic sequences, one of the main benefits of drilling horizontally is to reduce gas or water coning or cusping, for example in the Prudhoe Bay Field, in which over 20 horizontal wells have been drilled (Sherrard *et al.* 1987; Wilkinson 1988). There are many other potential applications in braided fluvial reservoirs.

Conclusions

Computer reservoir simulation modelling, now an essential tool for the engineer, has provided the impetus for advances in geological reservoir characterization. The question is: how can we adequately represent braided fluvial reservoirs in such models? At one end of the spectrum, sheet sands (although laterally variable) can be adequately mapped and modelled as 'layered' systems based on conventional geological approaches. For many engineering purposes, typical braided fluvial reservoirs can be considered to fall within this category. At the other end of the spectrum we encounter reservoirs composed of discrete but overlapping and inter-communicating sand bodies. Where the scale of this intercommunication is smaller than average well spacing, stochastic modelling techniques may be effective.

The geologist must not forget that, despite the recent interest in small scale reservoir characterization, large-scale features will dominate many recovery processes. Greater involvement by the geologist in improved dynamic understanding through the careful application of well testing, pressure profiling, production logging and reservoir monitoring should be beneficial. This will be one way of addressing the problem that, despite the amount of reservoir characterization research which is currently being pursued we cannot demonstrate that we are able to consistently economically recover significantly higher proportions of hydrocarbons-in-place than would have been possible ten years ago (Haldorsen & Damsleth 1991). However, we have a wealth of information from past performance of fields all over the world and need to learn to use it more effectively. Engineers have a vision of first identifying the likely depositional environment of a reservoir and then identifying analogous fields drilled on close spacing to define sand/shale continuity) with good core control and well-documented pressure – production history. Information from

such fields could then be used in a likely range of key reservoir description parameters to be used in models to assess development requirements for a new field and help predict its likely performance.

Finally, despite ever-increasing use of sophisticated computer modelling in both the engineering and geological fields, it is still essential to have a sound understanding of basic geological techniques, and also of the ultimate economic constraints governing field development.

Discussions with R. Lind and S. Berczi of Heinemann Oil Technology provided the starting points for several aspects of this synthesis. Sections on field development and geological input to simulation are partly abbreviated from course notes originally compiled in A. F. Corrigan, while contributions from J. Stiles improved the discussion of well test analysis and reservoir monitoring. A. Miall, A. Brayshaw and C. Braithwaite are also thanked for their helpful reviews of an earlier draft.

Principal abbreviations and units

B	billion
DST	drill stem test
EOR	enhanced oil recovery
GIIP	gas initially in place
M	thousand
mD	millidarcy
MM	million
RFT	repeat formation tester
SCF	standard cubic feet
SCF/D	standard cubic feet per day
STB	stock tank barrels
STB/D	stock tank barrels per day
STOOIP	stock tank oil originally in place
T	trillion
TDT	thermal decay time

References

ANON. 1990. Round table discussion on reservoir simulation. *Oilfield Review*, **2**, 24–33.

ABBOTS, I. L. (ed.) 1991. *United Kingdom Oil and Gas Fields, 25 Years Commemorative Volume.* Geological Society, London. Memoir 14.

ARCHER, J. S. 1983. Reservoir definition and characterisation for analysis and simulation. *Proceedings of the 11th World Petroleum Congress*, **PD6(1)**, 65–87.

—— 1987. Some factors influencing fluid flow in petroleum reservoir models. *In*: KLEPPE, J. *et al.* (eds).

—— & WALL, C. G. 1986. *Petroleum Engineering Principles and Practice.* Graham and Trotman.

ARONOFSKY, J. S., COX, T. F. & LANE, S.M. 1985. Reservoir simulation moves into third

generation. *Oil and Gas Journal*, **November**, 75–80.

ARPS, J. J. 1967. *A statistical study of recovery efficiency.* American Petroleum Institute Bulletin, **D14**.

ATKINSON, C. D., McGOWEN, J., BLOCH, S., LUNDELL, L. L. & TRUMBLY, P. N. 1990. Braidplain and deltaic reservoir, Prudhoe Bay Field, Alaska. *In*: BARWIS, J. H., McPHERSON, J. G. & STUDLICK, J. R. (eds) q.v., 7-29.

——, TRUMBLY, P. N. & KREMER, M. C. 1988. Sedimentology and depo-environments of the Ivishak sandstone, Prudhoe Bay Field, North Slope Alaska. *In*: *Giant oil and gas fields: a core workshop.* SEPM Core Workshop No. **12**, Houston, 561–613.

AUGEDAL, H. O., OMRE, H. & STANLEY, K. O. 1986. SISABOSA: a program for stochastic modelling and evaluation of reservoir geology. *In*: NITTEBERG, J. (ed.) *Proceedings of a conference on reservoir description and simulation with emphasis on EOR*, Institute for Energy Technology.

AYESTARAN, L. & KARAKAS, M. 1990. Layered reservoir testing. *Middle East Well Evaluation Review*, **9**, 22–47. Schlumberger Technical Services, Dubai.

——, NURMI, R. D., SHEHAB, G. A. K, & EL SISI, W. S. 1989. Well test design and final interpretation improved by integrated well testing and geological efforts. *Society of Petroleum Engineers Paper 17945 presented at Middle East Oil Technical Conference, Manama*.

BARKER, G. & VINCENT, P. 1988. Geological and reservoir engineering considerations for the N. Rankin gas recycling project. *Australian Petroleum Exploration Association Journal*, **28**, 54–66.

BARNES, A. L. 1989. Approaches to full field simulation. *Society of Petroleum Engineers Paper 19041 presented at Middle East Oil Technical Conference, Manama*.

BARWIS, J. H., MCPHERSON, J. G. & STUDLICK, J. R. (eds) 1990. *Sandstone Petroleum Reservoirs*. Springer Verlag, New York.

BEGG, S. H. & KING, P. R. 1985. Modelling the effects of shales on reservoir performance: calculation of effective vertical permeability. *Society of Petroleum Engineers Paper 13529 presented at Reservoir Simulation Symposium, Dallas*.

——, CHANG, D. M. & HALDORSEN, H. H. 1985. A simple statistical method for calculating the effective permeability of a reservoir containing discontinuous shales. *Society of Petroleum Engineers Paper 14271*.

BENZAGOUTA, S. & TURNER, B. 1992. Heirachial analysis of reservoir quality in the Buchan Oilfield (Abstract). *Braided rivers: form, process and economic applications; a two-day meeting held at the Geological Society of London*.

BESTON, N. B. 1986. Reservoir geological modelling of the North Rankin Field, Northwest Australia. *Australian Petroleum Exploration Association Journal*, **26**, 375–388.

BOWMAN, M., MCCLURE, N. M. & WILKINSON, D. W. 1993. Wytch Farm oilfield: deterministic reservoir description of the Triassic Sherwood Sandstone. *In*: PARKER. J. R. (ed.) *Petroleum Geology of NW Europe. Proceedings of the 4th Conference*. Geological Society, 1513–1518.

BRADLEY, N. B. (ed.) 1989. *Petroleum Engineering Handbook*. Society of Petroleum Engineers, Richardson.

BRITT, L. K., JONES, J. R., PARDINI, R. E. & PLUM, G. L. 1991. Reservoir description by interference testing of the Clayton Field. *Journal of Petroleum Technology*, **43**, 575–577.

BROOKS, J. & GLENNIE, K. W. (eds) 1987. *Petroleum Geology of North West Europe*. Graham and Trotman.

BULLER, A. T., BERG, E., HJELMELAND, O., KLEPPE, J., TORSÆTER, O. & AASEN, J. O. (eds) 1990. *North Sea Oil and Gas Reservoirs - II. Proceedings of the 2nd North Sea Oil and Gas Reservoirs Conference, Trondheim, Norway 1989*. Graham and Trotman.

BUSHELL, T. P. 1986. Reservoir geology of the Morecambe Field. *In*: BROOKS, J., GOFF, J. & VAN HOORNE, B. (eds) *Habitat of Palaeozoic Gas in N.W. Europe*. Geological Society, London, Special Publications, **23**, 189–208.

BUZA, J. W. & UNNEBERG, A. 1987. Geological and reservoir engineering aspects of the Statfjord Field. *In*: KLEPPE, J. *et al.* (ed.) q.v., 23–38.

CHANCELLOR, R. E. & JOHNSON, R. C. 1988. Geologic and engineering implications of production history from five Mesaverde wells in Central Piceance Creek Basin, Northwest Colorado. *Society of Petroleum Engineers Formation Evaluation*, **3**, 307–314.

CHIERICI, G. 1985. Petroleum reservoir engineering in the year 2000. *Energy Exploration & Exploitation*, **3**, 173–193.

CLEMENTSEN, M. R., HURST, A. R., KNARUD, R. & OMRE, H. 1990. A computer program for evaluation of fluvial reservoirs. *In*: BULLER, A. T. *et al.* (eds) q.v., 373–386.

CLIFFORD, H. J., GRUND, R. & MUSRATI, H. 1979. Geology of a stratigraphic giant: Messla oil field, Libya. *American Association of Petroleum Geologists Memoir*, **30**, 507–524.

COATS, K. 1989. Reservoir simulation. *In*: BRADLEY, N. B. (ed.) q.v., 48/1-48/20

COOKE-YARBOROUGH, P. 1991. The Hewett Field, Blocks 48/28-29-30, 52/4a-5a, UK North Sea. *In*: ABBOTS, I. L. (ed.) q.v., 433–442.

CORRIGAN, A. F., DAVIES, N., GUEST, W., KAYE, L. & MARTIN, J. H. 1990. *Advance reservoir geology: a North Sea perspective*. Joint Association for Petroleum Exploration Courses, **101**.

COWAN, G., OTTESEN, C. & STUART, I. A. 1993. The use of dipmeter logs in the structural interpretation and palaeocurrent analysis of Morecambe Fields, East Irish Sea Basin. *In*: PARKER, J. R. (ed.) *Petroleum Geology of NW Europe: Proceedings of the 4th Conference*, Geological Society, 867–882.

DAKE, L. P. 1978. *Fundamentals of Reservoir Engineering*. Elsevier.

DALTON, R. L. & MATTAX, C. C. 1990. Reservoir simulation. *Journal of Petroleum Technology*, **42**, 692–699.

DICKEY, P. A. 1989. Application of pressure measurements to development geology. *In*: MASON, J. F. & DICKEY, P. A. (eds) q.v., 105–108.

DRANFIELD, P., BEGG, S. H. & CARTER, R. R. 1987. Wytch Farm Oilfield: reservoir characterisation of the Triassic Sherwood Sandstone for input to reservoir simulation studies. *In*: BROOKS, J. & GLENNIE, K. W. (eds) q.v., 149–160.

EDWARDS, C. W. 1991. The Buchan Field, Blocks 20/5a and 21/1a. UK North Sea. *In*: ABBOTTS, I. L. (ed.) q.v. 253–259.

EHLIG-ECONOMIDES, C. A. 1987. Well testing in layered reservoirs. *In*: *North Sea Oil and Gas Reservoirs*, Norwegian Institute of Technology (Graham and Trotman), 269–276.

EXPLORATION STAFF OF THE ARABIAN GULF OIL COMPANY 1980. Geology of a stratigraphic giant—the Messlah oil field. *In*: *Second Symposium on the Geology of Libya, Tripoli, Sept 16–21, 1978, 521–536*.

FAYERS, F. J. 1991. The need for continued reservoir description and simulation for advanced recovery technologies in large fields. *Advances in Reservoir Technology: Characterisation, Modelling and Management, Edinburgh, February 1991*. Unpublished conference proceedings.

FELDER, R. D. 1988. Cased-hole logging for evaluating bypassed reserves. *Journal of Petroleum Technology*, **40**, 969–974.

FIELDING, C. R. & CRANE, R. C. 1987. An application of statistical modelling to the prediction of hydrocarbon recovery factors in fluvial reservoir sequences. *In*: ETHRIDGE, F. G. *et al.* (eds) *Recent developments in fluvial sedimentology*. Society of Economic Paleontologists and Mineralogists Special Publications, **39**, 321–327.

FISHER, W. G. 1989. Reservoir simulation. *In*: MASON, J. F. & DICKEY, P. A. (eds) q.v., 141–158.

FREYSS, H. P. & BURGESS, K. 1991. Overcoming lateral reservoir heterogeneities via horizontal wells. *Paper presented at the 6th European symposium on improved oil recovery, Stavanger, May*.

GARB, F. J. & SMITH, G. L. 1989. Estimation of oil and gas reserves. *In*: BRADLEY, N. B. (ed.). *Petroleum Engineering Handbook*. Society of Petroleum Engineers, Richardson. 40/1–40/38.

GARDINER, S., THOMAS, D. V., BOWERING, E. D. & MCMINN, L. S. 1990. A braided fluvial reservoir, Peco Field, Alberta, Canada. *In*: BARWIS, J. H., MCPHERSON, J. G. & STUDLICK, J. R. (eds) q.v., 31–56.

GATES, C. F. & BREWER, S. W. 1975. Steam injection into the D and E zone, Tulare Formation, South Belridge Field, Kern County, California. *Journal of Petroleum Technology*, **March**, 343–348.

GEEHAN, G. W., LAWTON, T. F., SAKURAI, S., KLOB, H., CLIFTON, T. R., INMAN, K. F. & NITZBERG, K. E. 1986. Geologic prediction of shale continuity, Prudhoe Bay Field. *In*: LAKE, L. W. & CARROLL, H. B. (eds) q.v., 63–82.

GILLESPIE, S. & SANDFORD, R. M. 1970. The geology of the Sarir Oil Field. *In*: *Proceedings of the 7th World Petroleum Congress*, Volume II, 181–197.

GREEN, C. & SLATT, R. M. 1992. Complex braided stream depositional model for the Murdoch Field Block 44/22 UK Southern North Sea. *Braided rivers: form, process and economic applications; a two-day meeting held at the Geological Society of London*. (Abstract).

GRINGARTEN, A. C. 1987. Type curve analysis: what it can and cannot do. *Journal of Petroleum Technology*, **January**, 11–13.

GUNDESØ, R. & EGELAND, O. 1990. SESIMIRA — a new geological tool for 3D modelling of heterogeneous reservoirs. *In*: BULLER, A. T. *et al.* (eds) q.v., 363–372.

GUNTER, J. M. & MOORE, C. V. 1987. Improved use of wireline tests for reservoir evaluation. *Journal of Petroleum Technology*, **39**, 635–644.

HALBOUTY, M. 1976. Needed: more coordination between earth scientists and petroleum engineers. *Society of Petroleum Engineers Paper 6107 presented at the Annual Fall Conference, New Orleans*.

HALDORSEN, H. H. 1986. Simulator parameter assignment and the problem of scale in reservoir engineering. *In*: LAKE, L. W. & CARROLL, H. B. (eds) q.v., 293–340.

—— & CHANG, D. M. 1986. Notes on stochastic shales; from outcrop to simulation model. *In*; LAKE, L. W. & CARROLL, H. B. (eds) q.v., 445–486.

—— & DAMSLETH, E. 1990. Stochastic modelling. *Journal of Petroleum Technology*, **42**, 404–412.

—— & —— 1991. Challenges in reservoir characterisation. *In*: *Advances in Reservoir Technology: Characterisation, Modelling and Management, Proceedings of a conference held on 21/22 February, Edinburgh*. Petroleum Science and Technology Institute.

—— & LAKE, L. W. 1984. A new approach to shale management in field scale simulation models. *Society of Petroleum Engineers Journal*, **August**, 447–457.

——, CHANG, D. M. & BEGG, S. H. 1987. Discontinuous vertical permeability barriers: a challenge to engineers and geologists. *In*: KLEPPE *et al.* (eds) q.v., 127–152.

HARRIS, D. G. 1975. The role of geology in reservoir studies. *Journal of Petroleum Technology*, **May**, 625–632.

—— & HEWITT, C. H. 1977. Synergism in reservoir management: the geologic perspective. *Journal of Petroleum Technology*, **July**, 761–770.

HARRIS, E. I. 1981. Production geology of the North Rankin gas field. *In*: *Energy Resources of the Pacific region*. American Association of Petroleum Geologists, Studies in Geology, **12**, 273–283.

HARRIS, N. B. 1989. Reservoir geology of the Fangst Group (Middle Jurassic) Heidrun Field, offshore Mid-Norway. *American Association of Petroleum Geologists Bulletin*, **73**, 1415–1435.

HAUGEN, S. A., LUND, Ø. & HOYLAND, L. A. (1988). Statfjord Field. development strategy and reservoir management. *Journal of Petroleum Technology*, **40**, 863–873.

HEWETT, T. A. & BEHRENS, R. A. 1988. Conditional simulation of reservoir heterogeneity with fractals. *Society of Petroleum Engineers Paper 18326 presented at the 63rd Annual Technical Conference, Houston*.

HILL-VAN BEEK, F. 1991. Reservoir technology development in the next decade. *In*: *Advances in Reservoir Technology: Characterisation,*

Modelling and Management, Proceedings of a conference held on 21/22 February, Edinburgh. Petroleum Science and Technology Institute.

HINDERAKER, L., BYGDEVOLL, J., BU, T., NYBRÅTEN, G. & KRAKSTAD, O. 1992. IOR resource potential of Norwegian North Sea sandstone reservoirs. *Journal of Petroleum Science and Engineering,* **7**, 3–14.

HOLLANDER, N. B. 1987. Snorre. *In*: SPENCER, A. M. *et al.* (eds) *Geology of the Norwegian Oil and Gas Fields.* Graham and Trotman, 307–318.

HORNE, R. N. 1990. *Modern Well Test Analysis: a Computer-aided Approach.* Petroway Inc., Palo Alto.

HUURDEMAN, A. J. M., BREUNESE, J. N., AL-ASBAHI, A. M. S., LUTGERT, J. E. & FLORIS, F. J. T. 1991. Assessment of halite-cemented reservoir zones. *Journal of Petroleum Technology,* **43**, 518–523.

JOHNSON, A. & SCANLON, M. E. 1991. Pulsed-neutron monitoring in the Bunter sands of the Esmond complex. *Society of Petroleum Engineers Formation Evaluation,* **6**, 327–333.

JOHNSON, H. D. & KROL, D. E. 1984. Geological modeling of a heterogeneous sandstone reservoir: Lower Jurassic Statfjord Formation, Brent Field. *Society of Petroleum Engineers Paper 13050 presented at Annual Fall Conference, Houston.*

—— & STEWART, D. J. 1985. Role of clastic sedimentology in the exploration and production of oil and gas in the North Sea. *In*: BRENCHLEY, P. J. & WILLIAMS, B. P. J. (eds) *Sedimentology: Recent Developments and Applied Aspects.* Geological Society, London, Special Publications, **18**, 249–310.

KEIJZER, J. H. & KORTEKAAS, R. F. M. 1990. Comparison of deterministic and probabilistic simulation models of channel sands in the Statfjord reservoir, Brent Field. *Society of Petroleum Engineers Paper 20947 presented at EUROPEC 90, The Hague.*

KETTER, F. J. 1991. The Esmond, Forbes and Gordon Fields, Blocks 43/8a, 43/13a, 43/15a, 43/20a, UK North Sea. *In*: ABBOTTS, I. L. (ed.) q.v., 425–432.

KHANTANIAR, S. & PETERS, E. J. 1992. Reservoir heterogeneity and unstable displacements. *Journal of Petroleum Science and Engineering,* **7**, 263–281.

KING, P. R. 1990. The connectivity and conductivity of overlapping sand bodies. *In*: BULLER, A. T. *et al.* (eds) q.v., 353–362.

KLEPPE, J., BERG, E. W., BULLER, A. T., HJELMELAND, O. & TORSÆTER, O. (eds) 1987. *North Sea Oil and Gas Reservoirs.* Norwegian Institute of Technology (Graham and Trotman).

KNUTSON, C. F. 1976. Modelling of non-continuous Fort Union and Mesaverde sandstone reservoirs, Piceance Basin, Northwestern Colorado. *Society of Petroleum Engineers Journal,* **August**, 175–188.

LAKE, L. W. & CARROLL, H. B. Jr (eds) 1986. *Reservoir Characterisation.* Academic Press, Orlando.

LASSETER, T. J., WAGGONER, J. R. & LAKE, L. W. 1986. Reservoir heterogeneities and their influence on ultimate recovery. *In*: LAKE, L. W. & CARROLL, H. B. Jr (eds) q.v., 545–559.

LIBSON, T. E., VACCA, H. L. & MEEHAN, D. N. 1985. Stratton Field, Texas Gulf Coast: A successful cased hole re-evaluation of an old field to determine remaining reserves and to increase production level. *Journal of Petroleum Technology,* **37**, 105–124.

LORENZ, J. C., HEINZE, D. M., CLARK, J. A. & SEARLS, C. A. 1985. Determination of meander-belt sandstone reservoirs from vertical downhole data, Mesaverde Group, Piceance Creek Basin, Colorado. *American Association of Petroleum Geologists Bulletin,* **69**, 710–721.

MAHER, C. E. 1991. The future for expert systems in applying reservoir technology. *In*: *Advances in Reservoir Technology: Characterisation, Modelling and Management, Proceedings of a conference held on 21/22 February, Edinburgh.* Petroleum Science and Technology Institute.

MALAVAZOS, M. & McDONOUGH, R. C. M. 1991. Pressure transient response in compartmentalised gas reservoirs: a South Australian field example. *Society of Petroleum Engineers Paper 23009 presented at Society of Petroleum Engineers Asia-Pacific Conference, Perth.*

MARTIN, J. H. & COOPER, J. A. 1984. An integrated approach to the modelling of permeability barrier distribution in a sedimentologically complex reservoir. *Society of Petroleum Engineers Paper 13051 presented at Annual Fall Meeting, Houston.*

——, EVANS, A. J. & RAPER, J. K. 1988. Reservoir modelling of low sinuosity channel sands: a network approach. *Society of Petroleum Engineers Paper 18364 presented at European Petroleum Conference, London.*

MASON, J. F. & DICKEY, P. A. (eds) 1989. *Oil Field Development Techniques: Proceedings of the Daqing International Meeting, 1982.* American Association of Petroleum Geologists Studies in Geology, **28**.

MATTHEWS, C. S. 1986. Transient, semisteady state and steady-state flow. *Journal of Petroleum Technology,* **38**, 385–387.

MATHEWS, J. L., EMANUEL, A. S. & EDWARDS, K. A. 1989. Fractal methods improve Mitsue miscible predictions. *Journal of Petroleum Technology,* **41**, 1136–1142.

MIALL, A. D. 1978. Lithofacies types and vertical profile models in braided fluvial deposits: a summary. *In*: MIALL, A. D. (ed.) *Fluvial Sedimentology.* Canadian Society of Petroleum Geologists Memoirs, **5**, 597–604.

—— 1988. Reservoir heterogeneities in fluvial sandstones: lessons from outcrop studies. *American Association of Petroleum Geologists Bulletin,* **72**, 682–697.

MILLER, D. D., McPHERSON, J. G. & COVINGTON, T. E. 1990. Fluviodeltaic reservoir, South Belridge Field, San Joaquim Valley, California. *In*: BARWIS, J. H. *et al.* (eds) q.v., 109–130.

MURPHY, P. J. 1990. Performance of horizontal wells in the Helder Field. *Journal of Petroleum Technology*, **42**, 792–800.

NASCIMENTO, O. S., BORNEMANN, E., JOBIM, L. D. C., CARVALHO, M. D., PIMENTEL, A. M., BONET, E. J., RODRIGUES, E. B., SANDOVAL, J. R. L., LASSANDRO, V., RODRIGUES, T. C. & HOCOTT, C. R. 1982. Aracas Field-reservoir heterogeneities and secondary recovery performance (abstract). *American Association of Petroleum Geologists Bulletin*, **66**, 612.

NYBRÅTEN, G., SKOLEM, E. & ØSTBY, K. 1990. II Reservoir simulation of the Snorre Field. *In*: BULLER, A. T. *et al.* (eds) q.v., 103–114.

O'BRIEN, D. G., BROWN, M. E. & LEDERER, M. C. 1984. Use of reservoir performance analysis in the simulation of Prudhoe Bay. *Society of Petroleum Engineers Paper 13217 presented at Annual Fall Conference, Houston*.

PAYNE, D. V. *et al.* 1991. Examples of reservoir simulation studies utilising geostatistical models of reservoir heterogeneity. In: LAKE, L. W., CARROLL, H. B. Jr & WESSON, T. C. (eds) *Reservoir Characterisation II*. Academic Press, San Diego, California, 497–523.

POSTON, S. W. & GROSS, S. J. 1984. Numerical simulation of reservoir sandstone models. *Society of Petroleum Engineers Paper 13135 presented at Annual Fall Conference, Houston*.

RICHARDSON, J. G. *et al.* 1977. Synergy in reservoir studies. *Society of Petroleum Engineers Paper 6700 presented at the Annual Fall Technical Conference, Denver*.

——, HARRIS, D. G., ROSSEN, R. H. & VAN HEE, G. 1978. The effect of small, discontinuous shales on oil recovery. *Journal of Petroleum Technology, November*, 1531–1537.

——, SANGREE, J. B. & SNEIDER, R. M. 1987*a*). Coning. *Journal of Petroleum Technology*, **39**, 883–885.

——, —— & —— 1987*b*. Braided stream reservoirs. *Journal of Petroleum Technology*, **39**, 1499–1500.

RITCHIE, J. S. & PRATSIDES, P. 1993. The Caister Fields, Block 44/23a UK North Sea. *In*: PARKER, J. R. (ed.) *Petroleum Geology of NW Europe: Proceedings of the 4th Conference*. Geological Society, 759–770.

ROBERTS, J. D., MATHIESON, A. S. & HAMPSON, J. M. 1987. Statfjord. *In*: SPENCER, A. M. (ed.). *Geology of the Norwegian Oil and Gas Fields*. Graham and Trotman, 307–318.

RUDKIEWICZ, J. L., GUÉRILLOT, D., GALLI, A. & GROUP HERESI 1990. An integrated software for stochastic modelling of reservoir lithology and property with an example from the Yorkshire Middle Jurassic. *In*: BULLER, A. T. *et al.* (eds) q.v., 399–406.

RUPP, K. A. *et al.* 1984. Design and implementation of a miscible water alternating gas flood at Prudhoe Bay. *Society of Petroleum Engineers Paper 13272 presented at Annual Fall Meeting, Houston*.

SANFORD, R. M. 1970. Sarir Oil Field, Libya - desert suprise. *In*: HALBOUTY, M. T. (ed.) *Geology of*

Giant Petroleum Fields. Memoir of the American Association of Petroleum Geologists, **14**, 449–476.

SCHLUMBERGER 1981. *RFT Essentials of Pressure Test Interpretation*.

—— 1989. *Cased Hole Log Interpretation Principles/Applications*.

—— 1992*a*. Reservoir characterisation using expert knowledge, data and statistics. *Oilfield Review*, **4**, 25–39.

—— 1992*b*. Trends in reservoir management. *Oilfield Review*, **4**, 8–24.

SHERRARD, D. W., BRICE, B. W. & MacDONALD, D. G. 1987. Application of horizontal wells at Prudhoe Bay. *Journal of Petroleum Technology*, **39**, 1417–1426.

SIMLOTE, V. N., EBANKS, W. J. Jr & ESLINGER, E. V. 1985. Synergistic evaluation of a complex conglomerate reservoir for EOR, Barrancas Formation, Argentina. *Journal of Petroleum Technology*, **37**, 295–305.

SIMPSON, R. E. & WEBER, A. G. 1986. Gasfield development - reservoir and productions operations planning. *Journal of Petroleum Technology*, **38**, 217–226.

SLATT, R. M. & HOPKINS, X. 1990. Scaling geologic reservoir description to engineering needs. *Journal of Petroleum Technology*, **42**, 202–212.

STANLEY, K. O., JORDER, K. RÆSTAD, N. & STOCKBRIDGE, C. 1990. I. Stochastic modelling of reservoir sand bodies for input to reservoir simulations, Snorre Field, northern North Sea, Norway. *In*: BULLER, A. T. *et al.* (eds) q.v., 91–102.

STARLEY, G. P., MASINO, W. H., WEISS, J. L. & BOLLING, J. D. 1991. Full field simulation for development planning and reservoir management at Kuparuk River Field. *Journal of Petroleum Technology*, **43**, 974–982.

STEWART, G. & AYESTARAN, L. 1982. The interpretation of vertical pressure gradients measured at observation wells in developed reservoirs. *Society of Petroleum Engineers Paper 11132 presented at the Annual Fall Meeting, New Orleans*.

STRUIJK, A. P. & GREEN, R. T. 1991. The Brent Field, Block 211/29, UK North Sea. *In*: ABBOTTS, I. L. (ed.) q.v., 63–72.

STUART, I. A. & COWAN, G. 1991. The South Morecambe Field, Blocks 110/2a, 110/3a, 110/8a, UK East Irish Sea. *In*: ABBOTTS, I. L. (ed.) q.v., 527–541.

THAKUR, G. C. 1991. Waterflood surveillance techniques — a reservoir management approach. *Journal of Petroleum Technology*, **43**, 1180–1192.

THOMAS, J. M. D. 1990. The movement of oil initially bypassed behind stochastic shale barriers. *In*: BULLER, A. T. *et al.* (eds) q.v., 437–444.

TIRATSOO, E. N. 1990. World oilfields - past, present and future. *In*: ALA, M., HATAMIAN, H., HOBSON, G. D., KING, M. S. & WILLIAMSON, I. (eds) *Seventy-Five Years of Progess in Oil Field Science and Technology*. Balkema, Rotterdam, 39–54.

Tollas, J. M. & McKinney, X. 1991. Brent Field 3-D reservoir simulation. Journal of Petroleum Technology, **43**, 589–596.

Van. B. T., Pajon, J.-L., Joseph, P. & Chautra, J.-M. 1991. 3D reservoir visualisation. *Journal of Petroleum Technology,* **43**, 1310–1314.

Van der Graaf, W. J. E. & Ealey, P. J. 1989. Geological modelling for simulation studies. *American Association of Petroleum Geologists Bulletin,* **73**, 1436–1444.

Wadman, D. H., Lamprecht, D. E. & Mrosovsky, L. 1978. Reservoir description through joint geologic-engineering analysis. *Society of Petroleum Engineers Paper 7531 presented at Annual Fall Conference, Houston.*

Wadsley, A. W., Erlandson, S. & Goemans, H. W. 1990. HEX - a tool for integrated fluvial architecture modelling and numerical simulation of recovery processes. *In*: Buller, A. T. *et al.* (eds) q. v., 387–398.

Weber, K. J. & Van Geuns, L. C. 1990. Framework for constructing clastic reservoir simulation models. *Journal of Petroleum Technology,* **42**, 1248–1253, 1296–1297.

Westaway, P., Wittman, M. & Rochette, P. 1979. Application of nuclear techniques to reservoir monitoring. *Society of Petroleum Engineers Paper 7776 presented at Middle East Oil Technical Conference, Manama.*

Wilkinson, J. P. 1988. Horizontal drilling techniques at Prudhoe Bay, Alaska. *Journal of Petroleum Technology,* **40**, 1445–1451.

Wood, A. R. O. & Young, M. S. 1991. The role of reservoir simulation in the development of some major North Sea Fields. *Society of Petroleum Engineers Paper 17613 presented at the International Meeting on Petroleum Engineering, Tianjin, China, November.*

Woodward, K. & Curtis, C. D. 1987. Predictive modelling of the distribution of production constraining illites - Morecambe Gas Field, Irish Sea, Offshore UK. *In*: Brooks, J. & Glennie, K. W. (eds) q.v., 205–215.

——, Wanli, Y. & Zhiwu, W. 1989. Exploitation of multizones by water flooding in the Daqinq Oil Field. *In*: Mason, J. E. & Dickey, P. A. (eds) q.v., 63–87.

Zhiwu, W., Qiming, W., Bohu, L., Chengjing, P. & Xiangzhong, L. 1989. Ways to improve development efficiency of Daqing Oil Field by flooding. *In*: Mason, J. F. & Dickey, P. A. (eds) q.v., 49–62.

Sedimentology and gravel bar morphology in an Archaean braided river sequence: the Witpan Conglomerate Member (Witwatersrand Supergroup) in the Welkom Goldfield, South Africa

W. P. KARPETA

Reservoir Geology Group, Paleo Services, Units B1–B3, Howe Moss Drive, Airport Industrial Park, Dyce, Aberdeen AB2 0GL, UK

Abstract: The Witpan conglomerate member is the lower, thicker, more channelized of the two auriferous conglomerates that comprise the Archaean 'A' Reefs (Aandenk Formation, Central Rand Group, Witwatersrand Supergroup) mined in the southern part of the Welkom Goldfield, Republic of South Africa. It is interpreted as the deposit of a degrading, gravelly, braided river system with well developed topographical differentiation. Three morphological elements have been identified in the Witpan Conglomerate member, namely Major Channels, Minor Channels and Terrace areas which are comparable to Levels 1, 2 and 3 of the modern Donjek River. Nine facies are present in the Witpan Conglomerate member combined into eight facies assemblages which show differing three dimensional architecture and relationship to channels. The four conglomeratic bar facies assemblages (FA1 to FA4) are interpreted as longitudinal, diagonal, transverse and side bars respectively and are combined to form compound bars. The three quartzitic channel fill facies assemblages (FA5 to FA7) represent active, slough and abandoned channel fills. The eighth facies assemblage (FA8) forms the interchannel terrace areas.

The distribution of gold mineralization in the Witpan Conglomerate member is related to sedimentological factors including the presence of massive gravels, the accessibility of these gravels to flood water and the formation of areas of confined, convergent flow. Hence the bar facies assemblages are the richest followed by channel fill facies assemblages with the interchannel facies assemblage having generally low gold concentrations. Of the bars, diagonal bars are the most favourable for gold mineralization followed by longitudinal bars then side bars with transverse bars being the lowest.

Most previous studies of the auriferous conglomerates ('reefs') of the Archaean Witwatersrand Supergroup have used vertical profile analysis (Miall 1977) to establish large scale changes in facies and gold distribution. Such studies have identified proximal to distal changes, or major lateral changes in conglomerate facies which have then been related to large scale gold mineralization (scales of hundreds to thousands of metres, Smith & Minter, 1979). Such studies have proved very useful in the modelling of broad scale gold distribution for mine planning and exploration (e.g. Minter 1978; Smith & Minter 1979; Buck 1983; Buck & Minter 1985).

However, despite the availability of laterally extensive underground exposures of reef, very few published studies have taken advantage of this by using architectural element analysis (Allen 1983; Miall 1985). By regular mapping of advancing stope facies, it is possible to interpret the three dimensional architecture of the reef

conglomerates. From comparisons with studies on modern gravelly braided rivers (Smith 1974; Hein & Walker 1977; Bluck 1979) it should be possible to reconstruct bar morphology and development in these reefs. Further, by examining the distribution of gold in these bar bedforms it may be possible to construct models of gold mineralization at intermediate scales (metres to hundred of metres, Smith & Minter 1979). Such models would be useful in predicting gold mineralization on the stope mining scale.

This paper documents the sedimentology and three dimensional architecture of the auriferous Witpan Conglomerate member (lower 'A' Reef) of the Aandenk Formation, Central Rand Group, Witwatersrand Supergroup, in the southern part of the Welkom Goldfield, Republic of South Africa (Fig. 1) and attempts to show that architectural element analysis can be used to predict intermediate scales of gold mineralization in such auriferous conglomerates.

From Best, J. L. & Bristow, C. S. (eds), 1993, *Braided Rivers*, Geological Society Special Publication No. **75**, pp. 369–388.

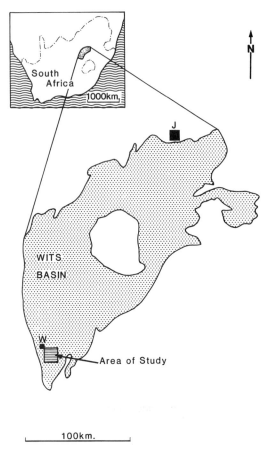

WITS.
BASIN

W.

Area of Study

100km.

Fig. 1. Locality Map showing area covered in this study (J, Johannesburg; W, Welkom).

Lithological classification

One problem encountered in describing the siliciclastic rocks of the Witwatersrand Supergroup has been their classification. Some authors (e.g. Minter 1978; Smith & Minter 1979) have used the conventional (Pettijohn *et al.* 1987) sandstone classification whilst others have used a classification resembling that used by Nagtegaal (1979) which allows for the diagenetic alteration of labile grains. Law *et al.* (1990) have questioned the usefulness of such classifications since these rocks are metamorphosed so that labile grains have been converted into phyllosilicates, and they have therefore suggested that a combination of mineralogy and sedimentary structures be used to 'reconstruct' lithology. This paper, however, uses a simpler, purely descriptive classification by referring to these quartzites as mature (less than 5% phyllosilicates), submature (between 5% and 25%

phyllosilicates) or immature (over 25% phyllosilicates) using maturity in the sense of compositional maturity (Tucker 1991) and totally ignoring the origin of these phyllosilicates whether depositional, diagenetic or metamorphic. The fine-grained clastic lithologies ('shales') are referred to in this paper as pelites.

Stratigraphic setting

The Witpan Conglomerate member is the lower, more channelized of the two auriferous conglomerates that comprise the 'A' Reefs in the southern part of the Welkom Goldfield, Republic of South Africa. The upper conglomerate is the sheet-like Uitsig Conglomerate member (Karpeta 1984). The 'A' Reefs occur within the Aandenk Formation of the Central Rand Group, Witwatersrand Supergroup (Fig. 2) and are Archaean in age (Allsop & Welke 1986). The Aandenk Formation consists of an overall upwards fining sequence up to 35 m thick, of predominantly polymictic, cobble and pebble conglomerates, submature to immature quartzites and thin pelite drapes showing an overall eastward palaeocurrent direction both above and below the 'A' Reef package (Fig. 3a). The 'A' Reef package is more mature and comprises a lower oligomictic, poorly gold mineralized small cobble conglomerate (up to 2 m thick) overlain by the Witpan Conglomerate member (up to 2 m thick) which is in turn overlain by parallel laminated, immature quartzites (between 0 and 2.5 m thick) and capped by the thin Uitsig Conglomerate member with its mature, trough cross-bedded quartzites. The 'A' Reef package has an overall southeast palaeocurrent direction (Fig. 3b).

Jordaan (1989) has suggested that the Aandenk Formation represents a westerly sourced, basin-marginal, alluvial fan sequence which was partially reworked by southeastward-flowing, axial braided river systems forming the 'A' Reefs themselves (Fig. 4).

A similar model was proposed by Kingsley (1987) for the overlying Eldorado Formation in the Welkom goldfield suggesting that similar basin fill styles were repeated in the upper part of the Witwatersrand Supergroup.

The Witpan Conglomerate Member

Lithology

The Witpan Conglomerate member consists of up to 2 m of well-sorted, clast-supported, oligomictic, large pebble conglomerates and subordinate greenish black (5GY 2/1), coarse

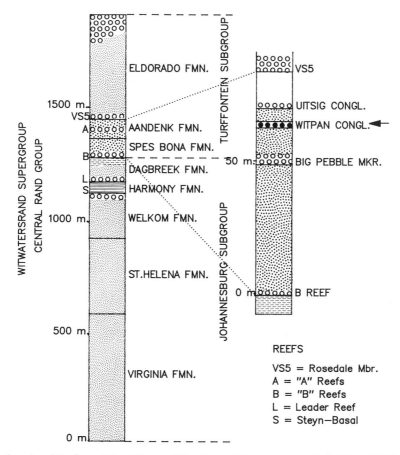

Fig. 2. Stratigraphy of the Central Rand Group, Witwatersrand Supergroup, in the Welkom Goldfield area.

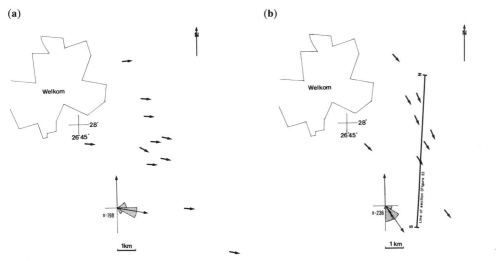

Fig. 3. (a) Palaeocurrent data for the Aandenk Formation. (b) Palaeocurrent data for the 'A' Reef package. (Each arrow represents the vector mean of more than ten cross-bedding measurements.)

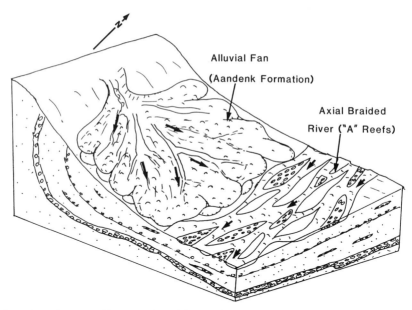

Fig. 4. Schematic environmental interpretation of the Aandenk Formation in the Welkom Goldfield (Adapted from Jordaan 1989).

grained, mature quartzites with minor olive grey (5Y 4/1) to dusky yellow (5Y 6/4), submature to immature, coarse to medium grained quartzites with pelitic drapes. Pebble sizes vary between small pebble and small cobble grade and have a mean diameter of 51 mm. Pebble compositions include vein quartz (77%), chert (8.5%), quartzite (13%) and altered volcanic lithologies (1.5%) and are typically well rounded (0.8).

Pyrite mineralization varies from poor (*c.* 2% of the matrix) to very good (*c.* 70% of the matrix) and comprises mainly rounded, compact, allogenic, detrital pyrite and rounded, porous 'mudball' pyrite up to 5 mm in diameter found concentrated on scour and accretion surfaces within the conglomerates and cross-bedding foresets in the quartzites. Authigenic crystalline pyrite of metamorphic origin is rare (Pyrite classification of Hallbauer 1986).

Gold forms discrete grains up to 50 μm in diameter with rounded morphologies suggesting a detrital origin. The gold to uranium ratio is 18:1.

Morphology and palaeocurrent data

The Witpan Conglomerate member is markedly channelized and three morphological elements have been identified comprising Major Channels, Minor Channels and Terrace areas (Table 1). The Major Channels consist of

irregular, low sinuosity, incised scours up to 120 m wide and 2 m deep infilled by conglomerates and mature to submature quartzites, and whose distribution appears to be controlled by footwall lithologies, being preferentially incised into underlying quartzites but rarely developed over footwall conglomerates or thick pelite sequences. These channels have bed relief indices (Smith 1974) averaging 2.9. The Minor Channels comprise high sinuosity, dendroidal scours up to 25 m wide and 0.7 m deep which are usually infilled with conglomerates, quartzites and pelites. Conglomerates commonly fill Minor Channels adjacent to Major Channels but quartzites predominate further away. Minor Channels are commonest around Major Channels and together they form 'channel complexes' up to 200 m wide. The location of these channel complexes appear to have been influenced by subtle tectonic downwarping (Fig. 5 and Karpeta 1984; Jordaan 1989). Terrace areas consist of areas up to 500 m wide where the Reef comprises a thin conglomerate lag. Overall gold mineralization is relatively high in the Major Channels and in conglomeratic Minor Channels, and low in the sandy Minor Channels and Terrace areas, except where 'carbon' seams are developed. Generally Terrace areas have poor gold mineralization.

Palaeocurrent data and channel orientations for the Witpan Conglomerate member (Figs 3b,

Table 1. *Morphological elements in the Witpan Conglomerate member*

Morphological element	Thickness	Width	Topographic level	Facies associations	Overall gold content	Interpretation
Major channels	Between 1 m and 2 m	<100 m	1	FA1–FA6	High	The main, permanently active, trunk streams
Minor channels	0.25 to 0.75 m	<25 m	2	FA1, F5-7	High to low	Episodically active during floods, abandoned during other times
Terrace	Less than 0.2 m	<500 m	3	FA8	Low	Interchannel areas occasionally reworked during very high floods

Table 2. *Witpan Conglomerate member facies*

Facies code	Description	Sedimentary structures	Interpretation	Gold content
Gm 51%	Massive, oligomictic clast supported conglomerates with mature matrix	Imbricate clasts, fining upwards and more rarely coarsening up units	Bar gravels and channel lags	High to low
Gt 11%	Trough cross stratified matrix supported conglomerates	Imbricate clasts trough cross bedded sets up to 50 cm	Channel scour and fill	Low
Gp 3.5%	Planar cross bedded, matrix supported conglomerates	Planar cross bedded with reactivation surfaces (isolated sets 1 m thick)	Linguoid/transverse bars and deltaic outgrowths from gravel bars	Low
St 24%	Trough cross bedded mature quartzites	Trough cross bedding pebble lags and pyrite stringers on scours (sets 20 cm)	Lower flow regime migrating dunes	Low to very low
Sp 3.5%	Planar cross bedded submature quartzites	Planar cross bedding with reactivation surfaces (sets 25 cm)	Delta outgrowths from emergent bars and migrating sand waves	Very low
Sr 5.5%	Ripple cross laminated sub-mature to immature quartzites	Ripple cross laminated and horizontal stratification	Ripples and horizontal bedding (lower flow regimes) in partially abandoned channels and emergents bar top sands	Very low
Fl 1%	Laminated and rippled pelitic partings	Lamination and ripple marked both linguoid and sinuous ripples	Waning flood deposits channel abandonment	Very low
Fc <0.5%	Laminated and rippled carbonaceous pelites	Lamination and ripple cross laminated shales convolute bedding and starved ripples	Deposits formed by density currents and suspension settling in lakes of standing water with algal growth	Very low
Cm very rare	Massive carbonaceous seams	Massive, occasional vertical filamentous structures	Fossilized plant material	Very high

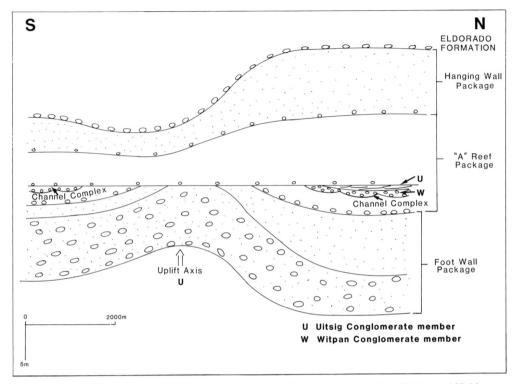

Fig. 5. Schematic cross-section of the Aandenk Formation in the southern part of the Welkom goldfield, showing syn-depositional upwarp axis controlling channel development.

8a & 9a) give an overall unimodal palaeoflow direction towards the southeast corresponding to that for the 'A' Reef package.

Facies

Nine facies have been identified in the Witpan Conglomerate member and are listed in Table 2. They have been given facies codes similar to those proposed by Miall (1977).

Facies Gm is the dominant facies in the Witpan Conglomerate member and comprises lenses and lags, up to 0.5 m thick, of massive to vaguely parallel stratified, moderately well-sorted, clast supported, oligomictic, medium to very large pebble conglomerates in a matrix of coarse-grained, pyritic, mature quartzite. In general, the conglomerates are massive but can show vague horizontal stratification associated with imbrication of clasts. Facies Gm is interpreted as bedload gravel that accumulated from clast-by-clast accretion during high flood discharges (Miall 1977). The quartzite matrix is interpreted as sand that infiltrated into the interstices of the gravel during lower discharges.

The gold content of this facies varies from high to low.

Facies Gt is a minor component in the Witpan Conglomerate member and consists of isolated sets, up to 0.5 m thick, of trough cross-stratified, matrix-supported, medium to large pebble conglomerates discordantly infilling scoop-shaped scour surfaces. Trough cross-stratification dips at between 15° to 20° and is defined by pebble size variations within the conglomerates. This facies is interpreted as the discordant infill of scour hollows and channels by coarse gravels (Miall 1977). These scours may have been formed by separation eddies or dissection of previously deposited sediments during falling stage (Miall 1977). The gold content of this facies is generally moderate to low.

Facies Gp is a minor facies in the Witpan Conglomerate member and comprises isolated sets of planar cross-stratified, matrix-supported, medium to large pebble conglomerates and pebbly quartzites, up to 1 m thick and 5 m across resting on planar to slightly scoop shaped scours. Foresets dip up to 20° and show alternations of pebble and sand grade sediments up to 18 cm thick with common low angle reactivation surfaces. This facies is interpreted as deposited by the migration of large, isolated, gravelly, three-dimensional bedforms with slip facies, such as transverse linguoid bars (Miall 1977; Hein & Walker 1978). The presence of reactivation surfaces suggests episodic migration due to fluctuating flood conditions (Collinson 1970). The gold content of this facies is generally moderate to low.

Facies St forms a major facies in the Witpan Conglomerate member and comprises stacked sets of trough cross-bedded, medium to coarse grained, mature quartzites with pyritic stringers and scattered small pebbles on scours. Sets are typically 0.2 m thick forming cosets up to 2 m thick and rest on scoop-shaped scours. This facies is interpreted as being produced by the migration of dune bedforms under lower flow regime conditions (Miall 1977; Allen 1982). The gold content of this facies is generally low.

Facies Sp forms a minor portion of the Witpan Conglomerate member and comprises isolated sets up to 0.3 m thick of planar cross-bedded, medium to coarse grained, mature to submature quartzites resting on planar surfaces. This facies is interpreted as being deposited by the migration of isolated, small scale sand waves (Miall 1977; Allen 1982) or bar side sand wedges (Boothroyd & Ashley 1975). The gold content of this facies is generally very low.

Facies Sr forms a minor part of the Witpan Conglomerate member and consists of drapes and lenses up to 0.3 m thick of ripple cross-laminated, medium grained, submature quartzites. It is interpreted as being deposited by the migration of current ripples under low flow regime conditions (Miall 1977; Allen 1982).

Facies Fl is a minor facies in the Witpan Conglomerate member and consists of thin laminated drapes of pelite up to 0.1 m thick. It is interpreted as being deposited by suspension settling of muds during very low flow conditions (Miall 1977). The gold content of this facies is very low.

Facies Fc forms a very minor part of the Witpan Conglomerate member, consisting of beds, up to 1 m thick, of laminated carbonaceous pelites with thin graded and ripple cross laminated, immature quartzite intercalations up to 1 cm thick. Convolute bedding and load casting is common. This facies is interpreted as the accumulation of muds by suspension settling in standing water with episodic inflows of sandy density currents (Sturm & Matter 1979). The highly carbonaceous nature of these pelites may be due to organic matter. The gold content of this facies is very low.

Facies Cm consists of thin seams up to 10 mm thick of carbonaceous matter and is rare in the Witpan Conglomerate member. It occurs mainly on scour surfaces at the base of and within the Major and Minor Channels and more rarely in the Terrace reef especially where they rest on footwall pelites. These 'carbon' seams have been interpreted as fossilized plants (Hallbauer 1975) that grew in the lower energy parts of the fluvial system. It is suggested that these plants would require a covering layer of water to protect them from desiccation and the effects of radiation. However, since the footwall lithologies of the Witpan Conglomerate member are generally very coarse grained, any standing water would drain rapidly away except where underlain by pelites (Karpeta 1991). This may explain the association between the 'carbon' seams and the underlying pelitic drapes. The gold content of this facies is high whether it is found in the Major or Minor Channels or even in the Terrace areas.

Facies assemblages

Eight combinations of facies occur in the Witpan Conglomerate member which show distinct three dimensional facies organization ('architecture') and relationships to the channels. These combinations are referred to as Facies Assemblages and are illustrated in Figs 6 and 7, and in Table 3. Four bar (FA1 to FA4), three channel fill (FA5 to FA7) and one interchannel facies assemblage (FA8) have been identified and represent the elements ('building blocks') from which the architecture of the Witpan Conglomerate member can be reconstructed. Both lateral and vertical changes between Facies Assemblages can be expected, corresponding to changes in bar geometry, bar-channel relationships and sediment and water discharge rates (Smith 1974; Hein & Walker 1978; Bluck 1979). It is these lateral and vertical changes in Facies Assemblages that can be used to interpret bar and channel evolution in the conglomerates.

Bar facies assemblages

Facies Assemblage 1 (Fig. 6a) consists of a central core of stacked lenses, each up to 0.5 m thick, of massive conglomerates (Facies Gm) and bounded by erosional, convex-up, bounding surfaces, the whole resting on a basal bounding surface. These stacked lenses occur within channels and are associated with increases in channel depths and widths. Conglomerate lenses usually show marked down-channel elongation of accretionary units, and a downstream decrease in clast size. Symmetrically

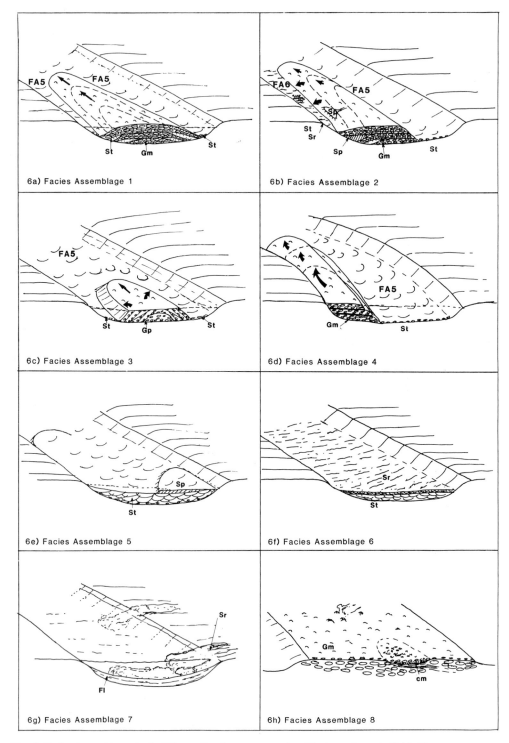

Fig. 6. Facies Assemblages in the Witpan Conglomerate member (Facies codes as in Table 2).

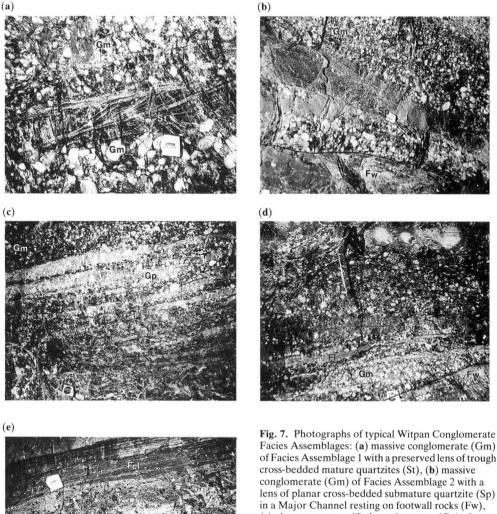

(a)

(b)

(c)

(d)

(e)

Fig. 7. Photographs of typical Witpan Conglomerate Facies Assemblages: (**a**) massive conglomerate (Gm) of Facies Assemblage 1 with a preserved lens of trough cross-bedded mature quartzites (St), (**b**) massive conglomerate (Gm) of Facies Assemblage 2 with a lens of planar cross-bedded submature quartzite (Sp) in a Major Channel resting on footwall rocks (Fw), (**c**) planar cross-stratified conglomerate (Gp) of Facies Assemblage 3 overlain by massive conglomerates (Gm) in a Major Channel, (**d**) alternating massive conglomerate (Gm) and laminated pelite (Fl) of a Facies Assemblage 4 on the edge of a Major Channel, (**e**) trough cross-bedded, pebbly mature quartzites (St) and laminated carbonaceous pelites (Fd) of Facies Assemblages 5 and 7 respectively, in a Minor Channel.

distributed on either side of this conglomerate core are lenses of trough cross-bedded mature quartzites (Facies St) showing down-channel cross-bedding orientations and rare across-channel oriented sets of planar cross-bedded submature quartzites (Facies Sp). These units range up to 40 m across and 100 m long in Major Channels but are much smaller, up to 10 m across and 25 m long, in Minor Channels. They

are associated with active channel fills (FA5) developed on both sides.

This facies assemblage is interpreted as gravel bars that accumulated by episodic accretion of bedload gravels during high flood stage (Facies Gm) followed by lower flood stage bar modification and emergence marked by bar-side sand wedges (Facies Sp, Rust 1975) or erosional remnants of channel dune migration (Facies St,

Table 3. *Facies assemblages in the Witpan Conglomerate Member (see also Fig. 7)*

Facies association	Dominant facies	Subordinate facies	Relationship to channels	Palaeocurrent growth direction	Dimensions	Gold content	Interpretation
FA1	Gm	St, Sp, Gt	Within channel	Symmetrical down-channel	100 m long 40 m wide	High	Longitudinal bar
FA2	Gm	St, Sp, Gt	Within channel or bank attached	Asymmetrical across-channel	150 m long 50 m wide	Very high	Diagonal bar
FA3	Gp	St, Fl	Within channel	Radial down-channel	15 m long 5 m wide	Moderate to low	Transverse bar
FA4	Gm	St, Sp, Fl	Attached to convex bank	Asymmetrical down-channel	20 m long 3 m wide	Moderate to high	Side bar
FA5	St	Sp	Within channel	Down-channel	100 m long 30 m wide	Moderate to low	Active channel fill
FA6	St, Sp, Sr	Fl, Cm	Within channel	Down and across channel	100 m long 30 m wide	Low except with Cm	Slough channel fill
FA7	Sr, Fl, Fc	—	Within minor channel	Variable	any length 25 m wide	Very low	Abandoned channel fill (lake)
FA8	Gm (thin)	Rare Cm	Interchannel terrace areas	Variable	areas up to 500 m across	Low except with Cm	Interchannel terrace

Miall 1977). The down-channel elongation and growth within these bars, the absence of well developed foresets and the symmetrical distribution of the sand lenses, suggest that they may represent longitudinal bars (Smith 1974; Hein & Walker 1977) formed under symmetrical flow conditions with relatively high sediment and water discharges. Gold mineralization in this facies assemblage is generally high with most gold concentrated in the lower part of the massive conglomerate core, especially towards the bar head. The upper part of the massive conglomerate core tends to show much lower gold concentrations possibly because of rapid emergence during waning flood conditions.

Facies Assemblage 2 (Fig. 6b) resembles FA1 in that it consists of a core of stacked lenses of massive conglomerates (Facies Gm), each bounded by an erosional, convex-up, bounding surface and resting on an erosional basal scour surface. However, unlike FA1, these stacked lenses show significant across-channel components of elongation and accretion together with a decreasing pebble size. Facies Assemblage 2 is generally only found in Major Channels and forms bar bedforms up to 50 m wide and 150 m long. Lenses of trough and planar cross-bedded quartzites (Facies St, Sp) are intercalated with the massive conglomerates but with distinctly asymmetrical distribution. Trough cross-bedding usually shows down-channel foreset orientations whereas the planar cross-bedding shows across-channel orientations. This facies assemblage is commonly associated with an active channel fill (FA5) developed on one side and an inner slough channel fill (FA6) developed on the other.

This facies assemblage is interpreted as a within-channel gravel bar active during high flood stage and modified during waning floods. The across-channel growth directions, the absence of foresets, the asymmetrical distribution of intercalated quartzites and the presence of an inner slough channel suggests a diagonal gravel bar (Smith 1974) which accumulated under asymmetrical flow conditions with relatively high sediment and water discharges (Hein & Walker 1977). As the bar became bank-attached at its upper end, a slough channel formed in which immature sands, silts and muds accumulated (Bluck 1979). Rare across-channel oriented sets of planar cross-bedded quartzites probably represent low stage bar-side sand wedges (Rust 1972). Gold mineralization in this facies association is concentrated in the lower part of the conglomerate core especially towards the bar head. Gold is also abundant in the

gravels associated with the inner or slough channels and are interpreted as concentrations produced by convergent flow over the bar (cf. bank hugger bar of Smith & Minter 1979).

Facies Assemblage 3 (Fig. 6c) is relatively rare in the Witpan Conglomerate member and comprises isolated, large scale sets up to 1 m high and 15 m long of planar cross-stratified gravels (Facies Gp) with low angle, internal reactivation surfaces and resting on a scoured, basal bounding surface. This facies assemblage is restricted to Major Channels associated with areas of significant channel widening or deepening and foresets commonly show radial, down-channel orientations. This facies assemblage is interpreted as isolated, gravelly, transverse, linguoid bars formed at high flood stage and partially modified during lower flood stage (Smith 1974). Transverse linguoid bars generally develop under lower sediment and water discharges than longitudinal or diagonal bars (Hein & Walker 1977). This facies assemblage generally has poor gold mineralization possibly due to lower discharge and divergent flow over the bar.

Facies Assemblage 4 (Fig. 6d) comprises a core of stacked lenses of massive gravels (Facies Gm) with internal bounding surfaces draped by rippled and laminated submature to immature quartzites and pelites (Facies Sr, Fl), and forming units up to 20 m long and 3 m across. This facies assemblage occurs mostly on the margins of Major and Minor Channels attached to convex banks and passing laterally into an active channel fill (Facies Assemblage 5). Elongation and growth directions are both across and down the associated channel.

This facies assemblage is interpreted as a side bar attached to the inner bank and growing into and down the channel (Smith 1974; Hein & Walker 1977). Such bars tend to form on inner convex banks in relatively low energy areas where the main flow is deflected against the outer bank (Smith 1974; Miall 1977). Gold mineralization in this facies assemblage is generally high in that part of the bar core adjoining the active channel but lower in the bar interior.

Channel fill facies assemblages

Facies Assemblage 5 (Fig. 6e) comprises stacked sets of trough cross-bedded, mature quartzites (Facies St) in cosets up to 2 m thick with a basal, medium to large pebble lag resting on an erosional basal bounding surface. Isolated sets of planar cross-bedded mature quartzites

(Facies Sp) and rare pelitic drapes (Facies Fl) also occur. This facies assemblage predominates in the Major and Minor Channels and occurs in units up to 30 m wide and 100 m long. Foreset directions within the trough cross-bedded quartzites indicate down-channel palaeoflow directions. This facies assemblage is interpreted as the fill of a channel that remained active throughout the flood cycle (an active channel) and hence show very little evidence of channel abandonment such as thick pelitic intercalations (Miall 1977). The stacked sets of trough cross-bedded quartzites reflect the migration of low flow regime dune bedforms in between-bar channels during low flood stage (Bluck 1974, 1979; Boothroyd & Ashley 1975). The isolated, planar cross-bedded sets are interpreted as transverse or linguoid sand bars that migrated down these channels (Collinson 1970). Gold mineralization is generally low in this facies assemblage and concentrated in the basal gravel lags. Abundant gold is recorded on concave channel margins which is attributed to reworking by channel edge vortices (Allen 1970, p. 139).

Facies Assemblage 6 (Fig. 6f) comprises a heterolithic, commonly fining-upwards, sequence of mature to submature, trough and isolated planar cross-bedded and ripple cross-laminated quartzites (Facies St, Sp, Sr) and laminated pelites (Facies Fl). Very rare carbonaceous seams are present (Facies Cm). This facies assemblage occurs in both Major and Minor Channels in units up to 30 m wide and 100 m long and is associated with Facies Association 2 diagonal bars and distal parts of Minor Channels. Foresets in the trough cross-bedded quartzites are oriented down-channel, whereas in the isolated planar cross-bedded quartzites are typically orientated across-channel. This facies assemblage is interpreted as the fill of a slough channel (Bluck 1979) formed in large channels during waning flood conditions. Such conditions are caused by a migrating bar cutting off one bar-flanking channel from active flow (e.g. diagonal bars). Minor Channels branching off from the Major Channels may also be partially abandoned during waning flood. Isolated planar cross-bedded sets are interpreted as bar-side deltas (Bluck 1979) formed by low flood stage flow over the bar. Gold mineralization in this facies association is very low except where diagonal bar gravels have prograded into such slough channels or where carbonaceous seams are present.

Facies Assemblage 7 (Fig. 6g) comprises sequence up to 1 m thick dominated by laminated carbonaceous pelites with thin graded and ripple cross-laminated immature quartzites (Facies Fc, Sr) and occur mostly in Minor Channels. Soft sediment deformation structures, including load-casted ripples, flame structures and pseudo-nodules, are common. This facies assemblage is interpreted as muds deposited by suspension settling in a lake in permanently abandoned channel system (Sturm & Matter 1979). Graded sandstone units may represent sporadic influxes of coarser sediment associated with flooding in the main part of the channel system. The presence of soft sediment deformation structures suggests rapid deposition possibly in a tectonically active environment (Reineck & Singh 1973). Gold mineralization in this facies assemblage is very poor.

Interchannel facies assemblages

Facies Assemblage 8 (Fig. 6h) consists of a thin laterally persistent lag, up to 15 cm thick, of massive, matrix supported, medium pebble conglomerate (Facies Gm) resting on a planar basal scour surface with very rare carbonaceous seams (Facies Cm) usually resting on pelitic partings in the footwall. Some of the pebbles in this conglomerate are anomalously large and of small cobble size while others show angular, facetted morphologies. This facies association is developed in the Terrace reef areas and is interpreted as an interchannel gravel lag produced by deflation and overbank sheet-flood reworking during maximum flood discharges (Williams & Rust 1969). The rare carbonaceous seams probably represent plant growth in standing pools of water. Gold mineralization in this facies association is generally very low with the exception of the carbonaceous seams which have very high gold contents. The high gold content of the 'carbon' seams (up to 100 times that of associated conglomerates) can be attributed to two possible mechanisms, mechanical trapping of detrital gold or chemical precipitation of gold from solution. Since interchannel Terrace areas appear to have been only rarely inundated with low energy flood waters, it seems unlikely that large amounts of detrital gold could have been brought in. Weir (1989) has suggested that gold in solution was precipitated by the plants that formed the 'carbon' seams. This mechanism could explain their anomalously high gold concentrations and lack of preferential top or bottom concentrations of gold in thick 'carbon' seams (Karpeta 1991). Watterson (1991) has shown that modern bacteria have similarly precipitated gold from solution in the Lillian Creek placer, Alaska.

Examples

Two of the stopes mined on the Witpan Conglomerate member on President Steyn Gold Mine Number 2 Shaft, are here described in detail to illustrate how architectural elements might be used to analyse these conglomerates.

Stope 1

Stope 1 comprises a NNW–SSE-trending Major Channel, up to 50 m wide and 2 m deep, and an irregular, meandering Minor Channel, up to 20 m across and 0.5 m deep, which cut across an area of Terrace Reef (Fig. 8a).

Within the Major Channel, a compound, within-channel gravel bar up to 100 m long and 30 m across, has been mapped. The bar comprises four stacked, massive conglomerate lenses (Facies Gm) with minor quartzites (Facies St), each separated by low angle bounding surfaces (Fig. 8b). The first two conglomerate lenses (Fig. 8c) show down channel growth directions with roughly symmetrical distributions of quartzite intercalations representing Facies Assemblage 1 and are therefore interpreted as stacked longitudinal gravel bar growth elements. Laterally, these conglomerates pass into stacked sets of trough cross-bedded, mature quartzites (Facies Assemblage 5) which are interpreted as active channel fill sands. The third and fourth conglomerate lenses show asymmetrical, across-channel growth directions (Facies Assemblage 2) suggesting that the bar became diagonal. On the eastern side of this bar, immature quartzites and pelites of Facies Assemblage 6 were mapped representing low flood stage, slough channel fills. During floods, however, gravels were still swept over the bar and into the slough. Algal mats grew in the quite water of the slough channel during low flood stage, now represented by 'carbon' seams (Facies Cm). Overall, gold mineralization (Fig. 8d) in this gravel bar is high, concentrated mainly in the lower bar core conglomerates and also in those bar conglomerates swept into the slough channel. The upper parts of the bar core gravels have low values.

In the Terrace area to the east, the Witpan Conglomerate member consists of a thin, matrix supported gravel lag, up to 15 cm thick, which is poorly gold mineralized. The Minor Channel, which cuts across this Terrace area, is infilled by massive conglomerates (Facies Gm) possibly representing simple longitudinal gravel bars and is generally well gold mineralized.

Stope 2

In Stope 2, the channel pattern is more complicated than in Stope 1 owing to the presence of 'islands' of coarse footwall cobble conglomerates which appear to have acted as riffles within the Major Channel and have nucleated the bars. The main feature of Stope 2 is a NNW–SSE-trending Major Channel up to 120 m wide and 2 m deep cutting across an area of Terrace. Branching off from this Major Channel and cutting across the Terrace area are three Minor Channels. The Major Channel can be divided into three areas, a northwestern diagonal bar complex, a central riffle and longitudinal bar area and a southeastern channel and point bar area (Fig. 9a).

In the northwestern area, the Major Channel is divided into several wide, shallow subchannels up to 0.5 m deep across a riffle of footwall cobble conglomerate and reunites into a 1.5 m deep channel on the other side (Fig. 9b). Initially, two sets of planar cross-stratified conglomerates, up to 0.5 m high and 30 m across, showing radial foreset orientations and reactivation surfaces, grew into the deeper part of the Major Channel beyond the riffle. These are interpreted as transverse, lobate bars (Facies Assemblage 3) that probably formed under relatively low sediment and water discharge conditions. The following stages of bar growth are marked by a series of four stacked lenses of massive conglomerates (Facies Gm) showing eastwards, across-channel dipping bounding surfaces often with mature and immature quartzite lenses and drapes preserved on them. The marked, across-channel growth directions and the preserved intercalations of submature and immature quartzites suggest that these massive conglomerate lenses accreted in a compound diagonal bar (FA2) prograding into a slough channel. Mapping of the bounding surfaces in this diagonal bar shows that they have irregular outlines possibly because of post-depositional bar modification (Fig. 9c). Overall, gold mineralization in this compound diagonal bar is moderate to high (Fig. 9d). However in the basal transverse bars (FA3), gold mineralization is low possibly because of the initial low discharge conditions. In the massive gravels of the diagonal bar (FA2), gold mineralization is high in those parts of the

(a)

(b)

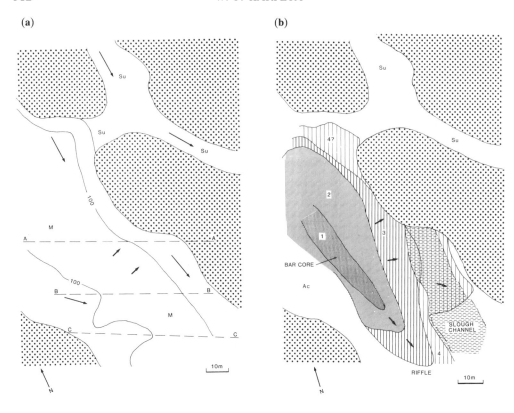

(c)

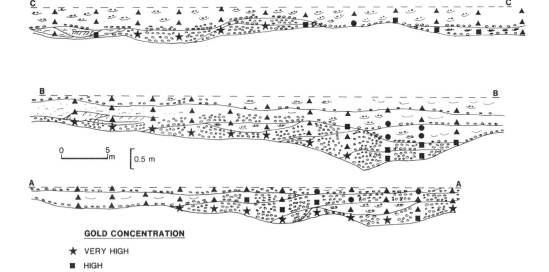

GOLD CONCENTRATION

★ VERY HIGH

■ HIGH

● INTERMEDIATE

▲ LOW

(d)

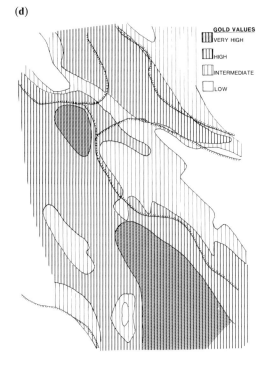

GOLD VALUES
⊞ VERY HIGH
⊞ HIGH
⊞ INTERMEDIATE
☐ LOW

Fig. 8. Bar development and gold mineralization in the Witpan Conglomerate member of Stope 1. (**a**) channel morphology; (**b**) bar development; (**c**) stope face sections; (**d**) gold distribution. (M, Major Channel; Su, Minor Channel; Ac, active channel; Sc, slough channel; 1, 2, 3, 4, bar growth stages; Long arrows, palaeocurrents from cross-bedding; Short arrows, bar growth directions; Stipple, interchannel Terrace areas.)

lenses in the slough channels but much lower in the rapidly emergent upper parts of the bar.

In the central area, the Major Channel narrows rapidly and is funnelled between two areas of Terrace, passing over a riffle of footwall cobble conglomerates. Downstream from this riffle is a simple, within-channel longitudinal bar (FA1) composed of four down-stream growing massive gravel lenses. Either side of this bar are two active channel fills (FA5) of trough cross-bedded mature quartzites. Either side of this constriction in the Major Channel, the Terrace areas are cut by Minor Channels, each up to 15 m wide and 0.5 m deep, which may have acted as overflow channels during floods. These Minor Channels have stacked massive conglomerate units probably representing simple longitudinal bars. Gold mineralization appears to be high in the longitudinal bars in both the Major and Minor Channels and is concentrated mainly in the lower part of the gravel lenses.

The southeastern part of the Major Channel consists of a fairly simple, curved channel, up to 50 m wide and 1.5 m deep. On the eastern, inner, convex bank of this channel, a simple side bar has accreted which consists of four downstream accreting, massive conglomerate lenses (FA4). These grade westwards into stacked, trough cross-bedded pebbly quartzites on the outer concave bank of the channel. Gold mineralization in this bar is relatively high.

Discussion

Morphological differentiation

The various morphological elements in the Witpan Conglomerate member resemble the topographical levels described by Williams & Rust (1969) in the Donjek River. The Major Channels of the Witpan Conglomerate member show evidence of continuous occupation and are therefore comparable with Level 1 of the Donjek River. This Level consists of the main, relatively continuously occupied channels which act as the principle sediment dispersal routes in the Donjek river (Williams & Rust 1969). The Minor Channels of the Witpan Conglomerate member show evidence of episodic occupation during flood events followed by abandonment during waning flood and resemble Level 2 of the Donjek River. This Level is generally active during peak flood and has few active channels at other times (Williams & Rust 1969). The Terrace area of the Witpan Conglomerate member appears to have been rarely flooded as

(a)

(b)

(c)

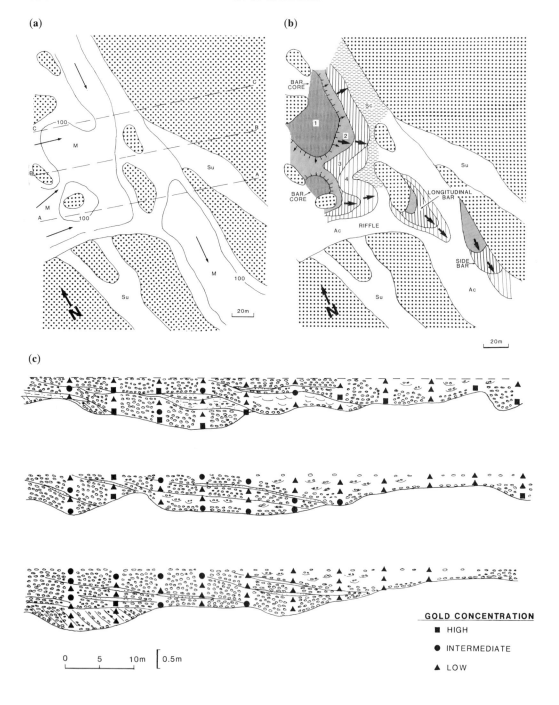

GOLD CONCENTRATION

■ HIGH

● INTERMEDIATE

▲ LOW

suggested by the matrix supported lags with occasional facetted pebbles indicative of long periods of subaerial exposure and abrasion by wind blown sand. These areas appear to correspond to Level 3 of the Donjek River which has only low energy flow at peak flood and is dry for most of the time (Williams & Rust 1969). Such topographical differentiation is commonly reported in modern, degrading braided river systems but is rare in aggrading systems (Miall 1977). The presence of topographic differentiation, together with the strong footwall control

(d)

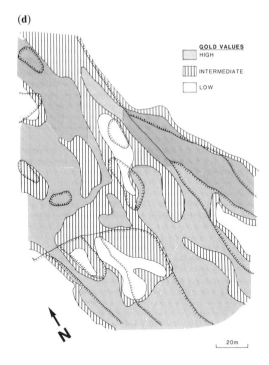

GOLD VALUES
▨ HIGH
▥ INTERMEDIATE
☐ LOW

N

20m

Fig. 9. Bar development and gold mineralization in Stope 2. (**a**) channel morphology; (**b**) bar development; (**c**) stope face sections; (**d**) gold mineralization. (Code letters as Fig. 8.)

on channel location and the erosional relationship with the footwall, all indicate that the Witpan Conglomerate member probably represents a degrading braided river.

Adams *et al.* (1978), Buck & Minter (1986) and Els (1991) have all stressed the importance of degradation in the formation of fluvial placers. Adams *et al.* (1978) indicated in their model study that placers are often produced by complex responses to changes in base level. They showed that an initial drop in base level in a fluvial basin would result in channel incision accompanied by the erosion and transport of large quantities of alluvial material within the basin. This event is followed by fluvial aggradation accompanied by the rapid deposition of poorly sorted alluvium in an unconfined, unstable braided river system (Adams *et al.* 1978). This is, in turn, followed by fluvial degradation accompanied by channel incision and placer formation producing concentrations of heavy minerals at favourable locations (Adams *et al.* 1978). A similar sequence of events can be postulated for the formation of the Witpan Conglomerate member where an initial base level drop possibly produced by tectonic or eustatic adjustment, resulted in the incision then rapid aggradation of an unconfined braided fluvial system which deposited the poorly sorted cobble gravels and coarse sands of the footwall.

This phase of rapid aggradation was followed by a phase of slow downcutting of fluvial channels into the footwall reworking and concentrating placer minerals. This phase of channel degradation produced the Witpan Conglomerate member.

Topographical differentiation appears to have had a strong control on the large scale distribution of gold mineralization in the Witpan Conglomerate member with the highest gold concentrations being found in the Major Channels and the conglomeratic Minor Channels (equivalents of Levels 1 and 2 of Williams & Rust 1969) and low concentrations in the sandy Minor Channels and Terrace areas (Levels 2 and 3 of Williams & Rust 1969). This association could be due to several factors including the availability of suitable conglomerate traps, the depth of incision and reworking, and the frequency of flood events in the various levels of the Witpan Conglomerate member. The lowest, most deeply incised, most regularly flooded gravel-rich levels carry the best gold mineralization.

Facies assemblages

Besides the bar types described by Smith (1974) and Hein & Walker (1978), Smith (1980) has also recognized two broader categories of gravel bars in braided rivers, namely simple bars and compound bars. Simple bars are relatively unmodified and show simple geometries, whereas compound bars show multiple episodes of deposition and extensive modification. In the Witpan Conglomerate member, simple bars are found mainly in the Minor Channels where in the Major Channels, the bars tend to show much more complex internal geometries and are therefore considered to be compound bars. Smith (1980) has suggested that simple bars tend to be found in streams where flows competent enough to move coarse bed load are relatively infrequent whereas compound bars occur in channels where such flows are frequent. Therefore, in the Witpan Conglomerate member, it is likely that the occurrence of simple bars in the Minor Channel reflects infrequent major flood events whereas the compound bars of the Major Channels indicate much more frequent flood events.

Gold mineralization at intermediate scale appears to be related to the distribution of bar types and channel fill sediments within the Witpan Conglomerate member. In general the bar facies assemblages (FA1 to FA4) carry the highest gold mineralization followed by the channel fill facies assemblages (FA5 to FA7) and then the terrace facies assemblage (FA8). This variation probably again reflects the availability of suitable open work gravel traps (Day & Fletcher 1991) and the frequency and strength of flood events bringing in placer gold.

The bar types can themselves be ranked according to their overall gold mineralization with diagonal bars (FA2) typically carrying the highest gold followed by longitudinal bars (FA1) then side bars (FA4) and finally transverse bars (FA3) having the lowest gold concentrations. It is probable that these transverse bars have low gold contents because they lack massive open work gravels (Facies Gm) and form under divergent flow conditions (Hein & Walker 1978) features which are less favourable for the formation of gold concentrations (Smith & Minter 1979).

The other three bar types (longitudinal, diagonal and side) all have stacked lenses of massive gravels (Facies Gm) which would act as favourable traps for detrital gold (Day & Fletcher 1991). However, only the lowest portions of each gravel lens are rich in gold. This association between the high gold values and the lowest part of the gravels may be due to the infiltration of gold down through the stacked conglomerates to the basal contact or because the upper parts of the gravel bar were emergent during gold trapping in the gravels. The former

mechanism is indicated by the occasional patchy high gold values within the gravels where they rest on preserved internal quartzite lenses. However, the second mechanism is considered more likely since it corresponds to the idea that heavy minerals are trapped after gravels have stopped moving during waning flood conditions (Day & Fletcher 1991) and the upper part of the gravel bars may therefore have been emergent at that time.

The variable gold contents of the longitudinal, diagonal and side bars also appear to reflect their relationships with adjacent channels. Side bars (FA3) are generally attached to the inner convex bank of a curved channel and therefore have only their outer sides in contact with the flood waters during emergence. Side bars also occur where the flow is thrown against the outer, concave bank and creates an area of divergent, low velocity flow next to the bar, limiting reworking and heavy mineral enrichment in the bar gravels. Longitudinal bars (FA1) and diagonal bars (FA2) have channels on both sides of the bar core making a greater area of openwork gravels accessible to reworking by floodwaters during emergence resulting in higher gold concentrations. In the Witpan Conglomerate member, diagonal bars (FA2) have higher gold concentrations than longitudinal bars, especially in those parts of the bar that have prograded across-channel. Such across-channel bar progradation is thought to have introduced openwork gravels into the slough channel during flood events and to have produced areas of convergent flow and extensive reworking in the confined area between the bar and the bank thus concentrating heavy minerals. This mechanism is similar to that suggested by Smith & Minter (1979) for mineral enrichment in bank-hugger bars.

Three factors are therefore thought to be significant in enriching detrital gold in gravel bars in the Witpan Conglomerate member:

(1) the presence of massive openwork gravels;
(2) the accessibility of these openwork gravels to flood events (i.e. open channels on either side of the bar);
(3) the presence of areas of convergent flow over these gravels.

For transverse bars (FA3), none of these factors apply, consequently gold mineralization is relatively low. In longitudinal bars (FA1), the massive gravel core is accessible on both sides to flood water and hence is relatively enriched in gold. In diagonal bars (FA2), both sides are accessible and an area of confined, convergent flow is formed during flood events leading to especial gold enrichment in these bars. Though side bars (FA4) have openwork gravel cores, they are generally only accessible to flood water on one side, and bank attached on the other, therefore gold mineralization is lower than longitudinal and diagonal bars.

Conclusions

The Archaean Witpan Conglomerate member (Aandenk Formation, Witwatersrand Supergroup) is interpreted as the deposit of a degrading, gravelly, braided river system showing well-developed topographical differentiation into three morphological elements, namely Major Channels, Minor Channels and interchannel Terrace areas. These elements represent different levels of the river system progressively occupied during flood cycles. Major Channels were permanently occupied throughout the flood cycle whereas Minor Channels show periodic abandonment during waning floods. Terrace areas were rarely invaded by floodwaters except during exceptionally high floods.

Architectural element analysis of the Witpan Conglomerate member has identified eight recurrent facies assemblages, four of which are interpreted as gravel bars, three as sandy channel fills and one as interchannel terrace gravel sheets. The four bar types correspond to the longitudinal, diagonal, transverse and side bars of modern gravelly braided rivers and are combined into compound bars showing more complex evolution. The three channel fills are interpreted as active, slough and abandoned channel fills. The terrace sheet gravels represent lags produced by deflation and reworking of interchannel areas by sheetfloods.

Broad scale gold mineralization in the Witpan Conglomerate member is related to the presence of topographical differentiation in the system, the Major Channels and gravelly Minor Channels having high gold values and the sandy Minor Channels and Terrace areas having low gold.

Intermediate scale gold mineralization is related to the facies assemblage present. High gold values require massive openwork gravels accessible to flood waters and the formation of areas of convergent flow over these gravels. Hence gold mineralization is highest in the gravelly bar facies assemblages and low in the sandy channel fill and interchannel terrace areas. Of the bars, diagonal bars have the highest gold contents followed by longitudinal and side bars with transverse bars showing the lowest gold mineralization.

Hence, by identifying the architecture of these conglomerates it is possible to predict the distribution of gold mineralization within them.

I would like to specially thank J. Hamman and S. Wright for their geological help, and J. Strauss and J. Jordaan for logistical assistance whilst collecting this data. I would also like to thank W. E. L. Minter for the inspiration for this study. Thanks go to W. Aitken for typing the original manuscript and to J. Andrews for drafting the figures. The manuscript was improved by the constructive comments of S. Buck, J. Noad and C. Bristow.

References

ADAMS, J., ZIMPFER, G. L. & McLANE, C. F. 1978. Basin dynamics, channel processes and placer formation: a model study. *Economic Geology*, **73**, 416–426.

ALLEN, J. R. L. 1970. *Physical Processes of Sedimentation*. George Allen and Unwin, London.

—— 1982. *Sedimentary Structures. Their Character and Physical Basis*. Development in Sedimentology, 30A and 30B. Elsevier, Amsterdam.

—— 1983. Studies in fluviatile sedimentation: bars, bar-complexes and sandstone sheets (Low-sinuosity braided streams) in the Brownstones (L. Devonian), Welsh Borders. *Sedimentary Geology*, **33**, 237–293.

ALLSOP, H. L. & WELKE, H. J. 1986. Age limits to the Witwatersrand Supergroup. *In*: ANHAEUSSER, C. R. & MASKE, S. (eds) *Mineral Deposits of Southern Africa*. Vols I and II. Geological Society of South Africa, 495–496.

BLUCK, B. J. 1974. Structure and directional properties of some valley sandur deposits in southern Iceland. *Sedimentology*, **21**, 533–544.

—— 1979. Structure of coarse grained braided stream alluvium. *Transactions of the Royal Society of Edinburgh*, **70**, 181–221.

BUCK, S. G. 1983. The Saaiplaas Quartzite Member: a braided system of gold- and uranium-bearing channel placers within the Proterozoic Witwatersrand supergroup of South Africa. *In*: COLLINSON, J. D. & LEWIN, J. (eds) *Modern and Ancient Fluvial Systems*. Special Publications of the International Association of Sedimentologists, **6**, 549–562.

—— & MINTER, W. E. L. 1985. Placer formation by fluvial degradation of an alluvial fan sequence: the Proterzoic Carbon Leader placer, Witwatersrand Supergroup, South Africa. *Journal of the Geological Society, London*, **142**, 754–764.

COLLINSON, J. D. 1970. Bedforms of the Tana River, Norway. *Geografisker Annaler*, **52A**, 31–56.

DAY, S. J. & FLETCHER, W. K. 1991. Concentration of magnetite and gold at bar and reach scales in a gravel-bed stream, British Columbia, Canada. *Journal of Sedimentary Petrology*, **61**, 871–882.

Els, B. G. 1991. Placer formation during pro-gradational degradation: the Late Archaean Middelvlei gold placer, Witwatersrand, South Africa. *Economic Geology*, **86**, 261–277.

Hallbauer, D. K. 1975. The plant origin of Witwatersrand "carbon". *Minerals Science and Engineering*, **7**, 111–131.

—— 1986. The mineralogy and geochemistry of Witwatersrand pyrite, gold, uranium and carbonaceous matter. *In*: Anhaeusser, C. R. & Maske, S. (eds) *Mineral Deposits of Southern Africa*. Vols I and II, Geological Society of South Africa, Johannesburg, 731–752.

Hein, F. J. & Walker, R. G. 1977. Bar evolution and stratification in the gravelly braided Kicking Horse River, B.C. *Canadian Journal of Earth Sciences*, **14**, 562–570.

Jordaan, M. J. 1989. Depositional setting of the Kimberley palaeoplacers in the south western part of the Late Archaean Witwatersrand Basin, South Africa (Ext. Abstr.) *OFS Goldfield Symposium, Geological Society of South Africa*, 29–31.

Karpeta, W. P. 1984. The sedimentology and strati-graphic setting of the 'A' Reef placers, Aandenk Formation, on President Steyn Gold Mine, Welkom, Orange Free State (Ext Abstr.) *Geokongres 84, Potchefstroom Univ. C.H.E.*, 61–62.

—— 1991. Hydrocarbon occurrences in the Vaal Reef and 'A' Reef placers: sedimentological controls and economic significance (Ext. Abstr.) *Carbon in Witwatersrand Reefs Symposium*, 57–59.

Kingsley, C. S. 1987. Facies changes from fluvial conglomerate to braided sandstone of the early Proterozoic Eldorado Formation, Welkom goldfield, South Africa. *In*: Ethridge, F. G., Flores, R. M. & Harvey, M. D. (eds) *Recent Developments in Fluvial Sedimentology*. Society of Economic Paleontologists & Mineralogists Special Publications, **39**, 359–370.

Law, J. D. M., Bailey, A. C., Cadle, A. B., Phillips, G. N. & Stanistreet, I. G. 1990. Reconstructive approach to the classification of Witwatersrand "quartzites". *South African Journal of Geology*, **93**, 83–92.

Miall, A. D. 1977. A review of the braided-river depositional environment. *Earth Science Reviews*, **13**, 1–62.

—— 1985. Architectural element analysis: a new method of facies analysis applied to fluvial deposits. *Earth Science Reviews*, **22**, 261–308.

Minter, W. E. L. 1978. A sedimentological synthesis of placer gold, uranium and pyrite in Proterozoic Witwatersrand sediments. *In*: Miall, A. D. (ed.) *Fluvial Sedimentology*, Canadian Society of Petroleum Geologists Memoirs, **5**, 801–829.

Nagtegaal, P. J. C. 1979. Sandstone-framework

instability as a function of burial diagensis. *Journal of the Geological Society, London*, **135**, 101–105.

Pettijohn, F. J., Potter, P. E. & Siever, R. 1987. *Sand and Sandstones*. Springer-Verlag, New York.

Reineck, H. E. & Singh, I. B. 1973. *Depositional Sedimentary Environments with Reference to Terrigenous Clastics*. Springer-Verlag, Berlin.

Rust, B. R. 1972. Structure and process in a braided river. *Sedimentology*, **18**, 221–245.

—— 1975. Fabric and structure in glaciofluvial gravels. *In*: *Glaciofluvial and Glacio-lacustrine Sedimentation*. Society of Economic Paleontologists & Mineralogists Special Publications, **23**, 238–248.

Smith, N. D. 1970. The braided river depositional environment: comparison of the Platte River and some Silurian clastic rocks, north-central Appalachians. *Geological Society of America Bulletin*, **81**, 2993–3014.

—— 1974. Sedimentology and bar formation in the Upper Kicking Horse River, a braided outwash stream. *Journal of Geology*, **82**, 205–223.

—— 1980. *A Short Course on Braided Stream Systems: Course Notes*. Rhodes Univ., Dept. of Geol.

—— & Minter, W. E. L. 1979. *Sedimentological controls of gold and uranium in local develop-ments of the Leader Reef, Welkom Goldfield and Elsburg No. 5 Reef, Klerksdorp Goldfield, Witwatersrand Basin*. Univ. Witwatersrand, Economic Geology Research Unit, Information Circular, **137**.

Stratten, T. 1975. Notes on the application of shape parameters to differentiate between beach and river deposits in South Africa. *Transactions of the Geological Society of South Africa*, **77**, 59–64.

Sturm, M. & Matter, A. 1978. Turbidities and varves in Lake Brienz (Switzerland): deposition of clastic detritus by density currents. *In*: Matter, A. & Tucker, M. E. (eds) *Modern and Ancient Lake Sediments*. Special Publications of the International Association of Sedimentologists, **2**, 145–166.

Tucker, M. E. 1991. *Sedimentary Petrology*. 2nd Edn. Publ. Blackwell Scientific, Oxford.

Watterson, J. R. 1991. Preliminary evidence for the involvement of budding bacteria in the origin of Alaskan placer gold. *Geology*, **20**, 315–318.

Weir, M. W. 1989. Significance of carbonaceous matter on gold and uranium distribution in Upper Witwatersrand reef conglomerates, President Steyn Mine (Ext. Abstr.). *O.F.S. Goldfield Symposium*, 53–57.

Williams, P. F. & Rust, B. R. 1969. The sedi-mentology of braided river. *Journal of Sedimentary Petrology*, **39**, 649–679.

Provenance of braided alluvial deposits of the Thari Formation, Rhodes, SE Aegean: evidence for major erosion of an ophiolite-bearing thrust sheet

LISA EDGINGTON & NEIL HARBURY

Research School of Geological and Geophysical Sciences, Birkbeck College & University College, Gower Street, London WC1E 6BT, UK

Abstract: The Middle to Upper Oligocene Thari Formation sediments in central and southern Rhodes, Greece were deposited adjacent to an active thrust front. They consist of clast-supported massive to horizontally stratified conglomerates, massive matrix-supported conglomerates interbedded with ophiolitic sandstone, and silty mudstone forming lenticular, discontinuous beds with common erosional contacts. Debris flow, stream channel, sheet flood deposits and the high gravel to sand ratios (90 : 10), suggest deposition by processes within a gravel-dominated braided alluvial system. Facies relationships demonstrate a clear proximal (NW) to distal (SE) variation across an alluvial fan. Provenance relationships based on 2400 clast counts show that the main constituents of the conglomerates in the north west area are rounded to well rounded pebbles and cobbles derived from an ophiolite sequence (80%) and include harzburgite, dunite, gabbro, serpentinite, and dolerite whilst the other major components, pelagic limestone and chert (20%), have an increasing importance to the south west of the area. These relationships suggest that the Thari Formation formed part of a flexural foreland basin-fill that developed adjacent to a deformed ophiolite stack eroded after early Paleocene to mid-Oligocene convergent tectonics.

Well exposed on the Island of Rhodes (Figs 1 and 2) are a series of nappes composed of Mesozoic–Early Tertiary, principally carbonate sequences, which formed the sedimentary cover of the Southern Tethyan margin and were stacked during Alpine Hellenide deformation in the Late Palaeogene. The stratigraphy of these sequences is described and interpreted as preserving a transition from a carbonate platform through slope to basin each with its own flysch cover (Hamilton 1840; Jaia 1912; Migliorini 1933; Mutti *et al.* 1970; Harbury & Hall 1988).

Two major sedimentary sequences cover the carbonate and flysch successions on Rhodes. The Middle Oligocene to Lower Miocene Vati Group of Mutti *et al.* (1970) rests with major unconformity on the underlying nappes and is in turn unconformably overlain by Neogene and Recent sediments (Figs 2 and 3).

The most detailed sedimentological and stratigraphical studies of the Vati Group were conducted by Mutti *et al.* (1970) during geological mapping of Rhodes. They consider the Vati Group to be a post-tectonic transgressive sequence commencing with fluvial deposits, represented by the Koriati Conglomerate and the lower member of the Thari Formation. In southern Rhodes these were followed by a rapid subsidence of the basin with subsequent deposition of the deeper water sediments of the Ag. Minas Marl and turbidites of the Messanagros Sandstone.

The objective of this paper is to improve our understanding of the sedimentary history and evolution of the Vati Basin based on facies analysis and provenance studies of the Upper Oligocene Thari Formation.

The Thari Formation

The outcrop of the Thari Formation is generally restricted to the northern and central parts of Rhodes and is dissected by two systems of faults, which strike NE-SW and WNW-ESE (Fig. 4). Many of the contacts of the Thari Formation with underlying and overlying sequences are faulted or poorly exposed. These faults truncate many of the sedimentary successions and complicate interpretation of previously formed structures and stratigraphy (Harbury & Hall 1988).

Despite the faulting, stratigraphic relationships of the Thari Formation are well defined. Where the base of the Thari Formation can be observed along the north west coast near Mandrico (Fig. 4) the Thari Formation unconformably overlies heavily-weathered dolerites. Elsewhere the Thari Formation rests on folded Laerma Member of the Katavia Flysch along the west coast near Monolithos (location

From Best, J. L. & Bristow, C. S. (eds), 1993, *Braided Rivers*, Geological Society
Special Publication No. 75, pp. 389–403.

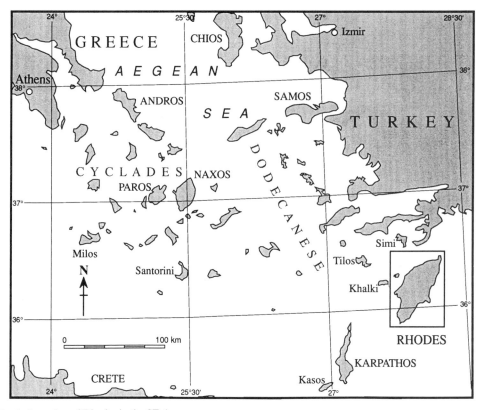

Fig. 1. Location of Rhodes in the SE Aegean.

11, Fig. 5). The Early–Mid Pliocene Levantinian deposits lie unconformably over the Thari Formation.

Although the Thari Formation is unfossiliferous, rare bioturbation is observed in the Artamiti area (Location 8, Fig. 5). Mutti *et al.* (1970) assigned a mid–late Oligocene age to the Thari Formation based on a correlation with the well-dated Ag. Minas Marl in the south of Rhodes. This interpretation is supported by the observation that the Thari Formation rests unconformably on the early Oligocene Laerma and Siana Members of the Katavia Flysch.

Mutti *et al.* (1970) proposed a type section for the Thari Formation measured immediately south of the Monastery of Artamiti. They identify a lower and upper member which they consider together to reach 500–600 m. In this area (Location 6, Figs 4 and 6) the Thari Formation consists of thick ophiolitic conglomerates and dark mudstones with thin ophiolitic sandstones. These mudstone and conglomerate facies are interpreted from this

study to have been deposited as turbidites in a moderately deep water environment. Thinly bedded, fine-grained sandstone and mudstone beds associated with massive clast-supported conglomerates and recognition of grading and classic Bouma sequences suggests deposition by turbidity currents. There was no evidence to suggest marine conditions and so these sediments may have been deposited as part of a lacustrine system developing in front of the propagating thrust sheet.

The data on which this paper is based is derived from the coarse clastic deposits which were deposited to the north and northwest of this 'type' section. These sediments are dominated by coarse conglomerates (90%) and minor sandstone and mudstones (10%) and are interpreted to have been deposited by a gravel-dominated, braided alluvial system. They may represent the lateral equivalent of the deeper water facies in the Artamiti area. The basis for this interpretation is presented in the following sections.

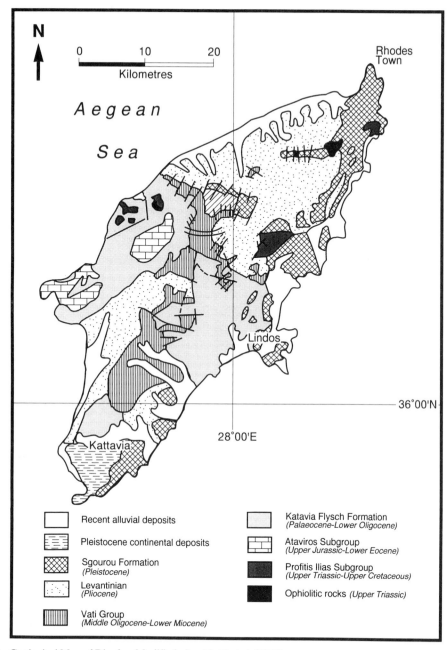

Fig. 2. Geological Map of Rhodes. Modified after Mutti *et al.* (1970).

Thari Formation lithofacies

Seven lithofacies have been distinguished in the Thari Formation (codes are from Miall 1978):

Clast-supported massive to horizontally stratified conglomerates (Gm);

Massive matrix-supported conglomerates (Gms);
Massive to parallel laminated sandstone (Sh);
Planar cross-laminated sandstone (Sp);
Scour fill sandstone (Ss);
Massive silt, mud (Fm);

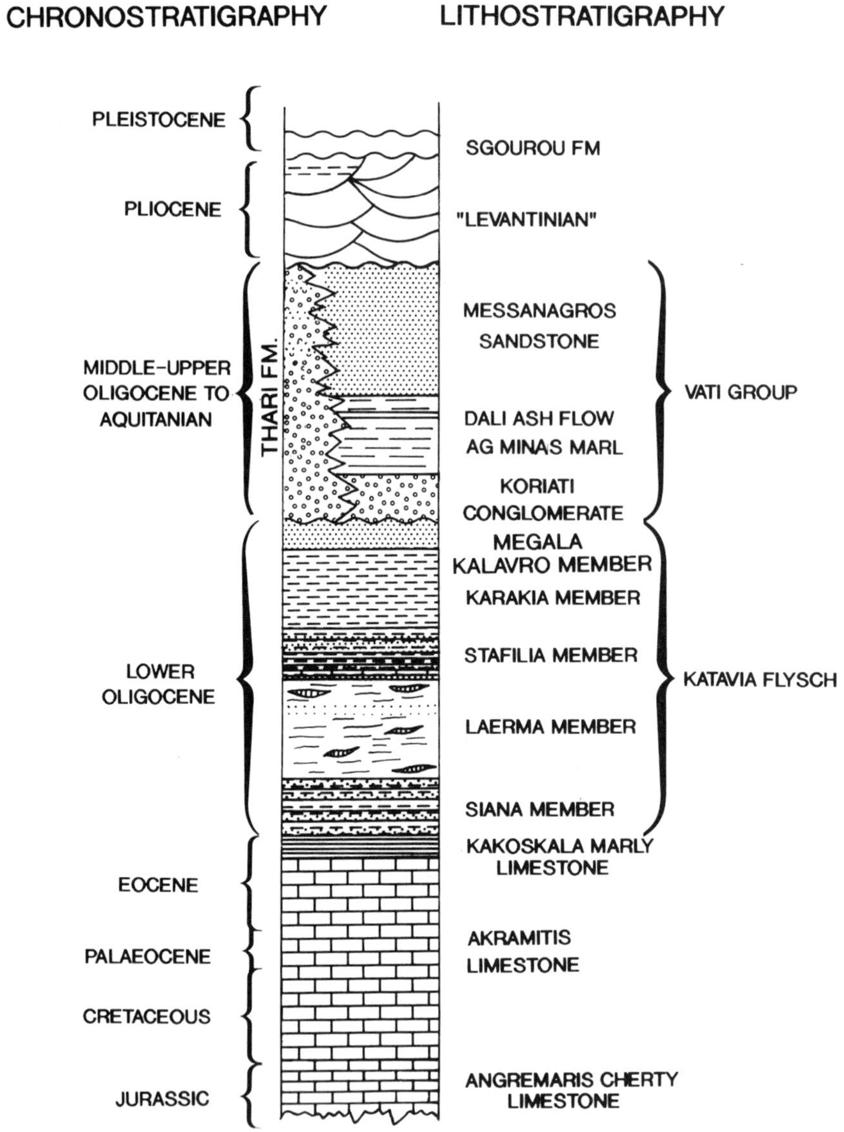

CHRONOSTRATIGRAPHY   LITHOSTRATIGRAPHY

Fig. 3. Stratigraphy of Rhodes. Modified after Mutti *et al.* (1970).

Finely laminated, ripple laminated silt, mud (Fl).

All these facies are predominantly dark brown to red in colour. Field photographs illustrating typical outcrop styles of the Thari Formation are shown in Fig. 7.

Lithofacies associations

For the purpose of description lithofacies can be described from four main areas (Fig. 5):

Road section near Kamiros Skala (location 1);
East of Mandrico (location 2);
Road section between Embonas and Apolona (location 5);
River section northeast of Laerma (location 6).

Road section near Kamiros Skala (location 1).
Massive, disorganized clast-supported polymict, polymodal channel-fill conglomerates (lithofacies Gm) are exposed along a 200 m road section near Kamiros Skala. Constituents are

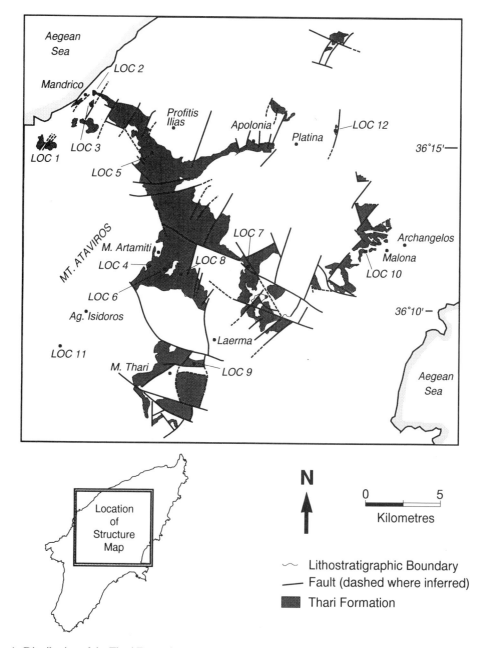

Fig. 4. Distribution of the Thari Formation in central and southern Rhodes.

subrounded to rounded clasts of dunite, gabbro, dolerite, harzburgite and limestone. A dark coarse to pebble grade ophiolitic sandstone matrix is observed between clasts. Clast diameters range in size from 2 cm to 24 cm and large outsize clasts reach up to 0.80 m (Fig. 7).

These conglomerate beds are 0.5–1.80 m thick extending laterally for 10–15 m. Channel margins are difficult to define but where identified (Fig. 8) channel-fills consist of either massive conglomerates or crudely stratified conglomerates. Crude stratification is picked

Fig. 5. Location map and sample sites.

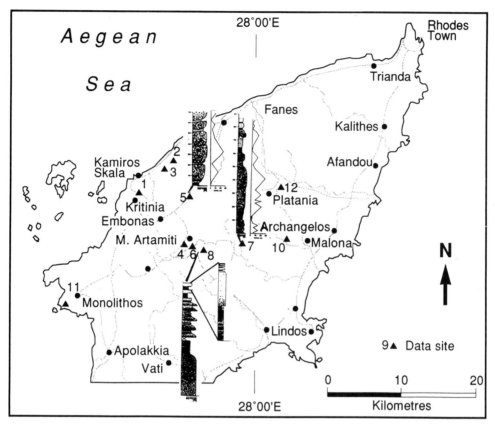

Fig. 6. Sketch logs of Thari Formation sections. At location 6 in the type area, the Thari Formation consists of thick ophiolitic conglomerates and dark mudstones with thin ophiolitic sandstones interpreted to have been deposited in a moderately deep water environment. The Thari examined at location 5 and 7 are dominated by coarse conglomerates and minor sandstone and mudstones interpreted to have been deposited by a gravel-dominated, braided alluvial system.

out by variations in the average clast size. Clast imbrication and preferred orientation of clasts is not well developed.

Poorly sorted, matrix-supported polymict, polymodal conglomerate (lithofacies Gms) is associated with lithofacies Gm and consists of subangular to subrounded clasts of gabbro, dolerite, harzburgite and limestone with a dark brown ophiolitic sandstone matrix. These conglomerates have irregular, non-erosive bases.

East of Mandrico (location 2). Massive clast-supported conglomerate (lithofacies Gm) is associated with matrix-supported conglomerate (lithofacies Gms) and subordinate dark ophiolitic sandstone (lithofacies Sh). Conglomerates have sharp non-erosive, non-channelized bases and lack internal structure. Clast-supported conglomerate beds grade upwards into sandstone.

Road section between Embonas and Apolona: (location 5). Excellent roadside exposures show clast-supported polymict, polymodal conglomerates (lithofacies Gm) deposited as sheets of gravel consisting of rounded to subrounded clasts of dolerite, gabbro, harzburgite and limestone interbedded with red sandstone (lithofacies Sh) and mudstone beds (lithofacies Fm). Towards the southwest the geometry of the sandstone and mudstone beds is lenticular. The discontinuous sandstone and mudstone beds are interbedded with conglomerates and individual depositional events are difficult to delineate (Fig. 9). The ratio of conglomerate to sandstone is approximately 90:10. Clast sizes range from pebble to boulder grade, and crude stratification is picked out by variations in average clast size. Gravel beds range from 0.8–1.5 m thick and extend laterally from 1 to tens of metres. Sandstone and mudstone beds are 0.2–0.5 m thick

Fig. 7. (**A**) Clast-supported polymict polymodal conglomerate with rounded to well rounded clasts of harzburgite, dunite, gabbro, dolerite and limestone within an ophiolitic sandstone matrix (scale 40 cm). (**B**) Clast-supported polymict, polymodal conglomerate. Main constituents are gabbro, dolerite and limestone. (**C**) Inverse grading within clast-supported conglomerate (scale 40 cm). (**D**) Stacked clast-supported conglomerates forming gravel sheets interbedded with thin beds of sandstone and rare mudstone.

and extend for only 1–2 m. Sandstone beds (lithofacies Sh) are commonly parallel laminated with either flat bases or follow the topography of the underlying bed. Tops of sandstone beds are sometimes scoured. Mudstone beds are massive (lithofacies Fm) to faintly laminated (lithofacies Fl), with flat non-erosive bases and flat to scoured tops.

River section northeast of Laerma (location 6). In this area units of massive to parallel laminated sandstone (lithofacies Sh), and scour fill sandstone (lithofacies Ss) form broad shallow scours. Planar cross-laminated sandstone (lithofacies Sp) is associated with finer grained granule to pebble grade clast-supported conglomerate (lithofacies Gm) and massive matrix-supported conglomerate (lithofacies Gms). Fine to coarse grained ophiolitic sandstone beds commonly fine upward into red thinly laminated mudstone beds (lithofacies Fl). Sandstone and mudstone beds range between 0.2 and 0.5 m thick and extend laterally over distances of 2–5 m.

Interpretation

High gravel to sand ratios (90 : 10), bed lenticularity and poor segregation of sand and gravel suggests that these sediments were deposited as part of a gravel dominated alluvial system. There is evidence from grain size changes and ratio of matrix-supported to clast-supported conglomerates for a transition from proximal to distal deposition on an alluvial fan complex from the northwest to the southeast.

Fig. 9. Road section between Embonas and Apolona (Location 5, see Fig. 5). Stacked clast-supported, poorly sorted conglomerates, sandstone and finely laminated silt/mud. These sediments are interpreted as gravel dominated braided river deposits.

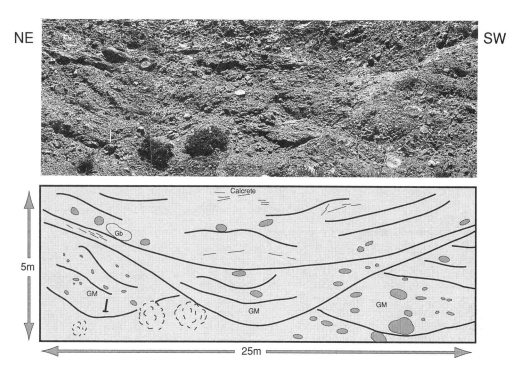

Fig. 8. Road section near Kamiros Scala (Location 1, see Fig. 5). Massive poorly sorted channel-fill conglomerates deposited by sediment gravity flow processes. Large out-sized clast (top left) has a diameter of 80 cm. These sediments are interpreted as braided deposits within a proximal semi-arid alluvial fan.

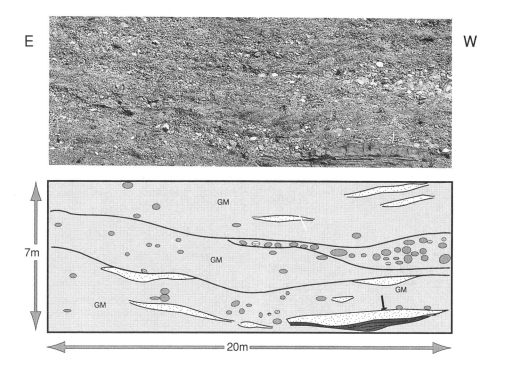

Channel-fill conglomerates deposited by sediment gravity flow processes in more proximal sediments in the NW of the island are dominated by massive poorly sorted, clast-supported conglomerates. Channels on the middle and upper levels of an alluvial fan are commonly filled by sediment gravity flows and gravel bed forms (Ramos & Sopena 1983; Miall 1978, 1985). The absence of fossils and reddened appearance to the sediments suggest subaerial deposition in a continental, semi-arid environment. Fine grained pebble to cobble grade, clast-supported conglomerate and minor sandstone and mudstone beds forming small scale fining upward cycles are interpreted as stream channel fill deposits. These are frequently associated with sediment gravity flow deposits on the more proximal portion of an alluvial fan complex.

Sheets of massive to crudely stratified conglomerates and thin sandstone and mudstone beds were deposited by sheet floods. Where lenticular, stacked, clast-supported, poorly-sorted conglomerates are separated by sandstone and rare mudstone beds, these are interpreted as stream channel deposits on the more distal portion of an alluvial fan. Clast-supported, massive to horizontally-stratified conglomerates, which are the most common lithofacies, are interpreted as longitudinal bar deposits moved during, or just after, high flow stage as sheets of gravel. During high water and sediment discharge these gravel bars, aggrade vertically and laterally downstream by the addition of clasts, to form longitudinal bars (Rust 1978). During reduced flow, deposition on the bar stops and flow is then active along lateral channels, and sometimes on top of bars. Lateral channels are filled with sandstone and mudstone during waning flow.

Provenance studies

Clast count data were obtained to quantify the lithological content and distribution of the rudaceous component of the Thari Formation. The provenance of the Thari is based on 2400 clast counts at 12 sample sites where suitable exposures permitted.

Sample collection

Clast count data was obtained using a 1 m² quadrat rule which provided a grid for 100 clast counts to be obtained. Identification of the lithology of a clast under each 10 cm × 10 cm grid node was made and tabulated. The quadrat was laid on conglomerates where clast diameters were in the range of 2 cm to 20 cm, to avoid clasts taking up too many grid cells and being repeatedly counted. This size range adequately encompassed all the lithological variety identified within the conglomerates of the Thari Formation.

Clasts counted during the early stages were retained to assess whether classifications remained consistent throughout the period of study, and that all reasonably common lithologies in the formation were represented.

Sample size

Data were obtained from 12 sample sites covering a wide area of the Thari Formation (Fig. 5) and a total of 2400 clast counts were obtained. For counts intended to determine the broad distribution of lithologies a minimum of 250–300 clasts is recommended (Bridgland 1986). There is some basis for choosing an optimum number of clasts for clast lithological studies. The likely accuracy of results can be demonstrated mathematically by calculating the 'standard error' at a 95% confidence level (i.e. to 2 standard deviations) and can be seen to vary according to count size. The calculation employs the equation:

$$\text{STD ERROR (95\% confidence level)} = 2\sqrt{(pq/n)}$$

where

> p = observed frequency (%)
> $q = 100 - p$
> n = number counted.

Dryden (1931) plotted curves for what he called 'probable error' for various observed frequencies against count totals (Fig. 10). This graph demonstrates that as the gradient of the curve increases, the accuracy increases rather more slowly as larger numbers of clasts are counted. Clearly the minimum number of clasts required is dependent on the degree of precision desired. A minimum of 250 or 300 takes the analysis above the 'sharp bend' of the 5% curve. However, there is no basis for considering that counts of this size will provide adequate representation of the proportion of rare components in a clast count. For example, the calculated standard error (95% confidence level) for a lithology with a frequency of 1% in a count of 300 is 1.14, i.e. larger than the frequency. This means that the sample size is too small to be 95% certain that a component representing 1% of the actual deposit will be encountered (Bridgland 1986).

Count size is very subjective. However,

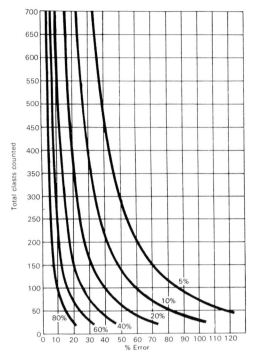

Y-axis label: Total clasts counted

X-axis label: % Error

Curve labels: 5%, 10%, 20%, 80%, 60%, 40%

Fig. 10. Standard error (95% confidence level) as proportion of observed frequency. After Dryden (1931).

Bridgland (1986) stated that if all reasonably common lithologies in a deposit are represented and the proportions of the more abundant lithologies are indicated then satisfactory results are likely to be obtained.

We are confident that the variety of lithological types and their proportion in the conglomerates of the Thari Formation reflect the real composition of the sediments.

Clast composition

Clasts identified in the conglomerates can be divided into ultrabasic, basic and sedimentary constituents (Fig. 11):

Ultrabasic:	harzburgite
	dunite
	serpentinite
Basic:	gabbro
	dolerite
	basalt
Sedimentary:	biomicrites
	calcarenite
	red chert.

Discussion

The harzburgites, dunite, gabbro, serpentinite and dolerite clast types recorded from the Thari Formation suggest erosion from an ophiolitic sequence (Fig. 12).

The most plausible source lies in the northern part of Rhodes, where partially serpentinised gabbro and peridotite outcrop are observed at a high structural level and rest with thrust contact on early Tertiary rocks (Mutti *et al.* 1970). As the present day distribution of the Thari Formation exceeds $750 \, km^2$, reaching a maximum thickness of 600 m, it seems likely that the original source area was a large ophiolitic body. Despite the only known occurrence being the small outcrops in north Rhodes, near Mandrico, Apolona and west of Kalithes, (Fig. 12) which rarely exceed several hundred metres in aerial extent, it is suggested that the ophiolitic source probably formed part of an originally extensive thrust sheet in the early Tertiary (Fig. 13).

There appears to be a progressive northwest to southeast increase in ultrabasic content of the conglomerates. The concentration of ultrabasic material in the SE area of outcrop suggests that rocks derived from specific levels of the ophiolite sequence formed dominant source areas of detritus during the development of the Thari Formation. Dolerite and gabbro clasts which might be expected to form the upper part of an ophiolitic body are more common towards the NW. Tectonic dismembering of the ophiolite might be invoked to explain the large proportion of ultrabasic lithologies (harzburgites and dunites) normally found below the petrological Moho reworked into the Thari Formation in some areas. Thrusting during emplacement of an ophiolitic nappe might alter original stratigraphic relationships. Jones & Robertson (1990) cite evidence for imbrication of ophiolitic sheets within the Pindos ocean basin of northern mainland Greece, prior to final obduction. Alternatively, gravity sliding during and after emplacement of an ophiolite may be a method of imbricating and disrupting the ophiolite stratigraphy (Searle & Cooper 1986). The small exposures of ultrabasic rocks observed on Rhodes do not allow differentiation between these two models.

Although the Thari Formation is dominated by ophiolitic detritus, limestone and chert clasts form a significant proportion of the clast types and in some instances may dominate the outcrop (e.g. St Georges Bay; location 11). Many of the limestone clasts contain Cretaceous planktonic foraminifera and this detritus, and the chert,

Fig. 11. (**A**) Granular gabbro. Plagioclase feldspar shows good lamellae twinning. Note anhedral interstitial crystals of clinopyroxene. Horizontal field of view 8 mm. (**B**) Basalt showing porphyritic texture and abundant zoned plagioclase feldspar. Note green cracked and altered clinopyroxene (centre left) and anhedral olivine crystals (centre right). Horizontal field of view 8 mm. (**C**) Serpentine with characteristic, non-orientated mesh work. Horizontal field of view 8 mm. (**D**) Calcilutite with Globorotalids planktonic foraminifera. Small spherical forms are calcitised radiolaria. Horizontal field of view 4 mm.

were probably derived from the pelagic limestone formations of the Profitis Ilias Subgroup (Mutti *et al.* 1970; Harbury & Hall 1988). This Upper Triassic–Upper Cretaceous basinal sequence was thrust on top of slope and platform sequences during the Late Eocene to early Oligocene.

Basalt and dolerite clasts are present in their greatest quantities in the NW area of outcrop. They show petrographic similarities with the basalts of the Triassic basement to the Profitis Ilias Subgroup and volcanic conglomerates of the Calopetri Conglomerate Formation, and the Thari Formation frequently rests with unconformable contact on these Mesozoic Formations (Harbury & Hall 1988).

Given the structural history of Rhodes, it is evident that the Thari Formation can be viewed as part of a flexural foreland basin fill (e.g. Beaumont 1982; Stockmal *et al.* 1986) that developed after early Palaeocene to mid-Oligocene convergent tectonics (Harbury & Hall 1988). Detritus was reworked from the

highest structural levels including a basinal carbonate sequence and an ophiolite thrust sheet. Other Vati Group formations in the south of the island consist from the base upwards of Koriati Conglomerate, Dali Ash Flow, Ag. Minas Marl and Messanagros Sandstone and represent fluvial, shallow water to deep water deposits respectively. The coarse nature of the ophiolitic detritus in the Thari Formation and the general absence of this material in the southerly parts of the Vati Group suggest the ophiolite nappe lay to the north of the area of the present day Thari Formation outcrop. Unfortunately there are no reliable bedforms or clast imbrication palaeocurrent indicators in the Thari Formation. However, a general decrease in clast size from northwest to southeast of the area of study supports a general north west to south east transport direction. There is a lack of good stratigraphic control within the continental facies of the lower part of the Vati Group and a general absence of sediments of this age from surrounding islands. These palaeogeographic

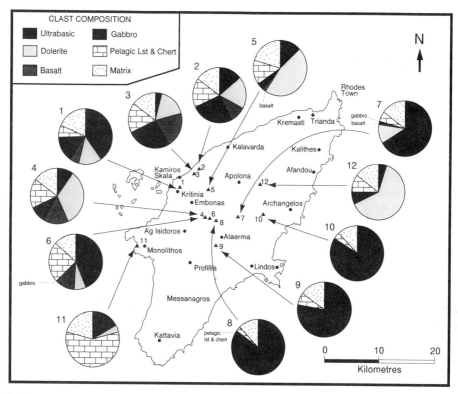

Fig. 12. Clast composition of the Thari Formation.

problems will not be resolved until a better correlation both within the Thari Formation and other parts of the Vati Group is established.

Conclusions

Traditional sedimentological field techniques have been used to describe sediments of the Thari Formation in central Rhodes. These sediments are interpreted to have been deposited as part of a gravel-dominated braided alluvial system that was intimately associated with an ophiolite sequence.

Debris flow, stream channel, and sheet flood deposits represent a gradual NW to SE proximal to distal alluvial fan deposition. Braided deposits within a proximal semi-arid alluvial environment are represented by predominantly poorly-sorted channel-fill conglomerates deposited by sediment gravity flow processes. Braided deposits in more distal portions are characterised by stacked clast-supported, poorly-sorted conglomerates forming gravel sheets.

A provenance study of the Thari Formation records sedimentation dominated by detritus derived from all levels of an ophiolite and Mesozoic basinal carbonate sequence. The ophiolitic source region lay to the northwest of the region of deposition which forms part of the stacked thrust sequence exposed on Rhodes. During sedimentation of the Thari Formation different levels of an ophiolitic sequence were exposed to erosion over the area of sedimentation suggesting that the ophiolite was dismembered prior to erosion. This distribution of ophiolitic detritus might be explained by imbrication of ophiolitic thrust slices during emplacement, or gravity sliding after emplacement of the ophiolite.

The Thari Formation can be viewed as part of a flexural foreland basin-fill (Fig. 13) that developed after early Palaeocene to mid-Oligocene convergent tectonics which accounted for the sedimentary history of the Vati basin.

The authors would like to thank J. Underhill and G. Nichols for their constructive comments on the manuscript. Field work was sponsored by Sun International Exploration and Production Company Ltd.

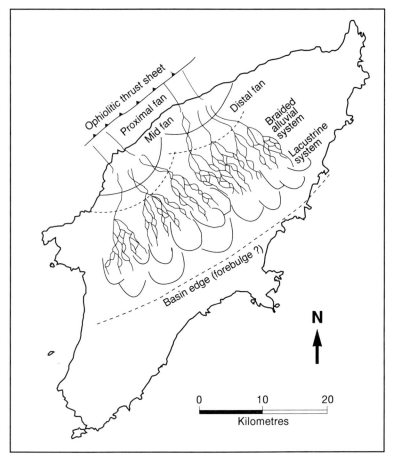

Fig. 13. Suggested palaeogeography during deposition of the Thari Formation where detritus was derived from the erosion of an ophiolitic thrust sheet.

References

BEAUMONT, C. 1981. Foreland basins. *Geophysical Journal of the Royal Astronomical Society*, **65**, 291–329.

BRIDGLAND, D. R. (ed.) 1986. *Clast Lithological Analysis.* Quaternary Research Association Technical Guide No. 3. Cambridge.

DRYDEN, A. L. 1931. Accuracy in percentage representation of heavy mineral frequencies. *Proceedings National Academy of Science USA*, **17**, 233–238.

HAMILTON, W. J. 1840. On a few detached places along the coast of Ionia and Caria and on the Island of Rhodes. *Proceedings of the Geological Society of London*, **3**, 293–298.

HARBURY, N. A. & HALL, R. 1988. Mesozoic Extensional History of the Southern Tethyan Continental Margin in the S.E. Aegean. *Journal of the Geological Society, London*, **145**, 283–30.

JAIA, G. 1912. L'Isola di Rodi. *Bolletin. della Societa Geografia Italiana*, **1**, 966–1003.

JONES, G. & ROBERTSON, A. H. F. 1990. Tectono-stratigraphy and evolution of the Mesozoic Pindos ophiolite and related units, northwestern Greece. *Journal of the Geological Society, London*, **148**, 267–288.

MIALL, A. D. 1978. Lithofacies Types and Vertical Profile Models, in Braided River Deposits. A summary. *Geological Survey of Canada*, **5**, 597–604.

—— 1985. Architectural-element analysis: a new method of facies analysis applied to fluvial deposits. *Earth Science Reviews*, **22**, 261–308.

MIGLIORINI, C. 1933. Cenni sull'isola di Rode. *Bolletino della Societa Geologia Italiana*, **52**, 40–61.

MUTTI, E., OROMBELLI, G. & POZZI, R. 1970. Geological studies on the Dodecanese islands. (Aegean Sea). *Annales Geologiques des Pays Helleniques*, **22**, 77–226.

RAMOS, A. & SOPENA, A. 1983. Gravel bars in low

sinuosity streams (Permian and Triassic, Central Spain). *Special Publication of the International Association of Sedimentologists*, **6**, 301–312.

RUST, B. R. 1978. Depositional models for braided alluvium. *In*: MIALL, A. D. (ed.) *Fluvial Sedimentology*. Geological Survey of Canada, **5**, 605–625.

SEARLE, M. P. & COOPER, D. J. W. 1986. Structure of the Hawasina window culmination, Central Oman Mountains. *Transactions of the Royal Society of Edinburgh: Earth Science*, **77**, 143–156.

STOCKMAL, G. S., BEAUMONT, C. & BOUTILIER, R. 1986. Geodynamic models of convergent margin tectonics. Transition from a rifted margin to overthrust belt and consequences for foreland basin development. *American Association of Petroleum Geologists Bulletin*, **70**, 181–190.

Debris provenance mapping in braided drainage using remote sensing

VICTORIA R. COPLEY & JOHN McM. MOORE

*Centre for Remote Sensing and Department of Geology,
Imperial College, London SW7 2BZ, UK*

Abstract: The NERC Geoscience community airborne remote sensing test site near Carboneras in southeast Spain is dissected by several flash flood drainage channels. These contain a variety of clastic debris types related to diverse source rocks in the catchment basins. As part of a larger study of source rock, regolith and drainage debris relationships, the spectral reflectance characteristics of debris types in braided flash flood channels have been used to map debris dispersion with remotely sensed imagery. The study is based upon 11 channel 7.5 m pixel Airborne Thematic Mapper (ATM) imagery acquired by NERC in May 1989. The objective of the research was to achieve optimum discrimination of channel debris types and to study the integration of distinctive source rock/regolith spectral signatures caused by progressive downstream mixing during transport.

Image processing enhances small spectral variations to improve discrimination of debris types. Imagery was masked to display only channel bed pixels and maximise spectral discrimination within drainage channels. Several enhancement techniques, including principal components and hue-saturation-intensity transformations, and decorrelation and contrast stretches, were then used to emphasise spectral differences among the debris assemblages in the channel beds. One of the most successful products is a selective principal components colour composite image. The image data are presented as a debris lithology distribution map.

Standard techniques for identifying debris provenance involve investigation of grain size parameters and rock type petrology. Distinctive quartz compositions of hydraulic gold mining sediment were used by James (1991) to develop a sediment mixing index for determination of mine tailings concentrations in fluvial deposits. East (1987) showed that the particle size properties of regoliths in a catchment of the Darling Downs, Australia, form statistical groupings which show a consistent spatial relationship to five landform types. For studies of contemporary processes, the use of trace metals and heavy minerals are reliable methods to map sedimentary units and to demonstrate sediment mixing. Sutherland (1991) used grain size characteristics to identify the possible source areas of fluvial suspended sediment within a drainage basin.

This paper presents an alternative method for identifying drainage debris provenance, based upon the spectral reflectance properties of different debris types. The objective of the research was to achieve the best discrimination of braided channel-bed debris units and to study the integration of distinctive source rock/regolith types caused by progressive downstream mixing during transport.

Study area

The study area is within the NERC Geoscience Airborne Remote Sensing Test Site near Carboneras in southeast Spain (Fig. 1). The district is dissected by braided drainage channels which contain water only during, and shortly after, flash floods, and are otherwise dry. The channels drain a complex thrust/wrench fault zone, and the debris composition in the separate channel beds is varied, reflecting the variety of source rocks. The major lithologies are black schist with vein quartz and Miocene molasse sediments (including marl and gypsum). Hornblende andesite and hydrothermally altered volcanics are also present. At upstream localities tributary bed material is dominated by the surrounding rock, but the situation becomes more complex downstream as selective erosion and mixing of the lithologies takes place.

Remote sensing

Airborne Thematic Mapper (ATM) linescan imagery of the study area was acquired by NERC in May 1989. The ATM scanner records digital data in eleven channels (ten channels in the visible and near- to mid-infrared parts of

From Best, J. L. & Bristow, C. S. (eds), 1993, *Braided Rivers*, Geological Society
Special Publication No. **75**, pp. 405–412.

405

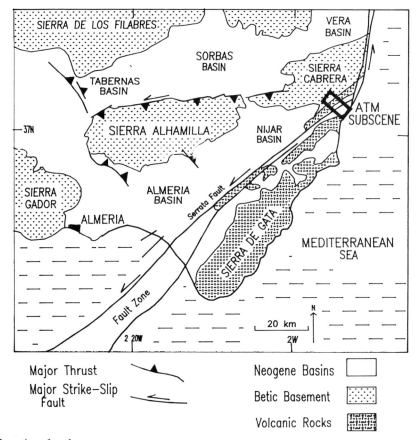

Fig. 1. Location of study area.

the electromagnetic spectrum and one in the thermal infrared portion) and is capable of providing spectrally similar data to Landsat Thematic Mapper, SPOT-HRV and other earth observation satellites (Cook & White 1989). ATM spatial resolution is much greater than these satellites because it flies closer to the ground. The nominal pixel size of the imagery used in this project is 7.5 m at nadir; this permits easy recognition of river beds, which contain 25 pixels at their widest. For each spectral band a pixel is assigned a digital number (DN) depending on the reflectivity (in the region of the electromagnetic spectrum being sensed) of the land cover at that location. The DN scale is from 0 to 255, where low values represent dark targets and high values indicate light targets.

Figure 2 shows the reflectance properties of rock types within the study area, as recorded by the ten reflectance channels of the ATM scanner. These spectral profiles (or signatures) are the basis for discriminating between rock

debris types using multi-band imagery. Varied source rocks yield spectrally distinct clastic debris types, and it is possible to trace material transported from upstream sources to the river estuary. Sediment mixing can therefore be evaluated, and fluvial processes inferred from a study of multispectral imagery.

Image masking

Figure 3(a) shows the poor quality discrimination of a monochrome air photograph for river bed debris types. Figure 3(b) is a digital simulation of a panchromatic air photo, obtained by averaging ATM bands 1 to 6; this image also has poor discrimination of the river bed debris. Unsatisfactory discrimination in the ATM image arises because the river pixel DN values occupy only a reduced segment (generally from DN 18 to 130) of the 0 to 255 dynamic range of the ATM sensor. The first objective of digital enhancement is therefore to improve the range of grey

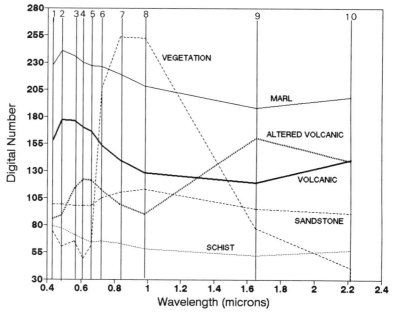

Fig. 2. Rock and vegetation spectral reflectance curves. Taken from ATM image. Vertical lines show midpoints of ATM channels.

tones in an image. This can be achieved by digitally spreading (contrast stretching) the 18 to 130 DN range across the full dynamic range (0 to 255) of a VDU. Visual discrimination of debris types is then significantly improved.

The image was first corrected for differential cross-swath illumination using an empirical regression equation (J. G. Liu, pers. comm.; based on the work of Danson 1987). The non-river bed pixels were suppressed (masked) by setting their DN values to zero, and the values of unmasked river bed pixels were then stretched across the range from 0 to 255.

Enhancement of river bed pixels

Although image masking utilizes the 0 to 255 DN brightness range for river bed pixels, and improves the display of debris types, the discrimination remains relatively crude. A variety of image enhancement techniques were used to refine the separation of debris types and to high-light subtle variations in debris spectral properties.

River bed gravel units show spectral variety across the entire ATM spectral range (bands 1 to 10; see Fig. 2). For this reason enhancement techniques were selected which would make use of debris spectral information. Consequently techniques such as simple band differencing and

band ratioing, which deal with only two spectral bands, were not attempted. (Differencing and ratioing are target-oriented operations which are used to look at a particular feature, for example iron minerals or vegetation, and are therefore inappropriate to this study which aims to enhance the diverse but delicate spectral properties of many river gravel types).

A variety of refined enhancement techniques were assessed. These included standard, and selective, principal components, hue-saturation-intensity transformations, and decorrelation stretches (see Drury 1987). The criterion used to determine the success of each of these image enhancement methods was ability to discriminate amongst the varied river bed gravel units. The enhanced images were compared with field data of debris lithological composition which had been collected at 21 localities in the study area. In relation to field information the best gravel discrimination was achieved by the selective principal components transformation. Of the enhanced images, this image compared most favourably, in terms of number of gravel units discriminated and accuracy of their spatial representation, with the field data obtained for lithological composition at different localities. The selective principal components technique, and its advantages over other techniques, are described below.

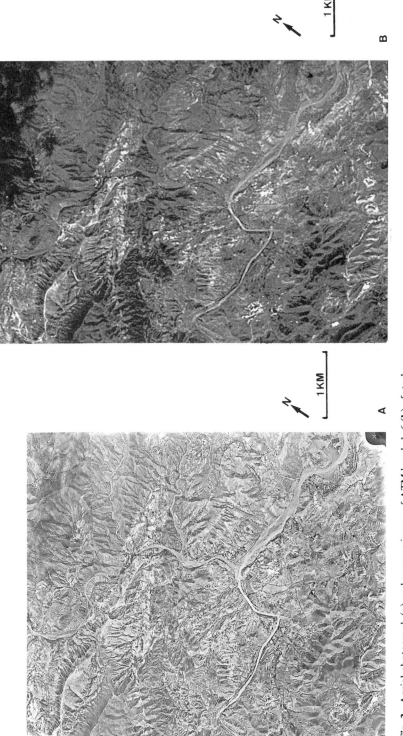

Fig. 3. Aerial photograph (**a**) and average image of ATM bands 1–6 (**b**) of study area.

Principal components analysis (PCA) of remotely sensed image data has been used for various mapping and information extraction purposes (e.g. Loughlin 1991; Crosta & Moore 1989). It is a mathematical transformation that generates new images, known as components or axes, which are linear combinations of the original multi-band image data. PCA allows the user to generate a set of images whose data relates to new orthogonal axes. The new images have no mathematical correlation with each other. Most of the total image data variance is allocated to the first principal component with decreasing variance going in each of the lower order components. Problems encountered with this standard PCA method include both the loss of information that is allocated to components not used (a problem experienced in this study) and difficulty in visually interpreting a colour composite made by combining standard PCA images. Chavez & Kwarteng (1989) put forward the technique of 'selective' PCA to reduce both of these problems.

Selective PCA uses only highly correlated subsets of images as input for transformation. By grouping the images PCA allocates most of the variance or information to the first component image data set because of the high degree of correlation among the input images. The second principal component highlights the major spectral feature, and is thus of crucial interest. The higher components are usually dominated by noise, because of the high interband correlation. It is the ability of a principal components transformation to enhance delicate spectral features in this way which makes it superior to other methods of image enhancement in discriminating river bed gravels. The subtle and rapid changes in river debris spectral characteristics associated with varying proportions of different lithologies are overlooked by hue-saturation-intensity transformations.

Decorrelation stretching, whilst involving a principal components transformation, does not separate spectral features or subdue confusing topographic shading. Thus a spectral feature of interest which may have been well expressed in one or two PC images is spread throughout decorrelation stretched images, and can be difficult to spot.

The selective PC colour composite image is easier to interpret than colour composites made from standard PCA images because in the selective PCA process, bands which are close to each other in the spectrum are used as a subgroup; the resultant colour composites look similar to colour composites made from untransformed bands. The selective PCA colour composite usually has more of the total variance than either an untransformed band or standard PCA composite.

Following the methodology described, principal component images were generated from each of the following triplets of ATM bands:

ATM (2, 3, 4)
ATM (5, 6, 7)
ATM (8, 9, 10).

These triplets all show a high degree of within-group correlation (Table 1). Triplets for PCA analysis should be formed from bands near to each other in the spectrum since this facilitates interpretation of colour composites made from the transformed bands. Nine bands were used in this study in order to make use of the full range of information recorded in each spectral region of the ATM. Band 1 was discarded because of atmospheric scattering effects, and Band 11 was not used since it records thermal emissivity and not reflectance.

Figure 4 shows images of the second principal component derived from each of the band triplets. These images have been enlarged to

Table 1. *Correlation matrix, for the river-bed subregion, of the ten reflective Airborne Thematic Mapper bands*

ATM Band	1	2	3	4	5	6	7	8	9	10
1	1.00									
2	0.84	1.00								
3	0.82	0.98	1.00							
4	0.81	0.96	0.99	1.00						
5	0.79	0.94	0.99	0.99	1.00					
6	0.60	0.70	0.81	0.84	0.88	1.00				
7	0.38	0.43	0.58	0.61	0.66	0.93	1.00			
8	0.30	0.34	0.50	0.54	0.59	0.88	0.98	1.00		
9	0.56	0.67	0.79	0.83	0.87	0.93	0.85	0.83	1.00	
10	0.69	0.83	0.91	0.94	0.95	0.90	0.73	0.68	0.95	1.00

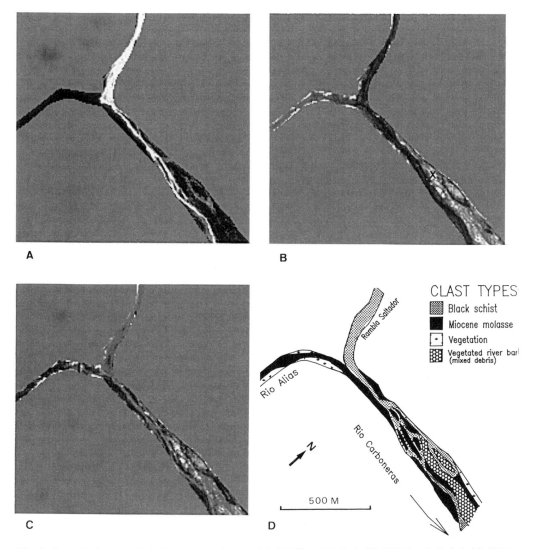

Fig. 4. Second selective principal component images: (**a**) ATM bands 2, 3, 4; (**b**) ATM bands 5, 6, 7; (**c**) ATM bands 8, 9, 10; (**d**) interpretation of composite principal component imagery.

show the confluence of the two major tributaries of the drainage network. The second principal component images of each of these triplets were combined to make a false colour composite image. The rationale for producing such an image is that it compresses all the spectral differences shown by the black and white images of Fig. 4(a–c) into a single colour image, and thus forms a convenient synthesis for debris mapping. An interpretation of this colour image is shown in Fig. 4(d).

Image-based drainage debris mapping

The images shown in Fig. 4(a–c) highlight different types of drainage debris. Images (b) and (c) show the varied lithological composition of the river bed material more effectively than image (a). The following discussion accounts for these differences in discrimination, and the distribution of debris. River names and flow direction are given in Fig. 4(d).

Figure 4(a) is the second principal component image obtained from ATM bands 2, 3 and 4. It highlights in white the schist debris being contributed to the Río Carboneras by the Rambla Saltador, whilst the Miocene molasse sediments which are contributed by the Río Alías are shown in black. Within this broad separation very little subdivision of debris type is achieved. The schist debris train forms the bed material of the main active channel in the Río Carboneras. This indicates that erosion may be currently more active in the Rambla Saltador drainage basin than the Río Alías catchment. Rainfall over the Rambla Saltador catchment, which drains the Sierra Cabrera hills, is likely to include an orographic rainfall increment in addition to any localised convectional rain. The nature of rainfall means that two contiguous runoff catchments may have different runoff histories, with flows recorded in one and not the other. It is therefore likely that Rambla Saltador catchment experiences higher rainfall totals than the Río Alías catchment, which drains a lower, more arid area, and that the high proportion of schist in the active channel represents the depositional consequences of out-of-phase floods (Reid *et al.* 1989). As well as being more prone to erosive forces, the schist in Rambla Saltador catchment is furthermore less resistant to erosion, and forms steep rectilinear slopes mantled by a plentiful rock debris.

An alternative reason for domination of the active main river channel by schist debris is the contrasting particle size of incoming sediment at the river confluence. Molasse debris from the Río Alías has a mean particle size of -1.22ϕ (2 mm) but schist debris reaches the river confluence with a mean particle size of -5.0ϕ (32 mm). Molasse debris may therefore be preferentially eroded from the active channel of the Río Carboneras.

The ATM bands most useful in vegetation diagnosis are bands 5, 6, and 7. This is because vegetation has its highest reflectance in the wavelength range of band 7, and band 6 occupies the wavelength range which allows it to be used for monitoring the 'red edge'. Band 5 provides a useful substractive, when used with band 7 in difference images, to extract pixels representing vegetation. Figure 4(b) is the second principal component from ATM bands 5, 6 and 7. The bright white pixels on this image represent grasses and shrubs which grow adjacent to and within the channel belt. This image provides further information about the 'dark' pixels of Fig. 4(a), which are seen to contain vegetation as well as molasse debris. Braiding of the active channel of the Río Carboneras on either side of a vegetated river bar can be clearly seen (point X).

Figure 4(c) shows the river braiding best,

although discrimination of the debris types within the braids is more difficult since the tones are not as distinctive as for images (a) and (b). This image is the second principal component of ATM bands 8, 9 and 10. The second PC image compresses spectral data from the near infrared and middle infrared regions of the electromagnetic spectrum. Rocks may display characteristic spectral reflectance behaviour at these wavelengths (Fig. 2) and ATM bands 8, 9 and 10 are therefore very useful for discriminating between rock types. The clastic debris types of the drainage channels are relatively unweathered and consequently preserve the reflectance characteristics shown by their source rocks. Image (c) shows that, within the main active drainage channel of the Río Carboneras, there is a series of narrower channels which appear to diverge around surfaces comprised of finer grained molasse debris. Although this braiding is seen in image (4a), image (4c) reveals the situation more fully and thus provides more information for inferring the nature of the fluvial processes at work. The white pixels in this image, like image (b), denote vegetation: channel-bordering shrubs and the vegetated mid-channel bar of the Río Carboneras are clearly shown.

PC colour composite imagery incorporates all the information given by the individual second principal component images. A three-band colour composite is the most comprehensive means of presentation for multichannel data (Cañas & Barnett 1985). The image obtained by compositing images 4a (blue), 4b (green) and 4c (red) represents the most successful visual product for mapping braided drainage debris terrain types and is in accordance with field observations. In this image, schist is highlighted in blue, molasse deposits in black, vegetation in yellow and the river bar in yellowish green. This type of image could also be transformed into a thematic map using classification techniques. Unfortunately, publication costs preclude reproduction of the PC colour composite image from this study, but an interpretation of the selective PC colour composite imagery is presented in Fig. 4(d).

An important constraining factor when using principal components analysis is that ancillary data relating to the site in question are needed for image interpretation purposes, since PCA is an empirical enhancement technique in which simple spectral information suitable for direct photo-interpretation is lost. The most effective way to verify PC images is by comparison with field information, simple band colour composites, or geological and vegetation maps.

Conclusions

Mapping debris using remote sensing has an advantage over traditional field-based provenance studies because of the synoptic coverage a remotely sensed image provides. A very intensive fieldwork programme would be required in order to produce, over such a large area, a debris distribution map with the level of detail of the images shown in Fig. 4. This study shows that digital enhancement and analysis of airborne remotely sensed imagery is an effective means of mapping braided drainage debris provenance in semi-arid areas which have dried-up, exposed river beds.

The value of multispectral digital image data compared with black and white aerial photographs has been demonstrated. Multispectral scanners such as the Airborne Thematic Mapper provide information which can be used to discriminate debris types much more effectively than do panchromatic photographs.

The digital form of remotely sensed imagery facilitates computer manipulation and image processing techniques can be applied to the data as a means to extract quickly and selectively information about earth surface materials. This information can be used to infer the nature of surface processes.

Airborne Thematic Mapper data is recommended for river bed studies since it provides the spatial and spectral resolution to map debris assemblages with sufficient detail (1 : 10 000–1 : 25 000 scale). The imagery used in this study has a pixel size of 7.5 m and in this case it is not possible to discern by eye in images debris types which occupy less than approximately four pixels ($15 \, m^2$ in area). Debris types must also be spectrally distinct if image processing is to be successful.

V.R.C. is grateful to NERC for sponsorship and for providing ATM data. Thanks to J. G. Liu for help with image processing.

References

CAÑAS, A. A. D. & BARNETT, M. E. 1985. The generation and interpretation of false-colour composite principal component images. *International Journal of Remote Sensing*, **6**, 867–881.

CHAVEZ, P. S. & KWARTENG, A. Y. 1989. Extracting spectral contrast in Landsat Thematic Mapper image data using selective principal component analysis. *Photogrammetric Engineering and Remote Sensing*, **55**, 339–348.

COOK, F. J. & WHITE, S. J. 1990. Overview of the 1989 NERC Airborne Remote Sensing Campaign. *In*: *Proceedings of the NERC Symposium on Airborne Remote Sensing. British Geological Survey, Keyworth, Nottingham 18–19 December 1990*, NERC, Swindon, 1–6.

CROSTA, A. P. & MOORE, J. McMM. 1989. Geological mapping using Landsat Thematic Mapper imagery in Almeria Province, South-East Spain. *International Journal of Remote Sensing*, **10**, 505–514.

DANSON, F. M. 1987. Estimating forest stand parameters using airborne MSS data. *In*: *Proceedings of the 13th Annual Conference of the Remote Sensing Society, University of Nottingham, 7–11 September 1987*, Remote Sensing Society, Nottingham, 46–54.

DRURY, S. A. 1987. *Image Interpretation in Geology*. London: Allen & Unwin.

EAST, T. J. 1987. A multivariate analysis of the particle size characteristics of regolith in a catchment on the Darling Downs, Australia. *Catena*, **14**, 101–118.

JAMES, L. A. 1991. Quartz concentration as an index of sediment mixing: hydraulic mine-tailings in the Sierra Nevada, California. *Geomorphology*, **4**, 125–144.

LOUGHLIN, W. P. 1991. Principal component analysis for alteration mapping. *In*: *Proceedings of the Eighth Thematic Conference on Geologic Remote Sensing, Denver, Colorado USA*, Environmental Research Institute of Michigan, Ann Arbor, 293–306.

REID, I., BEST, J. L. & FROSTICK, L. E. 1989. Floods and flood sediments at river confluences. *In*: BEVEN, K. & CARLING, P. (eds) *Floods: Hydrological, Sedimentological and Geomorphological Implications* John Wiley & Sons Ltd, 135–150.

SUTHERLAND, R. A. 1991. Selective erosion and sediment source identification, Baringo District, Kenya. *Zeitschrift für Geomorphologie*, **35**, 293–304.

Index